THE INFORMED ARGUMENT

A MULTIDISCIPLINARY READER AND GUIDE

◆

THIRD EDITION

◆

ROBERT K. MILLER
UNIVERSITY OF SAINT THOMAS

HARCOURT BRACE JOVANOVICH COLLEGE PUBLISHERS

FORT WORTH   PHILADELPHIA   SAN DIEGO   NEW YORK   ORLANDO   AUSTIN   SAN ANTONIO
TORONTO   MONTREAL   LONDON   SYDNEY   TOKYO

Acquisitions Editor: Stuart Miller
Manuscript Editor: Margie Rogers
Production Editor: David Hill
Designer: Suzanne Montazer
Art Editor: Avery Hallowell
Production Manager: Diane Southworth

Cover: © Obie Simonis, "The Balance Comes from Above."

Illustrations:

p. 42   MAXWELL HOUSE and 1892 are registered trademarks of Kraft General Foods, Inc. Reproduced with permission.

p. 44   This advertisement is provided courtesy of the U. S. Council for Energy Awareness, Washington, D.C.

p. 46   Reprinted by permission of the Beef Industry Council and Beef Board.

p. 47   Courtesy of the Ford Motor Company.

p. 48   Reprinted with Permission of Northwest Airlines.

p. 644   Imperial War Museum, London.

p. 645   Bundesarchiv, Koblenz.

p. 645   Bundesarchiv, Koblenz.

ISBN: 0-15-541456-9

Library of Congress Catalog Card Number: 91-65871

Printed in the United States of America

Preface for Students

♦

This book has been designed to help you argue on behalf of your beliefs so that other people will take them seriously. Part 1 will introduce you to the basic principles of argumentation that you need to evaluate the arguments you read and to compose arguments of your own. Part 2 will introduce you to strategies for evaluating your reading and to conventions for supporting arguments with information that you have acquired through that reading.

The readings gathered for you in *The Informed Argument,* Third Edition, should give you adequate information for writing on a variety of subjects. Part 3, "Cases for Argument," includes articles on twelve different topics, including a number of questions (such as "Should teenagers get plastic surgery?") that you may not have considered before. These articles were chosen to help get you started in argumentation with topics that easily lend themselves to discussion. The range of topics covered in the book is further broadened by Part 5, "Some Classic Arguments," nineteen important works from the history of ideas.

The readings that form the heart of the book are found in Part 4, "Sources for Argument." In this part of the book, you will find material on the same subject by several different writers. I hope that your reading in Part 4 will leave you better informed about the different subjects that are discussed. But whatever you learn about these subjects is a bonus. The purpose of *The Informed Argument* is not to turn you into an expert on gun control, global warming, or animal experimentation; it is to help you master skills that you can subsequently apply to subjects of your own choice long after you have completed the course in which you used this book.

In choosing the various essays for Part 4, I was guided by two basic principles. I tried to give equal consideration to opposing viewpoints so that you can better understand different sides of the issues in question. I also tried to include examples of different writing strategies. To fulfill these goals, I have included a mixture of old and new essays. You will find the date of original publication in boldface within the introductory note that comes immediately before every selection in Part 4. An essay can embody a strong argument or interesting point of view many years after it was written. On the other hand, an old essay can also include outdated information, so you should consider the age of each source when deciding the extent to which you can rely upon it.

If you read carefully, you will find that almost every written argument includes at least one weak point. This is because it is almost impossible to achieve perfection in writing—especially when logic is involved. One of the reasons people have been drawn to study philosophy is that some of the great minds of world civilization have occasionally composed arguments that are so brilliant they seem perfect. Most writers, however, usually have to settle for less than perfection, especially when time or space is limited. Experienced writers spend as much time revising their work as they possibly can, but they also know that they cannot expect to have the last word. In any written argument there is almost always going to be a point that has been overlooked or something that could have been better put. Therefore, don't feel that an argument automatically loses all credibility because you have discovered a flaw in it. Although you should be alert for flaws, especially in reasoning, you should consider the significance of the flaw in proportion to the argument as a whole. Some writers undermine their entire argument by contradicting themselves or making wild charges; others are able to make a strong argument despite one or two weak points.

I wrote this book because I saw that students often needed additional information before they could write well-supported arguments but did not always have time to do research. Some writers, however, enjoy doing their own research, and you may want to supplement your reading in this book with material that you have discovered on your own. Part 6, "A Guide to Research," discusses how to find sources in a library. Searching for your own sources will enable you to include recently published material within your arguments. If you discover unusual or surprising information, library research may also help make your arguments more interesting to readers who are already familiar with the material in *The Informed Argument*. The extent to which you decide to go outside the book, if at all, is something to be decided in consultation with your instructor. The book itself has been designed to make research an option rather than a necessity.

This edition includes thirteen essays written by students. These have been included so that you can see how other students have satisfied assignments similar to those you may be asked to undertake. These essays are intended to help you rather than impress you. As is the case with the reprinted essays by professional writers, some of the student essays are stronger than others. You should try to learn what you can from them, but you should not feel that they represent some sort of perfection that is beyond your grasp. All of the students in question are serious enough about writing that they will probably see things they'd like to change as soon as they see their essays in print, for revision is a never-ending task essential to good writing. I want to thank these students for giving me permission to publish their work and remind them that I hope they keep on writing. I also want to thank the many students who studied the first two editions of this book and helped me to see how it could be improved.

PREFACE FOR INSTRUCTORS

◆

The Third Edition of *The Informed Argument* continues to reflect my belief that students resent being asked to write on topics that seem trivial or contrived. Most of the readings are once again assembled into the equivalent of separate casebooks, six of which focus on important issues of the sort students often want to write about but lack adequate information to do so effectively. Instructors are free to treat each section either as a self-contained unit or as a springboard to further reading. To facilitate class discussion, every essay has its own editorial apparatus. This allows for much flexibility. Readings can be assigned in whatever sequence seems appropriate for a particular class. And there is plenty of material, so instructors can vary the assignments given to different classes without undertaking the work of an entirely new preparation.

The 87 selections, 52 of which are new to the Third Edition, are drawn from a variety of disciplines to help students master different types of writing and reading. Among the fields represented are biology, business, history, journalism, medicine, law, literature, philosophy, political science, psychology, and sociology. In selecting these readings I have been guided by three primary concerns: to provide students with model arguments, expose them to different points of view, and give them information for writing arguments of their own. I have also chosen pieces that require different degrees of experience with reading. Some of the pieces are easily accessible; others are more demanding. My goal was to give students an immediate point of entry into the issues in question and then encourage them to confront more difficult texts representative of the reading that they will be expected to undertake on their own in college.

Although I believe in the importance of writing across the curriculum, I also believe that literature should be part of the curriculum being written across. Consequently, the book still includes a section on literary criticism as a type of argumentation. The thematically organized sections in Part 4 are followed by Part 5, "Some Classic Arguments." This section increases the variety of readings made available to students through inclusion of such well-known essays as "A Modest Proposal" and "Letter from Birmingham Jail" as well as seldom-anthologized arguments by writers such as Émile Zola, Mahatma Gandhi, and Nelson Mandela.

The wish to increase the diversity of readings made available to students contributed to a new feature in this edition. Part 3, "Cases for Argument," addresses twelve different topics that can be used for class discussion or short writing assignments as an alternative to the assignments in Part 4. Other changes in this edition include the addition of material on critical reading to Part 2, "Working with Sources," and extensive revision of Part 6, "A Guide to Research."

Because books have become so expensive, I have designed *The Informed Argument* to satisfy the needs of students in a semester-long class and to be useful to them long afterward. Part 1 introduces students to the principles they need to understand for reading and writing arguments. I have tried to keep the explanations as simple as possible. Examples are provided for each of the concepts discussed, and student essays illustrate both inductive and deductive reasoning as well as the model for reasoning devised by Stephen Toulmin. In addition, two versions of the same student essay illustrate the importance of revision, and another student essay illustrates an expanded section on definition.

Part 2 discusses the evaluation, annotation, paraphrase, summary, synthesis, and documentation of texts. For easy reference, a gray border identifies the pages devoted to documentation. The major documentation styles in use across the curriculum are illustrated—not only those of the Modern Language Association (MLA) and the American Psychological Association (APA), which are discussed in detail, but also the use of documentary footnotes and a numbered system favored in scientific writing. MLA style is also illustrated by several student essays in Part 4 and by the model research paper in Part 6. To help students using APA-style documentation, original publication dates are printed in boldface within the headnotes for selections in Parts 4 and 5. Examples of APA-style essays, and other systems, are provided by one or more of the essays in Part 4.

Several of the suggestions for writing in Parts 4 and 5 encourage students to do library research. How to do so is discussed in Part 6, "A Guide to Research." In keeping with the book's multidisciplinary character, I use a search strategy that could be employed to locate material for many different courses. Although this information appears at the end of the book, it can be taught at any time.

Instructors new to *The Informed Argument* might also note that the book contains a total of thirteen student essays. Although student essays can be found in many textbooks, *The Informed Argument* includes essays that respond to sources that are reprinted in the book. I have included these essays because students often profit from studying the work of other students. Given the difficulty of arguing effectively and using sources responsibly, students using the Third Edition should welcome the chance to see how other students coped with assignments similar to their own.

In completing this book, I have contracted many debts. I would like to thank those colleagues who have offered comments and advice: Ruth Dorgan, Nancy Moore, and Al Young, University of Wisconsin at Stevens Point; Mary Joseph, York College; and Suzanne Webb, Texas Women's University. For their constant encouragement and support, I want to thank Phyllis and Robert Stanley Miller. William Warren Garitano deserves special thanks for his helpful and sage advice during many discussions of this project. And at Harcourt Brace Jovanovich, Eleanor Garner, Avery Hallowell, David Hill, Stuart Miller, Suzanne Montazer, and Margie Rogers deserve many thanks for their expert help.

CONTENTS

◆

P A R T   3

CASES FOR ARGUMENT   85

P A R T   4

SOURCES FOR ARGUMENT   133

Section 1 Mandatory Drug Testing: A Question of Privacy   133

P A R T 5

SOME CLASSIC ARGUMENTS   509

P A R T 6

A GUIDE TO RESEARCH   647

PART 1

AN INTRODUCTION TO ARGUMENT

———— ◆ ————

Argument is a means of fulfilling desire. That desire may be for something as abstract as truth or as concrete as a raise in salary. When you ask for an extension on a paper, apply for a job, propose a marriage, or recommend any change that involves someone besides yourself, you are putting yourself in a position that requires effective argumentation. In the years ahead, you may also have occasion to argue seriously about political and ethical concerns. Someone you love may be considering an abortion, a large corporation may try to bury its chemical waste on property that adjoins your own, or you may be suddenly deprived of a benefit to which you feel entitled. By learning how to organize your beliefs and support them with information that will make other people take them seriously, you will be mastering one of the most important skills you are likely to learn in college.

Working your arguments out on paper gives you the luxury of being able to make changes as often as you want until you are satisfied that your words do what you want them to do. This is an important benefit because constructing effective arguments requires that you think clearly without letting your feelings dominate what you say, and this can be difficult at times. But it can also be tremendously satisfying when you succeed in making other people understand what you mean. You may not always succeed in converting others to your point of view, but you can win their respect. This, in a way, is what argument is all about. When you argue for what you believe, you are asking others to believe in you. This means that you must prove to your audience that you are worth listening to. If you succeed this far, you may have won the argument even if you lose the vote on the particular issue at hand. Argumentation is intellectual self-assertion designed to secure consideration and respect, and it should not be confused with quarreling.

1

Bearing this in mind, you should always be careful to treat both your audience and your opponents with respect. Few people are likely to be converted to your view if you treat them as if they are fools and dismiss their beliefs with contempt. Reason is the essence of effective argumentation, and an important part of being reasonable is demonstrating that you have given consideration to beliefs that are different from your own and have recognized what makes them appealing. Since nobody likes a know-it-all, you should try not to be narrow minded or overly opinionated.

Similarly, you should avoid the temptation of arguing all things at all times. Most points can indeed be argued, but just because something can be argued does not necessarily mean that it *should* be argued. You won't be taken seriously if you seem to argue automatically and routinely. Argument should be the result of reflection rather than reflex, and argumentation is a skill that should be practiced selectively.

CHOOSING A TOPIC

The first step in written argumentation, as in all forms of writing, is choosing a topic. In doing so, you should be careful to avoid subjects that could be easily settled by referring to an authority, such as a dictionary or an encyclopedia. There is no point in arguing about how to spell "separate" or about what is the capital of Bolivia, because questions of this sort can be settled quickly and absolutely, having only one correct answer. Argument assumes the possibility of more than one position on the issue being considered. When you disagree with someone about anything that could be settled by simply checking the facts, you would be wasting your time to argue, even if you are sure you are right.

Almost all intelligent arguments are about *opinions*. But not all opinions lead to good written arguments. There is no reason to argue an opinion with which almost no one would disagree. An essay designed to "prove" that puppies are cute or that vacations can be fun is unlikely to generate much excitement. Don't belabor the obvious. Nearly everyone welcomes the arrival of spring, and you will be preaching to the converted if you set out to argue that spring is a nice time of year. If you've been reading T. S. Eliot, however, and want to argue that April is the cruelest month (and that you have serious reservations about May and June as well) then you may be on to something. You should not feel that you suddenly need to acquire strange and eccentric opinions. But you should choose a topic that is likely to inspire at least some controversy.

In doing so, be careful to distinguish between opinions that are a matter of taste and those that are a question of judgment. Some people like broccoli, and some people don't. You may be the world's foremost broccoli lover, dreaming every night of broccoli crops to come, but no matter how hard you try, you will not convince someone who hates green vegetables to head quickly to the produce department of the nearest supermarket. A gifted stylist could probably write an amusing essay on broccoli, in the manner of Charles Lamb or E. B. White, that would be a delight to read. But it is one thing to describe our tastes and quite another to insist that others share them. We all have likes and dislikes that are so firmly entrenched that persuasion in matters of taste is usually beyond the reach of what can be accomplished through the written word—unless you happen to command the resources of a major advertising agency.

Taste is a matter of personal preference. Whether we prefer green to blue or daffodils to tulips is unlikely to affect anyone but ourselves. Questions of judgment are more substantial than matters of taste because judgment cannot be divorced from logic. Our judgments are determined by our beliefs, behind which are basic principles to which we try to remain consistent. These principles ultimately lead us to decide that some judgments are correct and others are not, so judgment has greater implications than taste. Should a university require freshmen to live in dormitories? Should men and women live together before getting married? Should parents spank their children? All these are questions of judgment.

In written argumentation, questions of judgment provide the best subjects. They can be argued because they are complex, giving you more angles to pursue. This does not mean that you must cover every aspect of a question in a single essay. Because good subjects have so many possibilities, the essays that are written on them will take many different directions. Good writers sound like individuals, not committees or machines, and it is easier to sound like an individual when you address a subject about which many different things can be said. Moreover, in making an argument writers try to surprise readers with information—or an ingenious interpretation of information— that is not usually considered. If your audience consists of people who know almost nothing about your subject, then you may be able to build a convincing case by simply outlining a few basic points. But an educated audience will be converted to your view only if you move beyond the obvious and reveal points that are often overlooked. This is most likely to happen when the subject itself is complex.

It is important, therefore, to choose subjects that you are well-informed about or willing to research. This may sound like obvious advice, and yet it is possible to have an opinion with nothing behind it but a few generalizations that are impossible to support once you begin to write. You may have absorbed the opinions of others without thinking about them or may have prejudged a particular subject without knowing much about it. Nobody is going to take your views seriously if you cannot support them.

The readings that form Part 3 of this book were chosen to help you begin to argue. Those that form Part 4 were chosen to make you better informed on a number of important questions so that you can argue more effectively. After you have read six or seven essays on the same subject, you should be able to compose an argument of your own that will consider the various views you have encountered. But remember that being "better informed" does not always mean being "well informed." Well-educated men and women recognize how little they know in proportion to how much there is to be known. Don't suppose that you've become an expert on animal experimentation simply because you have spent a week or two reading about it. What you read should influence what you think, but as you read more, realize that controversial subjects are controversial because there is so much that could be said about them—much more than you may have realized at first.

DEFINING YOUR AUDIENCE

Argumentation demands a clear sense of audience. Good writers remember whom they are writing for, and their audience helps shape their style. It would be a mistake, for example, to use complicated technical language when writing for a general audience. But it would be just as foolish to address an audience of experts as if they knew nothing about the subject. As the writer you should always be careful not to confuse people. On the other hand, you must also be careful not to insult the readers' intelligence. Although awareness of audience is important in almost all types of writing, it is especially true in written arguments. A clear sense of audience allows you to choose the points you want to emphasize in order to be persuasive. Just as importantly, it enables you to anticipate the objections your readers or listeners are most likely to raise if they disagree with you.

In written argumentation, it is usually best to envision an audience that is skeptical. Unless you are the keynote speaker at a political convention, rallying the members of your party by telling them exactly what they want to hear, there is no reason to expect people to agree with you. If your audience already agrees with you, what's the point of your argument? Whom are you trying to convince? Remember that the immediate purpose of an argument is almost always to convert people to your point of view. Of course, an audience may be entirely neutral, having no opinion at all on the subject that concerns you. But by imagining a skeptical audience, you will be able to anticipate the opposition and offer counterarguments of your own, thus building a stronger case.

Before you begin to write, you should list for yourself the reasons why you believe as you do. Realize that you may not have the space, in a short essay, to discuss all of the points you have listed. You should therefore rank them in order of their importance, considering, in particular, the degree to which they would probably impress the audience for whom you are writing. Once you have done this, compose another list—a list of reasons why people might disagree with you. Having considered the opposition's point of view, now ask yourself why it is that you have not been persuaded to abandon your own beliefs. You must see a flaw of some sort in the reasoning of your opponents. Add to your second list a short rebuttal of each of your opponent's arguments.

You are likely to discover that the opposition has at least one good argument, an argument which you cannot answer. There should be nothing surprising about this. We may like to flatter ourselves by believing that Truth is on our side. In our weaker moments, we may like to pretend that anyone who disagrees with us is either ignorant or corrupt. But serious and prolonged controversies almost always mean that the opposition has at least one valid concern. Be prepared to concede a point to your opponents when it seems appropriate to do so. You must consider and respond to their views, but your responses do not always have to take the form of rebuttals. When you have no rebuttal and recognize that your opponent's case has some merit, be honest and generous enough to say so.

By making concessions to your opposition, you demonstrate to your audience that you are trying to be fair minded. Far from weakening your own case, an occasional concession can help bridge the gulf between you and your opponents, making it easier for you to reach a more substantial agreement. It's hard to convince someone that your views deserve to be taken seriously when you have belligerently insisted that he or she is completely wrong and you are completely right. Life is seldom so simple. Human nature being what it is, most people will listen more readily to an argument that offers some recognition of their views.

You must be careful, of course, not to concede too much. If you find yourself utterly without counterarguments and ready to concede a half dozen points, you had better reconsider the subject you have chosen. In a short essay, you can usually afford to make only one or two concessions. Too many concessions are likely to confuse readers who are uncertain about what they think. Why should they be persuaded by you when you seem half persuaded by your opponents?

Having a good sense of audience also means illustrating your case with concrete examples your audience can readily understand. It's hard to make people care about abstractions; good writers try to make the abstract concrete. Remember that it is often easy to lose the attention of your audience, so try to address its most probable concerns.

There is, however, a great difference between responding to the interests of your audience by discussing what it wants to know and twisting what you say to please an audience with exactly what it wants to hear. You should remember that the foremost responsibility of any writer is to tell the truth as he or she sees it. What we mean by "truth" often has many dimensions, and when limited space forces us to be selective, it is only common sense to focus on those facets of our subject that will be the most effective with the audience we are attempting to sway. But it is one thing to edit and quite another to mislead. Never write anything for one audience that you would be compelled to deny before another. Hypocrites are seldom persuasive, and no amount of verbal agility can compensate for a loss of confidence in a writer's character.

To better understand the importance of audience in argumentation, let us consider an example. The following essay was recently published as an editorial in a student newspaper.

TO SKIP OR NOT TO SKIP: A STUDENT DILEMMA

This is college right? The four-year deal offering growth, maturity, experience, and knowledge? A place to be truly independent? 1

Because sometimes I can't tell. Sometimes this place downright reeks of paternal instincts. Just ask the freshmen and sophomores, who are by class rank alone guaranteed two full years of twenty-four hour supervision, orchestrated activities, and group showers. 2

But the forced dorm migration of underclassmen has been bitched about before, to no avail. University policy is, it seems, set in stone. It ranks right up there with in-grown toe nails for sheer evasion and longevity. 3

But there's another university policy that has no merit as a policy and no place in a university. Mandatory Attendance Policy: wherein faculty members attempt the high school hall monitor–combination–college instructor maneuver. It's a difficult trick to justify as professors place the attendance percentage of their choice above a student's proven abilities on graded material. 4

Profs rationalize out a lot of arguments to support the policy. Participation is a popular one. I had a professor whose methods for lowering grades so irritated me I used to skip on purpose. He said, "Classroom participation is a very important part of this introductory course. Obviously, if you are not present, you cannot be participating." 5

Equally obvious, though not stated by the prof, is the fact that one can be perpetually present but participate as little as one who is absent. So who's the better student—the one who makes a meaningless appearance, or the one who is busy with something else? And who gets the points docked? 6

The rest of his policy was characteristically vague, mentioning that 7

absences "could" result in a lower grade. Constant ambiguity is the second big problem with formal policies. It's tough for teachers to figure out just how much to let attendance affect grade point. So they doubletalk.

According to the UWSP catalog, faculty are to provide "clear explanation" of attendance policy. Right. Based on the language actually used, ninety-five percent of UWSP faculty are functionally incapable of uttering a single binding statement. In an effort to offend no one while retaining all power of action, profs write things like (these are actual policies): "I trust students to make their own judgments and choices about coming, or not coming to class." But then continues: "Habitual and excessive absence is grounds for failure." What happened to trust? What good are the choices? 8

Or this: "More than three absences may negatively affect your grade." Then again, they may not. Who knows? And this one: "I consider every one of you in here to be mature adults. However, I reserve the right to alter grades based on attendance." 9

You reserve the right? By virtue of your saying so? Is that like calling the front seat? 10

Another argument that profs cling to goes something like, "Future employers, by God, aren't going to put up with absenteeism." Well, let's take a reality pill. I think most students can grasp the difference between cutting an occasional class, which they paid for, and cutting at work, when they're the ones on salary. See, college students are capable of bi-level thought control, nowadays. (It's all those computers.) 11

In summary, mandatory attendance should be abolished because: 1

1. It is irrelevant. Roughly the same number of students will either 1

skip or attend, regardless of what a piece of paper says. If the course is worth anything.

2. It is ineffective. It automatically measures neither participation, ability, or gained knowledge. That's what tests are for. Grades are what you end up knowing, not how many times you sat there to figure it out. 14

3. It is insulting. A college student is capable of determining a personal schedule, one that may or may not always meet with faculty wishes. An institution committed to the fostering of personal growth cannot operate under rules that patronize or minimize the role an adult should claim for himself. 15

4. It is arbitrary. A prof has no right and no ability to factor in an un- 16

realistic measure of performance. A student should be penalized no more than what the natural consequence of an absence is—the missing of one day's direct delivery of material.

5. It abolishes free choice. By the addition of a factor that cannot be fought. We are not at a university to learn conformity. As adults, we reserve the right to choose as we see fit, even if we choose badly. 17

Finally, I would ask faculty to consider this: We have for some time upheld in this nation the sacred principle of separation of church and state; i.e., You are not God. 18

> Karen Rivedal
> *Editor*

Karen chose a topic that would certainly interest many college students, the audience for whom she saw herself writing. Her thesis is clear: mandatory class attendance should not be required of college students. And her writing is lively enough to hold the attention of many readers. All this is good.

Unfortunately, Karen's argument also has a number of flaws. In paragraph 6 she offers what logicians call "a false dilemma." By asking, "So who's the better student—the one who makes a meaningless appearance, or the one who is busy doing something else?" she has ignored at least two other possibilities. Appearance in class is likely to be meaningful to at least some students, and cutting class may be meaningless if the "something else" occupying a student's attention is a waste of time. The comparison in paragraph 10 between reserving the right to lower grades because of poor attendance and "calling the front seat" is confusing. (In conversation after the initial publication of this essay, Karen explained to me that she was making a comparison between professors who "reserve the right to alter grades" and children who call "I got the front seat" when going out in the family car. I then pointed out that this analogy could easily be used against her. The driver *must* sit in the front seat, and surely whoever is teaching a class is analogous to the driver of a car rather than one of its passengers.) In paragraph 13 Karen claims, "Roughly the same number of students will either skip or attend, regardless of what a piece of paper says," but she offers no evidence to support this claim, which is really no more than guesswork. And since Karen herself admits that many students skip class despite mandatory attendance policies, her claim in paragraph 17 that required attendance "abolishes free choice" does not hold up.

But these lapses in logic aside, the major problem with this argument is that Karen misjudged her audience. She forgot that professors, as well as

students, read the school newspaper. Since students cannot change the policies of their professors, but professors themselves can usually do so, she has
overlooked the very audience that she most needs to reach. Moreover, not
only has she failed to include professors within her audience, but she has
actually gone so far as to insult them. Someone who is told that he or she is
"functionally incapable of uttering a single binding statement" is unlikely to
feel motivated to change. It's only in the very last paragraph of this essay
that Karen specifically addresses the faculty, and this proves to be simply
the occasion for a final insult. Although there may be professors who take
themselves too seriously, are there really that many who believe that they
are divine?

It's a shame that it's so easy to poke holes in this argument, because
Karen deserves credit for boldly calling attention to policies that may indeed
be wrong. Recognizing that her original argument was flawed, but still believing strongly that mandatory class attendance is inappropriate for college
students, Karen decided to rewrite her essay. Here is her revision.

Absent at What Price?
Karen Rivedal

This _is_ college, right? A place to break old ties,   1
solve problems, and make decisions? Higher education is,
I thought, the pursuit of knowledge in a way that's a
step beyond the paternal hand-holding of high school.
It's the act of learning performed in a more dynamic
atmosphere, rich with individual freedom, discourse,
and debate.

Because sometimes I can't tell. Some university   2
traditions cloud the full intent of higher education.
Take mandatory attendance policies: wherein faculty members attempt the high school hall monitor-college instructor maneuver. It's a difficult trick to justify as
professors place the attendance percentage of their
choice above a student's proven abilities on graded material.

This isn't to say that the idea of attendance it-   3
self is unsound. Clearly, personal interaction between
teacher and students is preferable to textbook teaching
alone. It's the mandatory attendance policy, within an
academic community committed to the higher education of
adults, that worries me.

Professors, however, offer several arguments to   4
support the practice. Participation is a popular one. I

had a professor whose methods for lowering grades so irritated me that I used to skip out of spite. He said,
"Classroom participation is a very important part of
this introductory course. Obviously, if you are not present, you cannot be participating."

Equally obvious, though, is the fact that one can   5
be perpetually present, but participate as little as one
who is absent. Participation lacks an adequate definition. There's no way of knowing, on the face of it,
if a silent student is necessarily a learning student.
Similarly, an instructor has no way of knowing for
what purpose or advantage a student may miss a class,
and therefore no ability to determine its relative
validity.

As a learning indicator, then, mandatory attendance   6
policy is flawed. It automatically measures neither participation, ability, or gained knowledge. That's what
tests are for. A final grade should reflect what a student ends up knowing, rather than the artificial consequences of demerit points.

Some faculty recognize the shortcomings of a no-   7
exceptions mandatory attendance policy and respond with
partial policies. Constant ambiguity is characteristic
of this approach and troublesome for the student who
wants to know just where he or she stands. It's tough
for teachers to figure out just how much to let attendance affect grade point. So they doubletalk.

This, for example, is taken from an actual policy: 8
"I trust students to make their own judgments and
choices about coming, or not coming, to class." It then
continues: "Habitual and excessive absence is grounds
for failure." What happened to trust? What good are
the choices?

Or this: "More than three absences may negatively   9
affect your grade." Then again, they may not. Who knows?
And this one: "I consider every one of you in here to be
mature adults. However, I reserve the right to alter
grades based on attendance."

This seems to say, what you can prove you have   10
learned from this class takes a back seat to how much I
think you should know based on your attendance. What the
teacher says goes—just like in high school.

Professors who set up attendance policies like   11
these believe, with good reason, that they are helping

students to learn by ensuring their attendance. But the securing of this end by requirement eliminates an important element of learning. Removing the freedom to make the decision is removing the need to think. An institution committed to the fostering of personal growth cannot operate under rules that patronize or minimize the role an adult should claim for himself.

A grading policy that relies on the student's proven abilities certainly takes the guesswork out of grade assigning for teachers. This take-no-prisoners method, however, also demands a high, some say unfairly high, level of personal student maturity. Younger students especially may need, they say, the extra structuring that a policy provides.   12

But forfeiting an attendance policy doesn't mean that a teacher has to resign his humanity, too. Teachers who care to can still take five minutes to warn an often absent student about the possible consequences, or let the first test score tell the story. As much as dedicated teachers want students to learn, the activity is still a personal one. Students must want to.   13

A "real-world" argument that professors often use goes something like, "Future employers aren't going to put up with absenteeism, so get used to it now." Well, let's take a reality pill. I think most students can differentiate between cutting an occasional class, which they paid for, and missing at work, when they're the ones on salary.   14

Students who intelligently protest an institution's policies, such as mandatory attendance requirements, are proof-in-action that college is working. These students are thinking, and learning to think and question is the underlying goal of all education. College is more than its rules, more than memorized facts. Rightly, college is knowledge, the testing of limits. To be valid, learning must include choice and the freedom to make mistakes. To rely on mandatory attendance for learning is to subvert the fullest aims of that education.   15

In revising her essay, Karen has retained both her thesis and her own distinctive voice. Such phrases as "the high school hall monitor–college instructor maneuver," the "take-no-prisoners method," and "let's take a reality pill" are still recognizably her own. But her argument is now more compelling. In addition to eliminating the fallacies that marred her original version, Karen included new material that strengthens her case. Paragraph 3 offers a much needed clarification, reassuring readers that an argument against a mandatory attendance policy is not the same as an argument against attending class. Paragraph 7 begins with a fairly sympathetic reference to professors, and paragraph 11 opens with a clear attempt to anticipate opposition. Paragraph 12 includes another attempt to anticipate opposition, and paragraph 13, with its reference to "dedicated teachers," is much more likely to appeal to the professors in Karen's audience than anything in the original version did. Finally, the conclusion of this essay is now much improved, and it successfully links the question of mandatory attendance policies with the purpose of higher education as defined in the opening paragraph.

DEFINING YOUR TERMS

If you want your arguments to be convincing, they must be understood by your audience. To make sure that your ideas are understandable, you must be careful to use words clearly. It is especially important to make sure that any terms essential to your argument are clear. Unfortunately, many writers of argument fail to define the words they use. It is not unusual, for example, to find a writer advocating gun control without defining exactly what he or she means by "gun control." Many arguments use words such as "censorship," "society," "legitimate," and "moral" so loosely that it is impossible to decide exactly what the writer means. When this happens, the entire argument can break down.

You should not feel that you need to define every word you use, but you certainly should define any important word your audience might misunderstand. When doing so, always try to avoid defining the word by using another term that is equally complex. For example, if you are opposed to the sale of pornography, you should be prepared to define what you mean by "pornography." It would not be especially helpful to tell your audience that pornography is "printed or visual material that is obscene" since this only raises the question: What is "obscene"? In an important ruling, the Supreme Court defined "obscene" as material that "the average person, applying community standards, would find . . . as a whole, appeals to the prurient interest," but even if you happened to have this definition at hand, you should ask yourself if "the average person" understands what "prurient" means—not to mention what the Court may have meant by "community standards." Unless you define your terms carefully, avoiding unnecessarily abstract language, you can end up writing an endless chain of definitions that require further explanation.

The easiest way to define a term is to consult a dictionary. However, some dictionaries are much better than others. For daily use, most writers usually refer to a good desk dictionary such as *The American Heritage Dictionary, The Random House Dictionary,* or *Webster's New Collegiate Dictionary.* A good general dictionary of this sort may provide you with an adequate working definition. But you may also want to consider consulting the multi-volume *Oxford English Dictionary*, which is available in most college libraries and is especially useful in showing how the usage of a word has changed over the years. Your audience might also appreciate the detailed information that specialized dictionaries in various subject areas can provide. Many such dictionaries are likely to be available in your college library. For example, if you are working on a paper in English literature, you might consult *A Concise Dictionary of Literary Terms* or *The Princeton Handbook of Poetic Terms*. For a paper in psychology you might turn to *The Encyclopedic Dictionary of Psychology,* or for a paper on a musical topic, *The New Grove's Dictionary of Music and Musicians.* There are also dictionaries for medical, legal, philosophical, and theological terms as well as for each of the natural sciences. When using specialized dictionaries, you will often find valuable information, but remember that the definition which appears in your paper should not be more difficult than the word or phrase you originally set out to define.

Instead of relying exclusively upon dictionaries, it is often best to define a term or phrase in words of your own. In doing so, you can choose among several strategies:

- You can give synonyms.
- You can compare the term with other words with which it is likely to be confused and show how your term differs.
- You can define a word by showing what it is *not*.
- You can provide examples.

Writers frequently use several of these strategies to create a single definition, and an entire essay could be devoted to writing such a definition. Here is an example written by a student.

Homicide

Geoff Rulland

You sit back in your lazy-boy, cold soda in hand,   1
grab the remote control and begin to flip through the
channels in search of something interesting to watch.
Something on the channel nine news catches your ear. You
listen intently as the newscaster informs you that a man
from a nearby town is being charged with homicide. A lot
of people would now sit back and continue the channel
scan thinking that the man was a murderer. Would that be
a safe assumption?

When someone is charged with homicide it doesn't   2
necessarily mean he or she is a murderer. Homicide is
classified in court as either "justifiable," "excusable," or "felonious." Murder, which falls into the class
of felonious homicide, is "the unlawful killing of a human being with malice aforethought," according to the
American Heritage Dictionary. This means that murder is
always wrong, but specifying that murder is an "unlawful
killing" implies that killing a human being is not always unlawful. A justifiable homicide would be a killing
committed intentionally without any evil design or under
the circumstance of necessity. For example, when a police officer is trying to catch a dangerous felon, using
a gun to wound and possibly kill could be justifiable.
An excusable homicide would be the killing of a human
being accidentally or in self-defense, such as in the
case of a burglar entering your home. Killing him may be
the only thing that will save you or your family. Manslaughter is another term often associated with killings
that aren't murders. The name gives the impression that
someone was brutally slain. Actually it is the accidental killing of one person by another, and it may have
been quite mild.

Black's Law Dictionary defines homicide as "the   3
killing of any human creature or the killing of one human being by the act, procurement, or omission of another." In other words, it's the killing of one person
by another in any manner. It doesn't matter if you hit a
person accidentally with your car, or if you purposely
shot someone, or if you hired a professional killer.
Black's then goes on to state the definition as "the act
of a human being in taking away the life of another human being." The Webster's New World Dictionary shortens
all of that down to "any killing of one human being by
another." The key word in this definition is "any." Webster's doesn't say how the killing must be done; it just
says that a person is killed.

Two words from the Latin language are the main com-   4
position of homicide. The first one is homo meaning man
and the other is caedere, which ties it to killing,
meaning to cut or kill. Homicida, meaning murderer, was
the form that was made from those two words which was

later changed in Latin to <u>homicidium</u>. After going
through the Old French language, the word then made its
way into English and into its present form, homicide.

Homicide is not necessarily a crime. Even though   5
all homicides result in the loss of life, sometimes committing homicide is a person's only choice. Homicide
shouldn't be immediately judged as murder or something
all out wrong. The word is "neutral" according to
<u>Black's</u> <u>Law</u> <u>Dictionary</u>. It merely states the act of
killing and pronounces no judgment on its moral or
legal quality.

With this in mind, the next time you hear of a ho-   6
micide on t.v. you should keep your mind open and neutral. Don't immediately form the opinion that it was a
murder, because a lot of the times you may be wrong. The
word merely states that a person was killed, not necessarily murdered.

In defining *homicide*, Geoff uses three of the strategies listed on page 12:
He provides examples of homicide; he compares homicide to such terms as
murder and *manslaughter*; and, by contrasting homicide with murder, he clar-
ifies what homicide is not. In addition to consulting two good desk dictionaries, *The American Heritage Dictionary* and *Webster's New World Dictionary*,
Geoff also took the trouble to consult a legal dictionary. *Black's Law Dictionary* confirmed his sense that homicide is a much broader term than murder,
and this became the central idea of his essay. Note also that, in paragraph 4,
Geoff reports the origin of the term. Any good dictionary will provide you
with some information of this sort, but you must be alert for it. A brief
etymology (or derivation) usually appears in italics at either the beginning or
end of dictionary definitions, and this information can often be helpful when
you are trying to understand a complex term. In *Webster's New World Dictionary,* for example, the definition of *homicide* begins:

[ME.; OFr.; LL. *homicidium,* manslaughter, murder < L. *homicida,* murderer <
homo, a man + *caedere,* to cut, kill]

Note that the little arrows establish the sequence of the word's history. In
this case, they are pointing away from Latin, not towards it, indicating the
Latin origin. (Arrows pointing to the right would indicate that the earliest
term came first, with others appearing in chronological order.) A key to
abbreviations used in a dictionary can be found by consulting its table of
contents. When you do so, you will probably find that your dictionary contains more information than you had realized.

Before leaving this essay, you might also note that it reveals a good
sense of audience. Writing for a class of students in freshman English, Geoff

recognized that many of his fellow students might find definition to be dry reading. To capture their attention, he begins with an imaginary anecdote addressed, in the second person, directly to readers. Compared with the thousands of essays that have begun "According to *Webster's* . . ." this introduction (with which the conclusion is subsequently linked) seems original and likely to encourage further reading. But you should not assume that this strategy would be appropriate for any audience or any writing occasion.

Understanding the meaning of *homicide* could be essential in an argument on capital punishment or gun control. When writing an argument, however, you will usually need to define your terms within a paragraph or two. Even if you cannot employ all the strategies that you might use in an extended definition, remember your various options and decide which will be most effective for your purpose within the space available. (For examples of essays that incorporate definition within argument, see pages 230, 377, and 595–96, and 609.)

In addition to achieving clarity, definition helps to control an argument by eliminating misunderstandings that can cause an audience to be inappropriately hostile or to jump to a conclusion that is different from your own. By carefully defining your terms, you limit a discussion to what you want to discuss. This increases the likelihood of your gaining a fair hearing for your views.

ORGANIZING YOUR ARGUMENT

If you have chosen your subject carefully and given sufficient thought to your audience and its concerns (paying particular attention to any objections that could be raised against whatever you wish to advocate), then it should not be difficult to organize an argumentative essay. Considering the various concerns discussed in the previous sections will provide you with what amounts to a rough outline, but you must now consider two additional questions: "Where and how should I begin my argument?" and "How can I most efficiently include in my argument the various counterarguments that I have anticipated and responded to?" The answers to these questions will vary from one essay to another. But while arguments can take many forms, formal arguments usually employ logic, of which there are two widely accepted types: inductive and deductive reasoning.

Reasoning Inductively

When we use *induction,* we are drawing a conclusion based upon specific evidence. Our argument rests upon a foundation of details that we have accumulated for its support. This is the type of reasoning that we use most frequently in daily life. We look at the sky outside our window, check the thermometer, and may even listen to a weather forecast before dressing to face the day. If the sun is shining, the temperature high, and the forecast favorable, we would be making a reasonable conclusion if we decided to dress lightly and leave our umbrellas at home. We haven't *proved* that the day will be warm and pleasant, we have only *concluded* that it will be. This is all we can usually do in an inductive argument: arrive at a conclusion that seems likely to be true. Ultimate and positive proof is usually beyond the writer's reach, and the writer who recognizes this and proceeds accordingly will usually arrive at conclusions that are both moderate and thoughtful. He or she recognizes the possibility of an unanticipated factor undermining even the best of arguments. A lovely morning can yield to a miserable afternoon, and we may be drenched in a downpour as we hurry home on the day that began so pleasantly.

Inductive reasoning is especially important in scientific experimentation. A research scientist may have a theory which she hopes to prove. But to work toward proving this theory, hundreds, thousands, and even tens of thousands of experiments may have to be conducted to eliminate variables and gather enough data to justify a generally applicable conclusion. Well-researched scientific conclusions sometimes reach a point where they seem uncontestable. It's been many years since Congress required the manufacturers of cigarettes to put a warning on every package stating that smoking can be harmful to your health. Since then, additional research has supported the conclusion that smoking can indeed be dangerous, especially to the lungs and the heart. That "smoking can be harmful to your health" now seems to have entered the realm of established fact. But biologists, chemists, physicists, and physicians are usually aware that the history of science, and the history of medicine in particular, is an argumentative history full of debate. Methods and beliefs established over many generations can be overthrown by a new discovery. Within a few years, that "new discovery" can also come under challenge. So the serious researcher goes back to the lab and keeps on working—ever mindful that truth is hard to find.

Induction is also essential in law enforcement. The police are supposed to have evidence against someone before making an arrest. Consider, for example, the way a detective works. A good detective does not arrive at the scene of a crime already certain about what happened. If the crime seems to be part of a pattern, the detective may already have a suspicion about who is responsible. But a good investigator will want to make a careful study of every piece of evidence that can be gathered. A room may be dusted for fingerprints, a murder victim photographed as found, and if the body is lying on the floor, a chalk outline may be drawn around it for future study. Every item within the room will be catalogued. Neighbors, relatives, employers, or employees will be questioned. The best detective is usually the detective with the best eye for detail, and the greatest determination to keep searching for the details that will be strong enough to bring a case to court. Similarly, a first-rate detective will also be honest enough never to overlook a fact that does not fit in with the rest of the evidence. The significance of every loose end must be examined to avoid the possibility of an unfair arrest and prosecution.

In making an inductive argument, you will reach a point at which you decide that you have offered enough evidence to support the thesis of your essay. When you are writing a college paper, you will probably decide that you have reached this point sooner than a scientist or a detective might. But whether you are writing a short essay or conducting an investigation, the process is essentially the same. When you stop citing evidence and move on to your conclusion, you have made what is known as an *inductive leap*. In an inductive essay, you must always offer interpretation or analysis of the evidence you have introduced; there will always be at least a slight gap between your evidence and your conclusion. It is over this gap that the writer must leap; the trick is to do it agilely. Good writers know that their evidence must be in proportion to their conclusion: The bolder your conclusion, the more evidence you will need to back it up. Remember the old adage about "jumping to conclusions," and realize that you'll need the momentum of a running start to make more than a moderate leap at any one time.

If you listen closely to the conversation of the people around you, the chances are good that you'll hear examples of faulty inductive reasoning. When someone says, "I don't like Chinese food," and reveals, under questioning, that his only experience with Chinese food was something called "hamburger chow mein" in a high school cafeteria, we cannot take the opinion seriously. A sweeping conclusion has been drawn from flimsy evidence. People who claim to know "all about" complex subjects often reveal that they actually know very little. Only a sexist claims to know all about men and women, and only a racist is foolish enough to generalize about the various racial groups that make up our society. Good writers are careful not to overgeneralize.

When you begin an inductive essay, you might cite a particular observation that strikes you as especially important. You might even begin with a short anecdote. A well-structured inductive essay would then gradually expand as the evidence accumulates, so that the conclusion is supported by numerous details. Here is an example of an inductive essay written by a student.

In Defense of Hunting
David Wagner

I killed my first buck when I was fourteen. I'd   1
gone deer hunting with my father and two of my uncles. I
was cold and wet and anxious to get home, but I knew
what I had to do when I sighted the eight-point buck.
Taking careful aim, I fired at his chest, killing him
quickly with a single shot.

I don't want to romanticize this experience, turn-   2
ing it into a noble rite of passage. I did feel that I

had proved myself somehow. It was important for me to
win my father's respect, and I welcomed the admiration I
saw in his eyes. But I've been hunting regularly for
many years now, and earning the approval of others no
longer seems very important to me. I'd prefer to emphasize the facts about hunting, facts that must be acknowledged even by people who are opposed to hunting.

It is a fact that hunters help to keep the deer   3
population in balance with the environment. Since so
many of their natural predators have almost died out in
this state, the deer population could quickly grow much
larger than the land can support. Without hunting, thousands of deer would die slowly of starvation in the
leafless winter woods. This may sound like a self-
serving argument (like the words of a parent who beats a
child and insists, "This hurts me more than it does you;
I'm only doing it for your own good"). But it is a fact
that cannot be denied.

It is also a fact that hunters provide a valuable   4
source of revenue for the state. The registration and
licensing fees we pay are used by the Department of Natural Resources to reforest barren land, preserve wetlands, and protect endangered species. Also there are
many counties in this state that depend upon the money
that hunters spend on food, gas, and lodging. "Tourism"
is our third largest industry, and all of this money
isn't being spent at luxurious lakeside resorts. Opponents of hunting should realize that hunting is the most
active in some of our poorest, rural counties--and
realize what hunting means to the people who live in
these areas.

It is also a fact that there are hundreds of men   5
and women for whom hunting is an economic necessity and
not a sport. Properly preserved, the meat that comes
from a deer can help a family survive a long winter.
There probably are hunters who think of hunting as a
recreation. But all the hunters I know--and I know at
least twenty--dress their own deer and use every pound
of the venison they salt, smoke, or freeze. There may be
a lot of people who don't have to worry about spending
$3.00 a pound for steak, but I'm not one of them. My
family needs the meat we earn by hunting.

I have to admit that there are hunters who act irresponsibly by trespassing where they are not wanted and, much worse, by abandoning animals that they have wounded. But there are many different kinds of irresponsibility. Look around and you will see many irresponsible drivers, but we don't respond to them by banning driving altogether. An irresponsible minority is no reason to attack a responsible majority.

6

I've listened to many arguments against hunting, and it seems to me that what really bothers most of the people who are opposed to hunting is the idea that hunters <u>enjoy</u> killing. I can't speak for all hunters, but I can speak for myself and the many hunters I personally know. I myself have never found pleasure in killing a deer. I think that deer are beautiful and incredibly graceful, especially when in movement. I don't "enjoy" putting an end to a beautiful animal's life. If I find any pleasure in the act of hunting, it comes from the knowledge that I am trying to be at least partially self-sufficient. I don't expect other people to do all my dirty work for me, and give me my meat neatly butchered and conveniently wrapped in plastic. I take responsibility for what I eat.

7

Lumping all hunters together as insensitive beer-drinking thugs is an example of the mindless stereotyping that logic should teach us to avoid. The men and women who hunt are no worse than anyone else. And more often than not, the hunting we do is both honorable and important.

8

David has drawn upon his own experience to make an articulate defense of hunting. He begins with an anecdote that helps to establish that he knows something about the subject he has chosen to write about. The first sentence in the second paragraph helps to deflect any skepticism his audience may feel at this early stage in his argument, and the last sentence in this paragraph serves as a transition into the facts that will be emphasized in the next three paragraphs. In the third paragraph, David introduces the evidence that should most impress his audience, if we assume that his audience is unhappy about the idea of killing animals. In paragraphs 4 and 5, he defends hunting on economic grounds. He offers a concession in paragraph 5 ("There probably are hunters who think of hunting as a recreation") and another concession in paragraph 6 ("I have to admit that there are hunters who act irresponsibly"). But after each of these concessions he manages to return smoothly to his own thesis. In paragraph 7 he anticipates an argument frequently made by people who oppose hunting and offers a counterargument that puts his opponents on the defensive. The concluding paragraph may be a little anticlimatic, but within the limitations of a short essay, David has made a fairly strong argument.

Reasoning Deductively

Sometimes it is best to rest an argument on a fundamental truth, value, or right rather than on specific pieces of evidence. You should try to be specific within the course of such an essay, giving examples to support your case. But in deductive reasoning, evidence is of secondary importance. Your first concern is to define a commonly accepted value or belief that will prepare the way for the argument you want to make.

The Declaration of Independence, written by Thomas Jefferson (pp. 528–32), is a classic example of deductive reasoning. Although Jefferson cited numerous grievances, he rested his argument on the belief that "all men are created equal" and that they have "certain unalienable Rights" which King George III had violated. This was a revolutionary idea in the eighteenth century, and even today there are many people who question it. But if we accept the idea that "all men are created equal" and have an inherent right to "Life, Liberty, and the pursuit of Happiness," then certain conclusions follow.

The right, value, or belief from which we wish to deduce our argument is called our *premise*. Perhaps you have already had the experience, in the middle of an argument, of someone saying to you, "What's your premise?" If you are inexperienced in argumentation, a question of this sort may embarrass you and cause your argument to break down—which is probably what your opponent had hoped. But whether we recognize it or not, we almost always have a premise lurking somewhere in the back of our minds. Deduction is most effective when we think about values we have automatically assumed and build our arguments upon them.

A good premise satisfies two requirements. In the first place, it is general enough that your audience is likely to accept it, thus establishing a common ground between you and the audience you hope to persuade. On the other hand, the premise must still be specific enough so that it prepares the way for the argument that will follow. It usually takes much careful thought to frame a good premise. Relatively few people have their values always at their fingertips. We usually know what we want or what our conclusion is going to be—but it takes time to realize the fundamental beliefs that we have automatically assumed. For this is really what a premise amounts to: the underlying assumption that must be agreed upon before the argument can begin to move along.

Because it is difficult to formulate an effective premise, it is often useful to work backwards when you are outlining a deductive argument. You should know what conclusion you expect to reach. Write it down, and assign to it number 3. Now ask yourself why you believe statement 3. This should prompt a number of reasons which you can group together as statement number 2.

And now that you can look both at your conclusion and at the immediate reasons that seem to justify it, ask yourself if there's anything you've left out—something basic that you skipped over, assuming that everyone would agree with that already. When you can think back successfully to what this assumption is, knowing that it will vary from argument to argument, you have your premise, at least in rough draft form.

This may be difficult to grasp in the abstract, so let us consider an outline for a sample argument. Suppose that the forests in your state are slowly dying because of the pollution known as acid rain—one of the effects of burning fossil fuel, especially coal. Coal is being burned by numerous industries not only in your own state, but in neighboring states as well. You hadn't even realized that there was a problem with acid rain until last summer when fishing was prohibited in your favorite lake. You are very upset about this and declare, "Something ought to be done!" But as you begin to think about the problem, you recognize that you'll have to overcome at least two obstacles in deciding what that something should be. Only two years ago, you participated in a demonstration against nuclear power, and you'd also hate to see the United States become more dependent upon foreign oil. So if you attack the process of burning coal for energy, you'll have to be prepared to recommend an acceptable alternative. The other question you must answer is "Who's responsible for a problem that seems to be springing from many places in many states?" Moreover, if you do decide to argue for a radical reduction in coal consumption, you'll have to be prepared to anticipate the opposition: "What's this going to do to the coal miners?" someone might well ask. "Will you destroy the livelihood of some of the hardest working men and women in America?"

You realize that you have still another problem. Your assignment is for a 750-word deductive argument, and it's due the day after tomorrow. You feel strongly about the problem of acid rain, but you are not an energy expert. Your primary concern is with the effects of acid rain, which you've witnessed with your own eyes. And while you don't know much about industrial chemistry, you do know that acid rain is caused principally by public utilities burning coal that has a high percentage of sulfur in it. Recognizing that you lack the expertise to make a full scale attack upon coal consumption, you decide that you can at least go so far as to argue on behalf of using low sulfur coal. In doing so, you will be able to reassure your audience that you want to keep coal miners at work, recognize the needs of industry, and do not expect the entire country to go solar by the end of the semester.

Taking out a sheet of paper, you begin to write down your outline in reverse:

3. Public utilities should not burn coal that is high in sulfur content.
2. Burning high sulfur coal causes acid rain, and acid rain is killing American forests, endangering wildlife, and spoiling local fishing.

Before going any farther, you realize that all of your reasons for opposing acid rain cannot be taken with equal degrees of seriousness. As much as you like to fish, recreation does not seem to be in the same league with your more general concern for forests and wildlife. You know that you want to describe the condition of your favorite lake at some point in your essay, because it gave you some firsthand experience with the problem and some vivid descriptive details. But you decide that you'd better not make too much of fishing in order to avoid the risk of sounding as if you care only about your own pleasure.

You now ask yourself what lies behind the "should" in your conclusion. How strong is it? Did you say "should" when you meant "must"? Thinking it over, you realize that you did mean "must," but now you must decide who or what is going to make that "must" happen. You decide that you can't trust industry to make this change on its own because you're asking it to spend more money than it has to. You know that as an individual you don't have the power to bring about the change you believe is necessary, but you also know that individuals become powerful when they band together. Individuals band together in various ways, but the most important— in terms of power—is probably the governments we elect to represent us. You should be careful with a term like "government" and avoid such statements as "The government ought to do something about this." Not only is the "something" hopelessly vague, but we don't know what kind of government is in question. Most of us are subject to government on at least three levels: municipal, state, and federal. Coming back to your topic, you decide to argue for *federal* legislation, since acid rain is being generated in several different states—and then carried by air to still others.

You should now be ready to formulate your premise. Since your conclusion is going to demand federal regulation, you need, at the very beginning of your argument, to establish the principle that supports this conclusion. You realize that the federal government cannot solve all problems; you therefore need to define the nature of the government's responsibility so that it will be clear that you are appealing legitimately to the right authority. Legally, the federal government has broad powers to regulate interstate commerce, and this may be useful to you since most of the industries burning coal ship or receive goods across state lines. More specifically, ever since the creation of Yellowstone National Park in 1872, the U.S. government has undertaken a growing responsibility for protecting the environment. Acid rain is clearly an environmental issue, so you would not be demanding anything new, in terms of governmental responsibilities, if you appealed to the type of thinking that led to the creation of a national park system in 1916 and of the Environmental Protection Agency in 1970.

You know, however, that there are many people who distrust the growth of big government, and you do not want to alienate anyone by appealing to Washington too early in the essay. A premise can be a single sentence, a full paragraph, or more—depending on the length and complexity of the argument. Since its function is to establish a widely accepted value which even your opponents should be able to share, it would probably be wise to open this particular argument with a fairly general statement. Something like: "We all have a joint responsibility to protect the environment in which we live and preserve the balance of nature upon which our lives ultimately depend." As a thesis statement, this obviously needs to be developed in the paragraph that follows. In the second paragraph you might cite some popular examples of joint action to preserve the environment, pointing out, for example, that most people are relieved to see a forest fire brought under control or an oil slick cleaned up before it engulfs half the Pacific coastline. Once you have cited examples of this sort, you could then remind your audience of the role of state and federal government in coping with such emergencies, and emphasize that many problems are too large for states to handle. By this stage in your essay, you should be able to narrow your focus to acid rain, secure in the knowledge that you have laid the foundation for a logical argument. *If* the U.S. government has a responsibility to help protect the environment, and *if* acid rain is a serious threat to the environment of several states, then it follows logically that the federal government should act to bring this problem under control. A brief outline of your argument would look something like this:

1. The federal government has the responsibility to protect the quality of American air, water, soil, and so on—what is commonly called "the environment."
2. Acid rain, which is caused principally by burning high sulfur coal, is slowly killing American forests, endangering wildlife, and polluting lakes, rivers, and streams.
3. Therefore, the federal government should restrict the use of high sulfur coal.

Once again, this is only an *outline*. An essay that made this argument, explaining the problem in detail, anticipating the opposition, and providing meaningful concessions before reaching a clear and firm conclusion, would amount to at least several pages.

By outlining your argument in this way, you have followed the pattern of what is called a *syllogism*, a three–part argument in which the conclusion rests upon two premises, the first of which is called "the major premise" because it is the point from which we begin to work to a specific conclusion. Here, for example, is a simple example of a syllogism:

MAJOR PREMISE: All people have hearts.
MINOR PREMISE: John is a person.
CONCLUSION: Therefore, John has a heart.

If the major and minor premises are both true, then the conclusion we have reached should be true. Note that the minor premise and the major premise share a term in common. In an argumentative essay, the "minor premise" would usually involve a specific case that relates to the more general statement with which the essay began.

A syllogism such as the one just cited may seem very simple. And it can be simple—if you're thinking clearly. On the other hand, it's even easier to write a syllogism (or an essay) that breaks down because of faulty reasoning. Consider the following example:

MAJOR PREMISE: All women like to cook.
MINOR PREMISE: Elizabeth is a woman.
CONCLUSION: Therefore, Elizabeth likes to cook.

Technically, the form here is *valid*. The two premises have a term in common, and if we accept both the major and minor premises, then we will have to accept the conclusion. But someone who thinks along these lines may be in for a surprise, especially if he has married Elizabeth confidently expecting her to cook his favorite dishes every night just as his mother used to do. Elizabeth may *hate* to cook, preferring to go out bowling at night or read the latest issue of the *Journal of Organic Chemistry*. You should realize, then, that while a syllogism may be valid in terms of its organization, it can also be *untrue*, because it rests upon a premise that can be easily disputed. Always remember that your major premise should inspire widespread agreement. Someone who launches an argument with the generalization that "all women like to cook," is likely to find he's lost at least half of his audience before he even makes it to his second sentence. Some generalizations make sense and some do not. Don't make the mistake of confusing generally accepted truths with privately held opinions. You may argue effectively on behalf of your opinions, but you cannot expect your audience to accept an easily debatable opinion as the foundation for an argument on behalf of yet another opinion. You may have many important things to say, but nobody is going to read them if alienated by your major premise.

You should also realize that there are many arguments in which a premise may be implied but not stated. You might have a conversation like this:

"I hear you and Elizabeth are getting married."
"Yes, that's true."
"Well now that you've got a woman to cook for you, maybe you could invite me over for dinner sometime."
"Why do you think that Elizabeth will be doing the cooking?"
"Because she is a woman."

The first speaker has made a number of possible assumptions. He may believe that all women like to cook, or perhaps he believes that all women are required to cook whether they like it or not. If the second speaker had the patience to continue this conversation, he would probably be able to discover the first speaker's premise. A syllogism that consists of only two parts is called an *enthymeme*. The part of the syllogism that has been omitted is usually the major premise, although it is occasionally the conclusion. Enthymemes usually result when a speaker or writer decides that it is unnecessary to state a point because it is obvious. Of course, what is obvious to someone trying to convince us with an enthymeme is not necessarily obvious to those of us who are trying to understand it. Although an enthymeme might reflect sound reasoning, the unstated part of the syllogism may reveal a flaw in the argument. When you encounter an enthymeme in your reading, you will often benefit from trying to reconstruct it as a full syllogism. Ask yourself what the writer has assumed, and then ask yourself if you agree with that assumption. One sign of a faulty deductive argument is that a questionable point has been assumed to be universally true, and we may need to discover this point before we can decide that the argument is either invalid or untrue.

Deductive reasoning, which begins with a generalization and works to a conclusion that follows from this generalization, can be thought of as the opposite of *inductive reasoning*, which begins with specific observations and ends with a conclusion that goes beyond any of the observations that led up to it. So that you can see what a deductive essay might look like, here is a short essay written by a student.

Preparation for Real Life
Kerstin LaPorte

In order for all children to reach their fullest   1
potential as adults, it is imperative that they be prepared for careers that will help them be productive members of society. Through the school system, taxpayers
are responsible for providing the educational opportunities for the development of minds, so that when these
students become adults, they too will be able to take
their turn for supporting the education of a future generation. But many property owners have grown increasingly angry over the continual raises in their taxes,
and this hostility is being expressed towards the school
system that these overtaxed people have to support.

Cuts in spending are made, but these cuts are not   2
reflected in the sports department. The costs of maintaining sports programs are immense. The money that is
taken out of the average annual school budget for the
equipment for training players, providing uniforms, and
paying coaches is more than most taxpayers realize. I
too am a taxpayer, whose taxes go up each year. It is my
view that this money would be better spent on more
up-to-date textbooks, lab equipment in the science department that is not outdated, the newest computer technology, adequate tools and machinery for the wood and
metal shops, and libraries that are stocked with the
necessary books and magazines to complement all academic

subjects. These investments will help a much larger percentage of the school population and develop skills in accord with public needs.

It would be a terrible loss to many people who gain   3
a great deal of satisfaction out of participating in sports activities if these activities were to be completely phased out. Therefore I advocate that sports programs for adolescents be community sponsored. Clubs, sponsored by participating members, local merchants, and private individuals, combined with fund raising, would provide all the sports activities that have no place in an academic field.

Proponents of school-sponsored sports would argue   4
that the children of lower income families would not be able to participate in a community club due to any costs this would incur. I firmly believe that if a student from a poor family has a special talent, clubs would probably vie for his membership, helping him or her with any financial deficiencies. Once the potential for a finely tuned athlete is seen, one who can help win the game or competition for the club, funding will be available for his or her recruitment.

The importance of physical fitness is not to be un-   5
derstated. Students need to be physically active in order to maintain mental and physical stamina. Therefore, a scaled-down physical education department must remain within the schools. If done for at least 30 minutes 3–5 times a week, aerobic exercise such as running, walking, and Jazzercize raises the heart rate sufficiently to promote physical fitness. It is not necessary to build pools, tennis courts, football stadiums, baseball parks, and basketball courts. Neither have I ever been able to justify the purchasing of cross-country skis, archery, weight lifting, and gymnastic equipment with academic funding. The maintenance of all the sport grounds and equipment involved, plus the replacement of broken or outdated equipment is also an added annual expense to the community.

Just as students who have similar interests form   6
clubs, which meet outside of school hours, students interested in further physical fitness can organize biking, skiing, or running clubs. This would involve the use of their own equipment, occur on their own time, and

fill the void left if sports training is taken out of the school curriculum.

If there were to be a major change in the approach to our sports programs, the existing buildings, equipment, and outdoor facilities in and around the schools must not be wasted. The clubs could lease those premises, and any member would be eligible to utilize the facilities during club hours. This would include student members, who could go and work out during their free hours if they wanted. In this manner, the costs would not detract from the academic necessities, and the facilities already built would not go to waste.   7

Opponents to my proposal might ask, what about funding for such extra-curricular activities as band, art, drama, and choir? There too, a very basic introduction to these fields is reasonable, just as scaled-down physical education would suffice. If a child shows promise of being a gifted musician, artist, actor, or singer, he or she can go on to obtain private instruction.   8

What about some of the academic subjects that seem unrelated to the job market, such as history, sociology, and psychology? Successful interaction between people depends on some knowledge of human nature, and these subjects are only on an introductory basis. As far as history goes, I would be scared to death to have a generation of voters go to the polls with no knowledge of the workings of government, ours or anyone else's, and unaware of the mistakes of the past, try to make wise decisions for the future.   9

As a future teacher, I have been reminded over and over again that it is imperative that I be a good role model for my students. Coaches of competitive sports are role models also. They promote healthy life styles by discouraging students from smoking and drinking. They do the best they can to make their students' experiences enjoyable by providing proper motivation and support. This need not end with the removal of the sports programs from the school. These same people can either stay in the teaching field in another capacity or work for the community clubs.   10

Yes, it is true that active daily training builds a particular responsibility and perseverance that will be   11

needed in "real life." However, this "daily training"
can be accomplished within the academic field also, and
will serve to engender the school spirit that pro sports
people feel is necessary in the educational environment.
Forensics, math competitions, essay contests, and history debates all contribute to build public speaking
ability, alleviate math anxiety, promote an increased
ability for self-expression in writing, which will aid
students' ability to synthesize and analyze information
and formulate informed opinions.

Extensive sports training through the school system   12
prepares a very small percentage of the school population for a successful future, as very few individuals
are lucky enough to go on to pro careers. Let's take the
money that goes for sports and use it to support an up-
to-date, academic education that will prepare all children for real life.

This essay has many strengths. The topic was well chosen, not only
because many people are interested in school sports, but also because Kerstin's view of sports is likely to inspire controversy—hence the need for her
argument. As already noted, good writers do not belabor the obvious. Writing this essay for an audience of students (with whom she shared an earlier
draft for peer review), Kerstin realized that many of her classmates believed
in the importance of school sports and that their convictions on this issue
could keep them from listening to what she had to say. She therefore adopted
a deductive strategy in order to establish some common ground with her
opponents before arguing that school systems should not fund sports. Her
opening paragraph establishes the premise upon which her argument is based:
the function of education is to help children "reach their fullest potential as
adults" and prepare them to become "productive members of society." Her
minor premise appears in paragraph 12: "Extensive sports training through
the school system prepares a very small percentage of the school population
for a successful future . . . " If we accept both the major and minor premise, then we should be prepared to accept the conclusion: "Let's take the
money that goes for sports and use it to support an up-to-date, academic
education that will prepare all children for real life."

As you can see from this example, deduction allows a writer the chance
to prepare the way for a controversial argument by strategically opening with
a key point that draws an audience closer, without immediately revealing
what exactly is afoot. With a genuinely controversial opinion, one must always
face the risk of being shouted down—especially with a potentially hostile
audience. Deductive reasoning increases the chance of gaining a fair hearing.

Of course, a writer who uses deduction should still remember to address those concerns most likely to be raised by opponents. In "Preparation

for Real Life," Kerstin begins paragraphs 4, 8, and 9 by anticipating opposition and then responding to it. She also makes a number of important concessions. In her third paragraph she concedes, "It would be a terrible loss to many people who gain a great deal of satisfaction out of participating in sports activities if these activities were to be completely phased out." The fifth paragraph begins by recognizing, "The importance of physical fitness is not to be understated." Paragraph 11 also begins with a concession: "Yes, it is true that active daily training builds a particular responsibility and perseverance that will be needed in 'real life'." And, in paragraph 10, Kerstin admits that coaches can be good role models. These are all concessions that should appeal to men and women who value sports. But Kerstin does not simply let these concessions sit on the page. In each case, she immediately goes on to show how the concession does not undermine her own argument. Whatever your own views on this topic may be, you should realize that concessions need not weaken an argument. On the contrary, they can strengthen an argument by making it more complex.

The moment at which writers choose to anticipate opposition will usually vary; it depends upon the topic, how much the author knows about it, and how easily he or she can deal with the principal counterarguments that others might raise. But whether one is writing an inductive or deductive argument, it is usually advisable to recognize and respond to the opposition fairly early in the essay. You will need at least one or two paragraphs to launch your own thesis, but by the time you are about one-third of the way into your essay, you may find it useful to defuse the opposition before it grows any stronger. If you wait until the very end of your essay to acknowledge that there are points of view different from your own, your audience may have already put your essay aside, dismissing it as "one-sided" or "narrow-minded." Also, it is usually a good idea to put the opposition's point of view at the beginning of a paragraph. By doing so, you can devote the rest of that paragraph to your response. It's not enough to recognise the opposition and include some of its arguments in your essay. You are a writer, not a referee, and you must always try to show your audience why it should not be persuaded by the counterarguments you have acknowledged. If you study the organization of "Preparation for Real Life," you will see that the author begins paragraphs 3, 4, 5, 8, and 11 with sentences that acknowledge other sides to the question of public funding for school sports. But in each case, she was able to end these paragraphs with her own argument still moving clearly forward.

One final note: Although it is usually best to establish your premise before your conclusion, writing an essay is not the same as writing a syllogism. In "Preparation for Real Life," the minor premise does not appear until the last paragraph. It could just as easily have appeared earlier (and actually did so in a preliminary draft). Writers benefit from flexibility and the ability to make choices depending upon what they want to say. When you read or write deductive arguments, you will find that relatively few of these arguments proceed according to a fixed formula determining exactly what must happen in any given paragraph.

Reasoning with the Toulmin Model

Although both inductive and deductive reasoning suggest useful strategies for writers of argument, they also have their limitations. Many writers prefer not to be bound by a prefabricated method of organization and regard the syllogism, in particular, as unnecessarily rigid. To make their case, some writers choose to combine inductive and deductive reasoning within a single essay—and other writers can make convincing arguments without the formal use of either induction or deduction.

In an important book first published in 1958, a British philosopher named Stephen Toulmin demonstrated that the standard forms of logic needed to be reconsidered because they did not adequately explain all logical arguments. Emphasizing that logic is concerned with probability more often than certainty, he provided a new vocabulary for the analysis of argument. In Toulmin's model, every argument consists of three elements:

> *claim:* the equivalent of the conclusion or whatever it is a writer or speaker wants to try to prove;
> *data:* the information or evidence a writer or speaker offers in support of the claim; and
> *warrant:* a general statement that establishes a trustworthy relationship between the data and the claim.

Within any argument, the claim and the data will be explicit. The warrant may also be explicit, but it is often merely implied—especially when the arguer believes that the audience will readily agree to it.

To better understand these terms, let us consider an example adapted from one of Toulmin's:

> CLAIM: Raymond is an American citizen.
> DATA: Raymond was born in Puerto Rico.
> WARRANT: Anyone born in Puerto Rico is an American citizen.

These three statements may remind you of the three elements in a deductive argument. If arranged as a syllogism, they might look like this:

> MAJOR PREMISE: Anyone born in Puerto Rico is an American citizen.
> MINOR PREMISE: Raymond was born in Puerto Rico.
> CONCLUSION: Raymond is an American citizen.

The advantage of Toulmin's model becomes apparent when we realize that there is a possibility that Raymond was prematurely born to French parents who were only vacationing in Puerto Rico, and he is now serving in the French army. Or perhaps he was an American citizen but became a naturalized citizen of the Soviet Union after defecting with important U.S. Navy documents. Because the formal logic of a syllogism is designed to lead to a conclusion that is *necessarily* true, Toulmin argued that it is ill-suited for working to a conclusion that is *probably* true. Believing that the importance of the syllogism was overemphasized in the study of logic, Toulmin argued that there was a need for a "working logic" which would be easier to apply in the rhetorical situations in which arguers most often find themselves. He designed his own model so that it can easily incorporate *qualifiers* such as "probably," "presumably," and "generally." Here is a revision of the first example:

CLAIM: Raymond is probably an American citizen.
DATA: Raymond was born in Puerto Rico.
WARRANT: Anyone born in Puerto Rico is entitled to American citi-
            zenship.

You should note that both the claim and the warrant have now been modified. You should also note that Toulmin's model does not dictate any specific pattern in which these three elements must be arranged, and this is a great advantage for writers. The claim may come at the beginning of an essay, or it could just as easily come after a discussion of both the data and the warrant. Similarly, the warrant may precede the data or it may follow it—or, as already noted, the warrant may be implied rather than explicitly stated at any point in the essay.

If you write essays of your own using the Toulmin model, you may find yourself making different types of claims. In one essay you might make a claim that can be supported entirely by facts. For example, if you wanted to argue that the stock market should be subject to greater regulation, you could define the extent of current regulation, report statistics from the stock market crash of 1987, and cite specific abuses such as scandals involving insider trading. In another essay, however, you might make a claim that is easier to support with a mixture of facts, expert opinion, and appeals to the values of your audience. If, for example, you wanted to argue against abortion, your data might consist of facts (such as the number of abortions performed within a particular clinic in 1991), testimony on which it is possible to have a difference of opinion (such as the point at which human life begins), and an appeal to moral values that you believe your audience should share with you. In short, you will cite different types of data depending on the nature of the claim you want to argue.

The nature of the warrant will also differ from one argument to another. In may be a matter of law (such as the Jones Act of 1917 which guarantees U.S. citizenship to the citizens of Puerto Rico), an assumption that one's data have come from a reliable source (such as documents published by the Securities and Exchange Commission), or a generally accepted value (such as the sanctity of human life). But whatever your warrant, you should be prepared to back it up if called upon to do so. No matter how strongly you may believe in your claim, or how compelling your data may be, your argument will not be convincing if your warrant cannot be substantiated.

It is important to realize that the Toulmin model for argumentation does not require that you abandon everything you've learned about inductive and deductive reasoning. These different systems of logic complement one another and combine to form a varied menu from which you can choose whatever seems best for a particular occasion. Unless your instructor specifies that an assignment incorporate a particular type of reasoning, you will often be able to choose the type of logic you wish to employ just as you might make any number of other writing decisions. And having choices is ultimately a luxury, not a burden.

For an example of a student essay that reflects the Toulmin model for reasoning, consider the following argument on the importance of studying history.

History Is for People Who Think
Ron Tackett

Can a person consider himself a thinking, creative,   1
responsible citizen and not care about history? Can an
institution that proposes to foster such attributes do
so without including history in its curriculum? Many
college students would answer such a question with an
immediate, "Yes!" But those who are quick to answer do
so without reflecting on what history truly is and how
and why it is important.

History is boring, complain many students. Unfortu-   2
nately, a lot of people pick up a bad taste of history
from the primary and secondary schools. Too many lower
level history courses (and college level, too) are just
glorified Trivial Pursuit; rife with rote memorization
of dates and events deemed important by the teacher and
textbooks, coupled with monotone lectures that could induce comas in hyperactive children. Instead of simply
making students memorize when Pearl Harbor was attacked
by the Japanese, teachers should concentrate on instilling an understanding of why the Japanese felt they had
no alternative but to attack the United States. History
is a discipline of understanding, not memorization.

Another common complaint is that history is unim-   3
portant. But even the most fanatic antihistory students,
if they were honest, would have to admit that history is
important at least within the narrow confines of their
own disciplines of study. Why be an artist if you are

merely going to repeat the past (and probably not as ex-
pertly, since you would have to spend your time formulating theories and rules already known and recorded in
Art's history)? Why write The Great Gatsby or compose
Revolution again? How could anyone hope to be a mathema-
tician, or a scientist, without knowing the field's history? Even a genius needs a base from which to build.
History helps provide that base.

      History is also important in being a politically   4
aware citizen. Knowing that we entered World War I on
the side of the Allies in part because Woodrow Wilson
was a great Anglophile, as some historians charge, is
not vital to day-to-day life. But it is important to
know that the economic reparations imposed on Germany
after the war set the stage for the rise of Hitler and
World War II and that that war ended with a Russian domination of Eastern Europe that led to the Cold War, during which political philosophies were formulated that
still affect American foreign and domestic policies.
This type of history enables citizens to form an intelligent world view and possibly help our nation avoid
past mistakes. Of course, this illustration is simplified, but the point is as valid as when Santayana said
that without history, we are "condemned to repeat it."
This does not mean that history will repeat itself exactly, but that certain patterns recur in history, and
if we understand the patterns of what has gone before,
perhaps we can avoid making the mistakes our ancestors
made.

      A person can live a long life, get a job, and raise   5
a family without having any historical knowledge. But
citizens who possess a strong knowledge of history are
better prepared to contribute intelligently to their
jobs and their society. Thus, knowing which Third World
nations have a history of defaulting on loans can help a
bank executive save his or her institution and its customers a great deal of grief by avoiding, or seeking exceptional safeguards on, such loans. And knowing the
history of U.S. involvement in Central and South America, from naval incidents with Chile in the 1890s to
trying to overthrow the Sandanistas in Nicaragua in the
1980s, can help Americans understand why many people and
nations are concerned about U.S. policies in the region.

More importantly, Americans cannot intelligently determine what those policies should be without a knowledge
of history.

Now, if history is important enough to be required   6
in college, how many credits are enough and what sort of
history should be taught? American, European, Eastern,
Latin American, or yet another? First, a course in American history must be required. Students can little appreciate the history of others, without first knowing
their own. Secondly, since we more and more realize that
we are members of a "global community," at least one
world history course should be mandated. Though there is
no magic number of credits that will ensure the student
becoming a thinking, creative member of society, history
can help fulfill the collegiate purpose of fashioning
men and women with the potential for wisdom and the
ability to critically appraise political, economic, and
moral issues. Thus, history should be a required part of
the college curriculum.

In arguing on behalf of history, Ron shows that he is well aware that many students would like to avoid history courses. Paragraphs 2 and 3 are devoted to anticipating and responding to opposition. Although Ron concedes that history can be boring if it is badly taught, and makes an additional concession at the beginning of paragraph 5, he still insists that all college students should be required to take at least two history courses. The *claim* of this essay is "history should be a required part of the college curriculum." The *warrant* behind this claim is a value that is likely to be widely accepted: a college education should help people to think critically and become responsible members of society. This warrant underlies the entire argument, but it can be found specifically in the last paragraph where Ron refers to "the collegiate purpose of fashioning men and women with the potential for wisdom and the ability to critically appraise political, economic, and moral issues" immediately before making his claim.

Providing *data* to support this claim presented the writer with a challenge, since it would be difficult to provide statistics or other factual evidence to prove that the claim fulfills the warrant. A reader might agree with the warrant and still doubt if requiring college students to study history would give them the ability to think critically about political and moral issues. Ron chose to support his claim by defining history as "a discipline of understanding, not memorization" and providing several examples of historical events that are worth understanding: the Japanese attack on Pearl Harbor, the consequences of World War I, and the nature of U.S. involvement in Central and South America. Additional support for the claim is provided by appeals to other values which Ron has assumed his audience to possess. Paragraph 3 includes an appeal to self-interest: knowing the history of your own field can save you from wasting time. This same strategy is employed in paragraph 5 where Ron suggests that the knowledge of history can lead to better job performance. All of the examples found within the essay are clearly related to the values that the argument has invoked, and within the limitations of a short essay Ron has done a good job of supporting his claim.

AVOIDING LOGICAL FALLACIES

An apparently logical argument may reveal serious flaws if we take the trouble to examine it closely. Mistakes in reasoning are called logical *fallacies*. This term comes from the Latin word for deceit, and there is some form of deception behind most of these lapses in logic. It is easy to deceive ourselves into believing that we are making a strong argument when we have actually lost our way somehow, and many fallacies are unintentional. But others are used deliberately by writers or speakers for whom "winning" an argument is more important than looking for truth. Here is a list of common fallacies that you should be careful to avoid in your own arguments and that you should be alert to in the arguments of others.

Ad Hominem Argument   An ad hominem argument is an argument that attacks the personal character or reputation of one's opponents while ignoring what he or she has to say. *Ad hominem* is Latin for "to the man." Although an audience may often consider the character of a writer or speaker in deciding whether it can trust what he or she has to say, most of us realize that good people can make bad arguments, and even a crook can sometimes tell the truth. It is almost always better to give a logical response to an opponent's arguments than to ignore those arguments and indulge in personal attacks.

Ad Misericordiam Argument   An ad misericordiam argument is an appeal to pity. Writers are often justified in appealing to the pity of their readers when the need to inspire this emotion is closely related to whatever they are arguing for and when the entire argument does not rest upon this appeal alone. For example, someone who is attempting to convince you to donate one of your kidneys for a medical transplant would probably assure you that you could live with only one kidney and that there is a serious need for the kidney you are being asked to donate. But in addition to making these crucial points, the arguer might also move you to pity by describing what will happen to the person who has been denied a needed transplant.

When the appeal to pity stands alone, even in charitable appeals where its use is fundamental, the result is often questionable. Imagine a large billboard advertising for the American Red Cross. It features a closeup photograph of a distraught (but nevertheless good-looking) man, beneath which in large letters runs this caption: PLEASE, MY LITTLE GIRL NEEDS BLOOD. Although we may already believe in the importance of donating blood, we should question the implications of this ad. Can we donate blood and ask that it be reserved for the exclusive use of little girls? Is the life of a little girl more valuable than the life of a little boy? Are the lives of children more valuable than the lives of adults? Of course, few people would donate blood unless they sympathized with those who need transfusions, and it may be unrealistic to expect logic in advertising. But consider how weak an argument becomes when the appeal to pity has little to do with the issue in question. Someone who has seldom attended class and failed all his examinations but then tries to argue, "I deserve to pass this course because I've had a lot of problems at home," is making a fallacious appeal to pity because the "argument" asks his instructor to overlook relevant evidence and make a decision favorable to the arguer because the instructor has been moved to feel sorry for him. You should be skeptical of any appeal to pity that is irrelevant to the conclusion or that seems designed to distract attention from other factors which you should be considering.

Ad Populum Argument   An ad populum argument, which means "argument to the crowd," plays upon the general values of an audience often to the point where reasonable discussion of a specific issue is no longer possible. A newspaper that creates a patriotic frenzy through exaggerated reports of enemy "atrocities" is relying on an ad populum argument. But the ad populum argument can also take more subtle forms. A politician may remind you that he was born and raised in "this great state," that he loves his children, and admires his wife—all of which are factors believed to appeal to the average man and woman but which nevertheless are unlikely to affect his performance in office. When a candidate lingers on what a wonderful family man he is, it may be time to ask a question about the economy.

Argument by Analogy   An analogy is a comparison that works on more than one level, and it is possible to use analogy effectively when reasoning inductively. To do this, you must be sure that the things you are comparing have several characteristics in common and that these similarities are relevant to the conclusion that you intend to draw. If you observe that isolation produces depression in chimpanzees, you could argue that isolation can cause a similar problem for human beings. The strength of this argument would depend upon the degree to which chimps are analogous to humans, so you would need to proceed with care and demonstrate that there are important similarities between the two species. When arguing from analogy, it is important to remember that you are speculating. As is the case with any type of inductive reasoning, you can reach a conclusion that is likely to be true but not guaranteed to be true. It is always possible that you have overlooked a significant factor that will cause the analogy to break down.

Unfortunately, analogies are often misused. An argument from analogy that reaches a firm conclusion is likely to be fallacious, and it is certain to be fallacious if the analogy itself is inappropriate. If a congressional candidate asks us to vote for him because of his outstanding record as a football player, he might be able to claim that politics, like football, involves teamwork. But because a successful politician needs many skills and will probably never need to run across a field or knock someone down, it would be foolish to vote on the basis of this questionable analogy. The differences between football and politics outweigh the similarities, and it would be fallacious to pretend otherwise.

Begging the Question   In the fallacy of "begging the question," a writer begins with a premise that is acceptable only to anyone who will agree with the conclusion that is subsequently reached—a conclusion often very similar to the premise itself. Thus, the argument goes around in a circle. For instance, someone might begin an essay by claiming, "Required courses like freshman English are a waste of time," and end with the conclusion that "Freshman English should not be a required course." It might indeed be arguable that freshman English should not be required, but the author who begins with the premise that freshman English is a waste of time has assumed what the argument should be devoted to proving. Because it is much easier to claim that something is true than to prove it is true, you may be tempted to beg the question you set out to answer. This is a temptation that should always be avoided.

Equivocation   Someone who equivocates uses vague or ambiguous language to mislead an audience. In argumentation, equivocation often takes the form of using one word in several different senses, without acknowledging that this has been done. It is especially easy to equivocate if you are addicted to abstract language. Watch out in particular for the abuse of such terms as "right," "society," "freedom," "law," "justice," and "real." When you use words like these, make sure you make your meaning clear. And make double sure your meaning doesn't shift when you use the term again.

False Dilemma   A false dilemma is a fallacy in which a speaker or writer poses a choice between two alternatives while overlooking other possibilities and implying that other possibilities do not exist. If a freshman receives low grades at the end of his first semester in college and then claims, "What's wrong with low grades? Is cheating any better?" he is pretending that there is no other possibility—for example, that of earning higher grades by studying harder, a possibility that is recognized by most students and teachers.

Guilt by Association   This is a fallacy that is frequently made in politics, especially toward the end of a close campaign. A candidate who happens to be religious, for example, may be maneuvered by opponents into the false position of being held accountable for the actions of all the men and women who hold to that particular faith. Nothing specific has been *argued*, but a negative association has been either created or played upon through hints and innuendos. Guilt by association may take the form of an ad hominem argument, or it may be more subtle. A careless writer may simply stumble into using a stereotype to avoid the trouble of coming up with a concrete example. But whatever its form, guilt by association is a fallacy in which prejudice takes the place of thought.

Ignoring the Question   When someone says, "I'm glad you asked that question!" and then promptly begins to talk about something else, he or she is guilty of ignoring the question. Politicians are famous for exploiting this technique when they don't want to be pinned down on a subject. But students (and teachers) sometimes use it too when asked a question that they want to avoid. Ignoring the question is also likely to occur when friends or lovers have a fight. In the midst of an emotional quarrel, criticism is likely to evoke remarks like, "What about you!" or "Never mind the budget! I'm sick of worrying about money! We need to talk about what's happening to our relationship!"

Jumping to Conclusions   This fallacy is so common that it has become a cliché. It means that the conclusion in question has not been supported by an adequate amount of evidence. Because one green apple is sour, it does not follow that all green apples are sour. Failing one test does not mean that you will necessarily fail the next. An instructor who seems disorganized the first day of class may eventually prove to be the best teacher you ever had. You should always try to have more than one example to support an argument. Be skeptical of arguments that seem heavy on opinion but weak on evidence.

Non Sequitur   This term is Latin for "it does not follow." Although this can be said of almost any faulty argument, the term "non sequitur" is usually applied more precisely. The most common type of non sequitur is a complex sentence in which the subordinate clause does not clearly relate to the main clause, especially where causation is involved. An example of this type of non sequitur would be "Because the wind was blowing so fiercely, I passed the quiz in calculus." This is a non sequitur because passing calculus should not be dependent on the weather. A cause-and-effect relationship has been claimed but not explained. It may be that the wind forced you to stay indoors, which led you to spend more time studying than you usually do, and this in turn led you to pass your quiz. But someone reading the sentence as written could not be expected to know this. A non sequitur may also take the form of a compound sentence: "Mr. Blandshaw is young, and so he should be a good teacher." Mr. Blandshaw may indeed be a good teacher, but not just because he is young. On the contrary, young Mr. Blandshaw may be inexperienced, anxious, and humorless. He may also give you unrealistically large assignments because he lacks a clear sense of how much work most students can handle. So watch out for non sequiturs the next time you register for classes.

Non sequiturs sometimes form the basis for an entire argument: "William Henderson will make a good governor because he is a friend of the workingman. He is a friend of the workingman because he was a plumber before he became a millionaire through his contracting business." Before allowing this argument to go any further, you should realize that you've been already asked to swallow two non sequiturs. Being a good governor involves more than being "a friend of the workingman." And there is no reason to assume that Henderson is "a friend of the workingman" just because he used to be a plumber. It may be over thirty years since he last saw the inside of a union hall, and he may have acquired his wealth by taking advantage of the men and women who work for him.

Post Hoc, Ergo Propter Hoc   If you assume that an event is the result of something that merely occurred before it, you have committed the fallacy of post hoc, ergo propter hoc. This is a Latin phrase which means "after this, therefore because of this." Superstitious people offer many examples of this type of fallacious thinking. They might tell you, "Everything was doing fine until the lunar eclipse last month; *that's* why the economy is in trouble." Or personal misfortune may be traced back to spilling salt, stepping on a crack, or walking under a ladder.

This fallacy is often found in the arguments of writers who are determined to prove the existence of various conspiracies. They often seem to amass an impressive amount of evidence—but the "evidence" is frequently questionable. Or, to take a comparatively simple example, someone might be suspected of murder simply because of being seen near the victim's house a day or two before the crime occurred. This suspicion may lead to the discovery of evidence, but it could just as easily lead to the false arrest of the meter reader from the electric company. Being observed near the scene of a crime proves nothing by itself. A prosecuting attorney who would be foolish enough to base a case on such a flimsy piece of evidence would be guilty of post hoc, ergo propter hoc reasoning. Logic should always recognize the distinction between *causes* and what may simply be *coincidences*. Sequence is not a cause because every event is preceded by an infinite number of other events, all of which cannot be held responsible for whatever happens today.

This fallacy can be found in more subtle forms in essays on abstract social problems. Writers who blame contemporary problems on such instant explanations as "the rise of television" or "the popularity of computers" are no more convincing than the parent who argues that all the difficulties of family life can be traced to the rise of rock and roll. It is impossible to understand the present without understanding the past. But don't isolate at random any one event in the past, and then try to argue that it explains everything. And be careful not to accidentally imply a cause-and-effect relationship where you did not intend to do so.

Slippery Slope   According to this fallacy, one step will inevitably lead to an undesirable second step. An example would be claiming that legalized abortion will lead to euthanasia or that censoring pornography will lead to the end of freedom for the press. Although it is important to consider the probable effects of any step that is being debated, it is fallacious to claim that men and women will necessarily tumble downhill as the result of any one step. There is always the possibility that we'll be able to keep our feet firmly on the ground even though we've moved them from where they used to be.

Straw Man   Because it is easier to demolish a man of straw than to beat a live opponent fairly, arguers are sometimes tempted to pretend that they are responding to the views of their opponents when they are only setting up a type of artificial opposition which they can easily refute. The most common form of this fallacy is to exaggerate the views of others or to respond only to an extreme view that does not adequately represent the arguments of one's opponents. If you reveal flaws in the position taken by someone who has called for abolishing Social Security, you should not think that you have defended that program from all its critics. By responding only to an extreme position, you would be doing nothing to resolve specific concerns about how Social Security is financed and administered.

UNDERSTANDING OTHER FORMS OF PERSUASION

Of the various forms of persuasive writing, logical argument is the most honorable. Although logic can be abused, its object is truth rather than manipulation. Whether we are writing a logical argument or simply trying to understand one, we have to be actively involved with ideas. To put it simply, we have to *think*. We may be influenced by what we know of the writer's credibility and whether he or she has touched our hearts within the argument as a whole. But behind any logical argument is the assumption that reasonable men and women should agree with its outcome—not so much because it is gracefully written (although it may be that), but because it is *true*.

There are other types of writing that rely upon an indirect appeal to the mind, exploiting what is known about the psychological makeup of an audience or its most probable fears and desires. Successful advertising is *persuasive* in that it encourages us to buy one product or another, but it is not necessarily logical. Few people have the money, time, or inclination to sample every product available for consumption. When we buy a particular mouthwash, toothpaste, soap, or soft drink—and even when we make purchases as large as a car—we may simply choose the cheapest product available. But bargain hunting aside, we are frequently led to purchase brands that advertising has taught us to associate with health, wealth, and happiness. A prominent greeting card company insists that we send their cards if we really and truly care about someone. Love has also been used as the justification for piling up extravagantly high phone bills. (After all, who wants to worry about money when doing something as noble as "reaching out to touch someone"?) One popular cigarette is associated with the masculinity of mounted cowboys, and another implies a dubious link with the women's movement. Almost no one really believes this sort of thing when forced to stop and think about it. But we often act without thinking, and this is one of the reasons why advertising has been able to grow into a billion dollar industry. Through the clever use of language and visual images, advertisers can lead people into a variety of illogical and possibly ruinous acts.

This, then, is the principal distinction between argument and persuasion: argument seeks to clarify thought, while persuasion often seeks to obscure it. Argument relies upon evidence or widely accepted truths and does not necessarily dictate any one particular course of action. Persuasion, on the other hand, can work altogether independent of the facts as we know them (such as how much money we can afford to spend before the end of the month), and it is almost always designed to inspire action—whether it is buying a new kind of deodorant or voting for the candidate with the nicest teeth. Persuasion is thus a form of domination. Its object is to make people agree with the will of the persuader, regardless of whether the persuader is "right" or simply selling his or her services by the hour.

Although argument may include an appeal to our emotions, persuasion is likely to emphasize such appeals. A persuasive writer or speaker knows how to evoke feelings ranging from love, loyalty, and patriotism to anger, envy, and xenophobia. An audience may be deeply moved even when nothing substantial has been said. With a quickened pulse or tearful eyes, we may find ourselves convinced that we've read or heard something wonderfully profound. But a few days later, we may realize that we've been inhaling the intoxicating fumes of a heavily scented gasbag, rather than digesting genuine "food for thought."

Analyzing Advertisements

Although persuasion is by no means limited to advertising, advertisements represent a form of persuasion which we regularly encounter in our daily lives. Recognizing that people are often bored by ads because there are so many of them, advertisers must be doubly persuasive: Before they can persuade us to buy a particular product or engage a specific service, advertisers must begin by persuading us to pay attention to the ad. Because advertisements cannot be taken for granted, advertising agencies have attracted some highly talented people, and a successful advertising campaign usually involves much planning. Different advertisements employ different strategies, and if you think about the ads you encounter, you will find that they often include more than one message. Consider the examples on pages 42 and 44.

At first glance, the advertisement for Maxwell House coffee (Figure 1) seems to appeal primarily through nostalgia. The opening line of the text tells us that the coffee in question is "inspired by the good old days." We then learn that Maxwell House 1892 is a "plain, old-fashioned coffee" produced "the old-fashioned way" of slow roasting beans "the traditional way" to make "an old style coffee." The illustration seems to reinforce the emphasis on "old-fashioned." Two women, evidently in the process of making

INTRODUCING A BRAND NEW COFFEE MADE WITH
STUBBORN OLD-FASHIONED PRIDE

¶ Introducing Maxwell House® 1892™ Slow Roasted Coffee—inspired by the good old
days and made that way, too. To coffee lovers everywhere it promises the unique taste experience
of the lusty flavor and aroma of plain, old-fashioned coffee—the kind that doesn't just
happen overnight.

¶ Thankfully Maxwell House has both the patience and experience to produce coffee the
old-fashioned way. And if all that experience has taught us anything, it is that
 slow roasting is the traditional way to extract the full flavor and aroma
of high grade beans. Slow roasting is a labor of love that can take
anywhere up to six times longer than is common practice these days.

¶ The result, however, is an uncommonly good cup of coffee—one
that is both lusty and satisfying without being bitter. So even though it
takes a little longer, and costs a little more to make an old style coffee as
good as Maxwell House® 1892,™ it's time and trouble well spent, as a trip to
your market will confirm.

© 1990 Kraft General Foods, Inc.

FIGURE 1.

homemade jam, are taking a coffee break. The sink, stove, and clothing suggest that the scene is taking place at least sixty years ago. The woman with
glasses looks serious—the sort of woman you could trust to roast your coffee
beans. The other woman smiles tentatively at us with a faintly melancholy
gaze, as if to suggest that she would enjoy her own coffee better if we would
remember to call home more often. Both women are wearing carefully ironed
aprons which have remained, somehow, spot-free.

But if the picture captures our attention by resembling a photograph from an old family album, a closer examination of the ad reveals that it does not persuade by nostalgia alone. It is, after all, introducing a new product, and it needs to appeal to readers who would be reluctant to give up their microwave ovens and actually work in a kitchen like the one pictured here. Although the woman with glasses seems to represent the "stubborn" and "plain" references in the text, she has a slightly wry expression suggesting that she realizes that "the good old days" were not altogether good. (This message is reinforced by the use of color in the ad as it originally appeared but which cannot be reproduced here: Although the illustration is primarily in the muted whites and browns of an old photograph, one of the women is wearing a rose-colored dress and the other a pale, pink apron—colors that suggest that the scene is a "rose-colored" vision of the past.) Readers who perceive this dimension of the ad might also note that this "plain, old-fashioned coffee" is also "lusty," a word that appears twice in the text. At this level, the ad might well appeal to a young sophisticate who is ready to settle down with something traditional as long as it isn't dull. While evoking the past, the ad thus also locates us within the present. It is designed to appeal both to people who long for the values of the past as well as to those who realize that nostalgia cannot be taken at face value.

Before turning away from this ad, you might note two other persuasive elements within it. The credibility of the claims is established by a reference to "the patience and experience" of the manufacturer. And by telling us that producing this coffee "costs a little more," the ad anticipates and responds to a possible reservation that may arise when we actually consider buying it.

If the ad for Maxwell House coffee appeals primarily through nostalgia for the past, the ad for nuclear energy (Figure 2) appeals primarily by evoking fears we may have about the future. The large image that dominates the page suggests oil that has been spilled. This image is likely to remind people of such terrible oil spills as the one off the coast of Alaska in 1989. Without explicitly saying so, the ad suggests that oil spills will continue to occur as long as we continue to pump and ship oil for our energy needs, and that this is a serious fear for anyone who cares about the environment. The image also directs our attention to the ad's principal claim: "Nuclear energy helps slow the flow of foreign oil." Within this context, "flow" has a double meaning. This key word relates to the image by conveying the idea of a threatening flow or spill, such as when the results of an oil spill flow into a harbor or onto a beach. In another sense, "flow" also conveys the idea of regular movement, as in the flow of a river. When something has been flowing for a long time, people may be inclined to take it for granted. But just as a river can go dry, so too can the flow of foreign oil become interrupted or even stop altogether. The text of the ad emphasizes that we rely too much upon the flow of foreign oil and that this reliance has put "America's national security and economy in danger." This fear was easy to evoke in 1990 when this ad appeared shortly after Saddam Hussein invaded Kuwait—hence the three references to the Middle East. But by using terms like "unrest" and

Nuclear energy helps slow the flow of foreign oil

Unrest in the Middle East has once again put America's national security and economy in danger.

We now import more than half of all the oil we use, much of it from the Middle East. But nuclear energy can help us reduce this excessive dependence on unstable sources. Our 112 nuclear electric plants already have cut foreign oil dependence by 4.3 billion barrels since the 1973 oil embargo, and continue to cut our oil imports by 740,000 barrels every day.

Nuclear energy is a clean and safe energy source that we can count on, one not endangered by turmoil in the Middle East.

For more information, write to U.S. Council for Energy Awareness, P.O. Box 66080, Dept. ME01, Washington, D.C. 20035.

U.S. COUNCIL FOR ENERGY AWARENESS

Nuclear energy means more energy independence.

© 1990 USCEA

FIGURE 2.

"turmoil" rather than by referring specifically to the war for Kuwait, the ad locates its claims within a broader context. There has been unrest within the Middle East for many years, and there is no reason to assume that this region will be free of turmoil in the years ahead.

The basic strategy of this ad becomes easier to understand when we consider that many people are afraid of nuclear energy because they believe it is unsafe and likely to do serious harm to the environment. Although the ad includes an address to which one can write for further information, it offers no evidence to support the claim that nuclear power is "a clean and safe energy source that we can count on." Nuclear energy is made to look good primarily by making oil look bad. This strategy can be effective to a degree, but it has certain limitations: Proving that something is bad does not in itself mean proving that something else is any better. If you do research upon nuclear energy, you may find that a well-documented case could be made for using it. On the other hand, you might find that there are serious risks involved in its production.

Three other ads are reprinted on pages 46–48. As an exercise in understanding persuasion, analyze at least one of them and determine what makes it appealing.

Recognizing Flaws in Persuasion

Just as some advertisements are more appealing than others, so are some ads more questionable than others. Many ads are relatively straightforward, but others may approach dishonesty. When analysing persuasion, wherever you encounter it and in whatever form, you should be alert not only for the various types of fallacious reasoning discussed earlier in this chapter, but also for the following flaws:

Bogus Claims   A claim can be considered "bogus" or false whenever a persuader promises more than he or she can prove beyond dispute. If a Chicago restaurant offers "fresh country peas" in the middle of January, you might want to ask where these peas were freshly picked. And if a large commercial bakery advertises "homemade pies," try asking whose home they were made in. You'll probably get some strange looks, because many people don't really expect words to mean what they say. But good writers become good writers in part because they have eyes and ears—eyes that see and ears that hear.

If a toothpaste promises to give your mouth "sex appeal," you'd still better be careful about whom you try to kiss. A claim of this sort is fairly crude, and therefore easily recognizable. But bogus claims can take many forms, some more subtle than others. A television advertisement for a new improved designer laxative may star an unnamed man in a white coat, with a stethoscope around his neck. The advertisement implies—without necessarily saying so—that the product in question is endorsed by physicians. Ads of this sort are also likely to speak vaguely of "recent studies," or better yet, "recent *clinical* studies," which are declared to prove a product's value. The product may indeed have value; on the other hand, it may be indistinguishable from its competition except in price and packaging. You might like it when you try it. But well-educated men and women should always be a little skeptical about promises from strangers.

When writing an essay, it is easy to fall into the habit of making bogus claims when reaching for generalizations to support your point of view. Im-

FIGURE 3.

itating the style of the advertisements with which they grew up, careless writers like to refer to those ever popular "recent studies" which conveniently seem to support whatever is being argued. Such phrases as "recent studies have shown" enable writers to avoid identifying who did the research. A recent study may provide the evidence to prove a point, but a good writer should be prepared to cite it, especially when the claim is surprising.

FIGURE 4.

It is one thing to write "Recent studies have shown that nutrition plays an important role in maintaining good health," for the generalization in this case enjoys wide acceptance. It would be something else altogether to toss off a claim like, "Recent studies have shown that Americans have the most nutritious diet in the world." A specific claim requires specific support—not

NOW YOU'LL HAVE TO BLAME SOMEONE ELSE IF YOU'RE LATE.

Say that a dog ate your pants. Or that you had a dental emergency. But whatever you say, don't say it was because of Northwest Airlines. It's not very likely, and truth is, no one will believe you anymore. Among the top five U.S. airlines, we have the best on-time performance this year. We know that in the dog-eat-dog world of business, sometimes there's no excuse for being late. For U.S. reservations, call your travel agent or call Northwest at 1-800-225-2525.

© 1990 Northwest Airlines, Inc.

NORTHWEST AIRLINES

FIGURE 5.

just a vague reference to an unidentified study. We cannot evaluate a recent study if we do not know how it was undertaken and where the results were published.

Writers who like to refer to "recent studies" are also fond of alluding to unspecified statistics, as in "statistics have shown," or "according to statistics." Statistics can be of great value, but they can also be misleading. Ask yourself if a statistic raises any unanswered questions, and note whether or not the source has been revealed. Similarly, you should turn a critical eye on claims like "It is a well-known fact that . . ." or "Everybody knows that. . . ." If the fact *is* well known, why is the writer boring us with what we already know? And if the fact is *not* well known, as is usually the case when lines of this sort are thrown about, then the writer had better explain how he or she knows it.

In short, if you want to avoid bogus claims, never claim anything that would leave you speechless if you were called upon to explain or defend what you have written.

Loaded Terms   Good writers have good diction; they know a lot of words, and just as important, they know how to use them accurately. They know that most words have positive or negative *connotations*—associations with the word that go beyond its standard definition or *denotation*. "Placid," "tranquil," or "serene" might all be used to describe someone who is "calm," but each word creates a slightly different impression. An experienced writer is likely to pause before choosing the adjective that best suits his or her subject.

A term becomes *loaded* when it is asked to carry more emotional weight than its context can legitimately support. A loaded term is a word or phrase that goes beyond connotation into the unconvincing world of the heavy handed and narrow minded. To put it simply, it is *slanted* or *biased*.

Loaded terms may appeal to the zealous, but they mislead the unwary reader and offend the critically minded. For example, when an aspiring journalist denounces the Bush "regime" in the school newspaper, he is taking what many men and women would consider a cheap shot—regardless of their own politics. "Regime" is a loaded term because it is most frequently used to describe military dictatorships. Even someone who is politically opposed to George Bush should still be clearheaded enough to speak of the Bush "Administration," which is the term best suited for a political discussion of the U.S. Presidency.

Like "regime," many words have such strong connotations that they can become loaded terms very easily. In the United States, for example, "Marxist" is almost always used as a type of rebuke. (And in some countries, "capitalist" is used in a similar way.) When most Americans hear that an idea is "Marxist," they become immediately hostile toward it. Nevertheless, when Salvador Allende became the democratically elected president of Chile in 1970, American newspapers seemed unable to report news from Chile without repeated references to "Marxist President Salvador Allende," as if "Marxist" was part of his job title. Even now, so many years after his assassination, "Marxist President Salvador Allende" can still be found making occasional appearances in the American press.

Within a particular context, a seemingly inoffensive word may become a loaded term. In order to manipulate reader response, a writer may sneak unnecessary adjectives into his or her work. A political correspondent may write, "Mr. D'Arcy, the wealthy candidate from Park Ridge, spoke today at Meryton High School." The candidate's income has nothing to do with the news event being reported, so "wealthy" is a loaded term. It's an extra word that serves only one function: to divide the candidate from the newspaper's audience, very few of whom are "wealthy." It would not be surprising if some readers began to turn against this candidate, regardless of his platform, simply because they had been led to associate him with a background that is alien to their own.

Do not make the mistake of assuming that loaded terms occur only in political discourse. They can be found almost anywhere, if you take the trouble to read critically and intelligently. You may even find some in your textbooks.

Misrepresentation   Misrepresentation can take many forms. Someone may come right out and lie to you, telling you something you know—or subsequently discover—to be untrue. In the course of writing a paper, someone may invent statistics or alter research data that point to an unwelcome conclusion. And then, of course, there is *plagiarism*—which means taking someone else's words or ideas without acknowledgment and passing them off as your own.

There are always going to be people who are tempted to lie, and there isn't much we can do about this except to keep our eyes open, read well, and choose our friends with care. But we ourselves can be careful to act honorably, and guidelines for working with sources appear in Part 2 of this book. There is, however, a common misrepresentation that must be understood as part of our introduction to the principles of argument and persuasion: dishonest writers will often misrepresent their opponents by twisting what others have said.

The most common way in which writers misrepresent opposing arguments is to oversimplify them. The ability to summarize what others have said or written is a skill that cannot be taken for granted, and we will turn to it shortly. There is always the possibility that someone may misrepresent an opponent accidentally—having failed to understand what has been said or having confused it in reporting it. But it is also possible to misreport others *deliberately*. A complex argument can be reduced to ridicule in a slogan, or an important element of such an argument could be entirely overlooked, creating a false impression.

Have the courage to ask for evidence whenever someone makes a questionable claim. And when you find it necessary to quote someone, make sure you do so not only correctly but also *fairly*. The concept of "quoting out of context" is so familiar that the phrase has become a cliché. But clichés sometimes embody fundamental truths, and here is one of them: quotations should be more than accurate; they should also reflect the overall nature of the quoted source. When you select a passage that truly represents the thesis of another's work, you can use it in good conscience—as long as you remember to put it in quotation marks and reveal to your readers where you got it. But if you fasten onto a minor detail and quote a line that could be misunderstood if lifted away from the sentences that originally surrounded it, then you are guilty of misrepresentation.

Bogus claims, loaded terms, and misrepresentation are almost always to be found in that extreme form of persuasion known as *propaganda*. Strictly speaking, propaganda means only the systematic use of words and images to propagate (or spread) ideas, but the abuse of propaganda within the last century has made the word widely associated with dishonesty. (For an extended definition of this term, see "The Purpose of Propaganda," by Adolf Hitler, pages 595–602.) Because the techniques of persuasion are easy to abuse, you should use them with great care. If you are trying to move an audience to action, you may find it useful to appeal to the heart as well as to the head, but you should try to avoid appealing to the heart alone. And when appealing to the mind, it is always more honorable to address your audience as thoughtful men and women than to subtly exploit their subconscious hopes and fears.

An essay or speech that works primarily by inspiring an emotional response is most likely to succeed only when an audience can be called upon for immediate action. If a senator can inspire her colleagues moments before a critically important vote, or an evangelist move a congregation to generosity just as the collection plate is about to be passed, then the results of such persuasion may be significant. But opportunities of this sort are rare for most writers. Almost everything we write can be put aside and reconsidered at another time. Irrespective of the ethical importance of arguing what is true and not just what is convenient, there is also a very practical reason for trying to argue logically: The arguments that carry the greatest weight are usually the arguments that are capable of holding up under analysis. They make more sense as we think about them, not less. Whereas persuasion relies upon impulse, argument depends upon conviction. Our impulses may determine what we do this afternoon, but our convictions shape the rest of our lives. If you make a genuinely logical argument, you may make some people angry with you, but you will not be accused of dishonesty. When you abandon logic for the techniques of persuasion, make sure that this is simply a change in writing strategy. Never write anything that you don't believe. This does not mean that there's anything wrong with writing fiction or satire. But it does mean that good writers shouldn't tell lies.

PART 2

WORKING WITH SOURCES

———— ◆ ————

READING CRITICALLY

Although reading can be a pleasure, and many people find it relaxing to read material that provides a temporary escape from daily concerns, serious reading requires an active response on your part. When reading in college, or in whatever profession you are preparing for, you need to think about what you read. To make sure that you understand the content of what you have read, you must be able to identify key points—such as an author's thesis—and any points where you had difficulty. But beyond working to understand the material before you, you should also be prepared to *evaluate* it. As students, you will sometimes find yourself confronted with more information than you can digest with ease. You will also find that different writers will tell you different things. When this happens, inexperienced readers sometimes become confused or discouraged. Being able to recognize what material deserves the closest reading, and what sources are the most reliable is essential to coping successfully with the many demands made upon your time as students. By reading critically, and reading often, you can acquire skills that will help you in almost any college course.

As you read the material collected in this book, you will find that some articles are easier to read than others. It would be a mistake to assume that the easiest material is necessarily the most reliable. On the other hand, it would also be wrong to assume that long, difficult articles are reliable simply because they are long and difficult. Whether you are preparing to write an argument of your own or simply trying to become better informed on an issue that has more than one side, you can benefit from practicing specific strategies for critical reading.

Previewing

Even before you begin to read, there are a few steps that you can take to help you benefit from the reading you are about to undertake. A quick preview, or survey, of a written text should give you an idea of how long it will take to read, what the reading will probably reveal, and how useful the reading is likely to be. When you glance through a newspaper, identifying stories that you want to read and others that you merely want to skim over, you are practicing a simple type of preview—one that is often guided primarily by your level of interest in various issues. But when previewing reading material in college, it is usually wise to ask yourself some questions that go beyond whether or not you happen to find a topic appealing.

How Long Is This Work?   By checking the length of a work before you begin to read, you can estimate how much reading time this material will demand based upon the speed and ease with which you normally read. The length may also be a clue in determining how useful a text may be. Although quantity is no sure guide to quality, a long work may contain more information than a short work. When reading an article in an anthology or in a magazine, you can quickly flip ahead to see where it ends. And when doing library research (discussed in Part 6 of this book), you can usually learn the length of a work before you even hold it in your hand. This information is included in periodical indexes and most book catalogs. (See the illustrations on pages 651 and 656.)

What Can I Learn From The Title?   Although a title may be too general to give you an idea of what to expect when you read the work in question, titles often reveal an author's focus. An article called "Drugs and the Modern Athlete" will differ in focus from one called "Drug Testing and Corporate Responsibility." Moreover, a title can often indicate the author's point of view. Examples within this book include "The Case Against Drug Testing," "All Animals Are Equal," and "The Dark Side of Competition in American Society."

Do I Know Anything About the Author?   Recognizing the names of established authorities in your field becomes easier as you do more reading, but written sources often include information that can help you estimate an author's credibility when that author is unfamiliar to you. A magazine article may identify the author at the beginning of the article, at the end of the article, or on a separate page (often called "Notes on Contributors") that can be found by consulting the table of contents. A book jacket will often include a biographical sketch of the author, and a list of her other works may appear at either the front or the back of the book. And anthologies often include introductory headnotes for the various writers they include. In a work such as *The Informed Argument*, headnotes can help you to discover if the author has any credentials appropriate for the topic at hand. The author may have already published other works on this subject. On the other hand, she may be writing about a topic that is not directly related to her field of expertise.

Suppose, for example, that you are about to read an argument on nuclear energy. By noting if the article was written by a utility executive or an environmental activist, you can prepare yourself for the sort of argument you are most likely to encounter. And if the article is written by a famous authority on child care, you might ask yourself if that author will be a credible authority on nuclear power plants. Remember, however, that experts can make mistakes, and an important argument can be written by someone new to the field. The best way to appraise an author's credibility is to read her work, noting how much evidence she provides to support her claims and how fairly she seems to treat other people.

What Do I Know About the Publisher?   An important work can be published by an obscure publisher, and a small magazine may be the first to publish an author destined to win a Pulitzer Prize. So the reputation of a publisher is not an automatic guide to the reliability of a source. But there are a few factors that can help you determine if a source is likely to be worthwhile. University presses usually expect a high degree of scholarship, and academic journals usually publish articles only after they have been examined by two or three other experts in that field. When you read an article from a popular magazine, you might consider if the nature of that magazine would determine what it is likely to publish. For example, an article on hunting in *Field & Stream* is almost certain to be very different from one on hunting in *Vegetarian Times*. If you read widely in periodicals, you will eventually find that some magazines and newspapers consistently reflect political positions that might be characterized as either "liberal" or "conservative." When you make a discovery of this sort, you can often make a pretty good guess about what kind of stand will be taken in an article from one of these periodicals. This guess can prepare you to note any bias within the article that should be considered when you evaluate it. But once again, remember that you are only making a preliminary estimate when previewing. The best way to judge a work is to read it carefully.

Is There Anything Else I Can Discover by Skimming Through the Material?   A quick examination of the text can identify a number of other features that can help you orient yourself to what you are about to read. Consider the length of the average paragraph; long paragraphs may indicate a densely written text that you will need to read slowly. Look to see if there are any special features, such as tables, figures, or illustrations that will give you visual aids. Look also to see if there are any subtitles. If so, they may provide you with a rough outline of the work in question and also indicate points where you may be able to take a break if necessary. Quickly reading the first sentence in every paragraph may also give you a sense of the work's outline. In some cases, a writer may actually provide you with a summary. Articles from scholarly journals are often preceded by an *abstract* (or summary) that can help you understand the article and estimate the extent to which it is likely to be of use to you. (See the examples on page 388.) Articles without abstracts may include a brief summary within the text itself; check the first few and last few paragraphs, the two positions where writers most often summarize their views. Finally, be sure to note if the work includes a reference list. Scanning a bibliography—noting both how current the research seems and how extensive it is—can help you appraise a writer's scholarship, and it can also alert you to other sources that you may want to read on your own.

Annotating

Marking a test with notes, or *annotating* it, can be a great help when you are trying to understand your reading. Annotation can also help you to discover points that you might want to question when you evaluate this work. One of the advantages of owning a book—or having your own photocopy of an excerpt from a book or magazine—is that you can mark it as heavily as you wish without violating the rights of others. But when you are annotating a text that is important to you, you will usually benefit from reading that text more than once and by adding new annotations with each reading.

Equipped with a yellow felt-tipped pen, some students like to "highlight" the passages that seem most important to them. If this technique has worked well for you, there is no reason why you should feel compelled to abandon it. But it has two disadvantages. One is that highlighting cannot be erased. Some students find themselves with yellow-coated pages because they were initially unable to distinguish between main points and supporting details—and were later unable to erase unnecessary highlighting when they came to understand the text better. A second problem is that highlighting pens usually make broad marks ill-suited for writing. Reading with a pen like this in hand means that you will need to reach for another pen or pencil whenever you want to add comments in the margin.

When reading, especially when reading a text for the first time, you might benefit from an alternative to highlighting. Try using a pen or pencil and simply make a small check (√) in the margin when a line seems important, an exclamation point (!) when you find surprising information or an unusually bold claim, and a question mark (?) when you have trouble understanding a particular passage or find yourself disagreeing with what it says. This simple form of annotation can be done very easily, and if you use a pencil, you will be able to erase any marks that you later find distracting.

When you are able to spend more time with a text, and want to be sure that you understand not only its content but also its strengths and weaknesses, then additional annotations are in order. Use the margins to define new words and identify unfamiliar allusions. Write comments that will remind you of what is discussed in various paragraphs. Jot down questions that you may subsequently raise in class or explore in a paper. By making cross references (like *cf.* ¶ *3* beside a later paragraph), you can remind yourself of how various components of the work fit together and also identify apparent contradictions within the work. Finally, whenever you are moved to a strong response—whether you are agreeing or disagreeing with what you have read—write that thought down before you lose it. An annotation of this sort can be useful when you are reviewing material before an exam, and it may very well be the seed from which a paper will later grow.

To give you an example of annotation, here is an annotated excerpt from Thoreau's "Resistance to Civil Government" (sometimes called "Civil Disobedience") the full text of which appears in Part 5, pp. 550–65. As you examine it, remember that most readers will annotate a text in different ways. Some annotations are more thorough and reflective than others, but no single response is ever likely to be a "correct" response against which your own annotation must be measured. As a general rule, however, you will often notice different aspects of a text when you reread it, so annotations are likely to accumulate in layers. Annotations have been reproduced here in both printing and handwriting in order to suggest how they accumulated during more than one reading.

Where Thoreau lived

He's thinking about slavery

Practically speaking, the opponents to a reform in Massachusetts are not a hundred thousand politicians at the South, but a hundred thousand merchants and farmers here, who are more interested in commerce and agriculture than they are in humanity, and are not prepared to do justice to the slave and to Mexico, *cost what it may.* I quarrel not with far-off foes, but with those who, near at home, co-operate with, and do the bidding of those far away, and without whom the latter would be harmless. We are accustomed to say, that the mass of men are unprepared; but improvement is slow, because the few are not materially wiser or better than the many. It is not so important that many should be as good as you, as that there be some absolute goodness somewhere; for that will leaven the whole lump. There are thousands who are *in opinion* opposed to slavery and to the war, who yet in effect do nothing to put an end to them; who, esteeming themselves children of Washington and Franklin, sit down with their hands in their pockets, and say that they know not what to do, and do nothing; who even postpone the question of freedom to the question of free-trade, and quietly read the prices-current along with the latest advices from Mexico, after dinner, and, it may be, fall asleep over them both. What is the price-current of an honest man and patriot to-day? They hesitate, and they regret, and sometimes they petition; but

Business mentality supports injustice

Why Mexico?

can anyone be absolutely Good?

"leaven" as in making bread

George & Ben "Founding fathers"

Mexico again. This must be important.

Mexican War (1846-47) very Controversial, Fought after Annexation of Texas, Mexico lost, In Peace Treaty, U.S. got all of California, Nevada, Utah + most of Arizona, New Mexico + Colorado for 15 million dollars. What a deal!

they do nothing in earnest and with effect. They will wait, well-disposed, for others to remedy the evil, that they may no longer have it to regret. At most, they give only a cheap vote, and a feeble countenance and God-speed, to the right, as it goes by them. There are nine hundred and ninety-nine patrons of virtue to one virtuous man; but it is easier to deal with the real possessor of a thing than with the temporary guardian of it.

? .

All voting is a sort of gaming, like chequers or backgammon, with a slight moral tinge to it, a playing with right and wrong, with moral questions; and betting naturally accompanies it. The character of the voters is not staked. I cast my vote, perchance, as I think right; but I am not vitally concerned that that right should prevail. I am willing to leave it to the majority. Its obligation, therefore, never exceeds that of expediency. Even voting *for the right* is *doing* nothing for it. It is only expressing to men feebly your desire that it should prevail. A wise man will not leave the right to the mercy of chance, nor wish it to prevail through the power of the majority. There is but little virtue in the action of masses of men. When the majority shall at length vote for the abolition of slavery, it will be because they are indifferent to slavery, or because there is but little slavery left to be abolished by their vote. *They* will then be the only slaves. Only *his* vote can hasten the abolition of slavery who asserts his own freedom by his vote.

I think voting is important. This is a bad comparison.

maybe

sounds Pretty cynical

I hear of a convention to be held at Baltimore, or elsewhere, for the selection of a candidate for the Presidency, made up chiefly of editors, and men who are politicians by profession; but I think, what is it to any independent, intelligent, and respectable man what decision they may come to, shall we not have the advantage of his wisdom and honesty, nevertheless? Can we not count upon some independent votes? Are there not many individuals in the country who do not attend conventions? But no: I find that the respectable man, so called, has immediately drifted from his position, and despairs of his country, when his country has more reason to despair of him. He forthwith adopts one of the candidates thus selected as the only *available* one, thus proving that he

Democrats nominated Polk at Baltimore Convention after Van Buren opposed annexation of texas.

?

True today?

I see the problem, but whats the solution??

is himself *available* for any purposes of the demagogue. His vote is of no more worth than that of any unprincipled foreigner or hireling native, who may have been bought. Oh for a man who is a *man,* and, as my neighbor says, has a bone in his back which you cannot pass your hand through! Our statistics are at fault: the population has been returned too large. How many *men* are there to a square thousand miles in this country? Hardly one. Does not America offer any inducement for men to settle here? The American has dwindled into an Odd Fellow,—one who may be known by the development of his organ of gregariousness, and a manifest lack of intellect and cheerful self-reliance; whose first and chief concern, on coming into the world, is to see that the alms-houses are in good repair; and, before yet he lawfully donned the virile garb, to collect a fund for the support of the widows and orphans that may be; who, in short, ventures to live only by the aid of the mutual insurance company, which has promised to bury him decently.

This sounds pretty racist to me. Did T fear immigrants?

Powerful speaker or leader who plays on Feelings.

Odd Fellows - secret fraternal organization like Masons - T is playing on name.

?

Friendliness

Poor-Houses

It is not a man's duty, as a matter of course, to devote himself to the eradication of any, even the most enormous wrong; he may still properly have other concerns to engage him; but it is his duty, at least, to wash his hands of it, and, if he gives it no thought longer, not to give it practically his support. If I devote myself to other pursuits and contemplations, I must first see, at least, that I do not pursue them sitting upon another man's shoulders. I must get off him first, that he may pursue his contemplations too. See what gross inconsistency is tolerated. I have heard some of my townsmen say, "I should like to have them order me out to help put down an insurrection of the slaves, or to march to Mexico,—see if I would go;" and yet these very men have each, directly by their allegiance, and so indirectly, at least, by their money, furnished a substitute. The soldier is applauded who refuses to serve in an unjust war by those who do not refuse to sustain the unjust government which makes the war; is applauded by those whose own act and authority he disregards and sees at nought; as if the State were penitent to that

no?

✓

sounds fair to me *

I wonder what Thoreau thought about women. Did they have a "duty" outside the home?

Through taxes, Thoreau points to Hypocrisy of average citizen. We pay for government action we disapprove of. (Is there any way around this?)

degree that it hired one to scourge it while it sinned, but not
to that degree that it left off (sinning) for a moment. Thus,   ✓
under the name of order and civil government, we are all
made at least to pay homage to and support our own meanness. After the first blush of (sin,) comes its indifference and
from immoral it becomes, as it were, *un*moral, and not quite
unnecessary to that life which we have made. *immoral = bad*

unmoral is ok?

The broadest and most prevalent error requires the most
disinterested virtue to sustain it. The slight reproach to which
the virtue of patriotism is commonly liable, the noble are
most likely to incur. Those who, while they disapprove of
the character and measures of a government, yield to it their
allegiance and support, are undoubtedly its most conscientious supporters, and so frequently the most serious obstacles
to reform. Some are petitioning the State to dissolve the   *Slavery?*
Union, to disregard the requisitions of the President. Why
do they not dissolve it themselves,—the union between
themselves and the State,—and refuse to pay their quota into
Back to   its treasury? Do not they stand in the same relation to the
money   State, that the State does to the Union? And have not the
again   same reasons prevented the State from resisting the Union,
which have prevented them from resisting the State?

How can a man be satisfied to entertain an opinion
Doesn't this   merely, and enjoy *it*? Is there any enjoyment in it, if his opin-
depend on the ion is that he is aggrieved? If you are cheated out of a single
neighbor and   dollar by your neighbor, you do not rest satisfied with
how badly   knowing that you are cheated, or with saying that you are
you need   cheated, or even with petitioning him to pay you your due;
the dollar?   but you take effectual steps at once to obtain the full amount,
and see that you are never cheated again. Action from prin-
ciple,—the perception and the performance of right,—changes| *yes*
things and relations; it is essentially revolutionary, and does
not consist wholly with any thing which was. It not only   *Thoreau's*
divides states and churches, it divides families; aye, it divides   *view of*
the *individual*, separating the (diabolical) in him from the (divine.)   *human*
nature, Link
yes!   Unjust laws exist: shall we be content to obey them,   *to sin above.*
or shall we endeavor to amend them, and obey them until
we have succeeded, or shall we transgress them at once? Men
generally, under such a government as this, think that they

Martin Luther
(1483-1546)
German Leader
of Protestant
Reformation

ought to wait until they have persuaded the majority to alter them. They think that, if they should resist, the remedy would be worse than the evil. But it is the fault of the government itself that the remedy *is* worse than the evil. *It* makes it worse. Why is it not more apt to anticipate and provide for reform? Why does it not cherish its wise minority? Why does it cry and resist before it is hurt? Why does it not encourage its citizens to be on the alert to point out its faults, and *do* better than it would have them? Why does it always crucify Christ, and excommunicate|Copernicus and Luther,/and pronounce Washington and Franklin rebels?

Such as
Civil War? Is
that what *I*
wants? (cf.
"why do they not
dissolve it
themselves"
above)

Nicolaus
Copernicus
(1473-1543)
Polish
Astronomer
who showed
that Earth
moves around
sun. Upset
people who
believed
Earth= center
of universe

He's over-
generalizing.
Sometimes
the government
does listen to
minorities -
at least today.

One would think, that a deliberate and practical denial of its authority was the only offence never contemplated by government; else, why has it not assigned its definite, its suitable and proportionate penalty? If a man who has no property refuses but once to earn nine shillings for the State, he is put in prison for a period unlimited by any law that I know, and determined only by the discretion of those who place him there; but if he should steal ninety times nine shillings from the State, he is soon permitted to go at large agai...

English money
(was it still in
circulation
after American
Revolution?
Ask in class)

Idealists
get treated
worse than
big crooks.

①

②

yes! ✱

If the injustice is part of the necessary friction of the machine of government, let it go, let it go: perchance it will wear smooth,—certainly the machine will wear out. If the injustice has a spring, or a pulley, or a rope, or a crank, exclusively for itself, then perhaps you may consider whether the remedy will not be worse than the evil; but if it is of such a nature that it requires you to be the agent of injustice to another, then, I say, break the law. Let your life be a counter friction to stop the machine. What I have to do is to see, at any rate, that I do not lend myself to the wrong which I condemn.

Three
distinctives
I get #3 but
1 + 2 are
hard to
visualize

③

SUMMARIZING

Summarizing a work is one of the best ways to demonstrate that you have understood it. And there will be many occasions when you will be required to summarize what others have said or written—or even what you yourself have said or written. This skill is especially important in argumentation. You will have to be able to summarize the main arguments of your opponents if you want to write a convincing argument of your own. And research papers will become ridiculously long, obscure, and unwieldy if you lack the ability to summarize your reading.

There is no clear rule to determine what passages are more significant than others. Every piece of writing must be judged on its own merits, and this means that you must consider every paragraph individually. The first sentence of a paragraph may be important if it introduces a new idea. Unfortunately for writers of summary (but fortunately for readers, who would be easily bored if every paragraph followed the same mechanical pattern) the first sentence may simply be a transitional sentence, linking the paragraph with whatever has preceded it. The *topic sentence* (also called the *thesis sentence*) is the single most important sentence in most paragraphs—the exception being the very short paragraphs that serve only as transitions. (Transitional paragraphs do not advance a new idea, but simply link together longer paragraphs devoted to ideas that are related, but not closely enough so that the paragraphs can flow smoothly together.) It is also important to realize that the topic sentence can occur anywhere in the paragraph.

As you read the material you want to summarize, limit yourself to marking no more than one or two sentences per paragraph. You should identify the topic sentence, and you may want to mark a line that contains an important supporting detail. At this point, you may choose to copy all the material you have noted onto a separate sheet of paper. But do not think that this means you have completed a summary. What you have are the notes for a summary: a collection of short quotations that are unlikely to flow smoothly together. A good summary should always be easy to read. So you must now take your notes and go to work shaping them into a clear, concise piece of writing.

Writers of summary must be prepared to *paraphrase*, which means to restate something you've read or heard into your own words. There are many different reasons for paraphrasing, and you've probably been practicing this skill since you were a child. We frequently paraphrase the words of others to soften unpleasant truths. Sometimes we may even be tempted to restate a relatively mild statement more harshly to make trouble for someone we don't like. But in writing summary, we should paraphrase only to make complex ideas more easily understandable. A paraphrase can be as long as the original material; under some circumstances, it may even be longer. So don't confuse paraphrase with summary. Paraphrasing is simply one of the skills that we call upon to write a coherent summary.

Reading over the quotations you have compiled, look for lines that seem longer than they have to be and ideas that seem unnecessarily complicated. Lines of this sort are likely subjects for paraphrase. As you restate these ideas more simply, you may also be able to include details that appeared elsewhere in the paragraph and seem too important to leave out. You should not have to restate everything that someone else has written, although there's nothing necessarily wrong in doing so. A summary can include direct quotation, so long as the quotations are relatively short and have a clarity that you yourself cannot surpass.

You should now reread your paraphrasing and any quotations that you have included. Look for gaps between sentences, where the writing seems awkward or choppy. Rearrange any sentences that would flow more smoothly once you have done so. Eliminate any repetition and add transitional phrases wherever they can help smooth the way from one idea to the next. After you have made certain that your sentences follow in a clear and easily read-able sequence and have corrected any errors in grammar, spelling, or syntax, you should have an adequate summary of the material you set out to cover. But you would be wise to read over what you have written at least one more time, making sure that the content accurately reflects the nature of whatever is being summarized. And be absolutely sure that any direct quotations are recognizable as such by being placed within quotation marks.

Writing summary requires good judgment. A writer has to be able to distinguish what is essential from what is not, and the judgment that sum-mary demands should be editorial only. If the material being summarized has a particular bias, then a good summary should indicate that that bias is part of the work in question. But *writers should not interject their own opinions into a summary of someone else's work.* The tone of summary should be neutral. You may choose to summarize someone's work so that you can criticize it later, but do not confuse summary with criticism. When summarizing, you are taking the role of helping another writer speak for herself. Don't let your own ideas get in the way.

Good summaries vary in length, depending on the length and complex-ity of the original material and on how much time or space is available for summarizing it. It's unusual, however, to need more than 500 words to sum-marize most material, and you may be required to summarize an entire book in less than half that. When summary is being used as a preliminary to some other type of work—such as argument or analysis—it is especially important to be concise. For example, if you are summarizing an argument before of-fering a counterargument of your own, you may be limited to a single para-graph. The general rule to follow is to try to do justice to whatever you are summarizing in as few words as possible and to make sure that you have a legitimate reason for writing any summary that goes on for more than a page or two.

Experienced writers know that summary is a skill worth practicing. If you find summary difficult, remind yourself that it combines two skills of fundamental and inescapable importance: reading and writing. Well-educated men and women must be proficient in both. Summarizing tests not only your ability to write simply and clearly, but also your ability to comprehend what you read. The selections in Parts 3 and 4 of this book will provide you with many opportunities for summarizing. You will also find an example of summary in the student essay by James McClain at the end of the section on mandatory drug testing (pp. 168–69).

SYNTHESIZING

Synthesis is closely related to summary, and it demands many of the same skills. The principal difference is that while summary involves identifying the major points of a single work or passage, synthesis requires identifying related material in two or more works and tying them smoothly together according to your purpose. Synthesis is often an extension of summary since writers may need to summarize various sources before they can relate these sources to one another, but synthesis does not necessarily require that a writer cover *all* the major points of the individual sources. You may go through an entire article or book and identify only one point that relates to another work you have read. And the relationships involved in your synthesis may be of various kinds. For example, two different authors may have made the same claim, or one might provide specific information that supports a generalization made by the other. On the other hand, one author might provide information that makes another author's generalization seem inadequate or even wrong.

When reading material that you may need to synthesize, always try to ask yourself: "How does this material relate to whatever else I have already read on this topic?" If you are unable to answer this question, consider a few more specific questions: Does the second of two works offer support for the first or does it reflect an entirely different thesis? If the two sources share a similar position, do they arrive at a similar conclusion by entirely different means or do they overlap at any points? Would it be easier to compare the two works or to contrast them? This process of identifying similarities and differences is essentially what synthesis is all about.

When you have determined the points that link your various sources to one another, you are ready to write a synthesis. To see how a synthesis can be organized, let us consider an example. Suppose you have read several articles on the subject of AIDS. The first article was by a scientist, the second by a clergyman, the third by a gay activist, and the fourth by a government official. You were struck by how differently these four writers responded to this epidemic. Although they all agreed that AIDS is a serious problem, each writer advanced a different proposal for fighting this disease. To write a synthesis, you would probably begin with an introductory paragraph that includes a clear thesis statement. In this case, it might be: "Although there is widespread agreement that AIDS is a serious problem, there is no consensus about how this problem can be solved." Each of the following four paragraphs could then be devoted to a brief summary of a different point of view. A final paragraph might emphasize the relationship of the several sources either by reviewing the major points of disagreement among them or by emphasizing one or two points about which everyone agreed. An outline for this type of synthesis would be something like this:

Paragraph one: Introduction
Paragraph two: Summary of first writer

Paragraph three: Summary of second writer

Paragraph four: Summary of third writer

Paragraph five: Summary of fourth writer

Paragraph six: Conclusion

Of course, any good outline should allow for some flexibility. Depending upon the material and what you want to say, your synthesis might involve fewer than six paragraphs or it might involve more. For example, if two of your sources were especially long and complex, there is no reason why you couldn't devote two paragraphs to each of these sources even though you were able to summarize your other two sources within single paragraphs.

An alternative method for organizing a synthesis involves linking two or more writers within paragraphs that focus on specific issues or points. This type of organization is especially useful when you have detected a number of similarities that you want to emphasize. Suppose that you have read six essays about abortion. Three writers favored legalized abortion for much the same reasons; three writers opposing abortion also used similar arguments. Your assignment is to identify the most common arguments made by people who favor legalized abortion and those made by people who oppose it. In this case, your outline for synthesizing this material might be organized like this:

Paragraph one: Introduction

Paragraph two: One argument in favor of abortion that was made by different writers

Paragraph three: A second argument in favor of abortion that was made by different writers.

Paragraph four: One argument against abortion that was made by different writers.

Paragraph five: A second argument against abortion that was made by different writers.

Paragraph six: Conclusion

During the course of your reading, you identified several other arguments both for and against legalized abortion, but you have decided not to include them within your synthesis since each of these points came up only within a single work and your assignment was to identify the most commonly made arguments on this subject. If you feel uneasy about ignoring these additional points, you can easily remind your audience in either your introduction or your conclusion that other arguments exist and you are focusing only on those most commonly put forward.

For an example of a synthesis written by a student, see the essay by Andrea Johnson at the end of the section on gun control (pp. 210–12).

AVOIDING PLAGIARISM

You are guilty of plagiarism if you take someone else's words or ideas without giving adequate acknowledgment. Plagiarism is one of the worst forms of dishonest writing, and you may be severely penalized for it even if you did not intend to do it.

The most obvious form of plagiarism is to submit someone else's paper as your own. No one does this accidentally. Another form of plagiarism is to copy long passages from a book or article and pretend that the words are your own. Once again, anyone doing this is almost certain to know that he or she is cheating.

But students sometimes plagiarize without intending to do so. The most common form of plagiarism is an inadequate paraphrase. Some students will read a passage in a book, change the wording, and then believe that they have transformed the material into their own work. *You must always remember that it is important to give credit to the* ideas *of others, as well as their words.* If you take most of the information another writer has provided and repeat it in essentially the same pattern, you are only a half-step away from copying the material word for word. Here is an example:

Original Source:

Hawthorne's political ordeal, the death of his mother—and whatever guilt he may have harbored on either score—afforded him an understanding of the secret psychological springs of guilt. *The Scarlet Letter* is the book of a changed man. Its deeper insights have nothing to do with orthodox morality or religion—or the universal or allegorical applications of a moral. The greatness of the book is related to its sometimes fitful characterizations of human nature and the author's almost uncanny intuitions: his realization of the bond between psychological malaise and physical illness, the nearly perfect, if sinister, outlining of the psychological techniques Chillingsworth deployed against his victim.

Plagiarism:

Nathaniel Hawthorne understood the psychological sources of guilt. His experience in politics and the death of his mother brought him deep insights that don't have anything to do with formal religion or morality. The greatness of *The Scarlet Letter* comes from its characters and the author's brilliant intuitions: Hawthorne's perception of the link between psychological and physical illness and his almost perfect description of the way Roger Chillingsworth persecuted his victim.

This student has simplified the original material, changing some of its wording. But he is clearly guilty of plagiarism. Pretending to offer his own analysis of *The Scarlet Letter*, he owes all of his ideas to another writer who is unacknowledged. Even the organization of the passage has been followed. This "paraphrase" would still be considered a plagiarism even if it ended with a reference to the original source (p. 307 of *Nathaniel Hawthorne in His Times*, by James R. Mellow). A reference or footnote would not reveal the full extent to which this student is indebted to his source.

Here is an acceptable version:

Paraphrase:

As James R. Mellow has argued in *Nathaniel Hawthorne In His Times, The Scarlet Letter* reveals a profound understanding of guilt. It is a great novel because of its insight into human nature—not because of some moral about adultery. The most interesting character is probably Roger Chillingsworth because of the way he was able to make Rev. Dimmesdale suffer (307).

This student has not only made a greater effort to paraphrase the original material, but he has also introduced it with a reference to the writer who inspired it. The introductory reference to Mellow, coupled with the subsequent page reference, "brackets" the passage—showing us that Mellow deserves the credit for the ideas in between the two references. And additional bibliographical information about this source is provided by the list of works cited which is included at the end of the paper. Turning to the bibliography we find:

Mellow, James. *Nathaniel Hawthorne in His Times*. Boston: Houghton, 1980.

One final caution: it is possible to subconsciously remember a piece of someone else's phrasing and inadvertently repeat it. You would be guilty of plagiarism if the words in question embody a critically important idea or reflect a distinctive style or turn of phrase. When you revise your rough draft, look for such unintended quotations; if you use them, show who deserves the credit for them, and *remember to put quoted material within quotation marks*.

DOCUMENTING YOUR SOURCES

"Documenting your sources" means revealing the source of information you report. You must provide documentation for:

- any direct quotation,
- any idea that has come from someone else's work, and
- any fact or statistic that is not widely known.

The traditional way to document a source is to footnote it. Strictly speaking, a "footnote" appears at the foot of the page, and an "endnote" appears at the end of the paper. But "footnote" has become a generic term covering both forms. Most writers prefer to keep their notes on a separate page since doing so is easier than remembering to save adequate space for notes on the bottom of each page. The precise form of such notes varies, depending upon the style manual being followed. Here is how a documentary footnote would look according to the style guidelines of the Modern Language Association:

A. *Bibliographic Form*

```
Manchester, William. American Caesar: Douglas MacArthur 1880–1964.
     Boston: Little, 1978.
```

B. *Note Form*

```
¹William Manchester, American Caesar: Douglas MacArthur 1880–
1964 (Boston: Little, 1978) 65.
```

The indentation is reversed, the author's name is not inverted, and the publishing data are included within parentheses. Also, the author is separated from the title by a comma rather than a period. A subsequent reference to the same work would follow a shortened form:

```
⁵Manchester 182.
```

If more than one work by this same author is cited, then a shortened form of the title would also be included:

```
⁷Manchester, Caesar 228.
```

Documentary footnotes require what many authorities now regard as unnecessary repetition, since the author's full name and the publishing data are already included in the bibliography. And many readers object to being obliged to turn frequently to another page if they want to check the notes. Some writers still use notes for documentation purposes. (You can find examples of such notes in the essays by Singer and Shurr in Part 4.) But most important style guides now urge writers to provide their documentation parenthetically within the work itself, reserving numbered notes for additional explanation or discussion that is important but cannot be included within the actual text without a loss of focus. Notes used for providing additional information are called *content* notes. (The essays by Singer and Shurr also include content notes, as do the essays by Hukill, Sedjo, and Ring which are found elsewhere in Part 4.)

The form of your documentation will vary, depending upon the subject of your paper and the requirements of your instructor. Students in the humanities are usually asked to follow the form of the Modern Language Association (MLA) or that recommended by *The Chicago Manual of Style*. Students in the social sciences are often expected to follow the format of the American Psychological Association (APA). And students in the natural sciences are usually required to use either a parenthetical system resembling that of the APA or else a system that involves numbering their sources. Make sure that you understand the requirements of your instructor, and remember that you can consult a specific manual in your field if you run into problems. Here is a list of manuals that can be found in many college libraries:

American Institute of Physics. Publication Board. *Style Manual for Guidance in the Preparation of Papers*. 3rd ed. New York: American Inst. of Physics, 1978.

American Chemical Society. *American Chemical Society Style Guide and Handbook*. Washington: American Chemical Soc., 1985.

American Mathematical Society. *A Manual for Authors of Mathematical Papers*. 7th ed. Providence: American Mathematical Soc., 1980.

American Psychological Association. *Publication Manual of the American Psychological Association*. 3rd ed. Washington: American Psychological Assn., 1983.

The Chicago Manual of Style. 13th ed. Chicago: University of Chicago Press, 1982.

Council of Biology Editors. Style Manual Committee. *CBE Style Manual: A Guide for Authors, Editors, and Publishers in the Biological Sciences*. 5th ed. Bethesda: Council of Biology Editors, 1983.

Gibaldi, Joseph, and Walter S. Achtert. *MLA Handbook for Writers of Research Papers*. 3rd ed. New York: Modern Language Assn., 1988.

Harvard Law Review. *A Uniform System of Citation*. 13th ed. Cambridge: Harvard Law Review Assn., 1981.

A detailed discussion of all of these styles is beyond the range of this chapter. But the following pages provide model entries for the most frequently used styles.

PARENTHETICAL DOCUMENTATION: THE MLA AUTHOR/WORK STYLE

Since 1984 the Modern Language Association has recommended that parenthetical documentation take the place of endnote or footnote citations. In MLA form, the author's name is followed by a page reference. It is not necessary to repeat within the parentheses information that is already provided within the text. If you are used to using footnotes for documentation, this format may seem a little strange at first, but it has the great merit of being easy to use and easy to understand. (Remember that additional information on these sources will be provided in a separate bibliography.)

A. A Work by a Single Author

```
Henry James often identified wickedness with sexual duplicity (Kazin
227).
```

or

```
Alfred Kazin has argued that Henry James identified wickedness with
sexual duplicity (227).
```

There is no punctuation between the author's name and the page reference when both are cited parenthetically. Note also that the abbreviation "p." or "pp." is not used before the page reference.

B. A Work with More Than One Author

```
Cleanth Brooks and Robert Penn Warren have argued that "indirection
is an essential part of the method of poetry" (573).
```

or

```
Although this sonnet may seem obscure, its meaning becomes clearer when
we realize "indirection is an essential part of the method of poetry"
(Brooks and Warren 573).
```

Note that when a sentence ends with a quotation, the parenthetical reference comes before the final punctuation mark. Note also that the ampersand (&) is not used in MLA style. When referring to a work by more than three authors, you should follow the guidelines for bibliographic entries and list only the first author's name followed by "et al." (Latin for *et alii*, "and others").

```
These works "derive from a profound disillusionment with modern life"
(Baym et al. 910).
```

C. A Work with a Corporate Author

When a corporate author has a long name, you should include it within the text rather than within parentheses. For example:

```
In 1980 the Council on Environmental Quality reported that there is
growing evidence of ground water contamination throughout the United
States (81).
```

rather than

There is growing evidence of ground water contamination throughout the
United States (Council on Environmental Quality 81).

Although both of these forms are technically correct, the first is
preferred because it is easier to read. Long parenthetical references
are unnecessarily intrusive, interrupting the flow of ideas.

D. *A Work with More Than One Volume*

When you wish to cite a specific part of a multivolume work,
include the volume number between the author and the
page reference:

As Jacques Barzun has argued, "The only hope of true culture is to make
classifications broad and criticism particular" (2: 340).

Note that the volume number is given in an arabic numeral, and a
space separates the colon and the page reference. The abbreviation
"vol." is not used unless you wish to cite the entire volume: (Barzun, vol. 2).

E. *More Than One Work by the Same Author*

If you cite more than one work by the same author, you need to
make your references distinct. You can do so by putting a comma
after the author's name and then adding a shortened form of the
title: (Hardy, *Mayor* 179). But your paper will be easier to read if
you include either the author or the title directly in the text:

Twain's late work reflects a low opinion of human nature. But when
Satan complains that all men are cowards (Stranger 184), he is only
echoing Col. Sherburn's speech in Huckleberry Finn (123—24).

F. *A Quotation within a Cited Work*

If you want to use a quotation that you have discovered in another
book, your reference must show that you acquired this material sec-
ondhand and that you have not consulted the original source. Use
the abbreviation "qtd. in" (for "quoted in") to make the distinction
between the author of the passage being quoted and the author of
the work in which you found this passage:

In 1835 Thomas Macaulay declared the British to be "the acknowledged
leaders of the human race" (qtd. in Davis 231).

G. A Quotation of Poetry

Identify line numbers when you quote poetry, but do not use the abbreviations "l." or "ll." These abbreviations can easily be confused with numbers. Write "line" or "lines" in your first citation of poetry; subsequent citations should include only the line numbers. Quotations of three lines or less should be included directly into the text of your paper. Separate the lines with a slash (/), leaving an extra space both before and after the slash:

```
Yeats returned to this theme in "The Second Coming": "The best lack all
conviction, while the worst / Are full of passionate intensity" (7-8).
```

Each line of longer quotations should begin on a new line, indented ten spaces from the margin.

PARENTHETICAL DOCUMENTATION:
THE APA AUTHOR/YEAR STYLE

The American Psychological Association requires that in-text documentation identifies the author of the work being referred to and the year in which this work was published. This information should be provided parenthetically, although it is not necessary to repeat any information that has already been provided directly in the sentence.

A. One Work by a Single Author

```
It has been argued that fathers can play an important role in the
treatment of eating disorders (Byrne, 1987).
```

or

```
Byrne (1987) argued that fathers can play an important role in the
treatment of eating disorders.
```

or

```
In 1987 Katherine Byrne argued that fathers can play an important role
in the treatment of eating disorders.
```

If the reference is to a specific chapter or page, that information should also be included. For example:

```
(Byrne, 1987, p. 93)
(Byrne, 1987, chap. 6)
```

Note that the abbreviations for page and chapter emphasize the distinction between the year of publication and the part of the work being referred to.

B. A Work with Two or More Authors

If a work has two authors, you should mention the names of both authors every time a reference is made to this work:

```
A recent study of industry (Bell & Freeman, 1991) argued that . . .
```

or

```
More recently, Bell and Walker (1991) have argued that . . .
```

Note that the ampersand (&) is used only within parentheses.

Scientific papers often have multiple authors because of the amount of research involved. In the first reference to a work with up to six authors, you should identify each of the authors:

```
Hodges, McKnew, Cytryn, Stern, and Kline (1982) have shown . . .
```

Subsequent references to the same work should use an abbreviated form:

```
This method was also used in an earlier study (Hodges et al., 1982).
```

If a work has six authors or more, this abbreviated form should be used even in the first reference. If confusion is possible because you refer to more than one work by the first author, list as many authors as necessary to distinguish between the two works.

C. A Work with a Corporate Author

When a work has a corporate author, your first reference should include the full name of the corporation, committee, agency, or institution involved. For example:

```
(United States Fish and Wildlife Service [USFWS], 1984)
```

Subsequent references to the same source can be abbreviated:

```
(USFWS, 1984)
```

D. A Reference to More Than One Work

When the same citation refers to two or more sources, the works should be listed alphabetically according to the author's name and separated with semicolons:

```
(Pepler & Rubin, 1982; Schesinger, 1982; Young, 1984)
```

If you are referring to more than one work by the same author(s), list the works in the order in which they were published.

```
The validity of this type of testing is now well established (Col-
lins, 1986, 1988).
```

If you refer to more than one work by the same author published in the same year, distinguish individual works by identifying them as "a," "b," "c," etc.:

```
These findings have been questioned by Walker (1983a, 1983b).
```

ORGANIZING A BIBLIOGRAPHY

Documenting your sources parenthetically or with notes allows you to reveal exactly which parts of a paper are supported by or owed to the works you have consulted. But a bibliography, which is a list of the sources consulted, is also essential so that readers can evaluate your research and possibly draw upon your sources for work of their own.

Works Cited in MLA Style

In an MLA style bibliography, the works cited are arranged in alphabetical order determined by the author's last name. MLA style requires that the author's first name be given. Every important word in the titles of books, articles, and journals is capitalized. The titles of books, journals, and newspapers are all underlined (italicized). The titles of articles, stories, and poems appear within quotation marks. Second and subsequent lines are indented five spaces (leave five spaces blank). Here are some examples:

A. A Book with One Author

```
Marcus, Steven. Engels, Manchester, and the Working Class. New York:
     Random, 1974.
```

Although it is important to give the author's full name, the book's full title, and the place of publication, you should use a shortened form of the publisher's name (Random House in this case) by citing one key term.

B. A Book with Two or Three Authors

```
Gilbert, Sandra M., and Susan Gubar. The Madwoman in the Attic: The
     Woman Writer and the Nineteenth-Century Literary Imagination.
     New Haven: Yale UP, 1979.
```

Note that the subtitle is included, set off from the main title by a colon. The second author's name is not inverted, and abbreviations are used for "University Press" to provide a shortened form of the publisher's name. For books with three authors, put commas after the names of the first two authors; separate the second two authors with a comma followed by "and."

C. An Edited Book

```
Garner, Helen, ed. A Book of Religious Verse. New York: Oxford
     UP, 1972.
```

D. A Book with More Than Three Authors or Editors

```
Clark, Donald, et al., eds. English Literature. New York: Macmil-
     lan, 1960.
```

Give the name of the first author or editor only and add the abbreviation "et al."

E. A Revised Edition

```
Carruth, Gorton. The Encyclopedia of American Facts and Dates. 8th
     ed. New York: Harper, 1987.
```

F. A Work in an Anthology

```
O'Brien, Patricia. "Michael Foucault's History of Culture." The New
     Cultural History. Ed. Lynn Hunt. Berkeley: U of California P,
     1989. 25-46.
```

Note that a period comes after the title of the selection but before the second quotation marks. A period is also used to separate the date of publication from the pages between which the selection can be found. No abbreviation is used before the page reference. (For a variation on this example, see the note on the bottom of p. 500.)

G. A Translated Book

Camus, Albert. Notebooks 1935–1942. Trans. Philip Thody. New York:
Knopf, 1963.

H. A Work in More Than One Volume

Daiches, David. A Critical History of English Literature. 2 vols. New
York: Ronald, 1960.

If the work has been published over several years, give the inclusive dates.

I. An Introduction, Preface, Foreword, or Afterword

Schorer, Mark. Afterword. Babbitt. By Sinclair Lewis. New York:
Signet-NAL, 1961. 320–327.

J. An Article in an Encyclopedia

Hunt, Roberta M. "Child Welfare." Encyclopedia Americana. 1985 ed.

For citing material from well-known encyclopedias, give the author's name first, then the article title. If material is arranged alphabetically within the source, which is usually the case, there is no need to include volume and page numbers. You should give the full title of the encyclopedia, the edition if it is stated, and the year of publication (e.g., "15th ed. 1986"). When no edition number is stated, identify the edition by the year of publication (e.g., "1985 ed."). If the author of the article is identified only by initials, look elsewhere within the encyclopedia for a list identifying the names these initials stand for. If the article is unsigned, give the title first. (Note: This same form can be used for other reference books, such as dictionaries and the various editions of *Who's Who*.)

K. A Government Publication

United States. Bureau of the Census. State and Metropolitan Data Book
1986. Washington: GPO, 1986.

For many government publications, the author is unknown. When this is the case, the agency that issued the publication should be listed as the author. State the name of the government (e.g., "United States," "Florida," "United Nations") followed by a period. Then give the name of the agency that issued the work, using abbreviations only if you can do so clearly (e.g., "Bureau of the Census,"

"National Institute on Drug Abuse," "Dept. of Labor") followed by a period. The underlined title of the work comes next followed by another period. Then give place of publication, publisher, and date. Most federal publications are printed in Washington by the Government Printing Office (GPO), but you should be alert for exceptions. (Note: Treat pamphlets just as you would a book.)

L. A Journal Article with One Author

Swann, Karen. "The Sublime and the Vulgar." College English 52
     (1990): 7–20.

The volume number comes after the journal title without any intervening punctuation. The year of publication is included within parentheses after the volume number. A colon separates the year of publication and the page reference. Leave one space after the volume number and one space after the colon.

M. A Journal Article Paginated Anew in Each Issue

Rosen, Michael J. "Is There a Midwestern Literature?" The Iowa Review
     20.3 (1990): 94–102.

In this case, the issue number is included immediately after the volume number, and the two are separated by a period without any intervening space.

N. An Article from a Magazine Published Monthly

Greenberg, Donald P. "Computers and Architecture." Scientific American Feb. 1991: 104–109.

Instead of citing the volume number, give the month and year of the issue. Abbreviate the month when it has more than four letters. (May, June, and July are spelled out.)

O. An Article from a Magazine Issued Weekly

Gallant, Mavis. "Overhead in a Balloon." New Yorker 2 July 1984:
     34–44.

The form is the same as for an article in a magazine that is issued monthly, but you add the date immediately before the month. Note that a hyphen between page numbers indicates consecutive pages. When an article is printed on nonconsecutive pages—beginning on page 34, for example, and continuing on page 78—give only the first page number and a plus sign: 34+.

P. An Article from a Daily Newspaper

Robinson, Karen. "The Line to Privacy Is Unlisted." <u>Milwaukee Journal</u>
    26 Mar. 1985, sunrise ed., sec. 2: 2.

If more than one edition is available on the date in question, specify the edition immediately after the date. If the city of publication is not part of the newspaper's name, identify the city in brackets after the newspaper title. Since newspapers often consist of separate sections, you should cite the section number if each section has separate pagination. If a newspaper consists of only one section, or if the pagination is continuous from one section to the next, then you do not need to include the section number. If separately paginated sections are identified by letters, omit the section reference but include the letter of the section with the page number (e.g., 7B or D19). If the article is unsigned, begin the citation with the title of the article; alphabetize the article under its title, passing over small words like "a" and "the."

Q. An Editorial

Wicker, Tom. "The Key to Unity." Editorial. <u>New York Times</u> 30 Jan.
    1991, natl. ed.: A15.

Editorials are identified as such between the title of the article and the title of the newspaper or magazine.

R. An Interview

Nelson, Veronica. Personal interview. 16 Aug. 1991.

If you interview someone, alphabetize the interview under the name of the person interviewed.

References in APA Style

In APA style, the reference list is arranged alphabetically, the order being determined by the author's last name. The date of publication is emphasized by placing it within parentheses immediately after the author's name. If a second or third line is necessary, such lines should be indented three spaces (leave three spaces blank).

A. Book with One Author

Choate, P. (1990). <u>Agents of influence</u>. New York: Knopf.

Note that the author's first name is indicated only by an initial. Capital letters are used only for the first word of the title and the first word of the subtitle if there is one. (But when a proper name appears within a title, it retains the capitalization it would normally receive. For example: *A history of ideas in Brazil.*) The name of the publisher, Alfred A. Knopf, is given in shortened form. A period comes after the parenthesis surrounding the date of publication, and also after the title and publisher.

B. *Book with Two or More Authors*

Youcha, G. & Seixas, J. (1989). <u>Drugs, alcohol, and your children: How to keep your family substance-free</u>. New York: Crown.

An ampersand is used to separate the names of two authors. When there are three or more authors, separate their names with commas and put an ampersand immediately before the last author's name.

C. *Edited Book*

Bottomore, T., & Nisbet, R. (Eds.). (1978). <u>A history of sociological analysis</u>. New York: Basic.

Give the names of all editors, no matter how many there are. The abbreviation for editors is "Eds."; it should be included within parentheses between the names of the editors and the date of publication. A single editor is identified as such by "Ed." in parentheses.

D. *Article or Chapter in an Edited Book*

Rickman, J. (1940). On the nature of ugliness and the creative impulse. In H. Ruitenbeek (Ed.), <u>The creative imagination</u> (pp. 97–121). Chicago: Quadrangle.

Do not invert the editor's name when it is not in the author's position. Do not put the title of the article or chapter in quotation marks. Use a comma to separate the editor from the title of the edited book. The pages between which the material can be found appear within parentheses immediately after the book title. Use "p." for page and "pp." for pages.

E. *Translated Book*

Beauvoir, S. de (1972). <u>The coming of age</u> (P. O'Brien, Trans.). New York: Putnam's. (Original work published 1970)

Within parentheses immediately after the book title, give the translator's name followed by a comma and the abbreviation "Trans." If the original work was published earlier, include this information at the end.

F. Revised Edition of a Book

Samuelson, P. A. (1980). <u>Economics</u> (11th ed.). New York: McGraw.

The edition is identified immediately after the title. Note that edition is abbreviated "ed." and should not be confused with "Ed." for editor.

G. Book with a Corporate Author

American Medical Association. (1982). <u>Family medical guide</u>. New York: Random.

H. Multivolume Book

Jones, E. (1953–57). <u>The life and work of Sigmund Freud</u> (Vol. 2). New York: Basic.

The volume number is included within parentheses immediately after the title. When a multivolume book is published over a number of years, list the years between which it was published.

I. Journal Article with One Author

Farber, N. (1990). The significance of race and class in marital de-cisions among unmarried adolescent mothers. <u>Social Problems</u>, <u>37</u>, 51–63.

Do not use quotation marks around the article title. Capitalize all important words in the journal title and underline. Put a comma after the journal title and then give the volume and page numbers. Abbreviations are not used for "volume" and "page." To distin-guish between the numbers, underline the volume number and put a comma between it and the page numbers.

J. Journal Article with Up to Six Authors

Korner, A., Zeanah, C. H., Linden, J., Berkowitz, R., Kraemer, H., & Agras, W. S. (1985). The relations between neonatal and later ac-tivity and temperament. <u>Child Development</u>, <u>56</u>, 38–52.

K. Journal Article Paginated Anew in Each Issue

Kupfer, D. J., & Reynolds, C. F. (1983). Sleep disorders. <u>Hospital Practice</u>, <u>28</u> (2), 101–119.

When each issue of a journal begins with page 1, you need to include the issue number in parentheses immediately after the underlined volume number.

L. *Article from a Magazine Issued Monthly*

Crump, M. (1991, February). You eat what you are. Natural History, pp. 46–50.

Within parentheses immediately after the author, include the month of issue after the year of publication. Use "p." or "pp." in front of the page number(s). Do not include the volume number. Follow the same form for an article in a magazine issued on a specific day, but add the date after the month:

Hazen, R. M. (1991, February 25). Why my kids hate science. News-week, p. 7.

M. *Article from a Newspaper*

Winslow, R. (1991, January 29). Medical costs soar, defying firms' cures. Wall Street Journal, p. B1.

Place the exact date of issue within parentheses immediately after the author. After the newspaper title, specify the page number(s).

N. *Government Document*

National Institute of Alcohol Abuse and Alcoholism. (1980). Facts about alcohol and alcoholism (DHHS Publication No. ADM 80–31). Washington DC: U.S. Government Printing Office.

List the agency that produced the document as the author if no author is identified. Within parentheses immediately after the document title, give the publication number which the government assigned to the document; it can usually be found on or near the title page and should not be confused with the call number which a library may have assigned to the document.

O. *Anonymous Work*

A breath of fresh air. (1991, April 29). Time. p. 49.

Alphabetize the work under the first important word in the title, and follow the form for the type of publication in question (in this case, a magazine published weekly). Use a short version of the title for the parenthetical citation in the text: ("Breath," 1991).

The Numbered System

In a numbered system the bibliography may be arranged in alphabetical order (determined by the authors' last names) or in the order in which the works are cited within the paper itself. Once this sequence is established, the items are assigned numbers in consecutive order beginning with 1, and these numbers are used as citations within the paper. There are many variations on the particular form of the bibliographical entries; authors of scientific papers should adopt the style recommended by the journal for which they are writing. But here are examples of two frequently used forms:

A. Biology

```
1. Ferris, F. G.; Beveridge, T. J. Functions of bacterial cell sur-
        face structures. Bioscience. 35:172–177; 1985.
2. Lewis, A. E. Biostatistics. New York: Reinhold; 1966.
```

Note that neither journal nor book titles are underlined. Quotation marks are not used for article titles. The year of publication appears at the end of the citation, and it is preceded by a semicolon.

B. Chemistry

```
(1) Silverman, M. P. J. Chem. Ed. 1984, 62, pp. 112–114.
(2) Bard, A. J. Chemical Equilibrium; Harper & Row: New York, 1966;
        pp. 17–28.
```

Note that journal titles are abbreviated, and article titles are not included.

Although the precise form of the bibliography will vary from discipline to discipline, certain features remain constant when a numbered system is used:

- Whenever the same source is cited, the same number is cited.
- Numbers appear on the same line as the text, and they are usually either underlined or italicized so that they can be distinct from other numbers in the text.

With these two points in mind, you should not confuse a numbered system of references with the use of numbered footnotes. When footnotes are used, numbers appear in consecutive order, each number is used only once, and numbers are raised above the line. When a numbered system of references is used, the same number appears whenever the source assigned that number is cited within the text, and the numbers will not necessarily be consecutive.

A numbered reference:

```
There are approximately 125,000 children at risk of developing Hun-
tington's disease (4).
```

or

```
There are approximately 125,000 children at risk of developing Hun-
tington's disease (4, p. 22).
```

A footnote:

```
There are approximately 125,000 children at risk of developing Hun-
tington's disease.⁴
```

For an example of a numbered system in use, see the essay by Timothy Paetsch (pp. 415–18) or consult an issue of *Science,* a journal that can be found in most libraries.

A CHECKLIST FOR DOCUMENTATION

Whether you document your sources by using footnotes or one of the recommended systems for parenthetical references, you should honor the following principles:

1. Remember to document any direct quotation, any idea that has come from someone else's work, and any fact or statistic that is not widely known.
2. Be sure to include all quotations in quotation marks.
3. Make sure that paraphrases are in your own words but still accurately reflect the content of the original material.
4. Remember that every source cited in a reference should have a corresponding entry in the bibliography.
5. Be consistent. Don't shift from the author/year system to the author/work system in the middle of your paper.
6. Try to vary the introductions you use for quotations and paraphrases and make sure that the material in question has been incorporated smoothly into your text. Read your first draft aloud to be better able to judge its readability.
7. When you mention authorities by name, try to identify who they are so that your audience can evaluate the source. (For example, "According to Ira Glasser, executive director of the American Civil Liberties Union, recent congressional legislation violates. . . .") But do not insult the intelligence of your audience by identifying well-known figures.
8. If in doubt about whether to document a source, you would probably be wise to go ahead and document it. But be careful not to over-document your paper. A paper that is composed of one reference after another usually lacks synthesis and interpretation.

PART 3

CASES FOR
ARGUMENT

◆

Many writers find that choosing a topic is one of the most difficult steps in writing. If you expect to be writing arguments, you can often identify topics by asking yourself how you react to the various news stories you hear on television or read in newspapers—not just large public questions that are reported in great detail (and likely to attract many other writers) but also smaller stories that receive less attention. The reading you do in college will usually be dominated by lengthy assignments designed to make you more knowledgeable in the fields you have chosen to study. Nevertheless, you should still try to read at least one newspaper or newsmagazine on a fairly regular basis. Doing so will contribute to your general knowledge of the world and provide you with a base of information upon which you can draw whether writing a paper or making informed decisions.

The dozen articles collected in Part 3 are intended to represent the sort of topics for argumentation that you might discover when you read a newspaper or magazine for information. Unlike most of the selections you will find in Part 4, the "cases for argument" are primarily informative rather than persuasive. They report information on topics that lend themselves to argumentation, but they are not arguments. Although you may occasionally detect some bias in the way information has been reported, you will find that each of the twelve cases provides information about which it is possible to have more than one type of reaction. As you read them, you should begin by identifying key points so that you could summarize each case if asked to do so. But you should also ask yourself what you think about the information that has been made available to you. Do not worry about whether your opinion is "correct" or whether you can defend it in detail. You are likely to have many opportunities to investigate these and other topics more thoroughly. Treat the following cases as an opportunity to practice those skills in critical thinking that are discussed in Part 2.

Because most people read only one newspaper on a regular basis, five of the following cases were taken from the same paper: *The Wall Street Journal*, which is widely recognized as one of the best newspapers in the country. The other cases have come from a selection of periodicals likely to be found in a public library. These range from mass-circulation newsmagazines such as *Time* to smaller but nevertheless influential magazines like *The New Republic*.

♦ CASE 1 ♦

KRYSTAL MILLER
School Dress Codes

A staff reporter for The Wall Street Journal, *Krystal Miller filed this story from Detroit after school authorities in that city decided to impose a dress code upon students. The following article was first published in the* Journal *on April 5, 1990. As you read it, try to understand not only the purpose of dress codes but also why some people are objecting to them.*

With a wardrobe that includes three leather coats, a Gucci gold-link necklace and two pairs of Gucci gym shoes, 15-year-old Melchishaua Person is considered the best-dressed student at Henry Ford High School. Her mother, who owns a costume-jewelry store, has spent $5,000 for her daughter's clothes as a reward for her B average. 1

Melchishaua is dismayed by the prospect of a dress code at school that would ban such trendy clothing. But all too literally, she may be dressed fit to kill. The desire to "bust fresh"—to dress at the height of teen-age fashion—has become dangerous at many of the nation's inner-city public schools. Yet many students, confident that if something violent happens it will happen to somebody else, resist dress codes as a blow to their culture and their freedom to express themselves in fashion. 2

Students have been beaten, shot and robbed of their leather and goose-down coats, thick gold chains, designer shoes and other prized items. A high-school student in New York was killed for his bomber jacket. Another, in Detroit, was found dead with his coat and shoes missing. More than 10 students have been wounded in Detroit in other clothing robberies near schools since last September. 3

Protest March

Alarmed officials of Detroit's schools plan to prohibit high-priced clothing and jewelry next fall. Similar codes have already been imposed, or will be, at schools in Baltimore, Chicago, Los Angeles, New York and New Haven. 4

The prohibitions enrage many students, though not all. Teen-agers here   5
have organized the Student Committee Against Dress Codes and held a protest march at Detroit's school administration building. "Anything can happen to you at any time," says Tamika Johnson, a 17-year-old senior at Henry
Ford. "The bottom line is that if my parents buy the clothes I have to be
able to wear them."

Dress codes as a deterrent to crime bother some adults. Mary Louise   6
Starks, who is in charge of psychological services for the Detroit school system, says they fail to address the roots of teen-age violence. "A dress code is
a temporary measure that is limited in scope," she says. "Students are committing these crimes because they don't have a sense of power and self-esteem.
They steal from their peers to gain control over another person."

Violators Sent Home

Such motivations, she believes, are unlikely to disappear when a dress code   7
is imposed. She also observes: "Our entire society has become extremely
materialistic. Greed is reflected from the highest public office to the streets."

Baltimore imposed its code last year after an outbreak of fights over   8
leather coats and gold chains. The code bans jewelry, leather and fur coats,
and designer jogging suits. Violators are sent home with a letter to their
parents. And students are now required to carry see-through book bags to
make it harder for them to conceal weapons at school.

"Violence isn't as bad as it was," says Jonathan Johns, 17, a senior at   9
Baltimore's Dunbar High School. "There's no way to prove it's all due to
the dress code, but I feel it's had a big impact." School officials say there
were only 15 assaults and robberies or attempted robberies in 1989, when the
code was established, down from 23 in 1988, and the number of incidents
involving guns fell to 35 from 55.

Tilton Elementary School in Chicago adopted a voluntary uniform of   10
navy blue and white last year after 12 students were robbed walking to or
from school. About half the school's 850 students wear the uniform. It may
become mandatory next September. "The code shows that you come to school
to learn and not to play, and it saves your parents money," says fifth-grader
LaDonna Wright, 10, who attends class in a white blouse and blue jumper.
"And people won't get killed or beat up for their clothes."

Nor will they at Mumford High School in Detroit, so far the city's   11
only public high school with a dress code. The code was imposed in 1986
after beatings and shootings of students for their Marc Buchanan brand leather
coats and jackets, Guess brand blue jackets and Adidas Top 10 gym shoes.

Today, the code prohibits those items as well as designer eyeglasses,   12
gold jewelry, designer purses, leather briefcases and about 30 other items. A
clause permitting officials to add to the list was recently invoked after several
Detroit youngsters were shot and robbed of Triple F.A.T. Goosedown coats.
The brightly colored coats, often with fur trim, cost as much as $250 each.

Violators of the Mumford code may be slapped with five day's suspen-   13
sion and a permanent blemish on their records. "The code has worked

marvelously well," says Mumford Principal Robert Oden. "Most kids don't think about the code anymore. It's become a way of life."

Students do think about it, however. "They have no right to tell us what to wear," says 16-year-old Windy Watson, a Mumford sophomore. "The school's job is to teach us, not tell us how to dress." She says many students violate the code regularly without being caught; she herself is carrying a contraband $154 Coach purse.

Some students at inner-city schools get money to buy expensive gear from drug dealing. But most others, or their parents, earn it from hard work.

Nicole Williams, a 17-year-old senior at Detroit's Cass Technical High School, often works as many as 35 hours a week at a McDonald's restaurant to pay for clothes and jewelry. She owns and wears to school a $202 pair of Guccis, a $68 pair of Used brand blue jeans and a $100 rhinestone-studded blue-jean jacket. "If they ban expensive clothes," she gripes, "a lot of students won't have anything to wear."

At Osborn High School in Detroit, 14-year-old Eric Harrington, a freshman, says he saves his allowance to pay for his clothing and jewelry. A Fila emblem adorns his $50 turtleneck sweater. "I like expensive clothes like Fila and Gucci," he says. "If I buy something I should be allowed to wear it."

Teen-age tastes change rapidly and differ from place to place. Bomber jackets (and gold-capped teeth) are hot in New York but not in Detroit. Chicago students prize athletic jackets with basketball and football team logotypes. Students in Los Angeles take special care in choosing colors: The wrong ones might invite attack by an unfriendly gang.

However varied the expression, the motivations for "busting fresh" seem universal. "First impressions are crucial," says Melchishaua Person, the well-dressed sophomore. "I feel better about myself when I look good. Everybody wants to look good." Robbed at Osborn High of his $130 goose-down coat, a 15-year-old student said he wore expensive clothes because otherwise he "probably wouldn't get a girlfriend."

Still, some students accept the codes as needed. "The reason the administration has made these rules is for our safety," says Christina Royal, 17, a junior at Crenshaw High School in Los Angeles, which has banned bandannas, baseball caps and other items associated with gangs. "I don't feel violated. It's for our own safety."

Marc Chambers, an 18-year-old senior at Pershing High School in Detroit, favors a code. Last year, he was robbed of his $500 full-length leather coat at gunpoint as he walked home from school. "A boy walked up to me and told me to take off the coat or he would bust a cap on [shoot] me," Marc says.

Miss Person's mother, Antreina Stone, is happy to give her daughter expensive clothing, but also says the code may be needed. "I'm in favor of a code if it will protect young people," she says. "Students can always wear their clothes on weekends and after school."

Says Frank Hayden, the Detroit school board member who proposed   23
the dress code: "I prefer that young people not be allowed to wear what they
want to my having to visit them in the hospital or attend another funeral."

QUESTIONS FOR DISCUSSION AND WRITING

1. Why have some public schools begun to impose dress codes? Is there any
   evidence that they can achieve their purpose? What are the principal objections to these codes? Summarize the two sides in this dispute.
2. Consider whether it is appropriate for a teenager to spend $202 on a pair
   of shoes—or for a mother to spend $5,000 on her daughter's wardrobe.
   Are such expenditures justifiable?
3. A 15-year-old student quoted in this story claims that he probably wouldn't
   get a girlfriend if he did not wear expensive clothes. Is this realistic? How
   important is clothing to teenagers?
4. Would you recommend a dress code for any of the schools you have
   attended? If so, what would it be like? Be prepared to defend your position.

♦ CASE 2 ♦

SUZANNE ALEXANDER

Fixed at a Price

First published in The Wall Street Journal *on September 24, 1990, the following
article was originally titled "Egged on by Moms, Many Teenagers Get Plastic Surgery: 'Dumbo' Ears, Banana Noses Can Be Fixed at a Price—and a Psychological
Cost." Although this title may be long, it provided newspaper readers with an efficient summary of what they could expect in the article. Suzanne Alexander is a
staff reporter on the* Journal. *As you read her article, try to understand not only
why cosmetic surgery is becoming more popular among teenagers but also why this
trend has alarmed some experts.*

As an eighth-grade graduation present, Kristina Olson got new ears from her   1
mother. Leigh Kane, at 17, got a new nose.

   Since last month, Danielle Borngiorno, 14, has had narrower hips and   2
thinner thighs. Her mother offered to pay for breast implants, too, but Danielle decided against that, for the time being. She is still considering chin and
nose work and a cheek implant. "Now, [it's] just like, let's go every week
and get something improved on. There are so many things you can do,"
says Danielle, who lives in Brooklyn, N.Y.

Why bother with padded bras and Clearasil when silicone and derma- 3
brasion promise permanence? Why spend one's adolescence brooding about
receding chins or big ears when it is so simple to have plastic surgery?

New, Young Clientele

To the dismay of at least some psychologists and medical doctors, cosmetic 4
surgery is now hardly more exotic than orthodontics among children whose
parents have the wherewithal to pay $600 or $6,000 for a surgical procedure
to improve on nature. Statistics don't exist, but many plastic surgeons say
their teen-age clientele has doubled in the past five years and now is as much
as 25% of their business.

Nose and ear jobs remain the most popular operations. But dermabra- 5
sion (sanding off layers of skin), breast augmentation and liposuction (fat
sucking) are coming on strong with kids, not just with middle-aged enter-
tainers like Phyllis Diller. Many Asian boys and girls, overeager to assimilate, seek to reshape the epicanthic fold in their eyelids. Some black youths,
a la Michael Jackson, see surgeons for narrower noses and thinner lips.

Observers critical of the phenomenon see in it pampered children who 6
can't tolerate the pain of being themselves. They see a society obsessed with
appearance and with narrow-minded notions of what constitutes beauty.

"I hear doctors defend the right of teens to have face-lift surgery and 7
eyelid surgery," says Frederick Stucker, chairman of the Otolaryngology—
Head and Neck Surgery Department at Louisiana State University, "but I
think we send the wrong message when we're willing to do it for teens."
Dr. Stucker maintains that a lot of operations are unnecessary because teen-
age acne, babyfat, and other "problems" usually disappear on their own as
kids get older.

Wanting It All

Adds Norman M. Cole, vice president of the American Society of Plastic 8
and Reconstructive Surgeons: "A real problem in our society is that parents
want everything for their children. Aesthetic surgery has become a commodity. 'I want my son to have a new stereo, car, nose and chin.' This is something that deserves some careful interrogation." Surgery to change racial
characteristics, Dr. Cole says, is "an inappropriate concession to Western
images. The Oriental eye in China is considered the most beautiful in the
world. It's a sad commentary . . ."

Cosmetic surgeons have their own interests in the matter, and some of 9
them argue that plastic surgery is a real boon to teenagers psychologically.
Insecurity, self-consciousness and a lack of self-esteem vanish once the bandages
come off. Surgery can take "years off a psychiatrist's couch," says Walter
Berman, a facial plastic surgeon in Beverly Hills, Calif.

"I did two kids [a 14-year-old girl and a 16-year-old boy] this week 10
who had a hereditary bagging of the upper eyelid," says Lori Hansen, a

plastic surgeon in Oklahoma City, Okla. "It made them look tired all the time. So we just took the extra skin and fat away. Things are so easily fixed now. We don't have to live with them."

But critics say that in many cases parents are to blame for wanting "perfect-looking" children, thus encouraging low self-esteem in their offspring. "We see it often," says Pearlman D. Hicks, a plastic surgeon in Long Beach, Calif. "The parent tells the kid, 'Your nose looks terrible. You don't even look like part of the family.' [Parents] plant the seed and get the kids worried."   11

Nose jobs, of course, are nothing new for teen-agers. But they once were a thing of the affluent and the disfigured. Now, middle-class people get them almost willy-nilly. They are a socially acceptable mid-course correction in the life of an adolescent. New procedures, like liposuction, have been introduced in the U.S. within the past 10 years and pull in a lot of patients.   12

Many teen-agers who have had cosmetic surgery say they are glad they did. Why put it off and prolong the agony when they are likely to have it done eventually anyway?   13

"My mom had the same problem. She had something done about it. I could have waited years, but I did it now," says Abigail Clawson, 15, speaking of her nose and chin jobs last April. Abigail, of Westlake Village, Calif., had a bump on her nose and a receding chin. Nobody ever teased her about her profile, but for some children, ridicule from schoolmates can be merciless: "Is that your nose or a banana?" the kids in Hartshorne, Okla., used to taunt Amanda Andrews, 13. For years, Amanda would come home from school weeping.   14

Explains Lorraine Hollis, Amanda's grandmother and legal guardian: "She had a great big snoot that slumped down—and a little, pointed chin. It gave her a witchy look." Ms. Hollis took Amanda in for rhinoplasty (nose surgery) on her 13th birthday a year ago this month. Now, Amanda says, "I'm happier. A lot more guys ask me out. Even those who teased me now say, 'You're looking better.' "   15

Kristina Olson, 20, of Indianapolis, used to hate to go to school because her "Dumbo" ears, as she refers to them, stuck out. "I couldn't enjoy life," says Kristina, who would sit in the back of the classroom and hold her hand over one ear while covering the other with her hair.   16

Finally, her mother took her in for otoplasty—which, in effect, pins back protruding ears—as a gift of "happiness and mental health." At the age of 16, Kristina entered a new school and "no one knew the history of my ears." Her self-esteem and self-confidence soared.   17

One young black woman, who doesn't want her name mentioned, thought her nose was too wide. While she didn't want to change all her racial features, the 19-year-old thought a smaller, narrower nose would "enhance" her beauty.   18

So, after white friends of hers had had rhinoplasties done and her own father had the surgery, the Los Angeles resident, now 21, decided to narrow her nose, too. "I don't think I'm trying to be white," although she realizes that "a lot of people see it that way."   19

Leigh Kane, of Glen Cove, N.Y., the boy who had the nose job at 17,   20
says he hadn't realized his nose was out of the ordinary until his mother told
him so two years ago. "I thought she was kidding. [She said] she noticed
that it was getting progressively worse as I got older," says Leigh, now 19.
Suddenly self-conscious, Leigh had a surgeon remove a bump on his nose
and fashion a new tip. And now he feels better about himself.

Despite the anecdotal evidence from satisfied young clients, medical   21
professionals worry that youngsters aren't prepared to cope with the perils—
physical and psychological—of cosmetic surgery.

"I think the psychological risk among teens is significantly higher than   22
it is among [the] more mature," says Dr. Cole. Often, teen-agers and their
parents have unrealistic expectations that changing appearance will solve deep-
seated problems that require psychiatric attention not cosmetic surgery.

Dr. Cole says that several years ago he performed rhinoplasty on a 16-   23
year-old girl who was ecstatic with the results at first but later returned com-
plaining that the nose job hadn't done the trick. She couldn't, however, articulate exactly what was bothering her. "I think psychologically . . . that
nose wasn't the problem," he says.

Since most surgical procedures are irreversible, operating on teen-agers   24
is a heavy responsibility. Patients are routinely told that things can't be put
back the way they were after the surgery has been done. Patients are counseled extensively before surgery, so they know the risks involved. In most
states, an 18-year-old can get plastic surgery without parental consent. Still,
some young patients and their families have regrets.

Dr. Cole says a colleague operated on the eyelids of an 18-year-old   25
youngster of Korean ancestry who panicked because his grandparents were
angry. "The family was insulted," Dr. Cole says. They felt that, in having
the surgery, the young man was rejecting his culture. He went back in des-
peration seeking to have the surgery undone, but of course it wasn't possible.

Doctors say that to be unhappy with one's physical appearance is sim-   26
ply a part of being a teen-ager, and that maturity can be the cure. Michael
Seifert, 14, of Los Angeles, has a bump on his nose and a father who is a
plastic surgeon. The son wanted surgery. The father refused on the grounds
that Michael is too young.

Lately, Michael has found a new girlfriend, who thinks the bump on   27
his nose gives him "character." He no longer wants to go under the knife.

QUESTIONS FOR DISCUSSION AND WRITING

1. According to this story, the number of teenagers seeking plastic surgery
   doubled between 1985 and 1990. What factors contributed to this rise?
   Can you think of any factors not mentioned in the story?
2. Why are some experts worried about the rising number of teenagers
   undergoing cosmetic surgery?
3. Were you ever self-conscious about your appearance as a teenager? Would
   you have undergone cosmetic surgery if that option was offered to you?
   Would you still do so after reading this story? Explain.

♦ CASE 3 ♦

ZACHARY CITRON

Tipping

The following article was originally published in The New Republic *on January 2, 1989, under the title "Waiting for Nodough"—a playful twist upon the title of an important play by Samuel Beckett,* Waiting for Godot. *The magazine provided no identification for Citron—often, but not always, a sign that the writer is a member of the staff. Unfamiliar with the author, experienced readers would nevertheless expect the piece to be sympathetic to the rights of working people since that would be consistent with the editorial policies of* The New Republic, *a biweekly magazine of ideas and commentary that usually reflect a liberal point of view.*

In the Third World, the tip is still alive and well. It serves as a small, mostly   1
harmless bribe, easing the enormous gap between a small wealthy elite and the impoverished urban masses. The kind of service you get from a railway porter, a shoemaker, even a government official will be in direct proportion to the gratuity paid. The same system prevailed in Europe until the postwar era, when professionalism finally crept into service jobs. Throughout most of the Continent, restaurants now use the service charge system, whereby a standard percentage of the price of a meal is automatically added to the check. In the United States, no more than one percent of all restaurants use a service charge. But that's up from virtually none a few years ago, and there is finally a movement among restaurant owners to fall in line with other modern industrialized societies and abandon the tip altogether.

Americans spent some $11.2 billion on gratuities in 1987. We seem to   2
like tipping in the same unreasonable way we like feet and quarts instead of meters and liters. A Gallup survey conducted in April 1987 reported that "in most situations a majority of consumers say they do not favor having a service charge added to their bill in lieu of tipping." Like their customers, restaurant owners prefer tipping because they feel it gives them control over the level of service. Most think that their wait staff would let standards slip if their tips—the bulk of their incomes in a job where the mandatory wage is $2.01 an hour—were coming to them automatically.

Waiters and waitresses have their own reasons for liking tips. Waiting   3
is considered something of a hardship post in a society that loathes the slightest whiff of servitude. Big tips help take away the pain. "The good people can make huge amounts of money: that's their reward, that's their incentive, that's their profession," explains Michael Olsen, a service industry expert at Virginia Polytechnic Institute and a committed supporter of the tip system.

Several fine dining establishments across the country have switched from   4
tipping to the service charge recently in the belief that waiters and waitresses, if not exactly professionals, deserve better than servants. Besides, restaurant owners say, intense competition among the wait staff can have bad side

effects, like backbiting and disregard for the interests of the restaurant as a whole. They argue that, even if waiting tables doesn't call for three years of graduate school, waiting is at least as likely as lawyering to engender an ethic of professionalism that assures a high standard of service.

Notwithstanding all this high-minded argumentation, the service charge   5
system might never have been discussed seriously in the United States had Congress not provided a strong incentive. For years the IRS has been trying in vain to crack down on underreported tips. They even issue bilingual booklets designed to help the help keep track of their incomes. But short of auditing every waiter and waitress in the country, the law is unenforceable. In 1981 an estimated 16 percent of tipping income was reported. According to a 1986 IRS report, the only type of income with a lower compliance rate was illegal income, at five percent.

So Congress decided to get tough with the restaurant industry. In 1982,   6
as part of the Tax Equity and Fiscal Responsibility Act (TEFRA), it came up with the ingenious ploy of putting the onus on owners to "allocate" tips among their waiting staff. The IRS settled on a ballpark figure—eight percent of gross restaurant revenues—as the minimum it would expect in declared tips. It was a partial success. The IRS reported a dramatic increase in the volume of declared tips: between 1982 and 1984 it picked up an extra $1.2 billion. . . .

Of course, the "minimum" soon became a maximum: waiters and   7
waitresses can sit tight as long as what they declare meets the mandatory eight percent. (Some establishments provide a computer program that does that calculation for them, thus dispensing with the messy business of actually counting the cash.) Meanwhile, Congress was getting even tougher on restaurants. It required owners to pay federal unemployment tax (1984) and Social Security tax (1988) on tipped income. The unintended result was to provide owners with a financial incentive to collude with the waiting staff to underreport tips. But the growing amount of congressionally mandated paperwork also provided an incentive, for reasons of administrative convenience, just to scrap the tip system altogether.

So switching to a service charge system is more talked about than ever   8
before. The trade journals have issued a flurry of surveys and editorials on the relative merits of the alternatives, and one, *Restaurant Business* magazine, has endorsed the service charge outright. In an editorial titled "The Service Charge Brouhaha," it argued that government involvement has given restaurant owners little choice.

Still, to a restaurateur, adopting a mandatory service charge has its   9
downside. One of the tip's historic strengths is that it keeps the waiting staff firmly at the front line in the battle to turn a profit. If things are going badly, the waiter is the first to know, and a tip gives him an incentive to do something about it. Also, what some call the Saturday Night mentality—the tendency among waiters to remember only the bumper weekend tips rather than the dry periods—suits bosses just fine. The service chargers are telling them to think again. Their package gives owners added clout as managers while

taking away their safe seat at the back of the house. It also offers a recovery plan for the industry's lobbyists: the beating the restaurant industry has taken on Capitol Hill over the last few years owes not a little to its image as a haven for tax cheats.

But this furious debate has so far been lost on the tip-giver. Let's face   10
it: as anyone who's ever stiffed a waiter or waitress can tell you, tipping is about power. Those fearful of change are sure to exploit our fears of higher restaurant checks, saucy waiters, and lost status.

QUESTIONS FOR DISCUSSION AND WRITING

1. Why do customers, restaurant owners, waiters, and waitresses prefer tipping instead of a fixed service charge?
2. What are the disadvantages of tipping? Why have some restaurants switched from tipping to the service charge?
3. Consider tipping from the customer's point of view. Does it have any disadvantages?
4. Have you ever worked as a waiter or waitress? If so, argue for or against an automatic service charge by drawing upon your personal experience as well as the information in this article.

◆ CASE 4 ◆

ROBERT L. ROSE

Is Saving Legal?

Robert L. Rose is a staff writer for The Wall Street Journal, *which published the following article on February 6, 1990, under the title "For Welfare Parents, Scrimping is Legal, But Saving Is Out." As you read the article, ask yourself how well the original title summarizes the problem discussed here. Try to understand how Grace Capetillo of Milwaukee broke the law and why she was prosecuted. Then be prepared to say whose side you are on.*

A penny saved is a penny earned. Usually.   1

Take the case of Grace Capetillo, a 36-year-old single mother with a   2
true talent for parsimony. To save on clothing, Ms. Capetillo dresses herself plainly in thrift-store finds. To cut her grocery bill, she stocks up on 67-cent boxes of saltines and 39-cent cans of chicken soup.

When Ms. Capetillo's five-year-old daughter, Michelle, asked for "Li'l   3
Miss Makeup" for Christmas, her mother bypassed Toys "R" Us, where the

doll retails for $19.99. Instead, she found one at Goodwill—for $1.89. She cleaned it up and tied a pink ribbon in its hair before giving the doll to Michelle. Ms. Capetillo found the popular Mr. Potato Head at Goodwill, too, assembling the plastic toy one piece at a time from the used toy bin. It cost her 79 cents, and saved $3.18.

Whose Money?

Ms. Capetillo's stingy strategies helped her build a savings account of more   4
than $3,000 in the last four years. Her goal was to put away enough to buy a new washing machine and maybe one day help send Michelle to college. To some, this might make her an example of virtue in her gritty North Side neighborhood, known more for boarded-up houses than high aspirations. But there was just one catch: Ms. Capetillo is on welfare—$440 a month, plus $60 in food stamps—and saving that much money on public aid is against the law. When welfare officials found out about it, they were quick to act. Ms. Capetillo, they charged, was saving at the expense of taxpayers.

Last month, the Milwaukee County Department of Social Services took   5
her to court, charged her with fraud and demanded she return the savings—and thousands more for a total of $15,545. Ms. Capetillo says she didn't know it, but under the federal program Aid to Families with Dependent Children, she was ineligible for assistance after the day in 1985 when her savings eclipsed $1,000.

Uncle Sam wanted the money back.   6

"Tax dollars are going to support a person's basic needs on the AFDC   7
program," says Robert Davis, associate director of the Milwaukee social services department. Federal rules, and the spirit of the program, don't intend for "people to take the money and put it in a savings account."

Welfare's Role

Ms. Capetillo's troubles began in 1988, when the social services department   8
discovered the savings account she had opened in 1984. The tipoff: The department had matched its records with those supplied by her bank to the Internal Revenue Service.

Next, the sheriff department's welfare fraud squad went into action.   9
Investigators contacted the M&I Bank two blocks from Ms. Capetillo's apartment and found she had "maintained over $1,000 consistently" in her savings account from Aug. 1, 1985 through May 31, 1988.

In an interview that May with investigators, Ms. Capetillo admitted   10
she hadn't reported the savings account to the department. After doing a little arithmetic, welfare officials figured she should repay $15,545—the amount of monthly aid she received after her bank balance passed $1,000. (The assistant district attorney later considered that harsh; he lowered the figure to $3,000.)

But the judge who got her case found it hard to believe Ms. Capetillo   11
was motivated by fraud. Indeed, for Ms. Capetillo, thriftiness had been a
way of life. Her father instilled the lessons of economizing, supporting his
nine children on his modest income from a local tannery.

After Michelle was born, Ms. Capetillo began drawing aid—and saving   12
in earnest. She says she rents the second floor of her father's duplex for $300
a month (though the welfare department says it suspects she was able to save
so much by skipping at least some rent payments). In the summer, she looks
for second-hand winter clothes and in the winter shops for warm-weather
outfits to snare out-of-season bargains. When Michelle's T-shirts grew tight,
her mother snipped them below the underarm so they'd last longer.

"She cared for her daughter well, but simply," says Donna Paul, the   13
court-appointed attorney who defended Ms. Capetillo. "With inflation, all
Grace could expect was for government aid to become more inadequate."

Now that Michelle is getting ready to enter the first grade, Ms. Cape-   14
tillo says she will no longer have to stay home to care for the child. She says
she plans to look for full-time work or go back to school to train to be a
nurse's aide.

But her round face, framed by shoulder-length black hair, still brightens   15
at the prospect of bargain-hunting. At her favorite supermarket, her eyes dart
from item to item. She spots the display of generic saltine crackers. "See
that? That's cheap," she pronounces, dropping a box in her grocery cart.

The total bill comes to $5.98, but Ms. Capetillo forgot the coupon that   16
entitles her to free bacon for spending more than $5. She pockets the receipt,
and vows to return for the bacon.

After the law caught up with her, Ms. Capetillo reduced her savings to   17
avoid having her welfare checks cut off. She bought her new washing machine, a used stove to replace her hotplate, a $40 refrigerator and a new
bedroom set for Michelle. But that didn't resolve the charge of fraud.

Finally, her day in court arrived. At first, Circuit Court Judge Charles   18
B. Schudson had trouble figuring out Ms. Capetillo's crime. To him, welfare
fraud meant double dipping: collecting full benefits and holding a job at the
same time.

After the lawyers explained the rules about saving money, he made it   19
clear he didn't think much of the rules. "I don't know how much more
powerfully we could say it to the poor in our society: Don't try to save," he
said. Judge Schudson said it was "ironic" that the case came as President
Bush promotes his plan for Family Savings Accounts. "Apparently, that's an
incentive that this country would only give to the rich."

The Limits of Aid

Others differ. County welfare worker Sophia Partipilo says Ms. Capetillo's   20
savings raise the question of whether she needed a welfare check at all. "We're
not a savings and loan," says Ms. Partipilo, who handled the case. "We don't
hand out toasters at the end of the month. We're here to get you over the
rough times."

Ms. Capetillo could have fought the charge. Her lawyer and even the   21
judge said later that there was a good chance a jury would have sided with
the welfare mother. Even the prosecutor admits that had she simply spent
the money, rather than saving it, she could have avoided a run-in with
the law.

But for Ms. Capetillo, going to court once was enough. She was so   22
frightened and her throat was so dry that the judge could barely hear her
speak. She pleaded guilty to "failure to report change in circumstance." The
judge sentenced her to one-year probation and ordered her to repay $1,000.

A few days later, Ms. Capetillo, who remains on welfare, returns from   23
a shopping trip and is met by Michelle. Banana in hand, Michelle greets her
mother with a smile and a gingerbread man she made at half-day kindergarten.

"Now you can see why I do what I do," says Ms. Capetillo.   24

QUESTIONS FOR DISCUSSION AND WRITING

1. Why did the Milwaukee County Social Services Department bring charges
   against Grace Capetillo?
2. How was Ms. Capetillo able to save more than $3,000 while on welfare?
   Her lawyer and the judge who heard this case believe that a jury may
   have sided with her. Whose side are you on?
3. According to this story, Grace Capetillo paid $300 a month in rent to her
   father. Is it right for parents to make their children pay rent? If so, under
   what circumstances?
4. In your opinion, how poor should someone be before being eligible for
   welfare? What assets, if any, would you allow someone to retain while
   receiving public assistance?

◆ CASE 5 ◆

BRETT PULLEY

A New Battle at Little Bighorn

First published in The Wall Street Journal *on October 15, 1990, the following article reports a conflict in Montana between Native Americans and admirers of George Armstrong Custer—a nineteenth-century army officer who died in battle near the Little Bighorn River, where a national park now honors his memory. Brett Pulley is a staff reporter for the* Journal. *As you read his article, try to determine why the conflict he reports is not simply a local dispute and why it was worth reporting on the front page of a major national newspaper.*

Last Stand Hill is a steep slope carpeted with buffalo grass, purple wildflow-   1
ers and legends. This is where, on a blistering hot June afternoon in 1876, Lt. Col. George Armstrong Custer and his Seventh Cavalry fell to Sioux and Cheyenne Indians. White marble markers designate where each of the 225 cavalrymen died.

Now, fresh battles are disturbing the cemetery-like calm here at Custer   2
Battlefield National Monument. From her National Park Service office near the bank of the Little Bighorn River, Superintendent Barbara Booher is wag-ing what some hope is her own last stand. Some Custer buffs are at war with her for leading a drive to place a $2 million memorial near the large granite obelisk that honors Mr. Custer and his men.

The dispute? The new memorial would honor the fallen Indians.   3

'Heroes' and 'Hostile Indians'

"They were the *enemy*," says Jerry Russell, president of the 700-member   4
Order of the Indian Wars. Another Custer buff, in the order's newsletter, asked: "What's next? A Shinto temple to the Japanese Air Force on the site of the Arizona? How about a posthumous Oscar to John Wilkes Booth at the Ford Theater for 'Outstanding Performance by an Actor'?"

Much of the ire is focused on Ms. Booher, the first Native American   5
to oversee the 760-acre park and Custer monument. Ms. Booher, whose parents are from the Northern Ute and Cherokee tribes, wants a more even-handed account in the tours and exhibits of what happened here.

"After all," she says, "Custer was only here for one afternoon. The   6
Indians were here for years."

Throughout the park, which is visited by 250,000 tourists a year, the   7
cavalrymen are referred to on historical markers and elsewhere as "fallen heroes" while the Cheyenne and Sioux are "hostile Indians." Ms. Booher plans to change that.

And instead of simply informing visitors how the "brave cavalrymen"   8
were left mutilated, Ms. Booher wants guides and museum pamphlets to

better explain that the Indians grew hostile because they were forcibly driven from their sacred homelands by gold-hungry miners and settlers.

The U.S. Senate is even considering changing the park's name to the more neutral Little Bighorn National Monument. Supporters of the change have argued for years that most battlefields aren't named for people, especially losers.   9

That would be a highly controversial move, but controversy has always surrounded the celebrated battle here and the flamboyant cavalry leader. Since no cavalrymen survived, details have been pieced together from accounts of surviving Indians and of cavalry troops who later discovered their comrades' bodies. Many early Indian accounts were lost through bad interpretation or dismissed as untrue. Myths and legends grew instead, leaving a forever-clouded account.   10

For his part, Mr. Custer has inspired hundreds of books and articles, more than a dozen movies and a television mini-series now in the works. Ronald Reagan even portrayed Custer once, in the 1940 movie "Sante Fe Trail."   11

But as history continues to romanticize Mr. Custer and his fallen troops, Native Americans have grown resentful that only a small, painted board honors the estimated 100 Indians who died here. Such sentiments sparked the movement to erect an Indian memorial.   12

Two years ago, Indian activist Russell Means led a band of Native Americans to the park, where they erected a flat metal Indian "monument" by pouring a concrete base atop the graves of the cavalry soldiers. Park administrators, to avoid a confrontation, stood by and watched. Weeks later, the makeshift monument was removed.   13

The incident incensed Custer loyalists. "Anyone else would have been arrested for that," says William Wells, a director of the Custer Battlefield Historical and Museum Association, who angrily watched as the memorial was erected. His 3,000-member, nonprofit group, which has no Indian members, operates the park museum and bookstore in cooperation with the park service.   14

The group is one of three nationwide organizations, with a total membership of 4,600, dedicated to preserving the memory of the Battle of the Little Bighorn—and to studying and upholding the legend and lore of their brash, golden-haired hero.   15

Some of those members are furious at Ms. Booher. "She's only in that position because she's a woman and an Indian," says Mr. Russell of the Order of the Indian Wars. "We won't rest until she's out."   16

"Now I know why my office has three windows," responds the soft-spoken, 49-year-old superintendent. "So I can see what's coming next." She labels her detractors "a dangerous few."   17

Updating Exhibits

Before her appointment in June 1989, Ms. Booher worked with the federal government in Anchorage, Alaska, including 10 years with the Federal   18

Aviation Administration and 10 with the Bureau of Indian Affairs. Her last eight years with the bureau were spent negotiating land-allotment programs for Native Alaskans.

During an executive trainee program with the bureau in 1989, she was   19
assigned to a two-week detail with the National Park Service in Denver. She impressed the park service regional director, Lorraine Mintzmeyer, who hired her for the job here. Ms. Mintzmeyer says Ms. Booher's heritage was a unique plus for the job, but adds, "I hired her for her ability."

Ms. Booher is working with outside museum curators and historians   20
to update and enhance the museum's exhibits. Sixteen of the exhibits focus on the cavalry and eight on the Indians; she would like to see that more balanced. This summer, for one of the battlefield tours, she hired a Native American guide who provided additional information on the life and customs of the Plains Indians.

She also has picked a fight with the museum association by asking it—   21
unsuccessfully—to sell the controversial book "Bury My Heart at Wounded Knee," which is prone to the Indian perspective, at the park's bookstore.

Careful Scrutiny

There's not much Ms. Booher does that hasn't caught the watchful eye of   22
one critic or another. She has been criticized, for instance, for hiring more Indians to work at the park. Recently, she received a congressional inquiry after a constituent complained she "is letting weeds grow up there" on Last Stand Hill.

That is true, but the weeds have always grown wild because the park   23
service maintains the hill in its natural state. "I haven't figured out whose fault the weeds were for the first 113 years," says Ms. Booher. "But this year, it's my fault."

The superintendent has her share of supporters. At the park service,   24
supervisors laud her work. And Democratic Rep. Ben Nighthorse Campbell of Colorado, whose ancestors fought Mr. Custer in the battle, says that "if these people who are out to get Barbara try to remove her, they're going to see another Indian uprising—right here in my office." He says Ms. Booher's leadership is needed to "bury the old-boy system" at the battlefield.

Area Indian tribes, even rival bands that hold longstanding grudges against   25
one another, have joined to support the Indian memorial and Ms. Booher. "We feel blessed to have Barbara," says Austin Two Moons, one of 10 members of a committee established by the National Park Service to help select a site and design for the proposed memorial.

The proposal for the memorial would place it 300 yards from the exist-   26
ing monument. A nationwide competition would be held to select a design. Legislation authorizing the memorial and its $2 million cleared the House two weeks ago without dissent. But the proposed amendment to change the park's name to the Little Bighorn National Monument could trigger extensive debate and delay Senate passage.

Many Custer supporters, like Mr. Wells, say they wouldn't mind the   27
Indian memorial if it were farther away from the cavalry monument and not
publicly funded. But even Mr. Wells says all of the controversy is strangely
appropriate for the publicity hungry George Armstrong Custer. "Custer will
always attract people and cause arguments," says Mr. Wells. "With all the
attention he still gets, George has got to be smiling in his grave."

QUESTIONS FOR DISCUSSION AND WRITING

1. Consider the analogy in paragraph 4 between Native Americans and the
   Japanese Air Force. Is it fair?
2. What would be the difference between calling this park Little Bighorn
   National Monument rather than Custer Battlefield National Monument?
3. Why is it difficult to determine exactly what happened at the Battle of the
   Little Bighorn?
4. According to the information reported in this article, how well qualified
   is Barbara Booher to superintend the park that is now her responsibility?
   Would you support her reappointment?

◆ CASE 6 ◆

JACOB V. LAMAR

The Immigration Mess

*Although written in February 1989—towards the end of a civil war in Nicaragua
that was of great concern within the United States—"The Immigration Mess" addresses questions that continue to trouble many Americans. How open should the
United States be to immigrants from other countries? And how well do we treat
immigrants once they are here? In writing this article for* Time, *staff writer Jacob
V. Lamar had access to information made available to him by* Time *reporters in
Washington, D.C., and Brownsville, Texas.*

Weary yet hopeful, their bodies battered but their spirits high, the families   1
while away the hours at the Casa Romero shelter for Central American refugees. They line up for a lunch of rice and beans, served from steaming
kettles; they mop the floors and shoot pool; they practice English phrases;
and they wait. And wait.

When they learn that their applications for political asylum in the U.S.   2
are finally about to be dealt with, they trek to a makeshift Immigration and
Naturalization Service post at the newly opened Port Isabel Processing

Center, 25 miles away. Two weeks ago, angry local officials forced the shutdown of an INS office in Harlingen to rid the town of 500 refugees who have been shoehorned into over-crowded shelters and camps since last year. At Port Isabel, the refugees, clutching their meager possessions, line up to be fingerprinted and questioned by immigration officials—and then wait some more to find out if they will be allowed to partake of the American Dream.

The hectic scene in southern Texas reflects the confusion of a U.S. im-   3
migration policy that is on the verge of being swamped by a virtual tidal wave of new arrivals. "We stand on the precipice of an enormous immigration crisis," says Wyoming Republican Senator Alan Simpson, who, with Democratic Congressman Romano Mazzoli of Kentucky, wrote the 1986 Immigration Reform and Control Act. It is a crisis with which the U.S., despite its cherished history as a nation of immigrants, is not prepared to cope. "We have no population policy," complains a State Department official. "No total concept on which to build."

The emergency springs primarily from Central America. Since last June,   4
30,000 Nicaraguans fleeing war and economic misery have flocked to the U.S. That number could be dwarfed by the tens of thousands expected to arrive in the U.S. in 1989. As a result of Moscow's liberalized emigration policies, some 50,000 Soviet citizens, primarily Jews and Armenians, will be allowed to leave the U.S.S.R. this year; most will be headed for the U.S. Several thousand of the 5 million Afghanistan refugees camped in Pakistan will also emigrate to the U.S.

The Immigration Reform Act is an example of the disarray of current   5
policy. Designed to control a huge influx of illegal immigrants, the law provided an opportunity for 3 million to 5 million aliens who had lived and worked in the U.S. since before 1982 to become permanent residents. It also established penalties for employers who knowingly hired illegal aliens, making it much more difficult for them to find jobs and provoking discrimination against job seekers who merely look like foreigners. But the law has not significantly reduced unauthorized immigration. The flow from the South continues at such a pace that the INS is embarking on what literally amounts to a last-ditch tactic: it will soon dig a 5-ft.-deep, 4-mile-long trench along the Mexican border near San Diego, in part to prevent fast-moving cars packed with illegal immigrants from racing across the boundary.

Moreover, the law has failed to forestall an epidemic of outright fraud   6
and abuse. The Western regional INS office, which covers California, Arizona, Nevada, Hawaii and Guam, has handed out $1 million in fines to heedless employers in the past two years. But with 400 agents in the region, the INS hardly has the manpower to wage a serious crackdown and thus goes after only the most blatant offenders—and many companies and illegal aliens are willing to take their chances. A survey by the University of California at San Diego's Center for U.S.-Mexican Studies, for example, found that some 41% of illegal aliens in the Southern California area admitted they had used fake information to obtain their jobs.

The U.S. is also wrestling with difficulties posed by the Soviet Union's   7
decision to nearly triple the number of exit visas it will grant its citizens this
year. Washington has long prodded Moscow for just such an opening to
émigrés. To accommodate the new Soviet arrivals, the Reagan Administration last year transferred 7,000 slots previously reserved for Asian immigrants to Soviet refugees, outraging advocates for Cambodian and Vietnamese
immigrants.

Efforts to devise a coherent immigration policy are hampered by the   8
political power of ethnic groups that have sunk deep roots in the U.S. Over
the past seven years, some 100,000 Irish natives entered the U.S. on tourist
visas, then stayed on after their allotted time expired. The Irish have complained that a 1965 immigration provision giving preference to family members of recent arrivals has helped Asians and Latinos while discriminating
against West Europeans. Two years ago, Irish-American activists took their
case to Congress and received an enthusiastic hearing. With the help of new
legislation pushed by powerful advocates like Senator Edward M. Kennedy,
some 3,900 Irish were granted additional visas to enter the U.S. in 1987.
Kennedy is now fighting for immigration legislation that will give preference
to those with valuable professional skills, high levels of education and a
knowledge of English, all conditions tailor-made for Irish immigrants.

The plight of the Central American refugees remains far more acute.   9
Recent court decisions have held that applicants for asylum have to be given
work-authorization documents, allowing them to seek immediate employment while the INS scrutinizes their pleas. But to stem a surge of arrivals
from Central America, the INS delayed granting work permits until asylum
applications could be processed and told the refugees to remain near their
point of entry until the paperwork was completed. The new regulations helped
turn the Rio Grande Valley into a giant alien way station.

At a packed Red Cross shelter a few miles from downtown Browns-   10
ville, the air is filled with the cries of babies and the smell of urine. Overcrowding and lack of sanitation in the area have contributed to an outbreak
of hepatitis. Refugee advocates are infuriated by the Federal Government's
inability to clear the bottleneck. Charges Roman Catholic Bishop John Fitzpatrick of the Brownsville diocese: "The INS is saying, 'Sorry, you can't leave
to work, but we can't feed you.' "

Meanwhile, harsh sentiment against the refugees is growing. "Nobody   11
knows who all these people are," says Brownsville trailer-court owner Bob
White. "They could be terrorists, or bandits, or typhoid carriers." Harlingen
Mayor Bill Card says his city decided to expel the INS from a registration
post to send a signal to the Bush Administration that the area needs more
help from Washington. Says he: "We have not been able to get the cooperation and attention of the Federal Government."

With the Federal Government straining under the budget deficit, it is   12
unlikely that the U.S. can afford to continue spending $382 million to pro-
vide welfare and medical care for refugees, some 75,000 of whom arrived last
year. Some experts believe the burden of caring for new residents could

become so heavy that slamming the door on the huddled masses seeking a better life in the U.S. may be inescapable. "In some fashion, we've got to ignore the promise of the Statue of Liberty," says Mazzoli. "The U.S.'s moral responsibility to accept immigrants is not unlimited."

Nevertheless, the beacon of hope for a better life in America burns   13 brightest for those who endure the most profound debasement and despair in their native land. While the U.S. today is ill-equipped to take them all in, the dream lives on. For that reason, the immigration wave is not likely to stop or even slow. "People aren't going to write their relatives and say, 'Don't come,'" argues Bishop Fitzpatrick. Nor, despite the burden, is the U.S. likely to turn its back on its history by hanging out a sign that reads NO VACANCY.

QUESTIONS FOR DISCUSSION AND WRITING

1. What world events prompted new waves of immigration to the United States in the late 1980s? Can you identify any events likely to encourage immigration that have occurred outside our borders since the first publication of this article in 1989?

2. Why did the 1986 Immigration Reform and Control Act fail to resolve the question of immigration to the United States?

3. What factors contributed to the crowded conditions in Brownsville, Texas, described in this article?

4. Immigration has played a great historical role in the shaping of the United States. In your opinion, how open should the United States be to new waves of immigration? Be prepared to support your position and to anticipate at least one argument likely to be raised by someone who disagrees with you.

5. How should immigrants be treated once they arrive in the United States? What rights should they have?

♦ CASE 7 ♦

WESTON KOSOVA

The Future of ROTC

Accompanying "Gays in Arms," a much longer article on gay people in the military, the following article was first published in the February 12, 1990, issue of The New Republic. *(For a description of* The New Republic, *see the headnote to Case 3.) As you read "The Future of ROTC," try to understand what factors have led to the reconsideration of a military policy that has been in place for many years—and why colleges are especially sensitive about this policy.*

Nineteen eight-nine was a bad year for ROTC. The faculty at the University of Wisconsin voted to recommend dismantling the program unless it changed the rules to admit gays and lesbians by 1993. Two students at Northwestern formed the Coalition for Equal Opportunity expressly to protest ROTC's anti-gay policy. Harvard voted to reinstate ROTC after 20 years of banishment (it kicked ROTC off campus in 1969 as a Vietnam protest) but then flip-flopped a week later. Now Harvard will consider taking ROTC back only when gays and lesbians are welcome. Yale voted not to take ROTC back for the same reason. At Iowa the law school refuses ROTC use of its buildings, and the Minnesota student-faculty senate made ambitious plans to launch a nationwide lobbying drive to force a change in Defense Department policy toward gays. 1

It's not the first time universities have taken on ROTC's ban on homosexuals. Students and faculty at the University of California have been criticizing the program since 1984. But the rules have changed since then. Anti-discrimination policies that previously protected the rights of women, minorities, and the handicapped have been amended at many schools to include gays and lesbians. At a handful of colleges a student can be disciplined, or even expelled, for saying something derogatory about a gay student. And there isn't a major university without its own "Ten Percent Society" or "Gay and Lesbian Student Alliance." ROTC's openly acknowledged rules against gays make it an easy target in the hypersensitive atmosphere on campuses today. 2

ROTC's policy is the same as the rest of the armed services: "Homosexuality is incompatible with military service." Gays can take the military science classes ROTC offers all university students, but they can't enroll as cadets in the program. This makes them ineligible for the scholarships the Air Force, Navy, and Army award to promising cadets. But a recruiter's ability to discover a potential cadet's sexual preference is limited to what he marks on his application. So it's not difficult for a gay simply to lie. And military paranoia about gays makes it easy for a gay cadet (or a heterosexual one, for that matter) to beg out of the military at any time with impunity—even after a four-year free ride through school—simply by claiming homosexuality. 3

Here's how: In exchange for taking one military science class a semes- 4
ter, attending periodic training camps, and serving four years of active duty
as an officer after graduation, ROTC pays for full tuition (or a hefty chunk of
it), books, lab expenses, plus $100 a month spending money. If for some
reason (lack of enthusiasm, poor test scores) a cadet on scholarship doesn't
win a commission, he must either pay back the scholarship in cash or serve
four years' active duty as an enlisted soldier. Unless he's gay. Or says he's
gay. Or says he's thought about becoming gay. In this case, he'll be honorably discharged from ROTC, and his commission will be canceled, along with
all further obligation to the service. Technically, scholarship cadets discharged for homosexuality are required to reimburse ROTC for the scholarship. But this isn't enforced. The Defense Department would rather eat the
cost of a cadet's training than weather the bad publicity a lawsuit would
invite.

Nobody will say how many ROTC cadets are tossed out each year for 5
being gay. (The Pentagon's statisticians conveniently lump together ejected
gay cadets with those disenrolled for "failure to meet weight standards,"
among other things. They claim that more specific records are not kept, but
that one can get the numbers by filing for them under the Freedom of Information Act.) But it's possible to make some reasonable guesses. Of the 20,178
Air Force cadets enrolled at colleges across the country last year, 1,155 of
them were disenrolled for various reasons. Suppose only ten percent of them
were gay. It costs an average of $39,598 to train each cadet. That's $4.5
million. Add in the scholarships that weren't repaid (another $13,465 per
person), and it jumps to $6 million. Run similar numbers for each of the
three ROTC branches, and all told the Pentagon is throwing away between $9
million and $18 million, along with a few hundred trained soldiers, sailors,
and airmen, every year.

The ACLU is preparing test cases with gay students ejected from ROTC 6
to challenge the policy. But the Pentagon may not be their only opposition.
Not all university administrators, even those at schools with anti-discrimination
rules, are eager to see ROTC leave—discrimination or not. ROTC brings a school
such as Wisconsin more than $2 million a year in scholarships and salaries.
And ROTC scholarships are strong incentives for attracting minority students,
a perpetual problem for Midwestern schools. Added to this are the millions
the Pentagon provides universities in research grants, which might be spoiled
by sour relations with ROTC. Wisconsin's faculty may have taken a strong
symbolic stand against ROTC discrimination, but the school's board of regents
isn't willing to take apart the program. Neither are the administrations at the
other schools. And there's another problem. Land grant universities such as
Wisconsin and Minnesota are required by law to offer military instruction.

ROTC officers disagree about how the controversy will be resolved. "I 7
don't think the protests will have any consequence on recruiting," says Army
ROTC spokesman Lt. Col. Cal Blake. The protests might even help recruiting, an Air Force ROTC recruiter told me, drawing students who otherwise
wouldn't have joined. But Capt. Gary Beck, head of Naval Sciences at

Wisconsin, disagrees. "This all has the potential to have a devastating effect on recruiting," he told a reporter for the student newspaper. In the long run, Beck may be right. And the problem doesn't end with recruiting. The Army, for example, counts on ROTC for more than 70 percent of its new officers. If ROTC-bashing replaces divestment as the next trendy campus crusade, the number of officers coming through the pipeline could drop radically.

In the meantime, ROTC officers are loath to talk about the possibility of gays among their ranks. Spokesmen for the program who were otherwise generous with time and answers suddenly went bureaucratic when I broached the subject. "We like officers to reflect society at large. We want women, minorities, and a good cross section in general," said one Army officer. Does that include gays? I asked. "Sir," he said, "if you'd like I can write down your question and I'll be glad to get back to you with an answer."   8

QUESTIONS FOR DISCUSSION AND WRITING

1. According to this article, how likely is the military to discharge cadets who identify themselves as homosexual?
2. What is the estimated financial cost of discharging these cadets? What do you imagine the human cost to be?
3. Do you see a contradiction within paragraph 5?
4. What incentives are there for universities to have ROTC on campus even if the program discriminates against gay people?
5. What is the military's rationale for making gay men and women ineligible for service? Do you agree?

◆ CASE 8 ◆

LIZ GALTNEY

Weekend Warriors

Only a year before thousands of Army reservists were called up for service in the Persian Gulf, U.S. News & World Report *published the following article in its issue of September 25, 1989. It predicted, "If the U.S. ever engages in another land war, even a small one, it will need part-time soldiers to fight it." As you read this article, try to understand why the fighting ability of the Reserves seemed doubtful at the time—a concern suggested by the original title, "The Sad State of Weekend Warriors."*

America's part-time soldiers have long been dismissed by their fellow warriors and many of their countrymen as poorly trained, ill-equipped and out of shape "weekend warriors." But the nation's second-string soldiers are now part of its first line of defense. If the U.S. ever engages in another land war, even a small one, it will need part-time soldiers to fight it. A combination of strategic assumptions that would reduce U.S. forces abroad and cut the size of the Regular Army have made the Reserves a critical part of the Pentagon's war plans. 1

The U.S. has promised its NATO allies that it will deliver 10 Army divisions within 10 days of the outbreak of a war in Europe. This so-called 10-plus-10 plan calls for Reserve troops to provide crucial "combat service" and "combat-service support" in the first days of a conflict. Army Reserve troops would serve as military police, doctors, combat engineers and in other support positions right away. Within two to three weeks of the start of a war, National Guardsmen would be thrown into battle to reinforce regular combat soldiers. 2

Despite the increased importance of the Reserves, the Regular Army continues to treat them like second-class soldiers. Too often, it is more interested in funding peacetime programs for active-duty soldiers or buying fancy weapons than arming and training the reservists who would fight another war. 3

Flunking Out

By any standard, reservists compare poorly with full-time soldiers. In 1987, only 65 percent of those who were tested passed the Army's Skill Qualification Test, which evaluates a soldier's proficiency in fighting skills, such as operating M1 tanks; 92 percent of the regular soldiers passed. Reservists failed at twice as many basic tasks, such as planting and sweeping mines, as active-duty soldiers. "No matter how well we do in peacetime training," says retired Col. Benjamin Covington, former president of the now defunct Army 4

Training Board, which studied more than 470 Reserve units, "the average Reserve unit will never be as combat-ready as its active-duty counter-part. Those who imply they will be as combat-ready are making a mistake." Gen. Bernard Rogers, a former supreme allied commander for Europe, believes the Soviets are keenly aware of the sorry state of America's weekend warriors.

The Army insists that Reserve soldiers will perform as well as regulars,   5 although it concedes that some units cannot meet even minimum requirements. Army officials say they are working on the problem. Gen. Colin Powell, who oversees all of the Army's National Guard and Reserve units as commander of the U.S. Forces Command at Fort McPherson, Ga., will become chairman of the Joint Chiefs of Staff on October 1. "Over all," Powell says, "the Reserves have improved over the last 10 years. Their readiness levels are higher, [but] the job is not done."

A Larger Role

The Army's dependence on the Reserves keeps growing, however. In an   6 effort to save money, the Pentagon is assigning more missions to part-timers—at the same time it cuts the Reserves' already limited funds for training and new equipment. Proposals to demobilize thousands of U.S. forces now stationed in Europe and in Korea could result in still greater reliance on Reserve units. President Bush has proposed withdrawing 30,000 American troops from Europe, most of whom would be active-duty Army soldiers. Over the next few years, some military officials say, the Army's 18 divisions (which contain 10,000 to 18,000 soldiers each) will probably be cut by at least one regular division, and perhaps by as many as two.

While guardsmen and reservists account for more than half the Army's   7 strength, the Air Force and Navy have Reserve forces of only 24 and 20 percent, respectively. The smaller, less labor-intensive services also have fewer people to train and, in some cases, a skilled labor pool on which to draw. The Air Force, for example, employs commercial pilots as reservists, since many of their skills are applicable to military planes.

In the Army Reserves, the demands of training are complicated by a   8 sluggish bureaucracy, officials say. Weekend warriors typically have less than one sixth the Regular Army's time to train, according to reports compiled by the Army and the General Accounting Office. Adds Capt. James Hohosh, who runs an Army Reserve artillery unit in Utah: "There isn't enough time to do it all."

Often, the Army fails to provide the training needed by Reserve and   9 National Guard units, leaving them to fend for themselves. In Georgia in 1987, for example, the Army replaced the aging M60A3 tanks of the 1/108 Armored Battalion's Delta Company with new M1 Abrams tanks. But the National Guard unit quickly discovered that many of the Army's three-month M1 training courses for active-duty soldiers were either full or available to reservists only at inconvenient times.

So Capt. Roosevelt Daniel, the company commander, and his trainer,   10
Sgt. 1st Class Jack Hawkins, set up their own training school—without formal Army approval. Says Daniel: "You can't get the job done sitting back
waiting around for somebody to get it done for you." Army officials argue
that certified programs generally provide better training than do-it-yourself
operations, but, a spokesman concedes, "it's better than no training at all."

Delta Company is the exception among Reserve and National Guard   11
units, however. Reservists sometimes can't even get their hands on such basic equipment as guns and gas masks, and training falls by the wayside. Although they would be sent to the front lines, most part-time units still depend
on hand-me-down goods from the Regular Army. Some units receive no
equipment at all. Army Reserve officials estimate that out of $900 million in
acquisitions authorized by Congress for the Reserves in recent years, $600
million has not yet been spent. Reserve officials blame the Regular Army for
foot dragging, and the evidence seems to support the charge. In fiscal 1987,
the five Army Reserve and National Guard commands had only 54 to 71
percent of essential equipment. "I wouldn't say the Army has neglected the
Reserves," says an Army spokesman. "It is probably caused by finite resources."

For field commanders, limited resources mean big problems. Sally Ma-   12
ria Bock, the former head of an Army Reserve chemical-decontamination
unit in Maryland, says equipment shortages forced her to keep her unit at
only 30 percent of its authorized strength. For three years, the unit could not
even obtain Korean War–era M-12 decontamination devices used to clean
bases and equipment of chemical agents. "It's difficult to look a soldier in the
eye and tell him the equipment is on its way," says Bock. "After you constantly tell them it's on its way, they finally say, 'Fine, so am I.' "

The Army further aggravates the problems of the Reserves by con-   13
stantly changing the missions of individual units. An infantry unit ordered to
become an armored company, for instance, must retrain all its foot soldiers
to operate tanks. Worse, as missions are added or changed, old ones are not
dropped, leaving part-time units overwhelmed by paper work and unprepared for the real work they would be called on to do in wartime. Army
brass acknowledge the problems this causes for unit commanders. Nevertheless, they estimate that a staggering 2,500 mission changes will be ordered
over the next five years.

No Substitute for Training

Even basic survival training is slipshod. Many units ignore survival training   14
altogether because it involves dirty grunt work, such as digging foxholes.
Yet the lack of survival skills can expose soldiers to needless risks. A GAO
report cites one unit's construction of "two fighting positions that could have
resulted in soldiers shooting at one another." Some reservists claim that
their lack of formal training isn't a problem because camaraderie is a far
better fighting tool than some of the formal training ordered by the Army

bureaucracy. "Camaraderie is our strength," insists Pat. Walsh, a Maryland National Guard helicopter pilot. "That kind of camaraderie is no replacement for training," replies James Webb, a former assistant secretary of defense for Reserve affairs. "All it means is that they'll help each other a lot in the POW camp."

Instead of field exercises that would help prepare units for the rigors of combat, reservists typically spend roughly half their limited training time on administrative tasks, according to GAO and Army studies. "Survival training for us," quips Lt. Robert Donohoo, a Utah-based reservist, "is to make sure our charts are filled out properly." A Georgia National Guard unit reports that an entire weekend drill was wasted when higher-ups ordered last-minute AIDS testing. Though Army officials agree that much of the paper work is unnecessary, they have done little to solve the problem, according to congressional sources. The Army, despite having spent 10 years and roughly $50 million, has failed to install a computer system that would help speed the mobilization of the Reserves in an emergency and eliminate much of the paper work. Because the Army failed to do the job, Congress recently reassigned the task to the National Guard.

Death from Exercise

Many weekend warriors are literally in no shape to fight. Roughly 20 percent of soldiers in the Reserve force are over 40 years old, and unlike active-duty soldiers, they are not required to stay fit. Some reservists say they are not concerned about the issue. Says Keith Harris, a helicopter instructor pilot in the Maryland National Guard, "It doesn't really matter if a guy is physically fit. If there's a real combat situation and 40-year-olds and 50-year-olds go into combat to save this country, by God, it won't matter if they can do only one push-up. As long as they can pull that trigger, they're going to go to war."

That kind of brave talk is not backed up by facts, however. In 1985, Webb forced the Army to conduct fitness examinations of Virginia National Guardsmen over 40 years old. According to Webb, only 29 percent of the participants passed the first phase of basic cholesterol, blood and other tests. Before the Army could complete a treadmill stress test, two guardsmen expired during the exercise. "Two guys died on the treadmill," says Webb, "and these were *combat* units!" Webb recalls that the Army, when asked to explain, responded by saying that it had fixed the problem by stopping the test. Webb, who conducted an extensive two-year study of the Reserves, says the Army repeatedly fought his attempts to identify and resolve problems. "They are always reluctant to turn over the rocks and look at the slugs."

In the end, the U.S. is still counting on nuclear weapons, not superior soldiers, to win its wars: The NATO doctrine of "flexible response" calls for going nuclear in the early days of a war in Europe, before Western troops are overrun by superior Warsaw Pact conventional forces. "We would go nuclear very early," says one Reserve official, describing the military's attitude toward part-time soldiers. "Why worry about the Reserves' problems?" But as the superpower confrontation in Europe ebbs and the Soviets press for the total elimination of nuclear weapons in Europe, and as the U.S. ponders how to combat new enemies in the terrorist camps of Lebanon and the mountains of Colombia, the caliber of the nation's fighting men may count for as much as or more than it ever has.

QUESTIONS FOR DISCUSSION AND WRITING

1. How does the Army compare with the Navy and Air Force in reliance upon reserve units? Why has the Army come to rely upon these units?
2. According to this article, how do reservists typically spend approximately half of their training time? What causes this time consumption?
3. How did reservists compare with regular soldiers when this article was first published? How did the Army defend itself from criticism?
4. Drawing upon the information in this article, as well as your knowledge of recent history, argue for or against major changes in Reserve training.

♦ CASE 9 ♦

ANONYMOUS

It's Over, Debbie

The following letter was written by a physician and first published in the January 8, 1988, issue of the Journal of the American Medical Society. *It prompted considerable discussion, including an editorial in* The New York Times. *As you read this letter, try to decide whether or not its anonymous author acted responsibly.*

The call came in the middle of the night. As a gynecology resident rotating   1
through a large, private hospital, I had come to detest telephone calls, because invariably I would be up for several hours and would not feel good the next day. However, duty called, so I answered the phone. A nurse informed me that a patient was having difficulty getting rest, could I please see her. She was on 3 North. That was the gynecologic-oncology unit, not my usual duty station. As I trudged along, bumping sleepily against walls and corners and not believing I was up again, I tried to imagine what I might find at the end of my walk. Maybe an elderly woman with an anxiety reaction, or perhaps something particularly horrible.

I grabbed the chart from the nurses station on my way to the patient's   2
room, and the nurse gave me some hurried details: a 20-year-old girl named
Debbie was dying of ovarian cancer. She was having unrelenting vomiting
apparently as the result of an alcohol drip administered for sedation. Hmmm,
I thought. Very sad. As I approached the room I could hear loud labored
breathing. I entered and saw an emaciated, dark-haired woman who appeared much older than 20. She was receiving nasal oxygen, had an IV, and
was sitting in bed suffering from what was obviously severe air hunger. The
chart noted her weight at 80 pounds. A second woman, also dark-haired but
of middle age, stood at her right, holding her hand. Both looked up as I
entered. The room seemed filled with the patient's desperate effort to survive. Her eyes were hollow, and she had suprasternal and intercostal retrac-
tions with her rapid inspirations. She had not eaten or slept in two days. She
had not responded to chemotherapy and was being given supportive care
only. It was a gallows scene, a cruel mockery of her youth and unfulfilled
potential. Her only words to me were, "Let's get this over with."

I retreated with my thoughts to the nurses station. The patient was   3
tired and needed rest. I could not give her health, but I could give her rest. I
asked the nurse to draw 20 mg of morphine sulfate into a syringe. Enough,
I thought, to do the job. I took the syringe into the room and told the two
women I was going to give Debbie something that would let her rest and to
say good-bye. Debbie looked at the syringe, then laid her head on the pillow
with her eyes open, watching what was left of the world. I injected the morphine intravenously and watched to see if my calculations on its effects would
be correct. Within seconds her breathing slowed to a normal rate, her eyes
closed, and her features softened as she seemed restful at last. The older woman
stroked the hair of the now-sleeping patient. I waited for the inevitable next
effect of depressing the respiratory drive. With clocklike certainty, within
four minutes the breathing rate slowed even more, then became irregular,
then ceased. The dark-haired woman stood erect, and seemed relieved.

It's over, Debbie.   4

QUESTIONS FOR DISCUSSION AND WRITING

1. What evidence led the physician to end Debbie's life? What unstated assumptions did the physician make?
2. Is there any information in this letter to suggest that the physician may
   have acted wrongly?
3. Did *JAMA* act responsibly in honoring this physician's request for ano-
   nymity, or should the name have been made public?
4. Under what circumstances, if any, would you support euthanasia?

◆ CASE 10 ◆

LAWRENCE E. JOSEPH
The Bottom Line on Disposables

*A freelance writer who specializes in business and the environment, Lawrence E.
Joseph published the following article in* The New York Times Magazine *on
September 23, 1990. As you read this article, try to understand not only what it
reveals about the environmental effects of disposable diapers but also how a major
corporation works to preserve sales when one of its products is under attack.*

Not since the automobile begat the suburb has a product so essential to the   1
American lifestyle become so maligned as a symbol of pollution and waste.
The disposable diaper, which during the 1970's and 80's became as indispensable to working parents as "Sesame Street" and strained carrots, is suddenly the environmental bad boy of the 90's. With the resurgence of the
ecology movement and the attendant rise of environmentally correct "green"
consumer products, change-and-chuck diapers are under attack by a loose
confederation of ecologists, politicians and health-care advocates.

The stigma extends to Procter & Gamble, which virtually invented the   2
throwaway diaper business and leads the $3.5 billion market with its Pam-
pers and Luvs brands. As a company devoted to providing the public with
the means to clean and care for itself—from Always feminine protection pads
to Zest deodorant soap—P.&G. cannot afford to have customers feeling guilty
about buying any of its products.

One day last spring in the Ivory Room, a plush private dining den at   3
P.&G. headquarters in the heart of downtown Cincinnati, a small group of
executives gathered to assess the problem. They helped themselves to the
sandwich buffet, passed around big plastic bowls of Pringles Cheez Ums
Potato Chips and Duncan Hines Chocolate Chip cookies, then settled in to
discuss the company's biggest public-relations challenge since the early 1980's,
when its Rely tampons were linked to toxic shock syndrome.

"We don't think mothers are willing to give up one of the greatest new   4
products of the postwar era," said Richard R. Nicolosi, the 42-year-old group
vice president in charge of P.&G.'s worldwide paper operations and the company's de facto diaper defender. He paused to blow steam off a cup of the
house coffee, Mountain Grown Folgers. "Why should they?"

For lots of reasons, say the critics, who are calling for a return to tra-   5
ditional, reusable cotton diapers. Citing estimates that range from 3.6 billion
to more than 5 billion pounds of discarded diapers a year, the anti-disposable
movement charges that the paper-and-plastic nappies are choking the nation's
landfills. They also claim that the waste products in the diapers threaten the
health of sanitation workers and, by leaching viruses and bacteria into ground
water, the health of surrounding communities.

Rallying to the cause, some two dozen states have enacted or proposed   6
legislation meant to discourage or tax the use of disposables. Beginning in
October 1993, subject to further study by the state's director of environmental control, Nebraska will ban all throwaway diapers not designed to decompose quickly. Eight other states, including California, Florida and New York,
are also considering bans.

Not that any of this has yet made a measurable impact on the roughly   7
9 percent of the nation's households that are home to a diaper-age child. Each
day, parents and babysitters reach for disposable instead of cloth more than
eight times out of ten. (In Western Europe, where P.&G. also has a major
presence, the number is often higher; the French use throwaways in 98 of
every 100 diaper changes.)

Still, the outcry over diapers comes at a time when Procter & Gamble,   8
America's foremost purveyor of personal-care products, is uncharacteristi-
cally vulnerable: its share of the diaper market has eroded from some 70
percent a decade ago to just below 50 percent today. During the same period,
the market share of Kimberly-Clark's Huggies has risen from less than 10
percent to more than 30 percent. In some metropolitan markets, meanwhile,
diaper delivery services appear to be making a comeback. The aging of the
population portends a declining birthrate, and P.&G. can ill afford a mass
defection to cloth diapers by the dwindling number of baby bottoms.

Which is why P.&G. is staging a P.R. counter-offensive under Nico-   9
losi, with the participation of another man at the lunch table, Gerald S. Gendell, manager of the corporate public affairs division. The methods include
lobbying state legislators and making speeches before consumer and environmental groups to tout the company's experiments in recycling and composting used disposables. And in a marketing move that is patently P.&G., the
company has produced two six-page, four-color brochures and mailed them
to more than 14 million households since the beginning of the year.

One of the pamphlets, called "Diapers and the Environment" and writ-   10
ten in patient, junior-high science text prose, seeks to put the environmental
uproar into perspective: "In repeated studies, experts have discovered diapers
make up less than 2 percent of total solid waste in municipal landfills. This
means, in the life of a landfill, diapers represent 7 weeks of a 10-year lifetime."

Attached to the brochure: discount coupons for Pampers and Luvs.   11

Nowhere is anti-disposable sentiment rooted more deeply than Seattle.   12
In this environmentally progressive city, where householders are charged
collection fees based on the size of their garbage cans, diapers are the subject
of a major political controversy.

"With disposable diapers, the first lesson a child learns is that when you   13
make a mess, you throw it into the garbage and it goes away. That message
is fundamentally wrong," declares Patricia Greenstreet, a Seattle attorney and
a former registered nurse.

The King County Nurses Association in Seattle, of which Greenstreet   14
is a director, has emerged as the most influential voice in the city's diaper
debate. The 2,400-member organization has distributed information leaflets
weighing the pros and cons of each type of diaper—with the scales tipping
toward cloth. Six of the eight Seattle hospitals with maternity wards have
already been persuaded to revert to cotton diapers. The other two intend to
join the fold soon. Nursing groups, hospitals and municipalities from some
30 states have asked the King County group for advice on shifting to cloth
diapers.

For Seattle's nurses, the issue is not the comfort of babies. Indeed, on   15
the subject of diaper rash—which diaper-delivery companies insist will occur
less frequently with cloth nappies—the Seattle nurses have taken no stand,
while the National Association of Pediatric Nurse Associates and Practitioners subscribes to the conclusion of a P.&G.-funded medical survey. This report, "Etiology of Diaper Dermatitis," found that disposable diapers containing
superabsorbent gel—Ultra Pampers is one such brand—keep babies drier.

Seattle's nurses fault disposables on ecological and public-health grounds.   16
Last year, with funding from the Seattle Solid Waste Utility, they commis-
sioned their own diaper study, concluding that disposables "burden our already overfilling landfills and utilize more nonrenewable natural resources
than reusable products. Furthermore, disposable diapers pose a potential risk
to solid-waste workers."

In King County, which includes Seattle and its environs, the county   17
council has held hearings on a proposed ordinance that would make it illegal
to place disposable diapers in trash cans unless the fecal matter has been removed. Such an ordinance was earlier adopted in Seattle proper, with the
endorsement of the King County Nurses.

The American Paper Institute, a trade association whose members in-   18
clude P.&G. and other disposable-diaper manufacturers, is calling for the county
to practice consumer education, rather than to police citizens' dustbins. P.&G.
has sent its own representatives to each hearing, and the company stands
ready to fight the anti-disposable fight throughout the land—municipality by
municipality, if need be. "Procter & Gamble will always be available to provide data and technical assistance on the diaper issue," says Scott Stewart, an
assistant to P.&G.'s corporate public relations director, Gendell.

P.&G. and the other manufacturers contend that there has not been a   19
single case of illness linked to diapers in landfills. The manufacturers also
point out that cloth diapers are not without their own environmental costs.
According to an Arthur D. Little study sponsored by P.&G., laundering a
cloth diaper, over its life cycle, consumes up to six times as much water as
is used in the manufacture of a disposable. Laundering cloth diapers also
supposedly creates nearly ten times as much water pollution as manufacturing disposables.

The Environmental Protection Agency has endorsed none of the var-   20
ious comparative studies. The E.P.A. "generally supports the use of cloth

over disposable diapers because disposables cause so much solid waste," says Lynda Wynn, a senior staffer on the Municipal Solid Waste Project at the E.P.A. in Washington. But, Wynn continues, the E.P.A. believes that until a scientifically valid "product life assessment" methodology is devised, no study can be considered definitive. Toward this end, the E.P.A. will assemble an advisory group of industry representatives, ecologists, and government experts to work out methods for evaluating the environmental impact of various types of solid waste.

For P.&G., having the jury still out is better than a presumption of guilt. The company was heartened by a recent report from the nonprofit National Resource Defense Council, an influential environmental organization. The N.R.D.C. concluded that, on ecological grounds, neither cloth nor disposables were clearly superior. Either choice imposes environmental costs, the report said.   21

In support of N.R.D.C.'s ongoing environmental research, P.&G.'s philanthropic foundation sent the council a $5,000 contribution earlier this year. The group politely returned the money.   22

The disposable-diaper controversy comes down to a philosophical question: Is the landfill half-empty or half-full?   23

All parties agree that throwaway diapers represent no more than 2 percent of the garbage carted to the nation's landfills each year. To the friends of disposables, 2 percent is a bearable load; for the antidisposable forces, the figure in unconscionably high.   24

Supposed solutions have emerged for reducing or eliminating the paper and plastic that disposable diapers leave behind. Nebraska, which abounds in potential landfill space, played Cornhusker politics in passing a law that would allow use of only "biodegradable" disposables in the state after 1993. Nebraska, of course, is a major corn-growing state. And cornstarch is a key ingredient of the plastic used in the so-called biodegradable brands; the best-publicized of these are Bunnies, made by American Enviro Products. The premise of such brands is that microbes will devour the cornstarch binders in the material, allowing the plastic polymer molecules to separate. Trace minerals that have been added to the plastic then oxydize the polymers into parafin, which in turn—the theory goes—breaks down in the soil. But critics contend that not even corn cobs will biodegrade in airless, sunless landfills—much less plastic-cornstarch composites.   25

Procter & Gamble, in its direct-mail campaign, has refuted the supposed ecological benefits of the biodegradables. The N.R.D.C., the Environmental Action Foundation and most other environmental groups are also skeptical. And the Environmental Marketing Task Force, a coalition of attorneys general from New York, Texas, Washington and a handful of other states, is investigating the marketing claims American Enviro is making for its Bunnies; the task force earlier this year filed suit in several states to bar the Mobil Corporation from advertising its Hefty trash bags as "degradable." Little wonder that legislators in Nebraska—which is not part of the task   26

force—have made their ban contingent on further study into the "environmental impact and fate" of biodegradables.

For its part, P.&G. is loudly advocating another type of ecological ex-   27
periment—a bit of guerrilla theater staged in the heart of enemy territory,
Seattle.

Each week Seattle's Baby Diaper Service Inc., in a contract with the   28
City of Seattle and underwritten by P.&G., sends its trucks to 722 households and 33 day-care centers to retrieve soiled disposables and haul them
back to a 7,500-square-foot recycling plant. There, in a joint project with a
company called Rabanco Recycling, workers load the dirty diapers into a
contraption resembling a giant food blender. The machine washes the nappies and separates them into their component parts: plastic, paper pulp and
absorbent gel. The plastic gets set aside for recycling; the paper pulp is sani-
tized. Although the project remains experimental, the pulp would be suitable
for selling to paper mills.

"High-grade pulp is the 'cash crop' of disposable diaper recycling," says   29
Nancy Eddy, a microbiologist who is supervising the project for Procter &
Gamble. But the company is still waiting for a market to develop for recycled plastic. "Though it can be used for flower pots, garbage bags and a host
of other uses, the prices for recycled plastic—when you can sell it at all—are
still way below the costs of recovery."

Even with a ready market for paper pulp, the plant at its current pro-   30
duction level would be unlikely to exceed revenue of about $150 per day.
"At this point we're just testing out the system," says Eddy. "Maybe it will
turn out to be more suited for other household paper products, even newspapers."

For Gene Anderson, who has been recycling disposable diapers in Se-   31
attle for a little over a year, P.&G.'s project is pure grandstanding. Anderson
is the 58-year-old proprietor of Anderson Diaper Service. "Procter & Gamble is filling up our landfills with billions of diapers a year and is trying to
take credit for saving the world from disposables!" complains Anderson.

Anderson Diaper Service lets customers choose between conventional   32
cloth delivery for about $48 per month and a disposable service for $50. For
the 1,400 customers on the recycling plan, Anderson Diaper twice a month
delivers new private-label disposables and collects the soiled ones. Back at
Anderson's laundering facility, the dirty disposables are cleaned in an industrial-
strength washing machine. A second machine then separates the pulp from
the two types of plastic—polypropylene liners and polyethylene backings.
Workers bale the plastic and store it against the day that a market emerges
for the material.

"I'm the only one who's actually been doing the job that everyone else,   33
including the Seattle Solid Waste Commission, just talks about," says Anderson. P.&G. officials like to point out that Anderson does not really recycle
anything; the plastic is sitting in a warehouse, and some of the valuable paper
pulp is washed down the drain. Anderson has heard it all before. "At least

we're keeping the plastic out of the landfill!" he says. "And the pulp's going into the sewage system, where it belongs."

So far, for all the sound and fury, the diaper debate has not hurt P.&G.   34
financially. In early July, a time when many blue-chip companies were reporting disappointing results, the company announced a fourth-quarter earnings increase of more than 66 percent. That capped a fiscal year in which earnings rose nearly 33 percent to $1.6 billion on revenue of $24.1 billion.

P.&G., in other words, can afford to discuss long-term solutions to its   35
public-relations quandary. Richard Nicolosi, whose paper-products division manages forests around the world, says the ultimate solution to the diaper dilemma may lie in the good earth.

"Though many people think of disposables as made of plastic, they are   36
actually about 65 percent high-grade paper pulp by weight," Nicolosi told the others at the table. "And that pulp can be composted. Inexpensively. Even profitably.

"European countries have been composting their refuse for more than   37
20 years," he continued. "The humus is then used to replace topsoil, fertilize tree farms and generally keep parks and roadways green. There's not a reason in the world we can't do the same thing."

Procter & Gamble last year conducted a five-week test project in St.   38
Cloud, Minn., with Recomp, a solid-waste composting company. Trucking disposable diapers each week from 3,000 households and day-care centers in St. Paul, 60 miles away, project engineers operated a system that shredded and recycled each diaper's plastic cover, then composted the soiled interior. According to Nicolosi, the composting costs in St. Cloud average about $50 per ton. While that is higher than the national-average landfill fee of about $30 per ton, it is well below the fees in metropolitan areas such as New York, where fees now often top $100 per ton.

Nicolosi wondered why more cities and towns, instead of opposing   39
disposables, are not putting them to work. "The real issue isn't what's consumed. The real issue is its destiny. Disposable diapers begin as trees, and they should end up as trees."

QUESTIONS FOR DISCUSSION AND WRITING

1. Why are environmentalists concerned about the use of disposable diapers?
2. What steps has Proctor & Gamble taken to protect future sales of Pampers and Luvs?
3. Are there any disadvantages to using cloth diapers?
4. How are "biodegradable" disposable diapers supposed to work? Is there any reason to believe that such diapers may not break down in landfills?
5. Are there any alternatives to discarding disposable diapers in landfills? How have European countries responded to this problem?

♦ CASE 11 ♦

BRUCE INGERSOLL

Range War

When first published in The Wall Street Journal *on June 6, 1990, "Range War" had three subtitles that alerted readers to what they could expect in the article: "Small Minnesota Town Is Divided by Rancor Over Sugar Policies," "Aided by U.S. Price Supports, Prospering Beet Growers Crowd Out Other Farmers," and "Son Can't Afford Dad's Farm." Bruce Ingersoll is a staff reporter for the* Journal. *As you read his article, try to understand why the local conflict he reports has national implications.*

Maynard, Minnesota. At the Lutheran Church here, some families refuse to worship in the same pew. Elderly farm women no longer get together once a week for coffee. Boyhood friends shun each other. 1

Resentments are eroding even the most enduring rite of rural life, the wave hello. Farmers sometimes pass on Chippewa County 17 without even a nod of acknowledgement. 2

What caused this rupture? Sugar. 3

Residents of this heartland hamlet (population 428) are embroiled in a modern-day range war, this one pitting the "beeters"—the sugar beet growers—against their grain-farming neighbors. Many farmers fume that the rich beeters are getting richer at their expense—thanks to preferential treatment by the federal government. 4

Across a broad swath of southern Minnesota and elsewhere, beeters, flush with sugar profits, are outbidding other farmers whenever land is rented or a farm is sold. They are driving up land prices and rents, and crowding less fortunate farmers off the land. "We've lost a whole generation of young farmers," asserts Owen Gustafson, a Maynard grain grower and a leader of Fair Farm Policy, a group protesting "inequities" of sugar subsidies. 5

A Very Sweet Deal

The protests extend to international trade negotiations and Congress, where the sugar program is under sharp attack as lawmakers debate the 1990 farm bill. Arguably, it's the sweetest deal in American agriculture: The government props up domestic sugar prices by curtailing imports of lower-cost sugar. Producers are guaranteed a "market stabilization price" of 22 cents a pound, about nine cents higher than the current world market price. 6

The result: Although some other crops are also subsidized, sugar beets often bring growers four times more per acre than wheat and corn. Large beeters here reap $100,000 to $200,000 each in annual sugar benefits. That's 7 not money from the government, but from consumers in the form of higher prices. Republican Sen. Richard Lugar of Indiana claims this "hidden tax" costs consumers $2.4 billion a year—although sugar growers contend the figure is far-fetched.

"That's super-welfare—that isn't a safety net," says Thomas Hammer, chief lobbyist for major sweetener users, which are allied with Fair Farm Policy in seeking cutbacks in sugar price supports.   8

Counters Irvin Zitterkopf, president of Southern Minnesota Beet Sugar Cooperative: "We aren't making as much as some of the people using our products, like candy makers and cereal people."   9

A Divided Family

For the farmers in this area, the debate taking place in Washington couldn't hit closer to home. "What we're trying to do is save our hides," says 51-year-old David Hovda, a Renville County cattle feeder. "They [the beeters] have really been endowed by the government. . . . They're going to drive us all out."   10

In Maynard and nearby Clara City and other small towns, widespread fear for the future, edged by envy of wealthy neighbors, is turning farmer against farmer, family against family—even dividing families.   11

Marvin Freiborg, a member of a large family of beet growers who himself worked with hogs, assailed the sugar program two months ago in a letter to the editor of the Clara City Herald. "I've kept quiet longer than I should have," he wrote. "I'm tired of watching the majority of beet growers outbid neighbors on land, expand their operations year after year, drive nice pickups, buy new equipment. . . ."   12

"My mom was just disgusted with me," says Mr. Freiborg, who had to give up his land last fall when his landlord raised the rent. "But I told the truth about what's happening. I had an awful lot of people call me, thanking me. They're just too timid to speak out."   13

The range war has been building for several years. It broke out into the open here when Mr. Gustafson, 39 years old, went to Washington early last year to protest the sugar program. He and his brother, Philip, have lost three pieces of rented land totaling 488 acres to higher-bidding beeters since 1985.   14

Driving home one night, Mr. Gustafson passes a gently swelling field, 160 acres of soft black earth under a canopy of stars. He and his brother had rented it for $63 an acre per year. It was sold last year, and the new owner rented it to a big beet grower from the town of Sacred Heart for more than $100 an acre. "There's no way we can pay that," he says. What's more, the Gustafsons aren't members of the local cooperative, so they can't profitably switch to growing sugar beets.   15

Accompanying Mr. Gustafson to Washington was an equally feisty neighbor, Ronald Carpenter, 43, who says that when he showed up at a land-rent auction here at LaRae's Cafe, alone among 20 beeters, "They laughed   16 at me. They knew I couldn't afford the cash rent. I bid just to run up the price."

Soon after the men returned from Washington, vandals broke into Mr. Carpenter's machine shed while he and his family slept. They dumped sugar into the gas tank of a tractor and spray-painted farm equipment with graffiti like this, still emblazoned on the side of his old pickup: "We Love Sugar."   17

On Maynard's main street, business at the Hair Affair, the beauty salon run by Mr. Carpenter's wife, Mary Ann, has fallen 50% from last year because of a boycott by some wives and daughters of beeters.   18

Her mother-in-law's coffee klatch has broken up. "She used to have coffee once a week with neighbor ladies," says Mrs. Carpenter. "They had been friends for 40 years. They just stopped calling."   19

The dispute is two-sided. "One farmer purposely sprayed herbicide so that the wind would drift it into the end rows of a beet field and kill the beets," says the Rev. Martin Scott Lucin, co-pastor of Immanuel Lutheran Church in Clara City.   20

Nobody is more troubled about the schism than the small-town ministers, who have been trying to help the antagonists better understand each other. In a sermon last year, the Rev. Ronald Duty, pastor of the Maynard Luthern Church, admonished his parishioners: "When we are jealous of another's prosperity or greedy for their land, instead of helping them to preserve their economic livelihoods . . . we do damage to the human community."   21

But for now, neither side is in the mood for reconciliation. Mr. Lucin recounts a farmhouse visit last year to a man dying of cancer: "He looked out the window and he vowed, 'The sugar beet guys aren't coming over here even after I'm gone.' "   22

Widespread Tensions

Wayne Schwitters, a Clara City beet grower, telling of a lost friendship with a local farmer, chokes up and looks away: "Him and I can't talk in church."   23

The rancor saddens Mr. Schwitters, one of the biggest beet growers in an area homesteaded a century ago by immigrant sodbusters, mostly from Scandinavia and Germany. "I feel sorry for those people raising corn and soybeans," says the 48-year-old farmer. "I think in reality corn and beans are way too cheap, and they are having a tough time."   24

Sugar also is making things tense in the Red River Valley along the Minnesota-North Dakota border. "Wheat farmers are starting to hate sugar beet growers," says Jacob Bakke, an elevator manager in Prosper, N.D. "It's unfair that they are just breaking even and the beet growers are making big bucks."   25

And in southern Louisiana, the expansion of sugar-cane planters is raising tempers in Cajun country. "These guys net more than I can gross per acre," complains Bill Burley, a soybean grower in Youngsville, La.   26

International Impact

Economic dislocations from the sugar program extend far beyond the Farm   27
Belt. To guarantee U.S. sugar cane and beet growers the market-stabilization
price, the government slashed imports of raw sugar to 1.25 million tons last
year from four million a decade ago. Critics of the sugar program say this
has deprived numerous sugar-producing nations in the Caribbean, Latin
America and Far East of export earnings, harmed their economies and caused
political instability, while increasing Third World demand for U.S. foreign aid.

At home, the sugar program has helped make possible the spectacular   28
rise of the high-fructose corn syrup industry—to the point that Americans
now consume more corn sweetener than refined sugar. The syrup industry
itself is not covered by the U.S. program. But by pegging their prices just
below the sugar support price, corn-sweetener producers captured not only
market share but huge profits.

Sugar producers contend that the program protects U.S. consumers from   29
wild swings in world sugar prices while shielding the producers from the
sugar-dumping practices of exporters, particularly the European Community, which heavily subsidizes production.

Broad Attacks

Minnesota and North Dakota beet growers say they wouldn't mind fending   30
for themselves in a free market, but only if all sugar producers were put on
equal competitive footing around the world.

The sugar program is under broad attack. At the urging of Australia,   31
the General Agreement on Tariffs and Trade has decreed U.S. sugar-import
quotas illegal. The Bush administration appears ready to phase out the sugar
program and other forms of protectionism in its quest for a breakthrough
GATT agreement to end trade-distorting farm subsidies.

In Congress, strong bipartisan support is building for an overhaul of   32
the sugar program, beginning with a 10% cut in sugar price supports.

Opposing change is Big Sugar's lobby and its phalanx of political-action   33
committees, long fabled on Capitol Hill for their generosity. From
1983 through mid-1989, sugar and corn-sweetener lobbyists supported their
pitches to members of Congress with $3.3 million in campaign contribu-
tions, according to an analysis of Federal Election Commission records
by Public Voice for Food and Health Policy, a Washington-based consumer
group.

The Fanjul Clan

That's a lot of money from about 10,000 beet growers in the Midwest and   34
the West; 1,000 cane producers, dominated by a few big sugar planters and
corporations in Florida, Louisiana and Hawaii; plus a handful of sugar pro-
cessors and corn refiners. But they can afford it.

Two of the biggest beneficiaries of the sugar program are the U.S.   35
Sugar Corp. and the Cuban-born Fanjul family of Palm Beach, Fla., led by
Jose (Pepe) Fanjul, who contributed $100,000 toward Republican campaigns
in 1988 alone, and his brother Alfonso, who is similarly generous toward
Democratic Party endeavors. Between them, U.S. Sugar, based in the sugar
mill town of Clewiston, Fla., and the Fanjul corporate empire control more
than 60% of Florida's cane acreage and produce more than 25% of the nation's cane sugar. Together they collected what the sweetener-users group
calls a "windfall" of $180 million in sugar benefits last year.

Here in southern Minnesota, beet growers such as Mr. Schwitters say   36
that other farmers could be growing beets if they hadn't passed up chances
to buy shares in the Southern Minnesota Beet Sugar Cooperative in 1974,
when it was organized, and four years later, when it was rescued from ruin
by a government-guaranteed $11.5 million bailout. For most farmers, the
cost of cooperative shares now is prohibitive. They therefore can't get into
sugar beets because the cooperative's processing plant in Renville is the only
one around.

Mr. Schwitters's rewards for taking the initial risk? A diamond-studded   37
stickpin in his tie. A 3,800-acre farming operation, including 1,700 acres of
beets. Seven hired hands and seven families of migrant farm workers. A big
house with two-story cathedral ceilings and a veranda where, his wife Jan
says, "it's fun to sit and see the crops coming up and the migrants working
out there."

'A Lot More Work'

Similarly rewarded are 330 other co-op shareholders. Last year, they reaped   38
an estimated $35 million in sugar price-support benefits.

A Fair Farm Policy study of Minnesota farm data calculates that the   39
beet growers made an average profit of $206.40 an acre from 1984 through
1988—about eight times what corn and soybeans brought in at $25.53 and
$25.94, respectively.

The beet growers say that profit figure is greatly exaggerated, although   40
Mr. Schwitters concedes that beeters earn more per acre than other farmers.
"By golly, if I didn't, I'd quit," he says. "It's a lot more work. It's a spe-
cialized crop."

The beet growers also maintain that local land prices and rents haven't   41
gone up nearly as much as the opposition says. "Yes, there are rents in excess
of $100" an acre, says William Rudeen, a beet grower near Bird Island, Minn.,
and current cooperative chairman. "But we're too small to have the impact
they say we have."

Subsidy Payments, Too

Their neighbors also are irritated that the beeters, in addition to sugar bene-   42
fits, also collect wheat and feed-grain subsidies for the part of their land devoted to those crops.

But while the government limits subsidized grain acreage each year to   43
try to prevent surpluses, beeters can plant as many beets as the Renville plant
can profitably process. The result: Sheltered from low-cost sugar imports,
they have expanded their beet acreage over 50% since the cooperative started.

The disparity deepens the local rifts, and merchants are under pressure   44
to take sides. "It's a tough fence to sit," acknowledges one farmer, Rolan
Ammermann. His father-in-law, a Clara City insurance agent, was aghast to
hear from a beet grower that Mr. Ammermann was baling oat straw for the
beeters' arch-foe, Ron Carpenter. Alarmed about appearances, his father-in-
law called him up. "It's got real tense for a while," says Mr. Ammermann.
"I just told him it's a business deal."

Also caught in the middle are landlords, including retired farmers and   45
widows. One young farmer, Randy Berends, has been all but dispossessed
because he can't afford to rent his retiring father's 320 acres at $105 an acre.
All he figures he can afford is $70.

"You can't blame the landlords for taking top dollar," he says. "It would   46
have been crazy for Dad to rent to me."

QUESTIONS FOR DISCUSSION AND WRITING

1. How is the federal government responsible for bitterness in rural Minnesota? Why have price supports for sugar made it difficult for some farmers
   to rent or buy land?
2. What are the arguments on behalf of federal price supports for products
   like sugar?
3. If raising beets is so much more profitable than raising other crops, why
   don't more Minnesota farmers switch to beets?
4. Who are the biggest beneficiaries of sugar supports? How have they sought
   to protect the sugar program from change?
5. How do you think the price of farm products should be determined—by
   the free market or by a system designed to protect farmers from swings
   in prices? Be prepared to respond to at least one argument likely to be
   raised by someone who disagrees with you.

♦ CASE 12 ♦

ROBIN WARSHAW

In the Bonds of Fraternity

A freelance journalist and author of a book on rape, Robin Warshaw published the following article in the August 21/28, 1989, issue of The Nation. *One of the oldest periodicals published in the United States,* The Nation *is known for editorial policies that usually express a liberal point of view. As you read this article, try to decide why the activities of fraternities and sororities should concern anyone besides college students.*

The theft of a few ledger books filled with personal jottings would be un-   1
likely to spark a police investigation in most places. But in the tiny village of
Hamilton, New York, where two shopliftings at the Busy Bee convenience
store might be considered a crime wave, the ledgerbook incident in April
triggered a local police probe. It also forced the town's main industry—as
Colgate University likes to call itself—to face the threat posed by an unsa-
vory fraternity scene badly at odds with the school's lofty intellectual mission.

The ledgers in question belonged to the college's oldest fraternity, Delta   2
Kappa Epsilon, or DKE (pronounced "Deke"), and were surreptitiously removed by persons unknown from a windowless building called the DKE
Temple. Photocopied excerpts were then sent to university administrators,
faculty and the press. The material was so repellent—racist, sexist, boastful
about sexual degradations and hazings, and crammed with passages reflecting
the group's mania for secrecy—that student rallies were held in protest. The
fraternity's defenders complained about the theft rather than the ledgers' content. DKE members have remained virtually silent publicly (the chapter president declined my request for an interview).

On Colgate's campus, the incident quickly snowballed into a debate   3
about Greek-letter groups at the 170-year-old school, where about 55 percent
of the 2,700 students belong to fraternities and sororities. The college, which
was all male until 1970, now has a nearly even split between men and women
students. Many of them agree with Marianne Weiss, a sorority member,
who says, "We live in a hick town in the middle of nowhere with a bunch
of cows. If there were enough alternatives, people wouldn't be going to the
Greek system." As it happens, Weiss's sorority was reprimanded last fall for
co-sponsoring a "jungle party" with a fraternity, three of whose members
attended in blackface. She doesn't defend that, but she also opposes making
DKE the campus scapegoat. "I think in the Greek-letter system there are
abuses," she says. "Those opinions [in the ledgers] are still common."

Last month, after an investigation, the college suspended DKE for   4
"hazing, blackballing and other infractions" for the 1989–90 academic year.
The faculty, witnesses to numerous testosterone-fired outrages on Fraternity

Row, voted overwhelmingly in May to abolish all fraternities and sororities by September 1994. However, only the school's board of trustees can impose such a ban; in July, it set up a special committee to review residential life and the role of fraternities and sororities.

The problem posed by Greek-letter organizations, especially fraterni-   5
ties, is not Colgate's alone. Nor is it one that is confined to small, rural campuses. Universities across the country are proclaiming diversity—social, sexual, ethnic, racial, economic and cultural—as the guiding spirit behind their pursuit of academic growth and excellence. At the same time, fraternities—whose members usually select one another on the basis of conformity to homogeneous group standards—are experiencing their highest membership levels ever. As a result, colleges find themselves trying to impart the bias-free goals of the 1990s to students who are clustering, in ever greater numbers, in the exclusionary communities of the 1950s. Those forces are clashing on more and more campuses.

Colgate president Neil Grabois, in his first year, may wish the DKE   6
crisis hadn't happened, but he's not avoiding it. "It's an opportunity to ask what we are and what we ought to be," says Grabois, who was previously provost of Williams College, which eliminated fraternities in the 1960s. "The question for us is, Are there features of the Greek-letter system which are either accelerating or accentuating trends in the culture that we would like to push against?" To those who would reply with an unequivocal "Of course," Grabois offers this caution: Before answering, he says, it's necessary to determine "what is specific about fraternities and not just sloshed 19-year-olds or sexually insecure 19-year-olds."

A look into the DKE ledgers may be helpful in drawing that distinc-   7
tion. The notes, scrawled in different handwritings, form a litany of odious attitudes and possibly criminal behavior. One entry, from January 1989, states: "watch your sexual practices—be careful of horrifying girls too much—University is very sensitive to anything sounding like rape. don't abuse women (too much)." Another reads: "This girl who me and X ganged—this babe and someone leaked it at dinner. That fuckin sucked." And from 1987, this description of a night of booze and sex: "going to have a crazy get together at the home of the virgin goddess [the DKE Temple] with imported fuel [slang for alcohol] and special guest star X the only female who is tits enough [DKE slang for "cool" enough] to do the subway shuffle [slang for a "train," or several men having sex with or forcing it from a woman, often when she is drunk]."

A list of what pledges must carry includes a "knife (long enough to   8
reach a Negro's Heart)." A passage written following new college rules for fraternity behavior bragged about stealing thirty cases of beer from the university pub—"a fitting rebuttal to the new regulations," a member wrote. Pages of meeting notes are also included. "You guys deserve beatings like we got," said one apparently older brother to younger ones. "It helps you understan[d]. You guys are pussies!" Another entry orders the beatings of two brothers. And from a list of reminders to members, these items: "if the

hazing goes wrong, we are finished"; "pledge banquet—within the next week, experimental road-trips—we have to find girls who will fuck"; "drug dealing—keep it *in the house*." [Emphasis in original.]

In baseball slang, to "deke" somebody means to fool him, decoy him.   9
Interesting, then, that fooling outsiders, especially college administrators, is a key element in the DKE writings, part of a group fealty that at times borders on the cultlike: "I've just finished reading the Record of what happened my freshman year when the House was threatened [suspended], and I realize how easy we have it now. But during that period things happened in the House for which we should be thankful—brotherhood became stronger than ever; unity was stronger than ever in the face of many adversaries; and secrecy was fine-tuned to an extent 'known only to our order.' Let us remember that, so that while we 'build our bridges' with the rest of the Colgate Community, while we adapt to new rules and attitudes, we . . . remember these words—the words my Pledge Father told me . . . DKE WILL ONLY CHANGE SO THAT DKE CAN REMAIN THE SAME." [Emphasis in original.] Nearly every passage carries the closing motto, "In the Bonds," above each DKE brother's signature.

Reading the excerpts, it's easy to understand how fraternity culture can   10
convince its members that a range of abuses—from marathon drinking-and-vomiting sessions to theft, beatings and even rape—are O.K. as long as the group sanctions them. "If these were working-class kids or poor kids in an inner-city ghetto, we'd call them a gang and we'd call them pathological," says Rhonda Levine, an associate professor of sociology at Colgate. Certainly, the reports of women who've been raped in fraternity houses nationwide show that what's sometimes called "wilding" when committed by poor or minority men is most often called "group sex" when the offenders have money and social status.

DKE has not been alone among Colgate fraternities in its transgres-   11
sions. Late last year, the alumni of Phi Gamma Delta closed their house due to rampant drug and alcohol abuse, vandalism and poor academic performance. Kappa Delta Rho was put on probation for rules infractions. In 1988, Delta Upsilon was disciplined for a function at which a member dressed as Hitler and two pledges went outside wearing T-shirts, one decorated with a swastika, the other with a Nazi slogan. Theta Chi and the sorority Gamma Phi Beta were suspended for the "jungle party" incident. In recent years, DKE has been suspended for fighting with Phi Delta Theta, Delta Upsilon for what college dean M. Lee Pelton calls "an out-of-control party" and Sigma Chi for violating university alcohol policy. (No wonder, on a recent visit, I saw a female student wearing a T-shirt with the plaintive message "Colgate University—The 4-Year Quest for the Sober Kiss.")

Anecdotal reports from students and faculty about fraternity culture are   12
just as damning. A letter written this spring by a Phi Gamma Delta member to the college administration described a paralyzing use of LSD, Ecstasy, cocaine and other drugs in his house, including a "drug olympics" held between members and pledges and a "tequila night" on which a record was

kept of shots consumed. On one occasion, the letter-writer drank thirty-three shots; the winner, he said, drank forty-three. When another member, sophomore Chris Chafe, quit the house in disgust over hazing, sexism and drug abuse, Chafe says, "People said, 'You're a fool, you're a whiner, you're an asshole. We went through it, you should be able to go through it. That's part of being in the house.' "

A female student told me of trips by the Alpha Tau Omega fraternity   13
pledges to Skidmore College at which, she had heard, a point system was applied to sex acts. The fraternity pledges would divide into teams and, by the end of the night, the team with the most points would win. I asked Michael Sippey, an A.T.O. member and vice president of the Interfraternity/Sorority Council, if the story was true. "It goes on. It bothers me," he says, but insists that the "tone" of the road trip has changed recently. Nonetheless, he says, "The concept is definitely warped." Other students report seeing freshman pledges return to the dorms from fraternity events incoherent from drinking or taking drugs and with bruises on their bodies. Professor Levine tells of one of her students found lying outside his fraternity house, unconscious from drinking.

"I think a lot of these guys are normal," says Adam Shyevitch, a senior   14
who favors abolishing the Greek-letter system. "One thing I've gotten out of this is that so many people don't have a clear image of when things are just wrong."

Those who defend the Greek-letter system, like senior Todd Betke, a   15
Phi Tau member and president of the Interfraternity/Sorority Council, argue against a ban at Colgate by saying the fraternities aren't exclusionary (since 55 percent of students belong) and don't foster sexism, racism, violence or other abuses. "There are incidents that people who are members of these institutions take part in, but that is not what the institutions stand for," Betke says.

And Betke's right. Most fraternity chapters stress social service over   16
socializing and virtually all have removed discriminatory language from their membership codes. Many houses cite as their chief assets their good works, the career importance of their alumni networks (George Bush and Dan Quayle were DKEs at their colleges) and what they call the "management skills" that their members learn. Still, it's not the blood drives, charity fund-raisers or improved résumé potential that brings in new members; it's an attraction to a culture that often seems to say, "Become one of us and you'll get loaded, you'll get laid, you'll become a man."

Yet, as Grabois asks, are such attitudes due to the specific nature of   17
fraternities? Certainly, young men sometimes form groups that express hostility toward women, African-Americans, homosexuals or anyone not exactly like themselves. These groups may be an informal cluster of friends or have a structure, as do fraternities, athletic teams and gangs. Fraternities, though, are especially dangerous because of the sheer number of men who join them (far greater than the number who belong to athletic teams);

because they are socially approved and even admired groups (as opposed to gangs); and because members must show unquestioning loyalty (unlike casual friends).

Despite all the "good deeds" news clippings that fraternities and their   18
alumni trot out, most fraternity cultures are still centered on proving manhood in accordance with three basic beliefs: that women are sex objects to be manipulated at will; that drinking and drug-taking are endurance sports; and that all nonmembers, be they other male students, professors or college administrators, are deficient weenies. Because fraternities are essentially closed shops, both morally and intellectually, members are unlikely to have those beliefs disputed in any way they will find convincing.

Some schools, including Colgate, have tried imposing reforms, but those   19
efforts have largely failed. However, the decision to eliminate Greek-letter systems altogether is still a hard one for most schools to make. "I don't think any campus is ever ready for it to happen," says James Reynolds, a psychology professor and chair of the Faculty Affairs Committee at Colgate. Schools worry that such bans will anger alumni and jeopardize donations as well as cause housing and recreation shortages that the colleges will then have to remedy. Nonetheless, Franklin and Marshall College in Lancaster, Pennsylvania, took the plunge last year. It withdrew all material support (a full-time administrator, use of facilities, programming and other aid), although most fraternities continue to maintain privately owned houses off campus. Despite the fears beforehand, alumni donations show a slight increase this year. Franklin and Marshall has increased social-event funding and may open a student entertainment center. "We're going to make the college programs and facilities the best we can," says its president, Richard Kneedler, "and the fraternities are not in our plans."

The fact that fraternities are flourishing on campuses today is not an   20
argument to allow them to exist. Although increased diversity at universities may frighten some students into retreating to reassuringly familiar and homogeneous groups, schools need not support such a backlash. Those fraternity members who are truly committed to public-service projects can volunteer directly, through the American Red Cross or literacy programs, while those interested in developing management skills can gain all they want in open-membership student government groups. In short, there is no benefit offered by most Greek-letter groups that does not already exist in a better form, or could not easily be developed, on any college campus. Amherst and Colby Colleges, like Franklin and Marshall, recently severed their Greek-letter systems. There's no reason that the same couldn't happen at other schools where scholarship and social diversity are valued and the inherently destructive influence of fraternities is finally recognized.

At Colgate, the question of eliminating the Greek-letter system remains   21
under review, but there are signs that more and more people feel the fraternity culture no longer has a place in a modern university. Says Professor Reynolds, "What has surprised me was the number of faculty who [previously] supported fraternities feeling the time has come for a change."

QUESTIONS FOR DISCUSSION AND WRITING

1. Why do people join fraternities and sororities at a school like Colgate? Why do you think students at larger schools decide to do so?
2. Why was DKE suspended at Colgate? Do you think that this penalty was fair?
3. Do colleges and universities have a mission that is likely to conflict with the purpose of fraternities and sororities? Why might fraternities be more controversial in the 1990s than they were in the 1950s?
4. Drawing upon the information in this article, and your own experience if you wish, defend or attack the Greek-letter system.
5. According to this article, Franklin and Marshall College increased funding for social events after it withdrew support from fraternities. Do schools have a responsibility to provide entertainment for students? If so, how much?

PART 4

SOURCES FOR ARGUMENT

◆

MANDATORY DRUG TESTING: A QUESTION OF PRIVACY

◆

JOHN J. BURT
Drugs and the Modern Athlete

John J. Burt is Dean of the College of Physical Education, Recreation, and Health at the University of Maryland. His belief in the importance of good health is evident in his books which include Education for Sexuality *(1970) and* Toward a Healthy Life Style *(1980), and in the following article which was first published in* **1987.**

Beset by a rapidly spreading moral malignancy, darkness has now fallen on   1
the road to intercollegiate athletics, a road that has in recent times been
potholed by behaviors that are dishonest, illegal, exploitative, and unhealthy.
Because these are values that colleges and universities were created to discourage, intercollegiate athletics are now endangered. Either these potholes
must be filled or the roads to athletics must be closed down. Indeed, we have

come to a time in history when young people are reporting that being an athlete—even a very good one—is no longer something to be proud of.

Hence, there is a great need today for athletes who can restore to athletics its powerful tradition—athletes who are honest and drug free and law abiding and healthy. This higher type of athletics needs its champions as it never did before, and there is no more essential and nobler task for the modern athlete—high school, college or professional—than to be seen and recognized as a star against the darkness of contemporary athletics.   2

One of the potholes requiring immediate attention is drug abuse among athletes—a problem that can only be solved by athletes helping athletes. To head this discussion in the right direction, let me begin with two observations. First, it should be noted that most athletes don't have a drug problem. In fact, 80 percent don't even use drugs ("The Substance," 1985). Second, the use of drugs among athletes does not appear to be greater than the use among students in general or society at large. The problem, then, reduces to the question: what's to be done for the small number of athletes who use drugs?   3

One option is to look the other way—consoling one's self with the knowledge that athletes are no worse than anyone else. This widespread attitude relieves the modern athlete of any responsibility toward those who use drugs. Going a step further, some drug-free athletes have assisted their drug-using friends in cheating on drug tests. Even worse, there have been reports of drug-free athletes treating other athletes by buying drugs for them.   4

A second attitude is one that compels athletes to help other athletes with their drug problems. In recommending this attitude, I ask you to consider the following cases. At one large and athletically powerful university, the team physician conducted exit interviews with all graduating athletes. Among these was a sub-group of drug users, all of whom had tested positive at some time during their college careers. Interestingly, these students, without exception, strongly supported the drug testing option. When an athlete at another university refused to be drug tested, the coach called him and his parents to a conference where it was explained that drug testing was a necessary condition for continuing on the team. This athlete transferred to another university, but both the athlete and his parents highly recommended the drug-testing university to a younger brother athlete.   5

Further, we have reports from a number of athletes who say that they strongly support drug testing for the reason that it permits them to say: no thank you, I can't use drugs; I am in a drug testing program for athletes. These examples point to some seldom recognized facts about drug-using athletes: (1) they understand that drug use is not in the best interest of either health or their athletic performance; (2) they need assistance in saying no to drugs; (3) they respect and appreciate those who help them to break away from drugs, but usually only after the fact; (4) they endorse drug testing as an effective option for dealing with the drug problem.   6

So let's discuss the drug testing option in more detail—beginning with the assumption that properly designed and properly conducted drug testing   7 programs, while a nuisance for the drug-free athlete, can be of great assistance to the drug-using athlete. Such programs, however, can only work when they have the support of well-informed athletes.

With respect to drug testing, there are at least two important questions facing the modern athlete: (1) What are my rights? and (2) What are my responsibilities? 8

The Rights of Athletes

Off the athletic field or outside the gymnasium, athletes have been too passive in the protection of their rights, and it is my hope that they will correct this situation and also that they won't put rights ahead of responsibilities. For example, athletes certainly have the right not to help each other with the drug problem; nevertheless, one would hope that they would feel some sense of responsibility to do so. If athletics are to be restored to a high level of public respect, a blending of rights and responsibilities will be required. 9

Regarding rights, the Fourth Amendment promises to athletes, like everyone else, that they will be left alone unless they raise suspicions of guilt. It forbids any intrusions on human dignity and privacy on the mere chance that incriminating evidence might be obtained. Since medical procedures— including urinalysis screening—may be regarded as a personal search capable of revealing incriminating evidence, the modern athlete should understand what the Fourth Amendment does and does not permit relative to personal searches. 10

The Fourth Amendment protects against *unreasonable* searches and seizures. Hence, the central issues regarding the legality of random drug testing of athletes evolves around the question: Is it reasonable? Since there can be no precise definition or mechanical application of "reasonableness," this becomes a complicated issue involving a balancing of the need for the search against the invasion of personal rights. 11

With reference to the reasonableness criteria, two types of searches have been allowed: (1) a search conducted pursuant to a warrant authorized by a detached magistrate and based on probable cause that a violation of law has occurred, and (2) a warrantless search conducted pursuant to public interest and safety. Random drug testing falls in the warrantless search category. 12

One type of warrantless search (called an administrative search) permits the personal searching of people at airports, the borders of our country, and at the entrance to courthouses and prisons. The Supreme Court has also ruled that administrative searches are reasonable in the sport of horse racing. For example, the State of New Jersey conducts an administrative search in which jockeys are required to submit to daily breathalyzer and random urine tests. In this case, the courts ruled that public interest in maintaining the integrity of a highly regulated sport outweighed the right of individual privacy. 13

In order for colleges and universities to make good on the claim that random drug testing of athletes is reasonable, at least three requirements pursuant to an administrative search would have to be met: 14

- The testing college or university would be required to justify the claim that intercollegiate sports—by their nature, conduct, and regulation—result in reduced privacy expectations for the athlete.

- The testing college or university would be required to identify a strong public interest in making testing imperative and to justify drug testing as a necessary condition for participation in sport.

- The testing college or university would be required to make good on the claim that they were unable to identify a less intrusive alternative mechanism by which its objective(s) might be achieved.

Regarding these requirements, the modern athlete should be familiar   15
with at least four arguments that are currently offered in favor of random drug testing of athletes as an administrative search.

Argument One: the random drug testing of athletes is "reasonable" because   16
there is a strong public interest in whether athletes are performing in full health. If the outcome of intercollegiate athletic contests were of no interest to anyone other than the players, if these contests were conducted in private, if no tickets or television rights were sold, if the behavior of athletes did not reflect upon the institutions that they represent, if these institutions were not held responsible for the health and safety of athletes, then drug testing clearly would be a violation of Fourth Amendment promises. A good argument can be made for a strong public interest in how hard athletes try and whether they perform in full health.

Argument Two: The random drug testing of athletes is "reasonable" because   17
intercollegiate sports are pervasively regulated and participation is a privileged choice. As an athlete, one receives, among other special considerations, immediate and first rate health care; special academic advising and tutelage; room and board; public visibility and travel opportunities; and for a small number, the chance to go on to professional sports. These are privileges not available to nonathletes. However, in company with these privileges, the athlete should clearly expect a reduction in privacy. This is because intercollegiate sports are pervasively regulated: e.g., training rules, including bed checks; training tables; frequent medical examinations; grade checks to determine eligibility; conference regulations; NCAA regulations; and a set of rules that govern the conduct of athletic contests.

Argument Three: The random drug testing of athletes is "reasonable" because   18
the aim of drug testing is to return the athlete to health rather than to collect evidence that is legally incriminating. Obviously this argument does not apply for those drug testing programs that specify punitive actions against athletes. However, a good argument can be made for an exception to privacy when the sole aim of drug testing is to return the athlete to health. In such programs, colleges and universities must agree to not voluntarily supply personally identifiable test results to any agency or person not connected with the health of the athlete. The results of a search legitimized for health reasons should not thereafter be used for punitive reasons.

Argument Four: The random drug testing of athletes is "reasonable" because   19
colleges and universities must reserve the right to conduct upon their athletes whatever
test it deems necessary to the protection of health and safety. Good athletic programs require that all athletes be medically certified as fit for competition, be
appropriately conditioned for competition, be outfitted with the appropriate
safety equipment, and be provided medical supervision. Moreover, good
athletic programs demand that athletes be disqualified from competition
whenever in the judgment of health authorities their continued participation
would constitute a threat to health.

To ensure informed judgments regarding the welfare of athletes, health   20
officials must not be denied the use of any important diagnostic test, no
matter how intrusive it might seem. And drug testing should be viewed and
treated like other medical procedures. The argument reduces to this: to prohibit the use of an effective screening test could clearly hamper the efforts of
health officials to protect the health and safety of athletes.

References

"The Substance Use and Abuse Habits of College Student-Athletes." (1985). College of Human
Medicine, Michigan State University.

QUESTIONS FOR MEANING

1. According to Burt, why do college athletes support drug testing programs?
2. What criteria need to be met if a drug testing program is to be considered
   "reasonable"?
3. Why does Burt believe that athletes have special responsibilities that offset
   their right to privacy?
4. What should be the purpose of drug testing?

QUESTIONS ABOUT STRATEGY

1. Consider Burt's use of figurative language in paragraphs 1–3. Is it effective?
2. Why does Burt acknowledge that "most athletes don't have a drug problem" before beginning his discussion of drug testing?
3. Should Burt have identified the universities he cites in paragraph 5?
4. Italics in print are the equivalent of underlining. Why does Burt put the
   four arguments on behalf of drug testing in italics? What does this show
   about his relationship to his audience?

AMERICAN SOCIETY FOR INDUSTRIAL SECURITY

Why Drug Testing Is Needed

*One of the many forms of argument is the "policy statement" with which an organization, institution, corporation, or government body outlines its stand on a particular issue and provides a rationale for that policy. The following statement was adopted in **1987** by the American Society for Industrial Security, a professional organization of men and women who do security work in private and public industry.*

The illicit drug trade in America has fast become a $110 billion annual business.[1] According to the Research Triangle Institute, a North Carolina-based research organization, drug abuse cost the U.S. economy $60 billion in 1983, nearly a 30 percent increase from the more than $47 billion estimated for 1980.[2]   1

No one seriously disputes that drug abuse in the workplace is a serious and growing problem for both public and private employers. Increasingly, the problem continues to contribute to the high rate of employee absenteeism, rising health care costs, a high rate of accidents, and the low productivity of our work force. It has been aptly called an American tragedy.   2

As a result, the American Society for Industrial Security (ASIS)—and its Standing Committee on Substance Abuse—is in favor of drug testing efforts by both business and government. We believe a comprehensive drug testing program puts drug abusers on notice that they will be held strictly accountable for their actions.   3

There Is Basis for Concern

Let there be no doubt that drug abuse in the workplace carries a heavy price tag for our society—one that translates not only into dollars but also into pain and suffering for innocent members of the public. The following are some examples of that price tag: 4

- Since 1975, more than fifty train accidents have been attributed to drug-impaired employees. In these mishaps, more than eighty people were injured, thirty-seven lost their lives, and property valued at more than $34 million was destroyed.[3]   5

- In 1979, a Conrail employee, while under the influence of drugs, lost control of his locomotive and crashed into the rear of another train. Two people lost their lives and damages exceeded $400,000.[4] The same scenario repeated itself only recently.   6

- A recent study by the U.S. Department of Justice found that more than 50 percent of all persons arrested in New York and Washington, DC,   7 for serious crimes were found to be using one or more illegal drugs. Cocaine seemed to be the drug of choice among those who were arrested.[5]

- Cocaine, once the drug of the rich and famous, now has a clientele of more than 4 million regulars, reaching from the assembly line to the boardroom of many of our major corporations.[6]   8

- Employees who use drugs are at least three times as likely to be involved in an accident, seven times as likely to be the target of garnishment proceedings, and often function at only 65 percent of their work potential.[7]   9

Presently, some 20 percent of all federal agencies and more than 25 percent of all Fortune 500 companies conduct some type of drug screening or testing program.[8] The utility, petroleum, and chemical industries—the first private employers to use drug testing—are now being joined by a multitude of other industries, including state and local governments, in screening or testing their employees for drugs.   10

Because of the sensitive nature of their work, airlines and railroads are also turning to drug testing programs as a way of filtering out employees who pose a danger to the public. Recently, they were joined by such corporate giants as AT&T, IBM, and DuPont. Drug testing, like going through metal detectors at today's airports, has become an unfortunate necessity.   11

ASIS views drug testing, when properly and lawfully applied, as a positive step towards combating drug abuse both at the workplace and in our society at large. ASIS also thinks that ultimately it is the public who stands to gain.   12

ASIS is cognizant that, if abused, drug testing can prove detrimental. But, in those few cases involving abuses, the courts have demonstrated both a willingness and an ability to intervene.   13

ASIS is also cognizant that drug testing by itself cannot rid the workplace or our society of drugs. Rather, it must be carried out in conjunction with educational and related programs, for our growing dependence on drugs poses a direct long-term threat to our society.   14

Need for Drug Prevention Programs

For drug testing to prove both meaningful and useful, it must be conducted in conjunction with educational, counseling, and treatment programs. Among other things, we recommend the following: 15

- *An active antidrug program.* Employers should establish clear, comprehensive, and well-documented policies concerning the use, possession, and sale of drugs at the workplace. The antidrug program should be publicized and include sanctions. It should encompass all strata of the work force.   16

- *Judicious use of screening and testing.* Both federal and local courts have 1⁷ upheld the validity of drug testing provided it is carried out at the preemployment stage; conducted for cause; or, within certain confines, conducted at random.

  The courts have also made it amply clear they will allow drug 18 testing where it is not discriminatory or abusive, has been published well in advance, is not used as a subterfuge to discourage union activities, is not clearly in violation of public policy, and is in compliance with any collective bargaining agreement or other contractual arrangement between an employer and his or her employees.

- *Use of employee assistance programs.* Attempts to rehabilitate otherwise 1⁹ good employees make both economic and political sense. Not only can it prove time-consuming to recruit, hire, and train a new employee, it can also prove costly in terms of dollars. Counseling and treatment can go a long way in helping employees who are addicted to drugs—provided employees also want to help themselves. A concerted effort should be made to assist them.

- *Education and training.* The ultimate goal should be to obtain a work 20 environment that is 100 percent drug-free. In addition to the aforementioned programs, this goal can be achieved through a continuous educational process involving films, free literature, training seminars, community involvement, counseling, incentives, etc. Keeping in mind that a drug-free workplace is a healthier and happier environment, a continuing drug education program results in better morale as well as financial benefits.

Conclusion

A drug-free workplace, though ideal, should be the goal of every business 21 and government agency in America. However, drug testing is only one of several steps that must be taken to achieve this objective. When incorporated into a comprehensive antidrug effort, drug testing can go a long way in combating drug abuse at the workplace.

Notes

1. "The Plague Among Us," *Newsweek,* June 16, 1986, p. 15.
2. "Battling the Enemy Within," *Time,* March 17, 1986, p. 53.
3. "Battling the Enemy Within," p. 53.
4. "Battling the Enemy Within," p. 53.
5. "Wide Drug Use Found in People Held in Crimes," *New York Times,* June 4, 1986, p. 1.
6. "The Plague Among Us," p. 15.
7. "Drug Abuse in the Workplace," *DEA/Registrant Facts,* 1985, p. 6.
8. Nell Henderson. "Drug-Testing Industry Flourishes," *Washington Business,* June 30, 1986, p. 1.

QUESTIONS FOR MEANING

1. What are some of the problems that occur in the workplace as a result of drug abuse?
2. Under what circumstances is drug testing legally feasible?
3. According to this policy statement, how has drug abuse changed during the past decade?
4. Vocabulary: scenario (6), cognizant (13), conjunction (14), sanctions (16), strata (16), subterfuge (18).

QUESTIONS ABOUT STRATEGY

1. What type of organization is employed in this policy statement?
2. Does this statement include any concessions?
3. How credible are the sources cited in this statement? Are there any claims that require additional support?
4. Is this statement more likely to appeal to management or to employees? To what sort of audience is it directed?

CHARLES MARWICK AND PHIL GUNBY
Fighting Drug Abuse in the Military

*Before drug testing became common in the worlds of sports and business, the armed services had begun to test military personnel—in part because many American soldiers returned to the United States with a habit of chronic drug use acquired during the Vietnam War. In the **1989** article reprinted here, Charles Marwick and Phil Gunby explain how the services test for drug use, and they also evaluate how successful these procedures have been in reducing drug abuse within the military. Their report was originally published in the* Journal of the American Medical Society, *for which they both write on a regular basis.*

In May, 1981, during night military exercises off Florida's Atlantic coast, a   1
Navy plane crashed on the aircraft carrier *Nimitz,* killing 14 persons, including the plane's pilot, and injuring 42.

Subsequently, it was found that the pilot had excessive levels of anti-   2
histamines in his blood—11 times more than the recommended therapeutic levels. These developments helped to stimulate a rapid expansion of the Navy's drug abuse screening program.

The Army and the Air Force also have acknowledged the problem and   3
screen their personnel at regular intervals for drugs of abuse. The Navy's drug screening laboratories collaborate with those of the other services.

Abuse Seems to be Declining

As a result, says the Department of Defense, use of illegal drugs among   4
members of the US military has dropped at least 80% since 1980. That estimate is based in large part on anonymous responses from 17,213 armed services members questioned in a worldwide survey conducted by the Pentagon.

In 1980, some 27% admitted recent illegal drug use.   5

Then, in 1982, the armed forces instituted widespread drug testing and   6
threatened those who tested positive with disciplinary action including possible less-than-honorable discharge from the service. A survey at the time
brought admissions of drug abuse within the past month from 19% of respondents. Three years later, 9% made such an admission.

In the latest survey, 5.3% of the 17,213 respondents said they had used   7
marijuana, cocaine, or other nonmedical drugs within the preceding 30 days.

Actually, testing for drug abuse in the military services dates back to   8
the early 1970s. That's when a Department of Defense survey revealed the
existence of widespread drug abuse among military personnel in Southeast
Asia and elsewhere.

Air Force, Army, Navy Respond

The Air Force, Army, and Navy began planning at that time to cope with   9
the problem (*JAMA*. 1975; 231:462). For example, the Navy established five
laboratories for screening personnel for abuse of drugs. These are located in
Norfolk, Va.; Great Lakes (Naval Training Center), Ill.; Oakland and San
Diego, Calif.; and Jacksonville, Fla.

All the Navy's drug screening laboratories operate in a standard man-   10
ner, says Capt. Michael L. Pratt, a veteran of 22 years' service and the com-
manding officer of the Jacksonville facility, which began as a seven-person
laboratory capable of screening fewer than 5000 samples a month. Today,
with an annual budget of $4.5 million, the Jacksonville laboratory is staffed
by 66 persons and handles more than 8000 samples a week using the most
sophisticated testing equipment available.

At an approximate cost of $12 per test, "this laboratory consistently   11
produces results that are rarely successfully contested in the courts," Pratt
says. It wasn't always this way. The road to accurate testing for drugs of
abuse was rocky for all the services.

Admissibility of Army, Air Force, and Navy results was argued in court   12
and the scientific validity of the testing procedures was questioned. Even the
constitutionality of drug testing itself was challenged.

Admittedly, there were errors. There were administrative and logistic   13
problems; early tests were frequently unable to identify and quantitate drugs
with certainty and this cast further doubts on the test results. All these problems were heightened for the Navy, for example, when the testing program
was suddenly expanded after the *Nimitz* accident.

But the Navy overcame these difficulties and over the years has devel-   14
oped a program that, Pratt says, is second to none and might well be a model
for drug screening elsewhere, including civilian testing. Urine specimens are
collected regularly from all servicemen and servicewomen in a random manner based on Social Security number. Screening and confirmation are kept as
two separate processes.

How Navy Screens

Screening is done by a sequence of two radioimmunoassays. Any specimen   15
reported positive by the initial radioimmunoassay must also be reported positive on a second radioimmunoassay or be discarded.

The specimen is then checked by gas chromatography–mass spectrom-   16
etry and must again be reported positive or the specimen will be discarded.
Gas chromatography–mass spectrometry yields extremely accurate results,
down to nanogram levels, Pratt says.

"We go to every length to make sure that any positive result is in fact   17
positive. To call a specimen positive because of some error along the line in
processing or testing is unacceptable," he says. "If there are any doubts about
the scientific validity of the results, we must call it negative. False negatives
happen all the time. But a positive must be truly positive."

A negative result is "not necessarily negative," Pratt says. "It may well   18
contain drugs but, since they are below the established cutoff level, we are
not allowed to call them [the results] positive." Cutoff levels are established
by the Department of Defense and revised from time to time.

The cutoff levels for cocaine and tetrahydrocannabinol were recently   19
lowered to take full advantage of the capability of mass spectrometry. They
are usually set high, Pratt says, to avoid the risk of a false positive.

How Air Force Screens

The Air Force Drug Testing Laboratory is at Brooks Air Force Base, San   20
Antonio, Tex. It is the sole Air Force laboratory for drug testing.

Like other Department of Defense laboratories, its staff uses the ra-   21
dioimmunoassay and gas chromatography–mass spectrometry tests to detect
minute quantities of drug residue and metabolites. More than 250,000 urine
samples are analyzed each year for evidence of marijuana, cocaine, amphetamines, barbiturates, opiates, and phencyclidine (PCP).

Specimens are tested first for drugs with the radioimmunoassay. Each   22
specimen that tests positive is submitted for confirmation by gas chromatography–mass spectrometry. A sample is not reported as positive unless it
tests positive for both the screening test and the confirmation test, the Air
Force surgeon general's office (Bolling Air Force Base in the District of
Columbia) says.

How Army Screens

Army laboratories in Wiesbaden, West Germany, and Honolulu, Hawaii, and   23
at Fort Meade, Md., have been commended for their quality assurance/qual-
ity control program. Quarterly inspections by civilian and military experts
have been performed since 1984 and cover all aspects of laboratory operations
including scientific and forensic acceptability of results reported, training
procedures, staff and equipment, and review of all positive results on an individual basis by toxicology experts.

Drug testing methods require limit of detection and limit of quantita-   24
tion controls in each batch of specimens. The forensic acceptability and re-
portability of a positive result depends both on the accuracy and statistical
supportability of the control and testing data.

The Armed Forces Institute of Pathology manages an external quality   25
control program where blind positive and negative samples are submitted in
a double blind manner through military installations to Army laboratories.
This procedure is used to determine the incidence of false-negative and false-
positive test results.

Officials say that results of this program show that, of the approxi-   26
mately 5000 spiked samples submitted per year, the laboratories correctly
identified more than 95% of these positive samples, for a false-negative rate
of less than 5%. The Armed Forces Institute of Pathology also submits more
than 13,000 negative samples a year, and no false-positive results have been
reported by an Army laboratory since 1983.

In addition to these external quality assurance/quality control efforts,   27
the Army has an in-house program. Thus, nearly one third of all samples
tested are quality assurance/quality control samples. The Army's contract
laboratories in North Carolina and Utah also come under these controls and
inspections.

Army officials emphasize that "a major requirement of any urinalysis   28
program is the accuracy with which the specimens are handled. It is essential
that a carefully controlled collection point be maintained. The individual giving the sample thus gains a degree of assuredness that the sample will be
tested accurately and reliably."

On the List for Testing

The Navy says drugs currently tested for include tetrahydrocannabinol; co-   29
caine; opiates such as codeine, morphine, and heroin; phencyclidine; the amphetamines; the barbiturates; and lysergic acid diethylamide (LSD). Not all
specimens are tested for all drugs.

The Navy is currently testing only 10% of specimens for any of the   30
barbiturates. Approximately half are tested for PCP and the other half for
LSD. Screening for LSD began only recently, Pratt says, and "surprisingly,
its popularity is increasing."

Errors and complications "happen all the time in anybody's labora-   31
tory," Pratt says. "So, if a batch of specimens looks wrong in some way,
we can pull another set of specimens from that batch and reprocess it. But
such retesting has to be done in groups. We are not allowed to take a single
specimen that may look as if it might be positive, say just a little bit below
the cutoff point, and rerun that. We would be accused of being discriminatory."

Of the 374,588 samples tested in fiscal 1988, a little over 2% were called   32
positive on screening and just under 2% were confirmed positive. This compares with 1983, when almost 8% of specimens were confirmed positive.

The figures indicate that since the expanded testing program has been   33
put in place, drug abuse in the Navy has been falling markedly. Pratt attributes the decline directly to the program. Says he: "It's very effective in
scaring the hell out of these guys."

QUESTIONS FOR MEANING

1. What statistics are offered by the Department of Defense in support of its
   drug testing programs?
2. What penalty could be faced by an armed services member who tests positive for drug use?
3. How does the testing procedure used by the Navy differ from that used
   by the Air Force?
4. What steps does the military take to review the efficiency of Army laboratories?
5. Vocabulary: collaborate (3), respondents (7), logistic (13), quantitate (13),
   toxicology (23), markedly (33).

QUESTIONS ABOUT STRATEGY

1. According to this article, drug testing has been an issue in the armed services since the early 1970s, yet the authors begin by reporting an incident
   from 1981. Why do they use the *Nimitz* episode for their introduction?
2. After devoting five paragraphs to reporting drug testing in the Navy,
   three to testing in the Air Force, and six to testing in the Army, the
   authors return to discussing the Navy in paragraphs 29–33. Why do they
   give so much attention to the Navy?
3. Do the authors recognize that the military has had any problems with its
   drug testing programs?
4. Why do you think the authors chose to end this article with a quote from
   Captain Michael Pratt? What effect does this quote have on your reading
   of the article as a whole?

ANNE MARIE O'KEEFE

The Case Against Drug Testing

As both a psychologist and a lawyer who specializes in health issues, Anne Marie O'Keefe is concerned not only with the problem of drug abuse but also with the legality of drug-testing programs. Her argument against mandatory drug testing was first published by Psychology Today *in* **1987**.

During 1986, the nation's concern over illegal drug use reached almost hys-   1
terical proportions. The U.S. House of Representatives passed legislation that, had the Senate agreed, would have suspended certain Constitutional protections and required the death penalty for some drug offenses. The President issued an executive order calling for the mass drug testing of federal employees in "sensitive" positions. Federal courts have deemed such testing to be illegal for some classes of federal workers; however, these decisions are still being appealed, and the administration is determined to forge ahead with its drug-testing program. And private employers have turned increasingly to chemical laboratories to determine who is fit for hiring, promotion and continuing employment. Between 1982 and 1985, the estimated proportion of Fortune-500 companies conducting routine urinalysis rose from 3 to nearly 30 percent—a figure expected to reach 50 percent by this year or next year.

While there are issues of legitimate concern about drug use and public   2
safety, the speed and enthusiasm with which many of our elected representatives and business leaders have embraced drug testing as a panacea has left many questions unanswered. Why did our national drug problem so rapidly become the focus of political and business decisions? Did this change reflect a sudden, serious worsening of the problem? Why did mass drug testing suddenly gain favor? Was it shown to be particularly effective in detecting and deterring illegal drug use? And finally, what are the costs of making employees and job applicants take urine tests?

Our country has a serious drug problem. The National Institute on   3
Drug Abuse (NIDA) estimates that nearly two-thirds of those now entering the work force have used illegal drugs—44 percent within the past year. But ironically, the drug-testing craze has come just when most types of drug use are beginning to wane. NIDA reports that for all drugs except cocaine, current rates are below those of 1979, our peak year of drug use.

Why the furor now? The drug-testing fad might be viewed as the prod-   4
uct of both election-year posturing and well-timed and well-financed marketing efforts by test manufacturers. During the 1970s, the relatively low-cost chemical assay (called EMIT) that promised to detect drugs in urine was first manufactured. In the beginning, these tests were used only by crime laboratories, drug-treatment programs and the military. By the early 1980s, a handful of private employers were also using them. But more recently, sales of drug tests have gotten a big boost from the attitudes and edicts of

the Reagan administration. On March 3, 1986, the President's Commission on Organized Crime recommended that all employees of private companies contracting with the federal government be regularly subjected to urine testing for drugs as a condition of employment. Then came the President's executive order on September 15, requiring the head of each executive agency to "establish a program to test for the use of illegal drugs by employees in sensitive positions." It remains unclear how many millions of federal workers will be subject to such testing if the President gets his way.

Strangely, drug testing is becoming widespread despite general agreement that the results of mass tests are often highly inaccurate. Error rates reflect both inherent deficiencies in the technology and mistakes in handling and interpreting test results. In a series of studies conducted by the federal Centers for Disease Control (CDC) and NIDA, urine samples spiked with drugs were sent periodically to laboratories across the country serving methadone treatment centers. Tests on these samples, which the labs knew had come from CDC, revealed drug-detection error rates averaging below 10 percent. However, when identical samples subsequently were sent to the same laboratories, but not identified as coming from CDC, error rates increased to an average of 31 percent, with a high of 100 percent. These errors were "false negatives," cases in which "dirty" urine samples were identified as "clean."   5

Independent studies of laboratory accuracy have also confirmed high error rates. One group of researchers reported a 66.5 percent rate of "false positives" among 160 urine samples from participants in a methadone treatment center. False-positive mistakes, identifying a "clean" urine sample as containing an illegal drug, are far more serious in the context of worker screening than are false-negative mistakes. This is because false positives can result in innocent people losing their jobs. Ironically, since the error rates inherent in the drug tests are higher than the actual rate of illegal drug use in the general working population, as reported by NIDA, the tests are more likely to label innocent people as illegal drug users than to identify real users.   6

Many of the false-positive results stem from a phenomenon known as "cross-reactivity." This refers to the fact that both over-the-counter and prescription drugs, and even some foods, can produce false-positive results on the tests. For example, Contac, Sudafed, certain diet pills, decongestants and heart and asthma medications can register as amphetamines on the tests. Cough syrups containing dextromethorphan can cross-react as opiates, and some antibiotics show up as cocaine. Anti-inflammatory drugs and common painkillers, including Datril, Advil and Nuprin, mimic marijuana. Even poppy seeds, which actually contain traces of morphine, and some herbal teas containing traces of cocaine can cause positive test results for these drugs.   7

Commercial testing companies almost always claim very high accuracy and reliability. But because these laboratories are not uniformly regulated, employers who buy their services may find it hard to confirm these claims or even to conduct informed comparative shopping. Companies that mass-market field-testing kits such as EMITs (which cost an estimated $15 to $25   8 per test) usually recommend that positive test results be confirmed with other laboratory procedures, which can run from $100 to $200 per test. But relatively few employers seem to be using the expensive back-up procedures before firing employees who test positive. Even when employers do verify positive results, employees who turn out to be drug-free upon retesting will already be stigmatized.

The tests have other critical failings, particularly their limited sensitivity   9
to certain drugs, a shortcoming the drug-test manufacturers readily admit. Consider cocaine, for example. Despite great concern in the 1980s over the use of concaine, the only illicit drug whose use is on the rise, this is the drug to which the tests are least sensitive since its chemical traces dissipate in a few days. Alcohol, which is legal but potentially detrimental to job performance, is also hard to detect, since traces disappear from within 12 to 24 hours. By contrast, urine testing is, if anything, overly sensitive to marijuana; it can detect the drug's chemical byproducts (not its active ingredient) for weeks after its use and can even pick up the residue of passive inhalation. Drug testing does not indicate the recency of use, nor does it distinguish between chronic and one-time use. Most important, though urinalysis can reveal a lot about off-the-job activities, it tells nothing about job performance.

Mass drug testing is expensive, but its greatest costs are not financial   10
and cannot be neatly quantified. The greatest costs involve violations of workers' rights and the poor employee morale and fractured trust that result when workers must prove their innocence against the presumption of guilt.

The most important cost of drug testing, however, may be the invasion   11
of workers' privacy. Urinalysis may be highly inaccurate in detecting the use of illegal drugs, but it can reveal who is pregnant, who has asthma and who is being treated for heart disease, manic-depression, epilepsy, diabetes and a host of other physical and mental conditions.

In colonial times, King George III justified having his soldiers break   12
into homes and search many innocent people indiscriminately on the grounds that the procedure might reveal the few who were guilty of crimes against the Crown. But the founders of our nation chose to balance things quite differently. An important purpose and accomplishment of the Constitution is to protect us from government intrusion. The Fourth Amendment is clear that "the right of the people to be secure in their persons . . . against unreasonable searches and seizures, shall not be violated. . . ." Searches are permitted only "upon probable cause, supported by Oath or affirmation, and particularly describing the place to be searched, and the persons or things to be seized."

The U.S. Supreme Court has ruled that extracting bodily fluids constitutes   13
tutes a search within the meaning of this Amendment. Therefore, except under extraordinary circumstances, when the government seeks to test an employee's urine, it must comply with due process and must first provide plausible evidence of illegal activity. People accused of heinous crimes are assured of this minimum protection from government intrusion. Because employees in our government work force deserve no less, most courts

reviewing proposals to conduct mass tests on such employees have found these programs to be illegal.

Unfortunately, workers in the private sector are not as well protected.   14
The Constitution protects citizens only from intrusions by government (county, state and federal); it does not restrict nongovernmental employers from invading workers' privacy, although employers in the private sector are subject to some limitations. The constitutions of nine states have provisions specifically protecting citizens' rights to privacy and prohibiting unreasonable searches and seizures. Several private lawsuits against employers are now testing the applicability of these shields. Local governments can, if they wish, pass legislation to protect private employees from unwarranted drug tests; in fact, San Francisco has done so. In addition, union contracts and grievance procedures may give some workers protection from mass drug testing, and civil-rights laws could block the disproportionate testing of minorities. Nonetheless, private employees have relatively little legal protection against mandatory drug testing and arbitrary dismissal.

Civil libertarians claim that as long as employees do their work well,   15
inquiries into their off-duty drug use are no more legitimate than inquiries into their sex lives. Then why has drug testing become so popular? Perhaps because it is simple and "objective"—a litmus test. It is not easily challenged because, like the use of lie detectors, it relies on technology that few understand. It is quicker and cheaper than serious and sustained efforts to reduce illegal drug use, such as the mass educational efforts that have successfully reduced cigarette smoking. And finally, while drug testing may do little to address the real problem of drug use in our society, it reinforces the employer's illusion of doing something.

Apparently some employers would rather test their employees for drugs   16
than build a relationship with them based on confidence and loyalty. Fortunately, there are employers, such as the Drexelbrook Engineering Company in Pennsylvania, who have decided against drug testing because of its human costs. As Drexelbrook's vice president put it, a relationship "doesn't just come from a paycheck. When you say to an employee, 'you're doing a great job; just the same, I want you to pee in this jar and I'm sending someone to watch you,' you've undermined that trust."

QUESTIONS FOR MEANING

1. What is meant by "false negatives," "false positives," and "cross-reactivity"?
2. What is revealed by the study conducted by the Centers for Disease Control which is discussed in paragraph 5?
3. What drug is urinalysis most likely to detect? What type of drug is it likely to overlook?
4. How does O'Keefe account for the rise in drug-testing? Why does O'Keefe believe the popularity of drug-testing is "ironic" and "strange"?
5. Vocabulary: furor (4), posturing (4), assay (4), stigmatized (8), quantified (10), morale (10), arbitrary (14).

QUESTIONS ABOUT STRATEGY

1. What concessions does O'Keefe make regarding drug abuse?
2. Why does O'Keefe provide the initials for the National Institute on Drug Abuse and the Centers for Disease Control within parentheses immediately after first using these names in paragraphs 3 and 5?
3. Why does O'Keefe report the price of widely used field-testing kits and the cost of laboratory procedures that are recommended for back-up testing?
4. Consider the quotation with which this essay ends. Is this an effective conclusion?

JOHN HORGAN

Test Negative

Specializing in questions involving how science touches the lives of citizens, John Horgan writes regularly for Scientific American. *In "Test Negative," which was first published in* **1990,** *Horgan examines the evidence that has been used to justify drug testing in the workplace, and he argues that the evidence does not hold up under analysis. As you read his argument, note that he discusses a study by the Research Triangle Institute that is cited in two other pieces reprinted in this section.*

More than eight million working Americans had their urine tested for illegal   1
drugs in 1989, and as many as 15 million will undergo such testing this year, according to the National Institute on Drug Abuse (NIDA). The fraction of companies that subject employees or job applicants to testing has jumped from 21 percent in 1986 to more than 50 percent last year, according to the American Management Association. The trend seems likely to continue: a majority of the respondents to a recent Gallup poll favored random drug testing of all workers.

What underlies the broad acceptance of a practice that conservative Su-   2
preme Court Justice Antonin Scalia has called a "needless indignity"? One factor may be the alarming statistics cited by testing advocates to demonstrate the high costs of drug abuse. Examination of some of these claims suggests that they do not always accurately reflect the research on which they are based. In fact, some of the data could be used to "prove" that drug use has negligible or even beneficial effects. Consider these examples.

• Last year President George Bush declared that "drug abuse among   3
American workers costs businesses anywhere from $60 billion to $100 billion a year in lost productivity, absenteeism, drug-related accidents, medical claims and theft." Variants of this statistic abound in discussions about drug abuse and are commonly repeated without qualification by the media. Yet all

such claims derive from a single study, one that "was based upon assumptions which need additional validation," according to an assessment last year by NIDA, the chief federal agency sponsoring research on substance abuse.

The study grew out of a survey of some 3,700 households by the Research Triangle Institute (RTI) in 1982. The RTI group found that the average reported income of households with at least one person who admitted to having *ever* used marijuana daily (20 days or more in a 30-day period) was 28 percent lower than the average reported income of otherwise similar households. The RTI researchers defined that difference in income as "loss due to marijuana use"; the total loss, when extrapolated to the general population, came to $26 billion. The researchers then added on the estimated costs of drug-related crime, health problems and accidents to arrive at a grand total of $47 billion for "costs to society of drug abuse." This figure—"adjusted" to account for inflation and population increase—represents the basis of Bush's statement, according to Henrick J. Harwood, who headed the RTI study and is now in the White House drug-policy office.

The RTI survey included questions on current drug use (at least once within the past month). Yet according to Harwood there was no significant difference between the income of households with current users of any illegal drug—including marijuana, cocaine and heroin—and the income of otherwise similar households. Does this mean that current use of even hard drugs— as opposed to perhaps a single marijuana binge in the distant past—does not lead to any "loss"? "You would be on safe ground saying that," Harwood replies.

• Officials of the U.S. Chamber of Commerce have testified before Congress and at national conferences on drug abuse that employees who use drugs are "3.6 times more likely to injure themselves or another person in a workplace accident . . . [and] five times more likely to file a workers' compensation claim." The pharmaceutical giant Hoffmann-La Roche, which is leading an antidrug campaign among businesses (and has a big share of the drug-testing market), also promulgates this claim in "educational" literature.

In fact, the study on which the claim is based has "nothing to do with [illegal] drug users," according to a 1988 article in the *University of Kansas Law Review* by John P. Morgan of the City University of New York Medical School. Morgan, an authority on drug testing, has traced the Chamber of Commerce claim to an informal study by the Firestone Tire and Rubber Company of employees undergoing treatment for alcoholism.

• In an interview with *Scientific American*, J. Michael Walsh, who heads NIDA's applied research division and is a strong supporter of workplace testing, singled out two studies that he said showed drug users are more likely to cause accidents, miss work and use health benefits. The studies were done at two utilities: the Utah Power and Light Company and the Georgia Power Company. The 12 workers in Utah and the 116 in Georgia who served as the primary research subjects were tested "for cause": they had either been involved in accidents, exhibited other "problem" behavior (commonly, high absenteeism) or submitted to treatment for alcoholism or drug abuse. Critics point out that it should not be terribly surprising if these subjects exhibited the cited traits at a higher-than-average rate.

What may be surprising is that, according to a report published by NIDA last year, Utah Power and Light actually "spent $215 per employee per year less on the drug abusers in health insurance benefits than on the control group." Those who tested positive at Georgia Power had a higher promotion rate than the company average. Moreover, Georgia workers testing positive only for marijuana (about 35 percent of all the positives) exhibited absenteeism some 30 percent lower than average. Nationwide, Morgan says, marijuana accounts for up to 90 percent of all positive findings, both because it is by far the most widely used illegal drug and because it persists in urine for up to a month (compared with two days for most other drugs).

• Perhaps the study most publicized of late by testing proponents involves employees of the U.S. Postal Service. The service tested 4,396 new hirees in 1987 and 1988 and—keeping the test results confidential—tracked the performance of positives (9 percent of the total) and negatives. By last September, the service reported, 15.4 percent of the positives and 10.5 of the negatives had been fired; the positives had also taken an average of six more sick days a year.

This study may be distorted by more subtle biases—related to race, age or gender—than those displayed by the utility studies, according to Theodore H. Rosen, a psychologist and a consultant on drug testing. Indeed, Jacques L. Normand, who headed the study, acknowledges that minority postal workers tested positive at a much higher rate than nonminority workers and that previous studies have shown minorities to have higher absenteeism.

Morgan points out, moreover, that the Postal Service study (like all those cited above) has not been published in a peer-reviewed journal. In fact, he says, only one study comparing the work of drug-test positives and negatives has passed peer review. Last year, in the *Journal of General Internal Medicine*, David C. Parish of the Mercer University School of Medicine in Georgia reported on a study of 180 hospital employees, 22 of whom had tested positive after being hired. Parish examined supervisor evaluations and other indexes and found "no difference between drug-positive and drug-negative employees" at the end of one year. He noted, however, that 11 of the negatives had been fired during that period and none of the positives.

• Proponents of testing often imply that drug use among workers is growing. A Hoffmann-La Roche brochure, for example, quotes Walsh pronouncing that "the problem of drug abuse has become so widespread in America that every company must assume that its employees will eventually be faced with a substance abuse problem." Yet in 1989 NIDA reported that illegal drug use has been decreasing for 10 years and that the decline has accelerated over the last five years. From 1985 to 1988 the number of current users (at least once in the last month) of marijuana and cocaine dropped by 33 and 50 percent, respectively.

To be sure, a subset of this group of current users is increasing: NIDA estimated that from 1985 to 1988 the number of people using cocaine at least once a week rose from 647,000 to 862,000 and daily users increased from 246,000 to 292,000. NIDA found that addiction to cocaine (including "crack") is particularly severe among the unemployed—who are beyond the reach of workplace testing.

Clearly, the U.S. has a drug-abuse problem. Could it be that neither   15
indiscriminate testing of workers—which could cost upward of $500 million this year—nor the dissemination of alarmist information by testing advocates is helping to resolve that problem?

QUESTIONS FOR MEANING

1. According to Horgan, what explains the increasing acceptance of drug testing in the workplace?
2. How did the Research Triangle Institute establish the economic cost of drug abuse? Why might additional research be necessary?
3. What flaws does Horgan detect in the studies by the Utah Power and Light Company and the Georgia Power Company?
4. Does this article include any evidence indicating that men and women who test positively for drug use may nevertheless perform well on the job?
5. Vocabulary: variants (3), binge (5), promulgates (6), dissemination (15), alarmist (15).

QUESTIONS ABOUT STRATEGY

1. Consider the title of this article. Can it be read in more than one way?
2. Why does Horgan quote Supreme Court Justice Scalia?
3. Paragraphs 3, 6, 8, 10 and 13 are all marked by black dots (sometimes called "bullets"). Why are they used, and what is their effect?
4. Does Horgan imply that Hoffmann-La Roche may not be a reliable source of information on the value of drug testing? Does he question the reliability of any other testing proponents?
5. What is the significance of the article by David C. Parish, cited in paragraph 12?

CRAIG HUKILL
Employee Drug Testing

Laws governing drug testing continue to evolve as the courts hear new cases. Court decisions, especially those of the Supreme Court, help to establish the circumstances under which testing can be required. Craig Hukill works in the Office of the Solicitor, U.S. Department of Labor. In **1989,** *he prepared the following summary of two significant cases for* Monthly Labor Review, *a journal published by the federal government. Hukill's summary provides information that can help employers and employees make informed decisions regarding drug testing in the workplace, but it does not argue on behalf of a specific policy that would apply to all cases.*

The Supreme Court recently upheld Government mandated and authorized   1
workplace drug testing against challenges that such testing violates the Fourth
Amendment's prohibition against unreasonable searches and seizures. In its
first two decisions on the propriety of drug testing, the Court held that employees may be tested for drug or alcohol use in situations where the Government's "compelling" interests in such tests outweigh employees' "minimal"
privacy interests. Thus, "safety-sensitive" railroad workers may be forced to
undergo testing when they are involved in certain accidents or rule violations, as may U.S. Customs Service workers who carry weapons or are involved in interdicting drugs.

In *Skinner* v. *Railway Labor Executives' Association,*[1] the railway group   2
sought to enjoin Federal Railroad Administration regulations that require blood
and urine testing of crew members involved in serious train accidents.[2] The
group also challenged regulations that permit, but do not require, urine and
breath testing of crew members involved in less serious accidents or rule
violations.[3] While conceding that collecting or analyzing a blood, urine, or
breath sample is a search to which the Fourth Amendment applies,[4] Justice
Anthony Kennedy rejected the railway association's challenges. Writing for
a seven-member majority, he stated that such a search is permissible if, depending on "all the circumstances surrounding the search and seizure and the
nature of the search and seizure itself," it is "reasonable."[5]

Under the Fourth Amendment, a search is usually not reasonable unless   3
it is conducted pursuant to a judicial warrant that is based upon probable
cause.[6] Justice Kennedy's opinion creates an exception to this rule because
"special needs, beyond the normal need for law enforcement, make the warrant and probable cause requirement impracticable."[7] According to Justice
Kennedy, a warrant generally is required to ensure that the search is authorized by law and will be narrowly limited. However, because the Federal
Railroad Administration's drug-testing regulations carefully circumscribe the
circumstances under which testing may be performed and narrowly define
their limits, he found that, on balance, a warrant would serve no useful

purpose. This is particularly true, he said, because requiring a warrant would impose a significant burden on the employer.

Even more important is the Court's determination that an employer   4
may compel a test even though it lacks probable cause or an individualized suspicion of drug or alcohol use. To reach this conclusion, the Court balanced the intrusion on employees' privacy, which it considered to be minimal, against the Government's interest in testing, which it considered to be compelling.

The Court found blood and breath tests to be minimally intrusive be-   5
cause they are routine in today's world and involve little risk, trauma, or pain. Urine tests were found to be somewhat more intrusive because excretory functions are "traditionally shielded by great privacy,"[8] However, this additional intrusiveness is reduced, the Court said, by procedures requiring samples to be taken in a medical environment by nonemployer personnel who do not watch. Finally, the Court also emphasized railroad workers' reduced expectations of privacy due to employment in a highly regulated industry. The Government, on the other hand, was found to have a compelling interest because of its need to deter drug and alcohol use in an industry where even a "momentary lapse can have disastrous consequences"[9] and because the Government must learn the causes of railroad accidents.[10]

The same day that *Railway Labor Executives' Association* was decided,   6
the Supreme Court upheld parts of a Customs Service drug-testing plan in *National Treasury Employees Union* v. *Von Raab.*[11] Under the plan, Customs Service employees are subject to urine testing for illegal drugs if they apply for promotions or transfers into other Customs Service jobs requiring them to be directly involved in drug interdiction, to carry firearms, or to handle classified material. Employees who are unable to offer a satisfactory explanation for a positive test result may be dismissed from their jobs.

Justice Kennedy, writing for a 5–4 majority of the Court, closely fol-   7
lowed the reasoning in *Railway Labor Executives' Association* that neither a warrant nor individualized suspicion is constitutionally required before drug testing may be performed. Applying the "special needs" balancing test, he held that suspicionless urine testing of employees who are involved in drug interdiction or who carry weapons is reasonable and therefore permissible. He did not rule on the reasonableness of the part of the Customs Service plan that requires testing of employees who handle "classified material," because he could not determine whether testing is limited only to those who are likely to handle "truly sensitive information."[12] Therefore, this portion of the case was remanded to the lower court.

The Court held that drug interdiction personnel and employees who   8
carry weapons have diminished expectations of privacy because they should reasonably expect their employer to inquire into their fitness for duty. At the same time, it held that the Government's interest is compelling because drug interdiction personnel are the "first line of defense against one of the greatest problems affecting the health and welfare of our population."[13] In addition,

it found that those who use drugs endanger their fellow workers and are susceptible to bribery and poor job performance.[14] Like the train operators mentioned in *Railway Labor Executives' Association*, employees who carry weapons perform jobs that become "fraught with . . . risks of injuries to others" if the employees' abilities are impaired, even momentarily, by drugs.[15]

Justice Antonin Scalia, who joined the majority in *Railway Labor Executives' Association*, dissented in *National Treasury Employees Union*. As he explained, the Federal Railroad Administration regulations at issue in *Railway Labor Executives' Association* are supported by ample evidence of substance abuse in the target class of employees.[16] Such evidence, he noted, is completely lacking in *National Treasury Employees Union*, where even the Customs Service admitted that it "is largely drug-free."[17] Similarly, he found speculative the Court's nexus between drug use and any injury to compelling public interests. Thus, he concluded, the "special needs" of the Customs Service for suspicionless testing do not outweigh employees' privacy interests.

While establishing a basic framework for analyzing drug-testing cases under the Fourth Amendment, the preceding two important decisions provide little guidance for deciding whether any particular testing scheme will withstand constitutional scrutiny. Instead, the Court's "special needs" balancing leaves the job of resolving such issues to the lower courts on a case-by-case basis. Many cases are likely to arise from challenges to Federal agencies' drug-testing plans under Executive Order 12564, which calls for a drug-free Federal workplace. Together with decisions already rendered in cases where employees have challenged agency testing plans, these new cases will generate a substantial body of case law in the near future.[18]

Notes

1. *Skinner* v. *Railway Labor Executives' Association*, 109 S. Ct. 1402 (1989).

2. 49 CFR § 219.201 (1987).

3. 49 CFR § 219.301 (1987).

4. The Fourth Amendment applies only to searches by the Government and its agents. In the situation at issue, the searches are performed by a private employer. Nevertheless, the Court found that the Fourth Amendment applies. When the employer performs testing that is mandated by the Government, it is acting as an instrument or agent of the Government. Even when it performs discretionary testing, it is doing so with the Government's encouragement, endorsement, and limited participation. Thus, the Government is sufficiently involved to implicate the Fourth Amendment. It is important to note that the propriety of drug testing plans *not* subject to the Fourth Amendment may be governed by Federal or State law. For example, § 8(a)(5) of the National Labor Relations Act, 29 U.S.C. § 158(a)(5) (1982), requires a private employer to bargain with its union before it implements a drug-testing plan for current employees, notwithstanding a broad management-rights clause in an existing collective bargaining agreement. See Johnson-Bateman, 295 N.L.R.B. No. 26, 1988–89 NLRB Dec. (CCH) § 16,236 (June 15, 1989).

5. *Skinner* v. *Railway Labor Executives' Association*, 109 S. Ct. at 1414.

6. *Id.*

7. *Id.*

8. *Id.* at 1418.

9. *Id.* at 1419.

10. Justice Stevens, in a concurring opinion, concluded that the Government's interest in determining the causes of accidents is the only basis upon which the challenged regulations may stand. He found unpersuasive the argument that alcohol and drug testing serves as a deterrent. In his view, employees not deterred by the potentially fatal consequences of operating a train under the influence of alcohol or drugs would not likely be deterred by the less onerous prospect of alcohol or drug testing. *Id.* at 1422 (Justice Stevens, concurring).

11. *National Treasury Employees Union* v. *Von Raab*, 109 S. Ct. 1384 (1989).

12. The Court did not define how employees who handle "truly sensitive information" differ from those who handle classified material, other than to indicate that they are less numerous.

13. *National Treasury Employees Union* v. *Von Raab*, 109 S. Ct. at 1392.

14. Justice Kennedy does not require the Customs Service to explain why, in light of such dangers, its plan does not require testing of persons who are not merely applicants, but are already employed in such positions. It could be argued that if the Customs Service's interests are as compelling as the Court found, then employees, as well as applicants, should be tested. See *National Treasury Employees Union* v. *Von Raab*, 816 F. 2d 170, 184 (5th Cir. 1987) (J. Hill, dissenting).

15. *National Treasury Employees Union* v. *Von Raab*, 109 S. Ct. at 1393.

16. See *Skinner* v. *Railway Labor Executives' Association*, 109 S. Ct. at 1407 n.1.

17. *National Treasury Employees Union* v. *Von Raab*, 109 S. Ct. at 1387.

18. For example, since March 21, 1989, when the Supreme Court issued its decisions in *Skinner* and the *Treasury Union* case, at least two courts of appeals have ruled on the propriety of agencies' random drug-testing schemes. See *Thomson* v. *Marsh*, No. 878 F. 2d 1431 (4th Cir. 1989), upholding the Army's plan to test civilian workers at a chemical weapons plant; and *Harmon* v. *Thornburgh*, No. 878 F. 2d 484 (D.C. Cir. 1989), prohibiting random testing of attorneys who conduct grand jury proceedings or who are assigned to prosecute criminal cases, but allowing testing of workers with access to top secret documents.

QUESTIONS FOR MEANING

1. In *Skinner* v. *Railway Labor Executives' Association*, why did Supreme Court Justice Kennedy decide that drug testing without a warrant could still be "reasonable" under the law?

2. In this same case, why did the Court decide that urine testing could be justified even though it is more intrusive than blood or breath testing?

3. What similarity does Hukill reveal between train operators and employees who carry weapons?

4. Why did Justice Scalia dissent in *National Treasury Employees Union* v. *Von Raab*?

5. Vocabulary: propriety (1), enjoin (2), circumscribe (3), interdiction (6), nexus (9), rendered (10).

QUESTIONS ABOUT STRATEGY

1. Although only ten paragraphs long, this article includes eighteen notes. What effect does this volume of notes have upon you as a reader?

2. How would you characterize the tone of the essay? Does Hukill betray any bias when he discusses Supreme Court decisions?
3. Consider the opening and concluding sentences of this article. Both sentences are emphasized by being placed in a key position. Why do they deserve this emphasis?

IRVING R. KAUFMAN
The Battle over Drug Testing

The recipient of many awards for distinguished service to the judiciary, Irving R. Kaufman has been a member of the New York bar since 1932 and a judge since 1949. He first came to national prominence as the judge who presided over the espionage trial of Julius and Ethel Rosenberg in the early 1950s. More recently, he was appointed chairman of the President's Commission on Organized Crime by Ronald Reagan in 1983. In the following essay, originally written for the New York Times *in* **1986,** *Kaufman defends the Commission's recommendation that drug testing be considered for appropriate use.*

All over America, the scenario is being acted out with increasing frequency. The players are remarkably diverse—an office manager in San Francisco, a police officer in Boston, even a Cabinet officer in the White House. Each of these individuals, and thousands more, has been asked to take a drug test at work. Some have acquiesced; others have refused. Those who have not yet confronted the issue personally would be well advised to consider it, for drug testing is shaping up as the premier issue in labor relations for the next decade.

"Scarcely any political question arises in the United States which is not resolved sooner or later into a judicial question," said Alexis de Tocqueville. Drug testing, for better or worse, is once again proving the veracity of the axiom. Opponents of drug testing in the workplace have pleaded their case not only on editorial pages but in the courtroom, where, typically, they denounce the practice as an invasion of privacy. The legal verdict remains uncertain, but it should be evident that drug testing is not a clear-cut issue; it may assume a multiplicity of forms in a variety of contexts, and nothing is served by reducing the debate to a series of slogans.

On Sept. 15, President Reagan signed an executive order calling for drug testing of a broad range of the Federal Government's 2.8 million civilian employees, earmarking about $56 million for the undertaking in the first year. The increased use of drug testing by governmental agencies and private employers—more than a quarter of the Fortune 500 companies test job applicants—is part of a larger trend in society's war on drug abuse, with a pronounced shift of emphasis to the drug user. But to inquire whether someone is for or against drug testing in the workplace is really to pose a question without content, the variables are so great. Is the drug test to be administered to Government workers—in which case the Fourth Amendment's protection from unreasonable searches and seizures must be satisfied—or to employees in private industry? Does a given company intend to test its employees at random or will a worker be asked to submit to urinalysis only when he exhibits some sign of drug abuse? Are employees to be included in the screening or only job applicants?

These important distinctions, however, have not prevented some em-   4
ployers and civil liberties groups from adopting blanket positions on drug testing. Those in favor insist that an employer has the right to demand a drug-free work force, and point to diminished productivity, increased accidents and absenteeism as the effects of drug abuse. Opponents of "jar wars"— the columnist William Safire's appellation—challenge its constitutionality in the case of public employees and its reliability in any context. More fundamentally, they claim that employers are not simply concerned with performance, but with enforcing a brand of morality; if an employee smokes a joint on the weekend, they reason, it is no concern to management as long as he performs competently come Monday.

The President first hinted that a major policy shift was in the works on   5
July 30, when he announced that he was considering widespread testing of Government employees, extending the existing testing procedures of such agencies as the Federal Bureau of Investigation, the Immigration and Naturalization Service, the Federal Aviation Administration, the Postal Service, the Drug Enforcement Administration and the military services. At a press conference, the President said he and his Cabinet had "pretty much agreed that mandatory testing is justified where the employees have the health of others and the safety of others in their hands." He also urged that "voluntary" drug testing be considered inside and outside the Government. As if to set an example, President Reagan and Vice President Bush underwent urinalysis, and 78 members of the White House senior staff were asked to participate in a "voluntary testing."

My experience as chairman of the President's Commission on Orga-   6
nized Crime, which fulfilled its mandate and disbanded last March, taught me just how sensitive a topic drug testing is with the public, and how quick the media can be to jump to conclusions. The commission examined every activity of organized crime, including money laundering, labor racketeering and misconduct by lawyers. But one conclusion stood out from the rest: drug trafficking is the lifeblood of organized crime, bringing in billions of dollars of revenues annually. Accordingly, the commission was determined to bring before the public proposals to combat drug abuse. The report we issued recommended that Federal agencies implement policies aimed at reducing drug use among their employees and consider including suitable

drug-testing programs where appropriate. It was also suggested that Government contracts not be awarded to companies that make no effort to detect and eliminate drug abuse among their workers.

For the next few days, the press reported that the commission had come   7
out in favor of mandatory drug testing for all Federal employees, and that it had asked the Government not to award contracts to private companies that do not administer across-the-board drug screening under any circumstances. The fact is the commission never intended to call for anything so severe. Above all, our recommendations were intended to launch a national debate. With that debate now full-blown, it would be inappropriate for me, as an active Federal judge, to express my conclusions about the legality of various drug-testing practices. Rather, my purpose here is to inform and to delineate the framework of the current debate.

Drug abuse has become an epidemic in America, so it should come as   8
no surprise that the problem has spilled over into the workplace. The National Institute on Drug Abuse reports that 65 percent of those entering the work force have used illegal drugs, 44 percent in the last year. In its study on drug trafficking, the President's Commission on Organized Crime reported that 20 million Americans use marijuana at least once a month and that 6 million use cocaine as often. A study by the Research Triangle Institute, a North Carolina business-sponsored research organization, found that drug use drained $60 billion from the nation's economy in 1983.

In justifying drug testing, employers may cite the need for reliable performance from those who hold the public safety in their hands, such as airline pilots and nuclear power plant operators. Less dramatic rationales are   9
offered when lives do not hang in the balance. Employers may claim an interest in the health and safety of employees, for instance, and the right to be free from the expense of workers who are not doing their jobs properly.

But is this really all that is behind the increasing popularity of drug   10
testing? Some, like the columnist Charles Krauthammer, have suggested that this screening is an attempt to improve behavior rather than production. Krauthammer labels testing an "extraordinary experiment in law enforcement," and regards it as a "sinister" form of "disguised and benign" social control. "It carries the threat of a real, material sanction, a sanction that hits you where it hurts, but doesn't quite put you in jail," he writes. "It jeopardizes your job, but not your liberty. And is administered not by guys in blue suits with guns, but in white coats and gloves—on orders not from a judge but from your boss." Ira Glasser, executive director of the American Civil Liberties Union, echoes that view.

The protests, however, have not dampened the enthusiasm of government   11
and business for drug testing. The precursor of all drug-detection programs was the Department of Defense's move in the 1970's to identify and treat returning Vietnam veterans addicted to heroin. Today, each branch of the military services administers drug tests. Where the nation's defense is deemed at stake, the courts have been most deferential. In the private sector, some of the most prestigious companies in the country require job applicants

to undergo urinalysis—including Exxon, the International Business Machines Corporation, Lockheed, Shearson Lehman Brothers, Federal Express, United Airlines, Trans World Airlines, Hoffman-La Roche, Du Pont, the American Telephone and Telegraph Company and The New York Times. Peter Ueberroth, commissioner of baseball, has made drug testing mandatory for players in the professional leagues, and the National Football League recently announced plans to test players for drug use three times a year.

The number of businesses that test not just applicants, but employees, 12 is also on the rise. Two Wall Street firms, Kidder, Peabody & Company, and Smith Barney, Harris Upham & Company, recently became the first brokerage houses to check employees for use of illegal drugs.

In the public sector, too, testing is catching on, not only in Federal 13 agencies but in a growing number of local police and fire departments. Last April, Francis M. Roache, the Boston Police Commissioner, announced that he would require the department's 2,400 employees to be tested for drugs at least once a year. Police chiefs in Houston and Los Angeles are also pressing for authority to conduct random drug tests.

Can the test results be trusted? A plethora of charges have been leveled 14 against the reliability of urinalysis, ranging from speculation that nasal sprays cause positive results to allegations of built-in racial bias because of the similarity between the chemical composition of the pigment, melanin, found in high levels in blacks and Hispanic people, and the active ingredient in marijuana. Others claim that positive tests may result from passive inhalation of marijuana smoke. But these assertions are spurious, according to J. Michael Walsh and Richard L. Hawks of the National Institute on Drug Abuse. Drug screening through urinalysis can be extremely accurate, they say, but much depends on the quality-control procedures followed by the laboratory and on the commitment to follow-up tests for all positive results.

The manufacturer of the most popular screening test, known as EMIT 15 (Enzyme Multiplied Immunoassay Technique) claims an accuracy rate of better than 95 percent under ideal circumstances. But opponents of testing maintain that even the slimmest margin of error is unacceptable. They also fear that standards will be lowered as laboratories compete for business and employers balk at expensive confirmation assays.

The accuracy issue is far from settled. Apparently, there is truth to the 16 assertion that certain kinds of widely available medications react in the same way as marijuana when analyzed. Syva, the manufacturer of the EMIT assay, warns that certain anti-inflammatory drugs can cause a false positive for marijuana, specifically the painkiller ibuprofen, found in Advil and other over-the-counter products. In addition, a person who eats enough food containing poppy seeds, which naturally contain morphine, could be surprised to find people asking questions about his heroin habit. Dr. Walsh of the National Institute on Drug Abuse, however, maintains that false positives can be virtually eliminated through proper confirmation and quality-control procedures. Unconfirmed positives, he emphasizes, should always be reported as negatives.

My expertise, however, is not as a scientist but as a judge. I turn, then,   17
to some of the emerging legal questions raised by drug testing, especially
when it is performed by the Government. The lawsuits have begun to reach
the courts, but it is still too early to say how the constitutional arguments
will ultimately fare.

Most of the legal issues surrounding drug screening in the workplace   18
are in flux, but participants in the current debate seem to agree on a few
general propositions. The first is that, unlike workers in private industry,
Government employees may claim the protection of the Fourth Amendment's prohibition against unreasonable searches and seizures. The second is
that private employers are not subject to the Fourth Amendment's strictures
(although they may be subject to other legal constraints) because the Bill of
Rights restrains only the actions of Government officials or those acting closely
in concert with them. Any discussion of the constitutionality of testing public employees for drugs, therefore, should begin with an examination of the
historical roots of the amendment.

The Fourth Amendment to the Constitution had its genesis in abuses   19
suffered by the colonists at the hands of Mother England. To protect its
mercantile empire, Parliament restricted trade between the colonies and areas
outside the empire by imposing prohibitive import duties on goods entering
the colonies from outside the empire. As a result, smuggling became widespread and was practiced by even the most respectable colonists. John Han-
cock, for example, was accused of smuggling in 1768. He defended himself
on the ground that the import duty was a form of taxation without representation.

The notorious Writ of Assistance was the principal enforcement mech-   20
anism for collection of duty fees. The writ was essentially a general warrant
for the King's custom inspectors indiscriminately to search homes and ware-
houses in order to insure that the Crown received all of the tribute to which
it was entitled. Today, the general search—its end, to ferret out evidence of
a crime; its means, virtually unrestricted—remains the paradigm of the kind
of governmental intrusion most reviled by the Fourth Amendment. The Fourth
Amendment teaches, then, that no matter how compelling the Government's
need to pursue a given policy, the individual's right to privacy must serve as
a check. As drug-testing programs begin to resemble the general search, their
legitimacy grows increasingly suspect.

The Fourth Amendment provides that the "right of the people to be   21
secure in their persons, houses, papers, and effects, against unreasonable searches
and seizures, shall not be violated, and no Warrants shall issue, but upon
probable cause, supported by Oath, or affirmation, and particularly describing the place to be searched, and the persons or things to be seized." By its
terms, the amendment covers much more than the wholesale warehouse
searches of the 18th century. All searches pursuant to a warrant must be
supported by probable cause, and there is an independent requirement of
reasonableness.

The landmark case of Boyd v. United States, decided in 1886, leaves   22
no doubt that a search may sometimes be reasonable even though conducted
without a validly issued warrant. For example, a police officer may search
the area immediately surrounding a lawfully arrested suspect for a weapon.
Similarly, an officer who observes suspicious conduct may stop and frisk a
suspect if he has reasonable grounds to believe the suspect is armed. But
wholesale drug testing of employees falls into a different category, for the
tests are often administered without suspicion of any particular individual,
and the odds are that any given person will be found free of drugs.

Under the emerging doctrine of the "administrative search," however,   23
courts sometimes allow broad-scale searches to be conducted without a warrant or individualized suspicion. Anyone who has flown on a commercial
airline in the last 15 years has been subjected to an administrative search in
the form of a cursory check of his person and belongings before boarding.
These searches, instituted by the Federal Aviation Administration pursuant
to Presidential order, fall within the ambit of the Fourth Amendment, but
have been held reasonable by the courts. The reasonableness inquiry turns on
a balancing test by the judge, who must weigh the urgency of the Government's reasons for conducting the search against the constitutionally protected interest in "the sanctities of a man's home and the privacies of life."

The United States Supreme Court first authorized an administrative search   24
in 1967, in a case involving housing inspection. The Court found that inspectors could assure compliance with the minimum standards of municipal
codes only by conducting periodic inspections of all structures. But, significantly, the Court did require the inspectors to obtain inspection warrants
before nonconsentual entry of a building.

In 1972, in a case involving the inspection of gun dealers, the Court   25
dispensed completely with the warrant requirement because of the highly
regulated nature of the firearms industry, where pervasive Government regulations and licensing reduced the dealers' legitimate expectation of privacy.
Unannounced periodic inspections were essential if the law was to serve as a
credible deterrent, the Court said. Clearly, though, it would contradict our
constitutional history to conclude that any search of commercial property
where the Government has a regulatory interest satisfies the Fourth Amendment. After all, the dreaded Writs of Assistance, which supplied the stimulus
to enact the Fourth Amendment, involved searches of commercial ware-
houses. The Court has acknowledged this by distinguishing between searches
of highly regulated industries, such as firearms, liquor and mining, on the
one hand, and ordinary businesses, on the other. Searches of the latter must
be accompanied by a warrant unless the proprietor gives his consent.

In some instances, the Court has extended the administrative search   26
doctrine to inspections of the individual. Administrative searches of persons
who have exhibited no behavior that would give rise to suspicion of illegal
activity have been approved at United States border areas, at entrances to
courthouses and, as mentioned, at airport departure gates. In addition, the

highly regulated nature of the horse-racing industry was the basis for upholding random, mandatory drug testing of jockeys by the United States
Court of Appeals for the Third Circuit last July. The lawsuit, filed by five
famous jockeys, including William Shoemaker and Angel Cordero, contested
the New Jersey Racing Commission's policy of drawing the names of several
jockeys from an envelope each day and requiring them to furnish urine samples after the last race that day. The court rejected the jockeys' insistence on
individualized suspicion before testing, instead embracing the racing commission's contention that searches in the highly regulated racing industry are
reasonable.

It must be noted that a search of the person is more akin to a search of   27
the home than to inspection of a commercial enterprise, for the Fourth
Amendment applies with its greatest vigor to intrusions upon the human
body. Still, a Federal Court of Appeals in California upheld preboarding
screening of all airplane passengers and their carry-on luggage because of the
indisputable need to prevent the hijacking of airliners. The court acknowledged the danger of airport searches being subverted into constitutionally
prohibited general searches for evidence of a crime, but was satisfied that the
inspections were to prevent hijacking rather than to prosecute individuals for
illegally possessing firearms.

The constitutional status of a drug-testing program, similarly, may hinge   28
in part on the purpose to which the program is put. If designed merely to
identify and rehabilitate drug users, as the President recently maintained, the
danger of a general search for evidence of crime is avoided. If criminal investigations or prosecutions were the primary purpose of the tests, one could
argue that the searches would be subject to the warrant and probable-cause
requirements of the Fourth Amendment. (It is further worth pointing out
that unlike possession and distribution of illegal drugs, use alone is not generally an indictable offense.) In the airport search case, the United States Court
of Appeals for the Ninth Circuit noted that authorities searched all passengers
and had no power to single out travelers. By analogy, a drug-testing program may appear more reasonable when it applies to all employees within a
given group, not just those who stir the boss's whimsy.

Some critics argue that it is a cramped notion of "consent" that deems   29
an employee's decision to submit to drug testing on pain of losing his job
"consensual," but the question of consent will invariably enter into the legal
calculus. In the airport case, the court emphasized the voluntary nature of
the search: only passengers who choose to board a plane are searched. In
another case, in which welfare benefits were conditioned on a case worker's
periodic visits to the home, the Supreme Court held that the visitation was
voluntary because the recipient was free to reject the conditions and forfeit
the payments. Whether the same logic will apply to permit a Government
employer to require workers to either submit to drug testing or find another
job remains to be seen.

Courts will also make inquiries into the intrusiveness of the method of   30
drug testing. When Fourth Amendment rights are implicated, the Government

is frequently required to employ the least restrictive means available to achieve its interest. Civil libertarians point out that to insure authenticity, workers must be observed while giving urine samples, creating embarrassment and humiliation. Furthermore, if grounds for individualized suspicion do exist, the basic rationale for the administrative search becomes attenuated. The Court approved administrative searches in housing inspections because it was impossible to tell from the outside whether any given house was in violation. But if a problem presents observable suspicious activity, counsel will surely argue that a blanket search subjecting everyone to governmental intrusion runs afoul of the Fourth Amendment's reasonableness requirement.

Few generalizations can be made from the small but growing body of legal precedent in drug testing cases. One observation that can be made, however, is that courts are extremely sensitive to the factual context surrounding the testing. Last year, for example, a United States District Court in Atlanta ruled that employees of a public utility who worked on high-voltage electric wires could be forced to submit to urinalysis. The tests were administered after an undercover agent planted among the workers by management reported that some of the employees had been smoking marijuana at work. The court found the tests reasonable in light of the extremely dangerous nature of the work and the careful nature of the investigation. 31

Similar considerations were present in one of the earliest drug testing cases to reach the courts. In 1976, a union representing 5,500 bus drivers challenged the constitutionality of the Chicago Transit Authority's requirement that bus operators submit to blood or urine tests following their involvement in a serious accident, or upon suspicion of drug or alcohol impairment. Here, again, the court found the intrusions reasonable, considering the transit authority's "paramount" interest in insuring that drivers are unimpaired. In the parlance of the Fourth Amendment, the interest in safety negated any "reasonable expectation of privacy." Several cases have upheld the testing of police and correction officers, whether conducted at random or "for cause." Last August, the New York State Supreme Court rejected a challenge to the testing of correction officers who drive prison vans and buses for New York City, citing the strong security and safety considerations involved in transporting prisoners. 32

But there have been dissenting voices, and notably articulate ones at that. On Sept. 18, Judge H. Lee Sarokin of Federal District Court in Newark ruled that mandatory urine testing of government employees, such as policemen and firefighters in Plainfield, N.J., violated the Fourth Amendment. Only a strong suspicion that a certain individual was using illegal drugs could justify testing a worker, the court held. And last year, Harold D. Vietor, chief judge of the United States District Court in Des Moines, reinstated a prison guard's pay, lost when he was temporarily discharged after refusing to take a urine test. Although prison officials had received an anonymous tip that the guard was using drugs, Judge Vietor determined that an individual's urine may not be tested unless the same kind of cause that is needed to search his house is present. Although the state pressed its need to identify drug 33 smugglers and keep its correctional staff drug-free, the court reasoned that the same logic could be used to support searching the guards' homes, or tapping their telephones. "There is no doubt about it," Judge Vietor wrote, "searches and seizures can yield a wealth of information useful to the searcher. (That is why King George III's men so frequently searched the colonists.) That potential, however, does not make a governmental employer's search of an employee a constitutionally reasonable one."

In another well publicized case, the Appellate Division of the New York   34
State Supreme Court ruled last summer that probationary teachers in a Long Island school district could not be compelled to submit to urinalysis. Without reasonable suspicion of drug abuse, the court said, the tests would be an unconstitutional invasion of privacy. "Strikingly absent from the record is even a scintilla of suspicion, much less a reasonable suspicion," the court noted.

Employers in the private sector are not subject to the Fourth Amend-   35
ment, but drug testing in this area will hardly go unchallenged. Workers may be able to raise privacy claims pursuant to local statutes, union agreements or even state constitutional provisions. For example, a computer program-mer sued the Southern Pacific Railroad in San Francisco in 1985 after she was discharged for refusing to submit to a drug test. Though her case is still unresolved, she has the benefit of an explicit right-to-privacy provision in the California Constitution.

Workers in private industry may also be able to challenge the accuracy   36
of test results in certain circumstances, aided by recently enacted ordinances, such as one passed in San Francisco. In another suit filed against Southern Pacific, an office manager was required to enroll in a rehabilitation program after urinalysis indicated the presence of cocaine. The manager contends that the test was a "false positive." For 28 days, according to his lawyer, he was isolated from his family at a drug clinic, although all follow-up tests were negative and doctors said there was no need for rehabilitation. For weeks after, the manager was required to attend drug-therapy meetings and to undergo regular testing. He obtained an injunction against further testing under a local ordinance, but was demoted the next day, prompting a second suit, which is being litigated.

Unfortunately, the debate on drug screening has been rich in emotion   37
and hyperbole. Not all proposals for drug testing are the brainchild of Big Brother or a knee-jerk reaction to saturation media coverage of drug abuse. Some screening programs may genuinely represent an effort to keep the workplace drug-free in order to insure safety and improve performance. But, though good intentions are reassuring, heightened sensitivity to concerns about privacy, accuracy and legality are indispensable.

QUESTIONS FOR MEANING

1. What does Kaufman mean when he describes drug testing as "part of a larger trend in society's war on drug abuse, with a pronounced shift of emphasis to the drug user"? Where has the emphasis usually been?

2. Why did the President's Commission on Organized Crime decide to focus attention on drug abuse? What were its recommendations?
3. What does "money laundering" mean in paragraph 6?
4. What was the Writ of Assistance, and how was it used against American colonists before the revolution? Why did the British use it? What effect did this writ eventually have on the American Constitution?
5. Can you explain what is meant by "probable cause" in paragraph 21?
6. Which businesses have the courts held it reasonable to search without a warrant?
7. Why did the courts hold that bus drivers can be required to submit to drug testing?
8. Vocabulary: acquiesced (1), veracity (2), axiom (2), contexts (2), appellation (4), delineate (7), sanction (10), deferential (11), plethora (14), spurious (14), flux (18), mercantile (19), notorious (20), ferret (20), paradigm (20), reviled (20).

QUESTIONS ABOUT STRATEGY

1. At what points in his essay does Kaufman recognize the views of people who oppose drug testing?
2. Why does Kaufman discuss airline baggage checks (in paragraphs 23 and 27)? Is he making an analogy between such searches and mandatory drug testing?
3. Where in this long essay does Kaufman most clearly summarize his own position?
4. Why does Kaufman devote so much space to reviewing various court cases? What effect did this review have upon your own view of mandatory drug testing?
5. How does Kaufman characterize the debate over drug testing? Why is it useful for him to present the debate from this point of view?

ONE STUDENT'S ASSIGNMENT

Summarize "The Battle over Drug Testing" by Irving Kaufman in approximately 500 words. Be sure to include each of the most important points made in this essay, and be careful to avoid letting your own opinion interfere with objectively summarizing what Kaufman has written.

A Summary of
Irving Kaufman's "The Battle over Drug Testing"
James A. McClain

Due to the increasing prevalency of drug abuse among workers, drug testing is on the rise and is becoming a major issue in labor relations. Knowing that this judicially controversial issue is complex, it would be well to outline and explain the current debate. 1

Those in favor of drug testing promote a workplace free of drug abuse because of the decreases in production and the increases in injuries and unexcused absences that accompany it. Advocates also say that testing for drugs by urinalysis produces reliable results and that false positives are minimized by proper laboratory procedures. Opponents of drug testing question its legality for public employees. They also say testing programs are affecting employees' personal lifestyles and argue that even the smallest percent error in test results is too much. However, these objections have not deterred more and more private businesses, federal agencies, and police and fire departments from testing employees and, in some cases, applicants also. 2

This increase in drug testing has spurred many legal questions. One involves public employees who claim immunity from testing under the Fourth Amendment's teaching "that no matter how compelling the Government's need to pursue a given policy, the individual's right to privacy must serve as a check" against unreasonable searches and seizures. But any conclusion about the legality of testing public employees needs to begin with a look at the amendment's history. The British precipitated it by using a general warrant prior to the American revolution to enter homes in random search of lawbreakers. If drug testing programs likewise end up 3 being searches without suspecting a certain individual, their legality will come into question and public employees may be able to obtain immunity.

Even so, under some circumstances courts do allow searches (like the inspecting of airline passengers and their baggage) to proceed without a warrant or individualized suspicion. The courts realize that a search of the person as at airports is explicitly addressed by the Fourth Amendment but are convinced the screenings are to locate hijackers and not to incriminate persons who may be doing something illegal such as smuggling cocaine. The constitutional status of drug-testing programs may thus depend upon their purposes. "If designed merely to identify and rehabilitate drug users . . . the danger of a general search for evidence of crime is avoided."   4

The question of consent is another legal controversy. Is it right to request that workers either bow to drug testing or look for other employment? Courts are also concerned about safety, which they feel overrides the right for privacy in some cases, as with bus drivers and airplane pilots. But in non-life-threatening situations the courts say that testing can be warranted only when it is almost certain that an individual is using drugs.   5

A final question concerns non-government employees. They're not able to find shelter under the Fourth Amendment but may be able to claim a right to privacy against drug testing because of state, local, or union provisions. These workers may also be able to oppose testing on the grounds of its accuracy.   6

Thus, although testing programs are designed to improve the workplace by keeping drugs out, their intrusiveness, reliability, and constitutionality also need to be carefully considered.   7

SUGGESTIONS FOR WRITING

1. When you were in high school, did you know any students who used drugs? If so, write an essay for or against the drug testing of students that incorporates your own experience or observations.
2. Does the school in which you are now enrolled have a policy regarding drug use by students? Write an argument for or against the current policy, or advocate a specific policy that you recommend for adoption.

3. Write an argument against testing athletes for drug use that will respond to each of John Burt's four arguments on behalf of drug testing.

4. Drawing upon information reported by Charles Marwick and Phil Gunby, write an argument for or against drug testing in the military.

5. Synthesize the arguments on behalf of drug testing in the workplace.

6. Both Anne Marie O'Keefe and John Horgan claim that drug use is declining in the United States. Do a research paper that will either support or challenge this claim.

7. Drawing upon the articles by Anne Marie O'Keefe and Irving Kaufman, write an essay defining the meaning of the Fourth Amendment.

8. Research court rulings since 1989, when Craig Hukill wrote his summary of recent cases. Summarize these rulings and argue whether the law is becoming more or less protective of individual rights.

9. Is there any alternative to drug testing? Write an argument on behalf of some other method besides testing for fighting drug abuse.

10. Do a research paper on what sophisticated testing can reveal about people besides whether they have used illegal drugs.

GUN CONTROL: TRIGGERING A NATIONAL CONTROVERSY

♦

JEANNE SHIELDS

Why Nick?

When people discuss controversial issues, they sometimes lose sight of how these is-sues affect individual lives. Gun control has been the subject of national debate for so many years that it may seem of interest only to men and women who are directly involved with guns: those who either own them, sell them, or work with them. But the abstract can become painfully real to anyone who becomes the victim of handgun violence, as this essay by Jeanne Shields reveals. After her son was murdered, Shields became active in the movement to control handguns. Her essay, which origi-nally appeared in Newsweek *in* **1978,** *is both a tribute to the memory of her son and an argument on behalf of stricter laws regulating the sale and possession of guns.*

If the telephone rings late at night, I always mentally check off where each 1
child is, and at the same time get an awful sinking feeling in the pit of my
stomach.

Four years ago, April 16, we had a telephone call very late. As my 2
husband answered, I checked off Pam in Long Beach (California), Nick in
San Francisco, David in New Brunswick (New Jersey) and Leslie outside
Boston. The less my husband spoke, the tighter the knot got in my stomach.
Instinctively, I knew it was bad news, but I wasn't prepared for what he had
to tell me. Our eldest son, Nick, 23, had been shot dead on a street in San
Francisco.

Nick was murdered at about 9:30 p.m. He and a friend, Jon, had come 3
from lacrosse practice and were on their way home. They stopped to pick
up a rug at the home of a friend. While Jon went in to get the rug, Nick
rearranged the lacrosse gear in the back of their borrowed Vega. He was shot
three times in the back and died instantly, holding a lacrosse stick.

Nick was the fourteenth victim of what came to be called the "Zebra 4
killers." Between the fall of 1973 and April 16, 1974, they had randomly
killed fourteen people and wounded seven others—crippling one for life. Four

men were subsequently convicted of murder in a trial that lasted thirteen months.

My son was tall, dark and handsome, and a good athlete. He was par- 5
ticularly good at lacrosse and an expert skier. Nick was an ardent photographer and wrote some lovely poetry. He was a gentle and sensitive man with
an infectious grin and the capacity to make friends easily. It was hard for me
to believe he was gone.

The generous support and love of our friends gave us the strength to 6
go on during those days. The calls and letters that poured in from those who
knew Nick were overwhelming. In his short life, Nick had touched so many
people in so many ways. It was both heartwarming and very humbling.

But always, running through those blurred days was the question. Why? 7
Why Nick? My deep faith in God was really put to the test. Yet, nothing
that I could do or think of, or pray for, was ever going to bring Nick
back.

Because Nick was shot two days after Easter, the funeral service was 8
filled with Easter prayers and hymns. Spring flowers came from the gardens
of friends. The day was mild, clear and beautiful, and a kind of peace and
understanding seeped into my aching heart.

No matter how many children you have, the death of one leaves a void 9
that cannot be filled. Life seems to include a new awareness, and one's philosophy and values come under sharper scrutiny. Were we just to pick up
the pieces and continue as before? That choice became impossible, because a
meaning had to be given to this vicious, senseless death.

That summer of 1974, the newspapers, magazines and television were 10
full of Watergate. But I couldn't concentrate on it or anything else. Instead I
dug hard in the garden for short periods of time, or smashed at tennis balls.

On the other hand, my husband, Pete, immersed himself in a study of 11
the gun-control issue. Very near to where Nick had died, in a vacant lot,
two small children found a gun—*the* gun. It was a .32-caliber Beretta. Police,
in tracing it, found that initially it had been bought legally, but then went
through the hands of seven different owners—most of whom had police records. Its final bullets, fired at close range, had killed my son—and then it
was thrown carelessly away.

Pete's readings of Presidential commission recommendations, FBI crime 12
statistics and books on the handgun issue showed him that our Federal laws
were indeed weak and ineffective. He went to Washington to talk to politicians and to see what, if anything, was being done about it. I watched him
wrestle with his thoughts and spend long hours writing them down on paper—the pros and cons of handgun control and what could logically be done
about the proliferation of handguns in this nation.

Through friends, Pete had been introduced in Washington to the Na- 13
tional Council to Control Handguns, a citizens' lobby seeking stricter Federal
controls over handguns. As Pete became more closely associated with the
NCCH as a volunteer, it became increasingly obvious that he was leaning
toward a greater involvement.

Consequently, with strong encouragement from me and the children,   14
Pete took a year's leave of absence from his job as a marketing executive so
that he could join NCCH full time. A full year and a half later, he finally
resigned and became the NCCH chairman.

The main adversaries of handgun control are members of the powerful   15
and financially entrenched National Rifle Association, macho men who don't
understand the definition of a civilized society. They are aided by an apathetic government which in reality is us, because we citizens don't make
ourselves heard loud and clear enough. How many people are in the silent
majority, who want to see something done about unregulated sale and possession of handguns? Why do we register cars and license drivers, and not do
the same for handguns? Why are the production and sale of firecrackers severely restricted—and not handguns?

I now work in the NCCH office as a volunteer. One of my jobs is to   16
read and make appropriate card files each day from a flood of clippings describing handgun incidents. The daily newspapers across the country recount
the grim litany of shootings, killings, rapes and robberies at gun point. Some
of it's tough going, because I am poignantly aware of what a family is going
through. Some of it's so appalling it makes me literally sick.

Some people can no longer absorb this kind of news. They have almost   17
become immune to it, because there is so much violence. To others, it is too
impersonal; it's always something that happens to somebody else—not
to you.

But anybody can be shot. We are all in a lottery, where the likelihood   18
of your facing handgun violence grows ever day. Today there are 50 million
handguns in civilian hands. By the year 2000, there will be more than 100
million.

So many families have given up so much to the deadly handgun. It will   19
take the women of this country—the mothers, wives, sisters, and daughters—to do something about it. But when will they stand up to be counted
and to be heard? Or will they wait only to hear the telephone ringing late at
night?

QUESTIONS FOR MEANING

1. Why is Shields especially interested in working for stronger *federal* controls in handguns? Does she present any evidence that such controls would
   save lives? Would gun control have saved the life of her son?
2. Describe the Shields family as they are presented in this essay. What sort
   of marriage do the parents seem to have? What are the children like? What
   type of home do you think they live in? How can you tell?
3. What is the National Council to Control Handguns, and what sort of
   work does the author of this essay do there? What is the object of this
   work?
4. Why does Shields believe that it will take "the women of this country—
   the mothers, wives, sisters, and daughters" to control handgun violence?

Is this a reasonable observation on the nature of violence in America? Or is it a simple case of sexual stereotyping? Does Shields support her conclusion, or does she contradict herself?

5. Vocabulary: ardent (5), proliferation (12), apathetic (15), litany (16), poignantly (16), and appalling (16).

QUESTIONS ABOUT STRATEGY

1. Why does Shields begin her essay with a description of her son's murder? And why does she repeat such small details as the specific car he was driving, and what he was holding in his hand when he died?

2. Shields writes lovingly of her son in paragraph 5, describing him as athletic, gentle, sensitive, friendly, and "tall, dark and handsome." How do you respond to this description when you read it? Does the description make Nick come alive for you? Does it make you more or less sympathetic to a mother's grief?

3. Shields acknowledges in paragraph 11 that the gun that killed her son was originally bought legally. What effect does this have upon her argument?

4. Does Shields ever say anything likely to offend the people she most needs to convince? Is this essay really designed to make an audience come to favor gun control, or does it have some other purpose?

5. How would you characterize the tone of this essay? Is there any evidence to suggest that Shields may have been too close to her subject to write about it effectively?

JOE FOSS
They Want To Take Our Guns

The recipient of a Distinguished Flying Cross and a Congressional Medal of Honor, Joe Foss served as Governor of South Dakota from 1954–58. From 1967–74, he appeared regularly on television as the host of The Outdoorsman. *In 1978, he served on the President's Council on Physical Fitness & Sports, and in 1979 he was a member of the White House Conference on Handicapped Individuals. Now President of the National Rifle Association, Foss has also served as Commissioner of the American Football League. "They Want to Take Our Guns" was first published in* **1988** *by* Conservative Digest.

Criminologists now estimate that every year some 650,000 American citizens   1
use a firearm in defense of their homes, their property, their family, their very lives. These are Americans just like you and me—men and women surprised in their dwellings or businesses or aroused from a deep sleep, possibly by the screams of a loved one. They will be threatened by robbery or rape or the many aspects of domestic terrorism we lump together and call "crime." They will have seconds to react, and they will instinctively choose self-preservation through the only means private citizens have available: They will reach for a firearm, in many instances a handgun purchased expressly for the purpose of self-defense. And each of these law-abiding American citizens will be well within their rights—both morally and according to the Constitution of the United States—when they do so.

It seems unthinkable that anyone would deny Americans the right to   2
defend themselves. Yet at this writing, Congress is being lobbied to do just that. Anti-gun organizations, aided by sympathetic media, continue to push for an ultimate ban on the sale of handguns. Never mind that more women, concerned for their safety, are purchasing self-defense firearms than ever before. Never mind that statistics show crime has continued to flourish—even increased—in cities with rigid handgun ordinances.

Yet the anti-gun push continues. It continues without regard for the   3
lives that would have been lost had thousands of law-abiding citizens been unable to use a personal firearm for self-protection. It continues without regard for public opinion. No national anti-gun measure has ever been approved by American voters. Just this year Nebraska citizens successfully circulated a petition that will place a "right to keep and bear arms" constitutional amendment on a state ballot this fall. And in Maryland, where anti-gun legislators rammed through a law banning handguns, the people have responded. Another successful petition drive will allow the people of Maryland an opportunity to overturn the ban at the voting booth.

Yet somehow the message isn't getting through. A deplorable   4
arrogance exists within the anti-gun camp, an arrogance that shows utter disdain for the reality of life and the will of people. The anti-gun crusade's

manipulation of lawmakers, the media, and even some police officials is totally lacking in principle.

For example, in the past several months groups like Handgun Control,   5
Inc., have paraded several high-ranking police officials in front of Congress and the public, prodding them to condemn the National Rifle Association, our nationwide efforts to protect America's Second Amendment rights, and firearms ownership in general. The police chief's message is this: Crime in America is flourishing because American citizens can legally obtain and own firearms. That's as absurd as saying that drunk driving is flourishing because American citizens can legally obtain and drive automobiles.

The propaganda emanating from these police chiefs serves little other   6
than their own political goals. It certainly does not reflect the viewpoint of most law-enforcement professionals, who agree that law-abiding citizens have a right and a need to protect their homes and families. The police can't be everywhere all the time, and any hardworking officer on the beat will be the first to tell you so. Therefore, when men like San Jose Police Chief Joseph McNamara claim to speak for law enforcement, it's much like one renegade general taking it upon himself to speak in behalf of the Pentagon. Now McNamara's ready to consider legalizing drugs. Police officers across America undoubtedly wince when this man claims to represent them.

The difference between thought and deed extends to the liberal media,   7
where famous columnists like Carl Rowan scream out in print for the abolishment of all handguns, yet reach for a pistol when intruders violate the privacy of *their* homes. Rowan now says he'll keep, and continue to use, a handgun to defend himself as long as crime is rife in America. Yet he still favors control for the rest of us.

The fact that Carl Rowan pushes for handgun laws and then chooses to   8
ignore them is representative of the overall anti-gun philosophy. In places where harsh anti-gun laws are in effect, including New York City and Washington, D.C., the rich, the powerful, and the influential are seldom without some means of self-protection. They use their money and prestige to step around the law, while lashing out at the sale of so-called "Saturday Night Specials," the only handguns our nation's elderly and poor can afford.

Crime doesn't prey upon the powerful and the protected. It seeks out   9
the weak and defenseless. Last year some 650,000 Americans decided they didn't want to become victims. Yet if the McNamaras and the Carl Rowans and the membership of Handgun Control, Inc., had been successful, these people would now be either the subject of glaring headlines or the small type in obituary notices. That's too great a price to pay so that a few vocal reformers may bask in their own smugness.

The battle lines have been drawn, and I must admit that the fight appears to be fast becoming bloody. I think it's a contest between idealism and   10
conservative common sense. On one side we have individuals like Senator Howard Metzenbaum (D-OH), a proverbial fountain of anti-gun legislation whose ways are deceitful, to say the least.

Metzenbaum sponsored the recent "plastic gun" legislation that, due to   11
the efforts of men like Senator James McClure (R-ID), cool heads in the
Justice Department, and our own NRA lobbyists, was eventually stripped of
its thinly disguised anti-gun designs.

The entire "plastic gun" fiasco is an excellent example of how the anti-   12
gun movement has been working its witchery. When the issue first arose,
we at the NRA took a common sense approach. For one thing, the entire
question was a moot point: There are presently no totally plastic guns being
manufactured. Some time in the future America will probably have the technology that enables us to make plastic guns, and then beefed up airport security, with instruments capable of detecting non-metal firearms, would
obviously best serve the safety of the American people.

But Metzenbaum was more interested in a *handgun ban*. He also wanted   13
more bureaucratic control over private firearms ownership. His "plastic gun"
bill would have banned millions of legitimate self-defense firearms and given
the federal government control over the transfer and trade of many of these
guns. His scheme was exposed, and the citizens of this country achieved a
common sense compromise.

Metzenbaum and his anti-gun comrades wasted little time in reviving   14
their crusade against our Second Amendment rights. Now, under the guise
of a national waiting-period law, the Ohio Senator and his sponsors want to
create a new and unbelievably cumbersome federal bureaucracy to preside
over firearms ownership in America. This new federal monstrosity would
decide who could purchase a handgun and when it could be purchased—if at
all. It would invade the privacy of law-abiding citizens with background checks.
This absurd waiting-period law would also allow the government to block
the sale, transfer, or trade of many firearms, and eventually result in gun
registration.

Most frightening of all, the measure would invalidate current state laws   15
that guarantee each law-abiding citizen the right to purchase a handgun for
sport or self-defense. As a result, a powerful few would gain control over
the freedom of millions of Americans—citizens who have never voted to
relinquish these rights. When I think of the impact of laws like these, I sense
democracy waning. And I renew my resolve to fight against these socialist
trends.

Whenever the gun prohibition issue is raised, our opponents cry out   16
that free and legal firearms ownership fosters crime. This is absurd. Criminals do not obtain their guns through legal channels. They do not stand in
the lines created by waiting-period laws. Criminals do not submit to background checks. They are not concerned about registration. Criminals operate
outside of the law. Doesn't it stand to reason that only the law-abiding obey
gun-control laws?

Therefore restrictions on handguns will only undermine the rights and   17
safety of honest citizens, and give criminals even greater opportunity to rape,
murder, and terrorize. So why doesn't common sense tell us to quit all this

anti-gun nonsense and begin attacking the real issues? Because firearms ownership isn't all that's on trial here.

We are at a crossroads in America, with one path drifting toward a   18
collective, sterile, carefully managed society, the other path reaffirming our
constitutional form of government and individual rights. The anti-gun faction is pushing for abolition of the liberties we cherish. That is why the National Rifle Association continues to fight for the right to keep and bear arms, reaffirming American individualism and the grass-roots strength of our system.

QUESTIONS FOR MEANING

1. Why does Foss believe that gun control will not reduce crime?
2. On what grounds does Foss base his opposition to legislation that would have restricted the manufacture and sale of plastic guns? And why does he oppose the waiting period proposed by advocates of gun control?
3. What does Foss mean when he says that America is at a "crossroads"? Paraphrase paragraph 18.
4. Vocabulary: utter (4), emanating (6), renegade (6), proverbial (10), fiasco (12), moot (12), guise (14).

QUESTIONS ABOUT STRATEGY

1. How convincing is the statistic cited in paragraph 1 and repeated in paragraph 9?
2. Examine paragraphs 2 and 8. Why does Foss refer to women, the elderly, and the poor?
3. Foss uses terms like "propaganda" (6), "scream" (7), "smugness" (9), and "socialist" (15). Are they appropriate for his argument?
4. Why does Foss criticize Senator Howard Metzenbaum? How do you respond to his characterization of Metzenbaum?

ROGER KOOPMAN
Second Defense

After graduating from the University of Idaho in 1973, Roger Koopman served as a congressional press secretary and administrative assistant before becoming a public relations specialist for the National Rifle Association's Institute for Legislative Action. He left the NRA in 1980 to pursue a business career in western Montana. A regular political columnist for the Bozeman Daily Chronicle, *he has published articles in many national magazines. "Second Defense" was first published in* **1990** *by Outdoor Life.*

Last year was a rough one for the right to keep and bear arms. Fueled by the   1
school-yard tragedy in Stockton, California, the Second Amendment's organized enemies have made great strides. Yet the erosion of our rights cannot be blamed on mere circumstance; the fault rests squarely in the laps of gun owners themselves, who for years have been employing every possible argument to defend their constitutional rights except the constitutional one.

In reality, we couldn't have played into the gun controllers hands more   2
if they had written the script! Consider, for example, our response to the current hysteria over so-called "assault rifles." We have argued, ad nauseam, that people should be "allowed the right" to own these firearms (whatever they are) because of the "legitimate uses" (whatever that means) for such guns, uses that include hunting, target practice, collecting, competitive shooting and self-defense. The predictable result? Whenever gun owners seem to be outnumbered by non-gun owners in a particular area, the legislatures and city councils have gone right ahead and banned these guns anyway, regardless of whether there are "legitimate uses" for them or not.

That's politics, and the process is, to say the least, a two-edged sword   3
that groups such as the National Rifle Association have lived by—and, at times, died by. Certainly no one would suggest that the battles the NRA fights shouldn't be fought. But the Constitution of the United States transcends politics, and its wisdom and truth are not dependent upon the nightly opinion polls on CNN News. The Constitution's Second Amendment does not speak in terms of "legitimate" and "illegitimate" uses for privately owned firearms. Rather, it proclaims, in simple and emphatic words, that a "free State" is secure only if the peoples' right to "keep and bear Arms" remains inviolate.

The gun control issue, then, is never a question of what the govern-   4
ment "allows" us to own. The Constitution states that government has *no authority* over the firearms ownership of the people. The people, not the government, possess an absolute right in the area of gun ownership. If you or I want to own an AR-15 or any other gun, it is none of the government's business *why* we want it, and certainly none of its business to presume that

we may be up to no good. In a free society, the salient question is *never* whether the government can trust the people, but always whether the people can trust their government. The history of the Second Amendment makes this point ever so clear. You could spend a lifetime studying the writings of the Founding Fathers and would never find among any of them the kinds of sentiments expressed by our 20th century gun controllers—sentiments that reflect a profound distrust for a free people. You would not find a single person among all of the founders of our nation who was worried about firearms in the hands of the citizenry. The very idea is preposterous.

What you *will* find is that there was a very widespread concern over firearms in the hands of the government, especially in the form of a federal "standing army." As great scholars of human history, our forefathers knew full well the threat to liberty posed by governments that developed a monopoly of force over the people. Thus, they authored the Second Amendment, guaranteeing that an armed citizenry (spoken of as the "militia") would always hold sway over the central government and would be a constant check against governmental excesses.

As with so many constitutional principles in this century, the essence of the Second Amendment has been turned upside down by an anti-gun establishment that reveres big government and distrusts the people. Make no mistake about it. What these folks stand for is a total reversal of our constitutional system, where rights and powers become vested *not* in the people, but in the government. They promote an alien, Old World mentality that turns the citizenry against itself by convincing us that we should "trust" the government and distrust our neighbor. Understood in this way, the issue becomes a lot larger than our opportunity to shoot a deer or plink a can. The issue is not guns; the issue is freedom, and it involves not just gun owners, but everyone—especially our children.

It's vitally important that we not allow the gun control lobby and its friends in the national media to paint us into a corner and narrowly define our position as "pro-gun." We are "pro-constitution" and "pro-freedom." And for goodness' sake, let's not fall into the trap of debating among ourselves what types of guns are "needed" and what guns can be outlawed; what gun-related freedoms are "necessary" and what ones we can afford to lose. Freedom is indivisible. Once we accept the notion that government has the right to deny *any* of our firearms rights, we have thrown in the towel and torn apart our Constitution.

If we are going to start winning these battles and regaining ground already lost, we must start framing the so-called "gun issues" in constitutional terms, and show how *every* citizen has a stake in the outcome. Even in states such as Montana, where I reside, the gun control lobby can carry the day by dividing and conquering the general populace with convincing, if thoroughly unconstitutional arguments. I am reminded of a proposal in the last legislative session that would have returned to Montana citizens at least a measure of their *rights* to carry firearms in a concealed fashion—something that the law enforcement community has always enjoyed the undisputed "right" to do. Following a heavy lobbying effort against the bill by some (not all) of these law enforcement people, legislators who should have known better were convinced to vote the measure down. Yet by doing so, they were essentially saying that law enforcement personnel (an arm of local and state government) possess firearms rights that the citizenry at large could be denied. The problem, of course, was that few, if any, of the legislators were made to look at the issue in constitutional terms.

In recent years, the battle lines on gun control have gradually shifted.   9
Defenders of the Second Amendment are now fighting not only the Liberal Left, but an increasing number of persons claiming to speak for the law enforcement community—our traditional ally! This is cause for real concern, not only strategically, but philosophically. Should current trends toward the polarization of law enforcement with the armed citizen continue, it raises an ominous specter: Are we moving toward a society that will be dominated by law and order "professionals" who reign supreme over a disarmed and once free people?

The advice of Larry Pratt, executive director of Gun Owners of Amer-   10
ica, is well worth repeating. Pratt warns that it is the natural tendency of government to concentrate power by "reserving for itself the monopoly of fire power." He also believes that sport shooting is a pleasant derivative of underlying constitutional principles, but it is not the reason the Founders wrote the Second Amendment. It was their deep concern over the power of government, with its standing military, that made them seek to guarantee for all time the right of every citizen to be armed.

The issue, indeed, is freedom. You will not find a single government   11
in the world today that would be able to enslave its people *if* those people enjoyed the unrestricted right to private gun ownership. It couldn't be done. China, on the other hand, tells us a very different story. It is not so much that an armed citizenry could have fought off the tanks in Tianamen Square as it is that an armed citizenry would have seen to it that the tanks were never there in the first place. The point is no less valid for this place we call America—the land of the free.

QUESTIONS FOR MEANING
1. Would Koopman accept any government restraints on the ownership of guns?
2. According to Koopman, why was the Second Amendment written into the Constitution?
3. In paragraph 7, Koopman claims "Freedom is indivisible." What does he mean by this?
4. Why did Koopman favor legislation in Montana that would have made it legal for citizens to carry concealed weapons?
5. Vocabulary: ad nauseam (2), transcends (3), salient (4), vested (6), polarization (9).

QUESTIONS ABOUT STRATEGY

1. Koopman begins his argument by claiming that opponents of gun control have ignored the constitutional argument that the Second Amendment protects the right to "keep and bear Arms." Is this claim convincing?
2. Consider how Koopman quotes the Second Amendment in paragraph 3. Why doesn't he quote the entire Amendment?
3. How fairly does Koopman characterize advocates of gun control?
4. Why does Koopman emphasize children at the end of paragraph 6? What is he implying here?
5. Koopman claims that opponents of gun control should describe themselves as "pro-constitution" or "pro-freedom" rather than "pro-gun." What is the difference? Has attention to language of this sort helped to shape the debate over any other public issues?

ROBERT J. SPITZER
Shooting Down Gun Myths

Like the preceding essay by Roger Koopman, the following essay by Robert J. Spitzer also concerns the Second Amendment: "A well regulated militia being necessary to the security of a free state, the right of the people to keep and bear arms shall not be infringed." Spitzer teaches political science at the State University of New York, College at Cortland. First published in 1985, this essay reviews important court rulings involving gun control.

The media event that began on Dec. 22, 1984, when subway rider Bernhard   1
Hugo Goetz responded to a demand for $5 from four youths with bullets from a .38-caliber revolver serves as a recent reminder that what historian Richard Hofstadter once labeled the "gun culture" is still tightly woven into the fabric of the American psyche. Much has been written about the political and criminological consequences of gun control, including the proliferation of weapons (especially cheap handguns), the effectiveness or ineffectiveness of various gun control measures and the almost staggering influence of the National Rifle Association in preventing stricter gun laws.

   Yet there has been surprisingly little public examination of the central   2
constitutional question pertaining to guns—namely, the meaning of the Second Amendment: "A well regulated militia being necessary to the security of a free state, the right of the people to keep and bear arms shall not be infringed." The oft-repeated cry of gun control opponents extolling the so-called individual "right to keep and bear arms" has been accepted by most of the public (a 1978 survey reported that 88 percent of Americans believe they have an individual right to bear arms) in large part because it has often

and stridently been repeated. A simple examination of how the courts have interpreted the Second Amendment shows, however, that those who think the Constitution gives them a right to tote a gun have not got a leg to stand on.

The Second Amendment admittedly has not received as much of the   3
Supreme Court's attention over the years as have other Bill of Rights issues, like free speech, free press and the right to counsel. But four cases provide the basis for understanding the Supreme Court's thinking on the matter over the last century.

The first Supreme Court ruling on the Second Amendment occurred in   4
a case called U.S. v. Cruikshank (1876). Speaking for the Court, Chief Justice Morrison R. Waite said the right "of bearing arms for a lawful purpose is not a right granted by the Constitution, nor is it in any manner dependent upon that instrument for its existence." The Cruikshank case established two principles: First, the Second Amendment does not afford an individual right to bear arms (as distinct from an individual's participation in a collective body or militia); second, the Second Amendment is not legally "incorporated"—that is, does not apply to the states through the due process and equal protection clauses of the 14th Amendment. The concept of "incorporation" is highly important in understanding the scope of the Second Amendment and the Bill of Rights as a whole. The process of incorporation has been the means by which the courts have extended constitutional protections to individuals in non-Federal cases. In 1876, none of the Bill of Rights had been incorporated; today, however, most of the constitutional protections we take for granted, like protection from unreasonable searches and seizures and the rights of free assembly and free exercise of religion, protect us because the Supreme Court "incorporated" them. The Court has never, however, "incorporated" the Second Amendment.

The second important court case was Presser v. Illinois (1886). In that   5
case, the Court reaffirmed Cruikshank, and stated that the Second Amendment does not apply to the states (is not "incorporated") and affirmed that though the states have the right to form militias, they are also free to regulate the circumstances under which citizens bear arms, within the parameters of state constitutions.

In an 1894 case, Miller v. Texas, the Supreme Court upheld the right   6
of states to regulate arms and said again that the Second Amendment did not apply to the states. The fourth and most important case came in 1939. U.S. v. Miller involved a challenge to Federal gun regulations stemming from the National Firearms Act of 1934. Speaking for a unanimous Court, Justice James C. McReynolds affirmed the right of the Federal Government to regulate firearms (in particular, transport and possession) and stated unambiguously that citizens possess a constitutional right to bear arms only in connection with service in a militia. Justice Miller also cited the Cruikshank and Presser cases as precedent, affirming the principles articulated in those cases.

The continued pertinence of the Miller case is indicated by two other   7
recent Supreme Court cases. In a 1972 case, Adams v. Williams, Justices

William O. Douglas and Thurgood Marshall issued a joint dissent in which they cited Miller and affirmed their view that the state could regulate firearms as it saw fit. The case itself, however, did not deal with the Second Amendment. In 1980, Justice Harry A. Blackmun commented in a footnote to his majority opinion (Lewis v. U.S.) that the Miller case represented the Court's thinking on gun control.

One final case warrants mention, though it was not reviewed by the   8 Supreme Court. On June 8, 1981, the village of Morton Grove, Ill., enacted an ordinance that banned the possession of handguns, except for police, prison officials, the military, collectors and others needing guns for their work. Residents who owned guns could keep and use them in licensed gun clubs, however. The ordinance was challenged by the National Rifle Association and their sympathizers. Both the Federal District Court and the Federal Court of Appeals rejected the arguments of the ordinance opponents. Both Federal courts said that the Second Amendment did not apply to the states, that there was no individual right to bear arms, that the Morton Grove ordinance was a reasonable exercise of authority and that the right to bear arms applies only to the maintenance of a well regulated militia (as was said in Miller).

The case of Quilici v. Village of Morton Grove was appealed to the   9 Supreme Court, but it declined to hear the case, leaving the lower Federal court ruling as the operative interpretation.

This recitation of cases demonstrates the Court's long recognition of   10 the right of the Government to regulate the ownership and use of firearms as it sees fit. The fact that sweeping national regulations have not been enacted is not due to a lack of constitutional authority, but rather to the political clout of gun control opponents and a gun "mythology" perpetuated in large part by gun enthusiasts.

Even if we examine the intentions of the founding fathers, it is clear   11 that their considerations in authorizing the Second Amendment lay with national defense. The citizen militia was considered the military force least threatening to democratic values and institutions. They feared the baneful consequences of a regular standing army, as European and earlier American history were replete with examples of tyrannies extended by such armies. Despite these fears, the founding fathers were also well aware of the military limitations of an army composed of part-time soldiers, and provision was made in the Constitution (Article I, Section 8) for both a militia and a standing army. The role of the citizen militia was formally supplanted in 1916 by the National Defense Act, which recognized the National Guard as the militia. And, of course, early fears of a standing army that would overthrow American democratic institutions never materialized.

Thus, the Second Amendment protects a "right to keep and bear arms"   12 only for service in a "well regulated militia" that has not been called up since the beginning of the 19th century. As Bill of Rights scholar Irving Brant observed, the Second Amendment "comes to life chiefly on the parade floats of rifle associations and in the propaganda of mail-order houses selling pistols to teen-age gangsters."

Many have applauded the actions of Bernhard Goetz as legitimate self-   13
defense, or as justifiable vigilantism. But even if we accept the propriety of
his actions, how do we disentangle his "right" to carry and use a gun from
the less ambiguous case of James Alan Kearbey, a 14-year-old junior high
school student who, on Jan. 21, entered his Goddard, Kan., school with an
M-1 rifle and a .357 magnum pistol (popularized in Clint Eastwood's film,
"Dirty Harry"). Kearbey shot and killed the school principal and wounded
three others. Goddard English teacher Darlene Criss ironically described the
town as "the safest place in America."

The Goetz case and the Kearbey case both argue for Government to   14
exercise its right to regulate the possession and use of firearms. But as the
merits of gun control are debated, it is time that we once and for all excised
erroneous references to an individual, constitutionally based "right" to
bear arms.

QUESTIONS FOR MEANING

1. Why does Spitzer believe that the Second Amendment does not guarantee
   an individual right to bear arms?
2. What is now recognized as the "well regulated militia" referred to in the
   Second Amendment?
3. What does Spitzer mean by "incorporation" in paragraph 4?
4. Of the various cases involving gun control that have been heard by the
   Supreme Court, which was the most important?
5. In paragraph 13, Spitzer asks how the "right" of Bernard Goetz to carry
   a gun can be separated from the right of James Alan Kearbey to do the
   same? Can you answer this question?
6. Vocabulary: psyche (1), stridently (2), articulated (6), baneful (11), replete
   (11), vigilantism (13), propriety (13), erroneous (14), excised (14).

QUESTIONS ABOUT STRATEGY

1. To what extent does Spitzer's argument rest upon his discussion of Supreme Court rulings?
2. Why does Spitzer discuss the case of Quilici v. Village of Morton Grove
   even though it was not heard by the Supreme Court?
3. How effective is the quotation from Irving Brant in paragraph 12?
4. What advantage is there to including the case of James Alan Kearbey in
   this argument? Why is this case "less ambiguous" than the Goetz case?

WILLIAM F. BUCKLEY, JR.
Ban the Guns?

Editor of the National Review *since 1955, and a syndicated columnist since 1962, William F. Buckley is one of the country's most prominent journalists. His many books include* God and Man at Yale *(1951),* Up from Liberalism *(1959),* Stained Glass *(1978), and* Racing through Paradise *(1987). He is also known to viewers of public television as the host of* Firing Line, *a weekly program focused upon the discussion of important public issues. The following article on gun control was first published as an editorial in* **1990.**

I have done a modest amount of hunting in my life, mostly in pursuit of   1
game, though my professional training was to hunt down Germans and Japanese. So that when a couple of weeks ago President Bush said that he certainly wasn't going to ban the importation of semi-automatic rifles, aware
that the debate had to do with the AK-47s and Uzi carbines being discussed
in California, I wondered just what animals Mr. Bush had in mind as logical
to hunt down with such weapons. I gave this a lot of thought, and suddenly
I remembered the scene in *Gunga Din* in which the wild Indians threw—was
it Cary Grant?—into a pit of poisonous adders. Well, he could certainly have
used an AK-47 in that situation, no question about it. In fact there are odd
situations in which odd forms of weaponry are useful.

The most frequently quoted Supreme Court decision ceding to the Fed-   2
eral Government the right to specify the species of weapons you can legally
go out and purchase was *United States* v. *Miller*, and that was back in 1939,
when the Court sustained the National Firearms Act of 1934, which required
the registration of sawed-off shotguns. Quoth the Court, "In the absence of
any evidence tending to how that possession or use of a shotgun having a
barrel of less than 18 inches in length at this time has some reasonable relationship to the reservation or efficiency of a well-regulated militia, we cannot
say that the Second Amendment guaranteed the right to keep and bear such
an instrument."

Now actually, the *Miller* decision didn't finish the argument. Second   3
Amendment zealots pointed out that rather than fight the case, the defendants (Miller and Layton) disappeared, and the result of this was that their
case was half-heartedly argued. A lawyer conversant with the empirical record of weapons use might have pointed out, for instance, that thirty thousand short-barreled shotguns had been purchased by the United States
Government and used in World War I as "trench guns" (and indeed, such
weapons were used in World War II and through the Vietnam War). Besides
which, legal students of the decision concede that the Court made the most
substantial concession in the controversy in that it spoke of legal and, deriv-
atively, illegal deprivations of the right of Miller to bear arms—and Miller
was not a member of the state militia. This undercut the argument of the

abolitionists that the Second Amendment to the Constitution is limited to protecting the state militias' right to bear arms.

In due course, George Bush retreated, but the problem of outlawing   4
guns that can fire several dozen rounds per minute has hardly gone away. All that criminals need do now is to order guns domestically.

Those people and organizations who are adamant in believing in the   5
basic right of the American citizen to bear arms, whether to kill game, or to wound and kill human beings bent on murder or rape, do much damage to their cause by taking voluptuarian pro-gun positions. Mr. Larry Pratt of the Gun Owners of America has said of the import ban, "It takes guns out of the hands of the citizens in the face of rising criminal rage in this country." Well, that is formally true, but also could be said of whatever the law is that denies to a citizen the right to buy a howitzer. Wayne LaPierre of the National Rifle Association spoke more reasonably when he said, "Today's action, we trust, will end the rush to come up with ill-conceived and ill-defined legislative proposals."

Well, it won't. There are those around the country, for whom Judge   6
Abner Mikva is the high priest, who believe that the way to stop people from killing other people is to stop the manufacture of the contrivances that are used to kill people. "Go after the criminal," said Mr. Bush, which is as sound a direction as you get from the best-trained pointer, who freezes when he spots a crouching pheasant in the brush. What you need to do then is to kill the bird, which means these days that you have to fire through a blanket of judicial and sentimental fog, of the kind that made us take ten years to execute Ted Bundy. On him, we should have used an AK-47 and pleaded guilty.

QUESTIONS FOR MEANING

1. Consider the quote, in paragraph 2, from the 1939 Supreme Court decision in *United States* v. *Miller*. What does it mean?
2. Why does Buckley believe that the Miller case could have been fought more effectively?
3. Does Buckley believe that the right to own firearms is absolute? Where does he stand on the debate over Uzi carbines and AK-47s?
4. Vocabulary: zealots (3), conversant (3), empirical (3), adamant (5), voluptuarian (5).

QUESTIONS ABOUT STRATEGY

1. Why does Buckley begin his editorial by referring to his personal experience as a hunter and as a soldier?
2. Discussing *Gunga Din,* a popular film from the 1930s, Buckley breaks off, in mid-sentence, to ask if it was Cary Grant who was thrown into a snake pit. Why didn't he check? What does he suggest by writing here in a conversational voice?

3. How would you describe Buckley's tone when he refers to Larry Pratt and Wayne LaPierre in paragraph 5?
4. In his concluding paragraph, Buckley introduces his support for capital punishment. Is this appropriate for his conclusion, or is he losing his focus?

SARAH BRADY

Killing Our Future

The head of Handgun Control, Inc., Sarah Brady became active in the fight for gun control after her husband was badly wounded in an assassination attempt upon Ronald Reagan during his first year as President. James Brady was shot in the head, the bullet going through his left eye and crossing his brain. Helping her husband to recover speech and movement through many years of hard work, she also traveled widely to speak on behalf of gun control. She lobbied in particular for national legislation that would require a waiting period after someone applies to buy a gun so that a background check can be made before the purchase is approved. The following 1990 article provides an example of the type of argument Brady made on behalf of the legislation that came to be known as the Brady Amendment.

As America enters the next decade, it does so with an appalling legacy of   1
gun violence. The 1980s were tragic years that saw nearly a quarter of a
million Americans die from handguns—four times as many as were killed in
the Viet Nam War. We began the decade by witnessing yet another President, Ronald Reagan, become a victim of a would-be assassin's bullet. That
day my husband Jim, his press secretary, also became a statistic in America's
handgun war.

Gun violence is an epidemic in this country. In too many cities, the   2
news each night reports another death by a gun. As dealers push out in search
of new addicts, Smalltown, U.S.A., is introduced to the mindless gun violence fostered by the drug trade.

And we are killing our future. Every day a child in this country loses   3
his or her life to a handgun. Hundreds more are permanently injured, often
because a careless adult left within easy reach a loaded handgun purchased
for self-defense.

Despite the carnage, America stands poised to face an even greater es-   4
calation of bloodshed. The growing popularity of military-style assault weapons
could turn our streets into combat zones. Assault weapons, designed solely
to mow down human beings, are turning up at an alarming rate in the hands
of those most prone to violence—drug dealers, gang members, hate groups
and the mentally ill.

The Stockton, Calif., massacre of little children was a warning to our   5
policymakers. But Congress lacked the courage to do anything. During the
year of inaction on Capital Hill, we have seen too many other tragedies brought
about by assault weapons. In Louisville an ex-employee of a printing plant
went on a shooting spree with a Chinese-made semiautomatic version of the
AK-47, gunning down 21 people, killing eight and himself. Two Colorado
women were murdered and several others injured by a junkie using a stolen
MAC-11 semiautomatic pistol. And Congress votes itself a pay raise.

The National Rifle Association, meanwhile, breathes a sigh of relief,   6
gratified that your attention is now elsewhere. The only cooling-off period
the N.R.A. favors is a postponement of legislative action. It counts on public
anger to fade before such outrage can be directed at legislators. The N.R.A.
runs feel-good ads saying guns are not the problem and there is nothing we
can do to prevent criminals from getting guns. In fact, it has said that guns
in the wrong hands are the "price we pay for freedom." I guess I'm just not
willing to hand the next John Hinckley a deadly handgun. Neither is the
nation's law-enforcement community, the men and women who put their
lives on the line for the rest of us every day.

Two pieces of federal legislation can make a difference right now. First,   7
we must require a national waiting period before the purchase of a handgun,
to allow for a criminal-records check. Police know that waiting periods work.
In the 20 years that New Jersey has required a background check, authorities
have stopped more than 10,000 convicted felons from purchasing handguns.

We must also stop the sale and domestic production of semiautomatic   8
assault weapons. These killing machines clearly have no legitimate sporting
purpose, as President Bush recognized when he permanently banned their
importation.

These public-safety measures are supported by the vast majority of   9
Americans—including gun owners. In fact, these measures are so sensible
that I never realized the campaign to pass them into law would be such an
uphill battle. But it can be done.

Jim Brady knows the importance of a waiting period. He knows the   10
living hell of a gunshot wound. Jim and I are not afraid to take on the N.R.A.
leaders, and we will fight them everywhere we can. As Jim said in his
congressional testimony, "I don't question the rights of responsible gun owners.
That's not the issue. The issue is whether the John Hinckleys of the world
should be able to walk into gun stores and purchase handguns instantly. Are
you willing and ready to cast a vote for a commonsense public-safety bill
endorsed by experts—law enforcement?"

Are we as a nation going to accept America's bloodshed, or are we   11
ready to stand up and do what is right? When are we going to say "Enough"?
We can change the direction in which America is headed. We can prevent the
1990s from being bloodier than the past ten years. If each of you picks up a
pen and writes to your Senators and Representative tonight, you would be
surprised at how quickly we could collect the votes we need to win the war
for a safer America.

Let us enter a new decade committed to finding solutions to the prob-   12
lem of gun violence. Let your legislators know that voting with the gun
lobby—and against public safety—is no longer acceptable. Let us send a signal to lawmakers that we demand action, not excuses.

QUESTIONS FOR MEANING

1. What explanation does Brady offer for rising gun violence in the United
   States?
2. When Brady writes "we are killing our future," what does she mean?
3. Does Brady endorse any specific forms of gun control besides a national
   waiting period before the completion of a handgun purchase?

QUESTIONS ABOUT STRATEGY

1. Brady mentions the wounding of her husband in paragraphs 1 and 10.
   And John Hinckley, the man who shot him while attempting to assassi-
   nate Ronald Reagan, is also mentioned in paragraph 6. Are these references appropriate for Brady's argument? What effect do they have upon
   you?
2. Consider the end of paragraph 5. Is it ironic or sarcastic?
3. In paragraph 7, Brady claims that authorities in New Jersey have been
   able to stop more than 10,000 felons from buying guns. Is she vulnerable
   to counterargument on this point?
4. Brady refers to gun-control laws as "public-safety measures." Why is it
   useful for her to characterize these laws in this way?
5. How effective is the conclusion of this argument? What does it reveal
   about Brady's sense of audience?

DON B. KATES, JR.
Against Civil Disarmament

*A graduate of Yale Law School, Don B. Kates, Jr., has worked as an Office of Educational Opportunity poverty lawyer and taught both criminal and constitutional law. During the last fifteen years, he has emerged as one of the most articulate opponents of gun control, a subject on which he has written for numerous magazines. In the following essay, which originally appeared in Harpers in **1978,** Kates argues that conventional attitudes toward gun control need to be rethought. He tries to show that the controversy over gun control has confused the traditional distinction between liberal and conservative views.*

Despite almost 100 years of often bitter debate, federal policy and that of 44   1
states continues to allow handguns to any sane adult who is without felony convictions. Over the past twenty years, as some of our most progressive citizens have embraced the notion that handgun confiscation would reduce violent crime, the idea of closely restricting handgun possession to police and those with police permits has been stereotyped as "liberal." Yet when the notion of sharply restricting pistol ownership first gained popularity, in the late nineteenth century, it was under distinctly conservative auspices.

In 1902, South Carolina banned all pistol purchases, the first and only   2
state ever to do so. (This was nine years before New York began requiring what was then an easily acquired police permit.) Tennessee had already enacted the first ban on "Saturday Night Specials," disarming blacks and the laboring poor while leaving weapons for the Ku Klux Klan and company goons. In 1906, Mississippi enacted the first mandatory registration law for all firearms. In short order, permit requirements were enacted in North Carolina, Missouri, Michigan, and Hawaii. In 1922, a national campaign of conservative business interests for handgun confiscation was endorsed by the (then) archconservative American Bar Association.

Liberals at that time were not necessarily opposed in principle to a ban   3
on handguns, but they considered such a move irrelevant and distracting from a more important issue—the prohibition of alcohol. To Jane Addams, William Jennings Bryan, and Eleanor Roosevelt (herself a pistol carrier), liquor was the cause of violent crime. (Before dismissing this out of hand, remember that homicide studies uniformly find liquor a more prevalent factor than handguns in killings.) Besides, liberals were not likely to support the argument advanced by conservatives for gun confiscation: that certain racial and immigrant groups were so congenitally criminal (and/or politically dangerous) that they could not be trusted with arms. But when liberalism finally embraced handgun confiscation, it was by applying this conservative viewpoint to the entire populace. Now it is all Americans (not just Italians, Jews, or blacks) who must be considered so innately violent and unstable

that they cannot be trusted with arms. For, we are told, it is not robbers or burglars who commit most murders, but average citizens killing relatives or friends.

It is certainly true that only a little more than 30 percent of murders are   4 committed by robbers, rapists, or burglars, while 45 percent are committed among relatives or between lovers. (The rest are a miscellany of contract killings, drug wars, and "circumstances unknown.") But it is highly misleading to conclude from this that the murderer is, in any sense, an average gun owner. For the most part, murderers are disturbed, aberrant individuals with long records of criminal violence that often include several felony convictions. In terms of endangering his fellow citizen, the irresponsible drinker is far more representative of all drinkers than is the irresponsible handgunner of all handgunners. It is not my intention here to defend the character of the average American handgun owner against, say, that of the Swiss whose government not only allows, but requires, him to keep a machine gun at home. Rather it is to show how unrealistic it is to think that we could radically decrease homicide by radically reducing the number of civilian firearms. Study after study has shown that even if the *average* gun owner complied with a ban, the one handgun owner out of 3,000 who murders (much less the one in 500 who steals) is not going to give up his guns. Nor would taking guns away from the murderer make much difference in murder rates, since a sociopath with a long history of murderous assault is not too squeamish to kill with a butcher knife, ice pick, razor, or bottle. As for the extraordinary murders—assassins, terrorists, hit men—proponents of gun bans themselves concede that the law cannot disarm such people any more than it can disarm professional robbers.

The repeated appearance of these facts in studies of violent crime has   5 eroded liberal and intellectual support for banning handguns. There is a growing consensus among even the most liberal students of criminal law and criminology that handgun confiscation is just another plausible theory that doesn't work when tried. An article written in 1968 by Mark K. Beneson, longtime American chairman of Amnesty International, concludes that the arguments for gun bans are based upon selective misleading statistics, simpleminded non sequiturs, and basic misconceptions about the nature of murder as well as of other violent crimes.

A 1971 study at England's Cambridge University confounds one of the   6 most widely believed non sequiturs: "Banning handguns must work, because England does and look at its crime rate!" (It is difficult to see how those who believe this can resist the equally simple-minded pro-gun argument that gun possession deters crime: "Everybody ought to have a machine gun in his house because the Swiss and the Israelis do, and look how low their crime rates are!")

The Cambridge report concludes that social and cultural factors (not   7 gun control) account for Britain's low violence rates. It points out that "the use of firearms in crime was very much less" before 1920 when Britain had "no controls of any sort." Corroborating this is the comment of a former head of Scotland Yard that in the mid-1950s there were enough illegal hand-guns to supply any British criminal who wanted one. But, he continued, the social milieu was such that if a criminal killed anyone, particularly a police-man, his own confederates would turn him in. When this violence-dampen-ing social milieu began to dissipate between 1960 and 1975, the British homicide rate doubled (as did the American rate), while British robbery rates acceler-ated even faster than those in America. As the report notes, the vaunted handgun ban proved completely ineffective against rising violence in Britain, although the government frantically intensified enforcement and extended controls to long guns as well. Thus, the Cambridge study—the only in-depth study ever done of English gun laws—recommends "abolishing or substan-tially reducing controls" because their administration involves an immense, unproductive expense and diverts police resources from programs that might reduce violent crime.

The latest American study of gun controls was conducted with federal   8
funding at the University of Wisconsin. Advanced computerized techniques allowed a comprehensive analysis of the effect of every form of state hand-gun restriction, including complete prohibition, on violence in America. Published in 1975, it concludes that "gun-control laws have no individual or collective effect in reducing the rate of violent crime."

Many previous studies reaching the same conclusion had been dis-   9
counted by proponents of a federal ban, who argued that existing state bans cannot be effective because handguns are illegally imported from free-sale states. The Wisconsin study compared rates of handgun ownership with rates of violence in various localities, but it could find *no correlation*. If areas where handgun ownership rates are high have no higher per capita rates of homicide and other violence than areas where such rates are low, the utility of laws designed to lower the rates of handgun ownership seems dubious. Again, the problem is not the "proliferation of handguns" among the law-abiding citi-zenry, it is the existence of a tiny fraction of irresponsible and criminal own-ers whom the law cannot possibly disarm of these or other weapons.

Far from refuting the Wisconsin study, the sheer unenforceability of   10
handgun bans is the main reason why most experts regard them as not worth thinking about. Even in Britain, a country that, before handguns were banned, had less than 1 percent of the per capita handgun ownership we have, the Cambridge study reports that "fifty years of very strict controls has left a vast pool of illegal weapons."

It should be emphasized that liberal defectors from gun confiscation are   11
no more urging people to arm themselves than are those who oppose ban-ning pot or liquor necessarily urging people to indulge in them. They are only saying that national handgun confiscation would bring the federal gov-ernment into a confrontation with millions of responsible citizens in order to enforce a program that would have no effect upon violence, except the neg-ative one of diverting resources that otherwise might be utilized to some effective purpose. While many criminologists have doubts about the wisdom of citizens trying to defend themselves with handguns, the lack of evidence

to justify confiscation requires that this remain a matter of individual choice rather than government fiat.

Nor can advocates of gun bans duck the evidence adverse to their position by posing such questions as: Why should people have handguns; what good do they do; why *shouldn't* we ban them? In a free country, the burden is not upon the people to show why they should have freedom of choice. It is upon those who wish to restrict that freedom to show good reason for doing so. And when the freedom is as deeply valued by as many as is handgun ownership, the evidence for infringing upon it must be very strong indeed.

If the likely benefits of handgun confiscation have been greatly exaggerated, the financial and constitutional costs have been largely ignored. Consider the various costs of any attempt to enforce confiscation upon a citizenry that believes (whether rightly or not) that they urgently need handguns for self-defense and that the right to keep them is constitutionally guaranteed. Most confiscationists have never gotten beyond the idea that banning handguns will make them magically disappear somehow. Because they loathe handguns and consider them useless, the prohibitionists assume that those who disagree will readily turn in their guns once a national confiscation law is passed. But the leaders of the national handgun prohibition movement have become more realistic. They recognize that defiance will, if anything, exceed the defiance of Prohibition and marijuana laws. After all, not even those who viewed drinking or pot smoking as a blow against tyranny thought, as many gun owners do, that violating the law is necessary to the protection of themselves and their families. Moreover, fear of detection is a lot more likely to keep citizens from constant purchases of liquor or pot than from a single purchase of a handgun, which, properly maintained, will last years.

To counter the expected defiance, the leaders of the national confiscation drive propose that handgun ownership be punished by a nonsuspendable mandatory year in prison. The mandatory feature is necessary, for otherwise prosecutors would not prosecute, and judges would not sentence, gun ownership with sufficient severity. The judge of a special Chicago court trying only gun violations recently explained why he generally levied only small fines. The overwhelming majority of the "criminals" who come before him are respectable, decent citizens who illegally carry guns because the police can't protect them and they have no other way of protecting themselves. He does not even impose probation because this would prevent the defendants, whose guns have been confiscated, from buying new ones, which, the judge believes, they need to live and work where they do.

These views are shared by judges and prosecutors nationwide; studies find that gun-carrying charges are among the most sympathetically dealt with of all felonies. To understand why, consider a typical case that would have come before this Chicago court if the D.A. had not dropped charges. An intruder raped a woman and threw her out of a fifteenth-floor window. Police arrived too late to arrest him, so they got her roommate for carrying the gun with which she scared him off when he attacked her.

Maybe it is not a good idea for this woman to keep a handgun for self-   16
defense. But do we really want to send her to federal prison for doing so?
And is a mandatory year in prison reasonable or just for an ordinary citizen
who has done nothing more hurtful than keeping a gun to defend herself—
when the minimum mandatory sentence for murder is only seven years and
most murderers serve little time?

Moreover, the kind of nationwide resistance movement that a federal   17
handgun ban would provoke could not be broken by imprisoning a few impecunious black women in Chicago. Only by severely punishing a large
number of respectable citizens of every race and social class would registers
eventually be made to fear the law more than the prospect of living without
handguns in a violent society. At a very conservative estimate, at least half
of our present handgun owners would be expected to defy a federal ban.*
To imprison just 1 percent of these 25 million people would require several
times as many cells as the entire federal prison now has. The combined federal, state, and local jail systems could barely manage. Of course, so massive
an enforcement campaign would also require doubling expenditure for police, prosecutors, courts, and all the other sectors of criminal justice administration. The Wisconsin study closes with the pertinent query: "Are we willing
to make sociological and economic investments of such a tremendous nature
in a social experiment for which there is no empirical support?"

The argument against a federal handgun ban is much like the argument   18
against marijuana bans. It is by no means clear that marijuana is the harmless
substance that its proponents claim. But it would take evidence far stronger
than we now have to justify the enormous financial, human, institutional,
and constitutional costs of continuing to ferret out, try, and imprison even a
small percentage of the otherwise law-abiding citizens who insist on having
pot. Sophisticated analysis of the criminalization decision takes into account
not only the harms alleged to result from public possession of things like pot
or guns, but the capacity of the criminal law to reduce those harms and the
costs of trying to do so. Unfortunately most of the gun-control debate never
gets beyond the abstract merits of guns—a subject on which those who view
them with undifferentiated loathing are no more rational than those who love
them. The position of all too many gun-banning liberals is indistinguishable
from Archie Bunker's views on legalizing pot and homosexuality: "I don't
like it and I don't like those who do—so it ought to be illegal."

---

*I reach this estimate in this fashion: Surveys uniformly find a majority of gun owners support
gun registration—in theory. In practice, however, they refuse to register because they believe
this will identify their guns for confiscation if and when a national handgun ban eventually
passes. In 1968, Chicago police estimated that two-thirds of the city's gun owners had not
complied with the new state registration law; statewide noncompliance was estimated at 75
percent. In Cleveland, police estimate that almost 90 percent of handgun owners are in violation
of a 1976 registration requirement. My estimate that one out of two handgun owners would
defy national confiscation is conservative indeed when between two out of three and nine out of
ten of them are already defying registration laws because they believe such laws presage confiscation.

The emotionalism with which many liberals (and conservatives as well)   19
react against the handgun reflects not its reality but its symbolism to people
who are largely ignorant of that reality. A 1975 national survey found a direct correlation between support for more stringent controls and the inability
to answer simple questions about present federal gun laws. In other words,
the less the respondent knew about the subject, the more likely he was to
support national confiscation. Liberals advocate severely punishing those who
will defy confiscation only because the liberal image of a gun owner is a
criminal or right-wing fanatic rather than a poor black woman in Chicago
defending herself against a rapist or a murderer. Contrary to this stereotype,
most "gun nuts" are peaceful hobbyists whose violence is exclusively of the
Walter Mitty type. Gun owners' views are all too often expressed in right-
wing terms (which does nothing for the rationality of the debate) because
twenty years of liberal vilification has given them nowhere else to look for
support. If only liberals knew it, handgun ownership is disproportionately
high among the underprivileged for whom liberals traditionally have had
most sympathy. As the most recent (1975) national demographic survey reports: "The top subgroups who own a gun *only* for self-defense include blacks
(almost half own one for this reason alone), lowest income group, senior
citizens." The average liberal has no understanding of why people have guns
because he has no idea what it is like to live in a ghetto where police have
given up on crime control. Minority and disadvantaged citizens are not about
to give up their families' protection because middle-class white liberals living
and working in high-security buildings and/or well-policed suburbs tell them
it's safer that way.

A final cost of national gun confiscation would be the vast accretion of   20
enforcement powers to the police at the expense of individual liberty. The
Police Foundation, which ardently endorses confiscation, recently suggested
that federal agencies and local police look to how drug laws are enforced as
a model of how to enforce firearms laws. Coincidentally, the chief topic of
conversation at the 1977 national conference of supporters of federal confiscation was enforcement through house searches of everyone whom sales records indicate may ever have owned a handgun. In fact, indiscriminate search,
complemented by electronic surveillance and vast armies of snoopers and
informers, is how handgun restrictions are enforced in countries like Holland
and Jamaica, and in states like Missouri and Michigan.* Even in England, as
the Cambridge report notes, each new Firearms Act has been accompanied
by new, unheard-of-powers of search and arrest for the police.

These, then, are the costs of banning handguns: even attempting an   21
effective ban would involve enormous expenditures (roughly equal to the
present cost of enforcing all our other criminal laws combined) to ferret out
and jail hundreds of thousands of decent, responsible citizens who believe

---

*According to the ACLU, St. Louis police have conducted 25,000 illegal searches in the past
few years under the theory that any black man driving a late-model car possesses a handgun.

Michigan court records indicate that almost 70 percent of all firearms charges presented
are thrown out because the evidence was obtained through unconstitutional search.

that they vitally need handguns to protect their families. If this does not terrorize the rest of the responsible handgun owners into compliance, the effort will have to be expanded until millions are jailed and the annual gun-banning budget closely seconds defense spending. And all of this could be accomplished only by abandoning many restraints our Constitution places upon police activity.

What would we have to show for all this in terms of crime reduction? Terrorists, hit men, and other hardened criminals who are not deterred by the penalties for murder, robbery, rape, burglary, et cetera are not about to be terrified by the penalties for gun ownership—nor is the more ordinary murderer, the disturbed, aberrant individual who kills out of rage rather than cupidity.   22

What we should have learned from our experience of Prohibition, and England's with gun banning, is that violence can be radically reduced only through long-term fundamental change in the institutions and mores that produce so many violent people in our society. It is much easier to use as scapegoats a commonly vilified group (drinkers or gun owners) and convince ourselves that legislation against them is an easy short-term answer. But violence will never be contained or reduced until we give up the gimmicky programs, the scapegoating, the hypocritical hand-wringing, and frankly ask ourselves whether we are willing to make the painful, disturbing, far-reaching institutional and cultural changes that are necessary.   23

QUESTIONS FOR MEANING

1. What states were the first to initiate gun control legislation, and what motivated them to do so? Who were the supporters of these early laws, and who were they trying to control? Why does Kates believe that it is important to remember the history of the movement for gun control as we argue about the possibility of additional legislation?
2. What does Kates mean by "company goons" in paragraph 2?
3. In paragraph 6, Kates summarizes two simple arguments and describes them as non sequiturs. Explain why the reasoning is faulty in both the examples he cites.
4. What types of people are the most likely to own handguns? Why do these people feel that they need guns? Why is it, according to Kates, that the average liberal cannot understand this?
5. According to this essay, what is the main reason why gun control cannot work?
6. Proponents of gun control have frequently advocated a mandatory year in prison for anyone illegally possessing a handgun. Why do such people insist that the penalty be mandatory? Why does Kates oppose this idea in particular?
7. Vocabulary: congenitally (3), aberrant (4), felony (4), milieu (7), dissipate (7), loathe (13), impecunious (17), pertinent (17), empirical (17), vilification (19), demographic (19), and cupidity (22).

QUESTIONS ABOUT STRATEGY

1. Why does Kates quote a chairman of Amnesty International in paragraph 5? Why is this more effective than quoting the president of the National Rifle Association? Similarly, why does he describe the poor black woman in Chicago? What does this tell us about his audience? What type of people is Kates trying to convince, and what is his basic strategy in doing so?
2. What basic values does Kates assume in making this argument? What does he think of "law"—what it can and cannot do?
3. Why does Kates compare gun legislation with laws designed to control marijuana? Why is he then able to argue that gun laws are even harder to enforce?
4. Does Kates ever resort to ridiculing his opponents, or does he consistently treat them with respect?
5. Does Kates offer any alternatives to gun control as a way of making America less violent? Is it his responsibility to do so in order to make a good argument?

WILLIAM R. TONSO
White Man's Law

A professor of sociology at the University of Evansville, William R. Tonso is the author of Gun and Society *(1982). Drawing upon the work of Don B. Kates and other sources, he argues that the demand for gun control is the result of prejudice against minorities and the poor. The following essay provides an example of his views. It was first published in* **1985**.

Chances are that you've never heard of General Laney. He hasn't had a brilliant military career, at least as far as I know. In fact, I'm not certain that he's even served in the military. General, you see, isn't Laney's rank. General is Laney's first name. General Laney does, however, have a claim to fame, unrecognized though it may be. 1

Detroit resident General Laney is the founder and prime mover behind a little-publicized organization known as the National Black Sportsman's Association, often referred to as "the black gun lobby." Laney pulls no punches when asked his opinion of gun control: "Gun control is really race control. People who embrace gun control are really racists in nature. All gun laws have been enacted to control certain classes of people, mainly black people, but the same laws used to control blacks are being used to disarm white people as well." 2

Laney is not the first to make this observation. Indeed, allied with sportsmen in vocal opposition to gun controls in the 1960s were the militant 3

Black Panthers. Panther Minister of Information Eldridge Cleaver noted in 1968: "Some very interesting laws are being passed. They don't name me; they don't say, take the guns away from the niggers. They say that people will no longer be allowed to have (guns). They don't pass these rules and these regulations specifically for black people, they have to pass them in a way that will take in everybody."

Some white liberals have said essentially the same thing. Investigative 4 reporter Robert Sherrill, himself no lover of guns, concluded in his book *The Saturday Night Special* that the object of the Gun Control Act of 1968 was black control rather than race control. According to Sherrill, Congress was so panicked by the ghetto riots of 1967 and 1968 that it passed the act to "shut off weapons access to blacks, and since they (Congress) probably associated cheap guns with ghetto blacks and thought cheapness was peculiarly the characteristic of imported military surplus and the mail-order traffic, they decided to cut off these sources while leaving over-the-counter purchases open to the affluent." Congressional motivation may have been more complex than Sherrill suggests, but keeping blacks from acquiring guns was certainly a large part of that motivation. . . .

There is little doubt that the earliest gun controls in the United States 5 were blatantly racist and elitist in their intent. San Francisco civil-liberties attorney Don B. Kates, Jr., an opponent of gun prohibitions with impeccable liberal credentials (he has been a clerk for radical lawyer William Kunstler, a civil-rights activist in the South, and an Office of Economic Opportunity lawyer), describes early gun control efforts in his book *Restricting Handguns: The Liberal Skeptics Speak Out*. As Kates documents, prohibitions against the sale of cheap handguns originated in the post-Civil War South. Small pistols selling for as little as 50 or 60 cents became available in the 1870s and '80s, and since they could be afforded by recently emancipated blacks and poor whites (whom agrarian agitators of the time were encouraging to ally for economic and political purposes), these guns constituted a significant threat to a southern establishment interested in maintaining the traditional class structure.

Consequently, Kates notes, in 1870 Tennessee banned "selling all but 6 'the Army and Navy model' handgun, i.e., the most expensive one, which was beyond the means of most blacks and laboring people." In 1881, Arkansas enacted an almost identical ban on the sale of cheap revolvers, while in 1902, South Carolina banned the sale of handguns to all but "sheriffs and their special deputies—i.e., company goons and the KKK." In 1893 and 1907, respectively, Alabama and Texas attempted to put handguns out of the reach of blacks and poor whites through "extremely heavy business and/or transactional taxes" on the sale of such weapons. In the other Deep South states, slavery-era bans on arms possession by blacks continued to be enforced by hook or by crook.

The cheap revolvers of the late 19th and early 20th centuries were re- 7 ferred to as "Suicide Specials," the "Saturday Night Special" label not becoming widespread until reformers and politicians took up the gun control cause during the 1960s. The source of this recent concern about cheap revolvers, as their new label suggests, has much in common with the concerns of the gun-law initiators of the post-Civil War South. As B. Bruce-Briggs has written in the *Public Interest*, "It is difficult to escape the conclusion that the 'Saturday Night Special' is emphasized because it is cheap and is being sold to a particular class of people. . . ."

Those who argue that the concern about cheap handguns is justified   8
because these guns are used in most crimes should take note of *Under the Gun: Weapons, Crime, and Violence in America*, by sociologists James D. Wright, Peter H. Rossi, and Kathleen Daly. The authors, who undertook an exhaustive, federally funded, critical review of gun issue research, found *no conclusive proof that cheap handguns are used in crime more often than expensive handguns*. (Interestingly, the makers of quality arms, trying to stifle competition, have sometimes supported bans on cheap handguns and on the importation of cheap military surplus weapons. Kates observes that the Gun Control Act of 1968, which banned mail-order gun sales and the importation of military surplus firearms, "was something domestic manufacturers had been impotently urging for decades.") But the evidence leads to one conclusion that cheap handguns are considered threatening primarily because minorities and poor whites can afford them.

Attempts to regulate the possession of firearms began in the northern   9
states during the early part of the 20th century, and although these regulations had a different focus from those that had been concocted in the South, they were no less racist and elitist in effect or intent. Rather than trying to keep handguns out of the price range that blacks and the poor could afford, New York's trend-setting Sullivan Law, enacted in 1911, required a police permit for legal possession of a handgun. This law made it possible for the police to screen applicants for permits to possess handguns, and while such a requirement may seem reasonable, it can be and has been abused.

Members of groups not in favor with the political establishment or the   10
police are automatically suspect and can easily be denied permits. For instance, when the Sullivan Law was enacted, southern and eastern European immigrants were considered racially inferior and religiously and ideologically suspect. (Many were Catholics or Jews, and a disproportionate number were anarchists or socialists.) Professor L. Kennett, coauthor of the authoritative history *The Gun in America*, has noted that the measure was designed to "strike hardest at the foreign-born element," particularly Italians. Southern and eastern European immigrants found it almost impossible to obtain gun permits.

Over the years, application of the Sullivan Law has become increasingly   11
elitist as the police seldom grant handgun permits to any but the wealthy or the politically influential. A beautiful example of this hypocritical elitism is the fact that while the *New York Times* often editorializes against the private possession of handguns, the publisher of that newspaper, Arthur Ochs Sulzberger, has a hard-to-get permit to own and carry a handgun. Another such permit is held by the husband of Dr. Joyce Brothers, the pop psychologist

who has claimed that firearms ownership is indicative of male sexual inadequacy.

Gun-control efforts through the centuries have been propelled by racist and elitist sentiments. Even though European aristocrats were members of a weapons-loving warrior caste, they did their best to keep the gun from becoming a weapon of war. It was certainly all right to kill with civilized weapons such as the sword, the battle ax, or the lance; these were weapons that the armored knights were trained to use and which gave them a tremendous advantage over commoners who didn't have the knights' training or possess their expensive weapons and armor. But guns, by virtue of being able to pierce armor, democratized warfare and made common soldiers more than a match for the armored and aristocratic knights, thereby threatening the existence of the feudal aristocracy.

As early as 1541, England enacted a law that limited legal possession of handguns and crossbows (weapons that were considered criminally dangerous) to those with incomes exceeding 100 pounds a year, though long-gun possession wasn't restricted—except for Catholics, a potentially rebellious minority after the English Reformation. Catholics couldn't legally keep militia-like weapons in their homes, as other Englishmen were encouraged to do, but they could legally possess defensive weapons—except, as Bill of Rights authority Joyce Lee Malcolm has noted in her essay "The Right to Keep and Bear Arms: The Common Law Tradition," during times "of extreme religious tension."

According to Malcolm, when William and Mary came to the English throne, they were presented with a list of rights, one of which was aimed at staving off any future attempt at arms confiscation—"all Protestant citizens had a right to keep arms for their defence." England then remained free of restrictive gun legislation until 1920 when, even though the crime rate was very low, concern about the rebellious Irish and various political radicals ushered in today's draconian gun laws. (Colin Greenwood, former superintendent of the West Yorkshire Metropolitan Police, has discovered in his research at Cambridge University that the English gun crime rate is significantly *higher* now than it was before that nation's strict gun laws were enacted.)

Alas, the European aristocracy wasn't able to control gun use, and at least in part, the spread of effective firearms helped to bring down aristocracy and feudalism. By contrast, in 17th-century Japan the ruling Tokugawa Shogunate was able to establish a rigidly stratified society that deemphasized the development of guns and restricted arms possession to a warrior aristocracy, the *samurai*. When Commodore Perry "reopened" Japan to the rest of the world in the middle of the 19th century, few Japanese were familiar with guns (the sword was the most honored weapon of the samurai) and the most common guns were primitive matchlocks similar to those introduced to Japan by the Portuguese in the middle of the 16th century. As post-Perry Japan modernized and acquired a modern military, it also quickly developed modern weaponry. But a citizenry without a gun-owning tradition was easily kept in place in a collectivist society where individuals were more susceptible to formal and informal social controls than are westerners.

The preceding are just samples of the political uses to which gun controls have been put throughout the world. Nazi Germany, the Soviet Union, and South Africa are modern examples of repressive governments that use gun control as a means of social control. Raymond G. Kessler, a lawyer-sociologist who has provided some of the most sociologically sophisticated insights into the gun control issue, suggests in a *Law and Policy Quarterly* article that attempts to regulate the civilian possession of firearms have five political functions. They "(1) increase citizen reliance on government and tolerance of increased police powers and abuse; (2) help prevent opposition to government; (3) facilitate repressive action by government and its allies; (4) lessen the pressure for major or radical reform; and (5) can be selectively enforced against those perceived to be a threat to government."

Of course, while many gun control proponents might acknowledge that such measures have been used in the ways Kessler lists, they would deny that the controls that they support are either racist or elitist, since they would apply to everybody and are aimed at reducing violence for everybody. Yet the controls that they advocate are in fact racist and classist in *effect*, and only the naive or the dishonest can deny their elitist *intent*.

Kessler has also written that while liberals are likely to sympathize with the poor and minorities responsible for much of this nation's violent crime, when they are victimized themselves, "or when they hear of an especially heinous crime, liberals, like most people, feel anger and hostility toward the offender. The discomfort of having incompatible feelings can be alleviated by transferring the anger away from the offender to an inanimate object—the weapon."

A perfect example of this transference is provided by Pete Shields, the chairman of the lobbying group Handgun Control Inc., whose son was tragically murdered with a handgun by one of San Francisco's Zebra killers—blacks who were killing whites at random in the early 1970s. This killing was carried out by a black man who was after whites—his own skin color and that of his victim were important to the killer—but in his grief, the white liberal father couldn't blame the criminal for this racist crime. So the gun was the culprit. The upshot is that we now have Handgun Control Inc., with its emphasis on the *weapon* used to commit a crime rather than the criminal. Yet blacks and minorities, who would be prevented from defending themselves, are likely to be harmed most by legislation proposed by Handgun Control Inc., the National Coalition to Ban Handguns, and other proponents of strict handgun controls.

Since the illegal possession of a handgun (or of any gun) is a crime that doesn't produce a victim and is unlikely to be reported to the police, handgun permit requirements or outright handgun prohibitions aren't easily enforced. And as civil liberties attorney Kates has observed, when laws are difficult to enforce, "enforcement becomes progressively more haphazard until at last the laws are used only against those who are unpopular with the police." Of course minorities, especially minorities who don't "know their place," aren't likely to be popular with the police, and these very minorities, in the face of police indifference or perhaps even antagonism, may be the most inclined to look to guns for protection—guns that they can't acquire legally and that place them in jeopardy if possessed illegally. While the intent of such laws may not be racist, their effect most certainly is.

Today's gun-control battle, like those of days gone by, largely breaks 21 down along class lines. Though there are exceptions to the rule, the most dedicated and vociferous proponents of strict gun controls are urban, upper-middle-class or aspiring upper-middle-class, pro-big-government liberals, many of whom are part of the New Class (establishment intellectuals and the media), and most of whom know little or nothing about guns and the wide range of legitimate uses to which they are regularly put. Many of these elitists make no secret of their disdain for gun-owners. For instance, Gov. Mario Cuomo of New York recently dismissed those who are opposed to the Empire State's mandatory seat-belt law as "NRA hunters who drink beer, don't vote, and lie to their wives about where they were all weekend."

On the other hand, the most dedicated opponents of gun control are 22 often rural- or small-town-oriented, working- or middle-class men and women, few of whom possess the means to publicize their views, but many of whom know a great deal about the safe and lawful uses of guns. To these Americans, guns mean freedom, security, and wholesome recreation. The battle over gun controls, therefore, has come about as affluent America has attempted to impose its anti-gun prejudices on a working-class America that is comfortable with guns (including handguns), seldom misuses them (most gun crime is urban), and sees them as protection against criminal threats and government oppression.

How right you are, General Laney. "All gun laws have been enacted to 23 control certain classes of people. . . ."

QUESTIONS FOR MEANING

1. Why does Tonso object to New York State's Sullivan Law?
2. What led England to adopt gun control in the 1920s?
3. According to this essay, what are the political motives that lead to gun control?
4. What does Tonso mean by "transference" in paragraph 19?
5. What is wrong with a law that is selectively enforced?
6. Vocabulary: impeccable (5), emancipated (5), agrarian (5), impotently (8), authoritative (10), collectivist (15), vociferous (21).

QUESTIONS ABOUT STRATEGY

1. Why do you think Tonso chose to begin this essay with a reference to General Laney when he realized that his audience was probably unfamiliar with this man?

2. Consider Tonso's use of sources in this essay. How well are they incorporated into Tonso's own argument? Which is the most effective?
3. Why does Tonso discuss both English and Japanese history?
4. How does Tonso characterize his opponents? Does he treat them fairly? What is the quotation from Mario Cuomo meant to illustrate?

JOSH SUGARMANN
The NRA Is Right

*Most of the debate over gun control has focused on whether there's a need to restrict handgun ownership. In the following essay, first published in **1987,** Josh Sugarmann argues on behalf of banning handguns altogether. A freelance writer living in New York, Sugarmann was communications director of the National Coalition to Ban Handguns from 1984 to 1986.*

One tenet of the National Rifle Association's faith has always been that handgun controls do little to stop criminals from obtaining handguns. For once, the NRA is right and America's leading handgun control organization is wrong. Criminals don't buy handguns in gun stores. That's why they're criminals. But it isn't criminals who are killing most of the 20,000 to 22,000 people who die from handguns each year. We are.   1

This is an ugly truth for a country that thinks of handgun violence as a "crime" issue and believes that it's somehow possible to separate "good" handguns (those in our hands for self-defense) from "bad" handguns (those in the hands of criminals).   2

Contrary to popular perception, the most prevalent form of handgun death in America isn't murder but suicide. An additional 1,000 fatalities are accidents. And of the 9,000 handgun deaths classified as murders, most are not caused by predatory strangers. Handgun violence is usually the result of people being angry, drunk, careless, or depressed—who just happen to have a handgun around. In all, fewer than 10 percent of handgun deaths are felony-related.   3

Though handgun availability is not a crime issue, it does represent a major public health threat. Handguns are the number one weapon for both murder and suicide and are second only to auto accidents as the leading cause of death due to injury. Of course there are other ways of committing suicide or crimes of passion. But no means is more lethal, effective, or handy. That's why the NRA is ultimately wrong. As several public health organizations have noted, the best way to curb a public health problem is through prevention—in this case, the banning of all handguns from civilian hands.   4

The Enemy Is Us

For most who attempt suicide, the will to die lasts only briefly. Only one   5
out of every ten people attempting suicide is going to kill himself no matter
what. The success or failure of an attempt depends primarily on the lethality
of the means. Pills, razor blades, and gas aren't guaranteed killers, and they
take time. Handguns, however, lend themselves well to spontaneity. Consider that although women try to kill themselves four times as often as men,
men succeed three to four times as often. For one reason: women use pills or
less lethal means; men use handguns. This balance is shifting, however, as
more women own or have access to handguns. Between 1970 and 1978 the
suicide rate for young women rose 50 percent, primarily due to increased use
of handguns.

Of course, there is no way to lock society's cupboard and prevent every   6
distraught soul from injuring him or herself. Still, there are ways we can
promote public safety without becoming a nation of nannies. England, for
instance, curbed suicide by replacing its most common means of committing
suicide—coal stove gas—with less toxic natural gas. Fifteen years after the
switch, studies found that suicide rates had dropped and remained low, even
though the number of suicide *attempts* had increased. "High suicide rates seem
to occur where highly lethal suicidal methods are not only available but also
where they are culturally acceptable," writes Dr. Robert Markush of the
University of Alabama, who has studied the use of handguns in suicide.

Most murders aren't crime-related, but are the result of arguments be-   7
tween friends and among families. In 1985, 59 percent of all murders were
committed by people known to the victim. Only 15 percent were committed
by strangers, and only 18 percent were the result of felonious activity. As the
FBI admits every year in its *Uniform Crime Reports,* "murder is a societal
problem over which law enforcement has little or no control." The FBI doesn't
publish separate statistics on who's killing whom with handguns, but it is
assumed that what is true of all murders is true of handgun murders.

Controlling the Vector

Recognizing that eliminating a disease requires prevention, not treatment,   8
health professionals have been in the forefront of those calling for a national
ban on handguns. In 1981, the Surgeon General's Select Panel for the Promotion of Child Health traced the "epidemic of deaths and injuries among
children and youth" to handguns, and called for "nothing short of a total
ban." It is estimated that on average, one child dies from handgun wounds
each day. Between 1961 and 1981, according to the American Association of
Suicidology, the suicide rate for 15- to 24-year-olds increased 150 percent.
The report linked the rise in murders and suicides among the young to the
increased use of firearms—primarily handguns. In a 1985 report, the Surgeon
General's Workshop on Violence and Public Health recommended "a complete

and universal ban on the sale, manufacture, importation, and possession of handguns (except for authorized police and military personnel)."

Not surprisingly, the American Public Health Association, the American Association of Suicidology, and the American Psychiatric Association, are three of the 31 national organizations that are members of National Coalition to Ban Handguns (NCBH).

Comparing the relationship between handguns and violence to mosquitos and malaria, Stephen P. Teret, co-director of the Johns Hopkins Injury Prevention Center, says, "As public health professionals, if we are faced with a disease that is carried by some type of vehicle/vector like a mosquito, our initial response would be to control the vector. There's no reason why if the vehicle/vector is a handgun, we should not be interested in controlling the handgun."

The NRA refers to handgun suicides, accidental killings, and murders by acquaintances as "the price of freedom." It believes that handguns right enough wrongs, stop enough crimes, and kill enough criminals to justify these deaths. But even the NRA has admitted that there is no "adequate measure that more lives are saved by arms in good hands than are lost by arms in evil hands." Again, the NRA is right.

A 1985 NCBH study found that a handgun is 118 times more likely to be used in a suicide, murder, or fatal accident than to kill a criminal. Between 1981 and 1983, nearly 69,000 Americans lost their lives to handguns. During that same period there were only 583 justifiable homicides reported to the FBI, in which someone used a handgun to kill a stranger—a burglar, rapist, or other criminal. In 1982, 19 states reported to the FBI that not once did a private citizen use a handgun to kill a criminal. Five states reported that more than 130 citizens were murdered with handguns for each time a handgun was justifiably used to kill a criminal. In no state did the number of self-defense homicides approach the murder toll. Last year, a study published in the *New England Journal of Medicine* analyzing gun use in the home over a six-year period in the Seattle, Washington area, found that for every time a firearm was used to kill an intruder in self-defense, 198 lives ended in murders, suicides, or accidents. Handguns were used in more than 70 percent of those deaths.

Although handguns are rarely used to kill criminals, an obvious question remains: How often are they used merely to wound or scare away intruders? No reliable statistics are available, but most police officials agree that in a criminal confrontation on the street, the handgun-toting civilian is far more likely to be killed or lose his handgun to a criminal than successfully use the weapon in self-defense. "Beyond any doubt, thousands more lives are lost every year because of the proliferation of handguns than are saved," says Joseph McNamara, chief of police of San Jose, who has also been police chief in Kansas City, a beat cop in Harlem, and is the author of a book on defense against violent crime. Moreover, most burglaries occur when homes are vacant, so the handgun in the drawer is no deterrent. (It would also probably be the first item stolen.)

Faced with facts like these, anti-control advocates often turn to the argument of last resort: the Second Amendment. But the historic, 1981 Morton Grove, Illinois, ban on handgun sale and possession exploded that rationale. In 1983, the U.S. Supreme Court let stand a lower court ruling that stated, "Because the possession of handguns is not part of the right to keep and bear arms, [the Morton Grove ordinance] does not violate the Second Amendment."   14

Criminal Equivocation

Unfortunately, powerful as the NRA is, it has received additional help from the leading handgun control group. Handgun Control Inc. (HCI) has helped the handgun lobby by setting up the perfect strawman for the NRA to shoot down. "Keep handguns out of the wrong hands," HCI says. "By making it more difficult for criminals, drug addicts, etc., to get handguns, we can reduce handgun violence," it promises. Like those in the NRA, HCI chairman Nelson T. "Pete" Shields "firmly believe(s) in the right of law-abiding citizens to possess handguns . . . for legitimate purposes."   15

In its attempt to paint handgun violence solely as a crime issue, HCI goes so far as to sometimes ignore the weapon's non-crime death tally. In its most recent poster comparing the handgun murder toll in the U.S. with that of nations with strict handgun laws, HCI states: "In 1983, handguns killed 35 people in Japan, 8 in Great Britain, 27 in Switzerland, 6 in Canada, 7 in Sweden, 10 in Australia, and 9,014 in the United States." Handguns *killed* a lot more than that in the United States. About 13,000 suicides and accidents more.   16

HCI endorses a ban only on short-barrelled handguns (the preferred weapon of criminals). It advocates mandatory safety training, a waiting period during which a background check can be run on a purchaser, and a license to carry a handgun, with mandatory sentencing for violators. It also endorses mandatory sentencing for the use of a handgun in a crime. According to HCI communications director Barbara Lautman, together these measures would "attack pretty much the heart of the problem."   17

HCI appears to have arrived at its crime focus by taking polls. In his 1981 book, *Guns Don't Die—People Do,* Shields points out that the majority of American's don't favor a ban on handguns. "What they do want, however, is a set of strict laws to control the easy access to handguns by the criminal and the violence prone—*as long as those controls don't jeopardize the perceived right of law-abiding citizens to buy and own handguns for self defense* [italics his]." Shields admits "this is not based on any naive hope that criminals will obey such laws. Rather, it is based on the willingness of the rest of us to be responsible and accountable citizens, and the knowledge that to the degree we are, we make it more difficult for the criminal to get a handgun." This wasn't always HCI's stand. Founded in 1974 as the National Council to Control Handguns, HCI originally called a ban on private handgun possession the "most effective" solution to reducing violent crime rapidly and was at one   18 time a member of HCBH. Michael Beard, president of NCBH, maintains the HCI's focus on crime "started with a public relations concern. Some people in the movement felt Americans were worried about crime, and that was one way to approach the problem. That's the problem when you use public opinion polls to tell you what your position's going to be. And I think a lot of the handgun control movement has looked at whatever's hot at the time and tried to latch onto that, rather than sticking to the basic message that there is a relationship between the availability of handguns and the handgun violence in our society. . . . Ultimately, nothing short of taking the product off the market is really going to have an effect on the problem."

HCI's cops and robbers emphasis has been endlessly frustrating to many in the anti-handgun movement. HCI would offer handgun control as a solution to crime, and the NRA would effectively rebut their arguments with the commonsensical observation that criminals are not likely to obey such laws. I can't help but think that HCI's refusal to abandon the crime argument has harmed the longterm progress of the movement.

Saturated Dresser Drawers

In a nation with 40 million handguns—where anyone who wants one can get one—it's time to face a chilling fact. We're way past the point where registration, licensing, safety training, waiting periods, or mandatory sentencing are going to have much effect. Each of these measures may save some lives or help catch a few criminals, but none—by itself or taken together—will stop the vast majority of handgun suicides or murders. A "controlled" handgun kills just as effectively as an "uncontrolled" one.

Most control recommendations merely perpetuate the myth that with proper care a handgun can be as safe as any other. Nothing could be further from the truth. A handgun is not a blender.

Those advocating a step-by-step process insist that a ban would be too radical and therefore unacceptable to Congress and the public. A hardcore 40 percent of the American public has always endorsed banning handguns. Many will also undoubtedly argue that any control measure—no matter how ill-conceived or ineffective—would be a good first step. But after more than a decade, the other foot hasn't followed.

In other areas of firearms control there has been increasing recognition that bans are the most effective solution. The only two federal measures passed since the Gun Control Act of 1968 have been bans. In each case, the reasoning was simple: the harm done by these objects outweighed any possible benefit they brought to society. In 1986, Congress banned certain types of armor-piercing "cop-killer" bullets. There was also a silver lining to last year's NRA-McClure-Volkmer handgun "decontrol" bill, which weakened the already lax Gun Control Act of 1968, making it legal, for instance, for people to transport unloaded "not readily accessible" handguns interstate. A last-minute amendment added by pro-control forces banned the future production and sale of machine guns for civilian use.

Unfortunately, no law has addressed the major public health problem.   24
Few suicides, accidental killings, or acquaintance murders are the result of
cop-killer bullets or machine guns.

Outlawing handguns would in no way be a panacea. Even if handgun   25
production stopped tomorrow, millions would remain in the dresser drawers
of America's bedrooms—and many of them would probably stay there.
Contrary to NRA fantasies, black-booted fascists would not be kicking down
doors searching for handguns. Moreover, the absolute last segment of society
to be affected by any measure would be criminals. The black market that has
fed off the legal sale of handguns would continue for a long while. But by
ending new handgun production, the availability of illegal handguns can only
decrease.

Of course, someone who truly wants to kill himself can find another   26
way. A handgun ban would not affect millions of rifles and shotguns. But
experience shows that no weapon provides the combination of lethality and
convenience that a handgun does. Handguns represent only 30 percent of all
guns out there but are responsible for 90 percent of firearms misuse. Most
people who commit suicide with a firearm use a handgun. At minimum, a
handgun ban would prevent the escalation of killings in segments of society
that have not yet been saturated by handgun manufacturers. Further increases
in suicides among women, for instance, might be curtailed.

But the final solution lies in changing the way handguns and handgun   27
violence are viewed by society. Public health campaigns have changed the
way Americans look at cigarette smoking and drunk driving and can do the
same for handguns.

For the past 12 years, many in the handgun control movement have   28
confined their debate to what the public supposedly wants and expects to
hear—not to reality. The handgun must be seen for what it is, not what we'd
like it to be.

QUESTIONS FOR MEANING

1. Why does Sugarmann believe that banning handguns would reduce the
   number of deaths that occur each year in the United States?
2. What causes of handgun violence are identified by Sugarmann?
3. What does Sugarmann mean by "strawman" in paragraph 15?
4. How does Sugarmann's position differ from the policy of Handgun Control Inc.?
5. Why is it that men kill themselves more often than women do even though
   women attempt suicide more frequently?
6. Vocabulary: tenet (1), prevalent (3), predatory (3), nannies (6), rationale
   (14), fascists (25), curtailed (26).

QUESTIONS ABOUT STRATEGY

1. Consider the title of this essay. Why do you think Sugarmann chose it?
2. Does Sugarmann make any concessions to opponents of gun control?

3. Why does Sugarmann link gun control with public health campaigns?
4. Sugarmann devotes five paragraphs to attacking an organization that is working to control handguns, an organization with which he might have forged an alliance. Was this wise? Did he have any choice?

ONE STUDENT'S ASSIGNMENT

Read all the essays on gun control in The Informed Argument *and draw them together by determining what are the major arguments for and against control. Try to show how the arguments of different writers relate to one another by making comparisons whenever possible. Limit your essay to between 750 and 1,000 words. Use MLA style parenthetical documentation.*

A Synthesis of Arguments on Gun Control
Andrea Johnson

Although the debate over gun control has recently   1
broadened to include regulating the AK–47 and other assault weapons (Buckley 186; Brady 188), most discussion
focuses upon whether or not it makes sense to restrict
the ownership of handguns.

Advocates of handgun control emphasize that hand-   2
guns are too easy to obtain and too easy to abuse. In
1976, Jeanne Shields estimated that there would be more
than 100 million handguns in the United States by the
year 2000, and she claimed, "We are all in a lottery,
where the likelihood of your facing handgun violence
grows every day" (173). More recently, Sarah Brady has
pointed out that nearly a quarter million Americans died
in the 1980s as the result of handguns (188). She argues
that "we must require a national waiting period before
the purchase of a handgun, to allow for a criminal-
records check" (189). But Josh Sugarmann believes that
Handgun Control Inc.––the organization that Mrs. Brady
now heads––is mistaken to believe that such regulations
as a mandatory waiting period would have any real impact
upon the rate of handgun violence. He calls for an outright ban upon handguns.

Sugarmann argues for a ban by claiming that handgun   3
violence is "a public health threat" rather than a crime
issue (204). He points out that most handgun deaths are
the result of suicides, accidents, and murders that are

not crime-related. If this is the case, then regulations designed solely to keep criminals from buying guns are not likely to accomplish much. Although Sugarmann and Brady differ in the solutions they propose, they agree that accidental deaths are a serious problem. According to Brady, "Every day a child in this country loses his or her life to a handgun. Hundreds more are permanently injured because a careless adult left within easy reach a loaded handgun purchased for self-defense" (188).

By emphasizing the number of handgun deaths that are not crime-related, advocates of gun control circumvent one of the major arguments made by opponents of gun control. Don B. Kates cites a 1975 study at the University of Wisconsin that concluded "gun-control laws have no individual or collective effect in reducing the rate of violent crime" (193). This may be because criminals are prepared to break the law. As Joe Foss points out, "Criminals do not submit to background checks. They are not concerned about registration. Criminals operate outside the law" (177). Both Kates and Foss also argue that owning a handgun can provide protection from crime.

Opponents of gun control also argue that restrictions upon the ownership of guns discriminate against the people who may need them most. Foss claims that rich and influential people can usually find a way to protect themselves, but that eliminating the sale of "Saturday Night Specials" would keep guns from "our nation's elderly and poor" (174). Kates points out that guns are often needed for self-defense by underprivileged people living in neighborhoods "where the police have given up on crime control" (196). William Tonso agrees with Kates and emphasizes that gun control laws are often "racist and elitist" (199).

Another argument against gun control is that the Second Amendment of the Constitution gives Americans the right to "keep and bear Arms." This argument is emphasized by Roger Koopman, but it is also made by Joe Foss. Both Koopman and Foss argue that gun control is undemocratic, and they imply that it could lead to the end of many freedoms traditionally cherished by Americans—an argument suggested by Kates when he warns against "the vast accretion of enforcement powers to the police at

the expense of individual liberty" (196). The ultimate
fear is that gun control could lead to a police state
like Nazi Germany because a repressive government has
disarmed its citizens (Tonso 202).

    Of all the arguments for or against gun control,   7
the constitutional question may be the most complex.
Koopman claims, "The Constitution states that government
has no authority over the firearms ownership of the people" (179). But Robert J. Spitzer points to a series of
cases in which the courts have recognized the legality
of various gun control laws. The most important of these
is U.S. v. Miller, a case the Supreme Court heard in
1939. On the other hand, William F. Buckley offers evidence to suggest that the decision in this case raises a
number of unresolved questions. Both Spitzer and Sugarmann also point to a law passed in 1981, banning handguns in Morton Grove, Illinois. This ordinance was
upheld in federal court, and the Supreme Court allowed
that decision to stand in 1983. Given the importance
that opponents of gun control attach to the Second
Amendment, the courts will probably need to consider additional cases that involve it.

    As for other guns, advocates of gun control are not   8
calling for new restrictions on the sale of rifles or
shotguns (Sugarmann 209) but they do want to stop the
sale of semiautomatic assault weapons to private citizens (Brady 189). William F. Buckley seems to favor restrictions on assault weapons even though he does not
endorse any type of handgun control. But opponents of
gun control like Joe Foss and Roger Koopman seem unwilling to accept any restrictions upon the sale and ownership of guns. Since there is no clear consensus among
either advocates or opponents of gun control, the debate
over this issue seems likely to continue for some time.

SUGGESTIONS FOR WRITING

1. Shields, Buckley, and Brady all draw upon personal experience in their
   arguments. If you have ever used a gun, or lived in a house where a gun
   was present, write an argument on gun control that begins with an account of your own experience.
2. What is your own opinion of gun control? Were you influenced by your
   reading in this unit? Summarize at least two of the arguments you have

read, and use these summaries as the foundation for a short essay of your own. Be sure to summarize the argument of at least one writer with whom you disagree, and then explain why you were not convinced by this argument.

3. Regardless of your own opinion on gun control, which essay in this unit is the most persuasive? Write an essay in defense of this writer, evaluating the techniques he or she used.

4. Write an essay explaining why advocates of gun control are especially concerned about handguns.

5. Drawing upon the arguments by Roger Koopman and Robert J. Spitzer, define the meaning of the Second Amendment.

6. Write an argument for or against restricting private ownership of semi-automatic assault weapons.

7. Both Joe Foss and Sarah Brady claim that public opinion is on their side. Who is right? Research to discover the results of at least two different polls and summarize their findings.

8. Do a research paper comparing the rate of violent crime in two states with significantly different gun laws.

9. Don Kates argues that "liberals" should oppose gun control. Respond with an argument designed to show why "conservatives" should favor it.

10. Both Kates and Tonso charge that gun control is racist. Do you agree? Write an essay in support of the position you take on this aspect of the controversy over gun control.

GLOBAL WARMING: IS IT REALLY A PROBLEM?

♦

MICHAEL E. MURPHY

What the Greenhouse Effect Portends

*"The Greenhouse Effect" is a phrase commonly used to describe why the earth may be growing warmer. According to this theory, increasing levels of carbon dioxide and other gases in the atmosphere are making the world warmer because they retain heat, something that a greenhouse is designed to achieve. But what might be desirable in a greenhouse could be disastrous elsewhere. The following selection outlines the projected consequences of global warming; it is excerpted from a slightly longer essay first published in **1989** by* America. *A judicial staff attorney for the California Court of Appeals, Michael E. Murphy holds a Ph.D. in geography.*

As winter approaches, bringing relief from seasonal fears of drought, the daunting questions of our degradation of the earth's atmosphere remain far from public consciousness. The onset of the 1988 drought coincided with the publication of the United Nations Bellagio Report on the "greenhouse effect," which, if not answering all questions, provided an authoritative statement of present knowledge. The report stirred only small ripples of interest in the sweltering July of 1988. Drought in the summer of 1989 was avoided in some parts of the United States that had a very wet May. Yet before cooler weather helps us forget what was in other areas a hot, dry summer, we may do well to consider the report's implication for the world our children will inherit—and for the future of our consumerist culture.

Among scientists studying the global warming trend, a sense of urgency has been building in the past decade. Three years ago a conference in Villach, Austria—jointly sponsored by the World Meteorological Organization, the United Nations Environment Program and the International Council of Scientific Unions—laid the groundwork for international cooperation through a series of broadly sponsored workshops. Last year a group of world authorities on the greenhouse effect met in Bellagio, Italy, to address the public-policy implications of scientific research. The Bellagio Report, published jointly by the World Meteorological Organization and the United

Nations Environment Program, is the product of their efforts. It represents an attempt of a representative group of acknowledged experts to survey, as a guide for action, the present state of scientific research on the global warming trend.

The report seeks to answer the layman's questions: What is the worst— 3 and the best—that may be expected? And what is most likely? The conclusions reveal that, whatever may be the uncertainties, the reality of the greenhouse effect is no longer doubted. The diagnosis of the problem, however, has shifted. Earlier concern focused on the buildup of carbon dioxide in the atmosphere due chiefly to the burning of fossil fuels. By retaining heat that would otherwise be radiated out into space, the increased level of carbon dioxide can significantly increase the temperature of the atmosphere. But recent studies have revealed that other trace gases with a remarkable capacity to retain heat—particularly methane, nitrous oxide and chlorofluorocarbons—may in combination have an effect roughly equal to that of dioxide. In the scientific literature, concern is now directed to this complex of carbon dioxide and other gases, generally described as "greenhouse gases."

The uncertainties stem in part from differing predictions of the amount 4 of greenhouse gases that society will continue to pump into the atmosphere. But there is also a range of opinion among scientists as to the sensitivity of the climate of these gases. A layman might be content to test the scientific waters to discern the prevailing current of opinion. The authors of the Bellagio Report, however, were reluctant to declare a consensus because they know that dissenting views have often been proven correct. The report considers three assumptions: a high climatic response to greenhouse gases suggested by "a few" studies, a moderate response predicted by "many" studies and a low climatic sensitivity indicated by "a few" studies. Similarly, it considers three possible trends in future emissions: An acceleration of present trends as the greenhouse effect gains a self-perpetuating momentum, a reduction in half of emissions by the year 2075 through a concerted global effort, and the continuation of present emission trends with a reduction only of chlorofluorocarbon emissions under the recent international protocol on the ozone layer.

The worst-case scenario is simply a vision of a climatic apocalypse. 5 Assuming an acclerated rate of emissions and a high climatic sensitivity, this predicts global warming at a rate of .8 degrees centigrade per decade in the next century, a rate that soon would push most forms of life on earth to the edge of survival. But the best-case scenario is also a cause for concern. It unites two optimistic assumptions that are unlikely to exist in unison—a low level of climatic sensitivity and a concerted world response to the problem. Under these implausibly benign circumstances, the global temperature would still increase at a rate of .06 degrees centigrade per decade, a rate somewhat faster than that experienced in the past century.

The most likely outlook, the scientists believe, is for a global warming 6 at a rate of .3 degrees centigrade per decade in the next century. This estimate, which assumes a moderate climate response and the continuation of present trends (other than for chlorofluorocarbons), would result in a total warming of 3 degrees centigrade or about 5.4 degrees Fahrenheit. In the scientists' professional judgment, there is a 50-percent chance that actual temperatures will vary above or below this level. A little reflection will show that a global warming of this magnitude is enough to represent one of the most important challenges facing humanity in the 21st century:

—For much of the temperate latitudes, it would spell more frequent drought. Higher summer temperatures would deplete soil moisture more rapidly, and changing patterns of summer rainfall might bring longer periods of dry weather.

—Unmanaged ecosystems, especially forests, would suffer most. In areas like Yellowstone Park and the Yosemite Valley near the edge of climatic zones, plant communities would sicken as climax species die faster than new species could establish themselves.

—In the semi-arid tropics, the current process of desertification would accelerate, forcing the migration of human populations.

—In the humid tropics, a region that is already often too hot and too wet, both temperatures and rainfall would increase. Increased temperatures would speed the process of evaporation that would lead to further rainfall through local convection currents.

—Throughout the world, sea level would increase almost three feet as a result of thermal expansion and melting of polar ice caps, flooding heavily populated delta regions and decimating salt-water marshes.

To bring the matter closer to home, July weather in New York City will be as hot as Miami is now, and St. Louis will be as hot as New Orleans. In California, summer water supplies will be cut by more than half, largely as a result of a smaller Sierra snowpack.   7

The report says that "the climate will continue to change, and the changes will persist indefinitely into the future." This guarded language recognizes that greenhouse gases may continue to accumulate in the atmosphere even if emissions are sharply reduced. Once again, the matter is hedged with uncertainty. If the world's forests could be restored by an ambitious reforestation program, they would absorb part of the carbon dioxide now being released into the atmosphere. The capacity of the oceans to absorb carbon dioxide also is a large and poorly understood variable. But weighing against any optimistic expectations is the possibility that the greenhouse effect could itself put in motion forces that would generate further change.   8

Consider the polar regions where tundra vegetation subsisting on permafrost soil is covered by snow for most of the year. The snow, being white, tends to reflect heat. If the snow cover is reduced by a climatic warming, the ground will assume a darker hue that absorbs much more solar energy. Partly as a consequence, the winter temperatures of the polar regions are expected to warm at a rate more than twice that of equatorial regions. At some point in the 21st century, this rapid warming could cause a general decline in tundra vegetation. Laboratory studies show that, as the vegetation decays, the peaty tundra ecosystem will release vast amounts of methane   9 causing further warming. One could sketch similar scenarios involving, for example, the retreat of arctic-pack ice or the death of temperate forests in the face of a warming trend. As it progresses, the greenhouse effect is likely to have some unpleasant surprises in store.

But will the public become aroused unless it can be told that the green-   10
house effect is occurring now? The matter has a complexity that resists simple answers. Over the past century average global temperatures appear to have risen .5 degrees centigrade. The four warmest years in this time were all in the 1980's; 1988 was one of the hottest on record. These statistics are consistent with predictions of the greenhouse effect based on laboratory tests and mathematical models. But proof is more difficult to obtain. To be sure of the matter, scientists must devise ways of distinguishing a greenhouse warming from a natural trend and gather adequate statistics for a meaningful analysis.

Three recent studies of temperatures in the upper stratosphere, how-   11
ever, have reported findings ominous enough to send a shiver of dismay through a father concerned about the world his children will inherit. By trapping heat in the lower atmosphere, the greenhouse effect should tend to cool temperatures in the upper atmosphere. Separate studies by Karen Labitzke of the Free University of Berlin, David Karoly of Monash University in Australia, and Mark Schoeberl of the Goddard Space Flight Center in Maryland have revealed a statistically significant cooling trend in the stratosphere. Though other explanations are possible, the cooling tends to confirm that the greenhouse has arrived.

The portentous significance of these findings lies partly in the knowl-   12
edge that ocean temperatures will delay—but not prevent—a warming trend. The surface of the ocean, which exerts a pervasive influence on weather, has a vast capacity to absorb heat. It will take decades for heat retained by the atmosphere to warm the ocean itself, creating a new thermal equilibrium between water and air. The consequence is that a warming effect that is only obscurely apparent today will be felt with full rigor a generation later when ocean temperatures have risen. My three grade-school children, who ask me what I mean by the greenhouse effect, may know from firsthand experience when they have children the same age.

A sense of urgency arises also from the long lead time needed to take   13
preventive action. In the past 70 years we have formed a way of life based on the profligate use of fossil fuels. It might take just as long, even if the popular will existed, to create a society relegating these fuels to minor uses. The climatic warming will, moreover, require the construction of new freshwater supply systems and coastal defenses, such as sea walls, dikes and drainage systems. The Public Works Department of the Netherlands estimates that investments in the order of several billion dollars will be needed to manage a one-meter increase in sea level. Such major public-works projects may have a planning and construction time of 20 to 40 years.

As the Bellagio Report indicates, there is much less controversy among   14
scientists about the greenhouse effect than might be gathered from stories in

the media. Testifying last June before the Senate Energy and Natural Resources Committee, NASA scientist James E. Hansen declared, "It is time to stop waffling so much and say that the evidence is pretty strong that the greenhouse effect is here now." But this view displays sophistication often lost on the press. An article on the summer drought in *The Christian Science Monitor* proclaimed, "It's too early to blame the changes on global warming." Though not necessarily wrong, the statement is misleading. The drought may have been caused by weather anomalies unrelated to the greenhouse effect, but it did highlight the global warming trend of the 1980's that very probably does reflect, in whole or in part, the greenhouse effect. As Syukuro Manabe of the National Oceanic and Atmospheric Administration observed, the hot summer days gave us a foretaste of things to come.

As we wait for greater certainty, opportunities to avert the greenhouse   15
are slipping away. But the problem seems to have been devised by a perverse fate to frustrate the mobilization of public concern. Even if the greenhouse effect is fully operative, any President would face great political risks in advocating a national policy responding to the challenge. The benefits of taking action now would not be felt within his term of office, or even his successor's term, but they would affect his grandchildren's generation. He could not be sure that a hot year would not be succeeded by several relatively cool and humid years. Political opponents would stress scientific uncertainties and call for further studies—a time-tested tactic for paralyzing action. And while no one doubts the reality of the problem, future studies could tend either to discount or to underscore its gravity.

Sensitive to the values of our times, the Bellagio Report assumes that   16
the greenhouse effect must be controlled within the context of continued economic growth. There are indeed some relatively painless (and partial) solutions. Chlorofluorocarbons, which account for about 25 percent of the greenhouse effect, can be eliminated through the use of substitutes. The technology exists for dramatic advances in energy efficiency, sometimes with net economic savings. West Germany today enjoys a standard of living comparable to that of the United States with half the energy consumption per capita. These steps to avert the greenhouse effect can be justified on other grounds. An end to chlorofluorocarbon use is demanded for protection of the ozone layer. And as we all know, lower energy bills would relieve the balance-of-payments deficit.

But easy solutions will carry us only so far. At some point, our efforts   17
to cut emissions are likely to encounter high costs or challenge cherished habits, such as our love of, and dependence upon, the automobile. An effective end to the problem will also require a degree of international cooperation that is hard to envisage. China plans a fivefold increase in coal-powered electric generating plants in the next 25 years. In the third world, the problem is peculiarly intractable because of poverty as well as politics. Where governments lack the resources for such elementary measures as sewage systems, it will not be easy to launch a concerted effort to cut greenhouse gas emissions. . . .

It does not matter how sensitive the world climate really is to green-   18
house gases. The writing is still on the wall. Laboratory tests, mathematical
models and weather statistics all tell us that the greenhouse effect is real and
will intensify. Even if global warming could be kept at a low rate of, say, .1
degree centigrade per decade, it will still have to end sometime. Sooner or
later, probably early in the next century but in any event in the near future
of the race, the buildup of greenhouse gases on the atmosphere will have to
end if humanity is to have a future. This will entail radical changes in our
materialistic civilization. By delay, we help assure that global warming will
be added to destruction of the rain forest, desertification of arid lands, depletion of topsoil, acidification of soil and extinction of species as one of the
most enduring legacies of our civilization to future generations.

QUESTIONS FOR MEANING

1. What was the purpose of the Bellagio Report, referred to in paragraphs
   1–4?
2. According to Murphy, how has the scientific perception of the greenhouse effect changed in recent years?
3. How does Murphy explain the uncertainties found in discussion of the
   greenhouse effect?
4. In the next century, what are the likely effects of even moderate global
   warming according to this essay?
5. Why does Murphy believe that we need to take action now even though
   the worst effects of global warming may not be apparent for many years?
6. Does Murphy make any specific recommendations that could help reduce
   the problem of global warming?
7. Vocabulary: discern (4), apocalypse (5), benign (5), temperate (6), portentous (12), relegating (13), anomalies (14), perverse (15), intractable (17).

QUESTIONS ABOUT STRATEGY

1. Writers of argument frequently try to link their concerns to the future of
   children. Murphy does so in paragraphs 1, 11, and 12. Is he exploiting an
   outworn convention, or are references to children appropriate when discussing global warming?
2. Murphy devotes much of his first four paragraphs to providing background information on the Bellagio report. Why do you think he did so?
   Is this strategy effective?
3. Does Murphy concede that there are any political difficulties that would
   need to be overcome somehow by men and women concerned about global
   warming?
4. Much of the debate over global warming involves speculation. How effectively does Murphy deal with the uncertain nature of his data?

CURTIS A. MOORE

Does Your Cup of Coffee Cause Forest Fires?

*How does global warming relate to other environmental concerns? And to what extent can it be caused by a variety of daily acts that might be taken for granted? These are among the questions addressed by Curtis A. Moore in the following article, first published in **1989** by International Wildlife. Moore served for eleven years as counsel to the U.S. Senate Committee on Environment and Public Works, and the article reprinted here is drawn from his research for a forthcoming book on threats to the environment.*

For years scientists have warned that the simplest of humanity's acts could have profound consequences. They were right: 1

- In April, 1980, an office worker in Schenectady, New York, sips a cup of steaming coffee served conveniently in a Styrofoam cup. In 1988 wildfires rage through Yellowstone National Park, the worst in two centuries.   2

- A peasant farmer in Brazil slashes two acres of tropical forest then sets it ablaze to make space for his crops. Two summers later, Hurricane Gilbert lumbers through the Caribbean, its 200-mile-per-hour winds leaving $7 billion in damages.   3

- A commuter in smog-choked Atlanta maneuvers his out-of-tune Chevrolet through backed-up rush hour traffic. Three years later, trees die on a North Carolina mountaintop.   4

- A retired factory worker in Dusseldorf, West Germany, flips on an electric reading light. Ten years later, millions are left homeless as monsoons flood Bangladesh.   5

Are such seemingly improbable cause-and-effect relationships really at work?   6

Increasingly, leading scientists are warning that they are. What's more, they speculate that even worse disasters may lie in wait for an unsuspecting humanity because of newly discovered interactions, or linkages, among pollutants.   7

"The problem is that so many things are changing at once," says Irving Mintzer of the Washington-based World Resources Institute. "The concentrations of trace gases are increasing while the global temperature is rising and the ozone layer is thinning. It's like playing football when the size of the field, the shape of the ball, the number of players, and the method of scoring change with every play."   8

Knowing that the Earth has gotten hotter, the ozone layer thinner and   9
ground-level pollution thicker, a panel of scientists convened by the U.S.
National Academy of Sciences two years ago warned against major unfore-
seen consequences. "We are pushing our climate and environment—the surroundings in which we live, work and play—into a region literally
unexperienced during the history of *Homo sapiens*," it cautioned.

Unusual climatic effects in 1988 seemed to confirm their predictions: 10

- Droughts and crop failures—the worst since Dust Bowl conditions of   11
  the 1930s—gripped not only the United States and Canada, but many
  other areas as well, including China and the Soviet Union.
- Forest fires in 1987 and 1988 in the United States left nearly 10 mil-   12
  lion acres blackened, the highest toll since the U.S. Forest Service
  began keeping records. At summer's end, standing timber in many
  areas contained less moisture than kiln-dried lumber.
- Local temperatures also soared. In Washington, D.C., readings ex-   13
  ceeded 90 degrees F on almost two of every three days during June,
  July and August. And it was hot everywhere: Moscow hit the 90s for
  five days running, while New Delhi peaked at 113 and Athens at 108.
- Within two weeks after Hurricane Gilbert slammed into Mexico,   14
  Hurricane Jean battered Nicaragua and Costa Rica, the first such storm
  in recorded history to hit Central America.
- In the Antarctic, an iceberg the size of Rhode Island shattered free.   15

These events of 1988 added to the growing body of circumstantial evi-   16
dence that the Greenhouse Effect—global warming caused by man-made pollution—had finally arrived.

Scientists knew that global average temperatures had already risen one   17
degree Fahrenheit over the last century. Then came the years of 1980, 1981,
1983 and 1987, which were the four hottest since records had been kept.

Such warming, according to scientific projections, is supposed to cause   18
ocean waters to expand, thus raising sea levels. In fact, measurements confirm that the ocean waterline has crept up 4 to 6 inches in the last century.

Other computer models predict that deep and mid-ocean temperatures   19
should begin to rise, and, sure enough, the only study done to date found an
apparent increase in the North Atlantic temperature of .2 to .3 degrees Celsius since 1958.

Finally, warming close to the Earth's surface is supposed to siphon heat   20
away from the stratosphere, 25 miles up, lowering temperatures there. Measurements confirm that this has happened, with a 2- to 3-degree C drop in
the last decade.

Evidence like this does not provide absolute scientific proof that an era   21
of global warming has indeed begun. In fact, scientists such as Alan Hecht,
director of the U.S. Government's National Climate Program, say it is highly

debatable. Nevertheless, an increasing number of individual researchers are concluding that global warming is exactly what is happening. According to climatologist James Hansen of the Goddard Space Institute, for instance, the chances are 99 percent that the hot years of the 1980s signaled the arrival of the Greenhouse Effect.

Even among scientists who consider Hansen's conclusion premature, virtually all agree that global warming will come sooner or later. Whatever the timing, such experts say, the environmental catastrophes of the last few years are consistent with projections for a hotter planet.

It is the interactions among pollutants which have the scientists most worried, however. Global warming, stratospheric ozone depletion, smog and acid rain, they fear, can become a witches' brew of troubles that feed off each other to produce other, even worse, disasters. Humanity, says Walter Broecker of Columbia University, is playing "Russian roulette."

These individual phenomena have been studied for years, some for a century or more. Each is disturbing in its own right.

The Greenhouse Effect

This is the name given to scientific predictions that air pollutants and other gases will raise Earth's temperature, perhaps by an average of nearly 10 degrees Fahrenheit. This pollution—37,000 pounds a year for every man, woman and child in the United States, according to figures compiled by the World Resources Institute—traps heat much like panes of glass in a hothouse.

Pollutants that cause warming include excess carbon dioxide (released when coal, oil, gas or even wood are burned), nitrous oxide (from smokestacks and auto tailpipes), methane (probably from rice paddies and livestock), and chlorofluorocarbons, or CFCs (from spray cans, foams and refrigerants).

Although motor vehicles and power plants account for nearly 75 percent of the carbon dioxide pollution from industrialized nations, tropical deforestation is also a major contributor. Burning one acre of primary forest as part of slash-and-burn agriculture systems in nations such as Brazil spews 400,000 pounds of carbon dioxide into the air. Moreover, when trees—which remove carbon dioxide from the air—are no longer alive, the buildup of Greenhouse gases accelerates.

Stratospheric Ozone Depletion

CFCs (better known as Freons, the name given them by their inventor, the DuPont Corporation) pose a dual threat. In the lower atmosphere CFCs trap heat, but higher aloft, these compounds destroy the ozone shield, a thin layer of gas which is all that stands between life on Earth and ultraviolet radiation so searing that it will explode unprotected cells on contact.

CFCs are put to hundreds of uses because they are relatively nontoxic, nonflammable and do not decompose near ground level. Refrigerators, air conditioners, spray-can propellants, foam cushions, insulation and containers such as cups and egg cartons are all manufactured using these Freon chemicals.

Because they are so stable, CFCs will last for up to 150 years. The CFC   30
gases rise slowly to about 25 miles where the tremendous force of the sun's
ultraviolet radiation shatters the CFC, freezing the chemical element chlorine. Once freed, a single atom of chlorine destroys about 100,000 molecules
of ozone before settling to the Earth's surface years later. Three percent, and
perhaps up to five percent, of the global ozone layer has already been destroyed by CFCs.

Researchers are particularly shaken by the effects of CFCs in the Antarctic and Arctic. At the South Pole, up to 50 percent of the ozone is destroyed each spring over an area the size of North America. Similar but less   31
severe losses occur over the Arctic as well, with the Soviet Union reporting
declines of up to 20 percent over Moscow and other high-latitude cities.

Scientists now know that at nearly 130 degrees Fahrenheit below zero,   32
temperatures in the stratosphere above Antarctica allow clouds of ice particles
to form. By providing an ice surface on which the CFCs can destroy ozone,
these clouds ignite a runaway reaction, the Freon equivalent of a nuclear
meltdown. The ozone destruction which would otherwise span years is completed within days.

Smog, or Ground-Level Ozone

Smog is formed when two pollutants—oxides of nitrogen and hydrocarbons—react with each other in the presence of sunlight. Hydrocarbons include chemicals ranging from gasoline fumes to industrial solvents. There are   33
hundreds of hydrocarbons, so there are hundreds, perhaps thousands, of
chemical byproducts from the reactions which occur in the air.

Collectively, this soup is known as smog. But most often, it is referred   34
to simply (and incorrectly) as ozone, its dominant and easiest-to-measure
ingredient. An unstable form of oxygen, ground-level ozone is chemically
the same as the gas which stops ultraviolet light 25 miles above the Earth's
surface.

Ozone in smog is an extraordinarily dangerous pollutant. Within seconds of entering the lungs, ozone has destroyed cell walls. After months of   35
exposure, the lungs of animals resemble those of smokers. If a single 14-ounce can could be filled with ozone, it could kill 14,000 people.

Government regulators worry most about ozone in cities because that   36
is where most people are. But the gas is also toxic to plants, and in the last
century levels of rural ozone have doubled. On average, they are now just
fractionally below the point at which plants, especially trees, begin to sicken
and die.

Acid Rain

The coal and oil burned by power plants contain sulfur which is converted   37
by oxidants into the acids which fall throughout much of eastern North

America and Europe. They poison lakes and streams, killing fish and other animal life.

Some scientists, including researchers at Harvard University, have cor-   38
related concentrations of acid pollutants with human illness and mortality, and concluded that the chemicals are responsible for up to 70,000 deaths a year just in the United States. Similar studies in Canada have reached comparable conclusions.

Acid compounds may also be killing the forests of eastern North Amer-   39
ica and Europe, possibly in combination with ozone. Forest declines were first discovered in Europe in the late 1970s, when they were dubbed *Waldsterben*, the German word for forest death. Since then, researchers have found similar, unexplained damage in both Canada and the United States, as well as in most other European nations.

Virtually every tree species in Central Europe has been affected. In North   40
America there are reports of extensive damage of some sort to white and yellow pine, red spruce, Fraser fir, yellow and sugar maple, birch, red maple and a wide variety of other species. Damage is so severe at the peak of North Carolina's Mt. Mitchell that Robert Bruck, a plant pathologist from North Carolina State University, terms it a "disclimax"—a collapse of the entire ecosystem.

In the past, scientists studied these atmospheric effects separately. Now,   41
they are discovering linkages among all four. "Whether or not it is atmospheric deposition in terms of ozone, in terms of acid rain, (or) in terms of global climate change . . . I believe we are looking at one giant phenomenon that is influencing many of our natural ecosystems," Bruck says.

The biggest concern of all is that these atmospheric ills, acting in con-   42
cert, will produce what scientists refer to as "surprises," dramatic and unexpected effects that are far more severe than the sum of the parts.

One way to illustrate these linkages is to examine what happens to a   43
common plastic-foam cup:

Step One: The cup contains one billion billion CFC molecules trapped in   44
tiny bubbles that give it shape and rigidity. Each of these molecules will last for up to 150 years. Neither burning in a trash incinerator nor burial in a landfill destroys the tough and resilient CFCs. Once freed from their plastic bubbles, the gases enter the air.

Step Two: The escaping CFCs begin to trap heat. The global average tem-   45
perature climbs.

Step Three: Arriving at a height of 25 miles after about 15 years, each of   46
the billion billion CFC molecules destroys 100,000 ozone molecules. The stratospheric ozone shield begins thinning, allowing more ultraviolet radiation to reach ground level. Human cancer rates escalate, and plants and animals living in the top microlayer of the ocean begin to die.

Step Four: The solar radiation also begins to sharpen the rate at which   47
lower-level smog is formed. As smog levels rise, forests already stressed by

extreme heat and drought begin to wither. With them, many endangered species disappear.

Meantime, the greater the concentration of ozone, the faster the rate at   48
which acid rain, snow and fog are formed. As ozone levels rise, acid begins falling nearer the pollution sources. This close-range fallout seems to be more toxic, so the rate at which plants and animals are killed also climbs. So does the level of poisonous metals that it releases from the soil.

Step Five: Because the smog and other ground-level pollutants are Green-   49
house gases, the rate at which heat is trapped rises yet another fraction. As it does, Arctic tundra thaws and decays, releasing trillions of pounds of methane, or natural gas, which is itself a Greenhouse gas.

Step Six: Methane begins rising through the air, trapping heat and accel-   50
erating global warming. These yet-higher temperatures cause even more methane to be released, setting up a vicious cycle in which methane leads to greater warming, and warming leads to more methane.

Step Seven: Finally entering the stratosphere, methane reacts to form water.   51
Because surface warming has lowered stratospheric temperatures, the water derived from methane freezes to form ice clouds. These clouds or other fine-particle pollution from power plants provide a solid surface for the ozone depletion reaction, accelerating both the processes of ozone destruction and surface warming.

Step Eight: As the ground level air temperatures rise, they begin heating   52
ocean surface waters. Initially, the hotter waters support a profusion of ocean life. But as nutrients—including the carbon dioxide dissolved in the ocean waters—are exhausted, there is a massive collapse, leading to exhaustion of the dissolved oxygen and still more deaths among marine plants and animals.

Step Nine: Finally, this chain of events culminates in utterly new "re-   53
gimes," as scientists like to call them—cases where the Earth no longer functions as it does today. In one scenario described by Walter Broecker of Columbia University, Europe becomes a frozen wasteland (as it did 12,000 years ago) because the warming Atlantic currents become so hot they break into hundreds of surface eddies.

Is this all science fiction?   54

No, says Ralph Cicerone of the National Center for Atmospheric Re-   55
search in Boulder, Colorado. "The numbers may or may not be right, but the principles are. When you add all this up, you want to dismiss it as baloney. But you can't."

The man who first concluded the CFCs would destroy the ozone layer   56
was F. Sherwood Rowland of the University of California at Irvine. He was also among the first to suggest the crucial role which cold plays in the Antarctic ozone hole and to predict that similar losses would be found over the North Pole as well. Rowland has been described as the man who has always been right.

Reflecting on the many recent atmospheric findings, Rowland recently   57
recalled the day he concluded that chemicals were destroying the ozone shield.
"There was no moment when I yelled 'Eureka,' " he said. "I just came home
one night and told my wife, 'The work is going very well, but it looks like
the end of the world.' "

QUESTIONS FOR MEANING

1. Why is Moore concerned about the interaction of global warming with
   other environmental problems?
2. What are CFCs, and what household products contain them?
3. Why is the ozone layer important? What evidence is there that it is being
   depleted?
4. According to Moore, why should we be concerned about smog—and especially the ozone content of smog?
5. Vocabulary: circumstantial (16), siphon (20), phenomena (24), deforestation (27), correlated (38), resilient (44), eddies (53).

QUESTIONS ABOUT STRATEGY

1. Paragraphs 1–5 suggest that individuals are responsible for global warming, often through daily acts that are usually taken for granted. Does he
   expect us to believe in the cause and effect relationships implied in these
   paragraphs, or is he simply trying to get our attention?
2. How alarming is the evidence in paragraphs 10–15? Overall, does Moore
   present sufficient evidence to justify his concern about the environment?
3. Does Moore admit, at any point, that evidence of global warming is not
   yet conclusive?
4. Consider the conclusion to this essay. Is the last line effective? Has Moore
   given readers any reason to take Rowland seriously?

ENRIQUE H. BUCHER
A Global Response to Climate Change

Writers concerned about global warming most often concentrate upon such projected effects as more frequent droughts caused by higher temperatures, the decline of plant life, and rising sea levels. But what would the health effects include? In particular, what tropical diseases might spread to parts of the world that now enjoy a temperate climate? This is the question addressed by Dr. Enrique Bucher, who works at the Centre for Applied Zoology at the University of Cordoba in Argentina. He wrote "A Global Response to Climate Change" for World Health, *a journal published by the World Health Organization [WHO]. His article was first published by that journal in* **1990**.

Although scientists are still not certain, it is reasonable to suppose that an   1
increase in the proportion of "greenhouse gases" in the atmosphere—carbon dioxide, methane and chlorofluorocarbon—could lead to global warming. What is certain is that there has been a steady increase in carbon dioxide in the atmosphere over the past 40 years or so. The other gases may have increased to an even greater extent. If present trends continue, by the year 2100 there could be a rise in sea levels of between one and three metres and, by the middle of the next century, an increase of between 2.5 and 5.5 degrees Centigrade in the planet's overall temperature, accompanied by a greater frequency of severe storms.

Such climatic changes could affect the epidemiological patterns of the   2
tropical diseases in several ways. Increases in rainfall and temperature, for example, could expand the areas of the world inhabited by malaria-carrying Anopheles mosquitos towards the poles. The disease would thus spread into areas where it has been eradicated. On the other hand, such an effect might be counterbalanced by a "drying-out" and further desertification of tropical regions, depriving large areas of the water conditions necessary for mosquito survival. But on the whole, increasing temperatures could be expected to increase the reproduction rates both of the parasites and their vectors and hence augment transmission of malaria.

Forest Habitat

In the case of leishmaniasis, continued exploitation of tropical forests could   3
lead first to an increase in the proportion of forest forms of the disease, as the parasites take advantage of greater access to potential human victims. As they are generally deprived of their forest habitat, though, the forest species would probably decline, a process hastened by a greater frequency of forest fires and loss of the soil moisture needed for forest regrowth. Urban forms of leishmaniasis, on the other hand, may spread into newly warmed-up areas towards the poles.

Chagas disease, or American trypanosomiasis, is to a large extent iso-   4
lated from the effects of climatic change, since the triatomine bugs that transmit it tend to live in poorly constructed rural houses, a habitat unlikely to be
affected by global warming. But if the global warming and decreased rainfall
lead to an expansion of semi-arid savannas, like the Gran Chaco of Argentina
and Paraguay, these areas might be invaded by peasant farmers culturally
adapted to semi-arid conditions. The result could be a replay of the sad cycle
of overgrazing, forest destruction and poverty typical of such areas elsewhere
in the world.

Poor housing, a concomitant of this scenario, would ensure the spread   5
of the triatomine bugs. As winter temperatures rose, there might also be a
lengthening of the insects' summer reproduction and disease transmission period in temperate areas like Argentina and Chile. As vegetation changed,
bugs with greater potential for transmitting the disease could in certain regions predominate over bugs with less or no disease-transmitting potential.

In Africa, diminished rainfall and subsequent progressive desertification   6
may restrict the areas of vegetation in which the tsetse fly vectors of sleeping
sickness (African typanosomiasis) live. Increased rainfall would have the opposite effect.

Large Scale Migration

The effects of global climatic change on schistosomiasis, a typically water-   7
related disease, would vary depending on local changes in water patterns.
Where these become more irregular, the breeding habits of the water snail—
the intermediate host of the schistosome worms—could be disturbed. On the
other hand, a growing water shortage could lead to large-scale human migrations and an increase in dam building for irrigation, two factors that could
accelerate the spread of the disease into new areas.

Another water-related disease, filariasis, might also be affected by global   8
warming. The blackfly vectors of onchocerciasis (river blindness) and the
mosquito vectors of lymphatic filariasis (elephantiasis) would reproduce more
quickly if there is a rise in the temperature and oxygen-content of water.

Generally speaking, increased temperatures would raise the reproduc-   9
tive rates of disease vectors, adding to vector control difficulties. As a consequence, the shorter generation times for these vectors could favour the
emergence of strains resistant to pesticides.

So what can be done? Unless galloping population growth, fuel burn-   10
ing and deforestation can be halted in time, the available evidence strongly
suggests that we will experience unprecedented changes in our environment.
There is no time to waste. Research will have to be organized on a far more
multi-disciplinary basis to explore the multi-faceted, interconnected web of
changes and their possible effects on tropical health. Planning in anticipation
of these changes will have to extend much further into the future, since short-
term, stop-gap solutions will be quickly overtaken by the rapid pace of events.

One topic of research should investigate how vectors and parasites are   11
likely to respond to changing conditions. Systems should be set up as soon

as possible to monitor changes in vector distribution and the incidence of disease so as to detect trends at their earliest stages. Adaptive strategies will have to be decided through coordinated national and international planning, in which tropical health concerns should be an integral part.

A Global Solution

In short, to deal with such a global problem, we need a global response. As   12 far as health and disease are concerned, who is more suited to organizing such a response than a global body like WHO?

QUESTIONS FOR MEANING

1. According to Bucher, what are some of the insect-transmitted diseases that may spread as a result of global warming?
2. Why is it possible that new strains of insects may emerge in response to global warming? Why might they be resistant to pesticides?
3. Why does Bucher believe that planning to control global warming must be global and long-term?
4. Vocabulary: epidemiological (2), parasites (3), concomitant (5), vectors (9).

QUESTIONS ABOUT STRATEGY

1. Bucher limits his focus to diseases likely to spread in Africa and South America. Is this an appropriate focus for a short article?
2. Does Bucher show any awareness that his audience may include readers who do not share his background in zoology?
3. As his last sentence reveals, Bucher addressed this argument to the World Health Organization [WHO]. By ending with a reference to this organization, has Bucher increased the effectiveness of his argument, or has he simply limited the number of readers who will feel compelled to respond to the problem of global warming?

ROBERT JAMES BIDINOTTO

What Is the Truth about Global Warming?

A staff writer for Reader's Digest, *which published the following article in* **1990**, *Robert James Bidinotto is experienced at writing about cultural and political controversies in terms that can be easily understood by a general audience. In his article on global warming, he offers both a summary of what the greenhouse effect means and an argument against adopting any expensive measures to prevent it until further research confirms that global warming is as threatening as environmentalists believe.*

In the summer of 1988, one of the century's worst heat waves gripped the   1
East Coast and had Midwest farmers wondering if the Dust Bowl had returned. On June 23, at a Senate hearing on global climate change, James Hansen, a respected atmospheric scientist and director of NASA's Goddard Institute for Space Studies, gave alarming testimony. "The earth is warmer in 1988 than at any time in the history of instrumental measurements," he said. "The greenhouse effect is changing our climate now."

Hansen's remarks touched off a firestorm of publicity. A major news   2
magazine speculated that the Great Plains would be depopulated. On NBC's "Today" show, biologist Paul Ehrlich warned that melting polar ice could raise sea levels and inundate coastal cities, swamping much of Florida, Washington, D.C., and the Los Angeles basin. And in his recent book, *Global Warming,* Stephen Schneider of the National Center for Atmospheric Research imagined New York overcome by a killer heat wave, a baseball double-header in Chicago called because of a thick black haze created by huge forest fires in Canada, and Long Island devastated by a hurricane—all spawned by the "greenhouse effect."

In Paris last July, the leaders of seven industrial democracies, including   3
President Bush and British Prime Minister Margaret Thatcher, called for common efforts to limit emissions of carbon dioxide and other "greenhouse gases." To accomplish this, many environmentalists have proposed draconian regulations—and huge new taxes—that could significantly affect the way we live. Warns Environmental Protection Agency head William Reilly: "To slow down the global heating process, the scale of economic and societal intervention will be enormous."

The stakes are high: the public could be asked to decide between envi-   4
ronmental catastrophe and enormous costs. But do we really have to make this choice? Many scientists believe the danger is real, but others are much less certain. What is the evidence? Here is what we know:

What Is the Greenhouse Effect?

When sunlight warms the earth, certain gases in the lower atmosphere, act-   5
ing like the glass in a greenhouse, trap some of the heat as it radiates back

into space. These greenhouse gases, primarily water vapor and including carbon dioxide, methane and man-made chlorofluorocarbons, warm our planet, making life possible.

If they were more abundant, greenhouse gases might trap too much   6
heat. Venus, for example, has 60,000 times more carbon dioxide in its atmosphere than Earth, and its temperature averages above 800 degrees Fahrenheit. But if greenhouse gases were less plentiful or entirely absent, temperatures on Earth would average below freezing.

Because concentrations of greenhouse gases have been steadily rising,   7
many scientists are concerned about global warming. Researchers at the Goddard Institute and at the University of East Anglia in England foresee a doubling of greenhouse gas concentrations during the next century, which might raise average global temperatures as much as nine degrees Fahrenheit.

What Is Causing the Buildup?

Nature accounts for most of the greenhouse gases in the atmosphere. For   8
example, carbon dioxide (CO_2), the most plentiful trace gas, is released by volcanoes, oceans, decaying plants and even by our breathing. But much of the *buildup* is man-made.

CO_2 is given off when we burn wood or such fossil fuels as coal and   9
oil. In fact, the amount in the atmosphere has grown more than 25 percent since the Industrial Revolution began around 200 years ago—over 11 percent since 1958 alone.

Methane, the next most abundant greenhouse gas, is released when or-   10
ganic matter decomposes in swamps, rice paddies, livestock yards—even in the guts of termites and cud-chewing animals. The amount is growing about one percent per year, partly because of increased cattle raising and use of natural gas.

Chlorofluorocarbons (CFCs), a third culprit, escape from refrigerators,   11
air conditioners, plastic foam, solvents and spray cans. The amount in the atmosphere is tiny compared with CO_2, but CFCs are thousands of times more potent in absorbing heat and have also been implicated in the "ozone hole."

What Does the Ozone Hole Have To Do with the Greenhouse Effect?

For all practical purposes, nothing. Ozone, a naturally occurring form of   12
oxygen, is of concern for another reason. In the upper atmosphere it helps shield us from ultraviolet sunlight, which can cause skin cancer. In 1985, scientists confirmed a temporary thinning in the ozone layer over Antarctica, leading to a new concern: if ozone thinning spreads to populated areas, it could cause an increase in the disease.

The ozone hole appears only from September to November, and   13
only over the Antarctic region, and then it repairs itself when atmospheric

conditions change a few weeks later. It also fluctuates; in 1988, there was little ozone thinning.

Ozone is constantly created and destroyed by nature. Volcanoes, for example, can release immense quantities of chlorine, some of which may get into the stratosphere and destroy ozone molecules.   14

But the most popular theory to explain the appearance of the ozone hole is that man-made chlorofluorocarbons release chlorine atoms in the upper atmosphere.   15

Despite thinning of upper atmospheric ozone over Antarctica, no increase in surface ultraviolet radiation outside of that area is expected. John E. Frederick, an atmospheric scientist who chaired a United Nations Environment Program panel on trends in atmospheric ozone, has dismissed fears of a skin-cancer epidemic as science fiction. "You would experience a much greater increase in biologically damaging ultraviolet radiation if you moved from New York City to Atlanta than you would with the ozone depletion that we estimate will occur over the next 30 years," he says.   16

Will Destruction of Forests Worsen the Greenhouse Effect?

When trees and plants grow, they remove CO_2 from the air. When they are burned or decay, they release stored CO_2 back into the atmosphere. In nations such as Brazil, thousands of square miles of tropical rain forests are being cleared and burned, leading many to be concerned about further CO_2 buildup.   17

Worldwide, millions of acres are planted with seedling trees each year, however; and new studies reveal that there has been no reliable data about the impact of forest destruction on global warming. Research by Daniel Botkin and Lloyd Simpson at the University of California at Santa Barbara and by Sandra Brown at the University of Illinois at Urbana shows that the carbon content of forests had been vastly overestimated, suggesting that deforestation is not as great a source of CO_2 as was once thought.   18

Can We Be Certain that Global Warming Will Occur?

Virtually all scientists agree that if greenhouse gases increase and all other factors remain the same, the earth will warm up. But "the crucial issue," explains Prof. S. Fred Singer, an atmospheric scientist at the Washington Institute for Values in Public Policy, "is to what extent other factors remain the same." Climatic forces interact in poorly understood ways, and some may counteract warming.   19

At any given time, for example, clouds cover 60 percent of the planet, trapping heat radiating from its surface, but also reflecting sunlight back into space. So, if the oceans heat up and produce more clouds through evaporation, the increased cover might act as a natural thermostat and keep the planet from heating up. After factoring more detailed cloud simulations into its   20 computer models, the British Meteorological Office recently showed that current global-warming projections could be cut in half.

Oceans have a major effect upon climate, but scientists have only begun   21
to understand how. Investigators at the National Center for Atmospheric Research attributed the North American drought in the summer of 1988 primarily to temperature changes in the tropical Pacific involving a current called El Niño—not to the greenhouse effect. And when ocean currents were included in recent computerized climate simulations, the Antarctic Ocean didn't warm—diminishing the likelihood that part of its ice sheet will break up and add to coastal flooding.

How heat travels through the atmosphere and back into space is an-   22
other big question mark for the global-warming theory. So is the sunspot cycle, as well as the effect of atmospheric pollution and volcanic particles that can reflect sunlight back into space. Such factors throw predictions about global warming into doubts.

So What Is the Bottom Line? Has the Earth Begun to Heat Up?

Two widely reported statistics *seem* to present a powerful case for global   23
warming. Some temperature records show about one degree Fahrenheit of warming over the past century, a period that has also seen a noticeable increase in greenhouse gases. And the six warmest years globally since record keeping began 100 years ago have all been in the 1980s.

As for the past decade, the increased warmth in three of its hottest   24
years—1983, 1987 and 1988—is almost certainly associated with El Niño events in the Pacific.

Paradoxically, the historical records of temperature change do not jibe   25
with the greenhouse theory. Between 1880 and 1940, temperatures appeared to rise. Yet between 1940 and 1965, a period of much heavier fossil-fuel use and deforestation, temperatures dropped, which seems inconsistent with the greenhouse effect. And a comprehensive study of past global ocean records by researchers from Britain and M.I.T. revealed no significant rising temperature trends between 1856 and 1986. Concludes Richard Lindzen of M.I.T.'s department of Earth, Atmospheric and Planetary Sciences, "The data as we have it does not support a warming."

Taking everything into account, few climatologists are willing to at-   26
tribute any seeming warming to the greenhouse effect. Last May, 61 scientists participating in a greenhouse workshop in Amherst, Mass., declared that "such an attribution cannot now be made with any degree of confidence."

Is There Any Other Evidence of Global Warming?

Atmospheric researchers use complex computer programs called General   27
Circulation Models (GCMs) to plot climate change. But a computer is no

more reliable than its input, and poorly understood oceanic, atmospheric and continental processes are only crudely represented even in the best GCMs.

Computer calculations do not even accurately predict the past: they fail to match historical greenhouse-gas concentrations to expected temperatures. Because of these uncertainties, Stephen Schneider says in *Global Warming,* it is "an even bet that the GCMs have overestimated future warming by a factor of two."

In time, the computer models will undoubtedly improve. For now, the lack of evidence and reliable tools leaves proponents of global warming with little but theory.

Should We Do Anything to Offset the Possible Warming Up of the Globe?

Fossil fuels now provide 90 percent of the world's energy. Some environmentalists have advocated huge tax increases to discourage use of coal and other fossil fuels. Some have suggested a gasoline tax. There are also proposals that the government subsidize solar, windmill and geothermal power; that some foreign debts be swapped for protecting fore s; and that worldwide population growth be slowed.

The buildup of greenhouse gases is cause for scientific study, but not for panic. Yet the facts sometimes get lost in the hysteria. Stephen Schneider confesses to an ethical dilemma. He admits the many uncertainties about global warming. Nevertheless, to gain public support through media coverage, he explains that sometimes scientists "have to offer up scary scenarios, make simplified, dramatic statements, and make little mention of any doubts we might have." Each scientist, he says, must decide the "right balance" between "being effective and being honest. I hope that means being both."

The temptation to bend fears for political ends is also ever present. "We've got to ride the global-warming issue," Sen. Timothy Wirth (D., Colo.) explained to a reporter. "Even if the theory is wrong, we will be doing the right thing in terms of economic and environmental policy."

But many scientists are troubled when inconclusive evidence is used for political advocacy. "The greenhouse warming has become a 'happening,' " says Richard Lindzen. To call for action, he adds, "has become a litmus test of morality."

We still know far too little to be stampeded into rash, expensive proposals. Before we take such steps, says Patrick J. Michaels, an associate professor of environmental sciences at the University of Virginia, "the science should be much less murky than it is now."

Further research and climatic monitoring are certainly warranted. If the "greenhouse signal" then emerges from the data, we can decide on the most prudent course of action.

QUESTIONS FOR MEANING

1. What is causing the buildup of carbon dioxide in the atmosphere? During what period has the buildup been especially dramatic?
2. How is methane released into the atmosphere?
3. According to Bidinotto, what natural phenomena could moderate the greenhouse effect?
4. Is there any evidence to suggest that burning fossil fuels does not lead to global warming?
5. What is the purpose of this argument? What does Bidinotto recommend?
6. Vocabulary: spawned (2), draconian (3), paradoxically (25), jibe (25) warranted (35).

QUESTIONS ABOUT STRATEGY

1. Bidinotto devotes most of his first three paragraphs to outlining concerns about global warming. What advantage does this type of opening offer?
2. At what point does the author first reveal that he believes concern about global warming may be exaggerated?
3. How useful are the subtitles included in this essay? What would be the effect of eliminating them?
4. In considering the views of scientists concerned about global warming, does Bidinotto give any reason likely to make readers question their credibility? How were you affected by paragraph 31?

PETER SHAW

Apocalypse Again

A 1958 graduate of Cornell, Peter Shaw received his Ph.D. from Columbia University in 1965. His books include The Character of John Adams *(1976),* American Patriots and the Rituals of Revolution *(1981), and* The War Against the Intellect: Episodes in the Decline of Discourse *(1989). Shaw, who describes himself politically as a "Former Liberal," published the following* **1989** *essay in* Commentary. *He is currently the Will and Ariel Durant Professor of the Humanities at Saint Peter's College.*

> Some say the world will end in fire,
> Some say in ice.
>
> Robert Frost

Predictions of the end of the world, as old as human history itself and lately   1
a subject of scholarly inquiry, have by no means abated in our own time.
Nor are those who believe in such predictions confined to isolated religious
sects, as was the case as recently as the 19th century. While such sects do
continue regularly to spring up and disappear, predictions of catastrophe have
become the virtual orthodoxy of society as a whole. Journalists, educators,
churchmen, and philosophers daily endorse one or another script foretelling
the end of individual life, of human civilization, or of the entire earth. Some
say the world will end in fire—through the conflagration of a nuclear holocaust; some say in ice—through the same event, this time precipitating a
"nuclear winter."

Fire and ice. We need only add earth and air to include within the apoc-   2
alyptic genre all four of the elements understood as basic by the Greeks, and
water to include the biblical account of the flood. Contemporary prophecies
of flood are stated in apparently scientific terms: as a result of global warming, the polar ice caps will melt and inundate the world's major cities. As for
earth and air, we anticipate the disappearance of the one thanks to the erosion
of farmland and shorelines, while the other is to be depleted of its ozone, if
not first saturated with carbon dioxide or poisoned by man-made pollutants.

Pagan man projected his fears outward; contemporary man internalizes.   3
Like biblical man (at least to that very limited extent) he holds himself, or
more accurately his own society, responsible for the coming end of the world.
Not only the disaster allegedly threatened by pollutants but every prospective
modern apocalypse stipulates man rather than the gods or nature as the primal cause. And the charge is always the same: whether it is to be by fire or
by ice, mankind faces extinction as a punishment for its impiety.

The continuities and discontinuities between ancient and modern imag-   4
inations of disaster would amount to no more than curiosities if it were the

case that superstitious fears had been replaced by rational ones. But it is not the case. On the contrary, given the best scientific understanding of reality available to early man, it made sense for him to ascribe natural disasters, present and future, to the gods. Later, it made sense for the Greeks to ascribe such disasters to some wayward or even malign characteristic of matter itself. Nor was Empedocles a simpleton for regarding the personification of the elements by gods as a persuasive account of reality. Would that our own conceptions of apocalypse were similarly founded on the best available scientific understanding. Instead, most if not all of the disasters currently being predicted have gained widespread credence *despite* a lack of scientific basis, or even in the face of definitive counterevidence.

Without question the most spectacular example of such a wholly suppositious theory has to do with the so-called greenhouse effect. The greenhouse effect itself, as every schoolchild knows, is simply the process by which the earth's atmosphere traps enough heat from the sun to create a habitable planet. As for the disaster scenario that bears the same name, it posits, in the words of a *New York Times* editorial, an increased "warming of the atmosphere by waste gases from a century of industrial activity." The *Times* goes on: 5

> The greenhouse theory holds that certain waste gases let in sunlight but trap heat, which otherwise would escape into space. Carbon dioxide has been steadily building up through the burning of coal and oil—and because forests, which absorb the gas, are fast being destroyed.

Now, aside from the mistaken assumption that forests worldwide are decreasing in size (they are not), the theory of a runaway greenhouse effect, otherwise known as global warming, presents even its advocates with a variety of internal contradictions. In the first place, the earth has a number of mechanisms for ameliorating fluctuations in global temperature: a significant rise in temperature, for example, leads to increased evaporation from the oceans; this is followed by the formation of clouds that shield the sun and then by a compensating drop in temperature. Too, if the greenhouse theory were valid, a global warming trend should be observable in records of temperatures soon after the jump in manmade carbon dioxide that is the result of modern industrial activity. Yet if there has been such a rise over the past one hundred years, it does not follow but precedes the onset of modern industrialism, and anyway it amounts to a barely detectable change of no more than one degree Fahrenheit over the entire period.   6

Here is a particularly significant problem for any hypothesis—the lack of evidence. Purveyors of the global-warming theory counter it by pointing to computer projections which show a catastrophic upward trend in the *next* century. Once again, however, a known problem presents itself: computer models, writes Andrew R. Solow, a statistician at Woods Hole Oceanographic Institution, "have a hard time reproducing current climate from current data. They cannot be expected to predict future climate with any precision."   7

Does any of this detract from the persuasive power of the global-warm-   8
ing theory? Apparently not. As in certain forms of religion, the less evidence,
the more faith. And in the resultant climate of belief (as it deserves to be
called), not only the lack of evidence but even outright counterevidence can
work to a theory's benefit. According to the late Leon Festinger, Henry W.
Riecken, and Stanley Schachter, the authors of the classic study, *When Prophecy Fails* (1956), "Although there is a limit beyond which belief will not stand
disconfirmation, it is clear that the introduction of contrary evidence can serve
to increase the conviction and enthusiasm of a believer." So it has been during the most recent phase of prediction, which itself represents a revival
of the great irruption of ecological warnings that dominated the early
1970's.

The central document in that earlier wave was *Limits To Growth,* a   9
report issued by the Club of Rome in 1972 foretelling a world-wide doom
brought on by the combined forces of "resource depletion," overpopulation,
pollution, and starvation. The future conjured up by computer simulation in
Limits to Growth bore a certain resemblance to the still more spectacularly
stated predictions of Paul Ehrlich in his 1968 book, *Population Bomb.* Ehrlich
had offered specific dates for specific catastrophes: 1983, for example, would
see a precipitous decline in American harvests and the institution of food
rationing, by which time a billion people worldwide would have already
starved to death. The Club of Rome, more cautiously, assigned likely years
for the exhaustion of specific resources: petroleum (1992), silver (1985), natural gas (1994), mercury (1985), tin (1987).

In 1982 one of the authors of the Club of Rome report had to admit   10
that his predictions were not coming true. Yet he was not repentant. There
may have been a postponement, a temporary reprieve, but man and the earth
still remained poised on the brink of cataclysm. Presumably Paul Ehrlich,
who never recanted, felt the same way. Just so have members of religious
sects always responded when their confidently predicted apocalypses pass
without incident.

True, the general public and even some members of the sect begin to   11
fall away after such disappointments; in our time, both Paul Ehrlich and the
Club of Rome did fade out of the spotlight. But instructively, and in contrast
to the sects studied in *When Prophecy Fails,* they did so without having been
exposed to the full glare of adverse publicity and ridicule that used to attend
the collapse of prophecy. Perhaps that is why so little time elapsed before the
public could be brought to credit similar predictions.

For even as the "population bomb" failed to explode on schedule, or   12
ecological disaster to strike, new predictions of not only global but galactic
proportions were being prepared. By the late 1980's these were receiving the
same respectful, credulous hearing as their forerunners, and were being promoted just as avidly by the press. In the case of nuclear winter, the most
publicized apocalypse, the cycle from prediction to publicity to disconfirmation took only a few years, from approximately 1985 to 1988; yet once again
the end came without bringing ridicule or discredit to the theoreticians.

Nuclear winter was at once a prediction of what would happen after a   13
nuclear war and the claim that an identical disaster, never detected in the
geological record, had already taken place once before, in the age of the dinosaurs. A giant explosion, the theory went, had been caused on earth by a
"nemesis" or "death star" wheeling in from far out in the universe and returning so quickly whence it had come as to be invisible to the most far-
seeing of modern telescopes. The clouds of dust kicked up by that explosion
had shielded the sun and thus caused the earth's vegetation to wither, bringing about the extinction of the dinosaurs by cold and starvation. The lesson for the mid-1980's was clear: intermediate-range nuclear missiles should
not be emplaced in Western Europe and disarmament should commence
forthwith.

As chance would have it, not long after the nuclear-winter theory gained   14
currency there was a giant volcanic eruption at Mount St. Helens in the state
of Washington. It was followed by the spreading of just such dark clouds as
had been described—but without any hint of the predicted effect on vegetation or climate. At about the same time, too, paleontologists demonstrated
that the dinosaurs could not possibly have been the casualties of a single,
catastrophic event, since they had disappeared over a period of some thousands of years. Finally, a check of some of the nuclear-winter projections
exposed gaping errors of math and physics.

As a result of these and other refutations of the theory, nuclear winter   15
died its own death-by-theoretical-starvation. But so quickly was its place
taken by similar predictions, similarly linked to geopolitical issues, that the
event seems to have almost entirely escaped notice. Nuclear winter remains
today in the public mind as a proven hypothesis, vying for popularity with
its mirror opposite, the greenhouse effect.

Actually, not so long ago (as the journalist John Chamberlain has pointed   16
out) we were being assured that we were living not in a warming but in a
"cooling world." In the 1970's, as *Science* magazine reported in 1975, mete-
orologists were "almost unanimous" that such a trend was taking place, and
that its consequences, especially for agriculture, were potentially disastrous.
Climatologists, according to *Fortune* magazine, warned that the cooling trend
"could bring massive tragedies for mankind." A decade later, all of this quite
forgotten, the opposite theory of global warming has drifted past the rocks
of evidentiary lack, tumbled safely through the falls of skepticism, and sailed
triumphantly onto the smooth lake of public respect.

The status of global warming as an unassailable, self-evident truth was   17
recently confirmed by the reaction to a scientific report that challenges its
assumptions. This report, compiled at the National Oceanic and Atmospheric Administration and duly described on the front page of the *New York
Times* and other newspapers, traces U.S. temperatures since 1895. It shows
that the putative one-degree rise in temperature worldwide over the past
hundred years, a figure widely accepted even by many of those skeptical of
the global-warming scenario, is wrong for the United States. As the *Times*
headline put it: "U.S. Data Since 1895 Fail to Show Warming Trend."

The reaction was immediate. All of the experts consulted by the *Times*   18
were in agreement that the report does not set back the global-warming theory by so much as an iota. Prominent among these experts was Dr. James
E. Hansen, director of the National Aeronautic and Space Administration's
Institute for Space Studies in Manhattan, a leading proponent of global warming
and the man who produced the data showing a one-degree rise in global
temperature. "We have to be careful about interpreting things like this," he
warned, and went on to explain that the United States covers only a small
portion of the earth's surface. Besides, the steadiness of the temperature readings could be a "statistical fluke." Note the implicit distinction here: we must
be "careful" in interpreting data that appear reassuring, but it is virtually our
duty to indulge any strongly felt premonitions of disaster even if they are
based on the flimsiest evidence, or none.

The concept of the "statistical fluke" could easily be applied to many   19
current predictions, but is not. Thus, the acidification of a number of freshwater lakes in the eastern United States is considered not a fluke but a definite
trend, even though it might be taken to fall well within the range of natural
fluctuations. Similarly, the disturbing deaths of numerous dolphins during
the summer of 1988 were traced to the same pattern of human depredation
of the environment supposed to be causing acid rain and other ecological
catastrophes. Later, it developed that the dolphins were killed by a so-called
"red tide" of algae—itself first seen as a man-created scourge but then conceded to be a natural phenomenon. Here, in other words, was a genuine
statistical fluke; but it was never labeled as such since it exonerated industrial man.

It does not give pause either to the catastrophists or to their credulous   20
promoters in the media that some predictions cancel out others. Dr. Hansen,
for example, suggests that the absence of a warming trend, as shown by the
new study, might be "the result of atmospheric pollutants reflecting heat
away from earth." Yet these are the same pollutant particles supposedly responsible for global warming in the first place. Now it develops that the
particles they carry with them counter the greenhouse effect. In fact, Dr.
Hansen is worried that "anti-pollution efforts are reducing the amount of
these particles and thus reducing the reflection of heat" away from the earth.
It is surely a measure of the power of catastrophic thinking that what may
have been the first public revelation of an actual decrease in man-made atmospheric pollutants should prompt the fear that such a decrease itself portends the direst consequences.

What all this suggests is that we have come to depend at any given   21
moment on a constant degree of threat. When times are bad—because of
war, depression, or real natural disasters—proximate fears tend to dominate
the imagination. When times are good—through the conquest of disease and
famine, the achievement of high employment, prosperity, and an upward
curve of longevity—apprehension has to be supplied from without. And during extended good times, a supply of fresh disasters is required as each one
comes progressively to lose its appeal. Air pollution, rising to disaster proportions in the Club of Rome report, declines in importance but is soon

succeeded by loss of the ozone layer, which will supposedly leave mankind vulnerable to the unfiltered rays of the sun and a consequent plague of, among other things, skin cancers and blindness. Continent-wide poisoning of fresh water through the eutrophication of lakes and streams from fertilizer runoff is forgotten only to be replaced by the threat of acid rain. Direct incineration of all mankind by atomic war cedes to a secondary stage of destruction by nuclear winter, and nuclear winter in turn to global warming.

This persistent and insistent imagining of disaster might be no more   22 than a sideshow were it not for its political dimension. But in the 1970's and 80's, successive waves of catastrophism followed and reflected episodes of defeat for radical political movements. The 70's wave succeeded the collapse of the New Left and engaged many of that movement's disillusioned supporters (as well, of course, as many people opposed or indifferent to the New Left). That of the 80's followed the worldwide discrediting of the economic, political, and moral record of Communism. It was as if sanguine hopes of an end to the cold war required a compensatory new fear, one that natural catastrophe alone could supply. And thus, soon after James Baker's nomination as Secretary of State, a bipartisan memorandum from members of the Senate Foreign Relations Committee called his urgent attention to the leading foreign-policy issue he would have to face, a "global problem of unprecedented magnitude." The issue was global warming.

It goes without saying that clean air and water, the retention of farm-   23 land and forests, a satisfactory ozone layer, and the avoidance of nuclear war are all desirable things. But the pursuit of these goals through the rhetoric of hellfire renders more immediate political concerns mundane and secondary. Many are the societies that have been distracted from the actual dangers they faced by the allure of disasters wholly imaginary. That consideration aside, though, our obsession with distant and unprovable catastrophe is so stultifying, from both the moral and the intellectual point of view, as to constitute a cultural disaster in its own right.

QUESTIONS FOR MEANING

1. What evidence does Shaw cite to support his claim that concerns about global warming are unreasonable?
2. Why is Shaw unconvinced by computer models that project future trends?
3. How does Shaw account for widespread belief in global warming despite the evidence he cites in support of his own case?
4. What does Shaw mean when he writes that concern about global warming is a "cultural disaster"? Paraphrase the last paragraph of this essay.
5. Vocabulary: abated (1), impiety (3), ascribe (4), personification (4), purveyors (7), precipitous (9), recanted (10), putative (17), sanguine (22).

QUESTIONS ABOUT STRATEGY

1. Consider the title of this essay. Does Shaw have any reason to emphasize the two words the title contains? Do you recognize an allusion in the title?

2. Shaw prefaces this essay with the first two lines of "Fire and Ice," a poem by Robert Frost. Why is this quotation appropriate for the argument that follows? How does Shaw link these lines to his own work?
3. What is the point of comparing global warming to other environmental concerns during the last twenty years? Reconsider paragraphs 9–16.
4. How would you describe the tone of this essay?
5. Does Shaw make any concessions likely to appeal to environmentalists?

WARREN T. BROOKES
The Global Warming Panic

If the earth is growing warmer, the world's economy is likely to change. In the United States, legislation to delay global warming would also have economic effects. Is such legislation necessary, or is concern over global warming exaggerated? The following essay addresses these questions. A 1950 graduate of Harvard, Warren T. Brookes is a syndicated columnist on the staff of The Detroit News. *The author of* The Economy in Mind *(1982), Brookes has written about financial issues for such publications as* National Review, Reader's Digest, The American Spectator, The Wall Street Journal *and* Forbes, *which published "The Global Warming Panic" in* **1989.**

On Nov. 7 the U.S. and Japan shocked environmentalists around the world   1
by refusing to sign a draft resolution at a Netherlands international conference on global climate change calling for the "stabilization" of emissions of carbon dioxide (CO_2) and other "greenhouse gases" by the year 2000. Instead, they made the conference drop all reference to a specific year, and to a specific CO_2 reduction target. The Bush Administration view was set forth by D. Allan Bromley, the presidential science advisor, in testimony to Senator Albert Gore's subcommittee on Science, Technology & Space: "My belief is that we should not move forward on major programs until we have a reasonable understanding of the scientific and economic consequences of those programs."

President Bush was immediately savaged by environmentalists, and by   2
politicians like Senator Gore (D–Tenn.). The Bush viewpoint does not sit too well with most of the media, either. Last January *Time* published a cover story on environmental catastrophes, declaring that greenhouse gases could create a climatic calamity. The *New York Times* weighed in a month ago with a story about how melting polar ice would flood the nations that can least afford to defend themselves, Third World countries like Bangladesh and India. Or perhaps you have seen the ads for Stephen Schneider's *Global Warming,* accompanied by a blurb from Senator Tim Wirth (D–Colo.). In his book

this well-known climatologist paints a future of seas surging across the land, famine on an epidemic scale and eco-system collapse.

Is the earth really on the verge of environmental collapse? Should wrenching changes be made in the world's history to contain CO_2 buildup? Or could we be witnessing the 1990s version of earlier scares: nuclear winter, cancer-causing cranberries and $100 oil? The calamitarians always have something to worry us about. Consider this: In his 1976 book, *The Genesis Strategy,* Schneider lent support to the then popular view that we could be in for another ice age, "perhaps one akin to the Little Ice Age of 1500–1850. Climatic variability, which is the bane of reliable food production, can be expected to increase along with the cooling."   3

At the very moment Bromley was testifying to Gore's subcommittee, MIT's prestigious *Technology Review* was reporting on the publication of an exhaustive new study of worldwide ocean temperatures since 1850 by MIT climatologists Reginald Newell, Jane Hsiung and Wu Zhongxiang. Its most striking conclusion: "There appears to have been little or no global warming over the past century." In fact, the average ocean temperature in the torrid 1980s was only an eighth of a centigrade degree (a quarter of a Fahrenheit degree) higher than the average of the 1860s. Ocean temperature is now virtually the same as it was in the 1940s. Since two-thirds of the buildup of CO_2 has taken place since 1940, the MIT data blow all of the global warming forecasts into a cocked hat. President Bush wisely told reporters: "You can't take a policy and drive it to the extreme and say to every country around the world, 'You aren't going to grow at all.' "   4

That is the central issue of the global warming debate, and it explains why the U.S. and Japanese position was supported by some 30 other developing nations which see that just as Marxism is giving way to markets, the political "greens" seem determined to put the world economy back into the red, using the greenhouse effect to stop unfettered market-based economic expansion.   5

In simplest terms, the earth's atmosphere does operate as a greenhouse. In addition to oxygen, nitrogen and water vapor, the atmosphere contains several gases that trap radiated heat, including methane and CO_2. Carbon dioxide is essential not only to warmth but to vegetation. It is also essential to life in another way: Without its heat-containing effect the planet would freeze, like the atmospherically naked moon.   6

Throughout most of human history that atmospheric blanket has held global temperatures at an average of about 60 degrees F., plus or minus 5 degrees F. During most of human history, the CO_2 concentration in that blanket has, until this century, hovered around 270 parts per million, although in earlier geologic epochs it reached as high as 20,000.   7

Over the last 100 years the CO_2 concentration has risen from 270 to today's level of 350. The culprit: man. Most of the greenhouse gas increase is the result of fossil fuel consumption. Add to that the rise in other man-generated trace gases—methane, nitrogen oxides and chlorofluorocarbons—and total greenhouse gases are now at 410 ppm. In other words, because of   8 the combined effect of these gases, we have already gone over halfway to a doubling of CO_2. Even so, there has been less than half a degree of warming in the last 100 years.

What do the environmental pessimists make of all this? The earliest versions of their computer "general circulation models" predicted that the earth would warm up by anywhere from 3 to 5 degrees Fahrenheit, by the year 2050. The most extreme scenarios warn of coastal flooding (from melting ice caps) and rising inland droughts. However, as the level of sophistication of the models has risen, these forecast effects have been steadily reduced to a new range of 1.5 to 2.5 degrees centigrade.

One major exception to this declining rate of doom is the model run by James Hansen of the National Aeronautics & Space Administration, who shocked a congressional hearing in June 1988 during the middle of a scorching near-nationwide drought, by saying he was "99% confident" the greenhouse effect is now here.

Even though the vast majority of the climatological community was outraged by Hansen's unproven assertions, environmental advocate Stephen Schneider notes in *Global Warming,* "Journalists loved it. Environmentalists were ecstatic. Jim appeared on a dozen or more national television news programs. . . ."

By the end of 1988, with Hansen and Schneider's enthusiastic support, global warming was deeply embedded in the public consciousness. Now over 60% of the public is convinced it will worsen, even as the evidence of that alleged trend is under increasingly sharp and solid scientific attack.

On the contrary, that attack has been used as a premise for even more immediate action. As one TV anchorman argued, "Even if we aren't sure it's true, shouldn't we take precautions and act now as if it were?"

Unfortunately, "taking such precautions" could well spell the end of the American dream for us and the world. Once CO_2 is in the atmosphere, we can't easily remove it. Since most of the forecast rise in the gas is a function of simple economic and population growth in the Third World, there is no realistic economic way to prevent a CO_2 doubling without slashing growth and risking a revolt of the have-not nations against the haves. The Washington, D.C.-based Center for Strategic & International Studies points out that, even though the U.S. is now the largest carbon fuel user, it's the developing countries that will quadruple their energy consumption by 2025. "By the middle of the next century, they will account for the bulk of the greenhouse gases emitted into the atmosphere, even if they succeed in doubling energy efficiency."

The Environmental Protection Agency finds that just to stabilize U.S. CO_2 emissions at present levels would force 30% taxes on oil and coal, while to meet environmentalists' demands for a 20% reduction in U.S. CO_2 emissions would require a tax of $25 per barrel on oil, and $200 a ton on coal, effectively doubling U.S. energy costs.

Unfortunately, the popular media don't seem to care. In May the national press erupted in a two-day firestorm when Hansen told Senator Gore's subcommittee that the Office of Management & Budget had censored his florid global warming testimony by adding the modest caveat, "These changes should be viewed as estimates from evolving computer models and not as reliable predictions."

Yet, at the moment of that testimony, 61 of the world's top climatologists, gathered for a five-day workshop in Amherst, Mass., were largely agreeing with OMB. *Science* magazine reported that most of the attendees were pleasantly surprised by OMB's efforts to control Hansen: "I can't say I agree with censorship, but it seems OMB has better people than I thought. I'd have to agree with their angle," said Rick Katz of the National Center for Atmospheric Research, one of the leading modelers.

Conference leader Michael Schlesinger, another top modeler (University of Illinois), agreed: "[Hansen's] statements have given people the feeling the greenhouse effect has been detected with certitude. Our current understanding does not support that. Confidence in its detection is now down near zero."

That conclusion was buttressed by one of the deans of U.S. climatology, Reid Bryson, a founder of the Institute for Environmental Studies at the University of Wisconsin, who said in July: "The very clear statements that have been made [by Hansen] that the greenhouse warming is here already and that the globe will be 4 degrees [centigrade] warmer in 50 years cannot be accepted."

On Dec. 24, 1988, Hansen received an unwelcome Christmas present in the form of a new research paper by one of the world's most universally respected climatologists, Thomas Karl, and two of his colleagues at the National Oceanographic & Atmospheric Administration, Kirby Hanson and George Maul. Their review of the best climatic record in the world—that of the 48 contiguous United States—concluded: "There is no statistically significant evidence of an overall increase in annual temperature or change in annual precipitation for the contiguous U.S. 1895–1987." As Karl says in an interview, "If there is a greenhouse warming effect, you can't find it in the U.S. records."

That news alone should have cooled off the global warming movement. But the environmentalists accepted Hansen's dismissal of the paper as "not significant" because the data covered only 1.5% of the earth's surface, not nearly enough to identify major trends.

But MIT meterologist Richard Lindzen says that Hansen's rebuttal is out of line. He points out that because of the law of large numbers—the fact that a large enough sample is likely to give an accurate picture of a larger population—"the absence of any trend in the record of the contiguous U.S. leads to the suspicion that all the trends in the global record may be spurious."

The major reason for this is that when you fully subject global temperature records (as Karl did the U.S. records) to adjustment for the effects of urbanization (cities are heat islands that artificially inflate temperature records), the global warming trend since 1800 has been only a third of a degree centigrade, and over the Northern Hemisphere land masses, no trend at all.

Here's another fact, noted by Hugh Ellsaesser of Lawrence Livermore   24
Laboratories, that should trouble the calamity theorists: Most of the past century's warming trend took place by 1938, well before the rise in CO_2 concentration. From 1938 to 1970 temperatures plunged so sharply a new ice age
was widely forecast. Furthermore, the warming trend since 1976 has been
just the opposite of that forecast by the greenhouse model, with *cooling* in
both the northern Pacific and North Atlantic.

In fact, the Northern Hemisphere shows no net change over the last 55   25
years, during which CO_2 concentration rose from approximately 300 to 350
ppm and other thermally active trace gases were in their steepest growth
phases.

In spite of this clear lack of correlated warming evidence, one of the   26
leading climate models now predicts that a 1% annual rise in CO_2 should,
over 30 years, produce a 0.7-degree centigrade warming. But when Patrick
Michaels of the University of Virginia applied that formula to the period
from 1950 to 1988, when greenhouse gases rose 1.2% per year, he found a
tiny 0.2-degree warming in land temperatures, where the model would have
predicted 1.3 degrees. When a model cannot come within 500% of explaining the past, it is useless as a predictor of anything.

As Reid Bryson concludes in a 1988 paper, "A statement of what the   27
climate is going to be in the year A.D. 2050 is a 63-year forecast. Do the
models have a demonstrated capability of making a 63-year forecast? No. A
6.3 year forecast? No. Have they successfully simulated the climatic variation
of the past century and a half? No. They are marvels of mathematics and
computer science, but rather crude imitators of reality."

The major weakness of the models is their assumption that the CO_2 28
buildup is the significant climate variable, and should *ceteris paribus* (all other
things being equal) generate warming. But, as it turns out, the *ceteris* are
decidedly not *paribus*.

One of those variables is cloud cover, which is at least 100 times more   29
powerful in affecting temperatures than greenhouse gases and is infinitely
variable. Yet, because cloud cover has been documented only for a decade or
so (by weather satellites), the models have little to go on. Until recently, the
modelers assumed that warmth gave rise to the kind of clouds that trap heat,
contributing still further to warming, in a vicious cycle. But in June 1988,
V. Ramanathan of the University of Chicago and a team of scientists at NASA
concluded from preliminary satellite data that "clouds appear to cool earth's
climate," possibly offsetting the atmospheric greenhouse effect.

The supreme irony is that this "cooling effect," most pronounced in   30
the Northern Hemisphere, coincides with the paths of coal-burning emission
plumes with their high concentration of sulfur dioxide. That confirms a long-
held thesis that sulfur dioxide creates "cool clouds." Of course, it is very
upsetting to an environmentalist to discover that a pollutant has a beneficial
side effect.

Sulfur dioxide emissions not only acidify rain, they combine with water   31
vapor to form what are known as "aerosols," which have the effect of

brightening clouds and making them reflect more heat away from the earth. Wisconsin's Reid Bryson described this effect as early as 20 years ago. Bryson's thesis was scorned at the time. But last June, Thomas Wigley, one of England's top climatologists and a global warming enthusiast, conceded in a paper in *Nature* magazine that sulfur dioxide cooling "is sufficiently large that the effects may have significantly offset the temperature changes that resulted from the greenhouse effect."

Michaels says this could also explain in part why U.S. daytime highs   32 (when brighter clouds have the most cooling effect) have actually declined substantially in the last 50 years, even as the nighttime lows have risen. "This should make you wonder," says Michaels, "why Hansen [and others] have only perturbed their models with CO_2, and not with SO_2 as well. If you only perturb the model with CO_2, it will predict the greenhouse warming effect. If you only perturb it with SO_2, you get an ice age."

Hugh Ellsaesser says the main reason the models have been so com-   33 pletely wrong in "predicting" the past is that they completely ignore the countervailing, thermostatic effects of the hydrological cycle of evaporation and condensation. Two-thirds of the predicted global warming is due not directly to CO_2's radiative power but to an indirect effect: Carbon dioxide warming supposedly causes a threefold amplification of water vapor surface evaporation into the atmospheric blanket.

But Ellsaesser says in the warmer, tropical latitudes, where the temper-   34 ature change from sea-level upward is most rapid, evaporation has the opposite effect. There, water vapor rises by deep convection in fast-rising towers. This in turn leads to more rapid condensation and precipitation, which then causes a drying and thinning of the upper atmosphere in a process called subsidence. "In the lower latitudes, a rise in CO_2 emissions will produce a 3-to-1 rise in greenhouse blanket *thinning* due to condensation. That's exactly the opposite of what the models predict," he says.

An eminent British scientist, Sir James Lovelock, says this hydrological   35 process "is comparable in magnitude with that of the carbon dioxide greenhouse, but in opposition to it." National Oceanographic scientist Thomas Karl agrees: "We will eventually discover how naive we have been in not considering CO_2's effects on cloud cover and convection. As CO_2 speeds up the hydrological cycle, more convection creates more clouds and more cooling. So, the greenhouse effect could turn out to be minimal, or even benign."

MIT's Richard Lindzen thinks that correcting for deep convection alone   36 could lower the global warming estimates by a factor of six. As a result, he says, "It is very unlikely that we will see more than a few tenths of a degree centigrade from this cause [CO_2] over the next century."

In the face of such mounting evidence, U.S. businesses may stop wor-   37 rying about devastating legislative enactments. That could be a mistake. As Nobel economist James Buchanan argues, what drives Washington policymaking is not economic or scientific realities but "public choice," the pursuit of power and funding.

The public choice potential of global warming is immense. Under a   38
global warming scenario, the EPA would become the most powerful government agency on earth, involved in massive levels of economic, social, scientific and political spending and interference, on a par with the old Energy
Department. Don't forget the energy crisis: During the 1970s, a great many
less-than-honest scientists confidently predicted the world was about to run
out of fossil fuels, and that by 1985, we'd be paying $100 a barrel for oil, or
more. We wasted billions on energy subsidies.

Senator Albert Gore is evidence of this public choice phenomenon. He   39
seems determined to run his next presidential campaign at least in part on
climate change, saving Mother Earth. Every year, at least one-sixth of the
U.S. is classified by the government's Palmer Index as being in drought.
Even though that index overstates the case, Gore could be looking at some
very big political states—maybe California or Texas or Iowa— where his
message will resonate with farmers and business. All he has to do is wait for
a warm spell, and capitalize on what mathematicians call noise in the statistics.

Patrick Michaels explains: "We know that the Pacific Ocean current   40
known as El Niño tends to warm and cool in two-year cycles. Just as its
warming cycle produced the 1987–88 droughts, in 1989 it cooled sharply,
making the U.S. much cooler and wetter than Hansen had forecast, and that
is likely to happen in 1990, again. But that means that 1991 and 1992 should
be warmer and drier than usual as the El Niño current warms. It won't
matter that this has nothing to do with global warming, the media will perceive it that way, and people will tend to believe it."

Bernard Cohen, a physicist at the University of Pittsburgh, warns, in a   41
1984 book: "Our government's science and technology policy is now guided
by uninformed and emotion-driven public opinion rather than by sound scientific advice. Unless solutions can be found to this problem, the U.S. will
enter the 21st century declining in wealth, power and influence. . . . The
coming debacle is not due to the problems the environmentalists describe,
but to the policies they advocate."

"Global warming" may well prove Cohen right.   42

QUESTIONS FOR MEANING

1. According to Brookes, what countries are most likely to increase production of greenhouse gases in the twenty-first century? Why would it be
   difficult to oppose industrial development in these countries?
2. Can you explain the concept of "heat islands" in paragraph 23?
3. What is meant by the "hydrological cycle"? Paraphrase paragraphs 33–35.
4. Vocabulary: bane (3), unfettered (5), florid (16), caveat (16), buttressed
   (19), perturb (32), convection (36), resonate (39), debacle (41).

QUESTIONS ABOUT STRATEGY

1. Consider the source cited in paragraph 4. Does it seem reliable? How credible are the other authorities cited by Brookes as he makes his case?
2. Review the numbers cited in paragraphs 7 and 8. Why does Brookes report that CO_2 concentration reached a high of 20,000 parts per million before reporting the increase within the last hundred years?
3. Writing in 1989, Brookes included a projection of weather patterns in the early 1990s. Did these projections prove accurate? How does your response to paragraph 40 influence your response to this argument as a whole?
4. Brookes claims that Americans "wasted billions on energy subsidies" (paragraph 38) and concludes his argument by raising fears about the influence of environmentalists upon public policy. What does this tell you about his sense of audience?

SHARON BEGLEY AND DANIEL PEDERSON
Fighting the Greenhouse

On the staff of Newsweek, *Sharon Begley and Daniel Pedersen collaborated upon the following article in* **1990**. *As its title suggests, "Fighting the Greenhouse" is focused upon attempts to prevent global warming. It describes a number of products and strategies for using energy more efficiently. Because Pedersen was based in London, and Begley in New York, the article also reports upon how the American response to global warming compares with action taken by the British government shortly before this selection was first published.*

Of course you know what it will take to save the world from the greenhouse effect. To cut emissions of carbon dioxide—the gas released when coal, gas or oil burn and the one responsible for more than half of the impending global warming—you'll have to turn down the heater in winter and break out the long johns. In summer, don't even *think* of air conditioning. Chuck your 100-watt bulbs, screw in 40s. Trade in the dishwasher and clothes dryer for a dish drainer and laundry line.

But wait. Human nature being what it is, scientists realize that if we depend on a penchant for sacrifice to forestall the greenhouse effect, we might as well start building sea walls to hold back the waters that will rise along with the thermostat. Surveys show that only about one fifth of those questioned would keep their homes warmer in summer or chillier in winter to help the environment. Luckily, though, conservation 1990s style doesn't mean freezing in the dark. From superwindows that leak no heat to fridges that work like giant Thermos bottles, "there is a host of technological changes we can make that will let us keep the amenities we're used to," says Eric Hirst of Oak Ridge National Laboratory.

Last week the World Resources Institute announced new data that sug-   3
gest the greenhouse threat is more serious than had been realized. Forty million to fifty million acres of tropical forests are disappearing each year, said WRI—50 percent faster than earlier satellite photos showed. Deforestation is second only to the burning of fossil fuels as a source of carbon dioxide (CO_2). Even without the new data, an international panel, convened at the urging of the Bush administration and 38 other countries, concluded last month that global warming will raise sea levels enough to inundate the plains of Holland and Bangladesh and obliterate the Maldives, among other disasters. It called for a 60 percent cut in CO_2 emissions. Conservation is the cheapest and fastest way to do that, at least until solar and wind power, which emit no CO_2, are widely available. Efficiency alone, calculates Christopher Flavin of Worldwatch Institute, could cut global CO_2 emissions 3 billion tons a year by 2010, from today's 5.6 billion.

Nations might start with that symbol of energy profligacy, air condi-   4
tioners. They use hydrocholorfluorocarbons (HCFCs) as the cooling fluid, and indirectly release CO_2 when electricity to run them is generated. HCFCs and CO_2 are greenhouse gases. But plug-in cooling needn't turn up the global thermostat. A model patented last year by Albers Technologies Corp. of Arizona cools air to 54 degrees Fahrenheit, dehumidifies it and removes contaminants. It uses water, not HCFCs, and draws half the electricity of conventional units. At $2,000 for a unit big enough to cool a 1,500-square-foot house, it costs about the same as current models. No American makers have expressed an interest—they don't want to fiddle with their product unless the government bans HCFCs. But last month a Saudi Arabian firm, Alessa Industries, agreed to turn out 25,000 every year beginning in 1992—and export 20,000 back to the United States.

Other breakthroughs are as close as the nearest window. During the   5
winter, windows in the United States leak about as much heat as is provided by the oil flowing through the Alaskan pipeline every year. Researchers led by Stephen Selkowitz at the Lawrence Berkeley Laboratory in California can fix that with a "superwindow." It has three layers of glazing and two coatings of metal oxides that cut heat loss; the space between the panes is filled with krypton and argon gases. Result: the window collects more heat on a winter's day than it leaks at night. Superwindows today cost about 30 percent more than moderately efficient ones; even better versions are about to leave the lab. This week Libbey Owens Ford will introduce special glass coatings that allow sunlight to penetrate better than it can through plain glass, providing low-tech solar heating to a room. And LBL is working on a "smart window" that changes electronically from clear, which allows sunshine in on cold days, to reflective, which diverts rays on scorchers. Similar chameleon-like glass for car sun roofs can keep out enough sunshine to drastically cut the need for air conditioning, and should be in models next year.

Researchers also have bright ideas for lighting, which accounts for al-   6
most 25 percent of U.S. electricity use. Replacing standard incandescents with
the best bulbs, compact fluorescents, can cut electricity use by as much as
two thirds. Last year Reno's Peppermill Hotel Casino installed about 1,000
fluorescents, and halved its lighting bill. Although fluorescents can cost 20
times as much as incandescents, they last 10 times longer, saving the consumer money, and emit light indistinguishable from incandescents. Since fluorescent bulbs draw less electricity, substituting one for an incandescent
prevents the emssion of up to 382 pounds of CO_2 that would otherwise be
emitted from power plants. Other gizmos helped the National Resources
Defense Council cut its office energy bill by more than half: occupancy sen-
sors use infrared or ultrasonic signals to detect motion, turning lights off
when no one is in the room. Because of such savings, Amory Lovins of the
Rocky Mountain Institute says, "this is not a free lunch. This is a lunch you
are *paid* to eat."

Even refrigeration can help stave off the greenhouse. In today's models,   7
a single unit lowers temperatures in the freezer and moves chilled air to the
fridge—which doesn't need to be as cold. At Oak Ridge, researchers think
that using different mixes of coolants and separate cooling loops could offer
energy savings of an additional 20 percent. And by replacing the CFC insulation with vacuum insulation as in a Thermos, refrigerators wouldn't
need CFCs.

Electric utilities have led the charge toward energy efficiency partly from   8
environmental concern, but largely because of the bottom line: it costs 30 to
50 percent less to cut demand for power than to build new generating capacity. Wisconsin Power Co. offers rebates for installing efficient refrigerators;
Southern California Edison will pay customers to install more efficient windows. New England Electric offers rebates to lighting dealers so they will
lower the price of fluorescents; it has also insulated more than 100,000 customers' hot-water tanks for free. CEO John Rowe says, "Conservation is
the heart of our environmental strategy." But, only 10 states let utilities earn
a return on investments in efficiency, hampering widespread adoption.

For next year the administration is requesting $213 million for the De-   9
partment of Energy's conservation research, which now receives $411 mil-
lion. The White House questions whether the United States will suffer from
global warming, and therefore opposes making possibly expensive changes
to control the greenhouse. But in a significant break with this wait-and-see
policy, Prime Minister Margaret Thatcher last month announced that Britain
would cut CO_2 growth 20 percent by 2005, stabilizing it at 1990 levels, if
other nations follow suit. How? Heavy reliance on energy efficiency is a
likely option. "You can cut carbon emissions 20, 30 percent without any
economic cost," says Michael Grubb of the Royal Institute for Economic
Affairs. Bringing all homes up to the latest standards for insulation, for example, would cut emissions nearly 9 percent, estimates Stewart Boyle of
Britain's Association for the Conservation of Energy. This week the West
German cabinet is expected to consider a proposal to cut carbon emissions

30 percent by 2010. Increasingly, as the world grapples with the uncertain threat of the greenhouse, the United States is being left out in the cold.

QUESTIONS FOR MEANING

1. According to this article, what is the easiest way to reduce the emission of carbon dioxide?
2. What evidence is there that industry is developing products that will make energy use more efficient?
3. Why is it that the United States could end up importing American-designed air conditioners from Saudi Arabia?
4. What motivates power companies to offer rebates to customers who improve the energy efficiency of their homes? How could more companies be encouraged to offer rebate plans?

QUESTIONS ABOUT STRATEGY

1. What is the function of paragraphs 1 and 2? Why do the authors open with a common perception of what energy conservation entails only to immediately call it into doubt?
2. In writing on a complex topic for a general audience, have the authors made any attempts to make their material easily accessible?
3. Can you identify any specific information in this article that would justify its publication in a weekly news magazine?
4. This article was originally published as a news story, not an editorial. Is it neutral or does it betray any bias?

ROGER A. SEDJO
Forests: A Tool to Moderate Global Warming?

Since trees absorb carbon dioxide from the atmosphere, environmentally-concerned people often wonder if planting more trees could prevent global warming. The following article on forests in a **1989** *issue of* Environment *explores the extent to which trees can help the planet. A Senior Fellow and Director of the Forest Economics Program at Resources for the Future in Washington, D.C., Roger Sedjo is the coauthor of* Postwar Trends in U.S. Forest Production Rate: A Global, National, and Regional View *(1981) and* The Long-term Adequacy of World Timber Supply *(1990).*

Earth's climate may be growing warmer in response to atmospheric accumulation of greenhouse gases, predominantly but not exclusively stemming from human-induced emissions of carbon dioxide (CO_2) into the atmosphere. Once in the atmosphere, CO_2 traps heat that would otherwise radiate into space.[1] Each year the Earth's atmosphere takes up approximately 2.9 billion tons of the 4.8 to 5.8 billion tons of carbon that are emitted from various sources. (CO_2 emissions are conventionally measured in terms of their carbon.) The rest is removed from the atmosphere by natural processes in carbon sinks—places like oceans or forests where carbon is removed from the atmosphere and stored. In addition, changes in land use that have eliminated terrestrial biomass, including tropical forests, have released into the atmosphere the carbon that was captive in the vegetation.

Humankind can respond to the prospective global climate change by adapting to the warming, attempting to limit the warming by preventing or mitigating the buildup of atmospheric carbon, or by some combination of the above. Forests can play a critical role in any attempt to mitigate the warming because they are able to capture and store large amounts of carbon from the atmosphere: During respiration and photosynthesis, green plants take in CO_2, release oxygen, and store carbon. Therefore, forests might be able to moderate or postpone the buildup of atmospheric carbon and thereby delay the advent of global warming. Such a delay would "buy" time for the development of viable substitutes for fossil fuels (e.g., solar energy, photovoltaics, and nuclear energy) as a permanent solution to the warming problem.

The increase in the amount of CO_2 in the atmosphere can be prevented or moderated in several ways. In addition to the obvious preventative approach of reducing the amount of carbon released into the atmosphere by dramatically reducing fossil fuel use and forest degradation, new carbon sinks can be created or existing ones expanded. Such carbon sinks could sequester the excess 2.9 billion tons of free CO_2 released into the atmosphere each year.

For example, it has been suggested that ocean plankton might be managed in such a way that they would sequester carbon and then conveniently sink to the bottom of the ocean.[2]

Because actively growing forests also sequester CO_2 from the atmosphere as part of the growing process, any increase in forest biomass constitutes a sink that will reduce the buildup of atmospheric CO_2. Mature forests, which experience negligible net growth, continue to hold stocks of carbon captive but do not sequester additional carbon; therefore they are neither sources nor sinks. Forests that are losing biomass volume—through burning, for example—release carbon into the atmosphere and are therefore net carbon sources.

4

The forest/carbon system can be viewed in terms of both stock and flow. Additions to and deletions from the carbon captive in forests are directly related to changes in the stock of forest biomass that occur through forest growth and destruction. While it would not be a permanent solution to the global warming problem, a buildup of forest stocks, via new plantations or spontaneous growth, might give us several additional decades in which to find other methods to limit CO_2 buildup and the consequent global warming. The possibility of forests becoming a major carbon sink is examined here.

5

While the temperate forests of the northern hemisphere may be roughly in carbon balance or provide a modest carbon sink, the declining tropical forests are a source of carbon.[3] If forest biomass is increased, more free CO_2 will be sequestered (see Table 1 on page 255).

6

Two factors have led to suggestions that massive reforestation could supply an additional carbon sink: the ability of forests to store large amounts of carbon and their importance in the global carbon cycle.[4] The ability of a forest to sequester carbon is directly related to its biomass growth. While most growth figures used by foresters represent only stemwood and ignore branches, roots, leaves, and the like, these latter should be included in an estimate of carbon sequestering and are included here. Carbon is also sequestered in litter on the forest floor although, since the decomposition rate is rather rapid, litter is likely to become neither a source nor a sink after a few years.

7

Land Area Requirements

In plantation forests on good sites in the southern United States and Pacific Northwest, stemwood can grow at about 15 cubic meters (m^3) per hectare each year with a minimum of silvicultural inputs.[5] If it is assumed that 1 m^3 of stemwood is associated with 1.6 m^3 of tree biomass (including stemwood, roots, branches, and so on), and that 1 m^3 of biomass contains 0.26 tons of carbon,[6] 1 hectare of new forest will sequester about 6.24 tons of carbon annually. Thus, about 465 million hectares of new plantations would be needed to sequester the estimated annual increment of 2.9 billion tons of free carbon.

8

The total worldwide area covered by forest plantations, both industrial and nonindustrial, was estimated at 90 million hectares in the mid-1970s; in

9

TABLE 1
The Potential of Forests as a Carbon Sink

SOLUTION	REQUIREMENT
Establishment of rapidly growing plantation forests	465 million hectares (ha) of new fast-growing forest (15 cubic meters [m^3] of stemwood per hectare per year)
Increasing the amount of forest biomass in existing forest area, either through increasing growth or decreasing harvest	Increased stemwood growth of $2.5 m^3/$ha/year on all existing 3,000 million ha of closed forest
Natural increases in forest growth and biomass as the result of climate warming	Spontaneous net expansion of 3.5 billion ha in natural slow-growing forests (from 4 billion ha to a total worldwide closed forest area of 7.5 billion ha)

Note: This table assumes that the net annual increase of atmospheric carbon is 2.9 billion tons per year.

1982, the United Nations Food and Agricultural Organization projected that by 1985 the total area of plantation forests in the tropics would be only 17 million hectares; and the most recent estimate puts total industrial plantations worldwide at about 92 million hectares, mostly in the northern industrial countries, with temperate climates (for example, the USSR, Japan, Western Europe, and the United States).[7] Protection forests where logging is restricted and other noncommercial forest plantations would add significantly to this total.

A large forested area—about 1.5 times the total forested area of the   10
United States and more than 15 percent of the world total of closed forests (forests in which the tree crowns are close enough to form an unbroken overhead canopy) would be required to sequester the free carbon. The enclosed portion of Figure 1 on page 256 encompasses an area that would be required for 465 million hectares. This area would approximate 75 percent of the nonforested land of the United States.

Clearly, to have a significant impact on global warming, plantations   11
would need to be established on an unprecedented scale. Even beyond the United States, it is questionable whether suitable land would be available to accommodate planting of this magnitude. Most of the land productive enough to support these forests lies either in the tropics or in the more southerly parts of the temperate climate zone and doubtless is already forested. However, some nonforested lands would surely be suitable for the establishment of forest plantations.

Another alternative would be to locate the plantations on less produc-   12
tive sites, perhaps in more northerly regions. In this situation, however, tree growth would be less rapid, and hence the total land area required and the

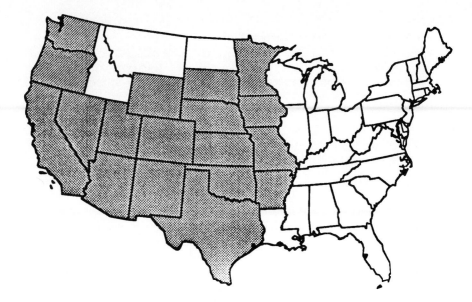

FIGURE 1.
465 million hectares of new closed forest, equivalent to the outlined area shown here, would be required to sequester all of the excess atmospheric carbon.

cost of establishing plantations would increase. In less productive sites, the total land area required could easily be several times that estimated above.

Economic Costs

The economic costs of undertaking an endeavor of this magnitude would be truly enormous. Recent estimates of established costs for forest plantation vary with the location from $230 per hectare to slightly more than $1,000 per hectare (all monetary sums are in U.S. dollars), with a mode around $400 per hectare.[8] Therefore, an initial investment cost of about $186 billion, excluding the cost of procuring the land, would be required for the establishment of 465 million hectares, the minimum area of new plantations required. While land purchase costs are also likely to vary with location, in the United States today they would average at least $400 per hectare for land with the necessary productivity and could cost as much as $1,000 per hectare.[9] Hence, startup costs for plantations in the United States would average at least $800 per hectare and possibly more.   13

If these conservative cost estimates are used, the minimum total cost of establishing 465 million hectares of carbon-sequestering plantations in temperate zones would be $372 billion, almost 10 percent of the U.S. annual gross national product (GNP). Total costs could be significantly higher, however, because highly productive agricultural lands that would demand   14 higher prices would almost certainly be required. Plantations could be located on less productive forest sites but, as noted, these sites would require larger areas, thus raising the costs of acquisition and planting. Realistically, total land procurement and plantation establishment costs would probably not be less than $500 billion. While this is a huge expenditure, society is clearly prepared to make expenditures of that magnitude for some purposes, such as the armed forces.

It should be stressed that the costs of obtaining the land are not simply   15
accounting costs that may be avoided by donations or expropriation: They represent real opportunities foregone. Land used as a carbon sink cannot be used to produce crops or livestock.

One promising possibility is to locate carbon-sequestering tree planta-   16
tions on the degraded lands of the tropics. In many parts of the tropics, these lands have little if any alternative use, and thus their cost is likely to be minimal. While large land areas are required, so too are they potentially available. Of degraded lands in the tropics, 758 million hectares, including 203 hectares of forest fallow in the humid tropics, have a potential for forest replenishment.[10] The huge volume of land area required, however, almost ensures that many low-productivity lands, perhaps in semi-arid regions, would be required, and thus the average cost per hectare necessary to establish plantations will be driven up.

In the tropics, the costs of establishing a plantation are similar to those   17
in the United States. Recent data from Indonesia indicate that plantation establishment costs on degraded grasslands are about $400 per hectare.[11] While productivity on degraded lands is sometimes low, annual growth rates of at least 15 m^3 are attainable on many sites in the tropics. If these cost and productivity figures are used as a low-cost starting point, and if the land is available at approximately no cost, the lowest total cost of establishing 465 million hectares of plantation forests can be estimated to be at least $186 billion. Taking everything (such as lower productivity, costs of land) into consideration, an estimate of at least $250 billion seems reasonable. While the economic cost would still be more than 5 percent of the annual U.S. GNP, it would be significantly lower than the total cost of a comparable carbon-sequestering plantation forest in the more temperate regions. Of course, these two courses are not mutually exclusive, and some mix of temperate and tropical sites might be optimal. In addition, wherever they are located, such forests would require significant follow-up protection and would incur additional maintenance costs.

Disposing of the Timber

A final factor that could affect the economic feasibility of using forests as a   18
carbon sink is disposal of the mature timber. The issue becomes less pressing if the purpose of the plantations is simply to buy time to develop a more adequate approach for dealing with carbon releases from fossil fuels. If

plantations were to be used for longer than a single rotation period of 20 to 50 years, however, this factor would become more pressing. If plantations are to continue to sequester high levels of carbon, it would be necessary to harvest mature trees to make way for a new, more rapidly growing second rotation. For example, it has been suggested that shorter rotations may be necessary to keep the level of sequestering high.[12] However, this suggestion ignores the problem of disposing of harvested timber. If the timber is simply treated as industrial wood, the large volumes harvested could severely disrupt world markets by depressing prices and generating a host of adverse impacts. In addition, anticipation of large volumes of timber from carbon-sequestering plantations would discourage tree planting and forest management elsewhere. Furthermore, much (but not all) industrial wood is quickly decomposed—for example, in the production of many paper products—and thereby the carbon-sequestering function is lost. If the timber is to maintain its carbon-sequestering function, it must remain undecomposed indefinitely. Additional costs would be involved in harvesting, transporting, inventorying, and preserving the timber. Assuming a harvest rotation of 30 years involving 450 m^3 per hectare and a harvest transportation cost of $15 per m^3, the total harvest-related costs would be $6,750 per hectare, exclusive of preservation and timber storage costs, which promise to be significant. This suggests that 30 years hence, costs for the 465 million hectares would amount to $3.14 trillion, plus substantial storage and preservation costs.

Intensive Forest Management

Another way to sequester excess atmospheric carbon might be to increase the biomass growth of the world's existing forests through improved forest management. To sequester all the excess atmospheric carbon, biomass growth for the 3,000 million hectares of existing closed forests would have to increase by an average of 4 m^3 per hectare per year, or about 2.5 m^3 per hectare for stemwood. This option would require an approximate doubling of the average forest growth rate in all of the world's closed forests, temperate and tropical. While intensive forest management has demonstrated its ability to increase forest productivity, a rapid increase in the total forest biomass—involving an approximate doubling of growth and an accompanying biomass accumulation—would be needed to sequester the excess carbon over the next several decades, even if emission levels remain the same.

19

Much of the increased productivity from intensive management is generated by operations introduced early in the growing cycle. These include planting, which insures a fully stocked stand; using genetically improved trees; controlling weeds for newly planted seedlings; and so forth. While these activities currently occur in the process of reforestation after a harvest, the pace at which they occur would need to accelerate dramatically to double the existing forest's growth rate and significantly increase biomass in the next few decades. Most of the increase in forest growth would have to come from increases induced in the already established stands.

20

The introduction of fertilizer is probably the most effective way to in- 21
crease growth during the growing cycle. Experiments have shown significant
responses to fertilization in older stands.[13] However, even if the growth rate
were to increase 80 percent in response to fertilization,[14] the efficacy of widespread fertilizer application to existing timber stands to accelerate growth and
carbon sequestering is questionable: Because much of the Earth's closed-for-
est inventory is now mature or "overmature," little net growth is biologically possible even if fertilizer were added.[15] Furthermore, a large fraction of
the world's forests are in cool northern climates where the potential growth
rate is constrained by the decreasing biomass productivity associated with
colder latitudes.[16] The burden of increasing overall average growth would
fall, therefore, upon the young and middle-aged stands in warmer climates,
but these stands are, in many cases, already growing relatively rapidly and
may already be managed.

In summary, while forest management can accelerate growth, much of 22
the advantage of forest management comes with initial forest establishment
and the early years of growth, rather than with existing, mature forest. It
thus appears unlikely that it would be technically feasible to double the growth
rate of the world's existing closed forest while simultaneously maintaining
and accumulating the increased biomass in a short period of time—for example, one or two decades.

Reduced Industrial Wood Harvests

If forests are to be useful in sequestering a greater amount of carbon, the 23
total forest biomass must ultimately increase. While dramatic increases in the
growth rates of many existing forests are unlikely to take place in the absence
of massive afforestation, forest biomass could be increased by lengthening
industrial timber rotations through a temporary reduction of the harvest. An
additional 1.5 billion m^3 of industrial stemwood (the current global annual
harvest) in the forests could be maintained if commercial harvesting completely ceased. The volume of biomass associated with this amount is roughly
2.4 billion m^3 (using a factor of 1.6 to include all biomass) and the carbon
captured therein would be about 600 million tons, or roughly 20 percent of
the annual excess of carbon. Of course, a substantial fraction of industrial
wood already remains in solid form and only decays slowly over many years.
Also, some nonstemwood parts of harvested trees (the root system) also decay slowly. Therefore, since so much of the biomass stays captured for some
time regardless of whether the trees are harvested, the actual net increase in
carbon captured from a no-harvest policy would probably be considerably
less—in the neighborhood of 300 million tons, or roughly one-tenth of the
excess atmospheric CO_2.

These findings suggest that even the extreme use of available techniques 24
to increase the biomass of existing forest area by either increasing growth or
reducing timber harvests is likely to have only a very modest effect on the
buildup of excess atmospheric carbon.

Natural Forest Expansion

A final mechanism by which forest stocks might conceivably increase is that   25
of a naturally generated buildup of forest biomass as the result of the global
warming process itself. In the Gaia Hypothesis, James E. Lovelock has suggested that the global environment can adapt to some degree to the changing
stresses placed upon the system.[17] One mechanism whereby the global "organism" might adapt to, and in part offset, a warming trend would be for
the warming to precipitate an expansion of some carbon-sequestering system, for example, the global forest system. Warmer temperatures, particularly at the higher elevations, perhaps in concert with enhanced rates of forest
growth brought about by the fertilization effects of increased CO_2 concentrations, might lead to an expansion of the forests into previously nonforested
areas. Depending upon how the lottery of temperature and precipitation
changes plays out, plausible outcomes of the greenhouse effect could be either
an increase or decrease in both the land area covered by and the biomass of
the world's forests. Clark S. Binkley, who is examining the implications of
the greenhouse effect for the industrial wood supply, has projected a considerable expansion of the world's exploitable boreal forests in response to global
warming.[18] His projections of total inventories, however, assumed that forest
inventories elsewhere would not change. While increased CO_2 levels will
probably cause forests to expand in some regions, they are likely to contract
in others. Roger A. Sedjo and Allen Solomon estimate the result of a doubling of CO_2 to be a modest net decrease in both total forest area and total
forest biomass.[19] However, one difficulty with both of these schemes (and
with most attempts to estimate how much warming affects the natural expansion of forest) is the inability to account properly for the changes in water
efficiency found with higher atmospheric CO_2 levels. Laboratory experiments suggest that plants may use water more efficiently in an atmosphere
with high CO_2 levels. Thus, a change in the regional temperature/precipita-
tion mix may be associated with higher CO_2 levels. However, the nature of
any potential change is, as yet, not well understood.

Since no current estimates are definitive, it may be instructive to esti-   26
mate the natural forest expansion that would be required to mitigate the buildup
of atmospheric CO_2 and to explore the plausibility of sufficient land areas
being available should the forest-expanding effect of warming be greater than
estimated. Assume for convenience that most of the expansion would take
place in such sparsely populated areas as the boreal forest, where there are
few competing human uses for land and relatively modest forest growth rates,
perhaps an average of 2 m^3 per hectare per year.[20] If we accept an adjustment
factor of 1.6 to account for the limbs, roots, and so on and an average of
0.26 tons of carbon sequestered per cubic meter of forest growth, roughly
0.83 tons of carbon per hectare will be sequestered annually. At this rate, a
net addition of 3.5 billion hectares of new forest would be required to sequester the excess carbon. This represents more than a doubling of the world's
area of closed forests and an increase in total forest area from the current 4

billion hectares to 7.5 billion hectares. The total forest area would be about 60 percent greater than the estimated 4.7 billion hectares that would exist today in the absence of significant human disturbance.[21]

The requisite 3.5 billion hectares of land is not available for naturally   27 generated boreal forest expansion. Such expansion could occur only if very large areas of nonboreal land were to become reforested. While some combination of forest expansion and increased forest growth could hypothetically be sufficient to sequester the excess atmospheric carbon, practical considerations suggest that natural processes are not likely to provide substantial near-term assistance to humans in mitigating CO_2 buildup, even under the most favorable conditions. This conclusion is reinforced by other considerations. For example, the modest rate of natural migration of forests ensures that any process of natural forest expansion would occur slowly, and even if an expansion of forest area should occur, it would at best coincide with and mitigate, rather than postpone, general global warming.

Carbon Sequestering Implications

If total global biomass increases, carbon sequestering will occur. As long as   28 a greater stock of biomass can be maintained, a higher level of carbon will be permanently sequestered. Carbon released by the burning of fossil fuels would simply be shifted from a fossil fuel to biomass residence. In a physical sense, a larger permanent stock of forest need not preclude industrial and fuel-wood harvesting at higher levels. As an example, a higher level of industrial and/or fuel-wood use need not exacerbate the atmospheric CO_2 problem if an increased stock of forest were established and maintained to "feed" that use. That is, the burning or destruction of biomass per se will not increase free carbon if the total stock of biomass is constant or rising.

The substitution of wood energy for fossil fuel energy would have the   29 advantage of decreasing the rate of carbon release from fossil fuels in the process of energy production. Thus, to mitigate global warming, less carbon from fossil fuels would ultimately need to find a nonatmospheric residence. This advantage could be maintained as long as the total stock of forest biomass did not decline. To meet this condition, the lands from which wood fuels are taken would need to be reforested to recapture the carbon freed by burning the wood. Thus, a continuous process of mature forest burning and new forest growth could sequester the carbon released in the wood burning.

The energy potential of the wood from the 465 million hectares of needed   30 plantation would be very large. In fact, one year's wood energy potential would be greater than the energy generated in two years by all the coal-fired power plants in the United States.[22] From an economic perspective, investments in energy forest plantations and power-generating equipment could offer some financial return. The output of the plantations would become feedstock in the power generation process and would replace high-priced fossil fuels. Thus, the basic question is, "How financially competitive can wood-burning power generation become as a substitute for the current fossil fuel modes of energy production?" Because wood is not now an important source of energy, it appears that the market does not, given present-day prices and technology, view wood energy as generally competitive with fossil fuel energy. If wood is now financially inferior, could its widespread use be justified, and perhaps subsidized, on the basis of global warming considerations?

Policy Options

Most proposals to mitigate the CO_2 buildup will involve some combination   31
of reducing tropical deforestation, conserving energy, and substituting other energy sources for fossil fuels. Nonetheless, these policies in themselves are unlikely to be sufficient to suspend the buildup of atmospheric CO_2. A policy to establish large areas of plantations, preferably in conjunction with a dramatic decrease in the rate of tropical deforestation, could contribute significantly to the postponement of the CO_2 buildup and hence delay global warming. While the costs would be high, they are not unprecedented; the U.S. defense budget annually operates in hundreds of billions of dollars.

Policy decisions, however, must always be made with great care. Al-   32
though a global warming mechanism exits in the greenhouse effect and concentrations of CO_2 and other greenhouse gases have clearly been rising for several decades, a definitive global temperature increase has not been documented. The global climate system is not totally understood. Hence, considerable uncertainty still exists. The global community is faced not only with the possibility of failing to act when it should act, but also with the possibility of acting when it need not. Because many of the proposed actions are very costly, prudence must be exercised.

Notes

1. See Jill Jäger, "Climatic Change: Floating New Evidence in the CO_2 Debate," *Environment*, September 1986, 6.

2. Roger Revelle, "Some Ideas and Conclusions from the Workshop," in N. J. Rosenberg, W. E. Easterling III, P. R. Crosson, and J. Darmstadter, eds., *Greenhouse Warming: Abatement and Adaption* (Washington, D.C.: Resources for the Future (forthcoming)).

3. R. P. Detwiler and Charles A. S. Hall, "Tropical Forest and the Global Carbon Cycle," *Science* 239 (1 January 1988):42–47.

4. Charles F. Cooper, "Carbon Storage in Managed Forests," *Canadian Journal of Forest Research* 13(1983):155–65; Sandra Brown, Ariel E. Lugo, and Jonathan Chapman, "Biomass of Tropical Tree Plantations and Its Implications for the Global Carbon Budget," *Canadian Journal of Forest Research* 16(1986):390–94; and Gregg Marland, "The Prospect of Solving the CO_2 Problem through Global Reforestation," DOE/NBB-0082 (Washington, D.C.: U.S. Department of Energy, Office of Energy Research, 1988).

5. P. Farnum, R. Timmis, and J. L. Kulp, "Biotechnology of Forest Yield," *Science* 219 (1983):694–702.

6. Brown et al., note 4 above.

7. J. P. Lanly and J. Clement, "Present and Future National Forest and Plantation Areas in the Tropics," *Unasylva* 31(1979):123; United Nations Food and Agriculture Organization, *Conservation and Development of Tropical Forest Resources,* Forestry Paper 37 (Rome: United Nations

Food and Agricultural Organization, 1982); and Sandra Postel and Lori Heise, "Reforesting the Earth," Worldwatch Paper 83 (Washington, D.C.: Worldwatch Institute, April 1988).

8. Roger A. Sedjo, *The Comparative Economics of Plantation Forests* (Washington, D.C.: Johns Hopkins Press for Resources for the Future, 1983), 161.

9. David Graham, Principal, Forest Investment Associations, Atlanta, Georgia, letter to the author, 24 May 1988.

10. Alan Grainger, "Estimating Areas of Degraded Tropical Lands Requiring Replenishment of Forest Cover," *International Tree Crops Journal* 5(1988):1–2.

11. Japan International Cooperative Agency, "Technical Guidance for Afforestation on the Grasslands in Benekat South Sumatra," ATA-186, JICA, Jakarta.

12. Cooper, note 4 above.

13. E. D. Ford, "The Dynamics of Plantation Growth," and E. K. S. Nambiar, "Plantation Forests: Their Scope and a Perspective on Plantation Nutrition," in G. D. Bowen and E. K. S. Nambiar, eds., *Nutrition of Plantation Forests* (London: Academic Press, 1984).

14. D. I. Beverge, "Wood Yield and Quality in Relation to Tree Nutrition," in G. D. Bowen and E. K. S. Nambiar, note 13 above.

15. For the USSR, see J. Holowacz, "Forests in the U.S.S.R.," *The Forestry Chronicle* 61, no. 5(1985):366–73; for China, see Dennis Richardson, "Forestry in China—Revisited," an unpublished manuscript; and for Canada, see G. M. Bonnor, "Canada's Forest Inventory 1981," Forestry Statistics & Systems Branch, Canadian Forestry Service, Department of Environment, Chalk River, Ontario, 1982, 79.

16. J. Zavitkovski and J. G. Isebrands, "Biomass Production and Energy Accumulation in the World's Forests," Paper presented at the Seventh International Forest Products Research Society Industrial Wood Energy Forum, 1983, Madison, Wisconsin, 1:12–22.

17. J. E. Lovelock, *Gaia: A New Look at Life on Earth* (New York: Oxford University Press, 1979).

18. C. S. Binkley, "The Impact of Climatic Variations on Agriculture: Introduction to the IIASA/UNEP Case Studies," in M. L. Parry, T. R. Carter, and N. T. Konijn, eds., *The Impact of Climate Variations on Agriculture, Volume I. Assessments in Cool Temperate and Cold Regions* (Dordrecht, the Netherlands: Kluwer Academic Publishers, 1988).

19. R. A. Sedjo and Allen Solomon, "Climate and Forests," in *Greenhouse Warming: Abatement and Adaption*, note 2 above.

20. P. Kauppi and M. Posch, "A Case Study of the Effects of CO_2-induced Climatic Warming on Forest Growth and the Forest Sector: A. Productivity Reactions of Northern Boreal Forests," in M. L. Parry, T. R. Carter, and N. T. Konijn, note 18 above.

21. E. Matthews, "Global Vegetation and Land Use: New High Resolution Data Base for Climate Studies," *Journal of Climate and Applied Meteorology* 22 (1983):474–87.

22. Estimate provided by Joel Darmstadter, Energy Division, Resources for the Future, Washington, D.C.

QUESTIONS FOR MEANING

1. What two factors have led to interest in reforestation as a response to global warming?
2. What are the advantages and disadvantages of planting forests on productive land in warm climates? Why not plant trees on less productive northern sites?
3. Does Sedjo anticipate any difficulties in disposing of the timber produced through reforestation?

4. What sort of management techniques can increase the efficiency of forests as carbon sinks?

5. Are there any advantages to burning wood rather than fossil fuels such as oil and coal?

6. Vocabulary: terrestrial (1), viable (2), sequester (3), negligible (4), hectare (8), silvicultural (8), optimal (17), host (18), feasible (22), boreal (26), requisite (27), exacerbate (26).

QUESTIONS ABOUT STRATEGY

1. How does Sedjo establish himself as an authority on this topic? Does he succeed in convincing you that he knows what he is talking about?

2. Why does Sedjo devote so much of his article to analyzing the costs that reforestation would entail? While emphasizing these costs, does he employ any strategy to suggest that they might nevertheless be bearable?

3. Consider the last sentence in paragraph 30. Is this question designed to inspire any particular response?

4. Where does Sedjo first state his thesis, and where does he restate it?

5. Although this article makes an argument for using forests to help delay the effects of global warming, the last paragraph calls for caution rather than action. Does this paragraph lead you to take Sedjo's argument more seriously or less?

BILL McKIBBEN
The End of Nature

Of the writers who have raised concern over global warming during the past decade, Bill McKibben is one of the best known. He is the author of The End of Nature, *a much-praised book published by Random House in* **1989.** *The selection provided here is taken from a long excerpt of the book published in* The New Yorker, *to which McKibben is a regular contributor. McKibben, who lives in the Adirondack Mountains of New York, has also published in* Rolling Stone, The Washington Monthly, *the* New York Times, *and the* New York Review of Books.

The single most talked-about consequence of a global warming is probably   1
the expected rise in sea level as a result of polar melting. For the last several thousand years, sea level has been rising, but so slowly that it has almost been a constant. In consequence, people have extensively developed the coastlines. But a hundred and twenty thousand years ago, during the previous interglacial period, sea level was twenty feet above the current level; at the height of the last ice age, when much of the world's water was frozen at the poles, sea level was three hundred feet below what it is now. Scientists estimate that the world's remaining ice cover contains enough water so that

if it should all melt it would raise sea level more than two hundred and fifty feet. This potential inundation is stored in the Greenland Ice Sheet (if it melts, it will raise the world's oceans twenty-three feet), the West Antarctic Ice Sheet (another twenty-three feet), and East Antarctica (more than two hundred feet), with a smaller amount—perhaps half a metre—in the planet's alpine glaciers. (Melting the ice currently over water, such as the sea ice of the Arctic Ocean, won't raise sea level, any more than a melting ice cube overflows a gin-and-tonic.) The East Antarctic is relatively safe; the direst fears of a rising sea came as the result of a 1968 study concluding that the Ross and Filchner-Ronne ice shelves, which support the West Antarctic Ice Sheet, could disintegrate within forty years. Subsequent investigations, however, seem to have demonstrated that such a disintegration would take at least two centuries, and probably more like five (though several investigators have speculated that it might become irreversible within the next century).

But the salvation of the West Antarctic does not mean the salvation of   2
Bangladesh, or even of East Hampton. A number of other factors may raise sea level significantly. Glaciers bordering the Gulf of Alaska, for example, have been melting for decades, and constitute a source of fresh water about the size of the entire Mississippi River system. And even if nothing at all melted, the increased heat would raise sea level considerably. Warm water takes up more space than cold water; this thermal expansion, given a global temperature increase of between one and a half and five and a half degrees Celsius, should raise sea level a foot, according to [National Aeronautics & Space Administration's] James Hansen. It is by now widely accepted that sea level will rise significantly over the next decades. The Environmental Protection Agency has estimated that it will rise between five and seven feet by 2100, and speculated about worst-case scenarios that might lead to an eleven-foot rise; the National Academy of Sciences has been more conservative; other researchers have turned in even scarier numbers. Suffice it to say that included in the range of guesses of almost every panel and scientist studying the problem is an increase in global sea level of better than three feet over the next century.

That may not sound like very much, but it means that the sea would   3
reach a height unprecedented in the history of civilization. The immediate effects of the swollen sea would be seen in a place like the Maldives. By most accounts, this archipelago of eleven hundred and ninety small islands about four hundred miles southwest of Sri Lanka is fairly paradisal. Its residents had never heard a gun fired in anger until last year, when a short-lived coup attempt was mounted by foreign mercenaries. They survived the downturn in the coir business (coir is an elastic fibre made from coconut husks); breadfruit and citron trees are abundant. But most of this happy nation rises only two metres above the Indian Ocean. If sea level were to rise one metre, storm surges would become an enormous, crippling danger; were it to rise two metres—well within the range of possibilities predicted by many studies—the country would all but disappear. In October of 1987, the Maldivian President, Maumoon Abdul Gayoom, went before the United Nations General Assembly. He described his country as "an endangered nation." The

Maldivians, he pointed out, "did not contribute to the impending catastrophe . . . and alone we cannot save ourselves." A map drawn a hundred
years from now may not show the Maldives at all, except as a danger to
mariners.

Other nations, though not extinguished, would be very badly hurt. A   4
two-metre rise in sea level would flood twenty per cent of the land in Bangladesh, much of which is built on the flood plains at the mouth of the Brahmaputra. In Egypt, such a rise would inundate less than one per cent of the
land, but that area constitutes much of the Nile Delta, where most of the
population lives. Nor is the danger only to the Third World. Several years
ago, the E.P.A. distributed a worksheet to allow local governments to calculate their future position vis-à-vis the salt water. In Sandy Hook, New
Jersey, for instance, add thirteen inches to the projected increase in sea level
to account for local geologic subsidence, for a net ocean rise, in the next
hundred years, of four feet one inch. In Massachusetts, between three thousand and ten thousand acres of oceanfront land worth between three billion
and ten billion dollars might disappear by 2025, and that figure does not
include land lost to encroaching ponds and bogs as the rising sea lifts the
water table. But storm surges would do the most dramatic damage: in Gal-
veston, Texas, ninety-four per cent of the land is within the plain that would
be flooded by the worst storms. Such surges are the reason that Holland built
many of its protective dikes. The most extensive barriers went up after the
winter of 1953, when a surge breached the existing dikes in eighty-nine places
along the central delta, killing nearly two thousand people and tens of thousands of cattle. Afterward, the Dutch decided to spend more than three billion dollars building new defenses.

As the Dutch effort indicates, much can be done to defend against in-   5
creases in sea level. The literature abounds with studies of how much it would
cost to protect coastal areas. The trouble is, spending the money to protect
the shoreline would lead to ecological costs harder to calculate but easy to
understand. Coastal marshes or wetlands exist in a nearly unbroken chain
along the Gulf and Atlantic Coasts of the United States. Protected from the
waves of the ocean by barrier islands or peninsulas, they are part land and
part water, and are home to an abundance of plants and animals. They are
more biologically productive than either the ocean or the dry land, in part
because tidal flows spread food and flush out waste; it is a cycle that encourages quick growth and rapid decay. These communities support an immense
variety of birds, fish, shellfish, and plants. Early settlers (with noble exceptions, like William Bartram) thought coastal marshes "misamal," and drained
or filled many of them. In recent years, federal and state authorities have
grudgingly begun to protect them. As King Canute demonstrated, however,
the ocean disregards governments, and as its level rises the area of the wetlands will dwindle. This is not axiomatic; if the marsh has room and time
enough to back up, it will, and the drowned wetland will be replaced by a
new one. But, as another recent E.P.A. report pointed out, "in most areas
. . . the slope above the marsh is steeper than the marsh; so a rise in sea

level causes a net loss of marsh acreage." That is, in many cases the marsh will run into a cliff it can't climb. In a number of places, the cliffs will be man-made. If I have a house on Cape Cod, and my choice is to build a wall in front of it or let a marsh come in and colonize my basement, I will probably build the wall.

Should the ocean go up a metre, at least half the nation's coastal wet- 6 lands will be lost one way or another. "Most of today's wetland shorelines still would have wetlands," according to the E.P.A. report to Congress. "The strip would simply be narrower. By contrast, protecting all mainland areas would generally replace natural shorelines with bulkheads and levees." The relentlessly practical authors add that "this distinction is important because for many species of fish, the length of a wetland shoreline is more critical than the total area." It's also important if you are used to the idea of the ocean meeting the land with ease and grace instead of bumping into an endless concrete wall.

There are other reasons to fear a sea-level rise. In normal times, the 7 water pouring out of a river pushes the ocean back. But in a drought the reduced flow creates a vacuum that the sea oozes in to fill. The "salt front" advances. In the drought of the nineteen-sixties, it nearly reached the point in the Delaware River where Philadelphia's water intake is located. During a drought, New York City must release vast quantities of water from its reservoirs on the upper Delaware to keep the salt front from creeping upriver. New Yorkers, however, continue to take showers and wash their hands. In the summer of 1985, city officials made up for the diminished flow from reservoirs by pumping water straight from the Hudson. This worked well— the water turned out to be considerably cleaner than many had expected— except that as the flow of the Hudson was reduced the salt front began to move up *that* river, and the town fathers of Poughkeepsie grew worried about *their* supply's getting salty. As the greenhouse warming kicks in, increased evaporation could steal from ten to twenty-four per cent of the water in New York's reservoirs, the E.P.A.'s 1988 report continues. In addition, a one-metre sea-level rise could push the salt front up past the city's water intake on the Hudson. In all, the report observes, "doubled carbon dioxide could produce a shortfall equal to twenty-eight to forty-two per cent of planned supply in the Hudson River Basin."

The expected effects of sea-level rise typify the many other conse- 8 quences of a global warming. On the one hand, they are of such magnitude that we can't grasp them. If there is significant polar melting, the earth's center of gravity will shift, tipping the globe in such a way that sea level might actually drop at Cape Horn and along the coast of Iceland. (I read this in the E.P.A. report and found that I didn't really know what it meant to tip the earth, though I was awed by the idea.) On the other hand, the changes ultimately acquire a quite personal dimension: Should I put a wall in front of my house? Does this taste salty to you? What's more, many of the various effects of the warming compound one another. If the weather grows hotter and I take more showers, more water must be diverted from the river, and the salt front moves upstream, and so on. The complications multiply almost endlessly (more air-conditioning means more power generated means more water sucked from the rivers to cool the generators means less water flowing downstream, et cetera ad infinitum). These aren't the simple complexities of, say, last summer, when everyone on the East Coast rushed to the beaches to escape the hot weather, only to discover a tide of syringes and fecal matter. These complexities are the result of throwing every single natural system into an uproar at the same time, so that none of nature's reliable compensations can be counted on. For example, at the same time that sea level is increasing, and the warmer air is gathering up more water vapor and presumably increasing the over-all precipitation, the temperature is continuing to go up. The result, the computer modellers say, will be greatly increased levels of evaporation; in many parts of the world, there will be a drier interior to complement the sodden coasts.

It's not simply a matter of heat. If the temperature rises, the number of   9 days with snow cover will likely fall. When the snow-melting season ends, more of the sun's energy is absorbed by the ground instead of being reflected back to space, and, as a result, the soil begins to dry out. In the greenhouse world, this seasonal change will begin earlier, because the snow will melt faster. In some areas, other weather changes may offset the evaporation. Roger Revelle, of the Scripps Institution, has estimated that flows in the Niger, the Sengal, the Volta, the Blue Nile, the Mekong, and the Brahmaputra would increase—probably with disastrous results in the last two cases—whereas flows might diminish in the Hwang Ho, in China; the Amu Darya and the Syr Darya, which run through the Soviet Union's principal agricultural areas; the Tigris-Euphrates system; and the Zambezi. The United States, as usual, has been most closely studied. America is blessed with ample water; on an average day, four trillion two hundred billion gallons of precipitation fall on the lower forty-eight states. Most of that water evaporates, leaving only about one trillion four hundred and thirty-five billion gallons a day, of which in 1985 only about three hundred and forty billion gallons a day were withdrawn for human use. It seems like more than enough. However, as anyone who has ever flown across the nation (and looked out the window) can attest, the water is not spread evenly. In its report to Congress, the E.P.A. notes that total water use exceeds average stream flow in twenty-four of the fifty-three Western water-resource regions, a difference made up by "mining" groundwater stocks and importing water. Much of the Colorado River's flow, for example, is damned, diverted, and consumed by irrigation projects and by the millions upon millions of people living in places that would otherwise be too dry.

And matters may get worse. After studying the temperature and   1(streamflow records, Revelle and the climatologist Paul Waggoner concluded that if a "conservative," two-degree-Celsius increase in temperature occurs, the virgin flow of the Colorado could fall by nearly a third; the same study predicts that if, as some of the computer models suggest, this temperature rise is accompanied by a ten-per-cent decrease in precipitation in the

Southwest because of new weather patterns, runoff into the upper Colorado could fall by forty per cent. Even if rainfall went *up* ten per cent, the runoff would still drop by nearly twenty per cent. Across the West, the picture is similar: in the Missouri, Arkansas, lower-Colorado, and Rio Grande irrigation regions, supply could fall by more than half. In the Missouri, Rio Grande, and Colorado basins, the estimated water needs in the year 2000 could not be met by stream flows after the expected climate changes. One model predicts a twenty-five-per-cent increase in the demand for irrigation water from the Ogallala Aquifer, the subterranean lake that irrigates the Great Plains and is already badly depleted.

A compelling question is what all this means for agriculture. The answer comes on several levels, the first being that of the individual plant. Quite apart from heat and drought, the simple increase of atmospheric carbon dioxide affects plants. Ninety per cent of the dry weight of a plant comes from the conversion of carbon dioxide into carbohydrates by photosynthesis. If nothing else limits a plant's growth—if it has plenty of sunshine, water, and nutrients—then increased carbon dioxide should increase the yield. And in ideal laboratory conditions this is what happens; as a result, some journalists have rhapsodized about "supercucumbers" and found other green linings to the cloud of greenhouse gases. But there are drawbacks. If some crops grow more quickly, farmers may need to buy more fertilizer, since leaves may become richer in carbon but poorer in nitrogen, reducing food quality not only for human beings but for nitrogen-craving insects, who may eat more leaf to get their fix. In the best case, direct effects of increased carbon dioxide on yield are expected to be small; the annual harvest of well-tended crops might rise about five per cent when the carbon-dioxide level reaches four hundred parts per million, all other things being equal.   11

But all other things won't be equal. All other things—moisture, temperature, growing season—will be different. It is an obvious point, but worth repeating: most of what we eat spends its growing life in the open air, "exposed," in the words of Paul Waggoner, "to the annual lottery of the weather." About fifty million acres of America's cropland and rangeland are irrigated, but even those fields depend on the weather over any long stretch. And we can't just stick the wheat crop under glass.   12

It is a tricky business trying to predict what changes in the weather will do to crops. A longer growing season—the period between killing frosts—surely helps; a lack of moisture surely hurts. If temperatures stay warm, plants grow nicely. If temperatures get really hot, they wither. (A long stretch above ninety-five degrees Fahrenheit, for instance, can sterilize corn.) The climate models are too crude to project with any precision what will happen in a given area, and too many variables make even the broadest predictions difficult. The severe droughts of the Dust Bowl years provide scant guidance: on the one hand, the technological revolution in agriculture has tripled yields since then, but on the other, as a government report notes, "the economic robustness associated with general multiple-enterprise farms has long since passed from the scene on any significant scale," and therefore "the current   13 vulnerability of our agricultural system to climate change may be greater in some ways than in the past." Most of the experts have simply thrown up their hands. The best guesses seem to be that the northern reaches of the Soviet Union and Canada will be able to grow more food and the Great Plains of the United States less—not so little that America couldn't feed itself but enough below present production so that United States food exports, which earn the country some forty billion dollars in a good year, might fall by seventy per cent. "It has been suggested," Stephen Schneider told the Senate energy committee last year, "that a future with soil-moisture change . . . would translate to a loss of comparative advantage of United States agricultural products on the world market"—a sentence to make an economist shiver on an August day.

This sounds like somewhat comforting news—as if we would still have enough to eat—but when computers are modelling something as complex as all of agriculture the potential for error is enormous (or the potential for accuracy is small). The effect of the heat and drought of 1988 made liars of most of the computer models in just a few weeks. They had concluded that the expected doubling of carbon dioxide in several decades might make the weather hot and dry enough to cut American corn and soybean yields as much as twenty-seven per cent, but in the summer of 1988, when the rains held off, the American corn crop fell thirty per cent—down by about two and a half billion bushels.

Even if, as seems likely, that heat wave had little to do with the greenhouse effect, we now have some idea what it will feel like once it is here. As of late August, the grain stored around the world amounted to only about two hundred and eighteen million metric tons—enough to last forty-seven days, and the lowest level since 1973. Worldwide consumption of grain outpaced worldwide production by sixty million metric tons last year. You can live with a budget deficit for quite a while, but when the food runs out there's no central bank to mint some more.

The thing to remember is that all these changes may be happening at once. It's hotter, and it's drier, and sea level is rising as fast as food prices, and hurricanes are strengthening, and so on. And not least is the simple fact of daily life in a hotter climate. The American summer of 1988, when no one talked about anything but the heat and how soon it would end, was only a degree or two warmer, on average, than what we were used to. But the models predict that summers could eventually be five or six or seven degrees warmer than the old "normal." Science has yet to devise a way of determining what percentage of people feel like human beings on any given August afternoon, or the number of work hours lost to the third cold bath of the day—or, for that matter, the loss of wit and civility in a population concerned mainly with keeping its shirts dry. These are important matters, and a future full of summers like that one is a grim prospect. Summer will come to mean something different—not the carefree season anymore but a time to grit one's teeth and get through. To anyone who lived through the 1988 heat it seems unlikely that people will simply get used to it.

A certain number of people who didn't get used to the heat died of it.   17
Public-health researchers have correlated mortality and temperature tables.
When the weather gets hot, they find, preterm births and perinatal deaths
both rise. Mortality from heart disease goes up during heat waves, and em-
physema gets worse. If, the E.P.A. notes, in its 1988 report to Congress,
"climate change encourages a transition from forest to grassland in some
areas, grass pollens could increase," worsening hay fever and asthma. "A
variety of other U.S. diseases indicate a sensitivity to changes in weather,"
the report continues. "Higher humidity may increase the incidence and severity of fungal skin diseases (such as ringworm and athlete's foot), and yeast
infections (candidiasis). Studies on soldiers stationed in Vietnam during the
war indicated that outpatient visits for skin diseases (the largest single cause
of outpatient visits) were directly correlated to increases in humidity."

That last sentence suggests that a useful place to look for information   18
about American weather might be Vietnam. There is nothing wrong with
the Vietnamese climate—it is not "better" or "worse" than the various
American climates, or the weather in Britain, or the cold of Canada. And
people have been able to move back and forth between all these zones, adapting to conditions. In fact, we often want to—a change of climate is perhaps
the single biggest inducement to travel. But now the climate is travelling. A
recent United Nations study estimates that sometime in the next century the
climate of Finland will have become similar to that of northern Germany,
that of southern Saskatchewan to northern Nebraska, of the Leningrad region to the western Ukraine, of the central Urals to central Norway, of
Hokkaido to northern Honshu, and of Iceland to northeast Scotland. If we
felt like keeping the weather we're accustomed to, it's we who would have
to move, travelling north ahead of the heat.

The list of miscellaneous circumstances that might result from changes   19
in the atmosphere looks to be infinite. In New York City, the heat of the
summer of 1988 softened asphalt and caused thousands of "hummocks"—
potholes in reverse—in the streets. "When it's over ninety degrees for a prolonged period of time, the problem is virtually out of control," Lucius Ric-
cio, of the New York City Bureau of Highway Operations, told the *Times*.
Steel expansion joints buckled along Interstate 66 around Washington, D.C.,
during the heat wave, and a hundred and sixty people were injured when a
train derailed in Montana, apparently because the heat warped the rails. Coupled with the physical predictions are endless political and financial conjectures. Francis Bretherton, of the National Center for Atmospheric Research,
told *Time* that if the Great Plains became a dust bowl and people followed
the seasonable temperatures north, Canada might replace the United States
as the Western superpower.

This game swings from the specific to the wildly speculative. There is   20
no easy way to say that something can't happen or is unlikely to happen;
forecasts have to be based on the past, and there is no longer a relevant past.
Jesse Ausubel, the director of programs at the National Academy of Engineers, told *Fortune* that it "may become difficult to find a site for a dam or

an airport or a public transportation system or anything designed to last thirty to forty years," and asked, "What do you do when the past is no longer a guide to the future?" We are left with a vast collection of "mights," and only one certainty: we have changed the world, and therefore some of the "mights" are inevitable. I find myself thinking often of some purple-martin chicks that Penny Moser found "cooked to death" near her Illinois farm in 1988's heat. This was an actual event and also a metaphor. The heat will cook the eggs of birds, and that destruction—and the hurricanes and the rising sea and the dying forests—will rob us of our sense of security. That the temperature had never reached a hundred degrees at the airport in Glens Falls, the city nearest my home, made it a decent bet that it never would. And then, in July of 1988, it did. There is no good reason anymore to say that it won't reach a hundred and ten degrees. The old planet is a different planet. There is no reason to feel secure, because there is no reason to be secure. . . .

But what about increasing efficiency—what about conservation? There is—no question—waste, even sixteen years after the energy crisis. For example, most of the electricity consumed by industry is used to drive motors; companies, anticipating expansion, tend to buy larger motors than they need; however, large motors are inefficient when they run at less than full speed. The latest edition of the *World Resources* yearbook estimates that if every industrial motor in the United States were to be equipped with available speed-control technology America's total electricity consumption would fall seven per cent. We must end waste, the sooner the better. But will this kind of action *solve* the problem? Consider a few numbers supplied by Irving Mintzer, of the World Resources Institute. He describes a "base case" scenario that "reflects conventional wisdom in its assumptions about technological change, economic growth, and the evolution of the global energy system." In this model, nations do not enact policies to slow carbon-dioxide emissions, nor do they provide more than minimal support for increased energy efficiency and solar research and development, though they do slow the rate of chlorofluorocarbon production. The result is an average global warming of up to 4.7°F. by the year 2000, and of up to 8.5°F. by 2030. This, Mintzer says, "is by no means the worst possible outcome." If the use of coal and synthetic fuels is encouraged, and tropical deforestation continues to increase, the planet would be doomed to an increase of up to 12.6°F. by 2030, and by 2075, to a nearly thirty-degree jump—a level with implications too sci-fi for us to imagine. The good news, such as it is, concerns Mintzer's "slow buildup scenario." In this one, strong international efforts to reduce greenhouse-gas emissions "eventually stabilize the atmosphere's composition." Coal, gas, and oil prices are markedly increased, per-capita energy use declines in industrialized countries, and governments actively pursue the development of solar energy. The world embarks on "massive" reforestation efforts. And so on. If all these heroic efforts had begun in 1980, by 2075 we would experience a warming of between 2.5°F. and 7.6°F., which is still "greater than any experienced during recorded human history."

Carbon dioxide and other greenhouse gases come from everywhere, so   22
the situation they create can be fixed only by fixing everything. Small substitutions and quick fixes are not the answer. One common suggestion is to
replace much of the coal and oil we burn with methane, since it produces
considerably less carbon dioxide. But . . . any methane that escapes unburned into the atmosphere traps solar radiation twenty times as efficiently
as carbon dioxide does. And methane does leak—from wells, from pipelines,
from appliances; some estimates suggest that as much as three per cent of the
natural gas tapped in this country escapes unburned. So converting from oil
to natural gas might make the situation worse. The size and complexity of
the industrial system we have built makes even small course corrections
physically difficult.

Not only is that system huge but the trend toward growth is incredibly   23
powerful. At the simplest level—population—the increase continues, if not
unabated, then only slightly abated. In some of the developing countries,
thirty-seven per cent of the population is under fifteen years of age; in Africa,
the figure is forty-five per cent. Without a static population, even the most
immediate and obvious goals, like slowing deforestation or reducing fossil-
fuel use, seem far-fetched. Over the last century, a human life has become a
machine for burning petroleum. At least in the West, the system that produces excess carbon dioxide is not only huge and growing but also psychologically all-encompassing. It makes no sense to talk about cars and power
plants and so on as if they were something apart from our lives—they *are*
our lives. Moreover, for any program to be a success we must act not only
as individuals and as nations but as a community of nations. The trouble is,
though, that some countries may perceive themselves to be potential winners
in a climate change. The Russians may decide that the chance of increased
harvests from a longer growing season is worth the risk of global warming.
And the United States, the Soviet Union, and China own about two-thirds
of the world's coal reserves, so any of them can scuttle progress. The possibilities of other divisions—rich nations versus poor nations, say—are large.
Every country has its own forms of despoliation to protect; the Canadians,
for instance, who complain loudly about their position as helpless victims of
American acid rain, are cutting down the virgin forests of British Columbia
at an almost Brazilian pace. And the fact that decisions must be made now
for the decades ahead means that, in the words of Richard Benedick, our
Deputy Assistant Secretary of State for Environment, Health, and Natural
Resources, "somehow, political leaders and government processes and bud-
get-makers must accustom themselves to a new way of thinking." Of all the
quixotic ideas discussed here, that may top the list.

The greenhouse effect is often compared to the destruction of the ozone   24
layer, another example of atmospheric pollution with global implications.
But the destruction of the ozone layer can and likely will be solved by our
ceasing to produce the chemicals currently destroying it. Though this step
won't end the problem overnight, it will take care of it eventually. And,

though the necessary international negotiations may be complex, steps like this are easy enough so that they will certainly be taken. Essentially, it's like controlling DDT. The problem of global warming, however, does not yield to the same sort of solution. With aggressive action—as Mintzer's numbers indicate—we can "stabilize" the situation at a level that is only mildly horrific, but we cannot solve it.

This is not to say that we should not act. We must act in every way   2!
possible, and immediately. We stand at the end of an era—the hundred years' binge of oil, gas, and coal which has given us both the comforts and the predicament of the moment. Even those countries which wouldn't object to a degree or two of warming for a longer growing season can't endure endless heating. The choice of doing nothing—of continuing to burn ever more oil and gas and coal—is not a choice. It will lead us, if not straight to hell, then straight to a place with a comparable temperature.

QUESTIONS FOR MEANING

1. Why might the oceans rise even if the world's great ice sheets do not melt?
2. What are the disadvantages to building dikes and seawalls to guard against rising sea levels?
3. How might global warming lead to the salinization of fresh water supplies?
4. What effects on agriculture are projected by McKibben? Why does a government report speculate that "the current vulnerability of our agricultural system to climate change may be greater in some ways than in the past"?
5. Why is McKibben concerned about the world's grain reserves?
6. In addition to considering environmental and economic effects of global warming, does McKibben suggest any possible effects upon human behavior?
7. Why is population growth a factor in planning a response to global warming?
8. Vocabulary: inundation (1), direst (1), archipelago (3), axiomatic (5), ad infinitum (8), attest (9), perinatal (17), quixotic (23).

QUESTIONS ABOUT STRATEGY

1. Is there any advantage in discussing the effects of rising sea levels upon the Maldives and Bangladesh before turning, as McKibben does, to possible effects on New Jersey and Massachusetts?
2. In paragraph 8, McKibben pauses to make a parenthetical observation: "I read this in the E.P.A. Report and found that I didn't really know what it meant to tip the earth, though I was awed by the idea." Why do you think he tells us this?
3. Does McKibben make you feel that global warming concerns you as an individual? If so, how did he achieve this effect?
4. In his last paragraph, McKibben insists upon the importance of action. But could his essay leave some readers feeling the situation is hopeless?

Has he gone too far in emphasizing the extent of the problem as he sees it? Or is all the information he provides essential for generating concern?

ONE STUDENT'S ASSIGNMENT

Write an essay on global warming that will define the degree to which you believe it is a problem and argue what, if anything, should be done to prevent future harm to the environment. Include material from at least three sources in The Informed Argument, *but do not use any other sources. Use APA style documentation. Since your sources will come from the textbook we are using in class, you do not need to include a reference list for this particular assignment.*

Trading Panic for Practicality

Pamela Pape

It's one hundred degrees as far north as Madison, Wisconsin. Farmers in Nebraska unhappily watch their crops wither on the stem. The elderly are dying of heat exhaustion in Indiana. Who wouldn't start to suspect that the earth's climate was getting warmer while living in such a sweltering hot box. In the 1980s, a string of summers just like these sparked quick belief in the greenhouse effect; however, evidence has not yet proved the existence of a global warming trend.   1

Simplified, the greenhouse effect works as its name suggests. Certain greenhouse gases, namely carbon dioxide, methane, nitrous oxide and chlorofluorocarbons (CFCs) let the sun's rays penetrate through to the earth as would the window panes in a greenhouse. However, these gases do not let heat radiate back out into space; hence, the simple equation: more greenhouse gases equal more heat in the atmosphere.   2

So where are these gases coming from? Burning fossil fuels is the main cause of carbon dioxide buildup (Bidinotto, 1990). That means that much of our lives is spent polluting the atmosphere, whether we're turning on the light after the alarm goes off, driving to and from work, or building a cozy fire to relax by. Our refrigerators, air conditioners, and hair spray all release CFCs into the air. And our cattle herds and cultivated rice paddies pass methane in their quiet way.   3

The result, concerned environmentalists fear, is an   4
extra-thick blanket of greenhouse gases which insulates
the earth. They point to the 1980s as proof of its influence. Severe drought, record highs, terrible hurricanes, world-wide crop failure, and devastating forest
fires all seemed to signal that the greenhouse effect
was tightening its grip (Moore, 1989). Further evidence
would include stratospheric cooling and ocean warming,
the former of which was discovered in two separate studies (Murphy, 1989).

But is the greenhouse effect entirely a man-made   5
menace? On the contrary, it is a natural phenomenon and
is, to a degree, essential to life on earth. "Without
its heat-containing effect the planet would freeze, like
the atmospherically naked moon" (Brookes, 1989, p. 243).
Volcanoes, oceans, swamps, and decaying plants all produce greenhouse gases which permeate the atmosphere, and
have done so for thousands of years. It would seem that
the danger would lie in enhancing this effect; it is not
inherently hazardous, or something we need to destroy.

As for all the incriminating evidence from the   6
1980s, how much importance does a decade hold in the
history of the world? Really, do ten hot years with
lousy weather prove anything conclusively? Random annual
variation or "noise" makes it difficult for scientists
to detect any trends. And while there are no studies to
refute stratospheric cooling, studies done at MIT suggest that the ocean isn't warming as it should according
to the greenhouse theory (Brookes, 1989).

What it all comes down to is that proponents of   7
global warming have taken their measurements and found a
net gain of one degree Fahrenheit in the average global
temperature over the last century (Moore, 1989). However, closer examination of the evidence shows that,
Between 1800 and 1940 temperatures appeared to rise. Yet
between 1940 and 1965, a period of much heavier fossil-
fuel use and deforestation, temperature dropped . . ."
(Bidinotto, 1990, p. 233). In addition, other scientists
calculated a rise of only one-third of one degree
Celsius in the last century when taking into account
the artificial inflation of statistics due to the
effects of urbanization (Brookes, 1989).

So is the earth warming or isn't it? Greenhouse   8
theorists predict alarming scenarios of what our future
holds. According to them, nothing short of apocalypse is
out of reach. Estimates vary, but the models describe
melting at the poles, innundation of cities close to sea
level, shifting weather patterns, and increasing desertification. However, these predictions are produced by
computer programs, which, in turn, are created by humans, who, though they are trying, have only a small
grasp of how the atmosphere works.

If the weather forecasters can't confidently tell   9
me whether it will rain or not tomorrow, how can they
tell me that New York will be in two feet of standing
water by 2010? There are just as many theories on the
other side: increased cloud cover will counteract the
warming trend; increased condensation will thin the
greenhouse blanket, etc. Each of these statements is
just as probable as any other.

The problem with these predictions is that they   10
really don't tell us anything useful. The real trouble
is that we don't understand how everything fits together. There are too many variables. The greenhouse effect grabs the headlines because cataclysm sells; the
scientific method doesn't (Brookes, 1989). Experimentation and true understanding lose out to the panicked acceptance of a scientific theory put in simplified terms
for easy public consumption. To make matters worse, politicians can jump on the environmentalists' bandwagon
and ride the global warming theory to a seat in the
capitol.

However, a simple awareness of the possible futures   11
associated with the greenhouse effect can foster positive action. For example, researchers are developing a
"smart window" which would electronically change in
response to need, reflecting the sun on hot days, and
allowing the rays to penetrate on cold days. Developing more efficient fluorescent bulbs and alternate in-
sulating systems for refrigerators (not using CFCs)
are two more practical advances (Begley & Pedersen,
1990).

In addition to these advances, there are alterna-   12
tives that we have not fully explored, or ceased to ex-

plore. Whether or not carbon dioxide emissions are
affecting the atmosphere, the fact remains that fossil
fuels are a finite source of energy. The government's
half-hearted attempts at funding research and development of solar, geothermal, wind, and nuclear (especially
fusion) energy are just putting off the inevitable.
Whatever happened to gasohol? It suffered an unnatural
death under the feet of the oil companies. Even minimal
changes in our lifestyles would help conservation efforts——the development of mass transit systems, for example. Our options are only limited by our imagination
and the government's determination.

 Instead of getting haunted by the greenhouse ghost,
let's direct ourselves at the heart of the matter. How
does the earth's climate work? What can we do to keep it
healthy? Developing alternatives is the way to keep our
options open. The future will come in its own time;
let's prepare ourselves as best we can to meet it.

SUGGESTIONS FOR WRITING

1. Drawing upon the argument by Michael Murphy, Enrique Bucher, and
   Bill McKibben, synthesize the projected effects of global warming.
2. Robert Bidinotto, Peter Shaw, and Warren Brookes all question the likelihood of global warming. Write a synthesis of their views.
3. Summarize the article by Roger Sedjo on the role of forests in moderat-
   ing global warming.
4. Both Curtis Moore and Roger Sedjo refer to the destruction of tropical
   rain forests. Do a research paper to determine the extent to which rain
   forests were destroyed during the 1980s and whether the remaining forests are still at risk.
5. How serious is the problem of ozone depletion? Drawing upon Curtis
   Moore, Robert Bidinotto, and your own research, write an argument
   for or against the need to restrict the use of choloroflurocarbons (CFCs).
6. Do research to determine how another industrialized nation, such as Great
   Britain or Germany, is responding to the threat of global warming. Write
   an argument focused upon what we can learn from this response.
7. Murphy, Moore, Bidinotto, Brookes, Shaw, and McKibben all cite James
   E. Hansen as a source in their arguments. Do research on Hansen and
   evaluate his credibility as a source.
8. Sharon Begley and Daniel Pederson suggest industry is developing new
   products that will encourage more efficient energy use. Write an argu-

ment focused upon whether we should change any of the ways we use energy in the United States.

9. Since the banning of fossil fuels is widely cited as a factor in the buildup of greenhouse gases, would increasing the use of nuclear energy help prevent global warming? Do research on nuclear energy and argue for or against its use.

10. Even if global warming proves to be an exaggerated fear, are there any steps that we should take to protect deteriorating coastlines and shrinking wetlands? Drawing upon the work of Bill McKibben, write an argument focused upon how these areas should be treated.

SECTION 4

ANIMAL EXPERIMENTATION:

DO RATS HAVE RIGHTS?

◆

JEAN BETHKE ELSHTAIN

Why Worry About the Animals?

The Centennial Professor of Political Science at Vanderbilt University, Jean Bethke Elshtain has also taught political science at the University of Massachusetts. She is the author of several books, including The Prism of Sex: Toward an Equitable Pursuit of Knowledge *(1980),* Private Woman: Women in Social and Political Thought *(1981), and* The Family in Political Thought *(1982). Elshtain, who has a Ph.D. from Brandeis University, published the following argument in a **1990** issue of* The Progressive, *where she serves as a member of the Editorial Advisory Board. Her work also appears in other periodicals including* Commonweal, The Nation, *and* Newsday.

These things are happening or have happened recently:

- The wings of seventy-four mallard ducks are snapped to see whether crippled birds can survive in the wild. (They can't.)
- Infant monkeys are deafened to study their social behavior, or turned into amphetamine addicts to see what happens to their stress level.
- Monkeys are separated from their mothers, kept in isolation, addicted to drugs, and induced to commit "aggressive" acts.
- Pigs are blowtorched and observed to see how they respond to third-degree burns. No pain-killers are used.
- Monkeys are immersed in water and vibrated to cause brain damage.
- For thirteen years, baboons have their brains bashed at the University of Pennsylvania as research assistants laugh at signs of the animals' distress.
- Monkeys are dipped in boiling water; other animals are shot in the face with high-powered rifles.

The list of cruelties committed in the name of "science" or "research"   2
could be expanded endlessly. "Fully 80 per cent of the experiments involving
rhesus monkeys are either unnecessary, represent useless duplication of previous work, or could utilize nonanimal alternatives," says John E. McArdle,
a biologist and specialist in primates at Illinois Wesleyan University.

Growing awareness of animal abuse is helping to build an increasingly   3
militant animal-welfare movement in this country and abroad—a movement
that is beginning to have an impact on public policy. Secretary of Health and
Human Services Frederick Goodwin complained recently that complying with
the new Federal regulations on the use—or abuse—of animals will drain off
some 17 per cent of the research funds appropriated to the National Institutes
of Health. (It is cheaper to purchase, use, and destroy animals than to retool
for alternative procedures.) One of the institutes, the National Institute of
Mental Health, spends about $30 million a year on research that involves pain
and suffering for animals.

The new animal-welfare activists are drawing attention in part because   4
of the tactics they espouse. Many preach and practice civil disobedience, violating laws against, say, breaking and entering. Some have been known
to resort to violence against property and—on a few occasions—against
humans.

Some individuals and groups have always fretted about human respon-   5
sibility toward nonhuman creatures. In the ancient world, the historian Plu-
tarch and the philosopher Porphyry were among those who insisted that human
excellence embodied a refusal to inflict unnecessary suffering on all other
creatures, human and nonhuman.

But with the emergence of the Western rationalist tradition, animals   6
lost the philosophic struggle. Two of that tradition's great exponents, René
Descartes and Immanuel Kant, dismissed out of hand the moral worth of
animals. Descarte's view, which has brought comfort to every human who
decides to confine, poison, cripple, infect, or dismember animals in the interest of human knowledge, was the more extreme: He held that animals are
simply machines, devoid of consciousness or feeling. Kant, more sophisticated in his ethical reasoning, knew that animals could suffer but denied that
they were self-conscious. Therefore, he argued, they could aptly serve as
means to human ends.

To make sure that human sensibilities would not be troubled by the   7
groans, cries and yelps of suffering animals—which might lead some to suspect that animals not only bleed but feel pain—researchers have for a century
subjected dogs and other animals to an operation called a centriculocordectomy, which destroys their vocal chords.

Still, there have long been groups that placed the suffering of animals   8
within the bounds of human concern. In the Nineteenth and early Twentieth
Centuries, such reform movements as women's suffrage and abolitionism
made common cause with societies for the prevention of cruelty to animals.
On one occasion in 1907, British suffragettes, trade-unionists, and their animal-

welfare allies battled London University medical students in a riot triggered by the vivisection of a dog.

Traditionally, such concern has been charitable and, frequently, highly sentimental. Those who perpetrated the worst abuses against animals were denounced for their "beastly" behavior—the farmer who beat or starved his horse; the householder who chained and kicked his dog, the aristocratic hunter, who, with his guests, slew birds by the thousands in a single day on his private game preserve.   9

For the most part, however, animals have been viewed, even by those with "humane" concerns, as means to human ends. The charitable impulse, therefore, had a rather condescending, patronizing air: Alas, the poor creatures deserve our pity.   10

The new animal-welfare movement incorporates those historic concerns but steers them in new directions. Philosophically, animal-rights activists seek to close the gap between "human" and "beast," challenging the entire Western rationalist tradition which holds that the ability to reason abstractly is *the* defining human attribute. (In that tradition, women were often located on a scale somewhere between "man" and "beast," being deemed human but not quite rational.)   11

Politically, the new abolitionists, as many animal-welfare activists call themselves, eschew sentimentalism in favor of a tough-minded, insistent claim that animals, too, have rights, and that violating those rights constitutes oppression. It follows that animals must be liberated—and since they cannot liberate themselves in the face of overwhelming human hegemony, they require the help of liberators much as slaves did in the last century.   12

Thus, the rise of vocal movements for animal well-being has strong historic antecedents. What is remarkable about the current proliferation of efforts is their scope and diversity. Some proclaim animal "rights." Others speak of animal "welfare" or "protection." Still others find the term "equality" most apt, arguing that we should have "equal concern" for the needs of all sentient creatures.   13

When so many issues clamor for our attention, when so many problems demand our best attempts at fair-minded solution, why animals, why now? There is no simple explanation for the explosion of concern, but it is clearly linked to themes of peace and justice. Perhaps it can be summed up this way: Those who are troubled by the question of who is or is not within the circle of moral concern; those who are made queasy by our use and abuse of living beings for our own ends; those whose dreams of a better world are animated by some notion of a peaceable kingdom, *should* consider our relationship with the creatures that inhabit our planet with us—the creatures that have helped sustain us and that may share a similar fate with us unless we find ways to deflect if not altogether end the destruction of our earthly habitat.   14

Dozens of organizations have sprung up, operating alongside—and sometimes in conflict with—such older mainline outfits as the Humane Society, the Anti-Vivisection League, and the World Wildlife Fund. Among the   15 new groups are People for the Ethical Treatment of Animals (PETA), Trans-Species Unlimited, In Defense of Animals, the Gorilla Foundation, Primarily Primates, Humane Farming Association, Farm Animal Reform, Alliance for Animals, Citizens to End Animal Suffering and Exploitation (CEASE), Whale Adoption Project, Digit Fund—the list goes on and on.

Some organizations focus on the plight of animals on factory farms, especially the condition of anemic, imprisoned veal calves kept in darkness and unable to turn around until they are killed at fourteen weeks. Others are primarily concerned with conditions in the wild, where the habitat of the panda, among others, is being destroyed or where great and wonderful creatures like the black rhinoceros and the African elephant or magnificent cats like the snow leopard or the Siberian tiger are marching toward extinction, victims of greedy buyers of illegal tusks or pelts. [16]

Another group of activists clusters around the use of animals in such profitable pursuits as greyhound racing, where dogs by the hundreds are destroyed once they cease "earning their keep," or in tourist attractions where such wonderfully intelligent social beings as the orca and the dolphin are turned into circus freaks for profit. In the wild, orcas can live for up to 100 years; in captivity, the average, sadly misnamed "killer whale" lasts about five. [17]

Those wonderful chimpanzees that have been taught to speak to us through sign-language also arouse concern. If the funding ends or a researcher loses interest, they are sometimes killed, sometimes turned over to the less-than-tender mercies of laboratory researchers to be addicted to cocaine, infected with a virus, or subjected to some other terrible fate. Eugene Linden describes, in his study *Silent Partners*, chimps desperately trying to convey their pain and fear and sadness to uncomprehending experimenters. [18]

Use of animals in war research is an industry in itself, though one usually shielded from public view. Monkeys are the most likely subjects of experiments designed to measure the effects of neutron-bomb radiation and the toxicity of chemical-warfare agents. Beginning in 1957, monkeys were placed at varying distances from ground zero during atomic testing; those that didn't die immediately were encaged so that the "progress" of their various cancers might be noted. [19]

Radiation experiments on primates continue. Monkeys' eyes are irradiated, and the animals are subjected to shocks of up to 1,200 volts. Junior researchers are assigned the "death watch," and what they see are primates so distressed that they claw at themselves and even bite hunks from their own arms or legs in a futile attempt to stem the pain. At a Government proving ground in Aberdeen, Maryland, monkeys are exposed to chemical-warfare agents. [20]

Dolphins, animals of exquisite intelligence, have been trained by the military in such scenarios as injecting carbon dioxide cartridges into Vietnamese divers and planting and removing mines. The Navy announced in April 1989 that it would continue its $30 million clandestine program, expanded in the Reagan years, to put dolphins to military use. The aim, *The* [21]

New York Times reported, is to use dolphins captured in the Gulf of Mexico to guard the Trident Nuclear Submarine Base at Bangor, Washington.

Several years ago, when I was writing a book on women and war, I came across references to the use of dogs in Vietnam. When I called the Pentagon and was put through to the chief of military history, Southeast Asia Branch, he told me that no books existed on the subject, but he did send me an excerpt from the *Vietnam War Almanac* that stated the U.S. military "made extensive use of dogs for a variety of duties in Vietnam, including scouting, mine detecting, tracking, sentry duty, flushing out tunnels, and drug detecting." Evidently, many of these dogs were killed rather than returned home, since it was feared their military training ill-suited them for civilian life.

Much better known, because of an increasingly successful animal-rights campaign, is the use of animals to test such household products as furniture polish and such cosmetics as shampoo and lipstick.

For years, industry has determined the toxicity of floor wax and detergents by injecting various substances into the stomachs of beagles, rabbits, and calves, producing vomiting, convulsions, respiratory illness, and paralysis. The so-called LD (lethal dose) 50 test ends only when half the animals in a test group have died. No anesthesia or pain killers are administered.

Dr. Andrew Rowan, assistant dean of the Tufts Unviersity School of Medicine, has offered persuasive evidence that such testing methods are crude and inaccurate measures of a product's safety. For one thing, a number of potentially significant variables, including the stress of laboratory living, are not taken into account, thus tainting any comparison of the effect of a given substance on human consumers.

The LD50 is notoriously unreproducible; the method for rating irritation is extremely subjective; and interspecies variations make test results highly suspect when applied to the human organism.

Most notorious of the "tests" deployed by the multibillion-dollar cosmetics industry is the Draize, which has been used since the 1940s to measure the potential irritative effects of products. Rabbits—used because their eyes do not produce tears and, therefore, cannot cleanse themselves—are placed into stocks and their eyes are filled with foreign substances. When a rabbit's eyes ulcerate—again, no pain killers are used—the cosmetics testers (who are usually not trained laboratory researchers) report a result. To call this procedure "scientific" is to demean authentic science.

Curiously, neither the LD50 test nor the Draize are required by law. They continue in use because manufacturers want to avoid alarming consumers by placing warning labels on products. More accurate methods available include computer simulations to measure toxicity, cell-culture systems, and organ-culture tests that use chicken-egg membranes.

The disdainful response by corporate America to animal-protection concerns seems, at least in this area, to be undergoing a slow shift toward new laboratory techniques that abandon wasteful, crude, and cruel animal testing. Several large cosmetics manufacturers, including Revlon, have only recently announced that they will phase out animal testing, confirming the claim of animal-welfare groups that the tests are unnecessary.

Among the nastier issues in the forefront of the "animal wars" is the   30
controversy over hunting and trapping.

It's estimated that about seventeen million fur-bearing animals (plus   31
"trash" animals—including pets—the trapper doesn't want) are mangled each year in steel-jaw leg-hold traps that tear an animal's flesh and break its bones. Many die of shock or starvation before the trapper returns. Some animals chew off part of a limb in order to escape. More than sixty countries now ban the leg-hold trap, requiring the use of less painful and damaging devices.

Protests against the manufacture, sale, and wearing of fur coats have   32
been aggressively—and successfully—mounted in Western Europe. In Holland, fur sales have dropped 80 per cent in the last few years. Radical groups in Sweden have broken into fur farms to release minks and foxes. An effort to shame women who wear fur has had enormous impact in Great Britain.

Similar campaigns have been mounted in the United States, but the fur   33
industry is waging a well-financed counterattack in this country. Curiously, the industry's efforts have been tacitly supported by some rights-absolutists within feminism who see wearing a fur coat as a woman's right. It's difficult to think of a greater *reductio ad absurdum* of the notion of "freedom of choice," but it seems to appeal to certain adherents of upwardly mobile, choice-obsessed political orthodoxy.

Hunting may be the final frontier for animal-welfare groups. Because   34
hunting is tied to the right to bear arms, any criticism of hunting is construed as an attack on constitutional freedoms by hunting and gun organizations, including the powerful and effective National Rifle Association. A bumper sticker I saw on a pickup truck in Northampton, Massachusetts, may tell the tale: MY WIFE, YES. MY DOG, MAYBE. BUT MY GUN, NEVER.

For some animal protectionists, the case against hunting is open and   35
shut. They argue that the vast majority of the estimated 170 million animals shot to death in any given year are killed for blood sport, not for food, and that the offspring of these slaughtered creatures are left to die of exposure or starvation. Defenders of blood sports see them as a skill and a tradition, a lingering relic of America's great frontier past. Others—from Nineteenth Century feminists to the Norman Mailer of *Why Are We in Vietnam?*—link the national mania for hunting with a deeper thirst for violence.

I am not convinced there is an inherent connection between animal kill-   36
ing and a more general lust for violence, but some disquieting evidence is beginning to accumulate. Battered and abused women in rural areas often testify, for example, that their spouses also abused animals, especially cows, by stabbing them with pitchforks, twisting their ears, kicking them, or in one reported incident, using a board with a nail in it to beat a cow to death.

But even people who recoil from hunting and other abuses of animals   37
often find it difficult to condemn such experiments as those cited at the beginning of this article, which are, after all, conducted to serve "science" and, perhaps, to alleviate human pain and suffering. Sorting out this issue is no

easy task if one is neither an absolute prohibitionist nor a relentless defender of the scientific establishment. When gross abuses come to light, they are often reported in ways that allow and encourage us to distance ourselves from emotional and ethical involvement. Thus the case of the baboons whose brains were bashed in at the University of Pennsylvania prompted *The New York Times* to editorialize, on July 31, 1985, that the animals "seemed" to be suffering. They *were* suffering, and thousands of animals suffer every day.

Reasonable people should be able to agree on this: that alternatives to   38 research that involves animal suffering must be vigorously sought; that there is no excuse for such conditions as dogs lying with open incisions, their entrails exposed, or monkeys with untreated, protruding broken bones, exposed muscle tissue, and infected wounds, living in grossly unsanitary conditions amidst feces and rotting food; that quick euthanasia should be administered to a suffering animal after the conclusion of a pain-inducing procedure; that pre- and post-surgical care must be provided for animals; that research should not be needlessly duplicated, thereby wasting animal lives, desensitizing generations of researchers, and flushing tax dollars down the drain.

What stands in the way of change? Old habits, bad science, unreflective   39 cruelty, profit, and, in some cases, a genuine fear that animal-welfare groups want to stop all research dead in its tracks. "Scientists fear shackles on research," intones one report. But why are scientists so reluctant to promote such research alternatives as modeling, in-vitro techniques, and the use of lower organisms? Because they fear that the public may gain wider knowledge of what goes on behind the laboratory door. Surely those using animals should be able to explain themselves and to justify their expenditure of the lives, bodies, and minds of other creatures.

There is, to be sure, no justification for the harassment and terror tactics used by some animal-welfare groups. But the scientist who is offended   40 when an animal-welfare proponent asks, "How would you feel if someone treated your child the way you treat laboratory animals?" should ponder one of the great ironies in the continuing debate: Research on animals is justified on grounds that they are "so like us."

I *do* appreciate the ethical dilemma here. As a former victim of polio, I   41 have thought long and hard for years about animal research and human welfare. This is where I come down, at least for now:

First, most human suffering in this world cannot be ameliorated in any   42 way by animal experimentation. Laboratory infliction of suffering on animals will not keep people healthy in Asia, Africa, and Latin America. As philosopher Peter Singer has argued, we already know how to cure what ails people in desperate poverty; they need "adequate nutrition, sanitation, and health care. It has been estimated that 250,000 children die each week around the world, and that one quarter of these deaths are by dehydration due to diarrhea. A simple treatment, already known and needing no animal experimentation, could prevent the deaths of these children."

Second, it is not clear that a cure for terrible and thus far incurable   43 diseases such as AIDS is best promoted with animal experimentation. Some

American experts on AIDS admit that French scientists are making more rapid progress toward a vaccine because they are working directly with human volunteers, a course of action Larry Kramer, a gay activist, has urged upon American scientists. Americans have been trying since 1984 to infect chimpanzees with AIDS, but after the expenditure of millions of dollars, AIDS has not been induced in any nonhuman animal. Why continue down this obviously flawed route?

Third, we could surely agree that a new lipstick color, or an even more   44
dazzling floor wax, should never be promoted for profit over the wounded bodies of animals. The vast majority of creatures tortured and killed each year suffer for *nonmedical* reasons. Once this abuse is eliminated, the really hard cases having to do with human medical advance and welfare can be debated, item by item.

Finally, what is at stake is the exhaustion of the Eighteenth Century   45
model of humanity's relationship to nature, which had, in the words of philosopher Mary Midgley, "built into it a bold, contemptuous rejection of the nonhuman world."

Confronted as we are with genetic engineering and a new eugenics,   46
with the transformation of farms where animals ranged freely into giant factories where animals are processed and produced like objects, with callous behavior on a scale never before imagined under the rubric of "science," we can and must do better than to dismiss those who care as irrational and emotional animal-lovers who are thinking with their hearts (not surprisingly, their ranks are heavily filled with women), and who are out to put a stop to the forward march of rationalism and science.

We humans do not deserve peace of mind on this issue. Our sleep should   47
be troubled and our days riddled with ethical difficulties as we come to realize the terrible toll one definition of "progress" has taken on our fellow creatures.

We must consider our meat-eating habits as well. Meat-eating is one of   48
the most volatile, because most personal, of all animal-welfare questions. Meat-eaters do not consider themselves immoral, though hard-core vegetarians find meat-eating repugnant—the consumption of corpses. Such feminist theorists as Carol Adams insist that there is a connection between the butchering of animals and the historic maltreatment of women. Certainly, there is a politics of meat that belongs on the agenda along with other animal-welfare issues.

I, for one, do not believe humans and animals have identical rights. But   49
I do believe that creatures who can reason in their own ways, who can suffer, who are mortal beings like ourselves, have a value and dignity we must take into account. Animals are not simply a means to our ends.

When I was sixteen years old, I journeyed on a yellow school bus from   50
LaPorte, Colorado, to Fairbanks, Iowa, on a 4-H Club "exchange trip." On the itinerary was a visit to a meat-packing plant in Des Moines. As vivid as the day I witnessed it is the scene I replay of men in blood-drenched coats "bleeding" pigs strung up by their heels on a slowly moving conveyer belt. The pigs—bright and sensitive creatures, as any person who has ever met

one knows—were screaming in terror before the sharp, thin blade entered their jugular veins. They continued to struggle and squeal until they writhed and fell silent.

The men in the slaughter room wore boots. The floor was awash in   51
blood. I was horrified. But I told myself this was something I should remember. For a few months I refused to eat pork. But then I fell back into old habits—this was Colorado farm country in the late 1950s, after all.

But at one point, a few years ago, that scene and those cries of terror   52
returned. This time I decided I would not forget, even though I knew my peace of mind would forever be disturbed.

QUESTIONS FOR MEANING

1. How do organizations like PETA differ from older, more mainstream organizations such as the Humane Society?
2. What is the purpose of a centriculocordectomy?
3. Proponents of animal experimentation often emphasize that it is essential to finding a cure for fatal diseases such as AIDS. How does Elshtain respond to this argument?
4. *Reductio ad absurdum* is Latin for reduction to an absurdity. Can you explain why insisting upon the right to wear a fur coat could be considered an absurd extention of the right to free choice? Paraphrase paragraph 33.
5. Vocabulary: espouse (4), exponents (6), eschew (12), hegemony (12), variables (25), tacitly (33), disquieting (36), ameliorated (42), eugenics (46), rubric (46).

QUESTIONS ABOUT STRATEGY

1. Elshtain opens her essay with a list of experiments that have caused animals to suffer. What advantage is there to this type of opening? Are there any disadvantages?
2. In paragraph 22, Elshtain mentions her research on women and war. Do the references to women in this essay limit its audience?
3. Consider the use of quotation marks in paragraph 37. What is the point of using them?
4. Where in this argument does Elshtain reveal what she wants? Would her recommendations work better elsewhere?
5. In paragraph 41, Elshtain describes herself as "a former victim of polio." Why do you think she shares this aspect of her life? How effective is her use of personal experience in paragraphs 50–52?

RON KARPATI

A Scientist: 'I Am the Enemy'

*A graduate of the UCLA medical school who did his pediatric training at Children's Hospital of Los Angeles, Ron Karpati is currently a fellow in pediatric oncology and bone marrow transplantation at the University of California, San Francisco. He published the following argument in a **1989** issue of* Newsweek, *where it appeared in "My Turn." A regular feature in* Newsweek, *"My Turn" provides a means for writers to reach a large audience by publishing their views in a national newsmagazine, but it is limited to approximately 1,100 words—the equivalent of a single page in the magazine. Working within the constraints of this space, Karpati offered a justification for the use of animals in medical research.*

I am the enemy! One of those vilified, inhumane physician-scientists involved in animal research. How strange, for I have never thought of myself as an evil person. I became a pediatrician because of my love for children and my desire to keep them healthy. During medical school and residency, however, I saw many children die of leukemia, prematurity and traumatic injury—circumstances against which medicine has made tremendous progress, but still has far to go. More important, I also saw children, alive and healthy, thanks to advances in medical science such as infant respirators, potent antibiotics, new surgical techniques and the entire field of organ transplantation. My desire to tip the scales in favor of the healthy, happy children drew me to medical research.

My accusers claim that I inflict torture on animals for the sole purpose   2
of career advancement. My experiments supposedly have no relevance to medicine and are easily replaced by computer simulation. Meanwhile, an apathetic public barely watches, convinced that the issue has no significance, and publicity-conscious politicians increasingly give way to the demands of the activists.

We in medical research have also been unconscionably apathetic. We   3
have allowed the most extreme animal-rights protesters to seize the initiative and frame the issue as one of "animal fraud." We have been complacent in our belief that a knowledgeable public would sense the importance of animal research to the public health. Perhaps we have been mistaken in not responding to the emotional tone of the argument created by those sad posters of animals by waving equally sad posters of children dying of leukemia or cystic fibrosis.

Much is made of the pain inflicted on these animals in the name of   4
medical science. The animal-rights activists contend that this is evidence of our malevolent and sadistic nature. A more reasonable argument, however, can be advanced in our defense. Life is often cruel, both to animals and human beings. Teenagers get thrown from the back of a pickup truck and

suffer severe head injuries. Toddlers, barely able to walk, find themselves at the bottom of a swimming pool while a parent checks the mail. Physicians hoping to alleviate the pain and suffering these tragedies cause have but three choices: create an animal model of the injury or disease and use that model to understand the process and test new therapies; experiment on human beings—some experiments will succeed, most will fail—or finally, leave medical knowledge static, hoping that accidental discoveries will lead us to the advances.

Some animal-rights activists would suggest a fourth choice, claiming   5
that computer models can simulate animal experiments, thus making the actual experiments unnecessary. Computers can simulate, reasonably well, the effects of well-understood principles on complex systems, as in the application of the laws of physics to airplane and automobile design. However, when the principles themselves are in question, as is the case with the complex biological systems under study, computer modeling alone is of little value.

One of the terrifying effects of the effort to restrict the use of animals   6
in medical research is that the impact will not be felt for years and decades: drugs that might have been discovered will not be; surgical techniques that might have been developed will not be, and fundamental biological processes that might have been understood will remain mysteries. There is the danger that politically expedient solutions will be found to placate a vocal minority, while the consequences of those decisions will not be apparent until long after the decisions are made and the decision making forgotten.

Fortunately, most of us enjoy good health, and the trauma of watching   7
one's child die has become a rare experience. Yet our good fortune should not make us unappreciative of the health we enjoy or the advances that make it possible. Vaccines, antibiotics, insulin and drugs to treat heart disease, hypertension and stroke are all based on animal research. Most complex surgical procedures, such as coronary-artery bypass and organ transplantation, are initially developed in animals. Presently undergoing animal studies are techniques to insert genes in humans in order to replace the defective ones found to be the cause of so much disease. These studies will effectively end if animal research is severely restricted.

In America today, death has become an event isolated from our daily   8
existence—out of the sight and thoughts of most of us. As a doctor who has watched many children die, and their parents grieve, I am particularly angered by people capable of so much compassion for a dog or a cat, but with seemingly so little for a dying human being. These people seem so insulated from the reality of human life and death and what it means.

Make no mistake, however: I am not advocating the needlessly cruel   9
treatment of animals. To the extent that the animal-rights movement has made us more aware of the needs of these animals, and made us search harder for suitable alternatives, they have made a significant contribution. But if the more radical members of this movement are successful in limiting further research, their efforts will bring about a tragedy that will cost many lives.

The real question is whether an apathetic majority can be aroused to protect its future against a vocal, but misdirected, minority.

QUESTIONS FOR MEANING

1. What evidence does Karpati cite to support his claim that animal experimentation is worthwhile?
2. Why does Karpati reject computer simulations as an alternative to animal testing?
3. According to Karpati, what are the likely effects of attempts to restrict the use of animals in research?
4. Vocabulary: vilified (1), apathetic (2), complacent (3), malevolent (4), placate (6), expedient (6).

QUESTIONS ABOUT STRATEGY

1. How do the title and opening line function within this essay? What is their purpose?
2. Karpati devotes the first half of his second paragraph to summarizing how opponents of animal-based research characterize scientists like himself. Does this strike you as a fair summary?
3. In paragraph 8, Karpati implies that people who are concerned about the suffering of animals are indifferent to the suffering of children. Is it logical to assume that the needs of animals and children necessarily conflict?
4. Within this short essay, Karpati limits himself to the topic of animal use in medical research. Is this a legitimate focus for a short essay? Does it ignore any other aspects of the controversy over animal experimentation?
5. Does Karpati make any concessions to the animal-rights movement?

JOHN G. HUBBELL

The "Animal Rights" War on Medicine

A 1950 graduate of the University of Minnesota, John Hubbell worked as a public relations specialist at Honeywell, Inc., before joining the staff of Reader's Digest *in 1955. Since 1960, he has been a roving editor of the* Digest, *which published the following article in* **1990**. *Hubbell's work has also been published in the* Saturday Evening Post *and* Catholic Digest.

In the predawn hours of July 4, 1989, members of the Animal Liberation 1
Front (ALF), an "animal rights" organization, broke into a laboratory at Texas
Tech University in Lubbock. Their target: Prof. John Orem, a leading expert
on sleep-disordered breathing.

The invaders vandalized Orem's equipment, breaking recorders, oscil- 2
loscopes and other instruments valued at some $70,000. They also stole five
cats, halting his work in progress—work that could lead to an understanding
of disorders such as Sudden Infant Death Syndrome (SIDS), or crib death,
which kills over 5000 infants every year.

An organization known as People for the Ethical Treatment of Animals 3
(PETA), which routinely issues press releases on ALF activities, quoted ALF
claims that biomedical scientists are "animal-Nazis" and that Orem "abuses,
mutilates and kills animals as part of the federal grant gravy train."

That was only the beginning of the campaign. A month later, on Au- 4
gust 18, animal-rights activists held statewide demonstrations against Orem,
picketing federal buildings in several Texas cities. The result: a flood of hate
mail to the scientist and angry letters to the National Institutes of Health
(NIH), which had awarded Orem more than $800,000 in grants. Finally PETA,
quoting 16 "experts," filed a formal complaint with the NIH which called
Orem's work "cruel" and without "scientific significance." The public had
no way of knowing that none of the 16 had any expertise in sleep-disordered
breathing or had ever been in Orem's lab.

NIH dispatched a team of authorities in physiology, neuroscience and 5
pulmonary and veterinary medicine who, on September 18, reported back.
Not only did they find the charges against Orem to be unfounded, but they
judged him an exemplary researcher and his work "important and of the
highest scientific quality."

Monkey Business

PETA first intruded on the public consciousness in 1981, during a notorious 6
episode in Silver Spring, Md. That May, a personable college student named
Alex Pacheco went to research psychologist Edward Taub for a job. Taub
was studying monkeys under an NIH grant, searching for ways to help stroke

victims regain use of paralyzed limbs. Pacheco said he was interested in gaining laboratory experience. Taub offered him a position as a volunteer, which Pacheco accepted.

Late that summer, Taub took a vacation, leaving his lab in the care of   7
his assistants. As he was about to return to work on September 11, an assistant called. Police, armed with a search warrant, were confiscating the monkeys; there was also a crowd of reporters on hand.

To his amazement, Taub was charged with 119 counts of cruelty to   8
animals—most based on information provided to the police by Alex Pacheco, who, it turned out, was one of PETA's founders.

After five years in the courts, Taub was finally cleared of all charges.   9
Yet the animal-rights movement never ceased vilifying him, producing hate mail and death threats. Amid the controversy the NIH suspended and later terminated Taub's grant (essentially for not buying new cages, altering the ventilation system or providing regular visits by a veterinarian). Thorough investigations by the American Physiological Society and the Society for Neuroscience determined that, in the words of the latter, the NIH decision was "incommensurate with the deficiencies cited." Yet a program that could have benefited many of the 2.5 million Americans now living with the debilitating consequences of stroke came to a screeching halt.

Wiped out financially, Taub lost his laboratory, though the work of   10
this gifted researcher had already helped rewrite accepted beliefs about the nervous system.

Dramatic Progress

The animal rights movement has its roots in Europe, where anti-vivisection-   11
ists have held the biomedical research community under siege for years. In 1875, Britain's Sir George Duckett of the Society for the Abolition of Vivisection declared: "Vivisection is monstrous. Medical science has little to learn, and nothing can be gained by repetition of experiments on living animals."

This sentiment is endlessly parroted by contemporary "activists." It is   12
patently false. Since Duckett's time, animal research has led to vaccines against diphtheria, polio, measles, mumps, whooping cough, rubella. It has meant eradication of smallpox, effective treatment for diabetes and control of infection with powerful antibiotics.

The cardiac pacemaker, micro-surgery to reattach severed limbs, and   13
heart, kidney, lung, liver and other transplants are all possible because of animal research. In the early 1960s, the cure rate for acute lymphocytic leukemia in a child was four percent. Today, because of animal research, the cure rate exceeds 70 percent. Since the turn of the century, animal research has helped increase our life-span by nearly 28 years. And now animal research is leading to dramatic progress against AIDS and Alzheimer's disease.

Animals themselves have benefited. We are now able to extend and   14
improve the lives of our pets and farm animals through cataract surgery,

open-heart surgery and cardiac pacemakers, and can immunize them against rabies, distemper, anthrax, tetanus and feline leukemia. Animal research is an unqualified success story.

We should see even more spectacular medical breakthroughs in the   15
coming decades. But not if today's animal-rights movement has its way.

Anti-Human Absurdities

In the United States, the movement is spearheaded by PETA, whose lead-   16
ership insists that animals are the moral equivalent of human beings. Any differentiation between people and animals constitutes "speciesism," as unethical as racism. Says PETA co-founder and director Ingrid Newkirk, "There really is no rational reason for saying a human being has special rights. . . . A rat is a pig is a dog is a boy." She compares the killing of chickens with the Nazi Holocaust. "Six million people died in concentration camps," she told the Washington *Post,* "but six billion broiler chickens will die this year in slaughterhouses."

Newkirk has been quoted as saying that meat-eating is "primitive, bar-   17
baric, arrogant," that humans have "grown like a cancer. We're the biggest blight on the face of the earth," and that if her father had a heart attack, "it would give me no solace at all to know his treatment was first tried on a dog."

The movement insists that animal research is irrelevant, that researchers   18
simply refuse to move on to modern techniques. "The movement's big buzz-word is 'alternatives,' meaning animals can now be replaced by computers and tissue cultures," says Bessie Borwein, associate dean for research-medicine at the University of Western Ontario. "That is nonsense. You cannot study kidney transplantation or diarrhea or high blood pressure on a computer screen."

"A tissue culture cannot replicate a complex organ," echoes Frederick   19
Goodwin, head of the U.S. Alcohol, Drug Abuse and Mental Health Ad-ministration (ADAMHA).

What do the nation's 570,000 physicians feel about animal research? A   20
1988 American Medical Association survey found that 97 percent of doctors support it, despite the animal-rights movement's propaganda to the contrary.

"Without animal research, medical science would come to a total stand-   21
still," says Dr. Lewis Thomas, best-selling author and scholar-in-residence at New York's Cornell University Medical College.

"As a human being and physician, I cannot conceive of telling parents   22
their sick child will die because we cannot use all the tools at our disposal," says pioneering heart surgeon Dr. Michael E. DeBakey of Houston's Baylor College of Medicine. "How will they feel about a society that legislates the rights of animals above those of humans?"

"The power of today's medical practice is based on research—and that   23
includes crucial research involving animals," adds Dr. Louis W. Sullivan, Secretary of the U.S. Department of Health and Human Services.

Radical Infiltration

How then have the animal-rights activists achieved respectability? By ex-   24
ploiting the public's rightful concern for humane treatment of animals.
ADAMHA's Goodwin explains: "They have gradually taken over highly respectable humane societies by using classic radical techniques: packing mem-
berships and steering committees and electing directors. They have insidiously
gained control of one group after another."

The average supporter has no idea that societies which traditionally   25
promoted better treatment for animals, taught pet care, built shelters and
cared for strays are now dedicated to ending the most effective kind of medical research. For example, the Humane Society of the United States (HSUS)
insists it is not anti-vivisectionist; yet it has persistently stated that animal
research is often unnecessary. It published an editorial by animal-rights proponent Tom Regan endorsing civil disobedience for the cause. Says Frederick
A. King, director of the Yerkes Regional Primate Center of Emory University, "HSUS flies a false flag. It is part of the same group that has attempted
to do severe damage to research."

PETA's chairman, Alex Pacheco, says that it is best to be "strategically   26
assertive" in seeking reforms while never losing sight of the ultimate goal:
"total abolition" of "animal exploitation." This strategy has worked. It has
taken the research community about ten years to realize that it is not dealing
with moderates. It is dealing with organizations like ALF, which since 1988
has been on the FBI's list of domestic terrorist organizations. And with Trans-
Species Unlimited, which trumpets: "The liberation of animal life can only
be achieved through the radical transformation of human consciousness and
the overthrow of the existing power structures in which human and animal
abuse are entrenched."

Consider some of the movement's "liberation activities":   27

• In the early hours of April 3, 1989, hooded animal-rights activists   28
broke into four buildings at the University of Arizona at Tucson. They smashed
expensive equipment, spray-painted messages such as "Scum" and "Nazis"
and stole 1231 animals. They set fire to two of the four buildings.

ALF took credit for the destruction, the cost of which amounted to   29
more than $200,000. Fifteen projects were disrupted. One example: 30 of the
1160 mice taken by ALF were infected with Cryptosporidium, a parasite that
can cause severe intestinal disease in humans. The project's aim was to develop an effective disinfectant for Cryptosporidium-contaminated water. Now,
not only is the work halted but researchers warn that, with less than expert
handling, the stolen mice could spread cryptosporidiosis, which remains
untreatable.

• On October 26, 1986, an ALF contingent broke into two facilities at   30
the University of Oregon at Eugene. The equipment the intruders smashed
and soaked with red paint included a $10,000 microscope, an electrocardio-
gram machine, an X-ray machine, an incubator and a sterilizer. At least 150

research animals were taken. As a result, more than a dozen projects were seriously delayed, including research by neuroscientist Barbara Gordon-Lickey on visual defects in newborns. An ALF statement called the neuroscientist a "butcher" and claimed that the animals had found new homes through "an intricate underground railroad network, much like the one used to transport fugitive slaves to the free states of the North in the last century."

Police caught up with one of the thieves: Roger Troen, 56, of Portland,   31
Ore., a member of PETA. He was tried and convicted. PETA denied complicity, but Ingrid Newkirk said that PETA would pay Troen's legal expenses, including an appeal of his conviction. PETA then alleged to the NIH that the university was guilty of 12 counts of noncompliance with Public Health Service policy on humane care and use of laboratory animals.

Following a lengthy investigation, investigators found all PETA's charges   32
groundless. "To the contrary," their report to the NIH stated, "evidence suggests a firm commitment to the appropriate care and use of laboratory animals."

But animal-rights extremists continued their campaign against Gordon-   33
Lickey. They posted placards urging students not to take her courses because she tortured animals. As Nobel Laureate Dr. David H. Hubel of Harvard University, a pioneer in Gordon-Lickey's field, says, "Their tactics are clear. Work to increase the costs of research, and stop its progress with red tape and lawsuits."

• Dr. Herbert Pardes, president of the American Psychiatric Associa-   34
tion, arrived in New York City in 1984 to take over as chairman of psychiatry at Columbia University. His office was in the New York State Psychiatric Institute, part of the Columbia Presbyterian Medical Center complex. Soon after, he noticed that people were handing out leaflets challenging the value of animal research. They picketed Dr. Pardes's home and sent him envelopes containing human feces.

Another Columbia scientist received a phone call on December 1, 1988,   35
from someone who said, "We know where you live. How much insurance do you have?" A few mornings later, he found a pool of red paint in front of his house. On January 4, 1989, a guest cottage at his country home burned down.

Devastating Results

How effective has the animal-rights movement been? Very. Although recent   36
polls reveal that more than 70 percent of Americans support animal research, about the same number believe the lie that medical researchers torture their animals.

According to ADAMHA's Frederick Goodwin, the movement has at   37
its disposal at least $50 million annually, millions of which it dedicates to stopping biomedical research. It has been especially successful in pressuring state legislatures, as well as Congress, which in turn has pressured the federal health establishment. As a result, new regulations are demoralizing many

scientists and driving up the cost of research. (For fiscal 1990, an estimated
$1.5 billion—approximately 20 percent of the entire federal biomedical-research
budget—may be needed to cover the costs of proposed regulation changes
and increased security.)

At Stanford University, a costly security system has had to be installed   38
and 24-hour guards hired to protect the animal-research facilities. As a consequence of the April 1989 raid at the University of Arizona at Tucson, the
school must now spend $10,000 per week on security, money that otherwise
could have been used for biomedical research.

Threats of violence to researchers and their families are having an effect   39
as well. "It's hard to measure," says Charles R. McCarthy, director of the
Office for Protection from Research Risks at the NIH. "But all of a sudden
there is a hole in the kind of research being done."

In the past two years, for instance, there has been a 50- to 60- percent   40
drop in the number of reports published by scientists using primates to study
drug abuse. Reports on the use of primates to learn about severe depression
have ended altogether.

And what of our future researchers? Between 1977 and 1987 there was   41
a 28-percent drop in the number of college students graduating with degrees
in biomedical science, and the growing influence of the animal-rights movement may add to that decline.

Stop the Fanatics

How are we to ensure that the animal-rights movement does not put an end   42
to progress in medical research?

1. Don't swallow whole what the movement says about horrors in our
   biomedical-research laboratories. With rare exceptions, experimental
   animals are treated humanely. Biomedical researchers know that an
   animal in distress is simply not a good research subject. Researchers
   are embarked on an effort to alleviate misery, not cause it.
2. There are many humane societies that are truly concerned with animal welfare and oppose the animal-rights movement. They deserve
   your support. But before you contribute, make sure the society has
   not been taken over by animal-rights extremists. If you are not sure,
   contact iiFAR (incurably ill For Animal Research), P.O. Box 1873,
   Bridgeview, Ill. 60455. This organization is one of medical research's most effective allies.
3. Oppose legislation at local, state and federal levels that is designed
   to hamper biomedical research or price it out of business. Your representatives in government are lobbied by the animal-rights movement all the time. Let them know how *you* feel.
4. Support HR 3270, the "Farm Animal and Research Animal Facilities
   Protection Act of 1989," introduced by Rep. Charles Stenholm (D.,
   Texas). This bill would make the kinds of break-ins and vandalism

ALF has been perpetrating a federal offense subject to a maximum of three years in prison and/or a fine of up to $10,000. Also support HR 3349, the "Health Facilities Protection and Primate Center Rehabilitation Act of 1989," introduced by Rep. Henry A. Waxman (D., Calif.). This bill makes criminal assaults on federally funded facilities a federal offense.

If we want to defeat the killer diseases that still confront us—AIDS, 43 Alzheimer's, cancer, heart disease and many others, the misguided fanatics of the animal-rights movement must be stopped.

QUESTIONS FOR MEANING

1. According to Hubbell, what sort of tactics are regularly employed by animal-rights activists? How have they become so influential?
2. Why has concern over the welfare of animals increased the cost of doing research?
3. In paragraph 41, Hubbell implies that the movement for animal rights could discourage students from majoring in biomedical science. Can you explain why that might be?
4. Vocabulary: exemplary (5), vilifying (9), incommensurate (9), patently (12), buzzword (18), replicate (19), insidiously (24), complicity (31).

QUESTIONS ABOUT STRATEGY

1. Hubbell begins his article with an example. Is it well chosen? Does it work as an introduction to the argument that follows?
2. How important is the last sentence in paragraph 4? How would the paragraph change if Hubbell dropped this sentence?
3. What is the function of paragraph 14?
4. How reliable are the authorities cited in paragraphs 18–23? Evaluating them strictly in terms of the information Hubbell provides about them, determine if any of these men seem more credible than others.
5. Hubbell devotes four of his five last paragraphs to making specific recommendations. Has his argument as a whole made this advice seem welcome? Are you inclined to follow any of it?

PETER SINGER

All Animals Are Equal[1]

Born in Melbourne, Peter Singer taught philosophy at University College, Oxford, and at New York University before returning to Australia, where he is now Professor of Philosophy and Director of the Centre of Human Bioethics at Monash University. His books include Democracy and Disobedience *(1974),* Practical Ethics (1979), Marx *(1980),* The Expanding Circle *(1981), and* The Reproduction Revolution: New Ways of Making Babies *(1982). He is best known for his work on behalf of animal rights. If the rise of the animal liberation movement can be traced to any single work it would be Singer's* **1973** *essay "All Animals Are Equal." Singer subsequently expanded his essay into a book,* Animal Liberation: A New Ethic for Our Treatment of Animals *(1975), the second edition of which was published in 1990. He has also coedited* Animal Rights and Human Obligations *(1975) and* Embryo Experimentation *(1990). As you read the following essay, you may find Singer's position surprising. But try to understand the reasoning that leads to it.*

In recent years a number of oppressed groups have campaigned vigorously for equality. The classic instance is the Black Liberation movement, which demands an end to the prejudice and discrimination that has made blacks second-class citizens. The immediate appeal of the black liberation movement and its initial, if limited, success made it a model for other oppressed groups to follow. We became familiar with liberation movements for Spanish-Americans, gay people, and a variety of other minorities. When a majority group—women—began their campaign, some thought we had come to the end of the road. Discrimination on the basis of sex, it has been said, is the last universally accepted form of discrimination, practiced without secrecy or pretense even in those liberal circles that have long prided themselves on their freedom from prejudice against racial minorities. 1

One should always be wary of talking of "the last remaining form of discrimination." If we have learnt anything from the liberation movements, we should have learnt how difficult it is to be aware of latent prejudice in our attitudes to particular groups until this prejudice is forcefully pointed out. 2

A liberation movement demands an expansion of our moral horizons and an extension or reinterpretation of the basic moral principle of equality. Practices that were previously regarded as natural and inevitable come to be seen as the result of an unjustifiable prejudice. Who can say with confidence that all his or her attitudes and practices are beyond criticism? If we wish to avoid being numbered amongst the oppressors, we must be prepared to rethink even our most fundamental attitudes. We need to consider them from the point of view of those most disadvantaged by our attitudes, and the practices that follow from these attitudes. If we can make this unaccustomed 3 mental switch we may discover a pattern in our attitudes and practices that consistently operates so as to benefit one group—usually the one to which we ourselves belong—at the expense of another. In this way we may come to see that there is a case for a new liberation movement. My aim is to advocate that we make this mental switch in respect of our attitudes and practices towards a very large group of beings: members of species other than our own—or, as we popularly though misleadingly call them, animals. In other words, I am urging that we extend to other species the basic principle of equality that most of us recognize should be extended to all members of our own species.

All this may sound a little far-fetched, more like a parody of other   4
liberation movements than a serious objective. In fact, in the past the idea of "The Rights of Animals" really has been used to parody the case for women's rights. When Mary Wollstonecroft, a forerunner of later feminists, published her *Vindication of the Rights of Women* in 1792, her ideas were widely regarded as absurd, and they were satirized in an anonymous publication entitled *A Vindication of the Rights of Brutes.* The author of this satire (actually Thomas Taylor, a distinguished Cambridge philosopher) tried to refute Wollstonecroft's reasonings by showing that they could be carried one stage further. If sound when applied to women, why should the arguments not be applied to dogs, cats and horses? They seemed to hold equally well for these "brutes;" yet to hold that brutes had rights was manifestly absurd; therefore the reasoning by which this conclusion had been reached must be unsound, and if unsound when applied to brutes, it must also be unsound when applied to women, since the very same arguments had been used in each case.

One way in which we might reply to this argument is by saying that   5
the case for equality between men and women cannot validly be extended to non-human animals. Women have a right to vote, for instance, because they are just as capable of making rational decisions as men are; dogs, on the other hand, are incapable of understanding the significance of voting, so they cannot have the right to vote. There are many other obvious ways in which men and women resemble each other closely, while humans and other animals differ greatly. So, it might be said, men and women are similar beings, and should have equal rights, while humans and non-humans are different and should not have equal rights.

The thought behind this reply to Taylor's analogy is correct up to a   6
point, but it does not go far enough. There *are* important differences between humans and other animals, and these differences must give rise to *some* differences in the rights that each have. Recognizing this obvious fact, however, is no barrier to the case for extending the basic principle of equality to non-human animals. The differences that exist between men and women are equally undeniable, and the supporters of Women's Liberation are aware that these differences may give rise to different rights. Many feminists hold that women have the right to an abortion on request. It does not follow that since these same people are campaigning for equality between men and women they must support the right of men to have abortions too. Since a man cannot

have an abortion, it is meaningless to talk of his right to have one. Since a pig can't vote, it is meaningless to talk of its right to vote. There is no reason why either Women's Liberation or Animal Liberation should get involved in such nonsense. The extension of the basic principle of equality from one group to another does not imply that we must treat both groups in exactly the same way, or grant exactly the same rights to both groups. Whether we should do so will depend on the nature of the members of the two groups. The basic principle of equality, I shall argue, is equality of consideration; and equal consideration for different beings may lead to different treatment and different rights.

So there is a different way of replying to Taylor's attempt to parody   7
Wollstonecroft's arguments, a way which does not deny the differences between humans and non-humans, but goes more deeply into the question of equality, and concludes by finding nothing absurd in the idea that the basic principle of equality applies to so-called "brutes." I believe that we reach this conclusion if we examine the basis on which our opposition to discrimination on grounds of race or sex ultimately rests. We will then see that we would be on shaky ground if we were to demand equality for blacks, women, and other groups of oppressed humans while denying equal consideration to non-humans.

When we say all human beings, whatever their race, creed, or sex, are   8
equal, what is it that we are asserting? Those who wish to defend a hierarchical inegalitarian society have often pointed out that by whatever test we choose, it simply is not true that all humans are equal. Like it or not, we must face the fact that humans come in different shapes and sizes; they come with differing moral capacities, differing intellectual abilities, differing amounts of benevolent feeling and sensitivity to the needs of others, differing abilities to communicate effectively, and differing capacities to experience pleasure and pain. In short, if the demand for equality were based on the actual equality of all human beings, we would have to stop demanding equality. It would be an unjustifiable demand.

Still, one might cling to the view that the demand for equality among   9
human beings is based on the actual equality of the different races and sexes. Although humans differ as individuals in various ways, there are no differences between the races and sexes *as such*. From the mere fact that a person is black, or a woman, we cannot infer anything else about that person. This, it may be said, is what is wrong with racism and sexism. The white racist claims that whites are superior to blacks, but this is false—although there are differences between individuals, some blacks are superior to some whites in all of the capacities and abilities that could conceivably be relevant. The opponent of sexism would say the same: a person's sex is no guide to his or her abilities, and this is why it is unjustifiable to discriminate on the basis of sex.

This is a possible line of objection to racial and sexual discrimination.   10
It is not, however, the way that someone really concerned about equality would choose, because taking this line could, in some circumstances, force

one to accept a most inegalitarian society. The fact that humans differ as individuals, rather than as races or sexes, is a valid reply to someone who defends a hierarchical society like, say, South Africa, in which all whites are superior in status to all blacks. The existence of individual variations that cut across the lines of race or sex, however, provides us with no defence at all against a more sophisticated opponent of equality, one who proposes that, say, the interests of those with I.Q. ratings above 100 be preferred to the interests of those I.Q.s below 100. Would a hierarchical society of this sort really be so much better than one based on race or sex? I think not. But if we tie the moral principle of equality to the factual equality of the different races or sexes, taken as a whole, our opposition to racism and sexism does not provide us with any basis for objecting to this kind of inegalitarianism.

There is a second important reason why we ought not to base our op-   11 position to racism and sexism on any kind of factual equality, even the limited kind asserts that variations in capacities and abilities are spread evenly between the different races and sexes: we can have no absolute guarantee that these abilities and capacities really are distributed evenly, without regard to race or sex, among human beings. So far as actual abilities are concerned, there do seem to be certain measurable differences between both races and sexes. These differences do not, of course, appear in each case, but only when averages are taken. More important still, we do not yet know how much of these differences is really due to the different genetic endowments of the various races and sexes, and how much is due to environmental differences that are the result of past and continuing discrimination. Perhaps all of the important differences will eventually prove to be environmental rather than genetic. Anyone opposed to racism and sexism will certainly hope that this will be so, for it will make the task of ending discrimination a lot easier; nevertheless it would be dangerous to rest the case against racism and sexism on the belief that all significant differences are environmental in origin. The opponent of, say, racism who takes this line will be unable to avoid conceding that if differences in ability did after all prove to have some genetic connection with race, racism would in some way be defensible.

It would be folly for the opponent of racism to stake his whole case on   12 a dogmatic commitment to one particular outcome of a difficult scientific issue which is still a long way from being settled. While attempts to prove that differences in certain selected abilities between races and sexes are primarily genetic in origin have certainly not been conclusive, the same must be said of attempts to prove that these differences are largely the result of environment. At this stage of the investigation we cannot be certain which view is correct, however much we may hope it is the latter.

Fortunately, there is no need to pin the case for equality to one partic-   13 ular outcome of this scientific investigation. The appropriate response to those who claim to have found evidence of genetically-based differences in ability between the races or sexes is not to stick to the belief that the genetic explanation must be wrong, whatever evidence to the contrary may turn up: instead we should make it quite clear that the claim to equality does not depend on intelligence, moral capacity, physical strength, or similar matters of fact.

Equality is a moral idea, not a simple assertion of fact. There is no logically compelling reason for assuming that a factual difference in ability between two people justifies any difference in the amount of consideration we give to satisfying their needs and interests. The principle of the equality of human beings is not a description of an alleged actual equality among humans: it is a prescription of how we should treat humans.

Jeremy Bentham incorporated the essential basis of moral equality into   14
his utilitarian system of ethics in the formula: "Each to count for one and none for more than one." In other words, the interests of every being affected by an action are to be taken into account and given the same weight as the like interests of any other being. A later utilitarian, Henry Sidgwick, put the point in this way: "The good of any one individual is of no more importance, from the point of view (if I may say so) of the Universe, than the good of any other."[2] More recently, the leading figures in contemporary moral philosophy have shown a great deal of agreement in specifying as a fundamental presupposition of their moral theories some similar requirement which operates so as to give everyone's interests equal consideration—although they cannot agree on how this requirement is best formulated.[3]

It is an implication of this principle of equality that our concern for   15
others ought not to depend on what they are like, or what abilities they possess—although precisely what this concern requires us to do may vary according to the characteristics of those affected by what we do. It is on this basis that the case against racism and the case against sexism must both ultimately rest; and it is in accordance with this principle that speciesism is also to be condemned. If possessing a higher degree of intelligence does not entitle one human to use another for his own ends, how can it entitle humans to exploit non-humans?

Many philosophers have proposed the principle of equal consideration   16
of interests, in some form or other, as a basic moral principle; but, as we shall see in more detail shortly, not many of them have recognised that this principle applies to members of other species as well as to our own. Bentham was one of the few who did realize this. In a forward-looking passage, written at a time when black slaves in the British dominions were still being treated much as we now treat non-human animals, Bentham wrote:

> The day *may* come when the rest of the animal creation may acquire those rights which never could have been witholden from them but by the hand of tyranny. The French have already discovered that the blackness of the skin is no reason why a human being should be abandoned without redress to the caprice of a tormentor. It may one day come to be recognised that the number of the legs, the villosity of the skin, or the termination of the *os sacrum,* are reasons equally insufficient for abandoning a sensitive being to the same fate. What else is it that should trace the insuperable line? Is it the faculty of reason, or perhaps the faculty of discourse? But a full-grown horse or dog is beyond comparison a more rational, as well as a more conversable animal, than an infant of a day, or a week, or even a month, old. But suppose they were otherwise, what would it avail? The question is not, Can they reason? nor Can they *talk?* but, *Can they suffer?*[4]

In this passage Bentham points to the capacity for suffering as the vital   17
characteristic that gives a being the right to equal consideration. The capacity
for suffering—or more strictly, for suffering and/or enjoyment or happiness—is not just another characteristic like the capacity for language, or for
higher mathematics. Bentham is not saying that those who try to mark "the
insuperable line" that determines whether the interests of a being should be
considered happen to have selected the wrong characteristic. The capacity for
suffering and enjoying things is a pre-requisite for having interests at all, a
condition that must be satisfied before we can speak of interests in any meaningful way. It would be nonsense to say that it was not in the interests of a
stone to be kicked along the road by a schoolboy. A stone does not have
interests because it cannot suffer. Nothing that we can do to it could possibly
make any difference to its welfare. A mouse, on the other hand, does have
an interest in not being tormented, because it will suffer if it is.

If a being suffers, there can be no moral justification for refusing to take   18
that suffering into consideration. No matter what the nature of the being,
the principle of equality requires that its suffering be counted equally with
the like suffering—in so far as rough comparisons can be made—of any other
being. If a being is not capable of suffering, or of experiencing enjoyment or
happiness, there is nothing to be taken into account. This is why the limit of
sentience (using the term as a convenient, if not strictly accurate, shorthand
for the capacity to suffer or experience enjoyment or happiness) is the only
defensible boundary of concern for the interests of others. To mark this
boundary by some characteristic like intelligence or rationality would be to
mark it in an arbitrary way. Why not choose some other characteristic, like
skin color?

The racist violates the principle of equality by giving greater weight to   19
the interests of members of his own race, when there is a clash between their
interests and the interests of those of another race. Similarly the speciesist
allows the interests of his own species to override the greater interests of
members of other species.[5] The pattern is the same in each case. Most human
beings are speciesists. I shall now very briefly describe some of the practices
that show this.

For the great majority of human beings, especially in urban, industri-   20
alized societies, the most direct form of contact with members of other species is at meal-times: we eat them. In doing so we treat them purely as means
to our ends. We regard their life and well-being as subordinate to our taste
for a particular kind of dish. I say "taste" deliberately—this is purely a matter
of pleasing our palate. There can be no defense of eating flesh in terms of
satisfying nutritional needs, since it has been established beyond doubt that
we could satisfy our need for protein and other essential nutrients far more
efficiently with a diet that replaced animal flesh by soy beans, or products
derived from soy beans, and other high-protein vegetable products.[6]

It is not merely the act of killing that indicates what we are ready to do   21
to other species in order to gratify our tastes. The suffering we inflict on the
animals while they are alive is perhaps an even clearer indication of our

speciesism than the fact that we are prepared to kill them.[7] In order to have meat on the table at a price that people can afford, our society tolerates methods of meat production that confine sentient animals in cramped, unsuitable conditions for the entire durations of their lives. Animals are treated like machines that convert fodder into flesh, and any innovation that results in a higher "conversion ratio" is liable to be adopted. As one authority on the subject has said, "cruelty is acknowledged only when profitability ceases".[8] So hens are crowded four or five to a cage with a floor area of twenty inches by eighteen inches, or around the size of a single page of the *New York Times*. The cages have wire floors, since this reduces cleaning costs, though wire is unsuitable for the hens' feet; the floors slope, since this makes the eggs roll down for easy collection, although this makes it difficult for the hens to rest comfortably. In these conditions all the birds' natural instincts are thwarted: they cannot stretch their wings fully; walk freely, dust-bathe, scratch the ground, or build a nest. Although they have never known other conditions, observers have noticed that the birds vainly try to perform these actions. Frustrated at their inability to do so, they often develop what farmers call "vices," and peck each other to death. To prevent this, the beaks of young birds are often cut off.

This kind of treatment is not limited to poultry. Pigs are now also being reared in cages inside sheds. These animals are comparable to dogs in intelligence, and need a varied, stimulating environment if they are not to suffer from stress and boredom. Anyone who kept a dog in the way in which pigs are frequently kept would be liable to prosecution, in England at least, but because our interest in exploiting pigs is greater than our interest in exploiting dogs, we object to cruelty to dogs while consuming the produce of cruelty to pigs. Of the other animals, the condition of veal calves is perhaps worst of all, since these animals are so closely confined that they cannot even turn around or get up and lie down freely. In this way they do not develop unpalatable muscle. They are also made anaemic and kept short of roughage, to keep their flesh pale, since white veal fetches a higher price; as a result they develop a craving for iron and roughage, and have been observed to gnaw wood off the sides of their stalls, and lick greedily at any rusty hinge that is within reach. 22

Since, as I have said, none of these practices cater for anything more than our pleasures of taste, our practice of rearing and killing other animals in order to eat them is a clear instance of the sacrifice of the most important interests of other beings in order to satisfy trivial interests of our own. To avoid speciesism we must stop this practice, and each of us has a moral obligation to cease supporting the practice. Our custom is all the support that the meat-industry needs. The decision to cease giving it that support may be difficult, but it is no more difficult than it would have been for a white Southerner to go against the traditions of his society and free his slaves; if we do not change our dietary habits, how can we censure those slaveholders who would not change their own way of living? 23

The same form of discrimination may be observed in the widespread 24 practice of experimenting on other species in order to see if certain substances are safe for human beings, or to test some psychological theory about the effect of severe punishment on learning, or to try out various new compounds just in case something turns up. People sometimes think that all this experimentation is for vital medical purposes, and so will reduce suffering overall. This comfortable belief is very wide of the mark. Drug companies test new shampoos and cosmetics that they are intending to put on the market by dropping them into the eyes of rabbits, held open by metal clips, in order to observe what damage results. Food additives, like artificial colorings and preservatives, are tested by what is known as the "LD$_{50}$"—a test designed to find the level of consumption at which 50% of a group of animals will die. In the process, nearly all of the animals are made very sick before some finally die, and others pull through. If the substance is relatively harmless, as it often is, huge doses have to be forcefed to the animals, until in some cases sheer volume or concentration of the substance causes death.

Much of this pointless cruelty goes on in the universities. In many areas of science, non-human animals are regarded as an item of laboratory equipment, to be used and expended as desired. In psychology laboratories experimenters devise endless variations and repetitions of experiments that were of little value in the first place. To quote just one example, from the experimenter's own account in a psychology journal: at the University of Pennsylvania, Perrin S. Cohen hung six dogs in hammocks with electrodes taped to their hind feet. Electric shock of varying intensity was then administered through the electrodes. If the dog learnt to press its head against a panel on the left, the shock was turned off, but otherwise it remained on indefinitely. Three of the dogs, however, were required to wait periods varying from 2 to 7 seconds while being shocked before making the response that turned off the current. If they failed to wait, they received further shocks. Each dog was given from 26 to 46 "sessions" in the hammock, each session consisting of 80 "trials" or shocks, administered at intervals of one minute. The experimenter reported that the dogs, who were unable to move in the hammock, barked or bobbed their heads when the current was applied. The reported findings of the experiment were that there was a delay in the dogs' responses that increased proportionately to the time the dogs were required to endure the shock, but a gradual increase in the intensity of shock had no systematic effect in the timing of the response. The experiment was funded by the National Institute of Health, and the United States Public Health Service.[9]

In this example, and countless cases like it, the possible benefits to mankind are either non-existent or fantastically remote; while the certain losses to members of other species are very real. This is, again, a clear indication of speciesism.

In the past, argument about vivisection has often missed this point, because it has been put in absolutist terms: would the abolitionist be prepared to let thousands die if they could be saved by experimenting on a single animal? The way to reply to this purely hypothetical question is to pose another: would the experimenter be prepared to perform his experiment on an orphaned human infant, if that were the only way to save many lives? (I say "orphan" to avoid the complication of parental feelings, although in doing so I am being overfair to the experimenter, since the nonhuman subjects of experiments are not orphans.) If the experimenter is not prepared to use an orphaned human infant, then his readiness to use nonhumans is simple discrimination, since adult apes, cats, mice and other mammals are more aware of what is happening to them, more self-directing and, so far as we can tell, at least as sensitive to pain, as any human infant. There seems to be no relevant characteristic that human infants possess that adult mammals do not have to the same or a higher degree. (Someone might try to argue that what makes it wrong to experiment on a human infant is that the infant will, in time and if left alone, develop into more than the nonhuman, but one would then, to be consistent, have to oppose abortion, since the fetus has the same potential as the infant—indeed, even contraception and abstinence might be wrong on this ground, since the egg and sperm, considered jointly, also have the same potential. In any case, this argument still gives us no reason for selecting a nonhuman, rather than a human with severe and irreversible brain damage, as the subject for our experiments.)

The experimenter, then, shows a bias in favor of his own species whenever he carries out an experiment on a nonhuman for a purpose that he would not think justified him in using a human being at an equal or lower level of sentience, awareness, ability to be self-directing, etc. No one familiar with the kind of results yielded by most experiments on animals can have the slightest doubt that if this bias were eliminated the number of experiments performed would be a minute fraction of the number performed today.   28

Experimenting on animals, and eating their flesh, are perhaps the two major forms of speciesism in our society. By comparison, the third and last form of speciesism is so minor as to be insignificant, but it is perhaps of some special interest to those for whom this paper was written. I am referring to speciesism in contemporary philosophy.   29

Philosophy ought to question the basic assumptions of the age. Thinking through, critically and carefully, what most people take for granted is, I believe, the chief task of philosophy, and it is this task that makes philosophy a worthwhile activity. Regrettably, philosophy does not always live up to its historic rule. Philosophers are human beings and they are subject to all the preconceptions of the society to which they belong. Sometimes they succeed in breaking free of the prevailing ideology: more often they become its most sophisticated defenders. So, in this case, philosophy as practiced in the universities today does not challenge anyone's preconceptions about our relations with other species. By their writings, those philosophers who tackle problems that touch upon the issue reveal that they make the same unquestioned assumptions as most other humans, and what they say tends to confirm the reader in his or her comfortable speciesist habits.   30

I could illustrate this claim by referring to the writings of philosophers in various fields—for instance, the attempts that have been made by those interested in rights to draw the boundary of the sphere of rights so that it   31 runs parallel to the biological boundaries of the species *homo sapiens,* including infants and even mental defectives, but excluding those other beings of equal or greater capacity who are so useful to us at mealtimes and in our laboratories. I think it would be a more appropriate conclusion to this paper, however, if I concentrated on the problem with which we have been centrally concerned, the problem of equality.

It is significant that the problem of equality, in moral and political philosophy, is invariably formulated in terms of human equality. The effect of this is that the question of the equality of other animals does not confront the philosopher, or student, as an issue in itself—and this is already an indication of the failure of philosophy to challenge accepted beliefs. Still, philosophers have found it difficult to discuss the issue of human equality without raising, in a paragraph or two, the question of the status of other animals. The reason for this, which should be apparent from what I have said already, is that if humans are to be regarded as equal to one another, we need some sense of "equal" that does not require any actual, descriptive equality of capacities, talents or other qualities. If equality is to be related to any actual characteristics of humans, these characteristics must be some lowest common denominator, pitched so low that no human lacks them—but then the philosopher comes up against the catch that any such set of characteristics which covers *all* humans will not be possessed *only by humans.* In other words, it turns out that in the only sense in which we can truly say, as an assertion of fact, that all humans are equal, at least some members of other species are also equal—equal, that is, to each other and to humans. If, on the other hand, we regard the statement "All humans are equal" in some non-factual way, perhaps as a prescription, then, as I have already argued, it is even more difficult to exclude non-humans from the sphere of equality.

This result is not what the egalitarian philosopher originally intended to assert. Instead of accepting the radical outcome to which their own reasonings naturally point, however, most philosophers try to reconcile their beliefs in human equality and animal inequality by arguments that can only be described as devious.

As a first example, I take William Frankena's well-known article "The Concept of Social Justice."[10] Frankena opposes the idea of basing justice on merit, because he sees that this could lead to highly inegalitarian results. Instead he proposes the principle that:

> . . . all men are to be treated as equals, not because they are equal, in any respect but simply because they are human. They are human because they have emotions and desires, and are able to think, and hence are capable of enjoying a good life in a sense in which other animals are not.

But what is this capacity to enjoy the good life which all humans have, but no other animals? Other animals have emotions and desires, and appear to be capable of enjoying a good life. We may doubt that they can think—although the behavior of some apes, dolphins and even dogs suggest that some of them can—but what is the relevance of thinking? Frankena goes on to admit that by "the good life" he means "not so much the morally good life as the happy or satisfactory life," so thought would appear to be unnecessary for enjoying the good life; in fact to emphasise the need for thought would make difficulties for the egalitarian since only some people are capable of leading intellectually satisfying lives, or morally good lives. This makes it difficult to see what Frankena's principle of equality has to do with simply being *human*. Surely every sentient being is capable of leading a life that is happier or less miserable than some alternative life, and hence has a claim to be taken into account. In this respect the distinction between humans and nonhumans is not a sharp division, but rather a continuum along which we move gradually, and with overlaps between the species, from simple capacities for enjoyment and satisfaction, or pain and suffering, to more complex ones.

Faced with a situation in which they see a need for some basis for the moral gulf that is commonly thought to separate humans and animals, but can find no concrete difference that will do the job without undermining the equality of humans, philosophers tend to waffle. They resort to high-sounding phrases like "the intrinsic dignity of the human individual."[11] They talk of the "intrinsic worth of all men" as if men (humans?) had some worth that other beings did not,[12] or they say that humans, and only humans, are "ends in themselves" while "everything other than a person can only have value for a person."[13]

This idea of a distinctive human dignity and worth has a long history; it can be traced back directly to the Renaissance humanists, for instance to Pico della Mirandola's *Oration on the Dignity of Man*. Pico and other humanists based their estimate of human dignity on the idea that man possessed the central, pivotal position in the "Great Chain of Being" that led from the lowliest forms of matter to God himself; this view of the universe, in turn, goes back to both classical and Judeo-Christian doctrines. Contemporary philosophers have cast off these metaphysical and religious shackles and freely invoke the dignity of mankind without needing to justify the idea at all. Why should we not attribute "intrinsic dignity" or "intrinsic worth" to ourselves? Fellow-humans are unlikely to reject the accolades we so generously bestow on them, and those to whom we deny the honor are unable to object. Indeed, when one thinks only of humans, it can be very liberal, very progressive, to talk of the dignity of all human beings. In so doing, we implicitly condemn slavery, racism, and other violations of human rights. We admit that we ourselves are in some fundamental sense on a par with the poorest, most ignorant members of our own species. It is only when we think of humans as no more than a small sub-group of all the beings that inhabit our planet that we may realize that in elevating our own species we are at the same time lowering the relative status of all other species.

The truth is that the appeal to the intrinsic dignity of human beings appears to solve the egalitarian's problems only as long as it goes unchallenged. Once we ask *why* it should be that all humans—including infants,

36

37

38

mental defectives, psychopaths, Hitler, Stalin and the rest—have some kind of dignity or worth that no elephant, pig, or chimpanzee can ever achieve, we see that this question is as difficult to answer as our original request for some relevant fact that justifies the inequality of humans and other animals. In fact, these two questions are really one: talk of intrinsic dignity or moral worth only takes the problem back one step, because any satisfactory defence of the claim that all and only humans have intrinsic dignity would need to refer to some relevant capacities or characteristics that all and only humans possess. Philosophers frequently introduce ideas of dignity, respect and worth at the point at which other reasons appear to be lacking, but this is hardly good enough. Fine phrases are the last resource of those who have run out of arguments.

In case there are those who still think it may be possible to find some   39
relevant characteristic that distinguishes all humans from all members of other species, I shall refer again, before I conclude, to the existence of some humans who quite clearly are below the level of awareness, self-consciousness, intelligence, and sentience, of many non-humans. I am thinking of humans with severe and irreparable brain damage, and also of infant humans. To avoid the complication of the relevance of a being's potential, however, I shall henceforth concentrate on permanently retarded humans.

Philosophers who set out to find a characteristic that will distinguish   40
humans from other animals rarely take the course of abandoning these groups of humans by lumping them in with the other animals. It is easy to see why they do not. To take this line without re-thinking our attitudes to other animals would entail that we have the right to perform painful experiments on retarded humans for trivial reasons; similarly it would follow that we had the right to rear and kill these humans for food. To most philosophers these consequences are as unacceptable as the view that we should stop treating non-humans in this way.

Of course, when discussing the problem of equality it is possible to   41
ignore the problem of mental defectives, or brush it aside as if somehow insignificant.[14] This is the easiest way out. What else remains? My final example of speciesism in contemporary philosophy has been selected to show what happens when a writer is prepared to face the question of human equality and animal inequality without ignoring the existence of mental defectives, and without resorting to obscurantist mumbo-jumbo. Stanley Benn's clear and honest article "Egalitarianism and Equal Consideration of Interests"[15] fits this description.

Benn, after noting the usual "evident human inequalities" argues, cor-   42
rectly I think, for equality of consideration as the only possible basis for egalitarianism. Yet Benn, like other writers, is thinking only of "equal consideration of human interests." Benn is quite open in his defence of this restriction of equal consideration:

> . . . not to possess human shape *is* a disqualifying condition. However faithful or intelligent a dog may be, it would be a monstrous sentimentality to attribute to him interests that could be weighed in an equal balance with those of

human beings . . . if, for instance, one had to decide between feeding a hungry baby or a hungry dog, anyone who chose the dog would generally be reckoned morally defective, unable to recognize a fundamental inequality of claims.

This is what distinguishes our attitude to animals from our attitude to imbeciles. It would be odd to say that we ought to respect equally the dignity or personality of the imbecile and of the rational man . . . but there is nothing odd about saying that we should respect their interests equally, that is, that we should give to the interests of each the same serious consideration as claims to considerations necessary for some standard of well-being that we can recognize and endorse.

Benn's statement of the basis of the consideration we should have for   43 imbeciles seems to me correct, but why should there be any fundamental inequality of claims between a dog and a human imbecile? Benn sees that if equal consideration depended on rationality, no reason could be given against using imbeciles for research purposes, as we now use dogs and guinea pigs. This will not do: "But of course we do distinguish imbeciles from animals in this regard," he says. That the common distinction is justifiable is something Benn does not question; his problem is how it is to be justified. The answer he gives is this:

. . . we respect the interests of men and give them priority over dogs not *insofar* as they are rational, but because rationality is the human norm. We say it is *unfair* to exploit the deficiencies of the imbecile who falls short of the norm, just as it would be unfair, and not just ordinarily dishonest, to steal from a blind man. If we do not think in this way about dogs, it is because we do not see the irrationality of the dog as a deficiency or a handicap, but as normal for the species. The characteristics, therefore, that distinguish the normal man from the normal dog make it intelligible for us to talk of other men having interests and capacities, and therefore claims, of precisely the same kind as we make on our own behalf. But although these characteristics may provide the point of the distinction between men and other species, they are not in fact the qualifying conditions for membership, or the distinguishing criteria of the class of morally considerable persons; and this is precisely because a man does not become a member of a different species, with its own standards of normality, by reason of not possessing these characteristics.

The final sentence of this passage gives the argument away. An imbe-   44 cile, Benn concedes, may have no characteristics superior to those of a dog; nevertheless this does not make the imbecile a member of "a different species" as the dog is. *Therefore* it would be "unfair" to use the imbecile for medical research as we use the dog. But why? That the imbecile is not rational is just the way things have worked out, and the same is true of the dog—neither is any more responsible for their mental level. If it is unfair to take advantage of an isolated defect, why is it fair to take advantage of a more general limitation? I find it hard to see anything in this argument except a defence of preferring the interests of members of our own species because they are members of our own species. To those who think there might be more to it, I suggest the following mental exercise. Assume that it has been proven that there is a difference in the average, or normal, intelligence quotient for two different races, say whites and blacks. Then substitute the term "white" for every occurrence of "men" and "black" for every occurrence of "dog" in the passage quoted; and substitute "high I.Q." for "rationality" and when Benn talks of "imbeciles" replace this term by "dumb whites"—that is, whites who fall well below the normal white I.Q. score. Finally, change "species" to "race." Now re-read the passage. It has become a defence of a rigid,· no exceptions division between whites and blacks, based on I.Q. scores, *not withstanding an admitted overlap* between whites and blacks in this respect. The revised passage is, of course, outrageous, and this is not only because we have made fictitious assumptions in our substitutions. The point is that in the original passage Benn was defending a rigid division in the amount of consideration due to members of different species, despite admitted cases of overlap. If the original did not, at first reading, strike us as being as outrageous as the revised version does, this is largely because although we are not racists ourselves, most of us are speciesists. Like the other articles, Benn's stands as a warning of the ease with which the best minds can fall victim to a prevailing ideology.

Notes

1. Passages of this article appeared in a review of *Animals, Men and Morals,* edited by S. and R. Godlovitch and J. Harris (Gollancz and Taplinger, London 1972) in *The New York Review of Books,* April 5, 1973. The whole direction of my thinking on this subject I owe to talks with a number of friends in Oxford in 1970–71, especially Richard Keshen, Stanley Godlovitch, and, above all, Roslind Godlovitch.

2. *The Methods of Ethics* (7th Ed.) p. 382.

3. For example, R. M. Hare, *Freedom and Reason* (Oxford, 1963) and J. Rawls. *A Theory of Justice* (Harvard, 1972); for a brief account of the essential agreement on this issue between these and other positions, see R. M. Hare, "Rules of War and Moral Reasoning," *Philosophy and Public Affairs,* vol. 1, no. 2 (1972).

4. *Introduction to the Principles of Morals and Legislation,* ch. XVII.

5. I owe the term "speciesism" to Dr. Richard Ryder.

6. In order to produce 1 lb. of protein in the form of beef or veal, we must feed 21 lbs. of protein to the animal. Other forms of livestock are slightly less inefficient, but the average ratio in the U.S. is still 1:8. It has been estimated that the amount of protein lost to humans in this way is equivalent to 90% of the annual world protein deficit. For a brief account, see Frances Moore Lappe, *Diet for a Small Planet* (Friends of The Earth/Ballantine, New York 1971) pp. 4–11.

7. Although one might think that killing a being is obviously the ultimate wrong one can do to it, I think that the infliction of suffering is a clearer indication of speciesism because it might be argued that at least part of what is wrong with killing a human is that most humans are conscious of their existence over time, and have desires and purposes that extend into the future—see, for instance, M. Tooley, "Abortion and Infanticide," *Philosophy and Public Affairs,* vol. 2, no. 1 (1972). Of course, if one took this view one would have to hold—as Tooley does—that killing a human infant or mental defective is not in itself wrong, and is less serious than killing certain higher mammals that probably do have a sense of their own existence over time.

8. Ruth Harrison, *Animal Machines* (Stuart, London, 1964). This book provides an eye-opening account of intensive farming methods for those unfamiliar with the subject.

9. *Journal of the Experimental Analysis of Behavior,* vol. 13, no. 1 (1970). Any recent volume of this journal, or of other journals in the field, like the *Journal of Comparative and Physiological Psychology,* will contain reports of equally cruel and trivial experiments. For a fuller account, see Richard Ryder, "Experiments on Animals," in *Animals, Men and Morals.*

10. In R. Brandt (ed.), *Social Justice* (Prentice Hall, Englewood Cliffs, 1962); the passage quoted appears on p. 19.

11. Frankena, *op. cit.* p. 23.

12. H. A. Bedau, "Egalitarianism and the Idea of Equality," in *Nomos IX: Equality,* ed. J. R. Pennock and J. W. Chapman, New York 1967.

13. G. Vlastos, "Justice and Equality," in Brandt, *Social Justice,* p. 48.

14. E. G. Bernard Williams, "The Idea of Equality," in *Philosophy, Politics and Society* (second series) ed. P. Laslett and W. Runciman (Blackwell, Oxford, 1962) p. 118; J. Rawls, *A Theory of Justice,* pp. 509–10.

15. *Nomos IX: Equality;* the passages quoted are on pp. 62ff.

QUESTIONS FOR MEANING

1. What is Singer's premise in arguing that animals deserve equal consideration with humans? Why can animals be said to have "interests"? Explain what Singer means by "equality."

2. What is "speciesism," and what two forms does it most commonly take?

3. Why have philosophers traditionally argued on behalf of "human dignity"? If you reject Singer's argument that "all animals are equal," explain why human beings have more "dignity" or "worth" than nonhuman animals. Try to answer the question that Singer poses in paragraph 38: Why can "infants, mental defectives, psychopaths, Hitler, Stalin, and the rest—have some kind of dignity or worth that no elephant, pig, or chimpanzee can ever achieve"?

4. Singer challenges the argument (represented by William Frankena in paragraph 34) that the ability to think distinguishes humans from other animals. Have you ever had experience with an animal that seemed to think?

5. Singer asks, "What is the relevance of thinking?" Is this a strange question for a philosopher to ask? How important is thinking to Singer himself? Is he contradicting himself?

6. What is the role of philosophy in the modern world? What are the responsibilities of philosophers, and how should they write? What is Singer's opinion of philosophy as practiced in most universities? Do you agree? If you have ever taken a course in philosophy, what did you learn from it? Would Singer have respected your teacher?

7. Judging from this essay, what philosopher seems to have had an especially strong influence on Singer in shaping his position regarding the rights of animals?

8. Vocabulary: latent (2), advocate (3), parody (4), refute (4), hierarchical (8), folly (12), insuperable (16), waffle (36), intrinsic (37).

QUESTIONS ABOUT STRATEGY

1. What is the function of paragraphs 1 and 2? Why does Singer wait until the end of the third paragraph before introducing the subject of "members of species other than our own—or, as we popularly though misleadingly call them, animals"? Explain why it can be misleading to call animals "animals." Why does Singer want us to reconsider our use of this term?

2. Explain the analogy that Thomas Taylor made between the rights of women and the rights of "brutes." Why does Singer go to the trouble of describing a work in which the idea of equality for women was ridiculed?

3. Singer was very much aware that he was arguing a point of view with which many people would disagree. At what points in his essay does he anticipate and respond to opposition?

4. What is the basic strategy of this argument? Where does Singer place the responsibility for assuming the burden of proof? To what extent does Singer's argument depend upon exposing the shortcomings of his opponents? If his opponents can be shown to reason badly, would it necessarily follow that Singer argues well? Distinguish between those paragraphs in which Singer analyzes the work of other philosophers and those in which he advances his own case.

5. What does this essay tell you about the type of audience Singer was writing for? What sort of political principle does Singer assume his audience shares with him? Is the logic of this argument strong enough to convince someone who did not share Singer's politics?

6. If you were to take Singer's argument and put it into the form of a syllogism, how would it read?

ROBERT WRIGHT
Are Animals People Too?

*First published in a **1990** issue of* The New Republic, *to which Robert Wright is a regular contributor, the following article surveys the ethical questions raised by the debate over animal experimentation. It also explores some of the political implications raised by this debate. When attempting to decide the extent to which animals are entitled to better treatment, Wright draws upon the work of Peter Singer, whose views can be found in the selection that begins on p. 299.*

I recently interviewed several animal rights activists in hopes that they would say some amusing, crazy-sounding things that might liven up this article. More often than not I was disappointed. They would come close to making unreservedly extremist pronouncements but then step back from the brink, leaving me with a quote that was merely provocative. For example, Ingrid Newkirk, co-founder of People for the Ethical Treatment of Animals (PETA), seemed on the verge of conceding that Frank Perdue is no better than Adolf Hitler—a proposition that technically follows her premise that animals possess the moral status of humans (and from references in animal rights literature to the ongoing "animal holocaust"). But she wouldn't go all the way. "He's the animals' Hitler, I'll give you that," she said. "If you were a chicken . . . you wouldn't think he was Mother Teresa." The other cofounder of PETA, Alex Pacheco, was not much more helpful. "You and I are equal to the lobsters when it comes to being boiled alive," he said, raising my hopes. But, he added, "I don't mean I couldn't decide which one to throw in, myself or the lobster."

The biggest disappointment was a woman who went by the pseudonym "Helen." She was a member of the Animal Liberation Front, a shadowy group that goes around breaking into scientific laboratories, documenting the conditions therein, and sometimes burning down the labs (minus the animals, which are typically "liberated"—taken somewhere else—in the process). Given all the intrigue involved in interviewing "Helen"—I had to "put out the word" that I wanted to talk with an ALF member, and when she called she always used a streetside phone booth and never left a number—I expected a rich encounter. This hope grew when I found out that she had participated in a recent lab-burning at the University of Arizona. But as professed arsonists go, Helen seemed like a very nice and fairly reasonable person. She was a combination of earnest moral anguish ("For the most part, people just aren't aware of how much suffering and death goes into what they eat and wear. . . . Most people just literally don't know") and crisp professionalism ("Whether I have any animosity toward [laboratory researchers] is irrelevant. . . . I just do everything I can to move them into a different job category"). And though her reverence for life may strike you as creepy—she picks up spiders off the floor and moves them outdoors, rather than squash them—it is not unbounded. She assured me that if termites were destroying her home, she would call the exterminator.

One reason for this general failure to gather satisfactorily extremist quotes   3
is that animal rights activists have become more media-savvy, developing a surer sense for when they are being baited. But another reason is my own failure to find their ideas extremist. Slowly I seem to be getting drawn into the logic of animal rights. I still eat meat, wear a leather belt, and support the use of animals in important scientific research. But not without a certain amount of cognitive dissonance.

The animal rights movement, which has mushroomed during the past   4
decade, most conspicuously in the growth of PETA (membership around 300,000), is distinguished from the animal welfare movement, as represented by, for example, the Humane Society of the United States. Animal *welfare* activists don't necessarily claim that animals are the moral equivalent of humans, just that animals' feelings deserve some consideration; we shouldn't needlessly hurt them—with pointless experimentation, say, or by making fur coats. And just about every thinking person, if pressed, will agree that animal welfare is a legitimate idea. Hardly anyone believes in kicking dogs.

But the truth is that animal welfare is just the top of a slippery slope   5
that leads to animal rights. Once you buy the premise that animals can experience pain and pleasure, and that their welfare therefore deserves *some* consideration, you're on the road to comparing yourself with a lobster. There may be some exit ramps along the way—plausible places to separate welfare from rights—but I can't find any. And if you don't manage to find one, you wind up not only with a rather more sanguine view of animal rights but also with a more cynical view of the concept of human rights and its historical evolution.

None of this is to say that a few minutes of philosophical reflection will   6
lead you to start wearing dumpling-shaped fake-leather shoes, sporting a "Meat is Murder" button, or referring to your pet dog as your "companion animal." The stereotype about the people who do these things—that they're ill at ease in human society, even downright antagonistic toward other humans—is generally wrong, but the stereotype that they're, well, *different* from most people is not. These are dyed-in-the-wool activists, and if they weren't throwing themselves into this cause, they would probably be throwing themselves into some other cause. (Pacheco, for example, had originally planned to become a priest.) Moreover, very few of them were converted to the movement solely or mainly via philosophy. Many will say that they were critically influenced by the book *Animal Liberation* (1975), written by the Australian ethicist Peter Singer, but reading Singer was for most of them merely a ratifying experience, a seal of philosophical approval for their intuitive revulsion at animal suffering. Pacheco received a copy of the book the same week he got grossed out while touring a Canadian slaughterhouse. He later gave a copy to Newkirk, who was then chief of Animal Disease Control for the District of Columbia. Around that time she spent a day trying to rescue some starving, neglected horses that were locked in their stalls and

mired in mud. That's when it hit her: "It didn't make sense. I had spent the whole day trying to get some starving horses out of a stall and here I was going home to eat some other animal." This gut perception is a recurring theme, as crystallized by Helen: "I just realized that if I wouldn't eat my dog, why should I eat a cow?"

Good question. And implicit in it is the core of the case for animal rights: the modest claim—not disputed by anyone who has ever owned a dog or cat, so far as I know—that animals are sentient beings, capable of pleasure and pain. People who would confine natural rights to humans commonly talk about the things we have that animals don't—complex language, sophisticated reasoning, a highly evolved culture. But none of these is important, for moral purposes, in the way that sheer sentience is.   7

One way to appreciate this is through a simple thought experiment [experiment 1]. Suppose there's a planet populated by organisms that look and act exactly like humans. They walk, talk, flirt, go to law school, blush in response to embarrassing comments, and discuss their impending deaths in glum tones. Now suppose it turns out they're automatons, made out of silicon chips—or even made out of flesh and blood. The important thing is that all their behavior—their blushing, their discussion of death—is entirely a product of the physical circuitry inside their heads and isn't accompanied by any subjective experience; they can't feel pain, pleasure, or anything else. In other words (to use the terminology of Thomas Nagel), it isn't like anything to be them.   8

Is there anything particularly immoral about slapping one of them in the face? Most everyone would say: obviously not, since it doesn't hurt. How about killing one of them? Again, no; their death doesn't preclude their future experience of happiness, as with real live humans, or cause any pain for friends and relatives. There is no apparent reason to bestow any moral status whatsoever on these creatures, much less the exalted status that the human species now enjoys. They have powerful brains, complex language, and high culture, but none of this makes them significant.   9

Now rearrange the variables [experiment 2]: subtract all these attributes and add sentience. In other words, take all the robots off the planet and populate it with non-human animals: chimps, armadillos, dogs, etc. Is there anything immoral about gratuitously hurting or killing one of these? Do they have individual rights? Most people would answer yes to the first question, and some would answer yes to the second. But the main point is that few people would quickly and easily say "no" to either, because these are harder questions than the robot question. Sentience lies at the core of our moral thinking, and language, intelligence, etc., lie nearer the periphery. Sentience seems definitely a necessary and arguably a sufficient condition for the possession of high moral status (experiments 1 and 2, respectively), whereas the other attributes are arguably necessary but definitely not sufficient (experiments 2 and 1, respectively).   10

The best way to get a better fix on exactly which traits are prerequisites for moral status is simply to try to explain why they *should* be. Take   11 sentience first. We all agree from personal experience that pain is a bad thing, that no one should have the right to inflict it on us, and consistency (part of any moral system) dictates that we agree not to inflict it on anyone else. Makes sense. But now try to say something comparably compelling about why great reasoning ability or complex language are crucial to moral status. Also, try to do the same with self-consciousness—our awareness of our own existence. (This is another uniquely human attribute commonly invoked in these discussions, but we couldn't isolate it in experiment 1 above because an organism can't have it without having sentience.)

If you accept this challenge, you'll almost certainly go down one of two   12
paths, neither of which will get you very far. First, you may try to establish that self-consciousness, complex language, etc., are the hallmarks of "spirit," the possession of which places us in some special category. This is a perfectly fine thing to believe, but it's hard to *argue* for. It depends much more on religious conviction than on any plausible line of reasoning.

The second path people take in asserting the moral significance of   13
uniquely human attributes is even less successful, because it leads to a booby trap. This is the argument that self-consciousness and reason and language give humans a dimension of suffering that mere animals lack: because we can anticipate pain and death; and because we know that death will represent the end of our consciousness forever; and because we recognize that threats to one citizen may represent a threat to us all—because of all this, the protection of human rights is essential to everyone's peace of mind; the torture or murder of anyone in town, as conveyed to the public via language and then reflected upon at length, makes everyone tremendously fearful. So a robust conception of individual rights is essential for the welfare of a human society in a way that it isn't for, say, the welfare of a chicken society.

Sounds nice, but it amounts to philosophical surrender. To rely com-   14
pletely on this argument is to concede that language, reason, and self-consciousness are morally important *only* to the extent that they magnify suffering or happiness. Pain and pleasure, in other words, are the currency of moral assessment. The several uniquely human attributes may revaluate the currency, but the currency possesses some value with or without them. And many, if not all, nonhuman animals seem to possess the currency in some quantity. So unless you can come up with a non-arbitrary reason for saying that their particular quantities are worthless while our particular quantities are precious, you have to start thinking about animals in a whole new light. This explains why Peter Singer, in *Animal Liberation,* readily admits that the human brain is unique in its ability to thus compound suffering.

Once the jaws of this philosophical trap have closed on the opponents   15
of animal rights, no amount of struggling can free them. Let them insist that language, reason, and self-consciousness *immensely* raise the moral stakes for humans. Let them add, even, that our sheer neurological complexity makes us experience raw pain more profoundly than, say, dogs or even mice do. Grant them, in other words, that in the grand utilitarian calculus, one day of solid suffering by a single human equals one day's suffering by 10,000

laboratory rats. Grant them all of this, and they still lose, because the point is that animals have now been *admitted* to the utilitarian calculus. If it is immoral, as we all believe it is, to walk up to a stranger and inflict 1/10,000 of one day's suffering (nine seconds' worth), then it is equally immoral to walk up and inflict one day's suffering on a single laboratory rat.

Actually, granting animals utilitarian value doesn't technically mean you   16
have to extend individual rights to them. As far as sheer philosophical consistency goes, you can equally well take rights away from humans. You can say: sure, it makes sense to kill 100 baboons to save the life of one human, but it also makes sense to kill a human to save the life of 100 baboons. Whatever you say, though, you have to go one way or the other, letting such equations work either in both directions or in neither. Unless you can create a moral ratchet called "human rights"—and I don't see any way to do it—you have to choose between a planet on which every sentient creature has rights and a planet on which none does.

And of course if no creature on earth has rights, then it can make sense   17
to kill a human not just for the sake of 100 baboons, but for the sake of two humans—or just in the name of the greater good. In other words, the logic used by animal rights activists turns out to play into the hands of the Adolf Hitlers of the world no less than the Albert Schweitzers. In *Darkness at Noon*, when Ivanov describes Stalin's rule as belonging to the school of "vivisection morality," Arthur Koestler is onto something more than good allegory.

Before figuring out whether to follow this logic toward vegetarianism   18
or totalitarianism, let's remove it from the realm of abstraction. Spending an evening watching videotapes supplied by PETA—such as *The Animals Film*, narrated by Julie Christie—is a fairly disturbing experience. This is partly because the people who made it gave it a subtle shrillness that reflects what is most annoying about the animal rights movement. There are man-on-the-street interviews conducted by an obnoxious, self-righteous interrogator demanding to know how people can own dogs and eat Big Macs; there is the assumption that viewers will find the late McDonald's founder Ray Kroc—a seemingly likable guy shown innocently discussing how he settled on the name "McDonald's"—abhorrent; there is a simple-minded anti-capitalist undercurrent (as if factory farmers in socialist countries spent their time giving foot massages to hogs); and there is grating atonal music meant to make the sight of blood more disturbing than it naturally is.

And that's plenty disturbing, thank you. Take, for example, the chick-   19
ens hung by their feet from a conveyer belt that escorts them through an automatic throat slicing machine—this the culmination of a life spent on the poultry equivalent of a New York subway platform at rush hour. Or consider the deep basketfuls of male chicks, struggling not to smother before they're ground into animal feed. There's also, naturally, the veal: a calf raised in a crate so small that it can't even turn around, much less walk—the better to keep the flesh tender. There are wild furry animals cut almost in half by steel-jawed traps but still conscious. There are rabbits getting noxious chemicals sprayed in their eyes by cosmetics companies.

And these are the animals that *don't* remind you of human beings.   20
Watching these portions of *The Animals Film* is a day at the zoo compared
with watching nonhuman primates suffer. If you don't already have a strong
sense of identity with chimpanzees, gorillas, and the like—if you doubt that
they're capable of crude reasoning, anticipating pain, feeling and expressing
deep affection for one another—I suggest you patronize your local zoo (or
prison, as animal rights activists would have it) and then get hold of a copy
of the ethologist Frans de Waal's two amazing books, *Peace-making Among
Primates* and *Chimpanzee Politics.* The commonly cited fact that chimps share
about ninety-eight percent of our genes is misleading, to be sure; a handful
of genes affecting the brain's development can make a world of difference.
Still, if you can watch a toddler chimp or gorilla for long without wanting
to file for adoption, you should seek professional help.

In videotapes that Helen helped steal in 1984 from the University of   21
Pennsylvania's Head Injury Clinical Research Center, anesthetized baboons
are strapped down and their heads placed in boxlike vices that are violently
snapped sixty degrees sideways by a hydraulic machine. Some of the baboons have what appear to be seizures, some go limp, and none looks very
happy. Some of the lab workers—as callous as you'd have to become to do
their job, perhaps—stand around and make jokes about it all. It's hard to say
how much scientific good came of this, because the scientist in question refuses to talk about it. But watching the tapes, you have to hope that the data
were markedly more valuable than what's already available from the study
of injured humans. In any event, the experiments were halted after PETA publicized the tapes (though ostensibly for sloppy lab technique, such as occasionally inadequate anesthesia, not because of the violent nature of the
experiments).

There are certainly many kinds of animal research that seem justified   22
by any reasonable utilitarian calculus. A case in point is the lab Helen helped
set afire at the University of Arizona. Among the researchers whose work
was destroyed in the attack is a man named Charles Sterling, who is studying
a parasite that causes diarrhea in both animals and humans and kills many
children in the Third World every year. There is no way fruitfully to study
this parasite in, say, a cell culture, so he uses mice, infecting them with the
parasite and thereby inducing a non-lethal spell of diarrhea. (The idea repeated mindlessly by so many animal rights activists—that there's almost
always an equally effective non-animal approach to experimentation—is
wrong.)

Sterling is one of a handful of workers in this area, and he figures, in   23
over-the-phone, off-the-cuff calculations, that all together they cause around
10,000 to 20,000 mice-weeks of diarrheal discomfort every year. The apparently realistic goal is to find a cure for a disease that kills more than 100,000
children a year. Sounds like a good deal to me. Again, though, the hitch is
that to endorse this in a philosophically impeccable way, you have to let go
of the concept of human rights, at least as classically conceived.

Then again, human rights isn't what it's classically conceived as being. It isn't some divine law imparted to us from above, or some Platonic truth apprehended through the gift of reason. The idea of individual rights is simply a non-aggression pact among everyone who subscribes to it. It's a deal struck for mutual convenience. 24

And, actually, it's in some sense a very old deal. A few million years ago, back when human ancestors were not much smarter than chimps, they presumably abided by an implicit and crude concept of individual rights, just as chimps do. Which is to say: life within a troop of, say, fifty or sixty individuals was in practical terms sacred. (Sure, chimps occasionally murder fellow troop members, just as humans do, but this is highly aberrant behavior. Rituals that keep bluster and small-scale aggression from escalating to fatality are well-developed. And when they fail, and death occurs, an entire chimp colony may be solemn and subdued for hours or longer as if in mourning.) At the same time, these prehuman primates were presumably much like chimps in being fairly disdainful of the lives of fellow species-members who didn't belong to the troop. At some point in human history, as troops of fifty became tribes of thousands, the circle of morally protected life grew commensurately. But the circle didn't at first extend to other tribes. Indeed, wide acceptance of the idea that people of all nations have equal moral rights is quite recent. 25

How did it all happen? In one of Singer's later and less famous books, *The Expanding Circle* (Farrar, Straus, & Giroux, 1981), whose title refers to exactly this process, he writes as if the circle's expansion has been driven almost Platonically, by the "inherently expansionist nature of reasoning." Once people became civilized and started thinking about the logic behind the reciprocal extension of rights to one another, he says, they were on an intellectual "escalator," and there was no turning back. The idea of uniformly applied ethical strictures "emerges because of the social nature of human beings and the requirements of group living, but in the thought of reasoning beings, it takes on a logic of its own which leads to its extension beyond the bounds of the group." 26

This, alas, is perhaps too rosy a view. The concept of human rights has grown more inclusive largely through raw politics. Had tribes not found it in their interest to band together—sometimes to massacre other tribes—they wouldn't have had to invent the concept of intertribal rights. Necessity was similarly the mother of moral invention in modern societies. Had the suffragists not deftly wielded political clout, men mightn't have seen the logic of giving women the vote. Had the abolition of slavery not acquired political moment in a war that slaughtered millions, slavery might have long persisted. 27

Certainly in advances of this sort an important role can be played by intellectual persuasion, by sympathy, by empathy. These can fuse with political power and reinforce it. South Africa today exemplifies the mix. President F. W. de Klerk may or may not truly buy the moral logic behind his 28 (relatively) progressive initiatives, but he definitely has felt the accompanying political pressure, ranging from international sanctions to domestic protest and unrest. On the other hand, behind those sanctions has been, among other things, some genuine empathy and some pure moral logic.

The bad news for animals is twofold. First, in all of these cases—women's rights; the abolition of slavery, ending apartheid—a good part of the political momentum comes from the oppressed themselves. Progress in South Africa never would have begun if blacks there hadn't perceived their own dignity and fought for it. Second, in all of these cases, empathy for the oppressed by influential outsiders came because the outsiders could identify with the oppressed—because, after all, they're people, too. With animal rights, in contrast, (1) the oppressed can never by themselves exert leverage; and (2) the outsiders who work on their behalf, belonging as they do to a different species, must be exquisitely, imaginatively compassionate in order to be drawn to the cause. To judge by history, this is not a recipe for success. It may forever remain the case that, when it comes time to sit down and do the moral bargaining, non-human animals, unlike all past downtrodden organisms, don't have much to bring to the table.

Notwithstanding these handicaps, the animal rights movement has made progress. America fur sales are by some accounts down (perhaps more out of fear of social disapproval than out of newfound sympathy). Some cosmetics companies have stopped abusing rabbit's eyes, finding that there are gentler ways to test products. And the university panels that administer federal laboratory regulations—designed to ensure that animal experimentation is worthwhile and not needlessly cruel—are undoubtedly, in the present climate, being at least as scrupulous as they've ever been (however scrupulous that is).

Even I—never quick to bring my deeds into sync with my words—am making minor gains. I hereby vow never again to eat veal. And it's conceivable that the dovetailing of moral concerns and health fears will get me to give up all red meat, among the most (formerly) sentient kind of flesh on the market. Also: no leather couches or leather jackets in my future. Shoes, yes, couches, no; the least we can do is distinguish between the functionally valuable and the frivolous. (Which also means, of course: people who wear fur coats to advertise their social status—which is to say all people who wear fur coats—should indeed, as the Humane Society's ads have it, be ashamed of themselves.) Finally, for what it's worth, I plan to keep intact my lifelong record of never eating pâté de foie gras, the preternaturally enlarged liver of a goose force-fed through a large tube.

But so long as I so much as eat tuna fish and support the use of primates in AIDS research, how can I still endorse the idea of human rights? How can I consider Stalin guilty of a moral crime and not just a utilitarian arithmetic error? One answer would be to admit that my allegiance to human rights isn't philosophical in the pure sense, but pragmatic; I've implicitly signed a non-aggression pact with all other humans, and Stalin violated the pact, which is immoral in this practical sense of the term. But I'd rather answer

29

30

31

32

that, yes, I think moral law should be more than a deal cut among the powerful, but, no, I haven't been any more successful than the next guy in expunging all moral contradictions from my life. I'll try to do what I can.

If there is a half-decent excuse for this particular contradiction, I suppose it is that human civilization is moving in the right direction. Given where our moral thinking was 200, 500, 5,000 years ago, we're not doing badly. The expanding circle will never get as big as Singer would like, perhaps, but if it grows even slowly and fitfully, we'll be justified in taking a certain chauvinistic pride in our species.   33

QUESTIONS FOR MEANING

1. Why does Wright believe that granting animals any consideration is the beginning of a "slippery slope?" Paraphrase paragraph 5. (For a definition of "slippery slope," see p. 39.)
2. According to Wright, why are "powerful brains, complex language, and high culture" morally insignificant when determining rights?
4. Where do "human rights" come from according to this essay? What role has politics played in the development of "rights"?
5. What two factors make the campaign for animal rights more difficult than earlier campaigns for various types of human rights?
6. Vocabulary: baited (3), cognitive (3), dissonance (3), sentience (7), gratuitously (10), utilitarian (15), ethologist (20), impeccable (23), aberrant (25), preternaturally (31), pragmatic (32).

QUESTIONS ABOUT STRATEGY

1. Wright begins his essay by discussing how he was disappointed by his interviews with animal rights activists. What is his motive in emphasizing that he found these people to be less extreme than he had anticipated?
2. Does Wright reveal any reservations about the animal rights movement despite the sympathy he comes to have for it?
3. How useful are paragraphs 8–10?
4. In paragraph 31, Wright makes a distinction between buying leather shoes and buying a leather sofa. Do you agree that we can make distinctions of this sort? How important is it to Wright's conclusion?
5. Consider the use of words like "suppose" and "perhaps" in paragraph 33. Would this essay be stronger if the conclusion were more emphatic?

DEBORAH G. MAYO

Against a Scientific Justification of Animal Experiments

*A magna cum laude graduate of Clark University, where she had a double major in philosophy and mathematics, Deborah Mayo has done extensive research on the use of statistics in science, economics, and philosophy. She received her Ph.D. from the University of Pennsylvania in 1979 and went on to teach philosophy at Virginia Polytechnic Institute and State University. She has received several fellowships from the National Endowment for the Humanities and published essays in numerous scholarly journals. "Against a Scientific Justification of Animal Experiments" was first published in **1983**. Drawing upon her training in logic and statistical testing, Mayo questions the scientific validity of experiments involving laboratory animals— thus moving the debate over animal experimentation beyond the questions of ethics and morality most often focused upon by other writers. Her essay also provides an example of APA style documentation.*

Introduction

Discussions of the treatment of animals typically focus on their use as food   1
and clothing, omitting the widespread use of animals in laboratory research. Animals serve as experimental subjects in teaching surgical operations; in testing the efficiency and safety of drugs, food, cars, household cleaners, and makeup; in psychological studies of pain, stress, and depression; and in satisfying the curiosity and desire of humans to learn more about biological processes. In so doing they are subjected to shocks, burns, lesions, crashes, stresses, diseases, mutilations, and the general array of slings and arrows of the laboratory environment.

If it is agreed that killing and torturing animals is prima facie wrong,   2
then additional justification is necessary in order to defend the sacrifice of millions of animals each year in research. The justification most frequently offered is that animal research provides increases both in scientific knowledge and in the health, safety, and comfort of humans. As Lowrance (1976) remarks:

> For most people, any qualms over jeopardizing the animals are more than offset by the desire to gain knowledge useful in alleviating human suffering (p. 52).
> . . . Few people would engage in such work were it not so essential (p. 54).

So closely is scientific experimentation associated with animal experimentation that those who oppose or criticize animal experiments are often taken to be opposing or criticizing science. One finds advocates of humane experimental methods labeled as anti-science and referred to as "those whose love of animals leads them into a hatred of science and even humanity . . ." (Lane-Petter, 1963, p. 472). The classic volume, *Experimental Surgery* (Markowitz et al., 1959) introduces the student to the Antivivisection Movement with the following remarks (emphasis added):

> It must be apparent . . . that ordinary antivivisectionists are immune to the usual methods of exposition by reasoned argument. *They strain at a dog and swallow a baby.* . . . They are an unfortunate evil in our midst, and we must accustom ourselves to their presence as we do to bad weather, and to disease.

The error in depicting critics of animal experiments as anti-science becomes clear when one begins to question the extent to which the purported scientific aims of these experiments are actually accomplished. For then it turns out that the experiments and not their critics are unscientific. However, humanists concerned with the treatment of animals too rarely question the scientific basis of animal experiments and fail to uncover dissent within the scientific community itself. To the philosopher's arguments that animal experimentation is morally indefensible, the animal researcher responds that they benefit humanity. But if the most common uses of animals in research can be shown to be neither significantly beneficial to humans nor scientifically sound, then any appeal to such benefits in justifying these uses is undermined. It is the purpose of this paper to undermine the justification of common types of animal experiments by questioning their practical and scientific relevance and validity. Those experiments that cannot be justified on scientific grounds can be no more justified than the frivolous killing and torturing of animals. In fact they are even less capable of justification, since such experiments block more fruitful uses of scientific resources.

Irrelevant Experiments

I shall first consider the relevance of animal experiments and then discuss various problems leading to their invalidity. In an important sense, invalidity is not separate from irrelevance, since invalid experiments are surely irrelevant ones. However, in this section I shall focus on experiments that are irrelevant because of the triviality or obviousness of the question they ask. Indeed, many experiments do not even have a specific question in mind at the outset. They are often carried out simply to see what will happen and after the results are in some sort of hypothesis is formulated. Whether the hypothesis has been formulated before or after the experiment is not reported in the description of the experiment. Yet, formulating the hypothesis on the basis of the experiment can be shown to lead researchers to conclude, wrongly, that something of relevance has been observed (see Mayo, 1981).

I must emphasize that the examples I here consider are not at all exceptional or unusual. On the contrary, each represents a basic type of experiment that is performed with minor variations on millions of animals each year. An examination of the *Psychopharmaceutical Abstracts,* in which summaries of published experimental results are reported, will attest to the triviality and repetitiveness of the great majority of inquiries. What is particularly disturbing about the irrelevant experiments mentioned here is the amount of pain and suffering they involve. That such irrelevant painful experiments are not rare even at present is made plain in Jeff Diner's (1979) *Physical and Mental Suffering of Experimental Animals,* in which research from 1975–1978 is reviewed. It must also be kept in mind that these experiments are examples of ones considered important enough to publish. It is fair to assume that, in reality, many more experiments with even less relevance are performed. I limit myself to considering only recent experiments, to make it clear that these are not atrocities of the past.

(i) Infant monkeys were blinded at the University of Chicago in order 5 to assess whether blindness inhibited social interactions as measured by facial expressions. The result: blind monkeys showed all normal facial expressions, except threat (Berkson & Becker, 1975).

(ii) Pigeons were starved to 70% of their weight in the City University 6 of New York. It was concluded that following starvation pigeons ate more than usual (*Journal of Comparative and Physiological Psychology,* Sept., 1971).

(iii) The Department of Psychology at the University of Iowa studied 7 the effects of brain lesions on the grooming behavior of cats. Cats underwent surgery to produce various types of brain lesions and films were taken of their subsequent grooming behavior. It was reported that:

> Statistical analyses of the grooming behavior shown on the films indicated that cats with pontile lesions and cats with tectal lesions spent less time grooming. . . . Other studies revealed that cats with pontile or tectal lesions were deficient in removing tapes stuck on their fur (Swenson & Randall, 1977).

(iv) At the Downstate Medical Center rats were surgically brain dam- 8 aged and then stimulated by pinching their tails. They were then offered substances to drink. It was reported that (Mufson et al., 1976):

> Brain-damaged animals during tail pinch-induced drinking trials are responsive to the sensory properties of the test liquid. Chocolate milk is consumed, but tap water is actively rejected. Tail pinch to sham-operated control rats failed to induce such behavior; instead, it induced rage behavior towards the hand that pinched the tail.

(Is it to be concluded from this that brain damage decreases rage at painful stimuli and increases the desire for chocolate milk?)

(v) The following experiment carried out at the George Washington 9 University Medical Center is a typical example of radiation research. Non-anesthetized rabbits had their heads irradiated while being restrained in "a Lucite restraining device." It is reported that "The developing skin, mucosal and eye lesions were recorded and often photographed, but no treatment was offered" (Bradley et al., 1977). The report continues to describe in detail the monstrous radiation-induced damage without drawing any conclusions.

(vi) An extremely widespread sort of experiment involves assessing the   10
effects of various drugs on "punished responding." Punished responding
typically involves first teaching an animal to perform some task such as pressing
a key by rewarding it with food, and later changing these rewards to punishments such as electric shocks. A number of such experiments have been carried out by Dr. J. E. Barrett using pigeons. Here, the "punishments" consist
of electric shocks administered through electrodes implanted around the pubis
bone. The results are rather inconclusive. It is reported that (Barrett & Witkin, 1976):

> The broad range of effects obtained in the present experiment make it difficult
> to readily characterize the effects of drug interactions on behavior.

(vii) At Emory University cats were used to study how two different   11
kinds of painful stimuli, foot shock and tooth shock, influence behavior. To
administer tooth shock, electrodes were implanted in the upper canine teeth
of the cats. Foot shock was administered by means of stainless steel rods that
formed the grid floor of the shuttle box in which the cats were placed. The
cats were trained to escape the shocks by jumping across a barrier. However,
when the cats were also subjected to the tooth shock, they were unable to
escape the foot shock. It was concluded that tooth shock exerted a stronger
influence than foot shock on behavior. The report regrets that (Anderson et
al., 1976):

> Since 14 mA was the maximum amount of current that could be generated by
> our apparatus, it was not possible to determine if foot shock levels greater than
> that would have led to escape responding.

(viii) The *British Journal of Ophthalmology* published the experiments of   12
Dr. Zauberman, which measured the number of grams of force needed to
strip the retinas from the eyes of cats. There was nothing said about how
this or similar experiments that were carried out could be relevant to the
problem of detached retinas in humans.

(ix) A good deal of research has as its goal the determination of the   13
effects of various operations on the sexual behavior of animals. For example,
for a number of years the American Museum of Natural History in New
York has conducted research on the effect of surgical mutilation on the sexual
behavior of cats. In 1969 cats raised in isolation had penis nerves severed.
The results of years of sex testing on these cats were overwhelmingly unsur-
prising: genital desensitization together with sexual inexperience inhibits the
normal sexual behavior in cats (cited in Pratt, 1976, p. 72).

Numerous other experiments by the same researchers were conducted   14
to determine the effect of surgically destroying the olfactory area on the brain
on sexual behavior in cats, monkeys, hamsters, rats, and mice. The conclusions from all of these experiments were reported to be "contradictory."

(x) Some experiments are rendered trivial or useless because they do no   15
more than repeat an experiment already performed numerous times. Even
worse is the continuous repetition of experiments whose relevance is dubious
in the first place. For example, there is the experiment that has been carried
out since the time of Claude Bernard, one of the founders of modern vivisection methods. This experiment involves sewing up the ends of the intes-
tines of dogs rendering them unable to defecate. Death has been observed to
follow in some cases between 5 and 11 days, in other cases between 8 and 34
days. To what use is such information to be put?

One of the reasons for continually repeating an experiment that has   16
already produced a result is that by using enough animals a result that is of a
sufficient degree of statistical significance can be obtained. It is thought that
the more observations the greater the evidence. However, this is based upon
a statistical fallacy. The more experiments needed in order to observe an
effect that is statistically significant, the smaller and more trivial the effect is.
With enough experiments, even a chance occurrence is rendered overwhelmingly significant, statistically speaking.

Invalidity of Experiments

Experimental investigations are multi-staged affairs involving a host of back-   17
ground variables, the gathering, modeling, and analyses of data and inferences based upon the data. At each stage a variety of flaws can arise to
render the experiment and inferences based upon it invalid. I shall consider
some of the most pronounced flaws that arise in carrying out animal experiments and making inferences from them in medical and pharmacological research. These flaws stem from the disparity between experimentally induced
conditions and conditions in humans, from within- and between-species differences, and from confounding variables before, during, and after experimental treatment. I consider each of these in turn.

Artificial Induction of Disease   One type of medical research involves as-   18
certaining whether certain pathological conditions in humans can be alleviated or cured by certain drugs. Animals are used as "models" upon which
to test these treatments. To do this it is necessary for the animal subject to
have the condition in question, and in order to bring this about healthy animals are made sick. To this end they surgically have organs removed or
damaged; they are injected with pathogenic organisms and cancer cells; they
have irritants applied to their eyes and shaved skins; are forced to inhale
various substances, and consume deficient diets. To produce such conditions
as fear, anxiety, ulcers, heart diseases, and shock, animals are stressed by
electric shocks or subjected to specially made pain devices, such as the Bla-
lock Press and the Noble-Collip Drum.

It turns out, however, that the conditions artificially induced have little   19
in common with the naturally occurring diseases in animals (when these exist) and much less in common with the diseases in man. This renders any

conclusions drawn on the basis of treating these induced conditions of little relevance for treating humans (or even animals in cases where the condition naturally occurs). Extrapolating results from animal research to humans also frequently fails because of an absence of comparative examples of diseases in animals (particularly with hereditary diseases). For example, ulcers do not occur naturally in animals, and cancer in animals is quite different from cancer in man.

It is for this reason that the usefulness of animals in cancer research has   20
been questioned. Most of the anticancer agents in use today have been tested in animals, most commonly rodents who have had tumors transplanted into them. This method, however, is of questionable validity. As noted in a review of testing anticancer drugs (*The Lancet,* April 15, 1972):

> Since no animal tumour is closely related to a cancer in human beings, an agent which is active in the laboratory may well prove to be useless clinically.

The situation would not be so serious if these agents were merely useless. In fact they are quite harmful, often causing side effects that may themselves precipitate further ills or even death. When researchers announce that a substance has been found to be effective in treating animal cancers, it is not revealed that the cell kinetics in animal cancers are vastly different than in humans. As the review above states:

> Animal tumours favored as test models have short doubling-times and a large proportion of cells in cycle with short generation-times. Probably, in many human cancers, intermitotic times are much longer and many cells are out of cycle. . . .

Since all anticancer agents in use have had their effectiveness assessed by animal tests, virtually all of them act only on rapidly dividing cells. This is one reason that treating human cancers (which typically do not divide rapidly) with these agents fails. The possibility of transplanting actual human cancers to animals is a suggestion which has been tried, but with poor results. As *The Lancet* review remarks, "This is hardly surprising, in view of the vastly different biochemical make-up of the animal model and of the human tumour which responds."

Hence, people are given drug after drug in the hope of arresting cancer   21
when in fact these drugs have been evaluated upon cancers and organisms "vastly different" from their own. It may be argued that no better method is available for treating cancer, and so for the time being it is the best that can be done. Such, however, is not the case. In the last 30 years or so new techniques have been developed which hold much promise. These new techniques involve testing anticancer agents on cultures of human cancer cells. This has the advantage of permitting the sensitivity of individual cancers to chemotherapy to be estimated, providing each patient with treatment custom-tailored to the type of cancer involved. This would prevent individuals from having to suffer the agonies of numerous trial agents that may be entirely

ill-suited for treating their particular strain of cancer. If these newer techniques are to be developed sufficiently, some of the attention presently given to animal testing will have to be channeled into these alternatives. Unfortunately, researchers have been reluctant to do so.

The need to induce pathological conditions in animals in order to test some treatment upon them gives rise to an additional area of medical research. This area involves experiments that have as their sole aim the determination of how various pathological conditions can best be brought about in animals. Although such research has provided means for inducing a number of conditions, cures for these conditions have not been forthcoming.

For instance, research has repeatedly been carried out in order to find ways of inducing peritonitis in dogs. Peritonitis is the painful condition suffered by humans after rupturing their appendices. Even after a standard method for producing this disease in dogs was available (i.e., surgically tying off the appendix and feeding the dog castor oil), further experiments to find improved methods were made. One such experiment is reported by Hans Ruesch in *Slaughter of the Innocent* (Ruesch, 1978, pp. 105–106):

> With each dog strapped down and his belly laid open, the 'surgeons'—subsidized by the American taxpayers who of course had never been asked for their consent—tied off and crushed the appendix, then cut out part of the intestinal tract and the spleen. With the intestinal system thus mutilated and unable to function normally, the dog was made to swallow a large dose of castor oil. The authors stated that thus 'a fatal, fulminating, diffuse peritonitis of appendical origin may be uniformly produced in dogs.'

There was no attempt to cure peritonitis, the aim having been merely to cause it. It was reported that the average survival time of the agonized dogs in this experiment was 39 hours.

Arguments to the effect that it is wrong to cause pain and suffering to animals are often rejected by claiming that animals simply do not suffer. Descartes, for example, asserted that the cries of an animal are no more significant than the creaking of a wheel. Ironically, it is precisely upon the assumption that animals *do* suffer from stress, fear, and pain in a manner similar to humans that the validity of much of animal experimentation rests. Few, if any, conditions are studied as widely in animals as are pain, stress, ulcers, fear, and anxiety. An enormous amount of data has been compiled about how to produce such conditions, a good deal of which arose from the research of Hans Selye (1956). To obtain this data, millions of animals, primarily rats, mice, rabbits, and cats were and continue to be subjected to burns, poisons, shocks, frustrations, muscle and bone crushing, exposure, and gland removal. However, as is generally the case with artificially induced conditions in animals, laboratory-induced stress and stress-related conditions have little in common with stress and stress-related diseases in humans. To support this claim, it is necessary to consider something about how these conditions are induced in the laboratory animal.

One of the tools developed in 1942 to aid Selye in his research on stress,   25
is the stress producing Noble-Collip Drum, named after its inventors, R. L.
Noble and J. B. Collip. The animals, locked and strapped (paws taped) inside
the revolving metal drum, are tossed about and in so doing are thrust against
iron projections in the drum. This treatment (often involving thousands of
tosses at a rate of 40 tosses a minute) crushes bones, tissues, and teeth, and
ruptures and scrambles organs. In assessing the considerable work of Selye,
the *British Medical Journal* (May 22, 1954, p. 1195) concluded that experimentally induced stress had little in common with conditions that humans develop. Ulcers brought about in animals subjected to a rotating drum differ
from ulcers in humans, not only because of a difference in species, but
because ulcers in humans stem from rather different origins (e.g., long-
term psychological stresses) than do those created in the laboratory through
physical torture. Unsurprisingly, treatments developed from Selye's stress
research (e.g., administering a hormone excreted by tortured animals,
ACTH) are of very dubious value. As one surgeon points out (Ogilvie,
1935):

> They [gastric and duodenal ulcers] never occur naturally in animals, and they
> are hard to reproduce experimentally. They have been so produced, but usually
> by methods of gross damage that have no relation to any possible causative
> factor in man; moreover, these experimental ulcers are superficial and heal rap-
> idly, and bear little resemblance to the indurated chronic ulcers we see in our
> patients.

The Noble-Collip Drum has been criticized not only as being inhumane, but
as being too crude to be scientifically useful. In what is considered a definitive review of experimentally produced shock, H. B. Stoner made this remark about it: "It is impossible to describe the effect of the injury and study
the injured tissue quantitatively. . . . The method seems altogether too crude
for modern purposes" (Stoner, 1961). Despite this, the Noble-Collip Drum
is still used in experiments on stress and shock. Typically, these experiments
attempt to test the effect of various drugs on the ability of unanesthetized
animals to withstand the trauma of the drum.

The most widely used means for bringing about stress, terror, anxiety,   26
and shock is administering electric shocks. A number of researchers are fond
of experiments in which animals are trained to avoid electric shocks by performing some task, such as pressing a lever, and thousands of such experiments are performed yearly. After the animal has learned this "shock
avoidance," frequently the experimental condition will be changed so that
what previously permitted the animal to avoid shock now delivers shock.
When such an experiment was performed on rhesus monkeys, it was found
to produce "conflict" followed by gastroduodenal lesions. Countless experiments of this sort are repeatedly performed simply to bring about stressful
conditions—without any attempt to treat these. When there is an attempt to
treat the induced stress-related condition, the results are often useless or

meaningless because of the disparity between natural and artificially induced conditions.

Electric shocks are also commonly used to induce aggression in ani-   2'
mals, mainly rats. When the restrained animals are given a sufficient number of shocks, they will bite, box, or strike each other. Then the effects of a number of drugs on shock–induced aggression are assessed. In one case, which is typical of such research, the effect of mescaline on rats in a shock–induced aggression situation was tested (Sbordone & Garcia, 1977). Although in some cases the drug appeared to increase aggression, it was also found that the same aggression was shown by.some nontreated rats. Hence, attributing the increased aggression to the drug is of questionable validity. Pratt (1976) describes the work of a prominent researcher in aggression studies, Dr. Roger Ulrich:

> Ulrich's work since 1962 . . . has consisted largely in causing pain to rats and observing the resulting aggressive behavior. This investigator would give painful foot-shocks to the rats through an electrified grid floor . . . (p. 61). Ulrich then introduced other distressing stimuli. . . . Bursts of intense noise (135 db, sustained for more than 1 min.) were introduced. The effects of castration were tried; . . . and finally one pair had their whiskers cut off and were blinded by removal of their eyes (pp. 61–62).

All of this aggression research has done little to control human aggression, which is rather different from the shock–induced aggression in rats. Ulrich himself has very recently come to question the usefulness of his past research. In a letter appearing in the *Monitor* he confesses (Ulrich, 1978):

> Initially my research was prompted by the desire to understand and help solve the problem of human aggression but I later discovered that the results of my work did not seem to justify its continuance. Instead I began to wonder if perhaps financial rewards, professional prestige, the opportunity to travel etc. were the maintaining factors.

Another condition that electric shocks are employed to induce is epilepsy. Monkeys are given electric shocks that produce convulsions similar to those caused by epilepsy and eventually drive them insane. The insane monkey is then given a variety of drugs with the hope of curing or controlling epilepsy. However, while the monkeys display behavior that appears similar to epilepsy in man, their shock–induced fits have little bearing on human epilepsy, which has rather different origins. Hence, inferences from such experiments to treating human epilepsy are of very questionable validity. Unsurprisingly, the animal-tested drugs have failed to cure or control epilepsy.

The development of drugs to prevent brain hemorrhages proceeds in a   28
similar manner. To evaluate the efficacy of drugs on animals, it is first required to create blood clots in the brains of test animals. To this end, their skulls are cracked by hammer blows, causing the brain to form blood clots. Drugs are then given to the animals to determine which seem to improve their wretched state. But blood clots from hammer blows are rather different

from those arising in humans, which are a gradual result of circulation problems or from long-term unhealthy eating and living habits.

In the interest of studying the effects of certain drugs on overeating (hyperphagia) researchers tested the drugs on rats that had overeaten (Wallach et al., 1977). However, in order to induce overeating in these rats they were forced to eat by painfully pinching their tails. The procedure was described as follows: "Tail pinch was applied for 10 minutes. Pressure was gradually increased until the animal either ate or became frantic." However, humans do not overeat because they are under pain or torture to do so. As such, the effects of drugs on the overeating of animals forced to overeat are irrelevant for assessing their effect on humans who overeat.   29

Underlying all these cases of induction of diseases is the assumption that by artificially creating a condition in animals that appears to resemble a pathological state in man, one can make inferences about the latter on the basis of treating the former. This assumption is often false because of the disparity between experimentally induced conditions in animals and the corresponding conditions in humans. Indeed, there is also likely to be a disparity between artificially produced disease in animals and its natural occurrence (if it exists) in that animal. An example of this is seen in the case of inducing a deficiency of vitamin E in mice. Because this deficiency brought about a syndrome similar to muscular dystrophy, it was theorized that vitamin E would be effective in treating muscular dystrophy in man. In 1961, researchers showed (Loosli, 1967) that hereditary muscular dystrophy in mice and the dystrophy brought about by a vitamin E deficiency in mice were fundamentally different. Hence, the inference that vitamin E is useful in treating muscular dystrophy (as opposed to vitamin E deficiency) is invalid not only for humans, but for mice as well. The researchers concluded that it is never certain that experimentally induced disease sufficiently copies an inborn error.   30

In addition to producing misleading inferences, the techniques of animal research are seen to be detrimental in that they take attention away from more fruitful methods, such as clinical observation of humans. In a 1978 address, Dr. Alice Heim, chairperson of the psychological section of the British Association for the Advancement of Science, remarked (*The Times,* September, 1978):   31

> Surely it is more valuable to work with disturbed human beings who seek help than to render cats and other animals 'experimentally neurotic'; then try to 'cure' them; and then try to draw an analogy between these animals and the immensely more complex *homo sapiens.*

Differences Between and Within Species   In addition to using animals as "models" for disease, animals are widely used to test the efficiency and safety of drugs and environmental substances by toxicologists and pharmacologists. The problem of differences between species is perhaps greatest in toxicological research. This problem often prevents the valid extrapolation of the results of animal tests to humans.   32

In experiments carried out to determine how poisonous various chemicals are, the classic measure of toxicity used is called the *median lethal dose,* abbreviated as LD_{50}. It is defined as the dose of a substance needed to kill 50% of a given species of animals. Each year, millions of animals, usually mice, are force-fed drugs, insecticides, floor polishes, food additives, lipsticks, and other chemical substances, and the dosage required to kill about half of them (within 14 days) is calculated. But the significance of the LD_{50} measure is far from clear.

The purpose of the LD_{50} test is to determine the degree to which substances are poisonous to humans. However, for a number of reasons it fails to provide such a determination. For one thing, many of the test substances are relatively innocuous and hence enormous quantities must be forced down the animals' throats to cause them to die. In such cases, the death is often caused simply by the damage done by the massive quantities and not the test substance itself. The calculated LD_{50}s for these substances have no bearing on the manner in which the substance is to be used by humans.

Having found the LD_{50}, experiments with increasingly lower dosages are made to ascertain the supposedly safe dosage of the drug (the LD_0). The next step is to extrapolate this safe dosage to humans. This extrapolation is made simply by multiplying the weight of the animal proportionately to the weight of humans. However, this safe level applies only to the test animal and it may differ radically for humans. This is particularly true when, as is often the case, the animal's death is attributable to the sheer volume of the substance. Extrapolating in this manner is also based on the assumption that the drug acts in a linear fashion—that twice the dosage means twice the effect. In fact, there is typically a threshold below which substances may have no real effect.

It might be thought that despite the differences between test animals and humans, that the LD_{50} may still provide a rank order of the degree of toxicity of substances. Such is not the case. One problem is that a substance with a low LD_{50} may be extremely poisonous over a long period of time, such as lead and asbestos. Hence, the LD_{50} is not useful for ascertaining the result of chronic exposure. In addition, it has been found that in different laboratories not only do the LD_{50} values differ, but the orderings differ as well. This arises from interspecies differences and a number of environmental factors that I shall take up later.

Scientists themselves have come to see the LD_{50} tests as clumsy and crude and lacking in reliability. In one study on four widely used household chemicals, it was found that the LD_{50}s in six laboratories differed both absolutely and relatively. It was concluded that "neither a particular method nor a single value may be regarded as a correct one" (Loosli, 1967, p. 120). Still, in the US, as in most countries, health agencies require that the LD_{50} be calculated for each of the thousands of new substances introduced each year.

Another test promoted by the FDA involves the use of rabbits' eyes to determine how dangerous various substances are to human eyes. In addition to cosmetics, detergents and pesticides are also tested in this way. In 1973,

Revlon alone used 1500 rabbits for eye and skin irritancy tests. As is usual for toxicity tests, no anesthesia is used since it is claimed to interfere with the results of the tests. The rabbits are immobilized in restraining devices for weeks, their eyes (which lack tear glands) being held open with clamps. In assessing the severity of eye irritants, the measure is not numerical, as with the LD$_{50}$. Rather, the eyes of the restrained rabbits are observed after several hours of having the irritant applied, and are described in terms of such categories as ulcerated cornea, inflamed iris, and gross destruction. Such crude determinations yield results that are unreliable and unmeaningful. In 1971, 25 of the best known laboratories jointly conducted a comprehensive evaluation of irritancy tests on rabbits. It was noted that "extreme variation" existed in the way the laboratories assessed the effects of irritants on rabbits.

The study (Weil & Scala, 1971) concluded that: 39

> The rabbit eye and skin procedure currently recommended by the Federal agencies . . . should not be recommended as standard procedure in any new regulations. Without careful reeducation these tests result in unreliable results.

As this was reported by the very laboratories that carry out such tests, it may be regarded as an understatement. Despite the acknowledged crudity and unreliability of these toxicity tests and measures, they are still routinely carried out, primarily as a means by which manufacturers can protect themselves and obtain the right to market new substances.

Underlying the use of animal models for pharmacological tests is the   40 presumption that it will be possible to extrapolate to humans. However, the vast differences that exist between species make the results from one species an unreliable indicator for another. There are a number of ways that substances can produce different effects in different animals. Chemicals act upon living things in five main stages: absorption, distribution, excretion, metabolism, and mechanism of action, and interspecies differences may arise during any of these. Even if the difference is quite small at each stage, they may accumulate to yield a large total interspecies discrepancy. These interspecies differences make inferences from animal experiments very much dependent upon which animal is used as the research model.

Richard Ryder (1975, p. 150) illustrates the gross differences between   41 species in the effectiveness of drugs by citing the following results. The effect of a 'Product X' was found to vary as follows:

SPECIES	BODY WEIGHT, MG/KG
Man	1
Sheep	10
Rabbit	200
Monkey	15.2

From these results it is clear that testing the substance on rabbits will be a poor indicator of its effectiveness in humans. Still, rabbits are a popular animal for this sort of testing.

Interspecies differences may lead to concluding that substances that are innocuous or beneficial in humans are harmful, and that substances that have insidious effects on humans are harmless. For example, penicillin is extremely poisonous to guinea pigs. Had penicillin been subjected to the routine animal tests, as new drugs presently are, it would never have been tried on humans. On the other hand, what is a deadly poison to humans, strychnine, may be safely consumed by guinea pigs. Similarly, a dose of belladonna that is fatal to humans is harmless for a rabbit, the often used laboratory animal. Morphine, while sedating most species, incites frantic excitement in cats, dogs, and mice. Arsenic, deadly for humans, can be safely consumed in enormous quantities by sheep. Still, foxes and chickens die from almonds, and parrots are poisoned by parsley. Tuberculin, which, because it cured TB in guinea pigs, was thought to also be a cure in humans, turned out to cause TB in humans. Digitalis, which because it was seen to produce severely high blood pressure in dogs was thought to be dangerous for humans, turned out to be a major treatment for humans with heart disease.

In certain species, aspirin is highly toxic and it has been seen to produce malformations in the fetuses of rats (*Newsweek,* Nov. 20, 1972). Other substances that are not teratogenic for humans, but are known to cause malformations in the offspring of laboratory animals, are adrenaline, insulin, and certain antibiotics. The converse is the case with drugs such as thalidomide, which was tested extensively in animals (e.g., the popular laboratory Wistar rat) without any adverse effects to the fetus, but which turned out to produce monstrous human babies. The thalidomide tragedy drove people to conclude that more animal testing was needed to protect the safety of humans, when, ironically, the tragedy was a product of animal testing. More specifically, it resulted from the invalidating factor of interspecies differences. After thalidomide was found to produce deformed humans, researchers tried repeatedly to produce similar effects on animals. One hundred fifty different strains and substrains of rabbits were tested, but with no malformations. Finally, it was found that such malformations could be produced in New Zealand white rabbits. One might ask what the point was in carrying out these experiments after thalidomide was already seen to produce malformed human fetuses. The teratogenic effects of a number of other drugs have also been shown not only to vary with species, but also with different strains of the same species.

It is interesting to note that the German drug company that marketed thalidomide, was, after being tried for two and a half years, acquitted on charges of having marketed a dangerous drug. The acquittal was based on the testimonies of numerous medical authorities who claimed that animal tests are never conclusive for making inferences about humans. Despite the failure of animal tests to reveal the danger of thalidomide, Turkish professor S. T. Aygun was able to discover its teratogenic properties through the use of chick embryos, and prevented its being marketed in Turkey. Thalidomide's dangers have also been revealed by testing it on sea-urchin eggs (Krieg, 1964). Much more on alternatives to animal testing may be found in Ruesch, 1978. Unfortunately, even those medical authorities who have come to see animal testing as scientifically unsound are reluctant to voice their views. The following remarks made by two doctors in 1976 express this point (Stiller & Stiller, 1976):

> In praxis all animal experiments are scientifically indefensible, as they lack any scientific validity and reliability in regard to humans. They only serve as an alibi for the drug manufacturers, who hope to protect themselves thereby. . . . But who dares to express doubts of our much-vaunted technological medicine, or even just to ask questions, without meeting the solid opposition from the vested interests of science, business, and also of politics and news media?

Confusion of Background Variables   Invalid inferences arise when what   45
is attributed to the experimental treatment actually arises from the influences of nontreatment variables. Animals even of the same species react differently under the same treatment as a result of nontreatment variables, both of the genetic and environmental kind. Different responses result from differences in the health of the animal, its age, sex, litter, and strain, its living conditions, stressful or painful stimuli, and even odors and the time of day. These variables arise before, during, and after the experimental treatment. I will now consider some ways in which these nontreatment variables may be confused with treatment variables and hence give rise to faulty inferences.

Animals that ultimately become subjects for research may start out with   46
very different characteristics. An experimental response may be the effect not of the experimental treatment in question, but of some former condition of the animal quite unrelated to the treatment. Hence, the background of experimental animals is of major relevance to the reliability of conclusions based upon them—a fact that is often ignored. How are research animals obtained, and how does their background influence the reliability of experiments made upon them?

Animals that find themselves in research laboratories may be of the   47
"specially bred" variety, or they may have arisen from a "random source," that is, from dealers or pounds. In the case of dogs and cats, the great majority come from random sources and are typically stray, unwanted, or stolen pets. For example, of the over 300,000 dogs used in biomedical research in the US in 1969, only about 40,000 were bred specially for the laboratory. By the time a random-source animal reaches the laboratory, an average of one month has been spent either in pounds, with dealers, in transport, or in the wild. Within this period the animal is subjected to poor diet and shelter, and a variety of stressful, unhygienic conditions. In an article in *Life* (February 4, 1966), the outrageous conditions maintained by dog dealers were exposed. The article reports:

> Unscrupulous dog 'dealers' taking advantage of the growing demand for dogs for vital medical research, are running a lucrative and unsavory business.

Laboratories now need almost two million dogs a year . . . . Some dealers keep
big inventories of dogs in unspeakably filthy compounds that seem scarcely less
appalling than the concentration camps of World War II. Many do not sell
directly to labs but simply dispose of their packs at auction where the going
rate is 30¢ a pound. Puppies, often drenched in their own vomit, sell for 10¢
apiece.

Unsurprisingly, as one researcher testified, 40% of the dogs obtained this
way die before they can even be used for research.

Hence, when such animals get sick or die upon receiving some treatment there is little reason to suppose the treatment was to blame. One researcher, testifying at a congressional hearing following the exposition in *Life,*
told of the following case. A drug had been condemned on the basis of an
experiment in which all the dogs receiving it died, but it turned out to be
distemper and not the drug that was responsible for the deaths (U.S. House,
1966). Nor have conditions improved much since the passage of the Laboratory Animals Welfare Act of 1966, which requires licensing and inspections. The rate of animal deaths prior to experimentation is still high. A more
detailed discussion of the human animal laws may be found in Pratt, 1976
and Ruesch, 1978.

Animals that arrive at the laboratory with infections often render results
equivocal. Experiments that are particularly vulnerable to the existence of
intercurrent infections are immunology, radiation, and carcinogenesis studies. Carcinogenesis, for example, is affected by the efficiency of immunological responses and rate of cell turnover, and both of these are affected by
indigenous pathogens.

To avoid the problem that the variability of the health of research animals presents, means by which animals are bred uniformly free of disease
have been developed. Strains of bacteriologically sterile animals, most often
rodents, are bred especially for use in the laboratory. These germ-free animals are born by cesarean section, raised in sterile surroundings, and fed
sterile foods. The germ-free condition of specially bred animals is advertised
as a major selling point in advertisements by suppliers of research animals.
One recent ad (*Laboratory Animal Science,* February, 1977) boasts "*New* Cesarean derived. Barrier reared CAMM RATS-Certified Pathogen Free."

However, the resulting "uniform biological material" as these animals
are often called, differs radically from normal animals. Animals raised in total
sterile conditions fail to develop immunologies that provide a natural defense
mechanism against disease. Hence, they are likely to be far more susceptible
to disease than their naturally bred counterparts.

By using specially bred animals that are biologically uniform there is
less variability in response, and as such, the results are claimed to be more
reliable. It is true that there will be more reliability in the sense of more
agreement among successive experiments with uniform as opposed to non-
uniform animals. However, there will not be more reliability in the sense of
accurately representing natural, random-bred, heterogeneous animal and

human populations. For this, uniformly bred animals provide extremely un-reliable models. It is true that uniform research animals yield less variability in response, and hence an effect may be detected with fewer animals. How-ever, the effect detected is not a reliable indicator of the effect that would arise in animals found in nature, much less in humans.

The demand for uniformity in research animals is, according to a prom- 53 inent researcher, M. W. Fox, often a "pseudo-sophistication." According to Fox, "Few investigators inquire or are aware of how the prior life history and environmental experiences of the animal may influence his ex-periment" (Fox, 1974, pp. 96–97). However, a knowledge of how the back-ground of the animal influences the experimental results is necessary to en-sure the validity of the experiment. Even when not bred to be germ-free, the laboratory animal may fail to develop the resistance to various stresses that it would in its natural habitat where it would normally be faced with a number of stresses. An example of such a natural stress is brought about when baby animals are left alone while their mothers go in search of food. Hence, the laboratory animal is apt to be less hearty than its natural counterpart.

For the most part, research animals are chosen not on the basis of how 54 appropriate they are for a given experiment—even when such information is available. Rather, they are selected for possessing such characteristics as tak-ing up little space, being inexpensive, being nocturnal, being docile and adaptable to laboratory environments. An advertisement for Marshall beagles (*Laboratory Animal Science,* February, 1977) boasts of having designed their research animal as one might design a car model. The ad reads:

> TRY OUT 1977 MODELS. Large selection of COMPACTS, MID SIZE & FULL SIZE MODELS. The Marshall Beagle is built with you in mind. All models feature sturdy unitized body construction and Easy Handling.

As a result, inappropriate animals are often used for detecting the effect of an experimental treatment. One way in which an animal may be inappropriate is if it tends to spontaneously generate the effect in question even when the experimental treatment is absent (i.e., in control animals).

Rats and mice, for example, tend spontaneously to develop a high in- 55 cidence of tumors. This renders them unsuitable for detecting tumors. Still, no animals are used as often as rats and mice for assessing the effect of nu-merous experimental treatments upon the production of tumors. The reason is that they are inexpensive and take up little room. Examples of recent ex-perimental treatments tested this way are saccharin and oral contraceptives. The *British Medical Journal* (October 28, 1972, p. 190) made the following remark concerning the report of the Council on Safety of Medicines on tests of oral contraceptives:

> The tables in the report show incidences of 25% of lung tumours and 17% of liver tumours in *control mice* and 26% adrenal tumours, 30% pituitary tumours, and 99% mammary tumours in *control rats*. It is difficult to see how experiments

on strains of animals so exceedingly liable to develop tumours of these various kinds can throw useful light on the carcinogenicity of any compound for man.

In this experiment, rats exposed to high dosages (up to 400 times the human use) of contraceptives were found to have more tumors than those not exposed. But this does not mean that the additional tumors were caused by the contraceptives, particularly given the high rate of tumors in untreated controls. The question of how many more tumors must be observed to conclude that treated rats differ significantly from untreated rats poses an important statistical problem. Given the high rate of tumors in controls, a rather high rate of tumors in a large sample of treated rats should be required. The report, however, does not indicate how many more tumors were observed. The Committee's report itself (Committee on Safety of Medicines, 1972) concludes that:

> . . . although a carcinogenic effect can be produced when some of the preparations are used in high doses throughout the life-span in certain strains of rat and mouse, this evidence cannot be interpreted as constituting a carcinogenic hazard to women when these preparations are used as oral contraceptives.

The report also notes that many animals died from the high dosage of the compound given.

The conclusion of this committee contrasts with the conclusions of the FDA with respect to the banning of DDT and the recently proposed banning of saccharin. In both cases the evidence consists of an increase of tumors observed in rats given extremely high doses of the substance in question. Without additional evidence, conclusions about the danger of these substances are ill-grounded, both because of the high doses and the high spontaneous rate of tumors in rats.

Even if the experimental effect observed does not result from a condition already present in the animal before entering the lab, it may arise from nontreatment factors introduced after entering the lab. Claude Bernard, the founder of modern animal experimentation, himself admitted that "The experimental animal is never in a normal state. The normal state is merely a supposition, an assumption." The animal is placed in an abnormal state because of the host of stressors it is confronted with.

Animals in the lab are deprived of their natural habitat, and often are terrorized by what they see even before they themselves are experimented upon. It is not uncommon for animals, particularly dogs, to be subject to devocalization prior to experimentation (sometimes referred to as "the anesthesia of the public"), which is itself a trauma. Also common is for an animal to be used for additional research after it has already undergone one or more experiments. (This practice, illegal in Britain, is legal in the US.)

When an animal is in fear or pain, all its organs and biochemical systems are affected. Measurement parameters such as blood pressure, temperature, metabolic rate, and enzyme reactions have been found to vary up to three times their normal value as a result of pain and stress (Hillman, 1970). Hence the value of any of these parameters measured following an experimental treatment may result not from the treatment, but from unrelated pain and stress to which the experimental animal has been subjected. As such, any experiment attempting to detect variations smaller than those already known to be attributable to experimental stress is invalidated. As one physiologist studying the effects of fear and pain notes, "It [experimental stress] is almost certainly the main reason for the wide variation reported among animals upon whom painful experiments have been done" (Hillman, 1970).

Animals may be stressed simply by being handled by the experimenter,   61 or by the order in which they are taken to the experimental room from the cage. When animals are taken one by one from a cage or pen, the last animals taken differ markedly from the first few taken because of the stress brought about from the changing composition of the cage or pen. As one researcher (Magalhaes, 1974, p. 103) states:

> Even apparently minor procedures such as successively removing rats from their colony cage for decapitation and subsequent biochemical analysis can have a marked influence on the results. One experimenter found that the corticosteroid measures obtained from the first few rats taken out of their cage were very much lower compared to those from the last few to be taken.

To avoid this problem, animals are sometimes experimented upon in their usual animal facility instead of removing them to the laboratory. But this gives rise to a number of other variables that tend to bias the experimental result, as the following notes (Magalhaes, 1974, p. 104):

> . . . the distress vocalizations, struggling and release of alarm odors during restraint (while taking blood samples, for example) may affect other animals that are to be sampled later, and from such animals 'later down the line' the samples might be qualitatively very different.

Experimental effects are also influenced by the manner in which the   62 experimental treatment is administered. For example, different results are likely to be obtained if a substance is forced-fed to an animal by a stomach tube as opposed to having it be eaten naturally. As we have already noted, the response may arise not from the substance administered, but from the large quantity the animal is forced to consume. As the toxicologist Dr. Leo Friedman points out: "We know that administration of *enough* of any substance in high enough dosage will produce some adverse effect" (Friedman, 1970). For example, massive amounts of common table salt cause birth defects in pregnant rats. However, there is no evidence that low doses of salt cause birth defects in humans.

There are a number of less obvious background variables that can arise   63 to confuse the effect of the experimental treatment, and hence lead to invalid inferences. Such variables include the time of day, the temperature of the room, and even the color of the clothing worn by the experimenter. Drug toxicity, for example, has been found to vary with the time of day at which animals are given the drug. Other time-dependent reactions are susceptibility to seizures and irradiation. Animals apparently have certain 24-hour rhythms, including periods of maximum activity and periods of minimum activity (Ader, 1974). Animals react differently to test treatments according to whether they occur during their period of maximum or minimum activity.

For example, it is known that restraining rats causes them to suffer   64
gastric lesions. However, when restraint occurs during the rats' periods of maximum activity, the rats are significantly more susceptible to the development of gastric lesions than those restrained during periods of minimum activity (Ader, 1974, p. 111). Presumably, being restrained during a period of maximum activity is perceived by the rat as being more stressful than being restrained during a period of minimum activity. It would seem likely, then, that rats restrained (as they are) for the introduction of some experimental treatment may show disturbances that are largely the result not of the treatment, but of the time of day. The influence of time also serves to explain some of the variation found between labs. After observing the significant effects of time, one researcher (Ader, 1974, p. 120, emphasis added) was led to conclude:

> . . . it does not seem facetious to ask how many discrepancies in the literature are attributable not to who is right and who is wrong, but to *when* the behavior was sampled.

Conclusion

The considerations I have discussed provide a strong argument against a sci-   65
entific justification of a great deal of animal experimentation; for they have identified numerous sources that often prevent such experiments from being scientifically relevant or valid. Often, an animal experiment is rendered irrelevant because the question it seeks to answer is trivial or obvious, or has already been answered countless times. Invalid experiments frequently arise from the disparity between artificially induced conditions in the laboratory and natural ones, from differences within and among species, and from a number of background variables whose effects are confused with experimental variables.

A few of these problems can be avoided to some extent, for example,   66
by being careful to control a large number of background variables. For the most part, however, these problems exist as limitations in principle to the beneficial use of animals in research. For instance, animals will never be able to produce tumors, ulcers, or a number of other pathological conditions in a manner that is similar to humans. The complex psychological problems humans face are not the sort of things that can be induced in laboratory animals.

The differences in drug toxicity in animals cannot be overcome, and accounting for the vast number of background variables is practically impossible.

Admittedly, it is possible to claim that animal experimentation is justifiable despite the fact that it is of no practical value. Ruesch (1978, p. 144) cites one such attempt made by Professor Leon Asher. According to Asher: 67

> . . . one might ask oneself whether it isn't a sacred case of conscience to follow the call toward the solution of the mysteries of life, and whether man shouldn't consider it a *religious duty* to satisfy the desire for exploration that Providence has placed in our hearts, without asking whether our research on life has any value for medical science or any other practical value.

However, not all actions that satisfy a "desire for exploration" may be considered permissible (much less a religious duty). Experimenting on humans may also satisfy such a desire, and one is likely to learn much more from humans than from animals. Surely, pointless inquisitiveness does not justify the infliction of pain and suffering, and both humans and animals have the capacity to suffer.

Increasing emphasis on research has also done harm to patient care. As   68
Ryder notes (1975, p. 75):

> A doctor's merit is no longer rated on how many patients he cures but on how many papers he publishes in learned journals. This has encouraged a great deal of trivial research and often there has been a decline in the standards of clinical care.

The employment of human data (which is available in great abundance) is one way to replace a good deal of medical, psychological, and toxicological research on animals with a more scientifically sound alternative.

Other promising alternatives to animal experiments are the use of tissue   69
cultures and mathematical models. Tissue culture involves cultivating living cells outside the organism, and has the advantage of permitting the growth of human as opposed to animal cells. Mathematical models, derived from theory or from past experiments, may be used to predict responses or effects from a variety of experimental conditions that are formulated mathematically. The strongest argument in favor of developing these alternatives is that much of animal experimentation is scientifically, and hence morally, indefensible.

References

Ader, R. (1974). Environmental variables in animal experimentation: The relevance of 24-hour rhythms in the study of animal behavior. In H. Magalhaes (Ed.), *Environmental variables in animal experimentation*. Lewisburg, Pennsylvania: Bucknell University Press.

Anderson, K. V., Pear, G. S., & Honeycut, C. (1976). Behavioral evidence showing the predominance of diffuse pain stimuli over discrete stimuli in influencing perception. *Journal of Neuroscience Research, 2,* 283–289.

Barrett, J. E., & Witkin, J. M. (1976). Interaction of D-Amphetamine with Pentobarbital and Chlordiazeopoxide: Effects on punished and unpunished behavior of pigeons. *Pharmacology, Biochemistry, and Behavior, 5,* 285–292.

Berkson, G. & Becker, J. D. (1975). Facial expressions and social responsiveness of blind monkeys. *Journal of Abnormal Psychology, 84,* 519–523.

Bradley, E. W., Zook, B. C., Casarett, G. W., Bondelid, R. O., Maier, J. G., & Rogers, C. C. (1977). Effects of fast neutrons on rabbits. *International Journal of Radiation, Oncology, Biology and Physics, 2,* 1133–1139.

Committee on Safety of Medicines. (1972). *Carcinogenicity tests of oral contraceptives.* London: H.M.S.O.

Diner, J. (1979). *Physical and mental suffering of experimental animals: A review of scientific literature 1975–1978.* Washington: Animal Welfare Institute.

Fox, M. W. (1974). Space and social distance in the ecology of laboratory animals. In H. Magalhaes (Ed.), *Environmental variables in animal experimentation* (pp. 96–105). Lewisburg, Pennsylvania: Bucknell University Press.

Friedman, L. (1970). Symposium on the evaluation of the safety of food additives and chemical residues: II the role of the laboratory animal study of intermediate duration for evaluation of safety. *Toxicology and Applied Pharmacology, 16,* 498–506.

Hillman, H. (1970). *Scientific undesirability of painful experiments.* Zurich: WFPA.

Krieg, M. B. (1964). *Green medicine.* Chicago: Rand McNally.

Lane-Petter, E. (1963). Humane vivisection. *Laboratory Animal Care, 13,* 469–473.

Loosli, R. (1967). Duplicate testing and reproducibility. In R. H. Regamey et al. (Eds.), *International symposium on laboratory animals* (pp. 117–123). Basel: Karger.

Lowrance, M. (1976). *Of acceptable risk.* Los Altos, California: Kaufmann.

Magalhaes, H. (Ed.), (1974). *Environmental variables in animal experimentation.* Lewisburg, Pennsylvania: Bucknell University Press.

Markowitz, J., Archibald, J., & Downie, H. G. (1959). *Experimental surgery* (4th ed.). Baltimore: Williams & Wilkins.

Mayo, D. (1981). Testing statistical testing. In J. C. Pitt (Ed.), *Philosophy in economics* (pp. 175–203). Dordrecht: Reidel.

Mufson, E. J., Balagura, S., & Riss, W. (1976). Tail pinch-induced arousal and stimulus-bound behavior in rats with lateral hypothalamic lesions. *Brain, Behavior and Evolution, 13,* 154–164.

Ogilvie, W. H. (1935, February 23). [Letter to the Editor]. *Lancet,* p. 419.

Pratt, D. (1976). *Painful experiments on animals.* New York: Argus.

Ragemey, R. H., Hennessen, W., Ikic, D., & Ungar, J. (Eds.). (1967). *International symposium on laboratory animals.* Basal: Karger.

Ruesch, H. (1978). *Slaughter of the innocent.* New York: Bantam.

Ryder, R. (1975). *Victims of science.* London: Davis-Poynter.

Sbordone, R. J., & Garcia, J. (1977). Untreated rats develop 'pathological' aggression when paired with a mescaline-treated rat in shock-elicited aggression situation. *Behavioral Biology, 21,* 451–461.

Selye, H. (1956). *The stress of life.* New York: McGraw.

Stiller, H., & Stiller, M. (1976). *Tierversuch und Tierexperimentator.* Munich: Hirthammer.

Stoner, H. B. (1961). Critical analysis of traumatic shock models. *Federation Procedings, 20,* Supplement 9, pp. 38–48.

Swenson, R. M., & Randall, W. (1977). Grooming behavior in cats with pontile lesions and cats with tectal lesions. *Journal of Comparative and Physiological Psychology, 91,* 313–326.

Ulrich, R. E. (1978, March). [Letter to the Editor]. *American Psychological Association Monitor*, p. 16.

Wallach, M. B., Dawber, M., McMahon, M., & Rogers, C. (1977). A new anorexigen assay: Stress-induced hyperphagia in rats. *Pharmacology, Biochemistry and Behavior*, *6*, 529–531.

Weil, M., & Scala, R. (1971). Study of intra-and inter-laboratory variability in the results of rabbit eye and skin irritations tests. *Toxicology and Applied Pharmacology*, *19*, 276–360.

QUESTIONS FOR MEANING

1. Is Deborah Mayo entirely opposed to animal experimentation? Would she ban all tests on animals?
2. What is Mayo's principal objection to the peritonitis experiment described in paragraph 23?
3. What's wrong with the eye tests described in paragraph 38?
4. Explain what LD_{50} means.
5. Does Mayo offer any explanation why scientists may be tempted to do trivial and even useless research?
6. Why is it important to know the background of any animal being experimented upon? What's wrong with using animals that have been specially bred for use in laboratories? What other variables can affect the results of an experiment?
7. What alternatives are there to animal experimentation? Does Mayo offer any specific evidence to suggest that such alternatives are feasible?
8. Vocabulary: purported (2), disparity (17), confounding (17), ascertaining (18), pathological (18), extrapolating (19), precipitate (20), kinetics (20), induce (22), toxicological (32), innocuous (34), linear (35), insidious (42), teratogenic (43), carcinogenesis (49), indigenous (49).

QUESTIONS ABOUT STRATEGY

1. Mayo argues that animal experimentation is bad science. Does she convince you that this is so? How "scientific" is her own argument? Does she sound as if she knows what she's talking about?
2. Does this essay ever seem emotional? In presenting detailed descriptions of experiments in which the suffering of animals is vividly portrayed, does Mayo ever advance her argument by playing upon the feelings of her audience?
3. Does Mayo ever repeat herself? If so, where? Is repetition justifiable in an essay of this length?
4. Why does Mayo break her essay into individually titled subsections?
5. Where in her essay does Mayo recognize the premise that supports arguments on behalf of animal experimentation? Are there any other points in the essay where Mayo represents her opponents' point of view?

EDWARD C. MELBY, JR.

A Statement from the Association for Biomedical Research

Edward C. Melby, Jr., is a veterinarian who received his D.V.M. from Cornell University in 1954. He was in private practice for several years before devoting himself to teaching and research. He taught laboratory animal medicine at the Johns Hopkins School of Medicine from 1962 to 1974, when he returned to Cornell as Professor of Medicine and Dean of the College of Veterinary Medicine. He is the author of the Handbook of Laboratory Animal Science, *Volumes 1–3 (1974–1976). As President of the Association for Biomedical Research, he offered the following testimony before a congressional committee in* **1981,** *when several laws that would restrict animal-based research were under serious consideration. Melby is currently vice president for science and technology assessment at SmithKline Beecham Corporation. He is also a consultant for the National Research Council and the National Institutes of Health.*

Mr. Chairman, Members of the Subcommittee, I am Edward C. Melby, Jr.,   1
President of the Association for Biomedical Research. I am also Dean of the Faculty and Professor of Medicine of the College of Veterinary Medicine at Cornell University. Prior to accepting that appointment in 1974, I served 12 years as a Professor and Director of the Division of Comparative Medicine of the Johns Hopkins University School of Medicine.

The Association for Biomedical Research (ABR), established in 1979,   2
represents nearly 200 universities, hospitals, medical schools, veterinary schools, research institutes, animal producers and suppliers, pharmaceutical, chemical, petroleum and contract testing companies. ABR's primary objective is to help assure the continuation of responsible biomedical research.

It is our understanding that we are here today to discuss the use of live   3
animals in medical research and laboratory testing. Perhaps one of the most significant steps taken in the past few years was the passage of the Laboratory Animal Welfare Act, Public Law 89-544, in 1966, for it marked a new era in research regulation. Amendments in 1970 as well as subsequently have broadened the Act to its present form known as the "Animal Welfare Act" and it now protects show horses, zoo and aquarium species, and other categories of animals as well as those used in laboratories. Ironically, the two largest categories of animals in the United States—largest by far—are not covered by the present Act; pet dogs and cats, and farm animals. It is important to understand this dichotomy perhaps best expressed through citing the numbers of animals involved. In FY 1980, 188,700 dogs were studied in research in the United States according to official U.S. Department of Agriculture figures. This can be compared to the over three billion—that is three billion—chickens raised for food each year in the United States or the

thirteen million—that is thirteen million—dogs killed each year by public pounds, municipal animal shelters, and "humane" societies, according to reliable estimates. There are believed to be about 35 million pet dogs in the United States at any moment, yet the Animal Welfare Act does not cover them. We will return to this point in a moment. But think about those numbers because it is important to put these data into proper perspective; 188,700 dogs studied in medicine and science compared to over thirteen million killed as unclaimed, unwanted dogs each year by towns and cities across America.

ABR was established precisely because no private, non-profit, non-governmental organization seemed to exist which would interact in *a positive way* with scientists, animal welfare organizations, science-based industries in medicine and health, universities and research institutions, and government regulators. ABR has, therefore, in its mere two years of existence, established lines of communication among these varied organizations and, in a more formal way, met with USDA officials to hold serious discussions on improving the Animal Welfare Act. These efforts are ongoing and have been very useful, we believe.   4

ABR here wishes to emphasize that it welcomes proposals, questions, and discussions with representatives of any interest in the field of animal use in biomedical research. Surprisingly, no animal welfare organization or "humane" society has presented any written proposal to us, nor has any legislator sought the views of the constituency ABR represents through contacting ABR. We hope such representations will be made in the future and assure the Subcommittee that ABR will respond thoughtfully and reliably to any consultation requested. We offer our services as a sounding board to all concerned with biomedical research.   5

The Subcommittee has expressed an interest in whether laboratory animals are studied unnecessarily or inappropriately. ABR has no reason to believe that in science as in politics or law, there is perfection. The difficulty with words like "unnecessary" or "inappropriate" is that what seems unnecessary to one person from one vantage point, may seem absolutely necessary to another from a different vantage point. Had a Pasteur or a Madam Curie in France, or a Fleming or a Lister in England, or a Salk or a DeBakey in the United States been prevented from following their studies on vaccines, X-rays, penicillin, antiseptics, polio or heart surgery because they were judged "unnecessary," these advances and concepts so taken for granted would not have been developed as they were. Verification of their results by a certain amount of replication was and is an essential part of the scientific process.   6

Having said that, it is clear to us that endless repetition and duplication without purpose is to be avoided. It is our opinion that the peer review system of the major granting agencies, such as the National Institutes of Health, the editorial review process for originality of thought by scientific journals, and the cost effectiveness of private industry, prevent most so-called "unnecessary" animal experiments. Those persons and organizations opposed to *all* studies of animals will, of course, consider all such studies as "unnecessary"—a view far from that of mainstream America, we believe.   7

Nevertheless, any improvements which would prevent unnecessary experiments without preventing those which turn out, sometimes unexpectedly, to have been very necessary, would be welcome. The Association for Biomedical Research believes that none of the legislative proposals now in the Congress succeed in making the distinction, but ABR is anxious to work toward this goal.

The use of techniques labelled by some as "alternatives" to animals is   8 as old as chemistry, physics, astronomy and modern science itself. Recent NIH studies have shown that roughly one third of its current budget is spent on research using mammals and about one fourth on research using humans themselves, the remainder being in research which studies neither people nor mammals directly. In other words, NIH's average yearly support over the last three fiscal years for projects which do not involve laboratory mammals constitutes 55% of total research dollars expended. Further in FY 1980, approximately 28% of NIH funds were committed to projects using neither humans or mammals. In dollars this translates into $704.8 million. This, combined with the finding that animal use declined by 40% in the decade 1968 through 1978 in the United States by a National Research Council-Institute of Laboratory Animal Resources survey published in 1980, must be taken by any reasonable person as strong evidence of science incorporating non-animal techniques as soon as they become scientifically reliable. So-called "alternatives" are consistently incorporated into research, education and testing requirements as the particular medical or scientific field warrants. In addition, the significant pressures of inflation on scientific endeavors have made acquisition and use of animals increasingly expensive. As a result, universities and private industry have experienced considerable motivation to replace animals with less expensive, non-animal techniques wherever possible. A significant percentage of industry's research and development budget is dedicated to the search for in vitro techniques as standard procedures. It must be emphasized, however, that the criterion of scientific excellence must remain the principal determinant of any research method. Where appropriate, alternatives to the use of living animals have and will continue to be developed; the benefits obtained through their precision and reproducibility certainly make alternatives a most attractive choice. Several of the present legislative proposals before the Congress in respect to these so-called "alternatives" are therefore redundant and, in our view, dangerous to the conduct of science by the time-tested, scientific peer review process in this country. The Soviet Union, it should be recalled, has still not recovered in medicine and biology from the period of "Lysenkoism" when the government dictated false biological information as a mandated approach to science.

The appropriate care, acquisition and maintenance of laboratory ani-   9 mals is of continuing interest and concern to all responsible scientists. ABR therefore supports efforts to amend those components of the Animal Welfare Act in need of improvement, to which I referred earlier. Indeed, ABR would recommend expansion of the present Act's coverage to pet dogs and cats, and those in municipal pounds or animal shelters, whose municipalities or owning organizations receive federal funds. ABR would be pleased to interact with Congressional sponsors of bills related to animal welfare to insure participation of the larger biomedical community, including the major research and teaching organizations and research-based industries of America.

We would be pleased to respond to any questions or comments you   10
may have, and hope that members of the Congress or their staff will contact our office at any time information from the biomedical perspective is required.

As part of these hearings, we wish to offer specific comment on four   11
bills (HR 556, HR 4406, HR 930 and HR 220) now under consideration by the Subcommittee on Science, Research and Technology. For purposes of clarity I list these according to the specific points identified by the Committee for review:

1. *Excessive, unnecessary, uneconomic or inappropriate use of animals in cur-*   12
   rent practice:

   Biomedical research institutions in this country operate under a   13
   peer review system comprised of before-the-fact reviews of applications and subsequent reviews of data and results in scientific meetings as well as by reviewers and editors of scientific journals. In 1966 the Animal Welfare Act (Public Law 89-547) was enacted. At about the same time, the scientific community sponsored an independent, peer review accreditation program under the auspices of the American Association for Accreditation of Laboratory Animal Care which now accredits some 440 institutions. Institutions now follow guidelines prescribed by the NIH Office of Protection of Research Risks, and a signed statement by each investigator is prepared in making application for research funds that principles for the proper use of animals are being followed.

   According to studies carried out under the auspices of the Na-   14
   tional Academy of Sciences–National Research Council, reported in 1980, there was a 40% decrease in total animal use in the decade 1968 through 1978. Although the reasons are varied, there is good evidence to indicate that the supply and use of healthier animals has reduced loss as well as variation in results and hence, reduced the need for confirmation through repetitive studies. Additionally, there has been the ongoing process of incorporating "new technologies" including tissue culture, computer modeling, in vitro diagnostic and assay instrumentation and, most recently, the advent of recombinant DNA techniques. This has been an ongoing process. For example, records of the College I head indicate that tissue culture techniques were introduced on this campus in the mid-1940's. The very nature of science requires that such new technologies be implemented as soon as they are demonstrated to be the equal or superior to existing techniques. Furthermore, economic pressures require that more effective substitutions be introduced wherever possible.

2. *Ways to promote more humane and appropriate use of animals, including*   15
   alternatives to animal use:

Concurrent with the enormous expansion of biomedical research   16
following World War II, the scientific community has made a major
commitment to the improvement of laboratory animal science. Indeed, an entirely new area of scientific specialization and the infrastructure to support it, has evolved to meet that need. Training
programs have evolved in both the two and four year colleges to
train animal technicians and technologists; a new specialty board recognized by the American Veterinary Medical Association, the
American College of Laboratory Animal Medicine, certifies veteri-
narians with advanced training and experience in that specialty; and
most institutions provide in-house training programs for animal
technicians and graduate students, many following the programs
fostered by the American Association for Laboratory Animal Science. Through these and related efforts the personnel directly involved in the care and use of laboratory animals have gained significant
understanding of the humane care and specialized requirements of
the various animal species used.

I believe it is important to repeat observations made earlier in this   17
testimony. So-called "alternatives" are consistently incorporated into
research, education and testing requirements as the particular medical or scientific field warrants. In recent years, the significant pressures of inflation on scientific endeavors have made acquisition and
use of animals increasingly expensive. As a result, universities and
private industry have experienced considerable motivation to replace
animals with less expensive, non-animal techniques wherever possible. It must be emphasized, however, that the criterion of scientific
excellence must remain the principle determinant of any research
method. Where appropriate, alternatives to the use of living animals
have been developed; the benefits obtained through their precision
and reproducibility certainly make alternatives a most attractive choice.
Both HR 930 and HR 220 have been written in such a manner as to
be a constructive force and we generally support that approach.

3. *Incentives for development of more and improved alternatives to animal use:*   18
The object of all research must be that of uncovering facts and   19
truths, regardless of the approach. In science there are enumerable
"incentives for excellence and accuracy," including various awards,
recognition by learned societies, research grant support, authorship
of books and scientific papers and perhaps most importantly, the
acceptance and recognition of one's peers. As mentioned previously,
alternatives to animal use have continually been developed, accepted
and implemented based upon scientific validity, improvement of effectiveness, cost reduction and efficiency. It is questionable whether
or not additional "incentives" can really be granted to stimulate
the development of meaningful alternatives to animal use, especially if this is carried out without reference to whether or not such
methods are scientifically useful in the understanding of human or

animal disease or for predicting safety of drugs. If the approach necess-
itates the use of animals, the scientist must be sensitive to the animal's requirements. It is our belief that the continuing progress
of scientific knowledge will continue, as it has in the past, to recognize, develop and implement such alternatives without artificial stim-
ulants.

4. *Responses from academic, private and public research institutions to prob-*   20
   lems raised by pending legislative proposals:

   In reviewing the several bills now before the Congress, two are   21
   particularly worthy of comment. HR 556 is, in our opinion, an intrusion into the scientist's ability to use a wide variety of approaches
   based upon experience, experimental design and intended objectives.
   To artificially require deviation from accepted scientific principles
   would create a situation not unlike the Lysenko era in the Soviet
   Union. As presented, the bill would mandate a wholesale diversion
   of 30% to 50% of *all* federal research funds from existing, peer reviewed projects, thus jeopardizing the entire scientific research program of the nation. As objectionable as that mandate might be, the
   fundamental issue with the approach taken by the bill is that it fails
   to recognize innovative and creative scientific inquiry, mandating restrictions on what have proven to be the most fruitful approaches to
   biological and medical research since the advancement of the germ
   theory of disease.

   HR 4406 proposes to amend the existing animal welfare act in a   22
   number of ways. Perhaps of greatest concern is the attempt to modify section 3(a) which would attempt to define "pain" in animals. It
   has been clearly demonstrated that the concept and interpretation of
   pain is exceptionally complex and clarification is not amenable by
   the sort of definition proposed. In section 10, we object strongly
   to the recommendation that inspectors be given authority to "con-
   fiscate or destroy" animals which, in the sole judgment of the in-
   spector, are "suffering as a result of failure to comply with any
   provision"—unless the institution's animal care committee is convened. In the day to day working situation of a complex institution
   such as the University I serve, such a provision for the convening of
   a committee for immediate action is clearly fraught with impossible
   problems. Furthermore, the scientific qualifications of individual
   "inspectors" is and will probably always remain a questionable
   aspect.

5. *Areas in which animal-based research or testing remains crucial to protection*   23
   or enhancement of human health:

   This topic must be addressed in a variety of ways and to ade-   24
   quately respond to the question would require a voluminous amount
   of data. I will, therefore, limit my observations but would be pleased
   to provide members of the Committee with additional information
   should that be helpful.

In the area of infectious disease, prior to advances in chemother-   2
apy and vaccines, such diseases were the cause of most deaths in the
industrialized world. Today, many have been reduced to the point
where infectious disease ranks among the lowest causes of death.
Biologic production and testing has always been dependent on animal use since only the complex, biologically interrelated systems of
the whole animal can respond in a fashion indicative to that of man.
Certain aspects of testing have been delegated to "alternatives" and
where proven efficacious, these practices will continue and expand.
Similarly, the toxic effects of many antibiotics and other chemotherapeutic agents have first been recognized through their application
in animals. This method of testing is the only one endorsed by the
FDA for human use and the USDA for animal use, for no acceptable
alternatives currently exist which embody the total host response
provided by animals. Relatively recent examples of the importance
of such testings and the use of a variety of systems are found in the
development of polio vaccine and the identification of thalidomide
as a teratogen.

In the underdeveloped countries, many infectious diseases still ac-   2
count for tremendous morbidity and mortality. According to the
1980 World Health Organization Summary Reports, 200,000,000
people are affected by schistosomiasis; 100,000,000 by leishumaniasis
with 400,000 new cases developing annually; 300–400,000,000 cases
of malaria which kills in excess of 1,000,000 children each year, and,
100,000,000 humans are affected by trypanosomiasis. It is estimated
that the morbidity from these four diseases alone is four times the
entire population of the United States. At the present time, there are
no alternatives to the use of animals in demonstrating the host response to these infectious agents. Any severe reduction in the use of
animals to continue important studies on these diseases, aimed at
treatment and prevention, would severely impede the progress being
made by many U.S. research institutions, including Cornell, thus
prolonging the suffering and death of millions of humans throughout the world.

In the United States, hepatitis B infection remains an important   2
cause of death and illness. Recent evidence indicates that infected
individuals demonstrate a very high rate of developing cancer of the
liver in later life. Outside of the United States, hepatitis is a major
contributor to human suffering. At the present time, Cornell University, under contract from NIH, is developing an important animal model for hepatitis B virus research and vaccine testing using
the feral woodchuck, *Marmota monax*. Should attempts be made to
eliminate the use of this or other valuable animal models for hepatitis
B research, it will severely impact the ability to develop a protective
vaccine for man.

In spite of significant progress in treatment and control, leprosy   28
remains a major world-wide disease with many cases occurring here
in the United States. To date, the only method for studying the
growth and establishment of infection of the causative agent is through
the use of the armadillo. Continued research in this disease will be
dependent on the use of this animal model.

The above examples are directed to human disease, yet it is important   29
to recognize that millions of domestic animals are saved in the United States
each year through the use of prophylactic vaccination. Recent United States
Department of Agriculture figures show that in 1970, for every 10,000 poultry sent to slaughter, 158 poultry had Marek's Disease. In 1979, as the result
of the development of a new vaccine, the incidence of Marek's Disease was
reduced to 11 per 10,000 poultry. As an example of other control measures,
in 1950, there were 1.4 cases of hog cholera per 10,000 animals. In 1979, this
figure was reduced to zero. Hog cholera has been virtually eliminated. In
1950, there were .86 cases of cattle tuberculosis per 10,000 animals slaughtered. This disease is transmissible to man. In 1979, cattle tuberculosis was
reduced to .008 cases per 10,000 thus decreasing the prevalence of this disease
by 1000-fold. A significant number of vaccines used in control of diseases of
animals were developed and tested at Cornell University, the most recent
being the canine parvovirus vaccine to protect against a new disease which
simultaneously occurred in several parts of the world in 1978. Recognizing
the tremendous number of dogs lost to this disease since 1978, and the significant distress this brought to animal owners, we question the wisdom of
mandating discontinuing the use of living animals in such research.

In the area of non-infectious disease, the major cause of mortality in the   30
United States is that of diseases associated with the cardiovascular system.
During the past three decades, animals have played an instrumental role in
the development of new surgical, therapeutic and electronic devices which
have played an enormous role in decreasing both mortality and morbidity.
As an example, it is estimated that 50,000 coronary bypass operations take
place annually in this country, thus relieving thousands suffering from pain
and for many, prolonging their lives.

Cancer ranks second, after cardiovascular disease, as a cause of death in   31
America. Tremendous advances have been made in cancer chemotherapy and
the public is just recognizing that permanent cures are now possible for many
forms of cancer. Granted, much remains to be done in solving the ravages
of this disease, but I must point out that all chemotherapeutic agents have
first been tested in animals for signs of toxicity. Indeed, animals remain the
key for further progress in our conquest of cancer.

Other diseases of significance in the United States have likewise bene-   32
fited from animal experimentation. Animal "models," or those animals in
which similar if not identical disease syndromes exist, obviously represent a
fertile source of investigation. In many instances, the information gained can

be of direct benefit to the animal populations involved, thus preventing death or improving the quality of their lives. As examples, one can cite spontaneous systemic lupus erythematosus, rheumatoid arthritis, and hemolytic anemia. In the field of endocrinology we have benefited immensely from the use of animals to delineate the growth changes and bodily responses altered through disorders of the endocrine system. Such studies have shed new light on diseases such as thyroiditis, pituitary giantism, Cushing's syndrome, Addison's disease, and many others. The isolation, purification, testing and synthesis of a number of hormones have significantly influenced the lives of millions. Again, because of the complexities of the systems involved, only living animals manifest the full range of physiologic changes needed to develop, test and produce such compounds.

In diseases of the central nervous system, significant advances have been   33
made in products such as lithium for patients with manic depression. At the present time, investigators at Cornell are testing several new synthetic lithium compounds in animals which promise to bring beneficial therapeutic effects without the severe toxicity currently encountered with the parent compound.

Chronic debilitating diseases, such as rheumatoid and osteoarthritis, have   34
benefited greatly from animal research. During the past two decades, surgical procedures developed in animals have led to the production and implantation of total hip joint prosthetic devices, knees, and other bone replacements in man. Such devices have provided pain-free locomotion in thousands of Americans who were previously immobile.

The examples cited above are chosen merely to illustrate the importance   35
of animal experimentation to relieve pain, suffering and death in both man and animals. The listing is representative of only a small portion of those diseases and disorders in which animals have made useful contributions to human medicine; most were selected because they are currently used or are under study at Cornell University; thus, I have personal knowledge concerning this work.

The Subcommittee should also be aware of the fact that, since World   36
War II, there have been 52 Nobel Prize winners in medicine and physiology. Thirty-seven of these awards were achieved with NIH grant awards. We have had 21 Nobel Prize winners in chemistry; twelve of these received NIH support. Within the past few days, this year's Nobel Prize recipients were announced. Their scientific observations and discoveries were made by utilizing animal models—non-human primates. The science being conducted in this country is perhaps the finest in the world. Congress must strive to preserve the right of scientific freedom to insure continued creativity and excellence.

In this correspondence I have intended to be informative, yet to con-   37
structively criticize the various bills currently before the Subcommittee on Science, Research and Technology. We are aware that under certain conditions our research animals are subject to painful procedures, yet we do every-

thing possible to minimize the number of such procedures and to use drugs to abrogate pain. Rest assured that we agree that alternatives to living animals should be employed whenever appropriate and that science will continue, as it has in the past, the development of new alternative methods. It is our opinion that enactment of HR 930 or HR 220 would promote such alternatives without disrupting biomedical research. We wish to emphasize to the Committee the significant past achievements in biomedical science, many of which have been accomplished through the use of living animals, and stress the importance of their use in ongoing and future studies. Attempts to reduce the use of animals through restrictive legislation or through the imposition of unnecessary bureaucratic authority which extends beyond the time-tested, peer review system, would seriously impede efforts to improve the lives of both man and animals.

On behalf of the Association for Biomedical Research, thank you for   38
permitting me to comment on these issues.

QUESTIONS FOR MEANING

1. Why does Melby believe that animal experimentation is already subject to sufficient control? Explain what he means by "peer review."
2. What pressures outside the research community affect the number of animals used in testing? How, in particular, does the economy affect animal experimentation?
3. What is the Association for Biomedical Research? What is its purpose and what exactly does it do? Does it seem like a reputable organization?
4. What specific accomplishments is Melby able to cite in support of animal experiments? How seriously do you take these achievements? Does Melby persuade you that American science is worthy of respect?
5. Vocabulary: dichotomy (3), verification (6), redundant (8), auspices (13), implemented (14), infrastructure (16), innovative (21), amenable (22), and delineate (32).

QUESTIONS ABOUT STRATEGY

1. Why does Melby begin by explaining who he is? Was this an appropriate way to begin? Under what circumstances might you begin an essay this way?
2. How does Melby present himself to the Committee? At what points in his testimony does he try to emphasize that he is a reasonable man?
3. How does Melby go about appealing to the animal lovers in his audience? Does he make any argument that would appeal to people who have pets? Why does he do this?
4. Does Melby present any information that caused you to reconsider your own position on this subject? If so, what was it? Try to explain why you found this point or points effective.

ALAN M. GOLDBERG AND JOHN M. FRAZIER
Alternatives to Animals in Toxicity Testing

Director of the Center for Alternatives to Animal Testing at Johns Hopkins University, Alan M. Goldberg is a council member of the National Academy of Sciences' Institute for Laboratory Animal Resources. At Johns Hopkins, he works with John M. Frazier who directs the center's In Vitro Toxicology Laboratory. Frazier's research is currently focused on working to decrease the number of animals used for chemical testing by developing measures of cell death in cultures. The following article, which reflects the nature of their research, was first published by Scientific American *in 1989.*

Each year thousands of chemicals undergo rigorous testing designed to evaluate their potential toxicity. Almost all of the tests take place in animals: the reactions of rats, rabbits and mice to chemicals are currently the best available predictors of the effects the substances will have on the human organism. The introduction of animal testing in the U.S. in the 1920's was a major advance in toxicity testing, and subsequent debates about the place of animals in testing were qualified by the absence of better alternatives.   1

In the past decade the issue of whole-animal toxicity testing has become more urgent and contentious. Animal-welfare advocates have decried the suffering of millions of animals, and industries bringing chemicals to the marketplace have begun to chafe at the costs and delays imposed by animal testing. Meanwhile, case histories such as that of thalidomide serve to remind the public and testing establishments alike of the perils of letting unsafe chemicals reach the marketplace. In answer to these concerns, toxicologists began exploring possible alternatives.   2

Their exploration has yielded a new methodology known as *in vitro* toxicity testing. Literally, *in vitro* means "in glass," but biologists interpret the term more broadly to mean research that does not involve intact higher animals. In vitro testing includes a battery of living systems—bacteria, cultured animal cells, fertilized chicken eggs, frog embryos—that can be employed to evaluate the toxicity of chemicals in human beings. Ultimately workers hope to be able to test chemicals in cultures of human cells from various organs and tissues so that the question of human toxicity can be answered more directly.   3

Several factors have paved the way for the introduction of in vitro testing. One is the growth of the science of toxicology itself. Today investigators understand much better how toxicological processes are begun and how toxic effects are expressed; they need not use the death or illness of an animal as an end point in their studies. Another factor has to do with technological   4 developments of the past few years. New options in culture techniques and bioanalytical tools allow workers to monitor toxicity with unprecedented thoroughness and precision at the cellular level rather than at the organismal level.

Yet the obstacles such efforts face are tremendous. Some are technical: singly or in combination, in vitro tests as yet cannot approximate the complexity of interactions that take place in a living animal. Some of the obstacles are bureaucratic: no framework has been established for approving in vitro test procedures or for incorporating the results of such tests into the evaluation of results from whole-animal, or in vivo, methods.   5

We believe in vitro tests will eventually be able to meet these challenges. Protocols for in vitro tests already exist that can complement the current panoply of whole-animal procedures and reduce the number of animals that are subjected to testing. It is not too soon to begin planning ways to integrate in vitro testing into toxicity testing as a whole.   6

Toxicity testing is one of the two major components of risk assessment, the process by which new substances are evaluated for their potential impact on human health and welfare. The other component is assessment of exposure. The exposure estimate indicates how many people will be exposed to a chemical in what concentrations, for how long and under what conditions. For a chemical to pose a risk of notable proportion, there must exist the likelihood of human exposure to the agent in quantities sufficient to produce adverse biological effects.   7

Toxicity testing is required for new chemicals introduced into the marketplace, old chemicals that are proposed for new uses and new mixtures of old or new chemicals. The main objectives of such testing are twofold. The first objective, known as hazard identification, involves determining which potential adverse effects—cancer, kidney damage, reproductive injury and so on—can ensue from exposure to a given chemical. The second objective is to provide data estimating the quantitative exposure-response relationship for the chemicals in human beings and other organisms.   8

The exposure-response relationship describes the likelihood of an organism's developing a particular adverse biological response as a function of its exposure to the chemicals. Such a relationship presumably exists for each of the hazards identified for a given chemical. It may vary, however, depending on how a person is exposed to the chemical—whether through ingestion, inhalation or contact with the skin. The age, genetic makeup and nutritional status of the person may play a role as well.   9

The LD50 test ("LD" stands for "lethal dose") is a classic example of an exposure-response test. A measure of acute lethality, the test was developed in the 1920's to determine the potency of digitalis and other medicinal preparations derived from biological materials. It provides a statistically accurate measure of the amount of a chemical that will produce 50 percent mortality in a population of animals, that is, the amount of the chemical that will kill half of them. Comparison of LD50 values for different agents gives   10 a measure of relative toxicity. A variation on the LD50 test is the ED50 (for "effective dose"), which measures the amount of a chemical that will produce a deleterious effect other than death in 50 percent of the population.

The Draize ocular- and skin-irritation tests are other classic indexes that   11
are widely used today. John H. Draize of the Food and Drug Administration standardized the protocol for the ocular-irritation test in the 1940's; it dictates specific procedures for measuring eye irritation in rabbits. A fixed dose of a chemical (.1 milliliter of a liquid or .1 gram of a solid) is placed in one of a rabbit's eyes; the other eye serves as a control. For the skin test, an area of the rabbit's hide is shaved and covered with the chemical being tested. In both tests there is a specific set of criteria for scoring irritation and inflammation.

The LD50 test and the Draize tests are probably the toxicity tests most   12
familiar to the public; they are also the ones singled out most frequently by animal-welfare activists. But chemicals are usually screened through many additional in vivo tests. These include acute toxicity tests other than the LD50 and subchronic and chronic toxicity tests that last anywhere from two weeks to two years. Such tests provide information on mechanisms of action, target organs, symptomatology and carcinogenicity (the ability to cause cancer) as well as lethality.

Other tests help to fill out the toxic profile of a chemical. Reproductive   13
and developmental toxicity tests evaluate chemicals' effects on reproductive success and their ability to cause developmental malformations, a property known as teratogenicity. Hypersensitivity procedures test for chemicals that may not directly damage the skin but may elicit instead an immunological response similar to the one produced by poison ivy. Phototoxicity testing determines whether sunlight will activate a test chemical and thus enhance skin irritation.

Studies of toxicokinetics are sometimes carried out to trace the absorp-   14
tion, distribution, metabolism, storage and excretion of a chemical. Such studies are quite useful when the same chemical exhibits differences in toxicokinetics in two animal species. Finally, neurological and behavioral tests monitor the effects of chemicals on cognitive functions in adult animals as well as in developing fetuses.

It is probably clear from this recitation of procedures that complete   15
toxicological evaluation of even one chemical is complicated, time-consuming and expensive. Testing a typical new chemical costs between $500,000 and $1.5 million, takes up to two or three years and may entail the sacrifice of thousands of animals. Furthermore, tens of thousands of products already on the market have never been tested thoroughly. The National Academy of Sciences observed recently that many of those substances might not have been evaluated at all.

Obviously, enormous benefits would accrue from toxicity tests that are   16
cheaper and faster than in vivo testing. Just as obviously, researchers will be hard-pressed to come up with a battery of in vitro tests that can match the

exhaustive screening possible with whole-animal procedures. Workers are making progress on roughly half a dozen categories of techniques.

The area of in vitro testing that has been pursued the longest and has been the best funded is that of genotoxicity: the ability of a chemical to damage genetic material. Genotoxicity encompasses substances that cause cancer, gene mutation and chromosomal abnormalities. Whole-animal tests for carcinogenicity are among the most expensive and time-consuming toxicity tests, which is probably why more than $70 million has been spent in the U.S. over the past decade to find in vitro alternatives. The in vitro tests currently available, such as the standard Ames bacterial assay, are widely used to screen for potential genotoxicity, but they cannot be expected to preempt whole-animal tests of chronic exposure, such as the rodent lifetime bioassay. 17

Another area of in vitro testing that has a relatively long history is cytotoxicity testing. Simply put, cytotoxicity assays evaluate the ability of a substance to kill cells. Some of these assays were developed for special purposes, such as screening drugs for the ability to kill cancer cells; others are meant for more general use. The number of methods available for distinguishing dead cells from live cells has increased rapidly in the past several years. In fact, the limiting factor on cytotoxicity testing is the number of cell types that can be cultured in vitro. 18

Two test systems have received considerable attention in the context of in vitro cytotoxicity testing: the total cellular-protein assay and the neutral-red uptake assay. In both tests cells cultured in plastic petri dishes are treated with various concentrations of a test chemical added to the culture medium. After 24 hours of exposure, the test chemical is washed out of the medium and an analytical reagent is added. In the case of the total cellular-protein test, a reagent called kenacid blue is added to the medium and reacts with proteins in the cells, imparting a blue color whose density can be measured. Healthy, rapidly growing cells contain more protein than dead ones; consequently, control cultures will be dark blue. Dishes in which cells have been killed by the test chemical will be progressively lighter in tone. 19

The concentration of the test chemical that produces 50 percent inhibition of protein content, known as the IC50, can be determined from the colors of the cell cultures and compared with the IC50's of known chemical toxins in order to rank the test chemical's relative toxicity. This assay can be automated to speed testing, and it can be performed in combination with enzymes that metabolize drugs so that the effects of chemical intermediates can be tested as well. 20

The assay measuring neutral-red uptake is not too different. Developed in its present form at Rockefeller University, the test is based on neutral red, a dye that is taken up from the culture medium and stored by living cells but not by dead ones. The amount of dye retained by the cells is an indication of the number of living cells. Again, an IC50 for the test chemical is established by linking cell mortality to the amount of the chemical the cells received. The assay is then quantified by comparing the IC50 with the IC50's of known toxins. 21

Although they may have only limited ability to predict tissue-specific 22
effects or effects resulting from tissue or organ interactions, cytotoxicity tests
do provide essential information on the intrinsic toxicity of pure chemicals,
mixtures and formulations. They can also be fairly good indicators of ocular
irritation, because cell death is a major cause of it. Corneal epithelial cells can
be subjected to cytotoxicity testing for ocular irritation, and in fact, such tests
are already used in product safety evaluation.

The Center for Alternatives to Animal Testing at Johns Hopkins Uni- 23
versity has identified more than 30 other in vitro tests that could be appropriate for testing ocular irritation. Some of these also test for cytotoxicity,
but others have different end points. Ray Tchao of the Philadelphia College
of Pharmacy and Science, for example, has devised a protocol to detect impairment of the so-called tight junctions between cells, junctions that are important in controlling the penetration of substances through the corneal
epithelial cell layer.

The so-called CAM test, pioneered by Joseph Leighton of the Medical 24
College of Pennsylvania and by Niels P. Lupke of the University of Müns-
ter, provides another in vitro measure of inflammation. In the CAM test,
part of the shell of a fertilized chicken egg is carefully removed to reveal the
delicate, veined chorioallantoic membrane (CAM) underneath. A test chemical is applied directly to the membrane; sometimes a Teflon ring is also
placed on the membrane to contain the chemical. Researchers look for inflammation of the membrane five minutes and 24 hours after the chemical
has been applied.

Several laboratories have also been exploring cultures of human epider- 25
mal cells as models of human skin. Some skin-cell culture methods are descended from skin-regeneration techniques developed for burn patients. The
skin-cell cultures can be tested for inflammation much as the membrane in a
CAM test is. Measuring the biological response to chemicals, however, is
easier in skin-cell cultures than it is in CAM tests.

In vitro tests are also being developed to monitor toxicity in particular 26
target organs. The question of target-organ toxicity is answered in vivo by
examining the organs of a treated animal for pathological changes. In vitro,
cells from specific organs must be cultured and tested. Considerable progress
has been made on in vitro screening for liver, blood, heart, kidney, lung and
nervous-system toxicity.

The techniques for culturing hepatocytes (liver cells) are particularly 27
well developed. Methods of in vitro hepatotoxicity testing, derived from experiments in liver research, involve isolated liver cells, liver slices and isolated, perfused whole livers. Human hepatocytes have already been used in
some tests; where the cells of other animals are used instead, in vitro target-
organ data can still reduce substantially the number of animals needed for
conclusive results. Enough tissue can be obtained from two or three animals
to conduct studies that would ordinarily require from 20 to 40 animals.

The purpose of these in vitro systems ranges from identifying chemicals 28
that specifically produce toxicity in the liver to determining the metabolic

kinetics of chemicals and the way in which they are excreted. Test systems based on rat hepatocytes can also evaluate cellular markers for potential toxicity. As more knowledge is obtained about the mechanisms of toxic action of chemicals in organ systems, new in vitro methods can be developed to test for these effects.

Progress has also been made in identifying in vitro systems for evaluating teratogenicity. The key to teratogenicity testing lies in establishing the relation between in vitro indexes of toxicological response and the complex process of differential toxicity in the developing organism, particularly in the human fetus. Although many of the alternative test systems proposed involve whole organisms—from the hydra or fruit fly to frog or rodent embryos—and therefore circumvent the problem of extrapolation between cell cultures and whole animals, the systems still have significant problems in predicting human teratogenicity.   29

In some cases, mathematical and computer models may be able to supplement the information provided by in vitro testing. Mathematical pharmacokinetic models are already helping toxicologists to estimate in vivo toxicokinetics from in vitro data. Computer-based "structure-activity" analyses attempt to correlate general toxicological responses with aspects of the molecular structure of the test chemical. Such methods are currently empirical, but they should improve as specific mechanisms of interaction are related to chemical structure.   30

The complexity of the exposure-response relationship seems, however, to rule out the possibility of making sound predictions from theoretical principles alone. The response of an organism to a given exposure of a chemical results from a diffuse array of interdependent processes at the molecular, cellular and organismal levels. In addition to the absorption, distribution, metabolism, storage and excretion of substances described by toxicokinetics, the outcome of an organism's exposure to a chemical also depends on toxicodynamics.   31

Toxicodynamics has to do with alterations in the biological system that are a consequence of the presence of a chemical in the system. At the molecular level such alterations are biochemical: they can, for example, inhibit an enzyme critical to normal cellular function. At higher levels of organization the alterations are manifested as tissue pathology or as clinical toxicity.   32

If a human being is exposed to a chemical, the toxicokinetic properties of the chemical determine whether the agent or one of its metabolites will ultimately reach a sensitive cellular or molecular target and initiate a biological response. If the reactive form of the chemical does reach the potential target, the toxicodynamics determine to what degree the agent will adversely affect the human being. The ultimate expression of pathology depends on the human organism's ability to repair toxin-induced damage at all levels of biological organization: the molecular and cellular levels as well as the levels of organs and tissues.   33

The toxicokinetics and toxicodynamics of a chemical and the ability of a biological system to effect repair all come to bear on the exposure-response   34 relationship. It is easy to see why it is challenging to predict human toxicity with anything short of a whole organism. Indeed, current predictive toxicology draws not just from whole-animal experiments and theory but from a historical data base, compiled over years of experience, that relates the results of in vivo testing to human epidemiological data and even in some cases to the outcome of accidental human exposure.

The foregoing discussion of toxicokinetic and toxicodynamic inter-   35
actions underscores the most obvious and important advantage of whole-animal testing: it provides an integrated biological system that serves as a surrogate for the complexities of human and other animal systems. In vivo tests have several other features that must be reckoned with. They can be used to assess the outcome of exposure by different routes (whether through ingestion, contact with the skin or inhalation) and over long periods (chronic toxicity tests can take a year or longer). In addition, whole-animal studies can be designed to determine whether or not particular toxic effects are reversible—an important parameter in risk assessment and risk management.

How might in vitro testing provide the same information? Would it be   36
necessary to have one in vitro test for every potential target-cell type in the body? How can in vitro tests evaluate toxicological responses that involve, say, immunological processes or blood pressure? How can they evaluate chronic toxicity or recovery from toxic insults? How can exposure by ingestion, inhalation or topical contact be simulated? These problems must be solved if in vitro tests are ever to replace in vivo testing completely.

Another potential stumbling block concerns the testing of human–cell   37
cultures, which, because it would eliminate the need for species extrapolation, is billed as one of the benefits of in vitro testing. There are a few hitches. Currently not all human cell types can be cultured; some types of cells "dedifferentiate" in vitro, that is, they take on the qualities of primitive, unspecialized cells instead of retaining the characteristics that identify them as muscle cells, spleen cells, colon cells and so on. Furthermore, the supply of normal human cells available for toxicological testing is somewhat limited. In order for human cells to be routinely employed in toxicity testing, some means of making them more readily available must be found.

These obstacles should be weighed against the disadvantages of whole-   38
animal testing that we have already mentioned: animal discomfort and death, species-extrapolation problems and excessive time and expense. In vitro tests could ameliorate all of these problems and several more. For example, whereas whole-animal testing is hard to standardize, the standardization of in vitro techniques is fairly straightforward. Furthermore, the dose of a chemical that is received by each cultured cell can be measured and controlled with precision, making it easier to establish the critical concentrations of toxins. Because much smaller quantities of a substance can be used, novel compounds available in limited amounts can be tested, and disposal problems are minimized if a compound turns out to be toxic.

It takes time to overcome the problems inherent in introducing any   39
new technology. It also takes time to gain acceptance for a new technology when the incumbent technology can boast a 50- to 60-year record of

empirical findings. Before any new in vitro test can become a regular, routine source of toxicological data, it will have to be validated. That means it must be shown to be reliable (to give consistent results in different laboratories and at different times in the same laboratory) and meaningful (to provide information that contributes to chemical safety evaluation). To promote acceptance, toxicologists must also begin to compile data bases for in vitro tests so that better predictions can be drawn from the results.

Contrary to a prevailing misperception, in vitro tests need not replace   40
existing in vivo test procedures in order to be useful. They can contribute to chemical safety evaluation right now. In vitro tests, for example, can be incorporated into the earliest stages of the risk-assessment process; they can be used to identify chemicals having the lowest probability of toxicity so that animals need be exposed only to less noxious chemicals. Such a procedure would reduce the number of animals tested and would also save time and the expense of research and development for products likely to fail subsequent safety evaluations. It is encouraging to note that several corporations have already implemented this approach in their testing strategies.

In any case, insisting on comprehensive replacement of existing tests   41
will only delay the implementation of in vitro methods indefinitely. In vitro toxicity testing will not replace animal testing in a single, quantum step. In fact, regulatory mechanisms do not yet exist for review and approval of new in vitro testing methodologies for chemical safety evaluation. With time, in vitro testing will become more firmly established, and it will eventually play a critical role in the safety-evaluation process. It is our hope that this goal will be attained with the support and encouragement of industry, regulatory agencies, the scientific community and animal-welfare advocates alike.

QUESTIONS FOR MEANING

1. What does *in vitro* testing mean? What is the Latin term for whole-animal testing?
2. According to Goldberg and Frazier, what factors have made in vitro testing more plausible? What advantages does it offer over testing on animals?
3. Are there any limits to in vitro testing?
4. What are the objectives of toxicity testing?
5. Approximately how many different types of in vitro tests may be available in some fields? Describe three of the tests reported by Goldberg and Frazier.
6. Vocabulary: contentious (2), protocols (6), panoply (6), deleterious (10), carcinogenicity (17), ocular (22), epidermal (25), extrapolation (29), empirical (30), immunological (36), quantum (41).

QUESTIONS ABOUT STRATEGY

1. In making a case for alternatives to animal testing, how have the authors established their credibility as scientists?

2. How useful is the background on LD50 and the Draize tests in paragraph 10? What does this paragraph tell you about the authors' sense of audience? Does their sense of audience remain consistent throughout the article?
3. Why do the authors point out that "in vitro tests need not replace existing in vivo test procedures in order to be useful" (paragraph 40)?
4. Consider paragraph 41. In writing their conclusion, have the authors used any strategies designed to draw diverse readers together?

ONE STUDENT'S ASSIGNMENT

Using APA style documentation, write an argument for or against animal-based research. Include material from at least one source in The Informed Argument *and at least two sources that you have located on your own. Because your paper will include material from outside the textbook we are using, remember to supply readers with an APA style reference list at the end of your essay.*

A Growing Shadow
Lisa Lemke

There is no doubt that scientific animal research has had a significant effect on the history of medicine and science and has resulted in many lifesaving achievements. Just a few of the most significant advancements include: the development of the rabies vaccine in 1885; the discovery of insulin in 1921; the discovery that penicillin fights bacterial infections in 1940; the development and testing of the polio vaccine in the 1950s; and the construction of the heart-lung machine and open heart surgery techniques also in the 1950s (Moore, 1989). No one can dispute the tremendous benefits to humankind that this research has provided. With the number of medical and scientific advancements that have been dependent upon animal research and the number of lives that have been saved as a result, it is difficult to justify elimination of such research.

One must, however, realize that this is the glamorous side of research; the reality of animal research is a harsh one--one of suffering and pain, and often, fruitless effort. Although society is grateful for the great medical miracles, miracles are few and far between. Millions upon millions of animals died for these

relatively few breakthroughs. Such a consideration does
not undermine their significance, but rather acknowledges their great cost. Thus a slim shadow is cast upon
the bright face of research.

This shadow grows a bit as research methods and fa-   3
cilities are closely examined. How is scientific research conducted? What exactly goes on behind bolted
laboratory doors? The answers to those questions can be
startling. While it is difficult to dispute the value of
research that led to insulin and a rabies vaccine, it is
not at all difficult to debate the necessity of some of
the research that is routinely performed. At the University of Oregon Dr. Barbara Gordon–Lickey has spent years
experimenting with cats. Gordon–Licky surgically rotated
cat's eyeballs in their sockets in an attempt to change
the way the animals' visual world was experienced. Other
cats had their eyes sewn shut to study visual regions of
the animals' brains. Although she claims that her work
may someday have a profound effect on the medical world,
even Gordon–Lickey concedes that there may be no practical applications to her experiments for years to come
(Barrett & Greene, 1989).

Experiments such as these have no useful purpose.   4
Scientists often find implications for humans, but implications don't really mean much in a scientific world
of facts and figures. Extrapolating results of animal
experimentation to humans is potentially dangerous. We
have seen this in the past with the thalidomide disaster. Although this morning–sickness drug was tested extensively on laboratory animals, it caused serious
deformities in thousands of fetuses born in Europe
(Mayo, 1983). This crisis occurred primarily in Europe,
but it remains a tragic example of the disastrous effects that generalizing results of animal experimentation to humans can have. Instead of needlessly
destroying animal lives, as well as wasting valuable
time and money performing experiments that may someday
have a possible practical application, scientists ought
to concentrate wholly on research designed to solve medical crises that exist today, such as AIDS and cancer.

Then there are those experiments that lead to star-   5
tling results that any layperson could have predicted.

In an experiment conducted by the American Museum of
Natural History, cats raised in isolation had nerves in
the penis severed. After years of this sex testing, the
scientists conducting the experiment were amazed to find
that "genital desensitization together with sexual inexperience inhibits sexual behavior in cats" (Mayo, 1983,
p. 327). Couldn't we guess that such traumas might have
had a negative effect on the sex life of a cat? It is a
gross waste of animal life as well as taxpayers' money
to conduct experiments that tell us what we already
know.

Some scientists cry for scientific freedom, but   6
shirk their own scientific accountability for the lives
they take and the treatment they give animals. If researchers need to exploit animals to conduct scientific
experiments and save the human race, they can at least
treat these animals with the respect they deserve by
providing humane care and maintaining mature and professional conduct when handling these animals.

There are laboratories which do strive to maintain   7
such standards in all aspects of research. The Laboratory for Experimental Medicine and Surgery in Primates
(LEMSIP) in Sterling Forest, New York, stands as a clear
example. Part of the New York University School of Medicine, it is the largest chimpanzee testing laboratory in
the country. Cages in the lab are kept meticulously
clean, and the staff is trained to nurture the animals
by treating them with kindness and even talking to them
(Barrett & Greene, 1989). This and other labs like it
deserve praise for their efforts towards making the laboratory a respectful and even caring institution.

But, just as not all animal rights activists are   8
bomb-toting extremists, not all laboratories are respectful or even humane institutions. Most people would
agree that "there is no excuse for such conditions as
dogs lying with open incisions, their entrails exposed,
or monkeys with untreated, protruding broken bones, exposed muscle tissue, and infected wounds, living in
grossly unsanitary conditions amidst feces and rotting
food" (Elshtain, 1990, p. 23).

These descriptions are horrifying enough, but con-   9
sider viewing on video tape the atrocities of the Uni-

versity of Pennsylvania Head Injury Clinic, a laboratory
that was funded by more than $1 million in taxpayers'
money (McArdle, 1985, p. 15). Baboons' heads were ce-
mented into metal helmets, the helmets were bolted into
a hydraulic jack, and the heads were thus thrust forward
at speeds high enough to smash the baboons' brains
against their skulls (Barrett & Green, 1989). Video
tapes recorded incredible violations of the Animal Welfare Act, disrespect for the animals, and blatant abuse.
Examples include: "use of nonsterile methods and the
smoking of cigarettes over open incisions . . . lack of
appropriate anesthesia and absence of post-injury relief" (McArdle, 1985, p. 17). Ironically, the experimental model was invalidated by introducing the
uncontrolled variable of a hammer and chisel to remove
baboons' heads from the apparatus (McArdle, 1985). Such
callous treatment is a dark cloud that extends the
shadow even further across the face of noble research.

And the horror is that while such treatment is not   10
the rule in laboratories, these are simply not isolated
incidents. The list of documented cruelty, abuse, and
neglect is long. The pictures, the video tapes, and the
descriptions disgust and enrage many people when they
are publicized. Why? Not because they are sob stories
exaggerated and exploited by animal rights activists,
but because they stand as harsh documented proof of the
cruelty expressed by fellow humans.

The necessity of animal research cannot be denied   11
in the age of such diseases as cancer and AIDS, but necessity does not justify the needless cruelty that occurs in some laboratories. America needs stronger laws
to prevent unnecessary and wasteful experimentation and
the abuse and neglect of laboratory animals. Perhaps
more importantly, the human race needs to adjust its attitude that animals are there for humans to use and exploit, then throw away. Animals used in research deserve
respect--respect in life, respect in death. "Humanity"
is what makes <u>Homo</u> <u>sapiens</u> human; without it we are no
more than animals.

References

Barrett, K. & Greene, R. (1989, September). Necessary evil?
    Redbook. pp. 160-1, 204, 206, 208.
Elshtain, J. (1990). Why worry about the animals? In R.
    Miller (Ed.), The informed argument (pp. 280-288). San
    Diego: Harcourt.
Mayo, D. (1983). Against a scientific justification of animal
    experiments. In R. Miller (Ed.), The informed argument
    (pp. 324-345). San Diego: Harcourt.
McArdle, M. (1985, Fall). Pain, outrage, and unrest at the
    University of Pennsylvania. The Humane Society News. pp.
    14-17.
Moore, M. (1989, Fall). Behind the headlines. University of
    Minnesota Health Sciences. pp. 2-6.

SUGGESTIONS FOR WRITING

1. Drawing upon Karpati, Hubbell and Melby, write an essay defending the use of animals in medical research.

2. Is all research equally valid? Can some experiments on animals be justified even if others cannot, or must one take an absolute position on this issue? If you think that some types of research are acceptable, write an essay that will define what is and what isn't permissible.

3. Is an elephant equal to a pig? Write an essay with the thesis that all animals are *not* equal. Make sure that you take the views of Peter Singer into account.

4. Interview someone who uses animals in either teaching or research, and then write a paper defending or attacking the way animals are used in your own school or community.

5. Jean Beth Elshtain raises the issue of how animals are used in the military. Write an argument focused upon this type of animal use, drawing upon your own research or personal experience.

6. Elshtain, Hubbell, and Wright all discuss People for the Ethical Treatment of Animals (PETA). Research this organization, and write an argument that will either support or question its tactics.

7. Synthesize the philosophical arguments for animal rights by drawing upon the essays by Peter Singer and Robert Wright.

8. What do religions teach regarding the relationships between human beings and animals? Write a paper defending or attacking animal experimentation according to Buddhist, Christian, Hindu, Jewish, or Moslem beliefs.

9. Can you oppose the use of animals in scientific research and still eat meat? Or is this a contradiction in your own values? Write an essay on

the relationship between eating animals and experimenting upon them. Is there a difference between these two activities that makes one defensible and the other not?

10. Mayo observes that animal experimentation is more restricted in Great Britain than it is in the United States. Do a research paper on the nature of the laws that protect animals in Britain and argue whether or not such laws would be desirable in our own country. Try to determine what effect British laws have had upon the practice of science. Is major research still being done in Great Britain, or has British law crippled the practice of science there?

11. Drawing upon the work of Goldberg and Frazier, write an essay defining the extent to which *in vitro* testing could replace specific examples of animal experimentation.

12. Thousands of cats and dogs are abandoned each year by owners who no longer wish to care for them. Some die slow deaths from starvation and disease. Others are rescued by humane societies which try to find new homes for them. If a new home cannot be found, the abandoned animal is either destroyed or sold to a research facility. Should unwanted pets be used for animal experimentation? Or are former pets entitled to special protection?

COMPETITION:
IS IT GOOD FOR YOU?

♦

ROSS WETZSTEON
The Winner Instinct

One of the issues on which men and women have often disagreed is the extent to which competition is healthy and productive. An editor and writer at The Village Voice *in New York City, Ross Wetzsteon argues that men are naturally competitive and that competition is fun—implying that women may not understand the pleasure that comes from competing. He wrote the following essay for* Redbook *in 1984.*

My wife used to hate playing cards with me. "You're too competitive," she   1
kept saying. "You get so intense, you can't just have fun—you always have
to win."

That didn't have anything to do with the way I felt, but try telling her   2
that. All I could do was deny that I'm competitive.

Then one rainy weekend in the country we played a vicious, back-and-   3
forth game of rummy, and when Kay finally edged me by three points, I
could see that her pleasure in winning was jeopardized by her fear that
I'd sulk.

"Now, don't get mad just because you lost," she said.   4

"Mad? That was the closest game I've every played!"   5

"You're just trying to prove you're not competitive."   6

"Not competitive? Then why was the game so much fun?"

She smiled cautiously as she gathered in the cards. "Now you're just   7
trying to pretend you don't care whether you won or lost."

"Of course I care, damn it, but don't you see? It's not winning or   8
losing that matters—it's the competition itself!"

I suddenly realized that when the subject had come up before, the only   9
reason I'd always denied being competitive was that Kay had made it seem
like such a dirty word. "Sure, women are just as ambitious and aggressive
as men," she had said once, "but we've been inhibited from expressing competitiveness. We were told when we were young that the only way we could

compete was for the attention of men—to compete in any other way was 'unfeminine.' But society defines competitiveness as a brutal, winning-is-everything attitude. So if by competition you mean imitating the macho way men behave—no, thanks."

My wife just couldn't see that competitiveness means a lot more to men   10
than that win-at-any-cost ethic. Listen to New York Mets' pitcher Tom Seaver, one of the most thoughtful athletes in America: "When we finally won the World Series, I realized I'd been wrong since boyhood. I'd always believed the thrill was in celebrating the victory. Now I saw that the thrill was in competition for its own sake." So I finally decided to admit that, yes, I'm very competitive, and what's more, I'm proud of it.

Now, I'm not going to deny that there are elements of adolescent in-   11
security or latent hostility or sexual rivalry in a lot of competition between men—all I'm saying is that there's another side to the story. Take male kidding around, for instance. I always tell my friend Arthur that he exaggerates so compulsively, he'll even tell people his summer house is at Six-Mile Harbor instead of Three-Mile Harbor. He comes right back at me: "You're putting on so much weight, pretty soon they'll have to give you your own zip code."

We indulge in so much of this typically male insulting humor that our   12
wives can be forgiven for thinking that beneath our surface joking there must be bitter rivalry. Believe me, we see the "oh-you-men" way they roll their eyes, but what we actually hear when we insult each other like this is one of the most reassuring things a friend can say: "I know all your faults—you can't hide a thing from me—but I like you anyway. I accept you the way you are." Still skeptical? Just let some guy who's not a close friend try to get away with that kind of one-upmanship.

Male competitiveness in our professional lives is often a way to show   13
our mutual respect. Sure, no one needs to be told that many men adopt a to-hell-with-the-bastards attitude in business; but far more often men also experience rivalry as a spur to achievement, as a means of being drawn to perform at the top of our abilities. I testified in a lawsuit a couple of years ago, and you would have thought the opposing attorneys would kill rather than let the other get the upper hand. But I overheard them talking after the decision. "I enjoy trying a case against you," one of them said. "You really keep me on my toes."

"Going up against you isn't any picnic," the other one answered. "I   14
know I've got to do my best just to stand a chance."

Can you tell which one won the case?   15

I've heard other men express the same feelings in any number of highly   16
competitive professions. "It's really sad," the owner of a newspaper where I once worked told me when a competing publication suddenly folded. "I ran a much better paper because of them. Now I'm afraid I'll get lazy." And while I'm not going to argue that men regret pulling off a deal against a competitor, their gratification is often less if they don't feel they were seriously challenged.

In sports the image of "winning is everything" is even more mislead-   17
ing. Most men I know get their real kick in sports not from winning but
from the fact that the playing field is one of the few places where compan-
ionship and challenge come together. In bowling or touch football or soft-
ball, stiff competition not only brings men closer together; it also encourages
them to do their best. This paradox at the heart of sports allows men to feel
both friendship and self-satisfaction, to share moments of pride. Of course,
there are nonstop competitors like John McEnroe, but there are also competitors like my friends Josh and Michael—anyone watching them play tennis
would think their lives were riding on the outcome. But after the match is
over, you can't tell who won—they both feel great. Competition has pushed
them to the limits of their abilities; they've done as well as they possibly
could; they've done something well together.

Still think winning is everything to men? Take my friend Fred, who   18
finally managed to beat his weekly tennis partner after losing something like
ten sets in a row. "You must feel terrific," I said.

"Yeah, I suppose so," he said offhandedly.   19

"What's wrong?" I asked.   20

"Well, to tell the truth," Fred said, "he was so far off his game, it   21
wasn't much fun."

I knew exactly how he felt—I play tennis so competitively that my   22
friends call my game "Death in the Afternoon," but I'd much rather play
way over my head and lose 2–6 than hack around and win 6–love.

So when my wife says that men can't relate to one another except com-   23
petitively, that it's a way to disguise their animosity or assert their superiority—no more apologies from me. I now argue that there's much more going
on, that men just as often use competition as a means of expressing acceptance or respect or sharing.

Take it from me—busting your butt to win has its own rewards, whether   24
you win or not. I came home from a tennis match one day absolutely glow-
ing. "You must have won," Kay remarked.

"Why do you say that?"   25

"You look so happy."   26

"Well, actually I lost," I said. "But he was so good, he made me play   27
better than I've ever played in my life."

QUESTIONS FOR MEANING

1. Why has competition become a "dirty word"? Why does Wetzsteon not
   only admit that he's competitive but also claim that he's "proud of it"?
2. Why does Wetzsteon believe that competition itself can be more rewarding than simply winning? Do you agree?
3. What does Wetzsteon mean when he writes of "the paradox at the heart
   of sports"?
4. Can you identify the allusion in the joking reference to the author's tennis
   game as "Death in the Afternoon"?

QUESTIONS ABOUT STRATEGY

1. What role does Wetzsteon's wife play in this essay?
2. In contrasting the way he and his wife feel about competition, does Wetzsteon ever use sexual stereotypes?
3. Where in his essay does Wetzsteon reveal he is aware that competition is not entirely admirable?
4. How effective is Wetzsteon's use of dialogue?

KATHERINE MARTIN

Is Winning Everything?

Athletics is one of the areas in which competition is most encouraged. But what happens when adults organize athletic competition for their children and pressure them to excel? The following essay written for Parents *magazine by Katherine Martin considers the potentially harmful effects of athletic competition on children. It was first published in* **1986.** *Martin's work has also appeared in such magazines as* Esquire, Ms, *and* Cosmopolitan. *The author of* Non-Impact Aerobics *(1987), she is now working as a screen writer in southern California.*

In the thick of a heated baseball game a young umpire is verbally harassed 1
by two vehement coaches. The boy tries his best on the next play but gets
more abuse from a parent restrained only by a hurricane fence. Exasperated,
he flops down on the ground while the coaches and a referee go at it with
each other.

A young boy afraid of batting is forced to stand at home plate while 2
his father deliberately throws pitches that hit him.

During a Little League game a mother storms down to the dugout and 3
belts her son across the head for being tagged out.

A football coach grabs the face mask of a youngster, yanks him spit- 4
close and screams obscenities at him.

A father beats his exhausted son to keep him running laps around a 5
track.

Twenty million children between the ages of eight and sixteen play 6
organized sports outside of school, and their experience in ballparks and on
playing fields has enormous impact on their physical, emotional, and social
development. Most of us believe that there's nothing more basic to the
American way of rearing young people than sports, but many have come to
realize that the world of sports for youth is not an entirely innocent or happy
one. In recent years adults have imposed unchildlike standards on children's
sports. In our zeal, we've overorganized, overregimented, overstructured,
and overtrained our kids. We've claimed their games for the serious business
of adult competition.

"That wasn't the case when there was a lot more spontaneous play," 7
says Barry Goldberg, M.D., associate clinical professor of pediatrics at Yale
University and pediatric consultant at the Institute of Sports Medicine and
Athletic Trauma at Lenox Hill Hospital in New York City. "Our society has
changed a great deal in the last twenty years. The small community is van-
ishing and there's less open space. People have to trek to playing fields. As a
result, organized teams have become a way to get kids together and, often,
they're patterned after professional and college sports.

"As adults intervene in children's games," warns Goldberg, echoing a 8
growing concern among youth sports experts, "we have to accept the responsibility for the end product."

That end product isn't always pretty. Over the past ten years, there 9
have been reports of children paralyzed and killed from "spearing" during
football games, and passing out from dehydration. One coach reportedly
injected oranges with amphetamines to get his ten- to twelve-year-old football players "up" for a game.

Many parents are transformed—and often not for the better—when they 10
see their youngsters in the thick of athletic competition. "When you first go
out to watch your child play sports, you see this biological extension of
yourself on the field and you feel some powerful emotions," says Rainer
Martens, Ph.D., and founder of the American Coaching Effectiveness Program (ACEP) and author of *Joy and Sadness in Children's Sports* (Human Kinetics Publishers). "Parents just aren't prepared for that. Suddenly, they find
themselves acting in ways they'd never think of at home—standing up and
screaming, 'You dummy! Catch the ball!' Behavior like this has a potentially
severe effect on children."

Speaking of these effects, psychologist Thomas Tutko, a leading au- 11
thority on youth sports and coauthor of the sobering book, *Winning Is Everything And Other American Myths* (Macmillan), comments, "I'm concerned about
how many good athletes are scarred by injury or burned out psychologically
by the time they are fifteen because they are unable to meet the insatiable
needs of their parents, their coach, their fans, or their own personal obsession. And I am concerned, too, about those kids who feel rejected because
of their limited athletic prowess.

"The effects may not be physically evident," continues Tutko, "but 12
failure in sports, or heavy-handed approaches by parents and coaches can
destroy a child's self-esteem, turn him away from a lifelong involvement in
physical activity, foster negative attitudes toward authority figures, and encourage hostile, aggressive behavior."

Our unfettered responses to our children as athletes can create insidious 13
pressures. In her twelve years of extensive research on the socio-psychologi-
cal aspects of competitive youth sports, Tara Scanlan, Ph.D., associate professor of kinesiology at the University of California, Los Angeles, found that
children experience intense stress when they perceive they're being pressured
to participate in an activity and when they worry about the performance
expectations and evaluations of their parents and coaches. "Kids are very

dependent on adults for feelings of their own competence and sense of self," says Scanlan. "It may not always seem so, since they may try to be stoic, tough little athletes who don't cry, but they process everything."

The implications for parents are clear. "As parents, we all have to walk   14
a very fine line between caring and creating pressure, between enthusiasm and going overboard," comments Bob Chandler, former all-pro football player, in the recent film, *The Winning Trap: Sports and Our Kids*. "We have to answer the question, What's in it for us? as honestly as we can, because unless we know what we want out of kids' sports we can't be truly effective in helping our children get what they want."

Before involving our children in team sports we need to look at our   15
own feelings about winning and losing, which may be colored by frustrations we feel in other areas of our lives, in our careers, or marital relationships. Our attitudes about sports may be charged, moreover, with memories of our own experiences as children, of our early successes or humiliations on the playing field.

"Before involving your child," says pediatrician Nathan Smith, a sports   16
medicine specialist at the University of Washington in Seattle and coauthor of *Kidsports* (Addison-Wesley), "ask yourself whether you're ready to be the parent of a loser, of a bench warmer. How would your responses differ if your child struck out or made a home run in a tie game? Would you be embarrassed if your child broke into tears after a tough loss or after making a mistake? Can you tolerate becoming a target for your child's displaced anger and frustration when there is no other outlet for disappointment and hurt?"

Or how would you feel if your child was benched during an important   17
game so that a child with less ability would have a chance to play? How would you react if an official made a questionable call against your child?

If we understand our own expectations and motivations, we can help   18
our children explore theirs. We will be ready to hear what they are saying, rather than what we want them to say. Why do they want to play? What do they expect the sport they have chosen to be like?

Although children learn very early the high value placed on sports by   19
society, when they play on their own, they tend to have a different perspective on sports than adults. They want to win, but winning is not their exclusive goal. In a ten-year study of more than a thousand children, sports psychologist Terry Orlick discovered that 90 percent of his young respondents would rather play on a losing team than warm a bench on a winning team. In fact, winning was at the bottom of their list. They wanted fun and excitement, and they wanted to improve their skills and be with friends.

"If sides are unequal, if rules give an advantage to one team, children   20
will negotiate to make it possible for either side to win," says another youth-sport expert, Vern Seefeldt, Ph.D., director of the Youth Sports Institute at Michigan State University. "That thrill of the unexpected is a major part of why children play sports. As adults we try to set up a distinct advantage for our team. We want to remove the element of uncertainty.

"When we were kids," Seefeldt continues, "we used to make up all   21
kinds of modifications to games, because we didn't always have the right
number of people for a team, or the use of a baseball diamond or a basketball
court. Now, as adults, we organize our children's games right down to the
letter of the rule, leaving them very little opportunity for innovation and
creativity, and depriving them of the process of arbitrating, negotiating, finding
solutions."

According to Tutko, "We actually cripple children psychologically when   22
we set up all the plays. They feel like machines. Sport can be a medium to
train children to be more responsible, but we have made winning take precedence over learning. That's so shortsighted. We could be teaching them
leadership skills by having them take turns running the team's calisthenics
and drills. We could teach them how to set up and run their own plays by
alternating team captains every practice."

To guide our children's involvement with sports, we must recognize   23
that they have different needs at different ages and that, at each stage, success
should be seen as an ongoing process of achieving potential.

QUESTIONS FOR MEANING

1. Why have sports for children become increasingly organized by adults?
2. When children play on their own, how do their games differ from those
   that are organized and supervised by adults?
3. Why do adults sometimes treat children unkindly when they fail to excel
   at sports?
4. What effects on children can result from an overemphasis on sports?
5. What should parents do before involving their children in organized sports?
6. Vocabulary: harassed (1), vehement (1), zeal (6), insatiable (11), unfettered
   (13), kinesiology (13), stoic (13), marital (15), innovation (21), precedence (22).

QUESTIONS ABOUT STRATEGY

1. What type of reasoning does Martin use to organize her material?
2. This essay originally appeared in *Parents* magazine. What evidence can you
   point to in the essay that shows Martin had her audience clearly in mind
   as she wrote?
3. Consider Martin's use of quotations. Do they help her to make her case?
   Could she afford to cut any of them?
4. Why does Martin identify Barry Goldberg, Rainer Martens, Thomas Tutko,
   Tara Scanlan, Bob Chandler, Nathan Smith, Terry Orlick, and Vern Seefeldt?

MARIAH BURTON NELSON

Who Wins? Who Cares?

A regular contributor to the Washington Post, Ms., *and* Women's Sports and Fitness, *Mariah Burton Nelson has also written for* Glamour, New Woman, Working Woman, Golf Illustrated, *the* Los Angeles Times, *and other periodicals. She graduated from Stanford University with a B.A. in psychology and later received a masters in public health from San Jose State University. She played basketball (center) for Stanford, for a French professional team, and for the New Jersey Gems of the Women's Pro Basketball League. The author of* Are We Winning Yet? How Women Are Changing Sports and Sports Are Changing Women *(1991), Nelson currently competes in rowing and swimming events. The following essay draws on Nelson's experience as an athlete as well as research for her book. When first published in **1990**, "Who Wins? Who Cares?" appeared alongside an argument against competition by Alfie Kohn, whose views are represented in this section by an essay that begins on p. 403.*

Competition can damage self-esteem, create anxiety and lead to cheating and hurt feelings. But so can romantic love. No one suggests we do away with love; rather, we must perfect our understanding of what love means.

So too with competition. "To compete" is derived from the Latin competere, meaning "to seek together." Women seem to understand this. Maybe it's because we sat on the sidelines for so long, watching. Maybe it's because we were raised to be kind and nurturing. I'm not sure why it is. But I've noticed that it's not women who greet each other with a ritualistic, "Who won?"; not women who memorize scores and statistics; not women who pride themselves on "killer instincts." Passionate though we are, women don't take competition that seriously. Or rather, we take competition seriously, but we don't take winning and losing seriously. We've always been more interested in playing.

In fact, since the early part of this century, women have devised ways to make sport specifically inclusive and cooperative. Physical educators of the 1920s taught sportswomanship as well as sport skills, emphasizing health, vigor, high moral conduct, participation, respect for other players and friendship. So intent were these women on dodging the pitfalls of men's sports that many shied away from competition altogether.

Nowadays, many women compete wholeheartedly. But we don't buy into the "Super Bull" mentality that the game is everything. Like Martina Navratilova and Chris Evert, former "rivals" whose rapport has come to symbolize a classically female approach to competition, many women find ways to remain close while also reaching for victory. We understand that trying to win is not tantamount to trying to belittle; that winning is not wonderful if the process of play isn't challenging, fair or fun; and that losing, though at times disappointing, does not connote failure. For women, if sports are power plays, they're not about power over (power as dominance) but power to (power as competence). Sports are not about domination and defeat but caring and cooperation.

"The playing of a game has to do with your feelings, your emotions, how you care about the people you're involved with," says University of Iowa basketball coach C. Vivian Stringer.   5

Pam Shriver has said of Steffi Graf, "I hope in the next couple of years that I get to be friends with her because it's just easier. It's more fun. I don't think it affects the competitive side of things."   6

Friendship has been a major theme of my sporting life as well, along with physical competence, achievement and joy. Though I've competed in seven sports from the high school to the professional level, I have few memories of victories or losses. I don't think winning taught me to be a gracious winner. I don't think losing readied me for more serious losses in life. Rather, my nearly 30 years of competition have taught me how to *play*, with empathy, humor and honesty. If another player challenges me to row harder, swim faster or make more clever moves toward the basket, the games take on a special thrill. But the final score is nearly irrelevant. Chris Evert once said the joy of winning "lasts about an hour."   7

I'm choosy about whom I compete with, and how. I don't participate in games in which "losers" are no longer allowed to play. Monopoly, poker, musical chairs, and single-elimination tournaments are a few examples. If playing is the point, then exclusion never makes sense. I also eschew competitions that pit women against men; they only serve to antagonize and polarize. I no longer injure myself in the name of victory. Nor, as a coach, will I allow players to get that carried away.   8

Some women, scarred by childhood exclusion, shamed by early "defeats," or sickened by abuses such as cheating and steroid use, still avoid competition. They're right to be wary. Although these things are more visible in men's sports, female athletes and coaches can also succumb to the "winning is the only thing" myth, committing myriad ethical and personal offenses, from recruiting violations to bulimia, in the name of victory.   9

But once one understands the spirit of the game, it's not a matter of *believing* that winning and losing aren't important, it's a matter of noticing that they're not. Women seem to notice. Most women can play soccer, golf, or run competitively and enjoy themselves, regardless of outcome. They can play on a "losing" team but leave the court with little or no sense of loss. They can win without feeling superior.   10

I think it's the responsibility of these women—and the men who remain unblinded by the seductive glow of victory—to share this vision with young players. Children, it seems to me, naturally enjoy comparing their skills: "How far can you throw the ball? Farther than I can? How did you do it? Will you show me?" It's only when adults ascribe undue importance to victory that losing becomes devastating and children get hurt.   11

Adults must show children that what matters is how one plays the game. It's important that we not just parrot that cliche, but demonstrate our com-   12 mitment to fair, participatory competition by paying equal attention to skilled and unskilled children; by allowing all children to participate fully in games, regardless of the score; and by caring more about process than results. This way, children can fully comprehend what they seem to intuit: that competition can be a way to get to know other people, to be challenged, and to have fun in a close and caring environment. To seek together.

Some of my best friends are the women and men who share a court or pool or field with me. Together we take risks, make mistakes, laugh, push ourselves and revel in the grace and beauty of sports. Who wins? Who cares? We're playing *with*, not *against* each other, using each other's accomplishments to inspire. 13

At its best, competition is not divisive but unifying, not hateful but loving. Like other expressions of love, it should not be avoided simply because it has been misunderstood. 14

QUESTIONS FOR MEANING

1. What is the origin of the word *competition*?
2. What distinction does Nelson make between different types of power?
3. Although Nelson enjoys competition, does she avoid any kind of games?
4. In paragraph 10, Nelson writes, "it's not a matter of *believing* that winning and losing aren't important, it's a matter of noticing that they're not." How does believing differ from noticing?
5. Vocabulary: tantamount (4), empathy (7), polarize (8), succumb (9), myriad (9), bulimia (9), ascribe (11), intuit (12).

QUESTIONS ABOUT STRATEGY

1. How does using definition, at the beginning of this essay, contribute to the purpose of the argument that follows?
2. Throughout this essay, Nelson implies that women and men compete differently. In your experience, is this a valid generalization? Are there any risks in making it?
3. Consider the analogy that Nelson makes, in paragraph 1, between competition and romantic love. Is this a good analogy? Why does Nelson return to the subject of love in paragraph 14?
4. How effective is the use of personal experience in this essay? Is it appropriate for the topic? Does Nelson rely too heavily upon it?

CHARLES R. DUKE

Giving the Competitive Edge to Students' Academic Achievement

A 1962 graduate of Plymouth State College, Charles R. Duke received his Ph.D. from Duke University in 1972. He has taught English at Murray State University, where he directed the West Kentucky Writing Project, and Utah State University. A specialist in English Education, he is the author of Creative Writing and English Teaching *(1974),* Teaching Fundamental English Today *(1976), and* Teaching Literature Today *(1979). The following article was first published in a* **1988** *issue of* NASSP Bulletin, *the journal of the National Association of Secondary School Principals.*

When the word "competition" is mentioned in connection with school, most people think of athletics.   1

In reality, competition permeates every aspect of the school environment. In fact, it may be the single most powerful influence on learning today. The factors that comprise the school experience for most young people—grades, teachers, peers, jobs, and self-identity—are all controlled in large measure by competition.   2

Athletic coaches have long been aware of the importance of instilling a sense of competition in their players; to a lesser extent, teachers also have recognized this influence and have tried to capitalize on it by organizing competitions in the classroom.   3

However, most of this competition does not come to the public's attention or bring recognition to students beyond the classroom.   4

Highlighting Academic Achievement

Many school districts are now seeking ways to highlight students' academic achievement in an effort to offset the public's perception that the only important student achievement is that which occurs on the playing fields on weekday nights. Considering the small percentage of students who actually demonstrate their achievements this way, it's not surprising that the public remains unaware of what else students may be learning or achieving.   5

To change this perception, some schools have decided to capitalize on the concept of competition, borrow from the success of athletics, and develop various academic contests that can showcase the talents of students, many of whom will never appear on the playing field.   6

School districts must proceed cautiously, however. Developing school/district academic competitions that benefit students and are not mere window dressing for the public requires some thoughtful assessment and plan-   7 ning. The SACI (School Academic Competition Inventory) offers a way to determine the potential in a school or district for an effective academic competition program.[1]

The School Academic Competition Inventory

1. Do the school/district's athletic achievements seem to overshadow academic achievements in the public's mind?   8
2. Does the academic climate within the school/district need improvement?
3. Could the student body, school staff members, and the public be made more aware of students' academic potential and achievements in the school/district?
4. Are there academic areas that need greater recognition by students, faculty members, administrators, and the public?
5. Do academic contests currently exist in the school or district?
6. Could the variety and number of competitions be increased or consolidated?
7. Are the contests coordinated throughout the school/district to ensure the quality and recognition of student achievement?
8. Are there potential sponsors for academic competitions?
9. Are there faculty members who might be willing to organize and run academic competitions?
10. Is there an individual who could monitor and/or coordinate school/district competitions?

If the majority of the responses to the SACI are positive, then educators   9
should consider developing strategies to emphasize the academic accomplishments of students in their schools.

Making Academic Achievement Visible

Initially, school leaders should look inside the school and examine present   10
practices. In most schools, some academic competitions already exist—most are run by departments. English departments feature literary contests, spelling bees, debate and speech tournaments, yearbook and journalism awards, and drama festivals.

Social studies departments offer opportunities to compete in essay writ-   11
ing contests. Science departments often arrange annual science fairs, and mathematics departments have problem-solving competitions.

Industrial arts, fine arts, and home economics typically have contests in   12
which completed projects are judged. Business departments stress performance via speed contests in typing, shorthand, and keyboarding skills. Music departments perhaps have higher visibility than many other academic departments because of competition in contests outside the school.

Such a list seems to suggest an abundance of academic competition within 13
a school. But often lacking in the midst of all this competition is some overall
coordination and public display of the achievements that these individual
competitions suggest.

If this is the case, educators should explore the feasibility of developing 14
an academic competition that might serve as a capstone event. This event's
purpose would be to highlight as many academic areas as possible without
diffusing the overall message: *recognition of students' academic achievement and
potential is a central mission of the school.*

In deciding if such an event is in the best interests of the school and 15
students, faculty members and administrators need to consider first the impact on students. At least five concerns should be addressed before any final
decision is made.

1. *Event Focus:* What will be the main focus of the event? Will it be interdis- 16
ciplinary or will it focus on only one or two academic areas?

Although arguments can be presented for either emphasis, the approach 17
likely to have the most impact on the school and the public is the interdisciplinary emphasis. Demonstrating students' abilities in a variety of academic
areas sends a strong message that academic achievement is a central element
across the school's curriculum.

2. *Competitive Skill:* What kinds of competitive skills will be called for in this 18
event: rote recall, general awareness, convergent and/or divergent thinking,
problem solving/decision making?

Since such an event should have a high profile for the public, what 19
kind of academic potential and achievement does the school want to highlight?

Central to the decisions here will be the time that can be provided for 20
the competition, the focus of the event itself, and whether or not there will
be any preliminary contests leading to the final event in which students can
demonstrate a variety of skills as well.

Given the nature of the public's current attitude toward education, or- 21
ganizers should look beyond rote recall to promote more emphasis on general awareness and problem-solving skills that can showcase students' abilities
to apply their academic knowledge and skills in various situations.

3. *Competition Entries:* Will the emphasis be placed on individual accomplish- 22
ment, team achievement, or a mixture? What degree of mastery must a student exhibit before being eligible to compete? The process of selecting students
for competition is always an important issue for adolescents.

Students and teachers need to know what the expectations are in this 23
area. Organizers should give careful attention to whether or not students of
varying academic skill and potential should be encouraged to participate and
what their chances of success may be. Of paramount importance is remembering that students who are required to participate in a competition for which
they are ill-prepared and which provides little guarantee for success will have
every right to regard academic competition as counter-productive to learning.

4. Sponsorship: Does the school want to retain control of the event or use   24
existing competitions established by outside agencies? The latter are regional
or national competitions that have standards, rules, procedures, and awards
already established.

A yearly listing of such competitions is available from the NASSP   25
Committee on National Contests and Activities.

Schools or districts who want to develop their own events have many   26
resources to draw upon. Competitions can even be matched to individual
interests or sponsors if necessary. Banks, newspapers, corporations, radio
and television companies, service organizations, unions, colleges, and universities are among the most likely candidates as sponsors.

With some careful attention to the focus of the event, educators should   27
gradually be able to build a coalition of sponsors. This coalition, in turn, will
give more impetus to promoting the interdisciplinary nature of the event and
will permit the event to grow from year to year while remaining responsive
to new academic thrusts in the school or district's curriculum.

5. Rewards: What will be the rewards for students who participate in the   28
event? How will judges be selected? For events of this nature to take on
significance in the minds of the participants as well as of the public, a substantial reward system must exist, and the rewards must be tied to a respected evaluation system that includes qualified judges. Therefore, organizers
will need to consider the availability of appropriate prizes and the selection
of judges.

The most appropriate form of reward is an academic scholarship awarded   29
in the name of one of the sponsors. Cash awards, bonds, or gift certificates
are acceptable, as are trophies and plaques. Winners also can be awarded
academic "letters" from their school or, if the competition involves several
schools, an appropriate badge that students can attach to their school jackets.

Selecting judges can become a politically sensitive issue, especially if   30
several schools are meeting for a districtwide competition. Here, the public
relations effect must be considered. Ideally, representatives from the sponsoring agencies—who do not have children competing—should serve as judges;
school superintendents and representatives from local colleges or universities
also are acceptable candidates.

Only as a last resort should school staff members be involved in the   31
judging process. This separation makes it easier for students and faculty
members to work together to prepare for the event, and the public perceives
the competition as a more objective event, one that clearly has the respect
and support of individuals outside the school.

Assuming that a decision is made to develop a capstone academic event,   32
ample time should be allowed, particularly in the first year, to attend to all
the details and to ensure that students, faculty members, and the public are
aware of the significance of the competition. Organizers should become familiar with some of the existing models for competitions and decide what
features, if any, should be incorporated into their own event.

Competition Across the Country

One of the more popular models of academic competition is the Academic   33
Olympiad, developed originally by the Mt. San Antonio Chapter of Phi Delta
Kappa in California. The goals of the Olympiad include the following:

- To confer visibility on scholarly performance through a competitive event
- To stimulate the academic efforts of high school students
- To recognize the scholarship of able students and the accomplishments of dedicated teachers
- To involve a large number of high school students without making excessive demands on their time
- To promote cooperation between school district representatives and university faculty members in the areas of curriculum and instruction.

One of the most recent and successful applications of the Olympiad   34
model can be found at Utah State University.[2] Seven school districts in northern
Utah cooperated with the university in developing the Olympiad. Each school
district pledged a minimum of $200 to participate and a team coach to coordinate a team from each of the participating schools.

The Utah State Office of Education endorsed the concept and provided   35
personnel to assist with test construction and judging. Officials at Utah State
University provided facilities and scholarships as well as technical and faculty
support. Additional gifts and grants came from businesses and individuals
and a $500 grant from Phi Delta Kappa International to the Utah State University Chapter served as seed money for the event.

The original Academic Olympiad took a year to plan. An executive   36
committee composed of representatives from each of the participating school
districts as well as from the university took major responsibility for the
planning.

Eleven subcommittees handled the key areas: finances, facilities, publicity and printing, rules and eligibility, recognition and awards, the Star Wars   37
competition, evaluation, and each of the selected academic areas: mathematics, language arts, social sciences, and the sciences.

Considerable time was devoted to preparing and validating the academic area tests and developing the various rules and procedures that teams   38
and coaches would follow.

Eighteen high schools from the seven participating districts met in the   39
spring of 1985 on the university campus for the full day of competition. Each
high school team included six members and three alternates who had been
selected for their knowledge and skills and who met the minimum grade
point distribution: two members with GPAs of 3.75 or above; two members
with GPAs of 3.0-3.74; two members with GPAs of 2.9 or lower. The three
alternates had to be distributed through the three ranges as well.

The grade point requirements were established to stimulate scholarship   40
among a broader range of students and to provide motivation for gifted but
low-achieving students to perform at higher academic levels.

After a morning of individual subject area tests and a luncheon, the   41
teams gathered for the Star Wars Competition, which is the culminating
competition for the Olympiad. In this event, the teams compete against each
other for team honors. The competition proceeds in six rounds of eight questions each, so each team member competes. The questions cover a wide range
of current events of state, regional, national, and international interest; mathematical problems; literary and historical figures, works, and events; scientific theories; etc.

Questions are given orally; students must respond in writing within 10   42
seconds. The correct answers are announced, and proctors keep a running
tally of each team's performance on large display boards so the audience and
teams can keep track of each team's status.

After the Star Wars competition, teams and individuals receive awards   43
ranging from scholarships, to individual winners in the various academic areas,
to trophies and plaques for team and school achievements. All team members
receive certificates of achievement. Coaches also receive awards based on their
teams' performances during the day.

No team goes home without substantial recognition. Press coverage is   44
extensive and cooperation from local newspapers and other media outlets has
been outstanding.

Since the 1985 event, the value of the prizes has escalated, particularly   45
in terms of scholarships, with academic departments at the university vying
to attract the students with the highest academic achievements during the
Olympiad.

Events like the Olympiad need not involve a large number of districts.   46
For instance, Wise County School District in Virginia conducts its own event
as part of the school system's Program of Academic Challenge for Excellence
(PACE).[3]

The Wise County program provides a year-long series of six academic   47
matches that culminate in an event similar to the Academic Olympiad. The
school district has discovered that this kind of competition attracts considerable interest and support from many taxpayers—over 73 percent in Wise
County—who do not have children in the schools but who are asked to
support the school's programs.

Wise County school officials also have discovered that interest in other   48
academic activities has increased to the point where the school system is adding special programs to meet the needs of its academically talented young
people.

In Kentucky an even more ambitious program has been underway since   49
1985. The Kentucky Academic Association (KAA) is a voluntary statewide
organization with two major functions: to establish and sponsor a statewide
system of academic competition and to monitor all competition in the state

and to assess its compliance with standards of educational soundness established by the association.

The association is governed by a 17-member board drawn from various geographic areas in the state as well as from professional organizations connected with the schools. The board sets policy and reviews the levels of academic competition in the state.   50

Any accredited public school in Kentucky as well as any private school that voluntarily complies with state accreditation standards and admission policies is eligible for membership in KAA. The Association offers three divisions for membership: high school (9-12), middle grades (6-8), and elementary (K-5). Schools pay nominal membership fees for each division in which they compete and are eligible to participate in all Association-sponsored competition held in the appropriate division.   51

The Association's main event is called the Governor's Cup Competition. It is a year-long, three-tiered (district, regional, and state) competition with those successful at one level advancing to the next. Four categories make up each level of the competition: 52

1. *Quick Recall*—teams of four students compete to provide factual answers to questions presented in a "college bowl" format.
2. *Creative Expression*—teams of four students work to solve a problem presented to them on the day of the competition.
3. *Written Assignment*—individual students take a written test in math, science, social studies, or language arts.
4. *English composition*—individual students are given a topic about which they must write a well-developed essay within a specified time.

A state champion is determined in each category (four champions in the written assessment category). In addition, the Association uses a point system to determine the school whose students collectively achieve the highest level of performance at the state level. That school receives the Governor's Cup. Any student of a member school is eligible to represent that school in the competition.   53

The Association also monitors each academic competition in Kentucky to be certain it meets the standards of educational quality that it feels all such competitions should achieve. The Association annually publishes a directory that lists all the approved academic competitions in the state. The directory also provides a calendar of events for all competitions, along with sponsors, locations, descriptions, and contact persons.[4]   54

Efforts such as the ones in Kentucky, Utah, and Virginia are being duplicated throughout the country. They clearly demonstrate that bringing the competitive edge to academic excellence results in respect and support for the basic mission of all schools: promoting academic potential and achievement among students.   55

References

1. Adapted from Melvin Zirkes and Robert Penna, "Academic Competitions—One Way To Improve School Climate." *NASSP Bulletin*, December 1984.

2. Varnell Bench and Oral L. Ballam, "Competition and Collaboration: An Academic Olympiad," *Phi Delta Kappan*, February 1986.

3. Ann Gregory and Jim D. Graham, "And Our Bonus-Round Question Is, 'Can Schools Spotlight Good Students?' " *The American School Board Journal*, August 1984.

4. For further information about the KAA, contact KAA, 1121 Louisville Road, Frankfort, Ky. 40601.

QUESTIONS FOR MEANING

1. Does Duke recommend the use of academic competition in any school? How could an administrator determine if an academic contest would be appropriate in her school?
2. What are the goals of an organized academic competition?
3. In paragraph 21, Duke recommends emphasizing "general awareness and problem-solving skills" because of "the nature of the public's current attitude toward education." What is he assuming about the public perception of education?
4. Does Duke recommend any steps to protect students from being injured by academic competition?
5. Vocabulary: permeates (2), feasibility (14), convergent (18), impetus (27), validating (38), proctors (42), accredited (51).

QUESTIONS ABOUT STRATEGY

1. How important is the competition inventory provided in paragraph 8? Was Duke right to devote so much space to it, or could he have simply referred readers to the article he cites in footnote number 1?
2. After discussing the Academic Olympiad sponsored by his own school, Utah State University, Duke goes on to discuss programs in Virginia and Kentucky. Is he losing his focus, or is there some reason for discussing these other programs?
3. Does Duke make any attempt to make academic competition seem like an appealing option for students who may not excel academically?
4. Duke claims that the programs he describes "demonstrate that bringing the competitive edge to academic excellence results in respect and support for the basic mission of all schools: promoting academic potential and achievement among students." Has his article provided enough evidence to support this claim?

Anthony R. Perry, Kevin M. Kane,
Kevin J. Bernesser, and Paul T. Spicker

Type A Behavior, Competitive Achievement-Striving, and Cheating Among College Students

Competition is often perceived as essential to academic success. But in their drive for success, are competitive students more likely to cheat? This is the question explored by a team of researchers at the University of Cincinnati, who published the follow-ing report of their findings in a **1990** *issue of* Psychological Reports. *As you read it, note that the authors divide their article into separate sections, following conven-tions common to publications in scholarly journals in the social and natural sciences. This article also provides another example of APA-style documentation.*

Summary.—The present study examined the cheating behavior in competitive and noncompetitive situations of 40 college students classified as Type A (16 women, 24 men) and 40 as Type B (19 women, 21 men). Type A-scoring students were more likely to cheat than Type B-scoring students irrespective of competition. The results suggest that in some situations, especially where ex-pectations for success cannot be met, Type A-scoring students may cheat to achieve success.

In the late 1950s, two cardiologists (Friedman & Rosenman, 1959) reported that the majority of their coronary heart disease patients showed a set of behavioral characteristics that they labeled the Type A behavior pattern. This purported relationship has generated considerable interest in recent years among both medical and psychological researchers. Clinical and epidemiological studies have demonstrated both prospectively and retrospectively that the Type A pattern is associated with at least twice the incidence of coronary heart disease relative to the noncoronary-prone pattern called Type B (Brand, 1978; Cooper, Detre, & Weiss, 1981; Friedman & Rosenman, 1974; Jenkins, Rosenman, & Zyzanski, 1974; Manuck, Kaplan, & Matthews, 1986; Matthews & Haynes, 1986). 1

Since it was first described by Friedman and Rosenman (1959), the Type A pattern has been characterized by extremes of impatience, aggressiveness and hostility, competitive achievement striving, and time urgency that are evoked by a variety of environmental situations (Glass, 1977, 1983; Kirmeyer & Biggers, 1988; Matthews, 1982). These major characteristics were captured in the following description of the Type A pattern provided by Friedman and Rosenman (1974): it is "an action-emotion complex that can be observed in any person who is aggressively involved in a chronic, incessant struggle to achieve more and more in less and less time, and if required to do so, against the opposing efforts of other things or other persons" (p. 67). 2

As the description suggests, competitive achievement-striving is an important component of the Type A pattern and has been viewed by some researchers as underlying the other characteristics (Carver & Humphries, 1982). For example, the Type A-scoring person's chronic sense of time urgency may be seen as growing out of an attempt to accomplish more and more in less time. The evidence for this orientation and its manifestations has come from a variety of sources. For example, several studies suggest that there is a relationship between the Type A pattern and measures of achievement motivation. Significant relationships have been found between scores on the student version of the Jenkins Activity Survey and scores on the Edwards (1957) measure of achievement motivation (see Glass, 1977). Matthews and Saal (1978) found no significant relationship between the Type A pattern and TAT measures of need for achievement. However, it should be noted that subjects who were very high in achievement motivation but who had little fear of failure also had high Type A scores on the Jenkins Survey. In a more recent investigation (Davis, Grover, Sadowski, Tramill, & Kleinhammer-Tramill, 1986), Type A scorers were shown to have a higher level of impact achievement motivation than Type B scorers, that is, Type A scorers reported being concerned with the effects of achievements rather than with the process of achieving.

Certainly, one would expect that having a positive psychological orientation toward achievement striving might result in greater actual achievement. There is, in fact, much evidence that supports this relationship. In an interview study of college students' Type A behavior and achievement striving conducted by Glass (1977), Type A-scoring students reported participating in more extracurricular activities, holding positions of leadership in these activities, and reported more academic honors in college than Type B-scoring students. A similar pattern, though nonsignificant, was also obtained for academic honors in high school. In addition, a greater proportion of Type A scorers reported being interested in subsequent graduate or professional school training as opposed to seeking employment immediately. Studies have also found relationships between Type A pattern and educational attainment as well as occupational and socioeconomic status (Mettlin, 1976; Waldron, 1978; Waldron, Zyzanski, Shekelle, Jenkins, & Tannenbaum, 1977).

Similarly, the Type A pattern has been related significantly to placing high importance on grades and achieving higher grades than Type B scorers in college. Grimm and Yarnold (1984) reported that Type A-scoring students set higher performance standards on college examinations than Type B scorers. In an investigation of physical attractiveness and academic achievement, Sparacino and Hansell (1979) found that Type A-scoring women reported higher GPAs and that study time was significantly related to their GPAs. Other studies have confirmed that Type A-scoring college students achieve higher academic success and report devoting more time to classes, studying, and academic and extracurricular activities than Type B scorers (Ovcharchyn, Johnson, & Petzel, 1981; Suls, Becker, & Mullen, 1981; Tang, 1988;

Waldron, Hickey, McPherson, Butensky, Gruss, Overall, Schmader, & Wohlmuth, 1980).

One question that arises from the research on the competitive achieve-   6
ment orientation of the Type A pattern is what strategies do they use in achieving their goals? In terms of academic success, the studies just described have shown Type A scorers to report they put forth greater effort than Type B scorers (e.g., devoting more time to studying). However, in some situations it may be that Type A scorers use other means to achieve their goals. Given their greater concern with success, it is possible that Type A scorers would be more likely to cheat to achieve success than Type B scorers. The present experiment examined this possibility among Type A- and Type B-scoring college students in both competitive and noncompetitive conditions. The method by which cheating was assessed was one in which subjects reporting higher than possible scores on a word-forming task were considered to have cheated. What was possible was judged by comparison with control groups treated identically except that the opportunity to cheat was eliminated, so cheating was not directly observed but was inferred probabilistically.

Method

Subjects   Subjects were 80 undergraduate students (40 women, 40 men) en-   7
rolled in introductory psychology courses at the University of Cincinnati who participated in exchange for course credit. Subjects' ages ranged from 18 to 27 yr., with a mean of 19.2 yr.

Materials   Form C of the Jenkins Activity Survey (Jenkins, Zyzanski, &   8
Rosenman, 1979) was administered to all subjects to measure Type A behavior. The experimental task was a word-forming task similar to that used by Cooper and Peterson (1980). On each of five cards (3- × 5-in.) were seven uppercase black letters. The letters on the cards (in the order of appearance) were (1) SGADBEE, (2) ODIFICL, (3) ETKPLAD, (4) KLOITWN, and (5) NAIGEVC.

Procedure   Prior to the experimental session, subjects were identified as   9
scoring either Type A or Type B estimated by a median split of the Jenkins Activity Survey scores ($Mdn = 247.5$, Type A scores ranged from 259 to 383, Type B scores ranged from 76 to 236). Subjects were than randomly assigned to one of the experimental conditions. During the experimental session the experimenter was unaware of the subjects' behavior pattern classification. Upon their arriving for the experimental session, the experimenter explained the word-forming task to the subjects. Subjects were told they would be given five cards, on each were seven randomly selected letters. Working with the letters on one card at a time, subjects were to use the letters to write down as many words as possible. Points were awarded for the number of letters used in each word; 2 points were given for a two-letter word, 3 points for a three-letter word, and so on. There was a time limit of 30 sec. per card.

In the no-competition groups, subjects participated individually. They   10
were told, "A score of 26.5 points per card is average for college students.
Try to score as many points as you can." In reality, pilot data★ and previous
research (Cooper & Peterson, 1980) showed that such a score was out of the
range in which subjects could be expected to score. In the competition groups,
subjects were tested in pairs. They were told, "A score of 26.5 points per
card is average for college students. The other person is your opponent. Try
to outscore him." For subjects in the groups without opportunity to cheat
(control groups), the experimenter scored the words. For subjects in the groups
with opportunity to cheat, the experimenter instructed the subjects to score
the words themselves and turn in their scores at the end of the session. Subjects were told they could keep the words they produced or throw them
away so subjects could cheat by employing inadmissible words and/or adding points to their scores.

Results

Preliminary analysis indicated the absence of sex differences; accordingly, these   11
data were pooled across sex of subjects for the subsequent analyses. Means
and standard deviations on the word-forming task were determined for each
subject in each experimental condition and are shown in Table 1.

A $2 \times 2 \times 2$ between-groups analysis of variance with the factors of be-   12
havior pattern (Type A, Type B), competition (yes, no), and opportunity to
cheat (yes, no) was computed on the word-forming scores. The analysis of
these data indicated significant main effects for the behavior pattern ($F_{1.72} = 8.18$,
$p < .006$, $\eta^2 = .07$) and for the opportunity to cheat ($F_{1.72} = 18.34$, $p < .0002$,
$\eta^2 = .17$). The two-way interaction between behavior pattern and opportunity to cheat was also significant ($F_{1.72} = 5.81$, $p < .02$, $\eta^2 = .06$). The significant main effects are best interpreted by the significant two-way interaction,
which showed that Type A-scoring students given the opportunity to cheat
scored significantly higher than Type A-scoring students given no opportunity to cheat or Type B scorers with or without the opportunity to cheat
($p < .05$) by the Tukey *HSD* procedure (Hays, 1981).

Discussion

The present investigation was designed to examine the possibility that   13
Type A-scoring individuals would be more likely to cheat to achieve success
than Type B-scoring students. This possibility was confirmed in a situation
in which subjects performed a word-forming task and were either given or
not given an opportunity to cheat. Results showed that Type A-scoring individuals were indeed more likely to cheat when they had the opportunity to

---

★Pilot data were collected from 5 graduate students and 5 undergraduate students enrolled at the
University of Cincinnati. The mean score on the word-forming task for this group was 14.6
(no competition, no opportunity to cheat).

TABLE 1
Mean Scores on Word-forming Task

GROUP	NO COMPETITION		COMPETITION	
	M	*SD*	*M*	*SD*
Type A Behavior Pattern				
Opportunity to Cheat	18.44	2.33	20.12	2.36
No Opportunity	13.78	4.80	14.04	2.24
Type B Behavior Pattern				
Opportunity to Cheat	14.60	3.98	15.50	4.74
No Opportunity	13.26	4.41	13.84	2.40

Note.—Higher scores are associated with greater cheating in the opportunity to cheat conditions.

do so, regardless of whether they competed against another person or performed alone.

Although cheating was not observed directly, several lines of research support the hypothesis that Type A-scoring students are more likely to cheat in some situations when given the opportunity. For example, Johnson (1981) showed that individuals with high achievement motivation are more likely than individuals with low achievement motivation to cheat on college examinations. Since this characteristic appears to be one of the central components of the Type A behavior pattern (Carver & Humphries, 1982; Matthews, 1982), it is logical to assume that Type A-scoring students would also be more likely to cheat to achieve success. In addition, Perry (1986) found that Type A-scoring students were more likely to violate traffic laws and consequently received more tickets for driving violations than Type B scorers. 14

It may be that, when Type A-scoring students are in situations in which their expectations for success cannot be reached by exerting additional effort, they will use other means. The present investigation provided such a situation. The expectation or success on the word-forming task was not possible given the time constraint. However, when Type A scorers were given the opportunity to cheat, they reported word-forming scores that were significantly higher than those of Type A scorers who were not given the opportunity to cheat. If cheating did not occur on the word-forming task, no difference should have been found between those groups. 15

In summary, a range of studies have shown that Type A-scoring individuals are more achievement-oriented than their Type B-scoring peers. Normally, Type A-scorers believe that by exerting sufficient effort they can overcome obstacles and reach their goals. The present findings suggest that in some situations Type A-scoring students may use other means for achieving success especially when their expectations cannot be met simply by putting forth greater effort. 16

References

Brand, R. J. (1978). Coronary-prone behavior as an independent risk factor for coronary heart disease. In T. M. Dembroski, S. M. Weiss, J. L. Shields, S. G. Haynes, & M. Feinleib (Eds.), Coronary-prone behavior. (pp. 11–24) New York: Springer-Verlag.

Carver, C. S., & Humphries, C. (1982). Social psychology and the Type A coronary-prone behavior pattern. In G. S. Sanders & J. Suls (Eds.), Social psychology of health and illness. Hillsdale, NJ: Erlbaum. (pp. 33–64).

Cooper, S., & Peterson, C. (1980). Machiavellianism and spontaneous cheating in competition. Journal of Research in Personality, 14, 70–75.

Cooper, T., Detre, T., & Weiss, S. (1981). Coronary prone behavior and coronary heart disease: a critical review. Circulation, 63, 1199–1215.

Davis, S. F., Grover, C. A., Sadowski, C. J., Tramill, J. L., & Kleinhammer-Tramill, P. J. (1986). The relationship between the Type A behavior pattern and process versus impact achievement motivation. Bulletin of the Psychonomic Society, 24, 441–443.

Edwards, A. L. (1957). Manual for the Edwards Personal Preference Schedule. New York: Psychological Corp.

Friedman, M., & Rosenman, R. H. (1959). Association of specific overt behavior pattern with blood and cardiovascular findings. Journal of the American Medical Association, 159, 1286–1296.

Friedman, M., & Rosenman, R. H. (1974). Type A behavior and your heart. New York: Knopf.

Glass, D. C. (1977). Behavior patterns, stress, and coronary disease. Hillsdale, NJ: Erlbaum.

Glass, D. C. (1983). Behavioral, cardiovascular, and neuroendocrine responses. International Review of Applied Psychology, 32, 137–151.

Grimm, L. G., & Yarnold, P. R. (1984). Performance standards and the Type A behavior pattern. Cognitive Therapy and Research, 8, 59–66.

Hays, W. L. (1981). Statistics. (3rd ed.) New York: Holt, Rinehart & Winston.

Jenkins, C. D., Rosenman, R. H., & Zyzanski, S. J. (1974). Prediction of clinical heart disease by a test for the coronary-prone behavior pattern. New England Journal of Medicine, 290, 1271–1275.

Jenkins, C. D., Zyzanski, S. J., & Rosenman, R. H. (1979). Manual for the Jenkins Activity Survey. New York: Psychological Corp.

Johnson, P. B. (1981). Achievement motivation and success: Does the end justify the means? Journal of Personality and Social Psychology, 40, 374–375.

Kirmeyer, S. L., & Biggers, K. (1988). Environmental demand and demand engendering behavior: an observational analysis of the Type A pattern. Journal of Personality and Social Psychology, 54, 997–1005.

Manuck, S. B., Kaplan, J. R., & Matthews, K. A. (1986). Behavioral antecedents of coronary heart disease and atherosclerosis. Arteriosclerosis, 6, 2–14.

Matthews, K. A. (1982). Psychological perspectives on the Type A behavior pattern. Psychological Bulletin, 91, 293–323.

Matthews, K. A., & Haynes, S. G. (1986). Type A behavior pattern and coronary risk: Update and evaluation. American Journal of Epidemiology, 123, 923–960.

Matthews, K. A., & Saal, F. E. (1978). The relationship of the Type A coronary-prone behavior pattern to achievement, power, and affiliation motives. Psychosomatic Medicine, 40, 631–636.

Mettlin, C. (1976). Occupational careers and the prevention of coronary-prone behavior. Social Sciences and Medicine, 10, 367–372.

Ovcharchyn, C. A., Johnson, H. H., & Petzel, T. P. (1981). Type A behavior, academic aspirations, and academic success. Journal of Personality, 49, 248–256.

Perry, A. R. (1986). Type A behavior and motor vehicle drivers' behavior. *Perceptual and Motor Skills, 63,* 875–878.

Sparacino, J., & Hansell, S. (1979). Physical attractiveness and academic performance: Beauty is not always talent. *Journal of Personality, 47,* 449–469.

Suls, J., Becker, M. A., & Mullen, B. (1981). Coronary-prone behavior, social insecurity and stress among college-aged adults. *Journal of Human Stress, 7,* 27–34.

Tang, T. L. (1988). Effects of Type A personality and leisure ethic on Chinese college students' leisure activities and academic performance. *Journal of Social Psychology, 128,* 153–164.

Waldron, I. (1978). Sex differences in the coronary-prone behavior pattern. In T. M. Dembroski, S. M. Weiss, J. L. Shields, S. G. Haynes, & M. Feinleib (Eds.), *Coronary-prone behavior.* (pp. 199–205) New York: Springer-Verlag.

Waldron, I., Hickey, A., McPherson, C., Butensky, A., Gruss, L., Overall, K., Schmader, A., & Wohlmuth, D. (1980). Type A behavior pattern: Relationship to variation in blood pressure, parental characteristics, and academic and social activities of students. *Journal of Human Stress, 6,* 16–27.

Waldron, I., Zyzanski, S. J., Shekelle, R. B., Jenkins, C. D., & Tannenbaum, S. (1977). The coronary-prone behavior pattern in employed men and women. *Journal of Human Stress, 3,* 2–19.

QUESTIONS FOR MEANING

1. What is the difference between Type A and Type B behavior patterns? What are some of the characteristics of Type A personalities?
2. Do people with the Type A behavior pattern enjoy any benefits? Are they at risk in any way?
3. How were students chosen to participate in the experiments described in this article?
4. How were the researchers able to infer that cheating had taken place even though it was not directly observed?
5. Vocabulary: prospectively (1), retrospectively (1), incessant (2), mean (7), constraint (15).

QUESTIONS ABOUT STRATEGY

1. What advantage is there to dividing an article like this into separate sections? What is the function of paragraphs 1–6?
2. How accurate is the summary that precedes this article? Could you make it any shorter?
3. This article was written for a professional audience with training in psychology. At what points, if any, did you have difficulty following it? How would you describe the authors' prose style?
4. Consider the author's list of references. How does it influence your evaluation of their work?

D. STANLEY EITZEN

The Dark Side of Competition
in American Society

*A 1956 graduate of Bethel College, David Stanley Eitzen returned there to give
the following speech in **1989**. Editor of* Social Science Journal *from 1978–84, he
is a sociology professor at Colorado State University. His many books include* Social Structure and Social Problems *(1974),* Sociology of American Sport
(1978), Diversity in American Families *(1987), and* Crime in the Streets and
Crime in the Suites: Perspectives on Crime and Criminal Justice *(1989).
"The Dark Side of Competition in American Society" is reprinted from* Vital
Speeches of the Day.

Some believe that competition is the behavioral equivalent of gravity, a nat-   1
ural and inevitable force. A student in one of my classes once remarked that
he was very competitive but that no one had ever taught him to be that way.
His argument was that competition is part of the DNA of the animal and
human worlds, with the best surviving. This is the credo of the Social Darwinists—that is, as people vie for a prize, honor, advantage, space, sex, or
whatever, excellence is rewarded, and progress is achieved. In the process,
the best minds and the best bodies win and rise to the top while the less able
lose and sink to the bottom. This logic has been used to justify social inequality with the able seen as deserving of their rewards and the failures
deserving of their lesser fate. This school of thought was prevalent in the
United States around the turn of the century and remnants are found today,
in the White House and Congress, sometimes in editorials, always among
racists, and even occasionally by academicians.

My argument is that if competition is "natural" among the human spe-   2
cies, so, too, is cooperation. Stated more strongly, I argue that cooperation
is more critical to human progress and to get the things we want than competition. A sports team composed of competitive individuals without teamwork is, by definition, relatively ineffective. The most notable human
accomplishments, such as the building of railroads or cathedrals, the forming
of a constitution, the damming of mighty rivers, and the overturning of
tyranny by a Gandhi or a Martin Luther King, Jr., are monuments to cooperative behavior.

My goal in this presentation is to analyze competition, this most central   3
value of American society, focusing on its negative consequences. I'll conclude by presenting some alternatives.

The Pervasiveness of Competition

Recall my student who said that no one ever taught him to be competitive.   4
Well, I believe that he was so immersed in a competitive environment that

he could not see it, just like a fish doesn't understand water because it does not know anything different. Let me elaborate.

Parents instill competition in their children at a young age. There is   5
evidence that first-borns tend to be more bowlegged than later-borns. I do not know the explanation for this but one possibility is that parents are so interested in showing off the prowess of their parenting *and* their progeny that they force their first child to walk earlier than they should. Having proven their point, parents are less demanding of later borns, at least with early walking. At a more blatant level, some parents enter their children in "diaper derbies" (crawling races for those under one year), beauty contests, baton twirling contests, and the like. Others enroll their preschoolers in music lessons, ballet lessons, swimming lessons, and other efforts to give their children a head start in the competitive world.

At the elementary school level, there are spelling contests, selection of   6
soloists or actors on the basis of tryouts, ability grouping based on test performance, and so on. Outside of school, there are community-sponsored competitions for the very young, such as in Florida where boys age five play tackle football for a three-and-one-half month season. Adults have organized triathalons (where the contestants participate in a three-part race involving swimming, bicycling, and running) for children as young as seven. The Cub Scouts have one event that epitomizes the American emphasis on competition—the Pinewood Derby. Each scout is given a block of wood and some wheels, from which they are to create a model racing car. Each scout (and his father, no doubt) works at making the fastest car. At the big event, of course, there is only one winner with the rest of the pack losers. Such an event is very American.

During the junior high and senior high school years, youth are exposed   7
even more to competition. At school, there is grading on the curve, trying out for athletic teams, cheerleader, debate, acting roles, competing for valedictorian, acceptance in top colleges, and intense competition for first chair for each instrument in band and orchestra. Outside of school there are community-based sports, including age-group swimming, elite music groups, beauty and talent contests, 4-H judging, and other forms of competition. An egregious example is the "punt, pass, and kick" contest sponsored by Ford Motor Company. In this contest, winners are selected at the local level and proceed through the various state and regional tournaments until a winner is found for each age category. In one year, there were 1,112,702 entrants in this contest and only six eventual winners. An interesting question is why an organization such as Ford would sponsor an event with six winners and 1,112,696 losers? This, too, is very American.

At the adult level, life is often a zero–sum situation where one wins at   8
the expense of others. The business world in a capitalist society, of course, is highly competitive (except among the large corporations where parallel pricing, shared monopolies, and government subsidies reduce competition substantially). At work, employees compete for limited promotions and salary raises. At my university, for example, each academic department ranks

its members from "best" to "worst" and the yearly raises are divided accordingly. One year the philosophy department refused to participate in this exercise, arguing that its members were uniformly excellent. The dean insisted that the faculty must be ranked or else no monies would be allocated to the department. Once again, this type of motivational scheme is very American

Even during leisure, many, if not most Americans engage in competitions, involving all manner of sports, participation in fantasy sports leagues, tryouts for community plays, music groups, gambling, art contests, county fair competitions for best quilt or pickles, and such competitions as the "Pillsbury Bakeoff," and "Mrs. USA." Finally, competition even intrudes into our most intimate of relationships. In families, there are sibling rivalries, parent-child competition, and even efforts by spouses (or lovers) to outdo the other. Eric Berne, the transactional analyst, wrote of the various "games people play" in relationships. One of those "games" employed even among lovers, he called, if you'll excuse his language, "Now, I've got you, you son of a bitch." Isn't it curious, that people in love would find themselves engaged in behaviors that elevate themselves by diminishing their partners.

The Positive Consequences of Competition

I'm sure that we are quite familiar with the arguments supporting competition, so I will merely list them. The two most common reasons given for competition are that it is a strong motivator and it pushes everyone to strive for excellence. These qualities have led American society to greater societal achievements in productivity than found in less competitive societies. This emphasis on competition and its justification of inequality, of course, fit nicely with capitalism.

The Negative Consequences of Competition

I am going to overlook the more obvious negative consequences of a highly competitive society such as war, the arms race, and imperialism. Similarly, I will not consider here the negative behaviors of corporations in a highly competitive environment such as fraud, misleading advertising, cheating, and the like. These are very important and I have written a book about these political and economic misadventures. Rather, I will focus here on the more subtle negative results of competition, ones that we might be more likely to miss.

One negative impact of the emphasis on competition is that it is unhealthy for individuals. In 1988 over $1 billion was spent in the United States for one drug—Zantac—which combats ulcers. Surely a major source of ulcers is the stress we face daily in our competitive environments. Similarly, those of us who are "Type A" are competitive, combative, impatient, overscheduled, teethgrinders. "Type B" people, in contrast, are relaxed, without a sense of urgency, and tolerant. They say the equivalent of "que pasa" a lot. With no expertise on this, I can only speculate that while the boundaries of temperament are encoded genetically, a competitive environment brings out the worst in Type A persons, which heightens their tendency for high blood pressure, stroke, and heart disease. These same people living in a less driven culture likely would live longer.

Another problem with competition is that, by definition, people are sorted into a very few "winners" and many "losers." What is the effect on a youngster's self-esteem when he or she is "cut" from the basketball team or when she or he rarely gets to play in games? What is the level of motivation for a junior high school student who is twenty-third chair flute in the school band? Will she or he strive ever more to achieve in music or give up?

When competition supersedes other values, it may be dysfunctional for the participants and even society. Several years ago, an experiment was made comparing ten-year-olds in the United States and Mexico. This experiment involved a marble-pull game. The investigator told pairs of children that they could obtain prizes by playing the game. The object of the game was for each player to pull a string that manipulated a marble holder so that the marble would drop into a goal at their end of the table. However, if both children pulled on their strings at the same time, the marble holder would break apart and neither child could win a prize. The children soon figured out that they could engage in a tug-of-war where no one would win or they could cooperate and take turns winning prizes. The Anglo-American children tended to choose the former route which meant no one won, while the Mexican children opted for the latter, where they shared prizes. Now which response was the more rational? My interpretation is that the American youth were possessed with an irrational competitive spirit that was dysfunctional. Let me give another illustration of how competition can have irrational consequences, this time looking at medical students. Norman Cousins, an especially keen observer of American life, has criticized the process whereby students are selected for and graduate from medical school. He says:

> [Since admission to medical schools is so competitive, grades have become] the most tangible measure on which the school can base its admission decisions. Grades may be an indication of ability to learn, but when they make students fiercely competitive, the end product is not necessarily good scholarship but more often a sharpening of academic predatory skills. . . . It is important to ask whether we really want to foster a barracuda psychology for young people who will have to carry the responsibility for maintaining the health and well-being of the American people. Do we really want them to be trained in an atmosphere that sharpens their teeth even more than it develops their minds?

When winning is the primary standard for evaluation, several negative outcomes result. Let me enumerate these, using sport for examples. First, in a competitive society there is a tendency to evaluate people by their accomplishments rather than their character, personality, and other human qualities. When "winning is everything," then losers are considered just that. One successful university basketball coach once counseled prospective coaches that if they wanted to be winners, then they should associate only with winners. Is this an appropriate guiding principle for conducting our lives?

Second, when winning is paramount, schools and communities orga- 16 nize sports for the already gifted. This elitist approach means that the few will be given the best equipment, the best coaching, and prime time reserved for their participation, while the less able will be denied participation altogether or given very little attention. If sports participation is a useful activity, then it should be for the many, not the few, in my view.

A third problem with the emphasis on winning is that parents may 17 push their children beyond the normal to succeed. Two examples make this point. Is it appropriate behavior for parents to hire a swimming coach for their twenty-two month old daughter, one who has the girl swim one-fourth of a mile three times a week, switching to one-half a mile three times a week when she turned two? This happened for a California youngster in 1980. The parents' goal is for this youngster to be an Olympic champion in 1992. In 1972 the national record for one-year-olds in the mile run was established by Steve Parsons of Normal, Illinois (the time was 24:16.6). Are these instances of child abuse or what?

A fourth problem with the primacy of winning is that coaches may 18 push their charges too hard. Coaches may be physically or emotionally abusive. They may limit their players' civil rights. And, they may play their injured athletes by using pain killers without regard for their long-term physical well-being.

Fifth, when the desire to win is so great, the "end may justify the means." 19 Coaches and players may use illegal tactics. Athletes may use performance enhancing drugs such as steroids and amphetamines to achieve a "competitive edge" or more subtly, but nonetheless unethical, using such means as blood doping or getting pregnant to get positive hormonal changes, and then having an abortion. Both of these practices occur among endurance athletes. As we all know, big-time college coaches in their zeal to win have been found guilty of exploiting athletes, falsifying transcripts, providing illegal payments, hiring surrogate test takers, paying athletes for nonexistent summer jobs, and illegally using government Pell grants and work study monies for athletes. So much, I would argue, for the myth that "sport builds character."

Sixth, when winning is all important, there may be a tendency to crush 20 the opposition. This was the case when Riverside Poly High School girls basketball team played Norte Vista several years ago. Riverside won by a score of 179–15 with one player, Cheryl Miller, scoring a California record of 105 points. Was the Riverside coach ethical? I think not. Moreover, what were the consequences of his actions on his team and on the players and community of Norte Vista? Will the Norte Vista girls be motivated to improve their performance or will this humiliating experience crush their spirit?

Seventh, many people in a competitive society have difficulty with 21 coming in second. In 1986, Kathy Ormsby, an excellent student and an All-American distance runner at North Carolina State, veered off the track during a race, ran away from the stadium and jumped off a bridge, suffering, as a result, a life-long paralysis. I can only speculate on her motives. I suspect that losing was so abjectly appalling to her that she could fathom no alternative but to end her life. This is an extreme example but it illustrates the intolerance some of us have for losers, even those who came close to winning. Let me illustrate this point with two examples. The Denver Broncos have made it to the Super Bowl three times but they have lost that big game each time. In the minds of the Bronco players, fans, as well as others across the United States, the Broncos were losers in each of those years even though they were second out of twenty-eight teams, which, if you think about it, is not too shabby an accomplishment. My other illustration involves a football team, composed of fifth-graders, in Florida. They were undefeated going into the state finals but lost there in a close game. At a banquet following that season each player on this team was given a plaque on which was inscribed a quote from Vince Lombardi:

> There is no room for second place. I have finished second twice at Green Bay and I never want to finish second again. There is a second place bowl game but it is a game for losers played by losers. It is and always has been an American zeal to be first in anything we do and to win and to win and to win.

In other words, the parents and coaches of these boys wanted them to 2never be satisfied with being second. Second is losing. The only acceptable placement is first.

Finally, when "winning is the only thing" the joy in participation is 2lost. I have observed that organized sports from youth programs to the professional level is mostly devoid of playfulness. When the object is to win, then the primacy of the activity is lost. In this vein, America's premier cross country skier, Bill Koch, has said:

> If 100 people enter a race that means there have to be 99 losers. The worst thing that you can teach children is that so many of them will be losers. Because then they won't even try. It's the striving, the attempt, the fight, that's the important thing.

In other words, it's the process that is primary, not the outcome. White water rafters and mountain climbers understand this. So, too, do players in a pickup touch football game. Why can't the rest of us figure out this fundamental truth?

Alternatives

I am not naive enough to think that we can eliminate competition in Amer- 24ican society. We will not become like the Hopi or the Zuni. Competition is built into the fabric of our society. I must admit, too, that I like competition, I thrive on it. But the problems inherent in competition bother me. I would like to find alternatives that would eliminate or at least diminish some of these problems. Let me provide a few possibilities for you to consider as you form families, become active in communities, and establish yourself in occupations.

Can we improve our competitive environment? I suggest that we shift from a competitive reward structure to an individualistic reward structure. The former is what we have—a system that rewards participants in relation to their competitors, such as grading on a curve or crowning a single winner. An individualistic reward structure, on the other hand, rewards individuals as they measure up to some absolute standard. The striving for excellence is still there but the number of winners is limitless. Grading according to a percentage is one example. Karate provides an excellent example as competitors strive to master different levels of achievement as symbolized by different colored belts. In my department in a research university, faculty members receive annual merit raises based mostly on the number of articles and books they publish annually. This system rewards the most prolific individual the most. Why can't we have a reward system based on a standard, which says that everyone who publishes at least one article a year in a refereed journal is judged as "excellent"? Those that publish one article every other year would be classified as "very good," and rewarded accordingly. Such a plan would encourage everyone in the department to be active scholars. The current system, in contrast, discourages some because they will never be labeled "excellent" and rewarded for that achievement. I believe that the department and individual faculty members suffer from our current practice.

The number of winners can also be maximized by rewarding different skills. Suppose, for example, that we engage in a two-mile race. Who might the winner be? In our society, the winner would be established by whomever is the fastest. But Gandhi said that "there is more to life than increasing its speed." Why not reward those who come closest to predicting their finishing time? Or, how about rewarding form, with judges evaluating the stride, arm swing, posture, and pelvic tilt of the runners? How about rewarding everyone who established a personal best? Why not have a number of categories with winners determined for each?

What about removing sports competition from schools? Schools in many European countries, for example, do not have sports. There are sports clubs in the community but the schools stay out of it, leaving the school day for education and not for the defeat of enemies on Friday evenings. This would free the facilities and equipment for maximum use by the students, not just the elite.

Let me conclude with a special example from the Special Olympics. A friend of mine observed a 200 meter race among three evenly matched 12-year-olds at a Special Olympics event in Colorado Springs. About twenty-five yards from the finish line, one of the contestants fell. The other two runners stopped and helped their competitor to his feet, brushed him off, and jogged together hand in hand to the finish line, ending the race in a three-way tie. The actions of these three, especially the two who did not fall, are unAmerican. Perhaps because they were retarded, they did not understand the importance of winning in our society. To them, the welfare of their opponent was primary. Can we learn this lesson from the retarded? My message is that the successful life involves the pursuit of excellence, a fundamental respect for others, even one's competitors, and enjoyment in the process. Competition as structured in our society with its emphasis on the outcome undermines these goals. I enjoin you to be thoughtful about the role of competition in your life and how it might be restructured to maximize humane goals.

QUESTIONS FOR MEANING

1. How does Eitzen define "Social Darwinists," and how do their beliefs relate to the idea of competition?
2. How could sports programs become elitist?
3. What does Eitzen imply about Native Americans such as the Hopi and Zuni?
4. What does Eitzen mean by an "individual reward structure"? Can you think of any other examples similar to those in paragraph 26?
5. Vocabulary: progeny (5), egregious (7), imperialism (11), encoded (12), dysfunctional (14), abjectly (21), fathom (21).

QUESTIONS ABOUT STRATEGY

1. Where does Eitzen first state his thesis? Where does he explain his purpose? Why might explicit statements like these be especially useful in a speech?
2. In paragraph 12, Eitzen admits to speculating upon a topic about which he has no expertise. How does this affect his credibility?
3. Consider the examples in paragraph 17. How does Eitzen expect readers to answer the question with which that paragraph ends?
4. Consider the use of "may" in paragraphs 17–20. Does it leave Eitzen open to counterargument?
5. At the end of paragraph 19, Eitzen implies that he has demolished "the myth that 'sports builds character.' " Has he?
6. How convincing are the alternatives suggested in paragraphs 27 and 28?

ALFIE KOHN
Incentives Can Be Bad for Business

A lecturer and writer in Cambridge, Massachusetts, Alfie Kohn has emerged as a leading critic of competition. He is the author of No Contest: The Case Against Competition *(1986) and* The Brighter Side of Human Nature: Altruism & Empathy in Everyday Life *(1990). His views on competition have also appeared in* The Humanist, Change, Psychology Today, The Los Angeles Times, Educational Leadership, New Age Journal, *and* INC. *magazine, which published the following article in* **1988.** *You will find that it has a slightly different focus from the other readings in this section, but that Kohn links his argument on incentive plans to the broader question of competition in the workplace.*

Whether they know it or not, most executives are Skinnerians. It was Harvard psychologist B. F. Skinner who popularized the theory of reinforcement, which holds that presenting a reward after a desired behavior will make that behavior more likely to occur in the future. To our pets we say, "Good dog!" and offer a biscuit. To our employees we say, "Good job!" and offer a performance bonus.   1

It seems to make sense. But research has been accumulating that shows   2
tangible rewards as well as praise can actually lower the level of performance, particularly in jobs requiring creativity. Study after study has shown that intrinsic interest in a task—the sense that something is worth doing for its own sake—typically declines when someone is given an external reason for doing it.

Author and sociologist Philip Slater put it starkly in his book *Wealth*   3
Addiction: "Getting people to chase money . . . produces nothing except people chasing money. Using money as a motivator leads to a progressive degradation in the quality of everything produced."

The problem is not with money per se, which most of us find desirable.   4
Rather, it is the fact that waving dollar bills in front of people leads them to think of themselves as doing work *only* for the reward. Performance tends to suffer as a result.

In one study, Teresa M. Amabile, associate professor of psychology at   5
Brandeis University, asked 72 creative writers to write some poetry. She gave one group of subjects a list of extrinsic reasons for writing, such as impressing teachers and making money, and asked them to think about their own writing with respect to those reasons. She showed others a list of intrinsic reasons: the enjoyment of playing with words, for example, and satisfaction from self-expression. A third group was not given any list. All were then asked to do more writing.

The results were clear. Those given the extrinsic reasons not only wrote   6
less creatively than the others, as judged by 12 independent poets, but the

quality of their work dropped significantly after this brief exposure to the extrinsic reasons.

This effect, according to other studies, is by no means limited to poets.   7
When young tutors were promised free movie tickets for teaching well, they took longer to communicate ideas, got frustrated more easily, and did a poorer job in the end than those who got nothing. In another study, a group of subjects who contracted in advance for a reward made less creative collages and told less inventive stories. Students who were offered a reward for participating in still another experiment not only did more poorly at a creative task, but also failed to memorize as well as the subjects who received no reward.

What's going on here? The experts offer three explanations for such   8
findings, and all of them have important implications for managers.

First, rewards encourage people to focus narrowly on a task, to do it as   9
quickly as possible, and to take few risks. "If they feel, 'This is something I have to get through to get the prize,' they're going to be less creative," says Amabile. The more emphasis placed on the reward, the more inclined someone will be to do the minimum necessary to get it. And that means lower-quality work.

The very fact of turning a task into a means for attaining something   10
else changes the way that task is perceived, as a clever series of experiments by Mark R. Lepper, a professor of psychology at Stanford University, demonstrated. He told a group of children that they could not engage in one activity they liked until they took part in another. Although they had enjoyed both activities equally, the children came to dislike the task that was a prerequisite for the other.

Second, extrinsic rewards can erode intrinsic interest. People who come   11
to see themselves as working for money or approval find their tasks less pleasurable and therefore do not do them as well. "Money may work to 'buy off' one's intrinsic motivation for an activity," says Edward L. Deci, a professor of psychology at the University of Rochester and a leading authority on the subject.

What's true of money is also true of competition, which, contrary to   12
myth, is nearly always counterproductive (see "No Contest," *Managing People*, November 1987). Deci put 80 subjects to work on a spatial-relations puzzle, and he asked some to solve it more quickly than those sitting next to them. Then each of the subjects sat alone—but secretly observed—in a room that contained a similar puzzle. It turned out that those who had been competing spent less time working on the task voluntarily—and later told Deci they found it less interesting—compared with those who didn't have to compete. The external prod of winning a contest, like that of a bonus, makes a task seem less enjoyable in its own right. Not surprisingly, what's seen as less enjoyable is usually done less well.

But there is a third reason that the use of external motivators can back-   13
fire. People come to see themselves as being controlled by a reward. They feel less autonomous, and this often interferes with performance.

There's no shortage of data showing that a feeling of freedom translates   14
into happier and more productive employees. In 1983–84, Amabile and Stan
Gryskiewicz, of the Center for Creative Leadership, in Greensboro, N.C.,
interviewed 120 research-and-development scientists, asking each to describe
one event from their work experience that exemplified high creativity and
one that reflected low creativity. The factor they mentioned most often, by
far, was freedom or its absence. Receiving a clear overall direction on a project is useful, the scientists said, but they worked best when they could decide
for themselves how to accomplish those goals.

Rewards are often offered in a controlling way, and to that extent, says   15
Deci's colleague Richard Ryan, they stifle productivity. He emphasizes the
enormous difference between saying, "I'm giving you this reward because I
recognize the value of your work," and "You're getting this reward because
you've lived up to my standards." Likewise for verbal feedback: the question
isn't whether you give enough of it, or even how positive it is. What matters
is how controlling the person perceives it to be.

This point was made in a study conducted by Deci, Ryan, and James   16
Connell. From questionnaires completed by several hundred workers in a
corporation that manufactured business machines, they found that those who
worked for controlling managers were less satisfied with their jobs and more
concerned with pay and benefits. The attitude seemed to be, "If you're going
to control me, I'm going to be alienated, and what I'm going to focus on is
money." In a related laboratory study, Ryan found that when subjects were
praised, told in effect, "Good, you're doing as you should," instead of simply letting them know how well they had done, motivation was low.

Does all this mean that employees should be paid less or ignored when   17
they do good work? Definitely not. Is it an argument for scrapping incentive
plans? Probably not. What the research indicates is that all incentive
systems—along with verbal feedback—should be guided by two clear principles. Higher-quality work, particularly on jobs requiring creative thinking,
is more likely to occur when a person focuses on the challenge of the
task itself, rather than on some external motivator, and feels a sense of
self-determination, as opposed to feeling controlled by means of praise or
reward.

Practically speaking, this means that incentives announced in advance   18
are more likely to undermine performance than are unexpected bonuses that
recognize an outstanding job after the fact. Particularly deadly are incentive
programs run as contests in which some teams (or individuals) will not receive bonuses no matter how well they perform. Managers need to consider
the impact of any incentive payment on the workers who *don't* receive it—
another hidden cost of rewards.

Provided these conditions are met—and everyone feels the system for   19
awarding bonuses is fair—incentives may not be harmful. But a supportive
workplace, one in which workers are allowed autonomy and are not only
informed about company goals but help determine them, may not even need
incentive systems.

The larger point is that innovation cannot be forced but only allowed   20
to happen. You can help create the conditions that allow it by playing down
the significance of rewards and playing up what employees find appealing
about the task itself. Effective supervisors take care of their subordinates'
financial needs but don't make a big deal about money and its relationship to
performance. Instead, they concentrate on the most powerful motivator that
exists: the intrinsic interest people have in solving problems. People are most
interested when their curiosity is aroused—when discrepancies exist between
what they thought was true and what they've just encountered—and when
they are challenged by a task that's neither so difficult as to be overwhelming
nor so simple as to be boring.

What's more, employees should be matched with the kind of work that   21
they find interesting. "In hiring we almost never look at intrinsic motivation," Amabile observes of most organizations. Yet having someone work
on the sort of problem to which he or she is naturally attracted is likely to
produce better results than using some artificial means to boost performance.

Of course, some tasks are universally regarded as dull. In these cases,   22
the idea is to get people to internalize the importance of doing them—to
transform external reasons into internal incentive. Deci and his colleagues
have recently turned their attention to this problem. Their findings suggest
that a manager should acknowledge that the task is boring, explain why it
needs to be done, and try to maximize a feeling of autonomy.

In another experiment, Deci and graduate student Haleh Eghrari had 90   23
subjects press a computer-keyboard space bar every time a dot of light appeared on the screen, a task most found uninteresting. The researchers admitted to one group that the activity wasn't much fun, but they explained
that it could be useful for learning about concentration. These individuals were praised for their performance afterward. A second group was told
that they "should attend to [the task] very carefully . . . since it will be for
your own good." Later they were informed that they had done well "as
[they] should." The third group was given only instructions without explanation.

As with the competition study, each subject was then left alone in a   24
room and given the option of continuing to play with the computer once the
experiment was over. Those in the first group chose to do this more often
and also did a better job at the task. "People need to experience a sense of
initiation," Deci explains, "so the less you're controlling and demanding, the
more they have a chance to feel that initiation themselves."

Self-determination, then, proves decisive with boring tasks as well as   25
with interesting ones. And it isn't only an autocratic environment that wipes
out feelings of autonomy. Even well-meaning managers can be controlling
in the way they praise or reward. Likewise, financial incentives can come to
seem so important that they reduce the attraction of the task itself. Lest managers squelch the very innovation they hope to create, rewards should be
used with caution.

QUESTIONS FOR MEANING

1. What does Kohn mean by "positive reinforcement"? Can you give an example from your own experience?
2. Throughout this article, Kohn makes a distinction between intrinsic and extrinsic rewards. What is the difference? Which are the most valuable in Kohn's view?
3. How does Kohn explain research findings that indicate performance can suffer when people compete for extra money?
4. What does the research of Edward L. Deci demonstrate about the effects of competition?
5. Why is Kohn opposed to contests or other incentive plans in which some employees receive no rewards?

QUESTIONS ABOUT STRATEGY

1. What kind of audience did Kohn probably envision when writing this piece? Is it directed towards employers, employees, or both?
2. How credible are the sources cited in this argument? Does Kohn provide any information that would enable readers to gauge the relative importance of the authorities he cites?
3. The focus of this article eventually broadens, moving from the specific topic of positive reinforcement to larger questions involving creativity, competition, and self-determination. How effective is this strategy?
4. Does Kohn offer any reassurance to readers who may fear that he is altogether opposed to incentive plans?
5. After you have read the response to this article published on pages 408–13, evaluate "The Author Replies" on pages 413–14. Does the exchange of views between Kohn and Peters suggest the need for any revision in the argument you have just read?

TOM PETERS
Incentives for Success

A management consultant with an M.B.A. and Ph.D. from Stanford, Tom Peters coauthored In Search of Excellence: Lessons from America's Best-Run Companies *(1982), the best-selling business book on record. In 1985, he coauthored* A Passion for Excellence: The Leadership Difference, *and in 1987 he published* Thriving on Chaos: A Revolutionary Agenda for Today's Manager. *His views on business have appeared in the* Wall Street Journal, *the* Harvard Business Review, Business Week, *and* Inc. *magazine, which in **1988** published the following response to the argument by Alfie Kohn reprinted on pages 403–406.*

A recent *New Yorker* cartoon pictures a blackboard bursting with obscure   1
mathematical formulations. One scientist, looking at the board, says to a
colleague, "Oh, if only it were so simple." I couldn't help recalling the cartoon as I read Alfie Kohn's article in the January issue of *Inc.*, "Incentives
Can Be Bad for Business."

Kohn clearly knows his field. From an academic perspective, his article   2
is superb. He musters compelling evidence to argue that—on the production
line or in the research lab—workers will respond most creatively if they have
a sense of autonomy, on the one hand, and if they value a task or a job for
its own sake, on the other. He is saying that intrinsic motivation is the key
to high performance, and I certainly agree.

Kohn further argues that companies can undermine worker creativity   3
by providing the wrong incentives—if, say, they put too much emphasis on
extrinsic rewards, such as money, prizes, and positive feedback. These kinds
of incentives, he says, lead employees to focus on performance that is quick,
riskless (that is, noninnovative), and geared strictly toward volume of output. If a company does use incentives, Kohn recommends that they emphasize quality of output, rather than quantity, and that they encourage self-
control (that is, innovation and risk taking). For similar reasons, Kohn argues
against establishing a competitive environment in a company. He particularly
abhors contests in which some people get no reward because other individuals or groups did better.

On a point-by-point basis, I have no quarrel with any of Kohn's argu-   4
ments. Moreover, I find him to be a thorough student of the arcane experimental literature on social psychology. But when it comes to the real world
of business, I worry that he leaves the wrong impression on a number of
scores.

Positive Reinforcement Is Better Than Negative

Kohn does a nasty disservice to Harvard psychologist B. F. Skinner by por-   5
traying him as a mindless advocate of "waving dollar bills in front of

people." To be sure, Skinner is the popularizer of positive reinforcement, but Kohn ignores his most important finding, one with huge implications for business, namely: positive reinforcement is much more beneficial than negative.

That's a key oversight because negative reinforcement (criticism) is far   6
and away the most common means by which American companies try to influence performance. They constantly tell people what they did wrong, rather than what they did right. Yet, as Skinner showed, negative reinforcement—even if well intended—seldom leads to improved performance. More often, it produces a) convoluted efforts to hide negative results and b) risk-averse behavior to a much greater degree than that which Kohn decries when criticizing the excesses of positive reinforcement.

Anyone who has spent time observing real-life business practices knows   7
that Skinner is absolutely right on this point. The great quality advocate, W. Edwards Deming, a statistician who has little truck with psychologists, is adamant in his agreement. He has said that the American propensity for negative performance appraisals is our number-one management problem. Nor is he being totally facetious when he contends that it takes half a year for the average manager to recuperate from his or her performance review.

And, by the way, Skinner would be the first to agree with Kohn that   8
"surprising" positive incentives work best. Skinner, after all, was the one who discovered that aperiodic (random, unexpected) "schedules of reinforcement" are much more powerful shapers of future behavior than periodic (routine, expected) schedules.

Business Problem Number One Is the Almost Total Absence of Positive Reinforcement

Although Kohn is correct about the pitfalls of positive reinforcement, he is   9
arguing in a vacuum. If only American business were having trouble because of too much emphasis on extrinsic motivation, resulting in the denigration of intrinsic motivation. Unfortunately, the much larger problem is the almost total absence of positive reinforcement in the average U.S. company, regardless of size.

Consider these two anecdotal, but typical, examples. One involves Sam   10
Preston, a recently retired executive vice-president at S. C. Johnson & Son Inc., which makes Johnson Wax among other products. Throughout his career, Preston would look for positive acts by employees. Whenever he stumbled on one, he would pen a quick note to the person responsible, concluding with the initials "DWD." Eventually the recipients figured out that "DWD" stood for "Damned Well Done." When I met Preston, he had just finished his round of retirement parties, and he spoke of his amazement as person after person came up, occasionally verging on tears, to thank him for a single "DWD" that he'd sent as much as 15 years earlier.

I heard a similar story from a man who had recently bought a quarry   11
in New England. Upon learning that a certain quarryman had cut an extraor-

dinary amount of rock the day before, the new owner had impulsively grabbed a walkie-talkie to offer congratulations and praise. Shortly thereafter, he was talking to another employee and learned that the quarryman had been on cloud nine for days. Turns out that this stellar, 25-year veteran of rock blasting had never before received a word of praise from the boss.

The plain fact is that, in America, workers and managers receive far too   12
little positive reinforcement for their contributions. The average employee faces a daunting array of hurdles and uncertainties. Simply to make it through the day is often worth a "well done." But that average person is not likely to receive even a doff of the cap from year to year, or decade to decade, let alone day to day. On a personal note, I must admit to Mr. Kohn that, despite having achieved a modicum of acclaim, I myself can never get enough of that wonderful stuff called positive reinforcement—and if you must schedule your applause in advance, it's jolly well fine with me.

Positive Reinforcement Need Not Be Quantity Based

Kohn cautions against rote behavior stemming from positive reinforcement,   13
but the real source of rote behavior is excessive attention to volume. What gets measured gets done, as the saying goes, and—at the vast majority of companies—what gets measured is volume. What gets overlooked is quality. The operative phrase is: "Don't improve it; ship it." That's a big problem, but what else can we expect when volume is all that we try to measure?

The solution, however, is not to abandon incentives, but to base them   14
on nonvolumetric factors as well. In this regard, I was delighted to learn recently that First Chicago Corp. is giving some of its managers bonuses based in part on their success in meeting certain "minimally acceptable performance" goals, as determined by customers.

Similarly, it was quality of service that helped Phil Bressler establish   15
himself as Domino Pizza's top franchisee in the important category of repeat business. Each of his stores would give out a volume-based award for best driver. Before the award was made, however, customers were asked to evaluate the driver's performance. If the quality of service didn't measure up, then no award.

The point is, there are ways to measure what was once thought to be   16
unmeasurable. You can keep score on quality, customer service, responsiveness, innovativeness, even customer listening. Moreover, the sheer act of keeping score will provide a positive stimulant to improvement. Job number two, I'd agree, is to get the right balance between intrinsic and extrinsic motivational factors, but first let's put some of these other missing indicators on the map.

And Then There Is the Little Matter of Equity, or Share and Share Alike

It's not easy to develop a good incentive system, and there are undoubtedly   17
thousands of ways to construct useless, even damaging, ones. To read Kohn's

article, you might think that bad incentive systems are the rule at most companies. The truth, however, is that most companies don't offer any incentives at all to their employees, except to a thimbleful of folks at the top.

A year and a century ago, in 1887, William Cooper Procter, president   18
of Procter & Gamble Co., said that the chief challenge of big business was to shape its policies so that each worker would feel he was a vital part of his company with a chance to share in its success. P&G's landmark profit-distribution plan divided profits between the company and its workers in the same proportion that labor bore the total cost. If wages were 50% of costs, the workers' bonuses would be a whopping one-half of profits. Sadly, P&G's example was not widely emulated, and today only 15% of the U.S. work force participates in such a profit-distribution or gain-sharing plan. A paltry 10% own stock in their companies, despite the generous ESOP incentives available since 1974.

The significance of this appalling record was suggested by a survey that   19
Daniel Yankelovich conducted in the early 1980s. U.S. and Japanese workers were asked to agree or disagree with the statement, "I have an inner need to do the best I can, regardless of pay." The U.S. workers, maligned by so many (especially their managers), outscored the Japanese. Then the two groups were asked a much more practical question: Who did they think would benefit most from an increase in worker productivity? This time, the tables were turned. Some 93% of Japanese workers thought that they would be the prime beneficiaries, while only 9% of the Americans felt that way. In other words, Japanese workers believe that increased productivity is a matter of self-interest—and the facts support them.

So Kohn may be right about the pitfalls of incentive systems, but he's   20
dead wrong in suggesting that bad incentive systems are a major problem for American business. The far greater—and more commonplace—sin is to ignore the worker's incremental contribution altogether.

Competition Is Still the Spice of Life

The ancient philosopher's line is that the world would have no beauty with-   21
out contrasting ugliness. For better or (sometimes certainly) for worse, comparison—which is to say, competition—is the chief motivator for individuals and groups, whether it takes place in teen beauty pageants, among Nobel-level scientists, or on the shop floor.

Now competition can go too far. I agree with Kohn that competition   22
may cause a worker to focus excessively on speed and what the guy next to him is doing, thereby losing sight of the intrinsic value (that is, quality) of the task at hand. I have seen the disastrous consequences of basing incentive pay on work group competition—especially when workers are not trained adequately, and when the company does not provide the time, the place, and the tools to work creatively on individual and team improvement.

On the other hand, I have also seen group competition work wonders   23
in a plant, under the right conditions. Look at New United Motor Manufac-

turing Inc. (NUMMI), the extraordinary joint venture between General Motors and Toyota. Its predecessor, a GM plant, was at the bottom of the heap in terms of productivity, quality, absenteeism, and numerous other performance indicators. Now, the 2,500-person operation scores at the top. The dramatic turnaround is mainly a result of employee involvement. Every worker is trained in at least a half-dozen jobs; each person must be good enough to train his or her colleagues; fellow hourly workers are team leaders; and the company provides all the training, tools, time, and space required for problem solving. Competition among teams is sky high, on the job and off, but meticulous preparation came first.

But, group competition aside, I think Kohn is focusing on a secondary   24
issue here. We face enormous business problems today, and they were not caused by too much competition. Rather they reflect the broad deterioration of the national economy—a consequence of the virtual absence of competition from World War II until about 1965. During that period, almost all of our major industries became tidy oligopolies, in no shape to compete with anyone.

Kohn decries the ill effects of copying, and too much distraction with   25
competition. I submit that it is far worse to ignore the competitive reality, and to refuse to copy at all. Consider the Ford Taurus, one of the biggest American product successes in decades. For years, Ford had systematically ignored or denigrated Japanese automobiles and, to some extent, European ones as well. In developing the Taurus, however, it did a complete about-face, purchasing hundreds of vehicles from around the globe. Following a copy-and-exceed strategy, Ford set out to best those vehicles on hundreds of features, from the inner workings of the engine to the ease of gas cap removability. That is, of course, precisely the strategy for which we once scorned the Japanese. Ironically, it is the same strategy with which the American (and then the Germans) surpassed the British in years gone by. The process may not be as creative as Kohn would like, and it certainly reflects an obsession with competition. But it works. And its success demonstrates once again that we have far more to fear from too little than from too much competition.

Let me just add a personal note in conclusion. Many years ago, I was a   26
Ph.D. student of management, and I read with pleasure almost every word of psychologist L. Edward Deci, whom Kohn so reveres. Intrinsic motivation and autonomy have been major, if not dominate, themes in all three of my books. And I acknowledge that the astonishing success of enterprises such as NUMMI are testimony to the importance of intrinsic motivation and self-control. For drawing attention to those issues, Alfie Kohn deserves two full and hearty cheers.

But I must withhold cheer number three, for I feel that, overall, Kohn   27
is addressing matters of secondary concern. Excessive emphasis on incentives and competition is simply not a widespread problem in American business. What we need is a lot *more* positive reinforcement, and a lot less of the negative kind, throughout the corporate landscape. And far from cautioning

companies about the dangers of incentives, we should be applauding those that offer their employees a bigger piece of the action. Likewise, we should welcome competition, whatever its source. We have competitive pressure to thank for the positive things that are happening in large companies these days, including the new willingness to copy from the best. Better that than the practices of inward-looking companies and workers, closed to ideas that were Not Invented Here. They are the ones who have made such a bungle of American economic performance worldwide over the past 20 years.

Life ain't simple, as that *New Yorker* cartoon suggested, and neither is   28
business. Kohn has much to say that is thoughtful and wise, and that ought to be heeded. But let's not ignore the forest for the trees.

ALFIE KOHN
The Author Replies

When Tom Peters argues   1
that the problem in the real world is too little positive reinforcement rather than too much, he is doing two things at once. He is describing what's going on, and he is prescribing what needs to be done instead. I have no quarrel with the first. But the cartoon phrase "Oh, if only it were so simple . . ." seems more appropriate to Peter's prescription—that we should just crank up the positive reinforcement—than to my review of the hidden problems with this tactic.

I do not dispute his argu-   2
ment that praise is better than punishment. Likewise, I say "amen" to his call for more goodies to find their way to workers instead of executives. The research shows quite clearly, however, that—when people feel controlled by praise, or when they come to think of themselves as working for extrinsic rewards—quality is likely to suffer. Peter's suggestion that we simply base those rewards on quality rather than quantity will not solve the problem. It may well be true that we have the capability to "keep score on quality," but it is clearly untrue that "the sheer act of keeping score will provide a positive stimulant to improvement."

The problem is not just   3
that an artificial incentive for doing a job well is a less effective motivator than intrinsic interest in the job. It's that the incentive can actually do substantial damage by eroding that interest. And the more a task involves creativity, the more a manager must take care

in handing out bonuses and praise. All else being equal, concentrating on the score is probably an *obstacle* to improved performance in the long run, at least for tasks more complicated than licking envelopes.

Up to this point in the discussion, though, my differences with Peters are probably more a matter of emphasis than of substance. I agree that workers ought to be recognized more for their efforts, and he agrees that rewards can stifle innovation. But we part company, and I think Peters parts company with the data as well, on the question of competition. As I tried to show in an earlier column ("No Contest," November 1987), the best amount of competition in a company—or anywhere else, for that matter—is none at all.

Even though it's well supported by the evidence, this fact flies in the face of everything we were raised to believe. It's hard to accept the painful truth that we are all made losers by the race to win, that excellence has nothing to do with beating others, that any win/lose arrangement not only is psychologically destructive and ruinous to relationships, but also inherently counterproductive.

A close reading of Peters's examples shows that the wonderful results he cites were not really a result of competition at all. Is social comparison or learning by observing use-

ful? In moderation, yes. But benefiting from others' example isn't at all the same thing as trying to defeat them. Does the Toyota-General Motors collaboration seem to be successful? If so, it's because of the employee involvement Peters describes. I'd be willing to bet that the workers (and their productivity) are thriving in *spite* of the additional element of group competition, not because of it.

It baffles me that someone with Tom Peters's expertise would help perpetuate the myth that "we have far more to fear from too little than from too much competition." What we have to fear is too little attention to quality, and competition is to quality as sugar is to teeth. Its effect on self-esteem is similar.

The research to back this up (which I review in my book, *No Contest: The Case Against Competition*) is so persuasive that I'd say the single most damaging mistake a company can make in devising an incentive plan is to set it up competitively. If a bonus is to be made available to employees, any individual (or, better yet, any team) that reaches a certain level of performance should receive that bonus. A contest sets us against one another, so that my success makes yours less likely. In reality, we have a great deal to fear from too much competition, and any amount is too much.

QUESTIONS FOR MEANING

1. According to Peters, how does Kohn misrepresent the beliefs of B. F. Skinner?
2. In what way do U.S. workers outscore their Japanese counterparts? What difference between U.S. and Japanese workers accounts for different degrees of productivity?
3. How can competition be useful in the workplace, and how could it benefit American industry?
4. Peters claims that Kohn addresses "matters of secondary concern." What does he identify as a matter of primary concern?
5. Vocabulary: abhors (3), arcane (4), convoluted (6), facetious (7), rote (13), emulated (18), meticulous (23).

QUESTIONS ABOUT STRATEGY

1. Peters opens and closes his argument with references to a cartoon in *The New Yorker*. Does he strike a light note at any other points in this article?
2. How would you describe Peters' attitude towards Kohn? If you were Kohn, how would you feel when reading this article?
3. Peters claims that Americans are much more likely to receive negative criticism rather than positive reinforcement at work. Based upon your own experience, does this seem like a reasonable generalization?
4. This counterargument is approximately 50% longer than the argument it was inspired by. Is the length appropriate, or would you recommend any cuts?

ONE STUDENT'S ASSIGNMENT

Write an argument for or against competition that will draw primarily upon your own personal experience. You might focus your essay on the effects of either competitive sports or academic competition for high grades. If you include any material from sources besides your personal experiences use one of the documentation styles favored by the Council of Biology Editors.

```
                  Competition: An Abused Privilege
                            Tim Paetsch


        Competition is a privilege. Although it does not          1
     guarantee triumph, it enables us to define personal
     goals and to pursue them, which is better than simply
     living from day to day. Even when we encounter failure,
     competition can be exciting and enjoyable. Therefore, we
     must view the basic principles of competition as benefi-
     cial. Unfortunately, this privilege is often abused.
```

When winning is an obsession rather than a goal, competition becomes an event filled with anxiety instead of pleasure. This can be seen often in high school sports—more often than we would like to believe. Many parents and coaches are putting too much pressure on young athletes, leading them to put even more pressure on themselves until they burn out.

Sports like wrestling are particularly vulnerable to the burnout dilemma because participants have no teammates to blend in with and help them accept defeat. When a wrestler screws up, all of the criticism and ridicule is directed at him alone.   2

I started to wrestle in fourth grade and enjoyed the sport for several years, but I eventually witnessed many cases of burnout. A wrestler in my home town had great success as a youngster, but in high school the coaches expected too much from him, causing him to quit the sport after his sophomore year. As seniors, two top-notch wrestlers didn't join their defending state champion team because "it's not worth it anymore." And Mark Schwab, a two-time Junior National Champion, nearly became a full-time beach bum because he was sick of wrestling.   3

Eventually, I also fell victim to burnout. Before entering high school I won several state titles and two regional national titles. I competed almost anonymously, with little coaching. When I became a high school wrestler, everything seemed to change. I had full-time coaches and fans with high expectations. I now had to perform in front of crowds of people who all knew me. If I lost, the day after the match, classmates would ask me, "What happened? How did you lose?" This led me to worry: "I can't screw up anymore, or else I'll have to keep answering to everyone in school." Eventually I began to avoid people whenever possible because I knew the topic of wrestling would immediately pop up. After high school I was so sick of the sport that I hung up my wrestling shoes and vowed never to wrestle again.   4

It's sad when pressure causes young athletes to relinquish all of the benefits of competition. What can be done to make athletic competition the enjoyable experience that it should be in high school?   5

First, coaches should make training seem less mo-   6

notonous. Training is a necessity in most sports, and it needs to be vigorous, but the usually loathed conditioning exercises are much more tolerable if coaches vary workouts. For example, rather than always sending the whole team out for a five mile run, a coach could break the team into partners or small groups and have continuous relay races with various exercises and drills. To provide incentive for the whole team, he could exempt them from some other exercises if everybody finishes in a given amount of time.

Second, we must help competitors realize that an opponent is not an enemy. One high school coach told me not to talk to any of my opponents because it would keep them uncertain of me and make them nervous. In other words, it would "psych them out." In actuality, I became just as nervous as my opponent. I was as uncertain of him as he was of me, and he seemed as inhuman as I. When I used to wrestle in kids' tournaments, I would find my opponent and talk to him before the match. Both of us were less nervous, making it easier for us to wrestle up to our ability. After the match we would go to the concession stand, have a couple of sodas, and there were no hard feelings. I see no reason why high school athletes couldn't do the same.

Third, we must limit the involvement of coaches at an actual competitive event. I realize that the coach is essential during the performance for some team sports, but in many cases he becomes overinvolved. Coaches often bark out so many instructions at an athlete that it only confuses and frustrates him. If a young athlete has not learned something in practice, he certainly cannot be expected to learn and execute it in a matter of seconds in the midst of competition.

Involvement of parents and friends also needs reform in some cases. Parents often see their kids as extensions of themselves competing, causing them to sometimes behave outrageously, belittling and embarrassing young competitors (1). Parents need to back off and let athletes compete for their own benefit. If you are a friend of an athlete, don't show over-concern when he or she loses or makes a mistake. The athlete would rather learn from the mistake and move on than have a sympathetic friend dwell upon a failure.

Finally, we must prevent competitors from putting   1
too much pressure on themselves. Having goals and striving for them is beneficial, but when a person cannot
fall asleep at night or vomits because he is so nervous
about how he will perform, then there is a definite
problem. Not only is the sport no longer enjoyable, but
performance is usually jeopardized. As Ross Wetzsteon
pointed out in "The Winner Instinct," the actual pursuit
of a goal is usually more exciting and rewarding than
its realization (2). Why ruin the process by turning
athletes into nauseated insomniacs? Coaches, parents,
and competitors must work together to prevent pressure
from building up so that athletes can enjoy pursuing
their goals even if they don't always achieve them.

References*

(1) Martin, K. 1986. Is winning everything? Pages 328–
    331 _in_ R. K. Miller, The informed argument. Harcourt
    Brace Jovanovich, San Diego.
(2) Wetzsteon R. 1984. The winner instinct. Pages 325–
    327 _in_ R. K. Miller, The informed argument. Harcourt
    Brace Jovanovich, San Diego.

SUGGESTIONS FOR WRITING

1. Drawing upon your own experience, as well as the essays by Katherine
   Martin, Mariah Burton Nelson, and D. Stanley Eitzen, write an argument for or against encouraging children to compete in sports.
2. To what extent is competition useful in the classroom? Drawing upon
   the essay by Charles Duke, write an argument for or against encouraging
   academic competition among high school students.

---

*This essay illustrates how numbered references can be used within an essay if they correspond correctly with the right source within the reference list at the end of the paper. Unlike numbered footnotes, in which the same number is never repeated within a single paper, numbered references allow for repeating the same number whenever the same source is cited. Thus, if Tim had wished to cite Martin's essay as support for another point he wanted to make, (1) would have appeared a second time within the text. The use of numbered references is limited mainly to scientific and technical writing, and their form can vary. Tim's reference list follows one of the forms recognized by the Council of Biology Editors in _CBE Style Manual: A Guide for Authors, Editors, and Publishers in the Biological Sciences._ You should note, however, that the _CBE Manual_ emphasizes that documentation styles vary from one journal to another, and writers planning to publish within a specific journal should follow the form that is used by that journal.

3. Is competition for good grades necessary for learning? Would you work equally hard in a class for which there would be no grade? Write an argument for or against grading.

4. The study conducted by Perry, Kane, Bernesser, and Spicker suggests that competition can lead to cheating. Are there any other reasons why students might cheat? Write an essay on cheating that will focus on either what causes it or what penalties are appropriate for it.

5. Alfie Kohn claims that competing for rewards can be counterproductive within the workplace. Drawing upon your own experience or research, write an argument that will support or challenge this view.

6. Compare the arguments by Kohn and Peters and determine if one is stronger than the other.

7. Write an essay on the positive and/or negative effects of competition in courtship.

8. Synthesize the arguments against competition made by Martin, Eitzen, and Kohn.

9. If you believe that competition can be good or bad depending on the situation, write an essay designed to establish the nature of healthy competition.

10. Do an informal survey among your friends and neighbors to determine how the people you know view competition. Try to speak to an equal number of men and women. Drawing upon your survey, write an essay that will support or challenge the claim that men are more competitive than women.

CENSORSHIP: WHO CONTROLS OUR CULTURE?

♦

GARRY WILLS

In Praise of Censure

A graduate of St. Louis University who received his Ph.D. from Yale in 1961, Garry Wills is widely recognized as a writer who applies the critical techniques of a scholar to the discussion of political and religious issues. For Inventing America *(1978), he won the National Book Critics Circle Award in 1979. His other books include* Nixon Agonistes *(1970),* Bare Ruined Choirs *(1972),* Confessions of a Conservative *(1979),* Reagan's America *(1987) and* Under God: Religion and American Politics *(1990). He also contributes to numerous periodicals, including the* New York Review of Books, Harper's, *and* Time, *which published the following essay in* **1989.**

Rarely have the denouncers of censorship been so eager to start practicing it.   1
When a sense of moral disorientation overcomes a society, people from the least expected quarters begin to ask, "Is nothing sacred?" Feminists join reactionaries to denounce pornography as demeaning to women. Rock musician Frank Zappa declares that when Tipper Gore, the wife of Senator Albert Gore from Tennessee, asked music companies to label sexually explicit material, she launched an illegal "conspiracy to extort." A *Penthouse* editorialist says that housewife Terry Rakolta, who asked sponsors to withdraw support from a sitcom called *Married . . . With Children,* is "yelling fire in a crowded theater," a formula that says her speech is not protected by the First Amendment.

But the most interesting movement to limit speech is directed at defam-   2
atory utterances against blacks, homosexuals, Jews, women or other stigmatizable groups. It took no Terry Rakolta of the left to bring about the instant firing of Jimmy the Greek and Al Campanis from sports jobs when they made racially denigrating comments. Social pressure worked far more quickly on them than on *Married . . . With Children,* which is still on the air.

The rules being considered on college campuses to punish students for   3
making racist and other defamatory remarks go beyond social and commer-

cial pressure to actual legal muzzling. The right-wing *Dartmouth Review* and its imitators have understandably infuriated liberals, who are beginning to take action against them and the racist expressions they have encouraged. The American Civil Liberties Union considered this movement important enough to make it the principal topic at its biennial meeting last month in Madison, Wis. Ironically, the regents of the University of Wisconsin had passed their own rules against defamation just before the ACLU members convened on the university's campus. Nadine Strossen, of New York University School of Law, who was defending the ACLU's traditional position on free speech, said of Wisconsin's new rules, "You can tell how bad they are by the fact that the regents had to make an amendment at the last minute exempting classroom discussion! What is surprising is that Donna Shalala [chancellor of the university] went along with it." So did constitutional lawyers on the faculty.

If a similar code were drawn up with right-wing imperatives in mind—   4
one banning unpatriotic, irreligious or sexually explicit expressions on campus—the people framing Wisconsin-type rules would revert to their libertarian pasts. In this competition to suppress, is regard for freedom of expression just a matter of whose ox is getting gored at the moment? Does the left just get nervous about the Christian cross when Klansmen burn it, while the right will react only when Madonna flirts crucifixes between her thighs?

The cries of "un-American" are as genuine and as frequent on either   5
side. Everyone is protecting the country. Zappa accuses Gore of undermining the moral fiber of America with the "sexual neuroses of these vigilant ladies." He argues that she threatens our freedoms with "connubial insider trading" because her husband is a Senator. Apparently her marital status should deprive her of speaking privileges in public—an argument Westbrook Pegler used to make against Eleanor Roosevelt. *Penthouse* says Rakolta is taking us down the path toward fascism. It attacks her for living in a rich suburb—the old "radical chic" argument that rich people cannot support moral causes.

There is a basic distinction that cuts through this free-for-all over free-   6
dom. It is the distinction, too often neglected, between censorship and censure (the free expression of moral disapproval). What the campuses are trying to do (at least those with state money) is use the force of government to contain freedom of speech. What Donald Wildman, the free-lance moralist from Tupelo, Miss., does when he gets Pepsi to cancel its Madonna ad is censure the ad by calling for a boycott. Advocating boycotts is a form of speech protected by the First Amendment. As Nat Hentoff, journalistic custodian of the First Amendment, says, "I would hate to see boycotts outlawed. Think what that would do to Cesar Chavez." Or, for that matter, to Ralph Nader. If one disapproves of a social practice, whether it is racist speech or unjust hiring in lettuce fields, one is free to denounce that and to call on others to express their disapproval. Otherwise there would be no form of persuasive speech except passing a law. This would make the law coterminous with morality.

Equating morality with legality is in effect what people do when they   7 claim that anything tolerated by law must, in the name of freedom, be approved by citizens in all their dealings with one another. As Zappa says, "Masturbation is not illegal. If it is not illegal to do it, why should it be illegal to sing about it?" He thinks this proves that Gore, who is not trying to make raunch in rock illegal, cannot even ask distributors to label it. Anything goes, as long as it's legal. The odd consequence of this argument would be a drastic narrowing of the freedom of speech. One could not call into question anything that was not against the law—including, for instance, racist speech.

A false ideal of tolerance has not only outlawed censorship but discouraged censoriousness (another word for censure). Most civilizations have expressed their moral values by mobilization of social opprobrium. That, rather than specific legislation, is what changed the treatment of minorities in films and TV over recent years. One can now draw opprobrious attention by gay bashing, as the Beastie Boys rock group found when their distributor told them to cut out remarks about "fags" for business reasons. Or by anti-Semitism, as the just disbanded rap group Public Enemy has discovered.   8

It is said that only the narrow-minded are intolerant or opprobrious. Most of those who limited the distribution of Martin Scorsese's movie *The Last Temptation of Christ* had not even seen the movie. So do we guarantee freedom of speech only for the broad-minded or the better educated? Can one speak only after studying whatever one has reason, from one's beliefs, to denounce? Then most of us would be doing a great deal less speaking than we do. If one has never seen any snuff movies, is that a bar to criticizing them?   9

Others argue that asking people not to buy lettuce is different from asking them not to buy a rocker's artistic expression. Ideas (carefully disguised) lurk somewhere in the lyrics. All the more reason to keep criticism of them free. If ideas are too important to suppress, they are also too important to ignore. The whole point of free speech is not to make ideas exempt from criticism but to expose them to it.   10

One of the great mistakes of liberals in recent decades has been the ceding of moral concern to right-wingers. Just because one opposes censorship, one need not be seen as agreeing with pornographers. Why should liberals, of all people, oppose Gore when she asks that labels be put on products meant for the young, to inform those entrusted by law with the care of the young? Liberals were the first to promote "healthy" television shows like *Sesame Street* and *The Electric Company*. In the 1950s and 1960s they were the leading critics of television, of its mindless violence, of the way it ravaged the attention span needed for reading. Who was keeping kids away from TV sets then? How did promoters of Big Bird let themselves be cast as champions of the Beastie Boys—not just of their *right* to perform but of their performance itself? Why should it be left to Gore to express moral disapproval of a group calling itself Dead Kennedys (sample lyric: "I kill children, I love to see them die")?   11

For that matter, who has been more insistent that parents should "in-   12
terfere" in what their children are doing, Tipper Gore or Jesse Jackson? All
through the 1970s, Jackson was traveling the high schools, telling parents to
turn off TVs, make the kids finish their homework, check with teachers on
their performance, get to know what the children are doing. This kind of
"interference" used to be called education.

Belief in the First Amendment does not pre-empt other beliefs, making   13
one a eunuch to the interplay of opinions. It is a distortion to turn "You can
express any views" into the proposition "I don't care what views you express." If liberals keep equating equality with approval, they will be repeatedly forced into weak positions.

A case in point is the Corcoran Gallery's sudden cancellation of an ex-   14
hibit of Robert Mapplethorpe's photographs. The whole matter was needlessly confused when the director, Christina Owr-Chall, claimed she was
canceling the show to *protect* it from censorship. She meant that there might
be pressure to remove certain pictures—the sadomasochistic ones or those
verging on kiddie porn—if the show had gone on. But she had in mind, as
well, the hope of future grants from the National Endowment for the Arts,
which is under criticism for the Mapplethorpe show and for another show
that contained Andres Serrano's *Piss Christ,* the photograph of a crucifix in
what the title says is urine. Owr-Chall is said to be yielding to censorship,
when she is clearly yielding to political and financial pressure, as Pepsi yielded
to commercial pressure over the Madonna ad.

What is at issue here is not government suppression but government   15
subsidy. Mapplethorpe's work is not banned, but showing it might have
endangered federal grants to needy artists. The idea that what the government does not support it represses is nonsensical, as one can see by reversing
the statement to read: "No one is allowed to create anything without the
government's subvention." What pussycats our supposedly radical artists are.
They not only want the government's permission to create their arti-
facts, they want federal authorities to supply the materials as well. Otherwise
they feel "gagged." If they are not given government approval (and money),
they want to remain an avant-grade while being bankrolled by the Old Guard.

What is easily forgotten in this argument is the right of citizen taxpay-   16
ers. They send representatives to Washington who are answerable for the
expenditure of funds exacted from them. In general these voters want to
favor their own values if government is going to get into the culture-subsidizing
area at all (a proposition many find objectionable in itself). Politicians, insofar as they support the arts, will tend to favor conventional art (certainly not
masochistic art). Anybody who doubts that has no understanding of a politician's legitimate concern for his or her constituents' approval. Besides, it is
quaint for those familiar with the politics of the art world to discover, with
a shock, that there is politics in politics.

Luckily, cancellation of the Mapplethorpe show forced some artists back   17
to the flair and cheekiness of unsubsidized art. Other results of pressure do

not turn out as well. Unfortunately, people in certain regions were deprived of the chance to see *The Last Temptation of Christ* in the theater. Some, no doubt, considered it a loss that they could not buy lettuce or grapes during a Chavez boycott. Perhaps there was even a buyer perverse enough to miss driving the unsafe cars Nader helped pressure off the market. On the other hand, we do not get sports analysis made by racists. These mobilizations of social opprobrium are not examples of repression but of freedom of expression by committed people who censured without censoring, who expressed the kinds of belief the First Amendment guarantees. I do not, as a result, get whatever I approve of subsidized, either by Pepsi or the government. But neither does the law come in to silence Tipper Gore or Frank Zappa or even that filthy rag, the *Dartmouth Review*.

QUESTIONS FOR MEANING

1. How does Wills define the difference between *censorship* and *censure*?
2. According to Wills, what is the purpose of free speech?
3. Why does Wills find it ironic when liberals oppose record labeling?
4. In paragraph 15 Wills writes, "The idea that what the government does not support it represses is nonsensical." Why does he believe this?
5. Vocabulary: reactionaries (1), defamatory (2), denigrating (2), imperatives (4), coterminous (6), opprobrium (8), subvention (15), masochistic (16).

QUESTIONS ABOUT STRATEGY

1. Consider the examples Wills cites in paragraph 5. If reported accurately, are either Zappa or *Penthouse* guilty of fallacious reasoning?
2. Could this argument appeal to readers who have different political and cultural values? Or is it likely to appeal only to either liberals or conservatives?
3. How effective is the comparison between Tipper Gore and Jessie Jackson in paragraph 12?
4. This argument contains references to many public figures. Does Wills make any attempt to explain who they are for the benefit of readers who may not recognize some of these names?
5. Why does Wills quote a sample lyric in paragraph 11? What impact did this example have upon you?

RANDY FITZGERALD
Our Tax Dollars for This Kind of Art?

Is the National Endowment for the Arts spending money wisely? And does it make sense for the federal government to be subsidizing the arts at all? These are the questions addressed by Randy Fitzgerald, a staff writer for Reader's Digest. *His argument was first published in* Reader's Digest *in 1990, when the National Endowment for the Arts was under attack for funding art that many Americans found offensive.*

What is the National Endowment for the Arts up to? First it gave Andres 1 Serrano $15,000 in taxpayers' money to produce a photograph of a crucifix submerged in a jar of his own urine. Serrano called this work "Piss Christ." Then the Endowment put up $30,000 to send an exhibition of Robert Mapplethorpe's photography on a nationwide tour. It included photos of nude children, a man urinating into another man's mouth, and a self-portrait of the photographer (who died of AIDS-related illness in March 1989) with a bullwhip protruding from his anus.

Last October, Congress reacted by voting to prohibit federal funding 2 for "obscene" works. But it left the final interpretation of obscenity up to Endowment officials.

In November an exhibit of art about victims of AIDS opened in New 3 York—with Endowment support. A catalogue accompanying the show attacked John Cardinal O'Connor of New York as a "fat cannibal" and a "creep in black skirts," and labeled St. Patrick's Cathedral "that house of walking swastikas." It fantasized about throwing Rep. William Dannemeyer (R., Calif.) off the Empire State Building and dousing Sen. Jesse Helms (R., N.C.) in gasoline and setting "his putrid ass on fire."

Newly installed National Endowment for the Arts chairman John 4 Frohnmayer suspended an Endowment grant of $10,000 for the AIDS exhibition, calling the show "too political." But a few weeks later, responding to howls of "censorship" from the arts community, he retreated and restored funding for the show, excluding the catalogue. Frohnmayer also promised to work for removal of the law barring taxpayer support for obscene works.

His capitulation was merely the latest example of how the Endowment 5 runs scared before a vocal coterie of artists who consider government grants an inalienable right. To head off taxpayer indignation over the Endowment's actions, officials of the agency cite its success stories: an insurance program for museums that allows priceless art from abroad to tour the United States; a design competition that resulted in the Vietnam Veterans Memorial in Washington; public broadcasting programs such as "Live From Lincoln Center;" and support for American folk art. But other recent grants stretch credulity.

A New Yorker was given $10,000 to study Thoroughbred race tracks 6 in the United States. Another grant gave $10,000 to investigate "public uses of abandoned Atlas missile silos." Another $8000 went to "explore and map the city of Newark, N.J." And $36,900 was awarded to the Society for American Baseball Research to ponder whether the "urban baseball park" will last into the next century.

"You're regarded as a philistine if you ask whether the public would approve of how its money is being spent on particular grants," says Paul Hasse, a former special assistant to the Endowment chairman. "The Endowment is extremely uncomfortable with public scrutiny." Adds Marvin Liebman, also a former assistant to the chairman. "The federal arts bureaucracy has total contempt for taxpayers."

Congress established the National Endowment for the Arts at the urging of President Lyndon Johnson to encourage greater creativity and promote wider access to the arts. But with the Endowment celebrating its 25th anniversary this year, it is time to ask whether taxpayers are getting their money's worth ($2.3 billion since 1965, $171 million for fiscal 1990). Even former officials contend that the agency may be the most cavalier with tax money of any agency in the federal government.

Grants are primarily determined by panels of artists, directors, arts administrators, critics, scholars, patrons and educators, all appointed by the Endowment. While these panels are supposed to base their recommendations on artistic quality and merit, rarely can they do so, given the hundreds of applications they must judge. As a result, award decisions often favor applicants known to the panelists—especially organizations and individuals who have already received grants.

Complaints of favoritism are frequent. Minnesota sculptor Raymond Bryan protests that the "rules on giving, largely unwritten, see to it that only an elite, allegedly avant-garde few get help."

Political-science professor Kevin Mulcahy of Louisiana State University agrees. In a study published in 1988 by the American Council for the Arts, Mulcahy noted that Endowment grants go largely to applicants in the Northeast, especially in New York City. And, said Mulcahy, the agency's peer-review system tends to serve the interests of well-connected artists while others are shut out.

There are appearances of conflict of interest throughout the Endowment's grant-making process. In 1988, for instance, of the eight orchestra representatives on the panel doling out tax dollars to symphonies, six received grants for their own orchestra companies, ranging from $44,000 to $286,000.

Under Endowment rules, panel members must leave the room when votes affecting them are taken. That so many panel members receive grants for their own endeavors anyway is described as coincidental by Endowment officials.

Last June, when the Endowment-backed Mapplethorpe exhibit was about to go on display at the Corcoran Gallery in Washington, D.C., numerous members of Congress objected to taxpayer funds promoting its sadomasochistic and homoerotic themes.

"I'm not saying Serrano and Mapplethorpe can't produce the trash they   15
call art," declared Rep. Richard Armey (R., Texas), who sent the Endowment a protest letter, signed by himself and 107 colleagues. "I'm just saying
the American taxpayer should not be forced to pay for it."

As a slap on the wrist, the House and Senate voted to cut the Endow-   16
ment's budget by $45,000—the exact amount given the Serrano and Mapple-
thorpe projects. Later, Congress added language banning federal support for
obscenity. Both actions have been denounced by the art establishment as
censorship.

But Samuel Lipman, a member of the Endowment's National Council   17
on the Arts from 1982 to 1988, sees the issue differently: "The acceptance of
public money implies an acceptance of a public responsibility. There is no
argument to be made for using public funds to support trash."

In the past two decades, America has experienced an unprecedented   18
"arts boom." The number of professional orchestras jumped from 149 to
271, major opera companies from 40 to 209, community arts organizations
from 125 to more than 2000. Part of the credit belongs to the Endowment,
which required institutional recipients to solicit up to $3 in private donations
for every federal dollar received.

But has the Endowment succeeded in its mission to expand public par-   19
ticipation in the arts while fostering artistic excellence? Government surveys
have found that arts-related events are attended primarily by people in upper
education and income groups—much as before the Endowment existed.

Furthermore, art cannot be improved merely by spending more money.   20
Says Hilton Kramer, formerly chief art critic for the New York Times: "The
Endowment has had absolutely no discernible effect on the creative side of
art. The greatest benefit has been enjoyed by the administrative officers of
the arts bureaucracy."

A 1989 Newsweek/Gallup poll disclosed that only 35 percent of Ameri-   21
cans endorse federal subsidies for art. So why is the government so deeply
involved?

Like other government programs, the subsidies are lauded most by the   22
people who benefit from them. As Pulitzer Prize-winning literary critic
Jonathan Yardley stated in the Washington Post: "Much of it is reverse
Robin Hood discrimination. Money is taken from middle- and lower-
income taxpayers and turned over to the enterprises that largely benefit the
well-to-do."

Congress does not seem inclined to eliminate the Endowment or sig-   23
nificantly reduce federal funding for the arts. Nor do members of Congress
try to dictate what artists may produce with their own resources. But Congress certainly has the responsibility to voice the public's concerns as it allo-
cates the public's money.

Doesn't it make more sense, for example, to take the tax money spent   24
on such grants as documenting high-school football in Texas or collecting
maps from the world's rapid rail systems and apply it instead to museum and
art preservation?

Besides, the idea that our artistic future depends on federal handouts   25
overlooks the complexity of creative motivation. As Robert J. Samuelson
noted in *Newsweek*: "Herman Melville did not require an Endowment grant
to write; Winslow Homer did not need a grant to paint." Adds novelist John
Updike, a past grant recipient: "I'm not sure the entire disappearance of the
Endowment would be a terrible loss.

To extend the Endowment's life for another three to five years, Con-   26
gress must pass reauthorizing legislation this year. Rep. Pat Williams (D.,
Mont.), chairman of the House subcommittee in charge of reauthorization,
concedes that Congress may be unable to reconcile the right of taxpayers to
determine how their money is spent with demands for artistic freedom. Declares Congressman Williams, a staunch Endowment supporter, "That places
its future in doubt."

Soon after being sworn in as its chairman, John Frohnmayer stated that   27
the Endowment must "serve the American people." He still has an opportunity to do so by ensuring that taxpayer money is spent in ways that don't
insult the vast majority of Americans. If the Endowment won't exercise
oversight, then Congress must.

QUESTIONS FOR MEANING

1. What are the two goals of the National Endowment for the Arts?
2. Who determines the awarding of NEA grants?
3. According to Fitzgerald, who benefits the most from public funding for
   the arts?
4. Where would Fitzgerald like to see the Endowment concentrate its funding?
5. Vocabulary: capitulation (5), coterie (5), philistine (7), cavalier (8), unprecedented (18), discernible (20), lauded (22).

QUESTIONS ABOUT STRATEGY

1. Why does Fitzgerald open his argument with such sensational examples?
   Is there any risk to this strategy?
2. Does Fitzgerald make any concessions that would appeal to supporters of
   the National Endowment for the Arts?
3. Consider the two authorities cited in paragraph 25. Based upon the information provided by Fitzgerald, are either of these sources especially credible?
4. After discussing John Frohnmayer in paragraph 4, Fitzgerald returns to
   him in paragraph 27. Is this a sign of faulty organization?

RICHARD A. POSNER
Art for Law's Sake

A judge on the United States Court of Appeals for the Seventh Circuit, Richard Posner is also a senior lecturer at the University of Chicago Law School, where he has taught since 1969. He is a 1959 graduate of Yale, who studied law at Harvard, where he headed the Harvard Law Review. *His books include* The Economics of Justice *(1981),* Law and Literature: A Misunderstood Relation *(1988), and* The Problems of Jurisprudence *(1990). "Art for Law's Sake" was first published in* **1989** *by* The American Scholar, *the journal of the Phi Beta Kappa Society.*

There is persistent, perhaps intensifying, controversy over offensive art. It is   1
well illustrated by the recent brouhaha over "Piss Christ." A photograph (which I have not seen) by Andres Serrano of a plastic crucifix immersed in a bottle of the artist's urine, "Piss Christ" won a prize funded by a federal grant, sparking proposals to attach conditions to public support of the arts that would prevent future public subsidies of blasphemous, obscene, or otherwise offensive works. The questions raised by the Serrano work were shortly afterward exacerbated by the removal from the Corcoran Gallery of an exhibition, also supported by public funds, of photographs by the late Robert Mapplethorpe on subjects homoerotic and, some have argued, sadomasochistic into the bargain. Among the photographs (which, again, I have not seen) is one that is reported to show a black man urinating into the mouth of a white man. But I shall concentrate on "Piss Christ," which poses the issue of public regulation of offensive art in a particularly useful way. Despite or perhaps because of my being a member of the judiciary, I do not want to discuss the legality of proposals to restrict public funding of offensive art. I want instead to discuss the larger philosophical and jurisprudential issues raised by such art. Concretely I want to argue that nowadays there is no objective method of determining what is art or what is offensive, and to consider whether, if this is right, it implies that offensive art should get a lot, or a little—or even no—protection from governmental interference, however that interference should be defined in this setting. For example, is it interference when the government grants, or when it withdraws, a subsidy to the arts?

When we say that lead is heavier than aluminum or that an automobile   2
is faster than a rickshaw, we make a statement that can be verified by methods independent of the tastes or personal values of the people doing the verifying. A Communist, a nudist, a Jehovah's Witness, and a follower of Ayn Rand will all agree on how to test such propositions and on how to interpret the test results. Such "observer independence" gives the propositions about lead and automobiles truth value, makes them objective. It is quite otherwise if we say that "Piss Christ" has, or does not have, artistic value. The problem is not that artistic value is not a thing which a work either has or has

not, for in this respect artistic value is no different from weight or speed, being like them an attribute or property rather than a thing. You don't take apart a Maserati and announce, "This is the carburetor and that is the speed." Similarly, "Piss Christ" is not a composite of urine, a bottle, a crucifix, a photograph, and artistic value.

But while it is possible to make objective measurements of physical properties such as weight and speed, it is not possible to make such measurements of artistic value, because people having different values and preferences do not agree and cannot be brought to agree on how to determine the presence of that attribute or even how to define it. A moralistic critic such as Tolstoy might think that the most important question about "Piss Christ" from an artistic standpoint is its likely effect on belief in Christianity. A Marxist critic might agree, and might further agree with Tolstoy that "Piss Christ" would undermine that belief, yet they would disagree about whether this made the work valuable or pernicious. Even if everyone to whom judges are willing to listen agrees that a work has no artistic value, we know from historical experience that it may; later generations may find such value in the work even though the artist's contemporaries did not. Conversely, a work highly valued in its time, or for that matter in later times, may eventually come to seem thoroughly meretricious. Artistic value is something an audience invests a work with, and as the tastes of audiences change, so do judgments of artistic value. About all that can be said in a positive vein is that the longer a work is held in high repute the likelier it is to continue to be held in high repute. This is the "test of time" that Samuel Johnson, David Hume, and George Orwell thought the only objective test of artistic merit. If, to take a concrete example, the Homeric epics are still being read more than twenty-five hundred years after they were composed, then chances are they will continue to be highly regarded for some time; their appeal is robust and resists cultural change.

So far, though, all we have established is an inductive generalization, not an explanation. We could try to figure out what such durable works as the *Iliad* and *Hamlet* and Raphael's madonnas and *The Marriage of Figaro* and the "Ode on a Grecian Urn" and the Louvre's "Winged Victory of Samothrace" have in common and call that the key to artistic value. But this sort of thing has been attempted for millennia without success, and it now seems clear that the quest is a snipe hunt, so diverse are the durable works of the Western tradition. Conceivably we might identify a *necessary* condition of artistic survival—that a work have a certain "omnisignificance" or, less portentously, a certain ambiguity or generality that enables it to be taken in different ways in different times and places. But the distinction between a necessary and a sufficient condition is critical here, for we would not concede artistic value to every work that crossed some threshold of ambiguity or generality. "Piss Christ" deals with a fundamental concern of humankind, religion, and does so in a distinctly ambiguous way. Serrano denies harboring any blasphemous intent and indeed claims—for all I know, with complete sincerity—that "Piss Christ" is a Christian commentary on the debasement of religion in modern America. The work may have artistic or even moral value, and then again it may not; it may soon come to be thought a worthless bit of trash. If it seems altogether too slight and ephemeral a work to have *any* chance of winning a secure niche in art history, let us remind ourselves that Marcel Duchamp's toilet seat, one of the objets trouvés of the Dadaist movement, has won such a niche along with Goya's disgusting painting "Saturn Eating His Children."

The conclusion to which I am driven is that ascriptions of artistic value   5 or valuelessness to "works of art"—especially to contemporary works of art— are arbitrary. And so with offensiveness, another property of, not a thing found in, a work. "Piss Christ" is no more a compound of urine, a bottle, a crucifix, and offensiveness than it is a compound of urine, a bottle, a crucifix, a photograph, and artistic value. Again this property, offensiveness, is largely, perhaps entirely, a matter of public opinion rather than of correspondence to or causation by something that is observer independent, something akin to the forces that determine weight and speed in accordance with the laws of physics.

This is not a problem when public opinion is united, as perhaps it is   6 over the offensiveness of certain particularly graphic or degrading types of visual obscenity. With specific reference to "Piss Christ" one might be tempted to argue that, while there may be no consensus on what is art, there is a consensus, in Western societies anyway, that the public display of excreta is offensive. Consensus is a highly fallible warrant of truth, yet we might grant it provisionally objective status, even when it is local and temporary—a consensus in our society today, although not in all others and perhaps not in ours tomorrow. But it is a mistake to suppose that there is a consensus concerning the offensiveness of public displays of excreta. If samples of diabetics' or addicts' urine, or the feces of sufferers from Crohn's disease or cancer of the colon were displayed at a medical convention, we would not think the display offensive. It is all a matter of context and purpose. The question of the offensiveness of "Piss Christ" is therefore connected to the question of its artistic value. Those who find the work artistically valuable will not be offended by the (photographic) presence of urine, which they will consider integral to the work's value. Those who find the work blasphemous and barren of artistic value will consider the display of urine gratuitous and hence, given our culture's feelings about excreta, offensive. A few people may find the work both offensive and aesthetic, as many find Ezra Pound's *Cantos* or Vachel Lindsay's *Congo*. Their judgment on whether "Piss Christ" should be suppressed will depend on how offensive, and on how aesthetic, they find it, and on their personal sense of the proper balance between art and insult.

All this (to turn now from philosophy to jurisprudence) would have   7 little or nothing to do with law if law had its own values, if it were morally autonomous. But for the most part it does not and is not. The law that entitles the victim of negligence to collect damages from the injurer is parasitic on—has no life apart from—social norms concerning what is careful and what is careless behavior. The prohibition in the First Amendment against government's abridging freedom of speech or freedom of the press, broadly conceived to include artistic as well as political and scientific expression, is parasitic in the same sense on social norms concerning artistic as well as other "speech" values and offensiveness and other speech harms such as violence. If a speaker urges a mob to lynch a prisoner because his guilt is so plain that a trial would be a waste of time and money, the speaker will be punishable for incitement to violence, because the danger of the speech will be felt to outweigh its value in drawing attention to the problematic character of due process. But if instead he writes a book urging the masses to rise up and liquidate the bosses, he will not be punishable because such books are thought to have some value and not to be very dangerous, although citizens of Communist states may want to dispute both points. If our society thought such books were dangerous, they would be suppressed. Practical considerations, rather than the text or the eighteenth-century background of the First Amendment, guide the application of the amendment to today's problems.

Certain forms of obscenity are considered by virtually everyone in our society (including many of the consumers of obscene works) to be completely worthless and highly offensive, and they are suppressed without much ado, although, it must be added, also without much success. But the consensus that condemns the extremely obscene does not extend to the class of works illustrated by "Piss Christ," which are thought valuable and nonoffensive by some, worthless and offensive by others, worthwhile but offensive by a handful. If there is no objective way to arbitrate such a disagreement, what should the courts do? More broadly, what are the implications for law of the kind of cultural relativism that I am describing?

There are three possibilities here, of which the first two reflect a desire to secure definiteness in law at any price. The first is to forbid *any* governmental interference with "art," no matter how offensive the "art." This approach does not escape subjectivity entirely; rather, it pushes inquiry back a stage, to the question of whether the work in question *is* art (and also to what counts as governmental "interference"). If a work is sufficiently offensive, it is classified as obscene, and therefore as non-art.

At the other extreme is the judicial-hands-off approach: Courts are the forum of principle, there are no principles to apply to questions of aesthetic merit and offensiveness, so let the political branches do what they want with these questions. Such an approach is likely to appeal to those who are especially protective of courts—who want the judges to shine and believe that the judicial escutcheon is tarnished when the judges mess in indeterminate questions such as artistic value and offensiveness.

The third possible approach, the intermediate or pragmatic, is to acknowledge that the problem of relativism, moral as well as aesthetic, so strikingly presented by a work such as "Piss Christ," is a general feature of American, and perhaps of any, legal controversy. Judges need not feel they must shy off merely because the issues raised by offensive art are spongy. That's just the way things are in law; the nature of the legal enterprise ensures that judges will frequently find themselves wrestling with indeterminate questions, because those are the questions least likely to be settled without recourse to lawsuits that have to be pressed all the way to the Supreme Court or to another high appellate court before the question can be answered. Judges struggle with such questions all the time yet somehow manage to retain that minimum of public respect which is indispensable to the effectiveness of a court system. They are unlikely to forfeit it if they venture—with appropriate caution—into the controversy that eddies around issues of value and taste in purported works of art. The significance of the qualification will, I hope, become clearer as I proceed.

The first thing to note about this venture is that although artistic value   12
is largely, perhaps entirely, unknowable, there is little doubt that art is valuable. If this seems a paradox, consider: The lesson of history is that many of the scientific theories in which we firmly believe today are almost certainly false, just as Euclidean geometry as a theory of spatial relations, the geocentric theory of the solar system, the luminiferous ether, the spontaneous generation of bacteria, and Newton's laws of motion are now known to be false after having been believed by the scientific community for centuries. Yet the fallibility of scientific theory does not lead a sensible person to doubt the existence, growth, or value of scientific knowledge. Even if every current scientific theory is someday falsified, we will still be able to make atomic bombs, fly airplanes, and immunize people against polio. Likewise it is a fact that art museums are thronged, that works of art command huge prices, that some people devote a lifetime to the study of art, and, more to the point, that many people would feel a profound sense of deprivation if the French Academy had succeeded in suppressing Impressionist art just as they feel that the world is a poorer place because so little classical Greek sculpture has survived.

If we grant that art has value and add that the censorship of art has a   13
dreadful historical record, we can derive, in order to guide judicial review of controversies over offensive art, a presumption in favor of letting the stuff be produced and exhibited to whoever is willing to pay the price of admission. The Supreme Court's recent decision in the flag-burning case illustrates the presumption. Flag burning is an offensive, inarticulate, and immature mode of political communication (at least when the flag is our own), but as long as one is burning a flag one bought and paid for, before a willing audience, the flag burning contributes, however feebly, to the marketplace of ideas without impairing anybody's property rights.

We can bolster the presumption in favor of a permissive judicial attitude   14
toward offensive art by noting that the "test of time" that is the closest we seem able to get to an objective measure of artistic value presupposes, like natural selection in the theory of biological evolution (which the test of time resembles), the existence of variety, from which history makes its selections. The whole thrust of censorship is to reduce variety, to suppress outliers, and by doing this it interferes with the test of time and impoverishes art's legacy to the future.

I don't mean "presumption" in any fancy lawyer's sense. I just mean   15
that judges should be highly suspicious of anything that smacks of censorship. But since it is only a presumption that I am defending, judges should
also be sensitive to arguments for rebutting it in particular cases, even at the
risk of occasionally being found guilty by history of the sort of folly illustrated by the audience that was scandalized when *The Playboy of the Western
World* was first performed in 1907 because Synge used the word "shift" for
a woman's slip. There is such a thing as worrying too much about history's
verdict on one's actions.

Consider a case in which the presumption in favor of freedom of artistic   16
expression was successfully rebutted. The case was decided by my court years
ago, and since it is quite over and done with, I can discuss it without violating professional proprieties.

The case, *Piarowski v. Illinois Community College,* involved a small ju-   17
nior college near Chicago that, being public, was subject to the constitutional
limitations on restricting free expression. The artist in the case, who was the
chairman of the college's art department, made an improbable effort to fuse
his two loves—the making of stained-glass windows and the art of Aubrey
Beardsley—by making stained-glass versions of some of Beardsley's illustrations from Aristophanes' comedy *Lysistrata.* The illustrations, like the comedy, are bawdy even by today's standards (how fitting that they should be
on public display in the Victoria and Albert Museum in London). They are,
of course, line drawings of white men and women—Greeks. To transpose
the drawings to the stained-glass medium, the artist in my case used pieces
of colored glass for each of the figures, and the colors had to contrast. He
made the innocent but, as it turned out, unfortunate choice of amber glass
for the women and white glass for the men. As a result, one of the stained-
glass windows depicts a brown woman, naked except for stockings, on her
knees, embracing in an attitude of veneration the huge white phallus of a
robed man. The other two windows depict brown women passing wind and
masturbating, respectively.

The artist hung the windows in the art department's annual exhibition   18
of faculty work, held in an alcove (the "gallery") off the main corridor of
the college (the "mall," as it is called), on the ground floor. As the college
has only one building, the exhibition was visible to all students, faculty, and
visitors, whether or not they wanted to see it—more especially as there is no
wall between the gallery and the mall. The first group to complain was the
cleaning staff, which was black. Most of the students in the college are black,
and they, too, were offended by the stained-glass windows and complained
to the president of the college, who ordered the artist to shift the display
from the first-floor corridor to a smaller exhibition room on the fourth floor,
a room normally used for exhibiting photographs but suitable for exhibiting
other works of art as well. When the artist refused, the president took down
the stained-glass windows and placed them in his office. The artist sued the
college, alleging a violation of the First Amendment.

Having studied photographs of Aubrey Beardsley's illustrations for   19
Lysistrata, I find the stained-glass pastiches to be essentially free of both artistic value and offensiveness. Beardsley's charm is on the line, and it is lost
when lines give way to chunks of colored glass. On the other hand, there
was no contention that the chairman of the art department was attempting a
commentary on race or sex; he was merely trying to use different colors,
vaguely human, to distinguish the figures in the windows from one another.
And the very crudeness of the windows neutralizes any obscene impact. For
the reasons stated earlier, however, I have no basis for confidence in my or
any other judge's ability either to evaluate the artistry of the stained-glass
windows or to gauge their offensiveness to a community in which Aubrey
Beardsley is not a household word.

A "hands-off relativist" might take the position that since issues of ar-   20
tistic and moral taste are not objective, the artist should have lost his suit
even if the college had refused to allow him to exhibit his stained-glass windows anywhere on (or for that matter off) the campus. This was not the
court's view, but neither did we think the Constitution *entitled* him to exhibit
his windows in the most public place in the college. The college's president
had offered an alternative place of exhibition that, while indeed less conspicuous, was by the same token less offensive. Racial sensitivities are a fact in
our society, and if, as I have argued, offensiveness ultimately is no more
objective than artistic value, neither is it less so. The college president's action seemed a reasonable compromise, and the court gave judgment for the
college. In so doing, we affirmed that "academic freedom" is a two-way
street. It is the freedom of a college to manage its affairs without undue
judicial interference no less than it is the freedom of the teacher or scholar to
teach or write or, in this case, create works of art without undue interference
by the state (for remember that this was a public college, and hence an arm
of the state). A further point worth making is that the power of a single
junior college to affect the art scene by shunting offensive works to less conspicuous places of exhibition is distinctly limited. But of course the example
might prove catching.

So particularistic and fact-specific—so pragmatic—a mode of adjudica-   21
tion that led to the judgment for the college, and that implies that the scope
of First Amendment protection may be different for works of art than for
political or scientific works, is not to everyone's taste. Lawyers have a predilection for rules, and there indeed are many occasions when hard-edged
rules are preferable to fuzzy standards, but controversies over offensive art
may not be one of them. It is not even clear that art would be helped rather
than hindered by a rule that forbade any and all public regulation of offensive
art. Such a rule—a rule that gave privileged status to the *flaunting* of offensive
art—might engender public hostility to art that would be out of all proportion to the benefits in artistic freedom gained. On the other hand, a rule that
gave government carte blanche to suppress art deemed offensive by any vocal, assertive, politically influential group in our diverse, teeming, and (let us

face it) rather philistine society could impair the future of art, a costly consequence. So perhaps the watchword in First Amendment cases having to do with art should indeed be *caution*.

QUESTIONS FOR MEANING

1. Why is it that art does not have what Posner calls "observer independence"?
2. What is the role of content and purpose in gauging "offensiveness"?
3. What is the difference between urging a mob to lynch a prisoner and writing a book calling for revolution?
4. Can you explain what Posner means by "cultural relativism" in paragraph 8?
5. Why is academic freedom "a two-way street"? Consider the example in paragraphs 17–20.
6. Vocabulary: blasphemous (1), exacerbated (1), homoerotic (1), jurisprudential (1), meretricious (3), millennia (4), portentously (4), ephemeral (4), ascriptions (5), gratuitous (6), escutcheon (10), impairing (13), pastiches (19), predilection (21).

QUESTIONS ABOUT STRATEGY

1. Why do you think Posner points out that he has not seen the controversial photographs he refers to in paragraph 1?
2. How does Posner establish his authority to be writing on this topic?
3. Consider the first sentence in paragraph 13. Why would Posner use a word like "stuff" after using a more formal voice in the first half of the sentence?
4. What function is served by alluding to the Impressionists in paragraph 12 and *The Playboy of the Western World* in paragraph 15?
5. In his conclusion, Posner calls for caution. Where has he prepared the way for this conclusion?

ROBERT BRUSTEIN
The First Amendment and the NEA

Drama critic for The New Republic, *which published the following essay in* **1989**, *Robert Brustein has had a distinguished career as both a critic and as a teacher of acting. Dean of the Yale School of Drama and Director of the Yale Repertory Theater Company from 1966–1979, Brustein has also taught at Vassar, Columbia, and Harvard. His articles have appeared in numerous periodicals, including* Harper's *and the* New York Times, *and they have been collected in such books as* The Third Theater *(1969) and* Who Needs Theatre: Dramatic Opinions *(1990).*

One of the troubling things underlying the current flap over the National   1
Endowment for the Arts is the belief that "no artist has a First Amendment right to a government subsidy." This is an assumption not just of moral absolutists on the right; it is being expressed by many liberals, including our own TRB★, who provides the quote. A recent cartoon by Jules Feiffer shows a wild-haired, scraggle-bearded artist raging against society, then concluding his tirade with the words "FUND ME." And Garry Trudeau's Mike Doonesbury covers his eyes when his wife, J.J., demands government subsidy for her "urinal art." Even among those who think the commonwealth will survive the works of Robert Mapplethorpe or Andres Serrano, some are questioning the judgment of the institutions that initially displayed them because they used government funds. It would seem that federal subsidy completely changes the ground rules governing freedom of artistic expression.

While some organs of the press—notably the *New York Times,* which   2
has covered the controversy superbly—recognize analogies between restraints on artistic freedom and on freedom of speech, I do not think the censorship threat is being properly appreciated, largely because it has been clouded by charges of obscenity and blasphemy. A consensus in Congress, and probably in society at large, seems convinced that the NEA should not be allowed to fund art that the majority finds unpalatable. Jesse Helms affirms that "if someone wants to write nasty things on the men's room wall, the taxpayers do not provide the crayon," while a letter signed by 27 senators and written on Alfonse D'Amato's stationary says, "This matter does not involve freedom of expression. It does involve whether taxpayers' money should be forced to support such trash."

In a cogently argued article in the *American Scholar,* Richard A. Posner   3
reminds us that "nowadays there is no objective method of determining what is art and what is offensive. . . . Even if everyone to whom judges are willing to listen agrees that a work has no artistic value, we know from historical experience that it may." I am not in a position to judge whether Serrano's "Piss Christ" or Mapplethorpe's homoerotic photographs represent art or

★Arbitrarily assigned letters that have traditionally designated an editorial column in *The New Republic.*

pornography. Along with most of their outraged critics, I haven't seen the exhibits. But even if posterity were to prove these works worthless, civil liberarians would be obliged to defend them, on the principle that if you are not prepared to protect bad speech, you are in a poor position to protect the good.

Already congressional proscription has widened to include not just "obscene or indecent materials," in the language of the ludicrous Helms amendment, but "material which denigrates the objects or beliefs of the adherents of a particular religion or non-religion" or "denigrates or debases or reviles a person, group, or class of citizens on the basis of race, creed, sex, handicap, age, or national origin." Were this to be adopted, which seems unlikely, a truly extraordinary amount of classical and contemporary art would be excluded from funding.   4

In fact, it is modern art itself—not just a crucifix dipped in urine—that represents the hidden target of the conservative backlash. Hilton Kramer is too sophisticated a critic to second Helms's fundamentalist religious prohibitions, and he is a well-known defender of high modernism, but his own position is not all that different. Opposed to government intervention in the arts through systematic programs of censorship, he nevertheless equates these with government intervention through systematic programs of support—citing such "antisocial" NEA-founded work as Richard Serra's *Tilted Arc*. What should the federal money support instead? Those artworks that Kramer calls "the highest achievements of our civilization." Invoking the same pious language, Samuel Lipman asks the NEA to reject "the latest fancies to hit the art market" and champion instead "the great art of the past, its representation in the present and its transmission to the future." (Compare Helms, pointing with pride to the paintings of pastoral North Carolina scenes on his walls: "I like beautiful things, not modern art.")   5

All this takes place in a rather grim historical context. Totalitarianism's campaign against "degenerate modern art," and its insistence that art be "the handmaiden of sublimity and beauty, and thus promote whatever is natural and healthy," is well known. The memory of it is still fresh. At this late date, we should be wary of the attack on the new and the "offensive." Conservatives would reply, of course, that the United States, unlike Nazi Germany or Stalinist Russia or Khomeini's Iran, is not calling for the suppression of offensive art, only its exclusion from federal funding. But the distinction between censorship and determining the distribution of taxpayers' dollars on moral grounds eludes me. It derives from the pernicious American tradition of letting the marketplace—rather than a Commissar of Culture or a Minister of Propaganda—function as the censor of the arts.   6

In short, the moral question of censorship is ultimately less threatening than the related political question with which I began: whether the federal government should be funding unpopular modern art at all. This issue was directly confronted in the original enabling legislation of the Endowment, which was created precisely to prevent politicians from voting directly on artists or projects. An unequivocal paragraph stated: "No department, agency,   7 officer, or employee of the United States shall exercise any direction, supervision, or control over the policy, determination, personnel, or curriculum, or the administration or operation of any school or other non-federal agency, institution, organization, or association." The NEA was thus intended as a buffer between Congress and the arts, with the legislators responsible for approving the budget and professional peer panels responsible for approving grants. Congress was never empowered to be a watchdog on the Endowment as it is, say, on HUD or the Pentagon. It was charged rather with guaranteeing the integrity of the grant-making procedure, however controversial. The decisions of the panels were rarely, if ever, overruled; and only 20 grants out of more than 85,000 were even questioned.

Today Congress seems to have forgotten that the original resolution of   8
the Endowment committed the federal government "to help create and sustain not only a climate encouraging freedom of thought, imagination, and inquiry, but also the material conditions facilitating the release of this creative talent." Contrary to current thinking, this placed the Endowment squarely under the protection of the First Amendment, guaranteeing free artistic expression on the same grounds as freedom of speech and freedom of the press. Of course some of these expressions were bound to enrage the majority. That is what we mean by dissent. But it is the very function of the First Amendment to defend unpopular minority opinion against the tyranny of majority constraint.

This fundamental purpose was soon undermined by know-nothing cries   9
of "elitism." If there is anything on which both right and left agree, it is the need for "populist" sovereignty of the majority over the arts. But popular taste has always been perfectly well represented by the market—by Broadway shows, best-selling books, platinum records, rock concerts, Hollywood movies. The National Endowment, by contrast, was designed as a countermarket strategy, not only to "create the material conditions facilitating the release of creative talent," but in the hope that by subsidizing cultural offerings at affordable prices, "the people," in Chekhov's words, "could be brought up to the level of Gogol rather than bringing Gogol down to the level of the people."

Critics like Kramer try to meet this argument by trying to discredit the   10
credentials of the professional panelists. "Professional opinion in the art world," he writes, "can no longer be expected to make wise decisions on these matters. . . . There is in the professional art world a sentimental attachment to the idea that art is at its best when it is most extreme and disruptive." It is certainly true that some artists like to flout prevailing codes of conduct. But even the high modernism that Kramer reveres was "extreme and disruptive," as good art often is. And the professional panel system, for all its flaws, remains the best we have. It is clearly preferable to the punitive grant procedures being prepared by our elected officials.

I was invited to participate on these panels a number of times, as a   11
drama critic and as director of a professional theater company. I joined other critics, directors, playwrights, theater artists, state council members, union

leaders, and related figures, and was consistently amazed at the quality and objectivity of their judgments. Naturally I had a stake in these meetings. Like others on the panel, my own theater was an annual candidate for funding, and grants were always preceded by evaluations. But like the others, I was obliged to leave the room when my theater was being discussed, and neither the grant amount nor the evaluation ration was disclosed until we were later officially informed.

To the charges that peer panels are old-boy networks rewarding like-   12
minded colleagues and excluding outsiders, or simply funding "the latest fancies to hit the art market," I can only reply that this was never my experience. The theater panels on which I served were composed of a great variety
of people, drawn from many aspects of the profession. There was usually
heated disagreement around the table. Often I disagreed with other panelists.
But what always impressed me was their capacity to accept arguments, and
fund theaters, that were fundamentally different in aesthetic from their own.
Our judgments were made not only on the basis of personal knowledge and
the quality of grant applications, but on the basis of the reports of anonymous on-site observers. And most astonishing was the panel's capacity to
evaluate, almost invariably correctly, the intrinsic worth of the applicant theater, rather than its extrinsic reputation among audiences and critics. It was
not at all unusual to see the grant of an establishment theater reduced because
it had gotten *too* fashionable, while a little-known experimental theater was
rewarded for taking risks.

In sum, these were self-interested, passionate theater people judging others   13
in a disinterested, dispassionate manner. They gave me heart about the capacity of normally egoistic professionals to perform a selfless civic duty. I
can't say if the professional panels in Opera/Music Theater, Dance, Literature, Art, and the other divisions of the Endowment function in the same
manner, but I suspect they do. At any rate, the peer system remains far
superior to the system proposed by the Congressional School of Criticism,
if only for understanding what most legislators do not understand: that "in
proportion as freedom is diminished," to cite the language of the NEA resolution, "so is the prospect of artistic achievement."

In the past 25 years, the National Endowment, however small its sub-   14
sidies (the Endowment accounts for less than five percent of the budget of a
normal-sized institution), has helped to support a great surge of artistic
achievement in this country. Its original declaration of purpose was one of a
few hopeful signs that America was coming of cultural age, an unusual legislative response to the Bowlders and Mrs. Grundys and Senator Claghorns
who invariably oppose anything creative and daring. These figures are once
again in the ascendant. But people of goodwill, rather than joining the moralistic brigade, must recognize that if you inhibit artistic expression, however
controversial, you threaten the rights of us all. They must recognize that
only government—in a time when other funding has grown increasingly restrictive and programmatic—can guarantee free and innovative art. And that

means acknowledging that, yes, every artist has a First Amendment right to subsidy.

QUESTIONS FOR MEANING

1. According to Brustein, what is the function of free speech?
2. Brustein claims that "a truly extraordinary amount of classical and contemporary art" would be excluded from funding by the amendment quoted in paragraph 4. Can you think of any examples that would support this claim?
3. Why isn't Brustein worried about whether the National Endowment for the Arts funds projects that will appeal to popular taste?
4. Explain the allusions to Bowlders and Mrs. Grundys in paragraph 14. What does it mean to bowlderize a text?
5. Vocabulary: tirade (1), unpalatable (2), proscription (4), sublimity (6), pernicious (6), unequivocal (7), flout (10), aesthetic (12), intrinsic (12), extrinsic (12).

QUESTIONS ABOUT STRATEGY

1. What is the point of showing agreement between liberals and conservatives in paragraph 1? How does this prepare the way for the argument that follows?
2. Consider the quotation from Senator Helms in paragraph 5. Why does Brustein include it? What is Helms assuming and what is Brustein implying?
3. How useful is the quotation in paragraph 7? Would a paraphrase have served as well?
4. Brustein draws upon his personal experience with grant funding in paragraphs 11 and 12. What does this add to his argument?
5. Has Brustein provided adequate support for his conclusions?

JOHN A. WILLIAMS
Prior Restraints

John A. Williams is the author of many novels. They include The Angry Ones *(1960),* Night Song *(1961),* Sissie *(1963),* The Man Who Cried I Am *(1967),* Mothersill and the Foxes *(1976), and* The Berhama Account *(1985). He has also published nonfiction, including a 1970 biography of Richard Wright,* The Most Native of Sons. *A 1950 graduate of Syracuse University, Williams has taught at the University of California, Santa Barbara, Boston University, and Rutger's University. The following argument on censorship was first published by* The Nation *in **1988**. It reflects Williams' own experience as a black writer who is concerned about how minorities are treated in the United States.*

In *The Media Monopoly* Ben Bagdikian notes that "in 1981 there were forty-six corporations that controlled most of the business in daily newspapers, magazines, television, books and motion pictures. Five years later the number had shrunk to twenty-nine." It is now 1988 and the shrinkage continues. In 1965 my editor at Little, Brown & Company, the late Harry Sions, told me that Time Inc.'s intended purchase of the company would make no difference in the quality of books Little, Brown produced. I didn't believe him, but I stayed with the house for a while anyway. We all know now that such takeovers have been bad news for writers. For one thing, they increase the importance of the dollar sign—always a mark of the censors. 1

But another element of censorship has emerged with the severe contractions of the publishing industry, and it is one black and other minority writers (and some white writers) have grumbled about for years. A dozen years ago I said in an interview, "PEN★ is so concerned with foreign authors and their plight, but how about the plight of black authors here?" The quote appeared in the June 7, 1976, edition of *Publishers Weekly*. The then secretary of PEN called me to say that PEN could not be responsible for "faddishness" in publishing. The possibility that a genteel sort of censorship lay hidden in the folds of a concern about "faddishness" did not occur to him—as it has not occurred to others. I saw no reason to pursue the issue, as I knew he did not believe one existed. The case has been made more legitimate, I think, by Irving Louis Horowitz's article "Monopolization of Publishing and Crisis in Higher Education" (*Academe*, November/December 1987). Horowitz has suggested that "the new monopolization has a direct bearing on the ability of publishing to satisfy a fundamental constitutional guarantee: free speech." He continues, "A free speech environment is more subtly eroded by different notions of appropriate profit goals that obtain in large and small firms." 2

Even before the domestic conglomerates took them over, publishing houses had become reluctant to accept works by black authors, so we cannot 3

★An international organization of writers.

realistically expect the foreign conglomerates to do any better. Quite possibly they will do worse, and the erosion of a free speech environment will continue.

Twenty years ago there were several black editors in publishing houses. 4 (That they are no longer in place may indicate that publishers do not feel them capable of editing books written by white writers.) True, they were mainly advisers to the major decision-makers, but they were there, and as a result there was some enthusiasm for the publication of black writers. That time is past, and I do not see it returning in my lifetime. I am not happy to have to write this, but the facts do tend to speak for themselves.

During that same brief period, newspapers and magazines also hired 5 minorities, but staffing to achieve a quota did not mean bigotry had died. Fifteen years ago, for example, *The New York Times* and the Associated Press were sued by minorities and women. Both settled out of court. More recently, last year, the New York *Daily News,* unwise enough to go to court in the face of ample evidence of discrimination against blacks, lost a suit to four black journalists who had charged it with discrimination. There is, of course, a clear, indisputable relationship between the media and the publishing industry.

It must be noticed, if rarely mentioned, that black reviewers and critics 6 are seldom asked to comment on works by white authors in the major review media. This, too, is censorship. PEN has a "Freedom-to-Write" committee. No one, however, actually bars an author's freedom to write; it is the freedom to publish, to be heard or read, that is at stake in both democratic and totalitarian states; it is the freedom to be judged on literary, and not only on racial or political, grounds. The problem here, though, is that the term "literary" can be used to exclude, especially by people who approach a work with a particular kind of historical, political and racial baggage but deny to others the right to bear the same freight. No doubt, this has always been true. No doubt, those who control this system still believe that minority writers either know nothing about it or else are fearful of what they do know and of the way that knowledge must reflect upon the controllers.

In *How We Live* (1968) Penney C. and L. Rust Hills inadvertently re- 7 vealed a contradiction concerning black writers that is still prevalent in publishing and in the media. They wrote: "It is not that Negroes are not writing or being published; but aside from Ellison and Baldwin, they have not yet produced the kind of writing that satisfies the complex contemporary literary tastes and sensibilities." In the book's appendix, however, they note: "The way students are now taught to read literature in our colleges and universities obscures from them what literature can tell us about ourselves and the way we live."

The clause "satisfies the complex contemporary literary tastes and sen- 8 sibilities" expresses a curiously incomplete thought. No doubt to have added "of white readers" would have been too obvious a declaration, too clearly a suggestion of literary prior restraint, first cousin to censorship. The contradiction emerges again in the complaint that the way students are taught "obscures from them what literature can tell us about ourselves." Since most black writers never make it into the textbooks that are used in colleges and universities, what white (and minority) students can learn about American life is limited.

The kind of censorship present in the publishing industry could not   9
exist without the support of critics, reviewers and academics. Addison Gayle Jr. characterizes academics as being in "control of the nation's cultural apparatus." They work together with "critics who, more often than not, peer out upon American society with a condescension usually reserved for idiots and half-wits." On the rare occasions when some academics do seek to widen the scope of literary study or when they describe its present limitations, they become anathema. *The Washington Post*'s Jonathan Yardley early this year described such efforts as being the work of "young fascists." Twenty-odd years ago the label would have been "radical" or "militant." What has happened to harden the language about what is essentially, in the case of Afro-American writers, censorship?

Actually, what we are witnessing is a hardening of attitudes about who   10
is going to send along the word. Some of this was already present in the 1960s. Reviewing Gwendolyn Brooks's *Selected Poems* for the *New York Herald Tribune*'s *Book Week* in October 1963, Louis Simpson wrote, "I am not sure it is possible for a Negro to write well without making us aware that he is a Negro." He continued, "On the other hand, if being a Negro is the only subject, the writing is not important." Simpson later apologized for this statement. The fact is that almost all white writers detail white life in their works. Fair enough—that is their experience. Black critics and reviewers in the main are not permitted to comment favorably or unfavorably on such depictions, though they surely hold vigorous opinions about them. There is no lack of white reviewers and critics, however, who can easily secure platforms from which they can create the impression that most of the writing done by black authors—writing from their experience—is really not very good and therefore warrants little consideration. Literary agents, most of whom are white, buttress this attitude with the general philosophy that black writers do not produce "commercial" work, do not make money and therefore do not make suitable clients. Some white writers find themselves tagged as uncommercial, and for that reason are also de facto censored.

Long before Simpson there was Robert Bone's *The Negro Novel in   11
America*, in which protest was viewed as inimical to "art." The literature of protest had been an honorable endeavor for writers for over a century. In the hands of black writers, however, critics saw it as tainted. And, most recently, in *The New York Times Magazine*, Saul Bellow is credited with this statement: "Who is the Tolstoy of the Zulus? The Proust of the Papuans? I'd be glad to read them." It will be noted that both groups are black. Bellow's questions prompt one to ask if, at the core of this statement, he is saying that black people have produced no literature worthy of his time. "Every intellectual," Ignazio Silone once declared, "is a revolutionary." He was wrong,

especially regarding this nation, where they seem to be growing more and more conservative.

I began this piece by discussing the effect of conglomerate takeovers on writing and on the right of free speech. I believe that censorship, intended or not, exists in publishing and affects black writers disproportionately, and that the publishing industry, in concert with the media and the academy, reinforces that second level of censorship created by profit-taking considerations. Sometimes this all comes together in the awarding of literary prizes. But the awarding of prizes cannot be separated from racist attitudes.

Recently, the names of forty-eight black writers—myself included—appeared on a statement in the press praising Toni Morrison and expressing concern that she has not received national recognition. As it was published, however, the statement was different from the one read to me over the phone. I was told it would deal, generally, with some of the concerns I've written about here. Literary awards were not mentioned. Everyone in or close to the publishing industry has heard gossip about publishing, editorial and authorial machinations at prize giving time. For example, I suppose that from now on, any mention of Toni Morrison's Pulitzer Prize will include reference to that letter, an inference of black literary maneuvering. Whenever "major" prizes are awarded to black writers, they tend to validate the individual but not in any way the body of Afro-American writing they cannot help but represent. That may be why James Baldwin never got a major award. Neither did Langston Hughes. Baldwin got publicity. Richard Wright and Chester Himes got very little of either. They all seemed to be men of the people, speakers for them. What is really under consideration here is power. Censorship is an exercise in power, however gently, however harshly it is exercised—and prizes can only be seen as accouterments of that power. At the heart of the need to display such power is the ancient conflict, always denied but deadly persistent: race and racism.

QUESTIONS FOR MEANING

1. How could corporate takeovers lead to censorship as defined by Williams?
2. Why have black writers been discriminated against?
3. According to Williams, who controls American culture?
4. What are the two levels of censorship that concern Williams?
5. Vocabulary: genteel (2), anathema (9), de facto (10), tainted (11), accouterments (13).

QUESTIONS ABOUT STRATEGY

1. Williams discusses publishing in the 1960s and 70s as well as in the 1980s. What purpose is served by discussing publishing over a twenty-year period?
2. Consider the quote from Saul Bellow in paragraph 11. What is Williams implying about Bellow?

3. In paragraph 8, Williams claims that "most black writers never make it into the textbooks that are used in colleges and universities." Judging from your own experience, does this seem like a reasonable claim?
4. Williams draws upon his own experience in paragraphs 1, 2, and 13. Has he done so effectively?

CARYL RIVERS

Rock Lyrics and Violence Against Women

*First published in **1985**, "Rock Lyrics and Violence Against Women" reflects concerns that have shaped other works by Caryl Rivers. A journalist whose articles have appeared in* Ms., McCall's, Saturday Review, *and the* New York Times Magazine, *Rivers is also the author of* Aphrodite at Midcentury: Growing Up Female and Catholic in Postwar America *(1973),* Intimate Enemies *(1987), and* Indecent Behavior *(1990). She has taught journalism at Boston University since 1966, and she is also a public affairs commentator for WGBH-TV in Boston.*

After a grisly series of murders in California, possibly inspired by the lyrics of a rock song, we are hearing a familiar chorus: Don't blame rock and roll. Kids will be kids. They love to rebel, and the more shocking the stuff, the better they like it.   1

There's some truth in this, of course. I loved to watch Elvis shake his torso when I was a teen-ager, and it was even more fun when Ed Sullivan wouldn't let the cameras show him below the waist. I snickered at the forbidden "Rock with Me, Annie" lyrics by a black Rhythm and Blues group, which were deliciously naughty. But I am sorry, rock fans, that is not the same thing as hearing lyrics about how a man is going to force a woman to perform oral sex on him at gunpoint in a little number called "Eat Me Alive." It is not in the same league with a song about the delights of slipping into a woman's room while she is sleeping and murdering her, the theme of an AC/DC ballad that allegedly inspired the California slayer.   2

Make no mistake, it is not sex we are talking about here, but violence. Violence against women. Most rock songs are not violent—they are funky, sexy, rebellious, and sometimes witty. Please do not mistake me for a Mrs. Grundy. If Prince wants to leap about wearing only a purple jock strap, fine. Let Mick Jagger unzip his fly as he gyrates, if he wants to. But when either one of them starts garroting, beating, or sodomizing a woman in their number, that is another story.   3

I always find myself annoyed when "intellectual" men dismiss violence against women with a yawn, as if it were beneath their dignity to notice. I   4 wonder if the reaction would be the same if the violence were directed against someone other than women. How many people would yawn and say, "Oh, kids will be kids," if a rock group did a nifty little number called "Lynchin,'" in which stringing up and stomping on black people were set to music? Who would chuckle and say, "Oh, just a little adolescent rebellion" if a group of rockers went on MTV dressed as Nazis, desecrating synagogues and beating up Jews to the beat of twanging guitars?

I'll tell you what would happen. Prestigious dailies would thunder on 5 editorial pages; senators would fall over each other to get denunciations into the Congressional Record. The president would appoint a commission to clean up the music business.

But violence against women is greeted by silence: It shouldn't be. 6

This does not mean censorship, or book (or record) burning. In a so- 7 ciety that protects free expression, we understand a lot of stuff will float up out of the sewer. Usually, we recognize the ugly stuff that advocates violence against any group as the garbage it is, and we consider its purveyors as moral lepers. We hold our nose and tolerate it, but we speak out against the values it proffers.

But images of violence against women are not staying on the fringes of 8 society. No longer are they found only in tattered, paper-covered books or in movie houses where winos snooze and the scent of urine fills the air. They are entering the mainstream at a rapid rate. This is happening at a time when the media, more and more, set the agenda for the public debate. It is a powerful legitimizing force—especially television. Many people regard what they see on TV as the truth; Walter Cronkite once topped a poll as the most trusted man in America.

Now, with the advent of rock videos and all-music channels, rock mu- 9 sic has grabbed a big chunk of legitimacy. American teen-agers have instant access, in their living rooms, to the messages of rock, on the same vehicle that brought them Sesame Street. Who can blame them if they believe that the images they see are accurate reflections of adult reality, approved by adults? After all, Big Bird used to give them lessons on the same little box. Adults, by their silence, sanction the images. Do we really want our kids to think that rape and violence are what sexuality is all about?

This is not a trivial issue. Violence against women is a major social 10 problem, one that's more than a cerebral issue to me. I teach at Boston University, and one of my most promising young journalism students was raped and murdered. Two others told me of being raped. Recently, one female student was assaulted and beaten so badly she had $5,000 worth of medical bills and permanent damage to her back and eyes.

It's nearly impossible, of course, to make a cause-and-effect link be- 11 tween lyrics and images and acts of violence. But images have a tremendous power to create an atmosphere in which violence against certain people is sanctioned. Nazi propagandists knew that full well when they portrayed Jews as ugly, greedy, and powerful.

The outcry over violence against women, particularly in a sexual con-   12
text, is being legitimized in two ways: by the increasing movement of these
images into the mainstream of the media in TV, films, magazines, albums,
videos, and by the silence about it.

Violence, of course, is rampant in the media. But it is usually set in   13
some kind of moral context. It's usually only the bad guys who commit
violent acts against the innocent. When the good guys get violent, it's against
those who deserve it. Dirty Harry blows away the scum, he doesn't walk up
to a toddler and say, "Make my day." The A Team does not shoot up sub-
urban shopping malls.

But in some rock songs, it's the "heroes" who commit the acts. The   14
people we are programmed to identify with are the ones being violent, with
women on the receiving end. In a society where rape and assaults on women
are endemic, this is no small problem, with millions of young boys watching
on their TV screens and listening on their Walkmans.

I think something needs to be done. I'd like to see people in the indus-   15
try respond to the problem. I'd love to see some women rock stars speak out
against violence against women. I would like to see disc jockeys refuse air
play to records and videos that contain such violence. At the very least, I
want to see the end of the silence. I want journalists and parents and critics
and performing artists to keep this issue alive in the public forum. I don't
want people who are concerned about this issue labeled as bluenoses and
bookburners and ignored.

And I wish it wasn't always just women who were speaking out. Men   16
have as large a stake in the quality of our civilization as women do in the
long run. Violence is a contagion that infects at random. Let's hear something, please, from the men.

QUESTIONS FOR MEANING

1. What distinction does Rivers draw between the rock music she enjoyed as
   a teenager and the type of rock she objects to today?
2. What does Rivers mean when she declares that television "is a powerful
   legitimizing force"?
3. According to Rivers, how does the portrayal of violence in rock differ
   from the way violence is usually portrayed in the media?
4. In paragraph 7, Rivers indicates that she is not in favor of censorship.
   What does she want?

QUESTIONS ABOUT STRATEGY

1. How does Rivers demonstrate that she is not a prude? Why is this strategy
   useful?
2. In paragraph 4, Rivers speculates upon how people would react if rock
   groups treated blacks and Jews like they treat women. How effective is

this comparison? How convincing is the prediction she offers in paragraph 5?

3. How were you affected by the evidence in paragraph 10? Does Rivers succeed in linking this evidence to her argument as a whole?

4. All but one of the sentences in paragraph 15 begin with use of the first person. Why do you think Rivers chose to begin so many sentences with the same word?

JON PARELES

Legislating the Imagination

A music critic for the New York Times *who specializes in popular music, Jon Pareles has also written for* Rolling Stone, Mademoiselle, Glamour, *and* Harper's Bazaar. *He published the following argument in* ***1990,*** *when several states were considering legislation that would require warning labels on recordings with lyrics that contain references that are either sexually explicit or likely to encourage violence. As you read "Legislating the Imagination," note that Pareles links the debate over labeling to the debate over the Helms amendment discussed earlier in this section by Robert Brustein.*

In South Korea and East Germany until recently, the government had to   1
approve every song, book, film, or play. In Singapore, the Undesirable Publications Act forbids song lyrics that make references to drugs or have obscene connotations. And if legislators in about a dozen states have their way, the United States will join such havens of enlightenment in allowing the power of the government to regulate the arts. What they're up to, in effect, is an attempt to regulate the imagination.

The Pennsylvania House of Representatives recently passed legislation   2
that prohibits the sale—to anyone—of recordings with lyrics on a number of rude topics unless their packages are labeled as follows: "WARNING: May contain explicit lyrics descriptive of or advocating one of more of the following: suicide, incest, bestiality, sadomasochism, sexual activity in a violent context, murder, morbid violence, illegal use of drugs or alcohol. PARENTAL ADVISORY."

The labels are to be fluorescent yellow and not readily removable. While   3
the Pennsylvania Senate considers the bill, similar measures are pending in Virginia, Arizona, Iowa, New Mexico, Illinois, Oklahoma, Delaware, and Kansas. A Missouri version adds "sodomy" to the possible offenses, while one in Florida, which adds "sexual activity" to the list, would prohibit selling stickered albums to minors. Unlike movie ratings, which are voluntarily

applied by film companies, the state laws would carry the threat of fines and jail terms for sellers of recordings.

It's not a free-speech issue, advocates say, just a label that provides   4
consumer information. That it also makes recordings look like radioactive waste barrels isn't their concern.

Whether or not they survive constitutional tests, the bills are the latest   5
fruit of the uproar raised over rock lyrics by the Parents' Music Resource Center, the Arlington, Virginia-based group that pressured recording companies into voluntarily placing "Explicit Lyrics—Parental Advisory" stickers on many potentially offensive albums—a few dozen of the nearly 3,000 albums released every year.

The group has always asserted that it does not advocate legislation and   6
quietly gave up its initial idea about citing lyrics for specific offenses, admitting the difficulties of interpretation. (In the group's newsletter, *The Record,* songs are categorized, targeted albums are still listed without explanations, and readers are urged to write their legislators about material they don't like.)

But the group's tactics—selective and often misleading excerpts from   7
lyrics, exaggeration of both the virulence and quantity of offensive material—are now being replayed in state legislatures, as legislatures strive to equate some recordings with pornography. In an election year an antismut crusade is always boffo.

Labeling is certainly a clever tactic. To be obscene, under Supreme Court   8
guidelines, a publication has to be pornographic through and through, without any "redeeming social value"—not one song of a dozen or some four-letter words. It also has to impress a reasonable adult—not just the "most susceptible" audience—as being geared exclusively to prurient interest. (Scare groups often posit a susceptible adolescent, on the brink of violence or suicide, as the typical rock listener. But beyond anecdotal cases, no research has established causal links between entertainment choices and actions.)

Labeling trickily sidesteps such stringent tests. Slap on a sticker because   9
somebody, sometime, might complain, and a whole album is categorized by its nastiest moment, no discussion necessary. Where criticism explains, examines, and sometimes condemns the meaning gleaned from lyrics—free speech at work—lists like those published by the Parents' Music Resource Center and the stickers proposed by legislators are blanket condemnations: The album is evil.

Hardly any albums—perhaps 2 Live Crew's *As Nasty as They Wanna*   10
Be, which is so raunchy that the group released an alternate (and poorly selling) version, *As Clean as They Gotta Be*—would fail the legal obscenity tests. But labeling would be more pervasive. The center's newsletter lists (without explanation) current albums by Aerosmith and Love and Rockets; neither performers nor manufacturers thought they needed labels.

Grouping categories together is ingenious. In all of rock, there are   11
probably fewer songs about bestiality than about molecular biology, unless Clifton Chenier's bayou classic, "I'm a Hog for You, Baby," counts. But a label doesn't distinguish between bestiality and adultery, a not infrequent topic in any narrative form; better slap a sticker on the Bible. Meanwhile,

why worry about interpretation? "Descriptive of or advocating" covers a lot of ground; antisuicide or antidrug songs would be targets along with their opposites. And somebody's going to have to explain to me the difference between morbid violence and other kinds.

Those yellow stickers would be scary in themselves. They'd be a lot   12
more prominent than package warnings on, for instance, cigarettes, which actually kill people. And since every country album—what's country music without booze or adultery?—along with nearly every opera (adultery, morbid violence, sadomasochism) or collection of patriotic songs (violence) will have a sticker, record stores will look awfully forbidding. That, in the end, seems to be the plan. Any leftover stickers could always be used on books.

Music, like the other arts, shares dreams, conjectures, and fantasies in   13
ways that aren't usually as simple as indoctrination. Art is fictive and ambiguous, and it's a way to explore both the ordinary and the forbidden in a symbolic realm where nobody gets hurt; the popular-culture marketplace strives to deliver a fabrication to fit every daydream. But music's amorphous playfulness makes some people nervous. They seem to assume that listeners can't distinguish between fantasy and reality—or, going even further, that fantasy overwhelms reality.

But is it that easy? William Bennett, the United States drug policy di-   14
rector, recently asserted that purposeful, forthright drug education programs don't "inoculate children against drug abuse." Record labelers, by contrast, insist that a line or two about drugs, pro or con, garbled over a loud beat, can send an impressionable child down the road to perdition.

Initiatives like the Pennsylvania bill and the Helms amendment that would   15
have prohibited federal financing of "obscene or indecent" art are attempts to rein in the public's fantasy life—to put certain areas of the imagination off limits, to equate a fleeting adulterous longing with violent murder or bestiality, to close down the mental playground where creativity flourishes alongside sinful daydreams.

George Clinton, mastermind of Parliament-Funkadelic, often leads his   16
audiences in a chant: "Think! It ain't illegal yet!" Not at the moment, but legislators are working on it.

QUESTIONS FOR MEANING

1. What is the difference between rating movies and putting labels on record albums?
2. According to Pareles, why has the Parents' Music Resource Center been guilty of misleading tactics?
3. How does labeling sidestep a difficult legal issue?
4. The Pennsylvania legislation, quoted in paragraph 2, groups together material that is "descriptive of" with material that advocates. Is there a difference between the two?
5. Vocabulary: connotations (1), havens (1), prurient (8), posit (8), amorphous (13), perdition (14)

QUESTIONS ABOUT STRATEGY

1. What purpose is served by linking rock to country music and opera?
2. Pareles implies that labeling records will lead to labeling books. Is his reasoning logical or fallacious?
3. Has Pareles made any attempts to be fair to his opponents?
4. In paragraphs 15 and 16, Pareles links listening to music to the value of thinking and imagining. Why is it useful for him to define the issue in these terms?

JAMES A. MICHENER
Are There Limits to Free Speech?

A 1929 graduate of Swathmore College, James A. Michener has been a prolific and highly successful writer for many years. He is best known for fiction that contains well-detailed descriptions of exotic settings such as Tales of the South Pacific *(1947), for which he won a Pulitzer Prize, and, more recently,* Alaska *(1988) and* Caribbean *(1989). In all, he has written more than forty books. A recipient of the U.S. Medal of Freedom who has served on the Board for International Broadcasting, Michener has frequently defended democratic ideals, including free speech. The essay reprinted here was first published by* Parade Magazine *in* **1990**.

I am a passionate defender of free speech for two reasons. First, I am a writer and exist as such only because as a U.S. citizen I am pretty much free to say and write what I think. The mighty First Amendment of the Bill of Rights ensures me that freedom. Second, in World War II, I helped to defend our nation and learned then to appreciate how precious all freedoms are.

But freedom of speech poses special problems. It can be difficult to define and quite often difficult to exercise. During my writing life, I have wrestled with such matters constantly. A few examples will illustrate how complicated the right to speak freely can be.

When I moved to Alaska in 1985 to write about that immense land, I was visited by the committees of three different groups. One group was Eskimo, one Athabascan Indian and one Metis (half-native, half-Caucasian). But all three delivered the same message. "You're free to write whatever you wish about Alaska, except for two forbidden subjects," they warned me. "We do not need anyone from the lower 48 to come up here and preach to us about either alcoholism or suicide. They are the scourge of our people, and we'll handle them without instructions from you."

One group wanted me to submit anything I wrote for its approval— and threatened me with serious consequences if I didn't. This posed a clear-cut problem: Either I wrote what I saw, or I submitted to censorship. Since I had no plans to write about the two forbidden subjects, I told the groups, "I suppose I'll be able to respect your wishes."

But when I reached farthest north and visited one Eskimo family after another who had lost a member to suicide, and I lived in Wainwright, a remote village where four high school students died in one day from drinking contaminated alcohol, I said: "All bets are off." Then I wrote into my novel the tragic story of an Eskimo girl I called Amy Ekseavik, who is a bright student expected to qualify early for college. The suicide of Amy's father, however, forces the girl to leave school to help out at home. Six months later, word trickles in to Desolation (my fictional name for a town much like Wainwright) that 15-year-old Amy has taken her father's gun, stepped outside her family's sod hut and committed suicide. These were stories about societal ills that had to be told, and to have surrendered to censorship—even of a benevolent kind—would have been wrong.

I am, of course, constantly mindful that freedom of speech has limits. Justice Oliver Wendell Holmes Jr. phrased one neatly: "The most stringent protection of free speech would not protect a man falsely shouting fire in a theater and causing a panic." Nor is libel against a fellow citizen permitted. Nor lying under oath. These are sensible limits to free speech, and I accept them.

The more difficult questions about the right vs. the responsibility of free speech arise in matters like the suicides of real-life Amy Ekseaviks. When does withholding such information from the public become suppression of free speech? And when does it take the form of common sense for the common good?

I remember the shock I received in the 1932 Presidential election when Franklin D. Roosevelt made a whistle stop in our little town in Colorado and allowed us to see something which had never appeared in a newspaper photograph or a newsreel: "Look! He can barely walk with braces on his legs." Those days of self-censorship are over, and I believe we are better off without them, although some of my friends in the media argue, "It was better in the old days. We didn't chew up our leaders so fast."

Now, to discuss some tough cases which perplex the nation today because they deal with the nitty-gritty of free speech:

Some years ago, I was asked to sign a document protesting government censorship of pornography. At first, I had no trouble signing it, for I agreed with the U.S. Supreme Court, which had refused to outlaw pornography generally but did allow censorship if the material had no redeeming social value. I do not like pornography. I have never patronized shops that sold it and certainly never wrote it myself—but I would not censor it, for I felt that infringing on the First Amendment could do the nation more serious harm than the circulation of a few lascivious picture books.

But as I was about to sign, a man more knowledgeable in this field than I showed me a display of obscene materials he thought ought to be censored. I wanted no part of them, but neither did I think they ought to be outlawed. Then he showed me others that presented a score of ways in which men could brutalize, even murder, women. These were hurtful to an orderly society, the products of sick minds and an invitation to abuse women. But should they be censored? I withheld judgment.

Finally, he showed me scenes of gross child pornography, and I was so   12
revolted by this abuse of children—before they reached the age at which they could form, inherit or consciously elect their patterns of sexual behavior— that I cried: "This filth should be outlawed, and the people who purvey it should be in jail!"

I still defend those three opinions. General pornography is distasteful   13
but not censorable. Sadistic materials denigrating women disturb me and probably ought not to be circulated, but I do not know my own mind as to their censorship. Child pornography should be outlawed, as it now is, and its perpetrators jailed.

One of the most perplexing censorship cases in recent memory in-   14
volved photographs by the late Robert Mapplethorpe on display in a Cincin- nati museum last spring. The exhibit contained more than a few shots of explicit homoerotic behavior, and whereas these photos had been viewed in other cities—Philadelphia posted a warning, then set them apart from the other photos—elected officials in Cincinnati found the show to be offensive by local moral standards. Arrests were made; indictments followed. (On Oct. 5, a jury acquitted the museum and its director of obscenity charges.)

How would I have handled this matter? I would not censor the show.   15
I would allow it to circulate and would even encourage interested patrons to judge it on its merits. But if I were a curator in a city where I knew local sensibilities might be offended—and where I might find myself in jail—I probably would not exhibit Mapplethorpe's photographs. Were I in a more liberal community (with job security), I'm sure I would exhibit them—copy- ing the Philadelphia tactic of keeping off to one side shots which should not be shown to schoolchildren.

Increasingly, the battles we are waging today over the freedom of speech   16
have to do with freedom of expression. One case involves a "rap band," 2 Live Crew, which specializes in staccato dialogue heavy with the grossest sexual emphasis. The band cut an album, *As Nasty As They Wanna Be,* which ridicules women as bitches and whores. It advocates that young men abuse their dates in appalling ways that cannot be specified in a family magazine.

A U.S. district judge in Fort Lauderdale ruled the album obscene. As a   17
result, a record-store owner was convicted of obscenity for selling it. And when 2 Live Crew performed in Hollywood, Fla., its sheriff decided that the judge's ruling empowered him to arrest Luther Campbell, leader of the band, for parading obscenity in public. His arrest, trial and recent acquittal resur- rect the complex debate over artistic freedom vs. a community's right to restrict sexual material.

How does a noncensorship man like me react? In my reverence for the   18
First Amendment, I would not censor the album. But I might be tempted to

try a citizen's arrest—not on the grounds of censorship, but because the lyrics are an incitement to the physical abuse and degradation of women.

The latest innovation in the suppression of free speech is called SLAPP   19 (for Strategic Lawsuit Against Public Participation). It works like this: Suppose that I am an aggressive land-developer who wants to convert your public park into condominiums. You, the concerned citizen, are opposed. So you write to the editor of your newspaper, opposing the park's conversion into high-rises. You have not defamed me or abused me. All you have done is exercise your right to free speech during a controversy.

But I am outraged at your intrusion into my plans and slap you with a   20 lawsuit charging libel, defamation, conspiracy, nuisance and other infractions of civil law. I also claim $250,000 in damages—and you find yourself with huge lawyers' fees staring you in the face.

There is little chance that my lawsuit against you could win in court.   21 In many such suits across the country, judges throw the cases out, for they are patently spurious. Yet when other public-minded citizens learn of the cost to you in worry and cash outlay, they are scared away from exercising their Constitutional right to join in a public debate.

There is a strong movement to outlaw frivolous SLAPPs, and the courts   22 are beginning to side with aggrieved citizens who have been abused or terrified by such suits. SLAPPs should be halted.

My last case is the most wrenching, for it involves deep-seated visceral   23 feelings: "Should the public burning of the American flag be outlawed?" This act is so repugnant to many loyal Americans that it produces outrage, and when the Supreme Court says that it should be seen merely as one more example of citizens exercising their freedom to express their views, allowed by the First Amendment, those offended cry, "Pass a Constitutional amendment outlawing it!" To do so would impair that part of the First Amendment which protects our freedom, and I must oppose it. As a defender of the remarkable pattern of government our nation has evolved, I deplore abuses which defame our flag, but I do not want to see it protected by tampering with our basic law. We can urge members of Congress to pass ordinary acts to achieve that purpose, and I hope they do. But leave the Bill of Rights alone.

I defend freedom of speech so vigorously because of personal experi-   24 ences. Three of my books have been banned by the nations about which I had written: South Africa, Spain and Poland. My novel *Hawaii* was so poorly received there, because I spoke openly of discrimination, that newspaper editorials advised me to leave the islands and never come back. And the chief of police in Jakarta, Indonesia, announced that he would publicly thrash me if I ever returned to his city. Heavy censorship has been part of my life, but I have lived to see opinion change. In all three nations where my books were banned, I have been invited back as an honored guest. As one critic said to me in Poland: "We still don't like parts of your book, but so many visitors tell us they visited Poland because of it, we have to redefine you as a friend."

More important is the fact that for the past 20 years I have served on   25
one U.S. government board or another, fighting communism and striving
to bring the freedom of speech to countries behind the Iron Curtain. This
has kept me informed as to the terrible things that can happen in a nation
like Romania, for example, when free speech is stifled. In one country after
another—first in Czechoslovakia, then Hungary—when tyrants were finally
overthrown, the people turned for democratic leadership to the writers, editors and poets who had fought to keep freedom of speech alive in their countries.

I suppose it always has been that way. Who, after all, were those free-   26
speaking prophets of the Old Testament who ranted against the evils of their
rulers but the editors and columnists of their day?

QUESTIONS FOR MEANING

1. How does Michener explain his own interest in censorship?
2. Does Michener identity any difficulties in answering the question posed
   by his title?
3. When writing about Alaska, why did Michener eventually ignore the re-
   quests of Eskimos?
4. What is SLAPP, and how does it work?
5. Vocabulary: scourge (3), benevolent (5), lascivious (10), purvey (12), sadistic (13), staccato (16), defamation (20), visceral (23).

QUESTIONS ABOUT STRATEGY

1. How does Michener protect himself from the possible charge that, in fa-
   voring free speech, he is protecting pornography?
2. In paragraph 18, Michener claims that he would not censor a 2 Live Crew
   album but he might attempt to arrest the band. Is this reassuring? Does it
   strengthen his case for free speech?
3. Does Michener make any attempt to link the importance of free speech
   with public issues that might interest a general audience?
4. Michener reports that three of his books were censored by foreign countries that subsequently invited him to visit as an honored guest. What is
   this information meant to show?
5. How effective is the comparison between Biblical prophets and newspaper
   columnists with which Michener concludes?

ONE STUDENT'S ASSIGNMENT

*Write an argument for or against "censorship" that is focused either on labeling re-
cord albums or on providing public funding for the arts. Include references to at least
two sources on censorship in* The Informed Argument *and at least two other
sources that you have discovered on your own through library research. At least one*

of these sources should represent a viewpoint different from your own. Use MLA
style documentation. Be sure to include an MLA style list of works cited.

Freedom to Listen
Patricia Lindholm

Rock'n'roll has had the power to incite controversy   1
ever since Elvis Presley woke up the nation with his gy-
rating pelvis in the 1950s. Recent years have shown that
rock'n'roll can also attract political attention. The
wives of a number of senators and government officials
in Washington, D.C., have used their influence to introduce a form of censorship to rock music—labeling based
on lyric content.

In May 1985, Mary Elizabeth "Tipper" Gore, wife of   2
Senator Albert Gore of Tennessee, and Susan Baker,
wife of Secretary of State James Baker, organized this
group of women into the Parents' Music Resource Center
(PMRC). According to Hendrick Hertzberg, staff writer
for <u>The New Republic</u>, Mrs. Gore's concern had been
prompted by her purchase of the soundtrack to Prince's
movie <u>Purple Rain</u> for her pre-teen daughter. When her
daughter mentioned a reference to masturbation in one of
the songs, Mrs. Gore chose to take action. The pressure
the PMRC exerted led to a series of Senate hearings and
culminated in an agreement with the Recording Industry
Association of America which specified that the words
"Explicit Lyrics – Parental Advisory" would be stickered
on recordings the PMRC deemed offensive (22).

When voicing her disapproval over the rock lyrics,   3
Mrs. Gore is practicing what Garry Wills calls "censure." "If one disapproves of a social practice, . . .
one is free to denounce that and to call on others to
express their disapproval" (421). I can respect Mrs.
Gore for recognizing something she judged harmful to her
child and for deciding to act on that feeling, but one
question remains: why did she buy a child the soundtrack
to a movie rated R, written by a performer well-known
for the sexual content of his music and concerts?

The PMRC claims to be filling a need in the record-   4
ing industry for in-depth consumer information by placing a label on the outside of recordings to warn

potential buyers of disturbing lyrics and subject matter. Susan Baker argues that

> the purpose of record labeling is simply to
> provide more information for consumers to en-
> hance their freedom of choice. . . . Responsi-
> ble labeling is not censorship. It is simply
> there to be used by those who choose to use
> it. It does not restrict access for those who
> feel it necessary. (9)

The rating system used for movies is employed by   5
the PMRC as a comparison with their proposal. But two
points should be raised in response: one, the movie
rating system is voluntarily done by the motion picture
industry, not by government legislation; and two, the
PMRC's speeches are full of such terms as "responsible
labeling" and "redeeming social value"--terms that are
very broad in meaning and can be applied in any manner
the user sees fit.

The problem of the uninformed consumer purchasing   6
questionable music is too broad to be resolved by labeling, which makes a value judgment about what is "objectionable." When one group decides they know best what
everyone wants, mistakes are often made. There are many
examples of one generation of readers censoring a
book, and the following generation looking back in
disbelief and embarrassment over the controversy. This
issue in music could easily cause the same reactions,
even if a recording is only being "labeled" not "censored."

Worried parents should realize that the consumer is   7
free to return a purchase for credit or refund in most
any store. To keep their doors open and their customers
happy, it seems reasonable that a store would be willing
to take back recordings found to be unsatisfactory to
the consumer. Sales clerks can also be helpful in describing particular performer's music and would likely
be much more informative than a generalized sticker
could be.

Children's exposure to such topics as violence and   8
sexual activity leaves everyone somewhat uneasy. But
young children are not going to pop into a music store
and pay $17.00 for the latest Motley Crüe compact disc.

A parent would probably be making the purchase and should be paying attention to what is being bought.

Labeling is certainly not going to keep a teenager 9 with spending money from purchasing a badly wanted recording. Teenagers like to test limits imposed by parents and society, and a recording labeled "objectionable" for that age group may have even more appeal if teenagers think they aren't supposed to have it. Besides, any teenager purchasing that type of recording will probably remove the cellophane wrapping (with the sticker) from the package before taking it home. Once again, parents should be watching what is influencing their children.

In short, the labeling itself will not be effec- 10 tive, as Mrs. Gore herself demonstrated by purchasing the soundtrack to an R-rated movie. Labels on both cigarette and alcoholic beverage containers state proven links between the consumption of these items and health problems, birth defects, and death. Yet millions of informed consumers choose to smoke and drink everyday and ignore the direct health risks these activities incur.

Nevertheless, the PMRC pressure is being felt na- 11 tionwide. The original brief "Explicit Lyrics – Parental Advisory" sticker is evolving in many state legislatures into a longer, more specific label. Now fluorescent yellow, the labels are many lines long and describe in no uncertain terms what might be heard on the recording-- "suicide, incest, bestiality, sadomasochism, sexual activity in a violent context, murder, morbid violence, illegal use of drugs or alcohol" (Pareles 449).

I find many rock lyrics personally offensive, espe- 12 cially those that describe violence against women, but it's my choice not to purchase the music and support the artist, just as it's someone else's choice to purchase it. When government legislation begins restricting our choices, it's time for us to speak up and protect our rights. The framers of the Bill of Rights set a standard for the future: let the people choose what they think is best for themselves. The First Amendment gives us the right to freedom of speech, which inherently includes music and other arts, not the restricted freedom of "approved" speech.

Don't let the PMRC fool you—labeling is a subtle   13
form of censorship. Widespread acceptance of this would
establish a dangerous precedent. Take it upon yourself
to do what you can to make sure mandatory labeling is
dropped—add your voice to those opposing labeling; support people with similar opinions who have access to the
public ear; at the very least, vote for those candidates
who reflect your views. Otherwise, it just may happen
you'll soon be hearing elevator music on your favorite
rock'n'roll radio station.

Works Cited

Baker, Susan. "The PMRC Responds: Responsible Labeling
     Is Not Censorship." Billboard Magazine. 14 Nov.
     1987: 9.
Hertzberg, Hendrick. "Tipper De Doo Dah." The New Repub-
     lic. 7 Dec. 1987: 22–23.
Pareles, Jon. "Legislating the Imagination." The In-
     formed Argument. Ed. Robert K. Miller. San Diego:
     Harcourt, 1992. (449–51).
Wills, Garry. "In Praise of Censure." The Informed Argu-
     ment. Ed. Robert K. Miller. San Diego: Harcourt,
     1992. (420–24).

SUGGESTIONS FOR WRITING

1. Are there limits to free speech in American colleges and universities?
    Should an administrator, professor, or student be penalized for using rac-
    ist or sexist language? Write an essay defining the extent to which you
    favor academic freedom at your own school.
2. Write a summary of the essay by Richard Posner.
3. Synthesize arguments by Gary Wills and James Michener on behalf of
    free speech.
4. Drawing upon Gary Wills, Robert Brustein, and John Williams, define
    what censorship means.
5. Wills, Fitzgerald, Brustein, and Michener all refer to the photographs of
    Robert Mapplethorpe. Locate a representative selection of his work and
    argue for or against providing public funding for a Mapplethorpe exhibit.
6. Research how the arts are subsidized in France, Germany, the Soviet
    Union, or Great Britain. Compare what you discover with what Bru-
    stein reports about arts funding in the United States.
7. Read one of the Michener novels that have been censored overseas: *Ib-
    eria, Poland,* and *The Covenant.* Identify any passages that could have given

offense to the Spanish, Polish, or South African governments. Then explain how you view these passages within the context of the book as a whole.

8. According to the National Council of Teachers of English, the most frequently censored books in American schools include: *Catcher in the Rye, The Grapes of Wrath, Nineteen Eighty-Four, Lord of the Flies, The Adventures of Huckleberry Finn, Brave New World, The Scarlet Letter, A Farewell to Arms, One Flew Over the Cuckoo's Nest,* and *One Day in the Life of Ivan Denisovich.* Read any of these books, then argue for or against its use in a senior high school English class.

9. Go to the public library and interview the librarian in charge of circulation. Ask if the library has ever been pressured into withdrawing a book from circulation. Ask also if the library keeps a record of complaints made against the books in its collection. If so, ask if you can see this record and use it for evidence in determining the extent to which censorship is an issue in your own community.

10. Can listening to music, watching television, or reading a book lead to acts of violence? Do research to see if labeling or censorship can be justified as a public safety measure.

SECTION 7

LITERARY CRITICISM: WHAT DOES A POEM MEAN?

◆

Stopping by Woods on a Snowy Evening

Whose woods these are I think I know.
His house is in the village though;
He will not see me stopping here
To watch his woods fill up with snow.

5   My little horse must think it queer
To stop without a farmhouse near
Between the woods and frozen lake
The darkest evening of the year.

He gives his harness bells a shake
10 To ask if there is some mistake.
The only other sound's the sweep
Of easy wind and downy flake

The woods are lovely, dark and deep.
But I have promises to keep,
15 And miles to go before I sleep
And miles to go before I sleep.

Robert Frost

The steaming horses think it queer

To   horse   must

The   to   to think it queer

To

We stop with not a farm house near

the woods an afrozen

Between a forest and a lake

The darkest evening of the year

She   her

He gives harness bells a shake

To ask if there is some mistake

the

The only other sounds sweep

downy

Of easy wind and falling flake.

The woods are lovely dark and deep

But I have promises to keep

That bid me

And miles to go before I sleep

And miles to go before I sleep

Facsimile of Robert Frost's handwritten draft of the last three stanzas of "Stopping by Woods on a Snowy Evening."

JOHN HOLMES

On Frost's "Stopping by Woods on a Snowy Evening"

Poet and educator John Holmes (1904–1962) graduated from Tufts College in 1929. He taught briefly at Lafayette College in Pennsylvania before returning to Tufts in 1934, where he taught poetry until his death twenty-eight years later. He was poetry critic for the Boston Evening Transcript, *and a reviewer for the* New York Times *and the* Atlantic Monthly. *His many books include* Address to the Living *(1937),* The Poet's Work *(1939),* Fair Warning *(1939),* Map of My Country *(1943),* The Symbols *(1955),* Writing Poetry *(1960), and* The Fortune Teller *(1961). His explication of "Stopping By Woods on a Snowy Evening" was originally published in* **1943.** *It demonstrates what an intelligent reader can learn from studying a poet's revisions.*

This facsimile [on the previous page] is a reproduction of the last three stanzas of "Stopping by Woods on a Snowy Evening" as Robert Frost worked it out. We know from the poet that he had just written the long poem, "New Hampshire," in one all-night unbroken stretch of composition, and that he then turned a page of his workbook and wrote this short poem without stopping. This fact has interesting implications. "New Hampshire" is a discourse in the idiomatic blank verse that is so peculiarly Frost's own style—the rhythms of natural speech matched to the strict but inconspicuous iambic pentameter, the beat always discernible but never formal. It is reasonable to suppose that after the hours spent in writing the long poem, in its loosened but never loose manner, he was ready, unconsciously, for a poem in strict pattern. He had also obviously had in his head for some time the incident on which the short poem was to be based, as well as the use he wished to make of it. He committed himself, as he has said, to the four-stress iambic line and to the *aaba* rime-scheme, in the first stanza, which he wrote rapidly and did not revise. He knew what he had seen, and he knew how he wanted to write it.   1

> Whose woods these are I think I know.
> His house is in the village though;
> He will not see me stopping here
> To watch his woods fill up with snow.

"That went off so easily I was tempted into the added difficulty of picking up my 3 for my 1-2-4 to go on with in the second stanza. I was amused and scared at what that got me into," Frost says. The facsimile shows what it got him into, how he got out of it, and how he achieved the poem as it meant itself to be written.   2

It began with what was the actual experience of stopping at night by some dark woods in winter, and the fact that there were two horses. He   3 remembered what he saw then. "The steaming horses think it queer." But the poem needs truth more than fact, and he cancels the line, and begins again, "The horse begins to think it queer," but doesn't like the word "begins," needing in the allowed space a word that will particularize the horse, so writes "The little horse must think it queer." Now he runs into a grammatical difficulty, which must somehow be solved before he gets on into the poem he already feels sure of. "I launched into the construction 'My little horse must think it queer that we should stop.' I didn't like omitting the 'that' and I had no room for 'should.' I had the luck to get out of it with the infinitive." This groping and warming-up has a kind of impatience, an urgency to get on with the poem, but not until all the parts are right. At this point the poet knew and did not know how the poem would end. He knew the feel, and the sense, and almost everything about the form—certainly enough to know when he got off the track.

Whether he revised the third line here or later we cannot know. But we   4
can see in several places in this poem his changes toward particularization. The line "Between a forest and a lake" is a notation, and "Between the woods and frozen lake" is a finished line of poetry. "A forest" is too big, too vague, but "the woods" is definite, and bounded; you get lost in a forest, but you can walk through and out of the woods, and probably you know who owns it—Vermonters do, as he has said in the first stanza. "A lake" has not the specific condition or picture of "frozen lake." This sort of revision, or what Frost calls, "touching up," is what makes a poem—this, plus the first inspiration. Either one, without the other, is unlikely to make a good poem.

The next stanza comes easier, because the rime-scheme has been deter-   5
mined, and one unexpected obstacle has been overcome. But once more there is a delay, as the poet makes a decision as to the "he" or "she"—and the more important and more interesting one about the falling snow. In writing "downy flake" for "fall of flake" the gain is great not only for accuracy of feeling and fact, but also for the music of the lines. The simple alliteration in "fall of flake" is canceled in favor of the word, one word, "downy," which blends with the vowel-chords a poet half-consciously makes and modulates as he goes. In this instance, it half-chimes with "sounds" and adds a rounder, fuller, and yet quieter tone.

Now the carry-over rime is "sweep," a fortunate one, really, and im-   6
portant to the final solution of the rime-scheme. It is not too much to assume, knowing all we know about the circumstances of the writing of this poem—the all-night composition of "New Hampshire," and the sudden urge to catch and shape still another saved idea—that the darker, more confident, more rapid strokes of the pen show the poet's growing excitement. The end is in sight. The thing he believed could happen will happen, surely now, and he must hurry to get it onto the page. This is the real moment of power, and any poet's greatest satisfaction.

"The woods are lovely dark and deep / But I have promises to keep."   7
The first two lines of the last stanza come fast, and flow beautifully, the crest of the poem's emotion and its music. We cannot know whether he had held

them in his head, or had swept up to and into them as he felt the destined pattern fulfilling itself.

Then, with success in sight, there comes an awkward and unexpected 8 stumble. He writes, "That bid me give the reins a shake," which may have been the fact and the action. But the rime is wrong. Not only has the rime been used in the previous stanza, but so has the image of the horse shaking his head and reins. Things are moving fast now, no doubt impatiently, but certainly with determination, shown in the heavy black lines of abrupt cancellation. He strikes out "me give the reins a shake," and writes above it, so the line will read, "That bid me on, and there are miles," and then the whole thing comes through! Of course! "Miles to go . . ."

That's what it was supposed to be—the feeling of silence and dark, 9 almost overpowering the man, but the necessity of going on. "And miles to go before I sleep." Then the triumph in the whole thing, the only right and perfect last line, solving the problem of the carried-over rime, keeping the half-tranced state, and the dark, and the solitude, and man's great effort to be responsible man . . . the repetition of that line.

"Stopping by Woods on a Snowy Evening" can be studied as perfected 10 structure, with the photostat manuscript to show that art is not, though it must always appear to be, effortless. It can be thought of as a picture: the whites, grays, and blacks of the masses and areas of lake, field, and woods, with the tiny figure of the man in the sleigh, and the horse. And it can be thought of as a statement of man's everlasting responsibility to man; though the dark and nothingness tempt him to surrender, he will not give in.

QUESTIONS FOR MEANING

1. What is the connection between "Stopping by Woods on a Snowy Evening" and the long poem "New Hampshire"?
2. Do you understand what Holmes means by "blank verse," "iambic pentameter," and "rime-scheme"? Identify any other vocabulary that seems peculiar to the analysis of poetry. If you have never studied poetry before, how can you find out what these terms mean?
3. Explain what Holmes means in paragraph 3 when he writes, "the poem needs truth more than fact."
4. According to Holmes, what are the two essential steps in the process of writing poetry?
5. What theme or themes does Holmes find in this poem?
6. Vocabulary: facsimile (1), idiomatic (1), inconspicuous (1), discernible (1), modulates (5).

QUESTIONS ABOUT STRATEGY

1. Why was it useful for Holmes to reproduce a partial facsimile of the original manuscript of "Stopping by Woods on a Snowy Evening"? If he had been unable to do so, what sort of changes would he have had to make in his essay?

2. How can studying the manuscript version of a poem help us to better understand the finished version? Explain why Frost deleted "steaming" and why two horses were turned into one "little" horse. Explain also why Frost changed "a forest" to "the woods" and "a lake" to "frozen lake." Do you agree with Holmes's interpretation of these changes? Could the changes mean anything else?
3. What does this essay reveal about the nature of literary criticism? How does reading critically differ from other types of reading?

JOHN CIARDI
Robert Frost: The Way to the Poem

The son of Italian immigrants, John Ciardi (1916–1986) taught English at Harvard from 1946 to 1953 and at Rutgers from 1953 to 1961, when he gave up teaching in order to be a full-time writer and poet. His many volumes of poetry include Homeward to America *(1940),* Other Skies *(1947),* Live Another Day *(1949),* If I Marry You: A Sheaf of Love Poems *(1958), and* In the Stoneworks *(1961). He is also the author of* How Does a Poem Mean?—*a highly respected book of criticism on the nature of poetry—and a fine translation of Dante's* Divine Comedy. *A fellow of the American Academy of Arts and Letters, Ciardi won many awards, most notably the Prix de Rome (1956–1957). As poetry editor for the* Saturday Review *from 1956 to 1972, he was in a position not only to encourage new poets but also to challenge conventional ideas about well-known poems. His columns were frequently controversial, as can be seen from the letters inspired by the following **1958** essay on Frost. At a time when many readers liked to see Frost as a grandfatherly nature poet, a sort of literary Norman Rockwell, Ciardi was one of the first critics to emphasize the element of despair that can be found in much of Frost's work.*

The School System has much to say these days of the virtue of reading widely, and not enough about the virtues of reading less but in depth. There are any number of reading lists for poetry, but there is not enough talk about individual poems. Poetry, finally, is one poem at a time. To read any one poem carefully is the ideal preparation for reading another. Only a poem can illustrate how poetry works.   1

Above, therefore, is a poem ["Stopping by Woods on a Snowy Evening"]—one of the master lyrics of the English language, and almost certainly the best-known poem by an American poet. What happens in it?—which is to say, not *what* does it mean, but *how* does it mean? How does it go about being a human reenactment of human experience? The author—perhaps the thousandth reader would need to be told—is Robert Frost.   2

Even the TV audience can see that this poem begins as a seemingly-simple narration of a seemingly-simple incident but ends by suggesting meanings far beyond anything specifically referred to in the narrative. And even readers with only the most casual interest in poetry might be made to note the additional fact that, though the poem suggests those larger meanings, it is very careful never to abandon its pretense to being simple narration. There is duplicity at work. The poet pretends to be talking about one thing, and all the while he is talking about many others.   3

Many readers are forever unable to accept the poet's essential duplicity. It is almost safe to say that a poem is never about what it seems to be about. As much could be said of the proverb. The bird in the hand, the rolling stone, the stitch in time never (except by an artful double-deception) intend any sort of statement about birds, stones, or sewing. The incident of this poem, one must conclude, is at root a metaphor.   4

Duplicity aside, this poem's movement from the specific to the general illustrates one of the basic formulas of all poetry. Such a grand poem as Arnold's "Dover Beach" and such lesser, though unfortunately better known, poems as Longfellow's "The Village Blacksmith" and Holmes's "The Chambered Nautilus" are built on the same progression. In these three poems, however, the generalization is markedly set apart from the specific narration, and even seems additional to the telling rather than intrinsic to it. It is this sense of division one has in mind in speaking of "a tacked-on moral."   5

There is nothing wrong-in-itself with a tacked-on moral. Frost, in fact, makes excellent use of the device at times. In this poem, however, Frost is careful to let the whatever-the-moral-is grow out of the poem itself. When the action ends the poem ends. There is no epilogue and no explanation. Everything pretends to be about the narrated incident. And that pretense sets the basic tone of the poem's performance of itself.   6

The dramatic force of that performance is best observable, I believe, as a progression in three scenes.   7

In scene one, which coincides with stanza one, a man—a New England man—is driving his sleigh somewhere at night. It is snowing, and as the man passes a dark patch of woods he stops to watch the snow descend into the darkness. We know, moreover, that the man is familiar with these parts (he knows who owns the woods and where the owner lives), and we know that no one has seen him stop. As scene one forms itself in the theatre of the mind's-eye, therefore, it serves to establish some as yet unspecified relation between the man and the woods.   8

It is necessary, however, to stop here for a long parenthesis: Even so simple an opening statement raises any number of questions. It is impossible to address all the questions that rise from the poem stanza by stanza, but two that arise from stanza one illustrate the sort of thing one might well ask of the poem detail by detail.   9

Why, for example, does the man not say what errand he is on? What is the force of leaving the errand generalized? He might just as well have told us that he was going to the general store, or returning from it with a jug of   10 molasses he had promised to bring Aunt Harriet and two suits of long underwear he had promised to bring the hired man. Frost, moreover, can handle homely detail to great effect. He preferred to leave his motive generalized. Why?

And why, on the other hand, does he say so much about knowing the   11
absent owner of the woods and where he lives? Is it simply that one set of details happened-in whereas another did not? To speak of things "happening-in" is to assault the integrity of a poem. Poetry cannot be discussed meaningfully unless one can assume that everything in the poem—every last comma and variant spelling—is in it by the poet's specific act of choice. Only bad poets allow into their poems what is haphazard or cheaply chosen.

The errand, I will venture a bit brashly for lack of space, is left gener-   12
alized in order the more aptly to suggest *any* errand in life and, therefore, life itself. The owner is there because he is one of the forces of the poem. Let it do to say that the force he represents is the village of mankind (that village at the edge of winter) from which the poet finds himself separated (has separated himself?) in his moment by the woods (and to which, he recalls finally, he has promises to keep). The owner is he-who-lives-in-his-village-house, thereby locked away from the poet's awareness of the-time-the-snow-tells as it engulfs and obliterates the world the village man allows himself to believe he "owns." Thus, the owner is a representative of an order of reality from which the poet has divided himself for the moment, though to a certain extent he ends by reuniting with it. Scene one, therefore, establishes not only a relation between the man and the woods, but the fact that the man's relation begins with his separation (though momentarily) from mankind.

End parenthesis one, begin parenthesis two.   13

Still considering the first scene as a kind of dramatic performance of   14
forces, one must note that the poet has meticulously matched the simplicity of his language to the pretended simplicity of the narrative. Clearly, the man stopped because the beauty of the scene moved him, but he neither tells us that the scene is beautiful nor that he is moved. A bad writer, always ready to overdo, might have written: "The vastness gripped me, filling my spirit with the slow steady sinking of the snow's crystalline perfection into the glimmerless profundities of the hushed primeval wood." Frost's avoidance of such a spate illustrates two principles of good writing. The first, he has stated himself in "The Mowing": "Anything *more* than the truth would have seemed too weak" (italics mine). Understatement is one of the basic sources of power in English poetry. The second principle is to let the action speak for itself. A good novelist does not tell us that a given character is good or bad (at least not since the passing of the Dickens tradition): he shows us the character in action and then, watching him, we know. Poetry, too, has fictional obligations: even when the characters are ideas and metaphors rather than people, they must be *characterized in action*. A poem does not *talk about* ideas; it *enacts* them. The force of the poem's performance, in fact, is precisely to act out (and thereby to make us act out empathetically, that is, to *feel out*, that is, *to identify with*) the speaker and why he stopped. The man is

the principal actor in this little "drama of why" and in scene one he is the only character, though as noted, he is somehow related to the absent owner.

End second parenthesis.   15

In scene two (stanzas two and three) a *foil* is introduced. In fiction and   16
drama, a foil is a character who "plays against" a more important character.
By presenting a different point of view or an opposed set of motives, the foil
moves the more important character to react in ways that might not have
found expression without such opposition. The more important character is
thus more fully revealed—to the reader and to himself. The foil here is the
horse.

The horse forces the question. Why did the man stop? Until it occurs   17
to him that his "little horse must think it queer" he had not asked himself
for reasons. He had simply stopped. But the man finds himself faced with
the question he imagines the horse to be asking: what *is* there to stop for out
there in the cold, away from bin and stall (house and village and mankind?)
and all that any self-respecting beast could value on such a night? In sensing
that other view, the man is forced to examine his own more deeply.

In stanza two the question arises only as a feeling within the man. In   18
stanza three, however (still scene two), the horse acts. He gives his harness
bells a shake. "What's wrong?" he seems to say. "What are we waiting for?"

By now, obviously, the horse—without losing its identity as horse—   19
has also become a symbol. A symbol is something that stands for something
else. Whatever that something else may be, it certainly begins as that order
of life that does not understand why a man stops in the wintry middle of
nowhere to watch the snow come down. (Can one fail to sense by now that
the dark and the snowfall symbolize a death-wish, however momentary, *i.e.,*
that hunger for final rest and surrender that a man may feel, but not a beast?)

So by the end of scene two the performance has given dramatic force   20
to three elements that work upon the man. There is his relation to the world
of the owner. There is his relation to the brute world of the horse. And there
is that third presence of the unownable world, the movement of the all-
engulfing snow across all the orders of life, the man's, the owner's, and the
horse's—with the difference that the man knows of that second dark-within-
the-dark of which the horse cannot, and the owner will not, know.

The man ends scene two with all these forces working upon him si-   21
multaneously. He feels himself moved to a decision. And he feels a last call
from the darkness: "the sweep/Of easy wind and downy flake." It would be
so easy and so downy to go into the woods and let himself be covered over.

But scene three (stanza four) produces a fourth force. This fourth force   22
can be given many names. It is certainly better, in fact, to give it many
names than to attempt to limit it to one. It is social obligation, or personal
commitment, or duty, or just the realization that a man cannot indulge a
mood forever. All of these and more. But, finally, he has a simple decision
to make. He may go into the woods and let the darkness and the snow
swallow him from the world of beast and man. Or he must move on. And
unless he is going to stop here forever, it is time to remember that he has a

long way to go and that he had best be getting there. (So there is something to be said for the horse, too.)

Then and only then, his question driven more and more deeply into himself by these cross-forces, does the man venture a comment on what attracted him: "The woods are lovely, dark and deep." His mood lingers over the thought of that lovely dark-and-deep (as do the very syllables in which he phrases the thought), but the final decision is to put off the mood and move on. He has his man's way to go and his man's obligations to tend to before he can yield. He has miles to go before his sleep. He repeats that thought and the performance ends.   23

But why the repetition? The first time Frost says "And miles to go before I sleep," there can be little doubt that the primary meaning is: "I have a long way to go before I get to bed tonight." The second time he says it, however, "miles to go" and "sleep" are suddenly transformed into symbols. What are those "something-elses" the symbols stand for? Hundreds of people have tried to ask Mr. Frost that question and he has always turned it away. He has turned it away *because he cannot answer it.* He could answer some part of it. But some part is not enough.   24

For a symbol is like a rock dropped into a pool: it sends out ripples in all directions, and the ripples are in motion. Who can say where the last ripple disappears? One may have a sense that he knows the approximate center point of the ripples, the point at which the stone struck the water. Yet even then he has trouble marking it surely. How does one make a mark on water? Oh very well—the center point of that second "miles to go" is probably approximately in the neighborhood of being close to meaning, perhaps, "the road to life"; and the second "before I sleep" is maybe that close to meaning "before I take my final rest," the rest in darkness that seemed so temptingly dark-and-deep for the moment of the mood. But the ripples continue to move and the light to change on the water, and the longer one watches the more changes he sees. Such shifting-and-being-at-the-same-instant is of the very sparkle and life of poetry. One experiences it as one experiences life, for every time he looks at an experience he sees something new, and he sees it change as he watches it. And that sense of continuity in fluidity is one of the primary kinds of knowledge, one of man's basic ways of knowing, and one that only the arts can teach, poetry foremost among them.   25

Frost himself certainly did not ask what that repeated last line meant. It came to him and he received it. He "felt right" about it. And what he "felt right" about was in no sense a "meaning" that, say, an essay could apprehend, but an act of experience that could be fully presented only by the dramatic enactment of forces which is the performance of the poem.   26

Now look at the poem in another way. Did Frost know what he was going to do when he began? Considering the poem simply as an act of skill, as a piece of juggling, one cannot fail to respond to the magnificent turn at the end where, with one flip, seven of the simplest words in the language suddenly dazzle full of never-ending waves of thought and feeling. Or, more   27 precisely, of felt-thought. Certainly an equivalent stunt by a juggler—could there be an equivalent—would bring the house down. Was it to cap his performance with that grand stunt that Frost wrote the poem?

Far from it. The obvious fact is that *Frost could not have known he was going to write those lines until he wrote them.* Then a second fact must be registered: *he wrote them because, for the fun of it, he had got himself into trouble.* 28

Frost, like every good poet, began by playing a game with himself. 29 The most useful way of writing a four line stanza with four feet to the line is to rhyme the third line with the first, and the fourth line with the second. Even that much rhyme is so difficult in English that many poets and almost all of the anonymous ballad makers do not bother to rhyme the first and third lines at all, settling for two rhymes in four lines as good enough. For English is a rhyme-poor language. In Italian and in French, for example, so many words end with the same sounds that rhyming is relatively easy—so easy that many modern French and Italian poets do not bother to rhyme at all. English, being a more agglomerate language, has far more final sounds, hence fewer of them rhyme. When an Italian poet writes a line ending with "vita" (life) he has literally hundreds of rhyme choices available. When an English poet writes "life" at the end of a line he can summon "strife, wife, knife, fife, rife," and then he is in trouble. Now "life-strife" and "life-rife" and "life-wife" seem to offer a combination of possible ideas that can be related by more than just the rhyme. Inevitably, therefore, the poets have had to work and rework these combinations until the sparkle has gone out of them. The reader is normally tired of such rhyme-led associations. When he encounters "life-strife" he is certainly entitled to suspect that the poet did not really want to say "strife"—that had there been in English such a word as, say, "hife," meaning "infinite peace and harmony," the poet would as gladly have used that word instead of "strife." Thus, the reader feels that the writing is haphazard, that the rhyme is making the poet say things he does not really feel, and which, therefore, the reader does not feel except as boredom. One likes to see the rhymes fall into place, but he must end with the belief that it is the poet who is deciding what is said and not the rhyme scheme that is forcing the saying.

So rhyme is a kind of game, and an especially difficult one in English. 30 As in every game, the fun of the rhyme is to set one's difficulties high and then to meet them skillfully. As Frost himself once defined freedom, it consists of "moving easy in harness."

In "Stopping by Woods on a Snowy Evening" Frost took a long chance. 31 He decided to rhyme not two lines in each stanza, but three. Not even Frost could have sustained that much rhyme in a long poem (as Dante, for example, with the advantage of writing in Italian, sustained triple rhyme for thousands of lines in "The Divine Comedy"). Frost would have known instantly, therefore, when he took the original chance, that he was going to write a short poem. He would have had that much foretaste of it.

So the first stanza emerged rhymed a-a-b-a. And with the sure sense 32 that this was to be a short poem, Frost decided to take an additional chance and to redouble: in English three rhymes in four lines is more than enough;

there is no need to rhyme the fourth line. For the fun of it, however, Frost set himself to pick up that loose rhyme and to weave it into the pattern, thereby accepting the all but impossible burden of quadruple rhyme.

The miracle is that it worked. Despite the enormous freight of rhyme, the poem not only came out as a neat pattern, but managed to do so with no sense of strain. Every word and every rhyme falls into place as naturally and as inevitably as if there were no rhyme restricting the poet's choices.   33

That ease-in-difficulty is certainly inseparable from the success of the poem's performance. One watches the skill-man juggle three balls, then four, then five, and every addition makes the trick more wonderful. But unless he makes the hard trick seem as easy as an easy trick, then all is lost.   34

The real point, however, is not only that Frost took on a hard rhyme-trick and made it seem easy. It is rather as if the juggler, carried away, had tossed up one more ball than he could really handle, and then amazed himself by actually handling it. So with the real triumph of his poem. Frost could not have known what a stunning effect his repetition of the last line was going to produce. He could not even know he was going to repeat the line. He simply found himself up against a difficulty he almost certainly had not foreseen and he had to improvise to meet it. For in picking up the rhyme from the third line of stanza one and carrying it over into stanza two, he had created an endless chain-link form within which each stanza left a hook sticking out for the next stanza to hang on. So by stanza four, feeling the poem rounding to its end, Frost had to do something about that extra rhyme.   35

He might have tucked it back into a third line rhyming with the *know-though-snow* of stanza one. He could thus have rounded the poem out to the mathematical symmetry of using each rhyme four times. But though such a device might be defensible in theory, a rhyme repeated after eleven lines is so far from its original rhyme sound that its feeling as rhyme must certainly be lost. And what good is theory if the reader is not moved by the writing?   36

It must have been in some such quandary that the final repetition suggested itself—a suggestion born of the very difficulties the poet had let himself in for. So there is that point beyond mere ease in handling a hard thing, the point at which the very difficulty offers the poet the opportunity to do better than he knew he could. What, aside from having that happen to oneself, could be more self-delighting than to participate in its happening by one's reader-identification with the poem?   37

And by now a further point will have suggested itself: that the human-insight of the poem and the technicalities of its poetic artifice are inseparable. Each feeds the other. That interplay is the poem's meaning, a matter not of WHAT DOES IT MEAN, for no one can ever say entirely what a good poem means, but of HOW DOES IT MEAN, a process one can come much closer to discussing.   38

There is a necessary epilogue. Mr. Frost has often discussed this poem on the platform, or more usually in the course of a long-evening-after a talk. Time and again I have heard him say that he just wrote it off, that it just came to him, and that he set it down as it came.   39

Once at Bread Loaf, however, I heard him add one very essential piece   40
to the discussion of how it "just came." One night, he said, he had sat down
after supper to work at a long piece of blank verse. The piece never worked
out, but Mr. Frost found himself so absorbed in it that, when next he looked
up, dawn was at his window. He rose, crossed to the window, stood looking
out for a few minutes, and *then* it was that "Stopping by Woods" suddenly
"just came," so that all he had to do was cross the room and write it down.

Robert Frost is the sort of artist who hides his traces. I know of no   41
Frost worksheets anywhere. If someone has raided his wastebasket in secret,
it is possible that such worksheets exist somewhere, but Frost would not
willingly allow anything but the finished product to leave him. Almost certainly, therefore, no one will ever know what was in that piece of unsuccess-
ful blank verse he had been working at with such concentration, but I for
one would stake my life that could that worksheet be uncovered, it would
be found to contain the germinal stuff of "Stopping by Woods"; that what
was a-simmer in him all night without finding its proper form, suddenly,
when he let his still-occupied mind look away, came at him from a different
direction, offered itself in a different form, and that finding that form exactly
right the impulse proceeded to marry itself to the new shape in one of the
most miraculous performances of English lyricism.

And that, too—whether or not one can accept so hypothetical a discus-   42
sion—is part of HOW the poem means. It means that marriage to the perfect
form, the poem's shapen declaration of itself, its moment's monument fixed
beyond all possibility of change. And thus, finally, in every truly good poem,
"How does it mean?" must always be answered "Triumphantly." Whatever
the poem "is about," *how* it means is always how Genesis means: the word
become a form, and the form become a thing, and—when the becoming is
true—the thing become a part of the knowledge and experience of the race
forever.

Letters to the Editor of the *Saturday Review*

Finding Each Other

The article "Robert Frost: The Way to the Poem," by John Ciardi (*SR* Apr.
12), is one of the most excellent pieces of explication I have had an opportunity to read. It is simple, thorough, and clear, and at the same time provocative response to the deepest and most far-reaching values in poetry. The
essay, just as it is, would be a boon to many students and teachers who
together are seeking to find each other as they attend to a poem.

Joseph H. Jenkins

Petersburg, Va.

Poking and Picking

Robert Frost's miracle, "Stopping by Woods on a Snowy Evening," comprises four stanzas, sixteen lines, 108 words. John Ciardi's analysis of it runs to ten full columns. This flushes an old question: Does such probing, poking, and picking really lead "The Way to the Poem"?

William L. Hassett

Des Moines, Ia.

Critical Absurdity

I have just discovered, by way of John Ciardi's analysis of Robert Frost's poem, "Stopping by the Woods on a Snowy Evening," that this charmingly simple, eloquent, lyrical little poem, long one of my favorites, is supposedly fraught with duplicity of meaning and symbolism, including a disguised death-wish, and that it is not at all about what it seems to be about.

This is really a new high in critical absurdity. If the presentation of this leading, cover-featured article were not so obviously straight-faced, I would have considered this a nice parody of much present-day "criticism." Who is Mr. Ciardi trying to kid? Or is he himself merely kidded? I am sure Mr. Frost must be highly amused or shaking his head in amazement at the awesome proportions his innocent poetic images have assumed ("By now, obviously, the horse has also become a symbol").

Mrs. Beverly Travers

New Orleans, La.

Enhance a Rainbow

It seems to us that when a poet uses the skill Frost employs in creating a mood, sharing an experience, one should accept it as given, without further analysis. One does not enhance a rainbow by subjecting it to a spectrometric analysis.

John G. Gosselink

Hartford City, Ind.

No Death-Wish

I was a little shocked when I read Ciardi's interpretation of the dark and snowfall in Frost's "Stopping by the Woods on a Snowy Evening" as a death-wish. I suppose every person must interpret poems like this in terms of his own experience. To me, it seems to say that there is a certain deep satisfaction in stopping to lose oneself in the contemplation of beauty. The experience itself is significant in that it brings the individual into a sense of relationship to basic reality. But one cannot escape too long into these subjective experiences. There is work to do; obligations must be met; one cannot spend his whole life escaping from these practical realities.

J. Josephine Leamer

Gardiner, Mont.

Superfluous Info

I am used to most magazines pointing out the obvious, but when *SR* tells me that a symbol stands for something else (John Ciardi's article on Robert Frost), I am really hurt. Chances are, if I thought a symbol was something other than something else, I wouldn't be reading *SR* or any other magazine.

Marjorie Duryic

Everett, Wash.

Simple Narrative

Why Mr. Ciardi had to pick such, as he himself states, "a simple narrative" to expound upon I'll never know. If one thought of poetry as Mr. C does, the joy of just reading beautiful poetry would be gone completely. One would begin to spend all his time searching for symbols and such.

H. Clay Barnard

Sausalito, Calif.

Penetrating Analysis

I have just finished reading John Ciardi's penetrating analysis of Robert Frost's familiar lyric. This is distinguished service in the cause of criticism. More articles like this and we *will* develop a poetry-reading America.

Sister Mary Denise, RSM

Dallas, Pa.

Its Essence

Through the years I've read "Stopping by the Woods on a Snowy Evening" many times and felt that with each reading I had extracted its meaning to the point where I felt certain that there was no more it could tell me. John Ciardi has exposed new and deeper meanings to me and, as an excellent teacher, has dissected and made clear its very essence.

Lloyd Rodnick

Detroit, Mich.

Heavy Limbs

Ciardi has some very interesting ideas. But wouldn't it be better to develop them in a separate essay? It seems to me that the literary woods is too full of heavy limbs falling upon little delicate branches.

Gary Thornburg

Losantville, Ind.

No Discords

Ciardi's calm, cleanly developed, and illuminating article on Frost's poem surely is a savory example of what his readers have clamored for all these months. In this essay one finds all of Mr. Ciardi's inspiring adherence to principles and none of those bubonic symptoms which many of his readers have denounced. Personally, I am pleased to find also fewer coinings of discordant and sometimes hideous compounds, an indulgence that often spoils the point of what Mr. Ciardi has to say.

Earl Clendenon

Chicago, Ill.

Frost's Analyst?

The business of equating this poem with all the current philosophical symbols that are in Ciardi's mind is, of course, Ciardi's privilege. But why should he speak as Frost's analyst?

Harvey Parker

Vista, Calif.

Pedantic Reparation

Ciardi very pedantically makes complete reparation for last year's storm-provoking criticism of Anne Morrow Lindbergh's delicate and deep poetry. Many college and high-school teachers will be able to use such an exhaustive analysis in the classroom.

Joseph A. McNulty

Philadelphia, Pa.

Self-Anointed Thor

After reading Ciardi's uncomprehending, clinical, anti-poetical "appreciation" of my friend Robert Frost's great lyric, I was so moved, in sundry unprintable ways, that I thought to write Robert: the essay reminded me throughout of a humorless pathologist slicing away with his microtome at a biopsy.

However, what I wanted to say "just came to me" and I simply "wrote it down"—on a Remington Noiseless which I use for all composition, including poetry. It took twenty minutes, from gag to madrigal—some twenty more to add an effort to refute Mr. Ciardi's contention that English is a knobby tongue to rhyme—and I forward the result to you, in the hope that you might print it as one (largely commercial) writer's testament that, to some of us, things do come, we do just write them down, and we know enough English to find little trouble in double-rhyming a ballad, even in what Mr. Ciardi regards as the difficult scheme of Frost's poem. I also felt J.C. should learn that "know," "here," "lake," and "sweep" hardly baffle an idle versifier—and Robert's variation of the ballad form is not beyond the reach even of typewriter poets like me.

Mr. Ciardi, neo-master of critique, finds it easy to demolish the avowedly amateur verses of Anne Lindbergh with his little mechanic's hammer; but he did not realize that when he undertook to acclaim a true poet his implement might bounce from the granite with predictable damage to the self-anointed Thor. Ciardi must be all Ph.D., and of the new academic sub-species.

Philip Wylie

Miami, Fla.

Stopping to Write a Friend on a Thick Night

In this week's *Saturday Review*
The first bit, Robert, deals with you.
At least, its author, John Ciardi
Tears a poem of yours in two

And shreds the halves. His toy lombard, he
Loads with treacle praise, and lardy,
Salutes your metaphor and tmesis
And fires again to call you hardy.

Art, to him, is just its pieces,
The obvious, his noblest thesis—
Who even calls down holocaust
On his own tongue—the mangling Jesus!

Your blanket snow's thus double-crossed
By one who should be blanket-tossed
And he has miles to go to Frost
And years to learn it's Frost he lost.

JOHN CIARDI
Letter to the Letter Writers

I have never known a magazine with *SR*'s knack for calling forth Letters to   43
the Editor. No one writing for *SR* need suffer from a sense that his ideas
have disappeared into the void: he will hear from the readers. I have been
hearing of late, and the charge this time, made by some readers, is that I
have despoiled a great poem in my analysis of Robert Frost's "Stopping by
the Woods on a Snowy Evening" (*SR* Apr. 12).

The Frost article was self-declaredly an effort at close analysis. I believe   44
the poem to be much deeper than its surfaces, and I set out to ask what sort
of human behavior it is that presents a surface of such simplicity while stirring such depths of multiple responses. It may be that I analyzed badly, but
the more general charge seems to be that all analysis is inimical to poetry,
and that general charge is certainly worth a closer look.

A number of readers seem to have been offended by the fact that the   45
analysis was longer than the poem, which, as one reader put it, "comprises

four stanzas, sixteen lines, 108 words" (rather technical analysis, that sort of word-counting), whereas my article ran to "ten full columns."

A first clear assumption in this reader's mind is the assertion that an analysis must not be longer than what it analyzes. I can see no way of defending that assumption. If there is to be any analysis at all, it is in the nature of things that the analysis be longer than the poem or the passages it analyzes. One hundred and eight words will hardly do simply to describe the stanzaic form and rhyme scheme of the poem, without any consideration of the nature of the rhyme problem. Analysis and the poem are simply enough tortoise and hare. The difference from the fable is that the poetic hare does not lie down and sleep. The unfabled tortoise, however, may still hope to crawl after and, in some sense, to mark the way the hare went.   46

The second assumption is that analysis obscures ("does not lead the way to") a poem, and amounts in fact to mere "probing, poking, and picking." The charge as made is not specifically against my article but against all analysis. The question may, therefore, be simply located: should poetry be talked about at all?   47

A number of readers clearly take the position that it must not be. "One should accept it (the experience of the poem) as given, without further analysis," asserts one reader. "One does not enhance a rainbow by subjecting it to spectrometric analysis." An unwavering position and an interesting figure of speech. I am drawn to that rainbow and fascinated by this use of the word "enhance." By "spectrometric analysis" I take the gentleman to mean "investigating the physical nature of" but said, of course, with an overtone of disdain at the idea of seeing "beauty" meaningfully through any "instrument." That disdain aside, however, one may certainly ask why detailed knowledge of the physical phenomena that produce a rainbow should "unenhance" the rainbow's emotional value. Is speculation into the nature of things to be taken as a destruction of nature?   48

Two years ago, looking down on Rome from the Gianiculum, I saw two complete rainbows in the sky at once, not just pieces of rainbows but complete arcs with both ends of each arc visible at once in a great bridge above the city. And in what way did it hurt me as part of my instant delight to register some sense of the angle at which the sun had to hit the atmosphere in order to produce such a prodigy? I must insist on remaining among those who are willing to learn about rainbows.   49

Such disdain seems to be shared by many of our readers. Mr. Philip Wylie, a man described to me as an author, filed the strongest, or at least the longest, of the recent objections. My "implement," as he sees it, bounces "from the granite (of the poem) with predictable damage to the self-anointed Thor. Ciardi must be all Ph.D., and of the new academic sub-species."   50

Not exactly factual, since I do not own a Ph.D., but fair enough: giving lumps is a time-honored literary game and anyone with a typewriter may play. Mr. Wylie's indignation is largely against my way of dealing with Mr. Frost's poem, and that is a charge I must waive—he may be right, he may be wrong; no score. One part of his charge, however, is a more general   51 anger at the idea that anyone should go into a detailed analysis of the rhyme scheme of a poem that "just came" to the poet. Once again the basic charge is that poetry is damaged by analysis. One should "just let it come."

Many others have joined Mr. Wylie in his defense of the untouchable-   52
spontaneous. "Get your big clumsy feet off that miracle," says one reader I find myself especially drawn to. "What good do you think you do," writes another, "when you tear apart a thing as lovely as Mr. Frost's poem?" Another: "A dissecting kit belongs in the laboratory, not the library." And still another: "If one thought of poetry as Mr. C does, the joy of just reading beautiful poetry would be gone completely. One would begin to spend all his time dealing with symbols and such."

I must, parenthetically, reject some of the terms of that last letter. "Be-   53
gin to spend *all* his time," is the writer's idea: that "all" is no part of mine. I shall pass the sneer contained in the phrase "symbols and such." But I cannot accept the responsibility for defending myself when misquoted. One reader, for example, accuses me of stating that a poem "is not at all about what it seems to be about." I can only reply that those are his terms, not mine, and that I have no thought of defending them.

It is that "all" in the first question, however, that locates the central   54
misunderstanding. "Once one begins to analyze," the assumption runs, "he begins to spend all of his time 'merely analyzing' and the analysis not only takes the place of the poem but leads to the poem's destruction."

Were there no misconception involved, this reader's anger would cer-   55
tainly be justified. What is misconceived is the idea that the analysis is intended to take the place of the poem. Far from it. One takes a poem apart only in order to put it back together again with greater understanding. The poem itself is the thing. A good poem is a hanging gull on a day of perfect winds. We sit below and watch it own the air it rides: a miracle from nature. There it hangs on infallible wings. But suppose one is interested in the theory of flight (as the gull itself, to be sure, need not be) and suppose one notices that the gull's wings can perform miracles in the air because they have a particular curvature and a particular sort of leading and trailing edge. And suppose he further notices that the gull's tail feathers have a great deal to do with that seemingly effortless mastery. Does that man cease to see the gull? Does he see nothing but diagrams of airflow and lift to the total damnation of all gulls? Or does he see the gull not only as the miracle of a perfect thing, but as the perfect thing in the enmarveling system of what encloses it?

The point involves the whole nature of perception. Do we "see" with   56
our eyes? I must believe that it is the mind that sees, and that the eyes are only the windows we see through. We see with the patterns of what we know. Let any layman look into a tide-pool and list what he sees there. Then let him call an imaginative biologist and ask the biologist what he sees. The layman will have seen things, but the biologist will see systems, and the things in place in those systems.

He will also see many things simultaneously. A basic necessity to all   57
poetic communication is what I have called *fluency* in an earlier article in these

pages. Fluency is the ability to receive more than one meaning, impression, stimulus—call it what you please—at the same time. Analysis must always fumble and be long-winded because it must consider those multiple impressions doggedly and one by one. If such itemized dealing accurately locates true elements of the poem, the itemization will have served its purpose, and that purpose must certainly be defended as one that has summoned some of the best minds of all ages. What analysis does, though laboriously, is to establish patterns one may see with.

But there then remains the reader's work. It is up to him, guided by   58
the analysis, to read the poem with the fluency it requires, and which analysis does not hope to achieve. Certainly, whatever is said here, poetry will be talked about and must be talked about. The one point of such talk, however, is to lead the reader more richly to the threshold of the poem. Over that threshold he must take himself. And I, for one, must suspect that if he refuses to carry anything as cumbersome as detail across that threshold, he will never furnish the house of his own mind.

QUESTIONS FOR MEANING

1. Explain the distinction that Ciardi makes between *how* a poem means and *what* a poem means. Paraphrase paragraphs 2, 38, and 42.
2. In paragraphs 3, 4, and 5, what does Ciardi mean by "duplicity"?
3. What is the topic statement of paragraph 11? Is this the premise that underlines Ciardi's approach to poetry?
4. According to Ciardi, what two principles are essential to writing good poetry?
5. Explain what Ciardi means by "foil" in paragraph 16.
6. Why does Ciardi believe that the horse in the poem is a symbol? Where does he define what he means by "symbol"?
7. What are the four dramatic forces that Ciardi identifies in "Stopping by the Woods on a Snowy Evening"?
8. How does Ciardi explain Frost's decision to end his poem by repeating "And miles to go before I sleep"? What technical problems did this decision solve for Frost, and why does Ciardi consider it a brilliant solution? What is the significance of the repetition?
9. Summarize the objections to Ciardi's essay that appear in the letters it inspired. What bothered people the most? Which is the best letter and which the silliest?
10. In responding to his critics, what did Ciardi identify as the major issue in the controversy over his interpretation of the poem? What is his response to this question? Had he anticipated it at any point in his original essay?
11. Explain what Ciardi means by "fluency" in the last two paragraphs of his "Letter to Letter Writers."
12. Vocabulary: epilogue (6), integrity (11), brashly (12), obliterates (12), spate (14), emphatically (14), haphazard (29), quandary (37), artifice (38),

germinal (41), lyricism (41), despoiled (43) inimical (44), disdain (48), prodigy (49), indignation (51), waive (51).

QUESTIONS ABOUT STRATEGY

1. What is the function of paragraph 1? How does it serve to prepare readers for the essay that follows?
2. Why are paragraphs 9 through 15 parenthetical to the primary purpose of Ciardi's essay?
3. Does Ciardi make any claims that he fails to support?
4. How useful is the analogy in paragraph 25? Did it help you to understand the nature of poetry?
5. Several of his critics complained that Ciardi's essay is too long. Do you agree? If so, what would you cut? How does Ciardi himself respond to this charge?
6. Which of Ciardi's critics makes an ad hominem argument? In responding to criticism, does Ciardi ever resort to sarcasm?
7. How effectively has Ciardi answered his critics? If you were amused by any of the letters to the editor, was Ciardi's rebuttal strong enough to win back your confidence in him?

HERBERT R. COURSEN, JR.

The Ghost of Christmas Past: "Stopping by Woods on a Snowy Evening"

Herbert R. Coursen, Jr., graduated from Amherst College in 1954 and received his Ph.D. from the University of Connecticut in 1965. Since 1964 he has taught English at Bowdoin College, where he became Professor of Creative Writing and Shakespeare. A former fighter pilot in the U.S. Air Force, Coursen has published in periodicals as diverse as Studies in Philology *and* Sports Illustrated. *He is the author of several works of criticism, including* The Rarer Action: Hamlet's Mousetrap *(1969),* Shaping the Self: Style and Technique in the Narrative *(1975), and* Christian Ritual and the World of Shakespeare *(1976). He has also written a novel,* After the War *(1980), and many volumes of poetry, including* Storm in April *(1973),* Fears in the Night *(1976), and* Walking Away *(1977). The following essay on Frost was first published in December* **1962**. *As you read it, you should be prepared to smile.*

Much ink has spilled on many pages in exegesis of this little poem. Actually, critical jottings have only obscured what has lain beneath critical noses all these years. To say that the poem means merely that a man stops one night to observe a snowfall, or that the poem contrasts the mundane desire for creature comfort with the sweep of aesthetic appreciation, or that it renders worldly responsibilities paramount, or that it reveals the speaker's latent death-wish is to miss the point rather badly. Lacking has been that mind simple enough to see what is *really* there. 1

The first line ("Whose woods these are I think I know") shows that the speaker has paused aside a woods of whose ownership he is fairly sure. So much for paraphrase. Uncertainty vanishes with the next two lines ("His house is in the village though;/He will not see me stopping here"). The speaker knows (a) where the owner's home is located, and (b) that the owner won't be out at the woods tonight. Two questions arise immediately: (a) how does the speaker know? and (b) how does the speaker know? As will be made manifest, only one answer exists to each question. 2

The subsequent two quatrains force more questions to pop up. On auditing the first two lines of the second quatrain ("My little horse must think it queer/To stop without a farmhouse near"), we must ask, "Why does the little 'horse' think oddly of the proceedings?" We must ask also if this *is*, as the speaker claims, the "darkest evening of the year." The calendar date of this occurrence (or lack of occurrence) by an unspecified patch of trees is essential to an apprehension of the poem's true meaning. In the third quatrain, we hear "harness bells" shook. Is the auditory image really an allusion? Then there is the question of the "horse's" identity. Is this really Equus Caballus? This question links itself to that of the *driver's* identity and reiterates 3 the problem of the animal's untoward attitude toward this evidently un-scheduled stop.

The questions have piled up unanswered as we reach the final quatrain   4
and approach the ultimate series of poetic mysteries to be resolved. Clearly,
all of the questions asked thus far (save possibly the one about the "horse's"
identity) are ones which any normal reader, granted the training in close
analysis provided by a survey course in English Literature during his sophomore year in college, might ask. After some extraneous imagery ("The woods
are lovely, dark and deep" has either been established or is easily adduced
from the dramatic situation), the final three lines hold out the key with which
the poem's essence may be released. What, to ask two more questions, are
the "promises" which the speaker must "keep," and why are the last two
lines so redundant about the distance he must cover before he tumbles into
bed? Obviously, the obligations are important, the distance great.

Now, if we swing back to one of the previous questions, the poem will   5
begin to unravel. The "darkest evening of the year" in New England is December 21st, a date near that on which the western world celebrates Christmas. It may be that December 21st *is* the date of the poem, or (and with
poets this seems more likely) that this is the closest the poet can come to
Christmas without giving it all away. Who has "promises to keep" at or near
this date, and who must traverse much territory to fulfill these promises?
Yes, and who but St. Nick would know the location of *each* home? Only he
would know who had "just settled down for a long winter's nap" (the poem's
third line—"He will not see me stopping here"—is clearly a veiled allusion)
and would not be out inspecting his acreage this night. The unusual phrase
"fill up with snow," in the poem's fourth line, is a transfer of Santa's occupational preoccupation to the countryside; he is mulling the filling of countless stockings hung above countless fireplaces by countless careful children.
"Harness bells," of course, allude to "Sleighing Song," a popular Christmas
tune of the time the poem was written in which the refrain "'Jingle Bells!
Jingle Bells!" appears; thus again we are put on the Christmas track. The
"little horse," like the date, is another attempt at poetic obfuscation. Although the "rein-reindeer" ambiguity has been eliminated from the poem's
final version, probably because too obvious, we may speculate that the animal is really a reindeer disguised as a horse by the poet's desire for obscurity,
a desire which we must concede has been fulfilled up to now.

The animal is clearly concerned, like the faithful Rudolph—another   6
possible allusion (post facto, hence unconscious)—lest his master fail to complete his mission. Seeing no farmhouse in the second quatrain, but pulling a
load of presents, no wonder the little beast wonders! It takes him a full two
quatrains to rouse his driver to remember all the empty stockings which
hang ahead. And Santa does so reluctantly at that, poor soul, as he ponders
the myriad farmhouses and villages which spread between him and his own
"winter's nap." The modern St. Nick, lonely and overworked, tosses no
"Happy Christmas to all and to all a good night!" into the precipitation. He
merely shrugs his shoulders and resignedly plods away.

QUESTIONS FOR MEANING

1. What interpretations of the poem does Coursen reject?
2. On what "evidence" does Coursen base his claim that "Stopping by Woods on a Snowy Evening" is about an overworked Santa Claus? Could anyone take this argument seriously?
3. Identify the allusion in the essay's title. What famous writer wrote about "the Ghost of Christmas Past"?
4. Vocabulary: exegesis (1), mundane (1), aesthetic (1), paramount (1), latent (1), quatrains (3), auditing (3), apprehension (3), auditory (3), reiterates (3), extraneous (4), adduced (4), traverse (5), obfuscation (5), myriad (6).

QUESTIONS ABOUT STRATEGY

1. At what point in this essay did you first become aware that you were reading a parody? Rereading the essay, can you find any clues that you originally overlooked?
2. How does Coursen's diction contribute to the essay's humor? Can you identify any comic shifts in style?
3. How does Coursen account for discrepancies between his thesis and the language of the poem itself?
4. What is the point of this essay? Is Coursen ridiculing the nature of literary criticism, or is he simply making a good-humored joke? How would you describe his tone?

WILLIAM H. SHURR

Once More to the "Woods": A New Point of Entry into Frost's Most Famous Poem

Born in Evanston, Illinois, William H. Shurr attended Loyola University in Chicago, where he graduated in 1955, but remained to continue his study of philosophy and theology. He received his Ph.D. from the University of North Carolina at Chapel Hill in 1968, and has taught English at Washington State University and the University of Tennessee. His books include Prose and Poetry of England *(1965) and* The Mystery of Iniquity: Melville as Poet 1857–91 *(1972). His essay on Frost was first published in the* New England Quarterly *in **1974**. As you read it, you should be careful to note the way in which Shurr draws upon earlier critics and incorporates their views into his essay while still advancing a thesis of his own.*

"Stopping by Woods on a Snowy Evening" may be the best-known poem   1
ever written by an American. It is surely one of the most commented upon—
so much so that readers, critics, and the author himself frequently pleaded
for a moratorium to criticism. Only the promise of a truly new "point of
entry" can justify still another expenditure of effort, readers' and writer's, on
the subject. The argument that follows presents a new interpretation of the
poem based on a study of Frost's specific diction and its provenance. The
interpretation thus established generates two insights: that Frost, in this poem,
is responding negatively to one of the most profound and typical elements in
the American experience; and that several other early poems, which Frost
was always careful to popularize, can now be linked to a coherent series of
statements. This cluster of poems documents a significant moment of change
in the evolution of Frost's consciousness and of American consciousness generally.

Commentary of Robert Frost's "Stopping by Woods on a Snowy Eve-   2
ning" is already extensive enough for us to determine something like a *stemma*
of critical traditions. The most common interpretation, thematically, has been
that the poem is an ethical statement concerning social commitments and
obligations to which a man must listen. This obvious view responds to the
attention-soliciting repetition with which the poem ends. Louis Untermeyer
was one of the earliest to put this interpretation into writing. Reginald Cook,
Robert Dolye, D. J. Lepore, and Stanley Poss have continued to accept this
reading as adequate.[1]

---

[1] See Louis Untermeyer's *Come In* (New York, 1943), later amplified and published as *The Pocket Book of Robert Frost's Poems* (New York, 1956), 192. Reginald L. Cook, *The Dimensions of Robert Frost* (New York, 1958). John Robert Doyle, *The Poetry of Robert Frost: As Analysis*

The second major tradition of interpretation was strikingly stated by 3
John Ciardi in his 1958 article in *The Saturday Review:* "Can one fail to sense
by now that the dark and snowfall symbolize a deathwish, however momentary, i.e., that hunger for final rest and surrender that a man may feel, but
not a beast?" The insight had been anticipated a decade earlier by Wellek and
Warren in *Theory of Literature,* where *sleep* was seen as a "natural symbol"
for *death*. It continues as a tradition in Leonard Unger and William Van
O'Connor, in John Lynen, Lawrance Thompson, and James Armstrong. Lloyd
Dendinger, more recently, has seen the lure of death operating thematically
in the poem, but proposes the "lure of wilderness" typical in American letters as even more basic to the poem.[2] One must note however that Frost
objected strongly to Ciardi's thesis: "That's all right, but it's hardly a death
poem."[3]

These two interpretations can stand together. Ciardi conflated them in 4
his *Saturday Review* article by saying that the speaker in the poem is finally
recalled from the attractive power of the death wish by his sense of belonging
to the world of man; the social side of his nature prevails over the psychic
lure of the depths.

A third tradition of interpretation can be discerned in which the "dark 5
woods" stand out as the central symbol to be explicated. Robert Langbaum
used the terminology of theological existentialism when he analyzed the poem
as a "momentary insight into the nonhuman otherness of nature." John Ogilvie rightly discerned that imagery of the dark woods is pervasive in Frost's
early poetry; for him the woods symbol implied the poet's desire for isolation and his need to explore the inner self. George Nitchie, surveying the
whole range of Frost's poetry, read this poem as a "yearning back to Eden
. . . an imagined withdrawal from the complicated world we all know into
a mysterious loveliness symbolized by woods or darkness."[4] One finds a
vagueness in all of these readings, as if they were not based on sufficient
evidence to make the readings definite or persuasive.

Finally, one may mention a fourth tradition of interpreting the poem. 6
This is a blatant allegorization, particularly of the first stanza. I know whose

---

(Johannesburg, Witwatersrand, and New York, 1965), 195. D. J. Lepore, "Setting and/or Statement," *English Journal*, LV, 624–626. Stanley Poss, "Low Skies, Some Clearing, Local Frost,"
New England Quarterly, XLI, 438–442.

[2] John Ciardi, "Robert Frost: The Way to the Poem," *Saturday Review*: 40 (April 12, 1958), 15ff.
Rene Wellek and Austin Warren, *Theory of Literature* (New York, 1949, 1955); the passage rele-
vant to Frost can be found on 194–195 of the first edition and 179 of the second edition. Leonard
Unger and William Van O'Connor, *Poems for Study* (New York, 1953), 600. John F. Lynen,
The Pastoral Art of Robert Frost (New Haven: Yale Univ. Press, 1960). Lawrance Thompson, *Fire
and Ice: The Art and Thought of Robert Frost* (New York, 1961), 27. James Armstrong,
"The 'Death Wish' in 'Stopping by Woods,' " *College English*, XXV, 440–445. Lloyd N. Dendinger, "The Irrational Appeal of Frost's Dark Deep Woods," *Southern Review*, II, 822–829.

[3] Quoted in Louis Mertins, *Robert Frost: Life and Talks—Walking* (Norman, 1965), 371.

[4] Robert Langbaum, "The New Nature Poetry," *American Scholar*, XXVIII, 323–340. John T.
Ogilvie, "From Woods to Stars: A Pattern of Imagery in Robert Frost's Poetry," *South Atlantic
Quarterly*, LVIII, 64–76. George W. Nitchie, *Human Values in the Poetry of Robert Frost* (Durham,
1960).

woods these are; He made them; His house is in the village; the village church. This makes the poem a religious allegory of fairly simpleminded type. If done with some irony it could take its place beside the successful spoof of symbol hunting generally, Herbert Coursen's "proof" that the speaker is really Santa Claus and that he must get on with the distribution of toys he has promised to all good children.[5] But the allegory is presented seriously. Although I have not seen this tradition in print, each year students have assured me that it was the quasi-official interpretation whenever they came 'round, dutifully, almost ritually, to "doing" the poem again in secondary school English classes. The curious thing about this interpretation is that it bears some similarity to the one which I am about to propose. Allegory is too blunt an instrument to use for analysis here, but there is convincing evidence that the poem is the record of a religious experience; or, since it is more precise to be more general here, say rather that the poem is a record of the mind's encounter with transcendence. Emerson achieved it, and on very nearly the same New England ground. His experience is joyfully recorded in the first chapter of *Nature*. In the first two paragraphs he lays down two conditions for this experience, "solitude" and "reverence"—conditions which are also prominent in the poem by Frost. The experience itself is recorded thus:

> In the woods, is perpetual youth. . . . In the woods, we return to reason and faith. There I feel that nothing can befall me in life—no disgrace, no calamity (leaving me my eyes), which nature cannot repair. Standing on the bare ground,— my head bathed by the blithe air, and uplifted into infinite space,—all mean egotism vanishes. I become a transparent eye-ball. I am nothing. I see all. The currents of the Universal Being circulate through me; I am part or particle of God.

The notion of "transparence" is repeated frequently in the essay, for example   7 in Chapter 6: "If the Reason be stimulated to more earnest vision, outlines and surfaces become transparent, and are no longer seen; causes and spirits are seen through them."[6] In similar woodland circumstances Frost's mind also threatens to become transparent, but his reaction is different. As he later told a questioner, "I thought it was about time I was getting the hell out of there."[7]

An analysis of the structure of Frost's poem shows that line 13, "The   8 woods are lovely, dark and deep," is central. From the first line, irrelevancies tug at his attention: the curious question of the *ownership* of these woods (Emerson would have dismissed the question by asserting that nobody owns the landscape), the sudden attention to the trivial subject of the horse's re-

---

[5]"The Ghost of Christmas Past: 'Stopping by Woods on a Snowy Evening,' " *College English,* XXII, 236ff.

[6]I quote from the splendid edition of *Nature* by Merton M. Sealts, Jr., and Alfred R. Ferguson (New York, 1969), 8, 24.

[7]Quoted in Mertins, 304.

sponse to a pause in their journey, and finally the abrupt shift to auditory sensation in the analysis of the sound of snow falling. In other words, there is only one assertion in the poem about the subject most under consideration: "The woods are lovely, dark and deep." All of Frost's attention to the actual woods is concentrated here; it is here that the subject itself is finally able to gain ascendancy over the side issues which attempt to snag the mind on its route towards this center. A major effect with which criticism of the poem must concern itself is the tension created by the actual subject of the poem and the speaker's resistance to it for three-fourths of the poem. When the assertion is finally made, its diction assumes supreme importance.

The speculation that this resistance is primarily to the lure of death is   9
finally inadequate. Whatever associations with death the words "sleep" and "dark" may have, they also are appropriate to another area of experience to be set forth in a moment. A more problematical aspect of the death-wish interpretation is the existence in the poem of a concrete symbol of death, a symbol which is not at the center of focus. If death appears in the poem, it is represented by the "frozen lake" mentioned almost casually in line 7. This symbol takes its meaning from well-documented facts in Frost's life. Frost's early obsession with suicide usually took the form of death by drowning, and according to his family the lake of this poem was between the Frost farm and the nearest town of West Derry, a drive which the poet often had to take.[8] This information underlines the statement of the poem that while the speaker may feel caught between the lure of death and *something else* ("Between the woods and frozen lake"), it is the something else represented by the woods that mainly occupies his attention. If *lake* is associated in his mind with *death,* what then, does the more central assertion about the *woods* mean?

The "new point of entry" mentioned in my title, and which brings   10
many of these materials together, involves a climactic phrase from a poem by Henry Vaughan, "The Night." The phrase reads "A deep but dazzling darkness." It will be seen to have immediate correspondences with line 13 of Frost's poem. "The woods are lovely, *dark* and *deep,*" prepared for earlier by "The *darkest* evening of the year" in line 8. Vaughan's poem works in the tradition of mystical theology which conceives of the soul's ascent to God as a passage through various well-defined stages of illumination until the final stage is reached in which the brightness is so intense that the seeker's senses and mind are blanked out, as it were by overstimulation. When the soul is wrapped in this dark night or cloud of unknowing, it knows, paradoxically, that it has arrived at the right place, at its spiritual center. The night becomes luminous, a deep but dazzling darkness which is God. One of the traditional sources for this notion of Divine Darkness is Dionysius the Aeropagite, in his *De Mystica Theologia* (I,i):

> As for thee, dear Timothy, I counsel that in the earnest exercise of mystical contemplation thou leave the senses and the operations of the intellect and all

[8] See Lawrance Thompson, *Robert Frost: The Early Years, 1874–1915* (New York, 1966), 548.

things that the senses or the intellect can perceive, and all things in this world
of nothingness or that world of being: and that, thine understanding being laid
to rest, thou ascend (as far as thou mayest) towards union with Him whom
neither being nor understanding can contain. For by the unceasing and absolute
renunciation of thyself and all things, thou shalt in pureness cast all things aside,
and be released from all, and so shalt be led upwards to the Ray of that Divine
Darkness which exceedeth all existence.

Throughout his poem, Vaughan works with these same paradoxes of darkness and vision and the finding of oneself in the total abandonment of the
self. His final stanza reads:

> There is in God (some say)
> A deep, but dazzling darkness; As men here
> Say it is late and dusky, because they
>   See not all clear;
> O for that night! where I in him
> Might live invisible and dim.

The stanza sketches two alternative responses possible for one who approaches this kind of night. The practical New Englander (Frost) may say,
equivalently, "it is late and dusky," and escape back to the brightly lit interior of home and family. The anglican mystic (Vaughan) stays with the experience and relishes the slow and dangerous knowledge it provides.

    The question of biography must remain subsidiary to literary analysis,   11
but there is much in Frost's early life to explain his resistance to this kind of
experience. His mother, always something of a religious fanatic, was a devoted Swedenborgian during Frost's early boyhood. Among the stories she
told the children were those of the Biblical Samuel, Joan of Arc, and Swed-
enborg himself, all of whom were granted direct auditory communication
from the supernatural world. His mother encouraged the sensitive young
boy to develop his own gifts of second sight and second hearing. When he
actually began hearing the sound of voices from another world, "he almost
scared himself out of his wits,"[9] a phrase that corresponds with Frost's own
later statement of his desire to get "the hell out of there" when something
similar seemed about to occur.

    The question remains, of course, whether Frost knew this passage from   12
Vaughan. The answer can be a confident "yes," merely on the basis of Frost's
well-known competence in the documents of his trade. But we can come
closer. No fewer than three writers must have thrust Vaughan's lines upon
his attention with new freshness, shortly before Frost came to write his own
poem. The year before, Herbert J. C. Grierson published his famous anthology *Metaphysical Lyrics and Poems of the Seventeenth Century*.[10] The volume,

---

[9] Thompson, *Robert Frost*, 36.

[10] The book was published by Oxford University Press in 1921. It is from this edition that I have
cited Vaughan's "The Night" above.

which included Vaughan's "The Night," was to start a renascence of interest in the Metaphysical Poets. T. S. Eliot, that same year, wrote his essay on the Metaphysical Poets as a review of this book, and published it the first of many times in the London *Times* Literary Supplement (October 20, 1921). Frost was very much aware of what Eliot was doing, as he would be for several years to come. He could hardly have ignored a book of poems that was promising to revise the official history of English letters. But a second book was also available which put Vaughan's poem explicitly in the mystical tradition and in the context of "Divine Darkness" literature. This was Evelyn Underhill's *Mysticism,* a sensitively written book full of marvelous quotations, so popular that it went through twelve editions between 1911 and 1930. Miss Underhill's emphasis was on the Anglican mystical tradition, in which Eliot (again) was becoming so totally interested. Miss Underhill cites the final stanza of Vaughan's "The Night" on the same page that she quotes the passage from Dionysius the Aeropagite introduced above.

In the absence of actual records, it always seems tendentious to propose "probable" sources for a particular literary work. But the question of sources is not crucial in this instance. A more fertile source of investigation (as in the case of the Freudian criticism which posits a death wish here) is the more general question of *provenance:* analogous areas of human experience where similar diction is employed. The three authors mentioned above provide, then, a possible source for Frost's diction, and a certain analogue to both experience and diction. Frost, in the central statement of this poem, employs the vocabulary characteristic of this same kind of mysticism.   13

A well-known source of Frost's early thought provides a still richer trove of analogues. This is William James. Frost already knew the writings of the noted psychologist when he sought admission to Harvard as a special student in 1897. James was on leave of absence when Frost was there, but one of his professors used James's shorter *Psychology* as his text. Frost used this text, as well as James's *Talks to Teachers on Psychology,* when he was a teacher at the Plymouth Normal School in 1911–1912.[11] Frost himself said in 1932, "The most valuable teacher I had at Harvard I never had. . . . He was William James. His books meant a great deal to me."[12]   14

In James's *The Varieties of Religious Experience* (1902), Frost would have found the same vocabulary of mysticism used by Vaughan, though not the citation from the poet himself. In Lectures XVI and XVII, for example, James quotes from Henry Suso, German mystic of the fourteenth century, on the state of the soul in mystical rapture, "lost in the stillness of the glorious *dazzling obscurity* and of the naked simple unity. It is in this modeless *where* that the highest bliss is to be found." A night-time experience, close to Frost's in "Stopping by Woods," is also quoted: "The perfect stillness of the night was thrilled by a more solemn silence. The darkness held a presence that was all the more felt because it was not seen. I could not any more have doubted   15

---

[11] Thompson, *Robert Frost: The Early Years;* see 231–232, 239–241, 372.
[12] Lawrance Thompson, *Robert Frost: The Years of Triumph, 1915–1938* (New York: 1970), 643.

that *He* was there than that I was. Indeed, I felt myself to be, if possible, the less real of the two." To select a final citation, among many that relate to the vocabulary of Frost's poem, James quotes St. Teresa of Avila on the mystic's sense of nothingness, the threat of abandonment of one's being. The metaphors of wakefulness and sleep are especially pertinent: "In the orison of union, the soul is fully awake as regards God, but wholly asleep as regards things of this world and in respect of herself. During the short time the union lasts, she is as it were deprived of every feeling, and even if she would, she could not think of any single thing."[13] The provenance of Frost's imagery is, now, quite clear. The words and images do not characterize Freud's descriptions of the death wish; they are found, however, throughout a large range of literature which attempts to describe a particular kind of mystical experience, an encounter with the Absolute in which man's own sense of selfhood is threatened with annihilation.

This kind of imagery, for this kind of terrifying experience of transcendent being, is deeply rooted in the human mind. In Greek mythology, high in the genealogy of the pre-divine entities, Sleep is the child of Night. One step further back, according to Hesiod's *Theogony,* is the father of Night, Chaos, the formlessness from which everything originates. Both Sleep and Night are mentioned in Frost's poem, as is also, by the implications of my argument, the Father of them all. One must point out, for those who espouse the death-wish interpretation, that Erebus is *another* child of Chaos, the sister of Sleep, and represents in mythological thought a distinctly different approach to the origin of all being. If we can reduce the statements of Frost's speaker here to mythological thought-patterns, they fall clearly into line with what I have been proposing. Frost's repeated line at the end of the poem, "And miles to go before I sleep," emphasizes his preference for other things, other "promises" he has made to himself, before he is ready to face this Night which exposes the sleeper to the infinite abandonment of forms, Chaos.   16

What all of these considerations lead to is the conclusion that "Stopping by Woods" is a decisive poem in the mental development of Robert Frost. It clearly describes the goal of a road not taken. This is the road of the holy man, whose goal is absorption in transcendent being. In determining the parameters of his genius Frost came upon this area, as is clearly shown by the vocabulary of this poem. Where the earlier Transcendentalists found in this experience the goal of their desires, Frost's later American draws the line and retreats. The poem is a statement of resistance to a particular kind of experience which the speaker finds radically uncongenial. Frost is on territory too personally threatening to cultivate as his own field of creative endeavor.[14]   17

---

[13] *The Varieties of Religious Experience* was published in New York by Longmans, Green and Co., 1902; I quote from the edition published in New American Library of World Literature, 1958, 322, 67, 313.

[14] Eban Bass has recently discerned a grouping of Frost's poems which he calls the "poetry of fear." He finds, though, that the fear remains enigmatic. See *American Literature,* XLIII, 603–615.

Frost has several poems which verge upon the edge of this same em-   18
blematical night, where one knows that one will lose himself, and where the
mystic trusts he will finally find himself and a total transforming wisdom as
well. This cluster of poems has its own dramatic structure. We may sketch
it lightly, with some well-known poems, to show the general curve; many
more poems could be plotted along the points on this graph. The poems
chosen are the ones Frost came back to again and again in his public readings.
Several years earlier, in "An Old Man's Winter Night," the subject of the
poem is vaguely troubled by a sense of presences in the night. But because
of aloneness and feeble old age he is unable to confront them directly: "One
aged man—one man—can't keep a house,/A farm, a countryside. . . ." Here
is the beginning of the fear that will develop of the formlessness that lies
outside of artificially established human boundaries. Another poem from the
same volume (*Mountain Interlude,* 1916) confirms Frost's own preferences for
the earthly and the particular. The famous "Birches" expresses a conscious
choice of one direction over another as proper for human cultivation: "Earth's
the right place for love:"[15]

> I'd like to go by climbing a birch-tree,
> And climb black branches up a snow-white trunk
> *Toward* heaven, till the tree could bear no more,
> But dipped its top and set me down again.

In other words, there is an unwillingness to cope with the experience of
transcendence expressed several years before the moment in July, 1922, when
"Stopping by Woods on a Snowy Evening" was written. A few years later
in *West-Running Brook* (1928), Frost printed "Acquainted with the Night."
The speaker is again alone, again it is night. He feels totally isolated in a
lifeless city and a loveless universe. A sign of the powerful feeling locked in
this poem is the fact that it is held together by a tight terza rima, a form
unusual in Frost. Panic, caused by a perception of limitlessness, is very close
to the surface. Again, in "Desert Places" (1936), in a setting similar to that
of "Stopping by Woods," the speaker has a sense of a universe that is no
longer inhabited, whether these be the vast interstellar spaces or his own
spaces "so much nearer home." In these poems the reason for his earlier
rejection of the transcendent experience is developed: it is as if acceptance
would have set him loose to wander in total isolation in the infinite formlessness of the universe. A final note to the explanation of Frost's resistance
to the transcendent experience, as he recorded it in "Stopping by Woods," is
stated in "Design" (from *A Further Range,* 1936). This is another closely knit
poem, a well-designed sonnet more tightly unified by the use of only three
rhymes. The "design" or providence which brings the moth and the dimpled
spider together on the diseased flower is probably the "design of *darkness* to

---

[15] A similar reading of "Birches" is offered by Anna K. Juhnke, "Religion in Robert Frost's
Poetry: The Play for Self-Possessions," *American Literature,* XXXVI, 153–164.

appall." The negative vastness that tenants the universe probably shapes things malevolently. One who perceived transcendence in this way could hardly be expected to cry, with Henry Vaughan, "O for the night. . . ."[16]

QUESTIONS FOR MEANING

1. How does Shurr justify writing this essay? What are the two new insights into the poem that he claims to offer?
2. What are the four traditional approaches to "Stopping by Woods on a Snowy Evening" that Shurr rejects? Why does he find these interpretations to be inadequate?
3. What does Shurr mean in paragraph 6 when he states that "Stopping by Woods on a Snowy Evening" is "a record of the mind's encounter with transcendence"?
4. Who was Ralph Waldo Emerson, and what was his experience in "the woods"?
5. What support does Shurr offer for his claim that Frost must have been familiar with "The Night" by Henry Vaughan?
6. Explain the concept of "Divine Darkness" discussed in paragraphs 10 and 15.
7. Who were the Transcendentalists, alluded to in paragraph 17?
8. In what sense is "Stopping by Woods on a Snowy Evening" a religious poem? According to Shurr, what is it that Frost rejects in this poem? Has he rejected God?
9. Vocabulary: moratorium (1), expenditure (1), provenance (1), *stemma* (2), conflated (4), psychic (4), theological (5), existentialism (5), ascendancy (8), paradoxically (10), subsidiary (11), tendentious (13), analogues (14), pertinent (15), orison (15), espouse (16), uncongenial (17), emblematical (18), terza rima (18), malevolently (18).

QUESTIONS ABOUT STRATEGY

1. Why does Shurr begin his essay by summarizing earlier interpretations of the poem?
2. How good is Shurr's research? Does he convince you that he has made a thorough study of the poem and the criticism it has inspired?
3. Why is it important for Shurr to link Frost to Emerson and James—and not just to Henry Vaughan?
4. Why does Shurr conclude his argument by comparing "Stopping by Woods on a Snowy Evening" with several other poems by Frost?

---

[16] Some other poems of Frost that might be considered as part of this same cluster are "A Passing Glimpse," "Beeches," and "For Once, Then, Something,"—all of which state a choice of a circumscribed area of poetic inquiry in place of a limitless one. "Come In" is also interesting as a definite refusal to enter the dark woods.

N. ARTHUR BLEAU

Robert Frost's Favorite Poem

*As the essays in this section have revealed, literary criticism is often argumentative. Critics often disagree about the meaning of literature, and the greatest controversy is frequently provoked by the most familiar poems and stories. Many critics would argue that a work of art has a life of its own that is independent of the author's intentions. But to know something of the circumstances under which a work is composed can sometimes help us to understand it. In forming your own judgment of "Stopping by Woods on a Snowy Evening," you may want to consider the following post-script: a **1978** narrative account of a conversation between Frost and one of his admirers which had occurred many years earlier.*

Robert Frost revealed his favorite poem to me. Furthermore, he gave me a 1
glimpse into his personal life that exposed the mettle of the man. I cherish
the memory of that conversation, and vividly recall his description of the
circumstances leading to the composition of his favorite work.

We were in my hometown—Brunswick, Maine. It was the fall of 1947, 2
and Bowdoin College was presenting its annual literary institute for students
and the public. Mr. Frost had lectured there the previous season; and being
well received, he was invited for a return engagement.

I attended the great poet's prior lecture and wasn't about to miss his 3
encore—even though I was quartered 110 miles north at the University of
Maine. At the appointed time, I was seated and eagerly awaiting his entrance—armed with a book of his poems and unaware of what was about to
occur.

He came on strong with a simple eloquence that blended with his stat- 4
ure, bushy white hair, matching eyebrows, and well-seasoned features. His
topics ranged from meter to the meticulous selection of a word and its varying interpretations. He then read a few of his poems to accentuate his message.

At the conclusion of the presentation, Mr. Frost asked if anyone had 5
questions. I promptly raised my hand. There were three other questioners,
and their inquiries were answered before he acknowledged me. I asked, "Mr.
Frost, what is your favorite poem?" He quickly replied, "They're all my
favorites. It's difficult to single out one over another!"

"But, Mr. Frost," I persisted, "surely there must be one or two of your 6
poems which have a special meaning to you—that recall some incident perhaps." He then astonished me by declaring the session concluded; where-
upon, he turned to me and said, "Young man, you may come up to the
podium if you like." I was there in an instant.

We were alone except for one man who was serving as Mr. Frost's 7
host. He remained in the background shadows of the stage. The poet leaned
casually against the lectern—beckoning me to come closer. We were side by
side leaning on the lectern as he leafed the pages of the book.

"You know—in answer to your question—there is one poem which   8
comes readily to mind; and I guess I'd have to call it my favorite," he droned
in a pensive manner. "I'd have to say 'Stopping by Woods on a Snowy
Evening' is that poem. Do you recall in the lecture I pointed out the importance of the line 'The darkest evening of the year'?" I acknowledged that I
did, and he continued his thoughtful recollection of a time many years before. "Well—the darkest evening of the year is on December twenty-sec-
ond—which is the shortest day of the year—just before Christmas."

I wish I could have recorded the words as he reflectively meted out his   9
story, but this is essentially what he said.

The family was living on a farm. It was a bleak time both weatherwise   10
and financially. Times were hard, and Christmas was coming. It wasn't going
to be a very good Christmas unless he did something. So—he hitched up the
wagon filled with produce from the farm and started the long trek into town.

When he finally arrived, there was no market for his goods. Times   11
were hard for everybody. After exhausting every possibility, he finally accepted the fact that there would be no sale. There would be no exchange for
him to get a few simple presents for his children's Christmas.

As he headed home, evening descended. It had started to snow, and his   12
heart grew heavier with each step of the horse in the gradually increasing
accumulation. He had dropped the reins and given the horse its head. It knew
the way. The horse was going more slowly as they approached home. It was
sensing his despair. There is an unspoken communication between a man and
his horse, you know.

Around the next bend in the road, near the woods, they would come   13
into view of the house. He knew the family was anxiously awaiting him.
How could he face them? What could he possibly say or do to spare them
the disappointment he felt?

They entered the sweep of the bend. The horse slowed down and then   14
stopped. It knew what he had to do. He had to cry, and he did. I recall the
very words he spoke. "I just sat there and bawled like a baby"—until there
were no more tears.

The horse shook its harness. The bells jingled. They sounded cheerier.   15
He was ready to face his family. It would be a poor Christmas, but Christmas is a time of love. They had an abundance of love, and it would see them
through that Christmas and the rest of those hard times. Not a word
was spoken, but the horse knew he was ready and resumed the journey
homeward.

The poem was composed some time later, he related. How much later   16
I do not know, but he confided that these were the circumstances which
eventually inspired what he acknowledged to be his favorite poem.

I was completely enthralled and, with youthful audacity, asked him to   17
tell me about his next favorite poem. He smiled relaxedly and readily replied,
"That would have to be 'Mending Wall.' Good fences do make good neighbors, you know! We always looked forward to getting together and walking
the lines—each on his own side replacing the stones the winter frost had

tumbled. As we moved along, we'd discuss the things each had experienced during the winter—and also what was ahead of us. It was a sign of spring!"

The enchantment was broken at that moment by Mr. Frost's host, who   18 had materialized behind us to remind him of his schedule. He nodded agreement that it was time to depart, turned to me and with a smile extended his hand. I grasped it, and returned his firm grip as I expressed my gratitude. He then strode off to join his host, who had already reached the door at the back of the stage. I stood there watching him disappear from sight.

I've often wondered why he suddenly changed his mind and decided to   19 answer my initial question by confiding his memoir in such detail. Perhaps no one had ever asked him; or perhaps I happened to pose it at the opportune time. Then again—perhaps the story was meant to be related, remembered and revealed sometime in the future. I don't know, but I'm glad he did—so that I can share it with you.

A Note by Lesley Frost

For many years I have assumed that my father's explanation to me, given   20 sometime in the forties, I think, of the circumstances round and about his writing "Stopping by Woods" was the only one he gave (of course, excepting to my mother), and since he expressed the hope that it need not be repeated fearing pity (pity, he said, was the *last* thing he wanted or needed), I have left it at that. Now, in 1977, I find there was at least one other to whom he vouchsafed the honor of hearing the truth of how it all was that Xmas eve when "the little horse" (Eunice) slows the sleigh at a point between woods, a hundred yards or so north of our farm on the Wyndham Road. And since Arthur Bleau's moving account is so closely, word for word, as I heard it, it would give me particular reason to hope it might be published. I would like to add my own remembrance of words used in the telling to me: "A man has as much right as a woman to a good cry now and again. The snow gave me its shelter; the horse understood and gave me the time." (Incidentally, my father had a liking for certain Old English words. *Bawl* was one of them. Instead of "Stop crying," it was "Oh, come now, quit bawling." Mr. Bleau is right to say my father bawled like a baby.)

QUESTIONS FOR MEANING

1. Summarize the experience that led Frost to write "Stopping by Woods on a Snowy Evening."
2. Of the various critics included in this section, who would be the most likely to use Bleau's testimony to reinforce his own interpretation of the poem?
3. Does the biographical information reported in this essay change your own perception of the poem?
4. What does this essay reveal about N. Arthur Bleau? What was he like in 1947? What was he like thirty years later?

5. Vocabulary: mettle (1), accentuate (4), droned (8), pensive (8), meted (9), enthralled (17), audacity (17), opportune (19).

QUESTIONS ABOUT STRATEGY

1. How important is the note by Lesley Frost supporting the substance of Bleau's report? Would you take Bleau seriously without this reinforcement? If so, why? If not, why not?
2. Lesley Frost describes Bleau's essay as "moving." Do you agree? How would you describe the style and pace of this essay? How good is Bleau's writing?
3. What is the function of paragraph 9? Why does it come at this point, after Bleau has already quoted Frost in paragraphs 6 and 8?

ONE STUDENT'S ASSIGNMENT

Study "Stopping by Woods on a Snowy Evening" and read at least one essay about the poem in The Informed Argument. *Demonstrate that this essay does not entirely explain the poem by offering an interpretation of your own. When writing about the poem, be careful to support whatever you claim with evidence from the poem itself. Use MLA style documentation.*

A View of the Woods
Kim Bassuener

Like any great poem, "Stopping by Woods on a Snowy   1
Evening" by Robert Frost has a number of possible meanings. According to one famous interpretation, this poem
is about death and despair (Ciardi 470). This is a valid
interpretation, but I think that it is too narrow. Part
of the delight of reading poetry is discovering the variety of meanings which can be derived from any one
poem. Another way of reading "Stopping by Woods on a
Snowy Evening" is to see it as a poem about how far man
has come from nature.

In the very first line, the narrator reflects,   2
"Whose woods these are I think I know." His uncertainty
about who owns the woods suggests that whoever owns them
does not visit them often or does not take enough pride
in them to let other people know that he owns them.
Frost continues to convey the distance between owner and

woods in the second line: "His house is in the village though." It is clear that the owner prefers civilization and people to nature. The third line also supports this idea: "He will not see me stopping here" emphasizes that the owner of the woods is removed from them. It is almost as if the poem is saying that the owner does not really own these woods which he cannot even see. The last line of the first stanza, "To watch his woods fill up with snow," uses "his" ironically. After the way the first three lines imply a sense of casual and remote ownership, the "his" in line 4 cannot be taken seriously. Nature is filling up the woods with snow, and we can only watch what ultimately seems to belong to nature, not man.

The second stanza further states how far away man has come from nature with "My little horse must think it queer" (5). The reader should ask why a horse would think it strange to stop by some woods. One of nature's creatures, a horse should love to be out in nature. Instead, it thinks it odd "To stop without a farmhouse near" (6). This shows that man has taken this animal from nature and made it dependent upon civilization. The horse would feel comfortable only if a farmhouse was nearby, and perhaps this is why it is "little." 3

Frost reminds us about the animal's confusion in the third stanza: "He gives his harness bells a shake / To ask if there is some mistake" (9–10). Thoroughly domesticated, the horse cannot understand why its master would want to stop by woods. The next two lines in this stanza contrast with the last two lines of the second stanza. Although we have already been told that the lake is "frozen" (7) and that this is "The darkest evening of the year" (8), the narrator now seems to forget that nature is potentially dangerous. "The only other sound's the sweep / Of easy wind and downy flake" (11–12) makes nature seem harmless and even comforting. The narrator seems to feel detached from the scene, like someone watching a snow storm on television. Any forest animal would know that this is no night to play with. A cold, dark, snowy night is no time to get sentimental about nature. But the poor human being cannot comprehend the true power of what he is only visiting. 4

The last stanza continues to portray the traveler   5
as a detached observer. When the narrator observes, "The
woods are lovely, dark, and deep" (13), he seems to see
nature as something scenic—like a picture on a wall. He
would like to look longer, but other values are more important to him: "But I have promises to keep / And miles
to go before I sleep / And miles to go before I sleep"
(14–16). His life is someplace else. He is not a part of
the scene that has briefly caught his attention.

When everything in the poem is taken into consid-   6
eration, it seems safe to believe that Frost could have
written this poem to show a conflict between man and nature. Although the man in the poem seems able to find
pleasure in looking at nature, he is too far removed
from it to be able to understand what he is looking at.

Work Cited*

Ciardi, John. "Robert Frost: The Way to the Poem." The
        Informed Argument. Ed. Robert K. Miller. San Diego:
        Harcourt, 1992. 467–74.

SUGGESTIONS FOR WRITING

1. Write an explication of "Stopping by Woods on a Snowy Evening,"
   drawing upon at least three of the essays in this unit.
2. Explicate one of the following poems. Do research if you wish, but make
   sure your interpretation explains the language of the poem you have chosen and not just the feelings it has inspired within you.

---

*This citation follows the MLA form for a work in an anthology as given on p. 75. An alter-
native form recommended by the MLA is to give the complete data of the article's original
publication as well as the complete data for the source in which it has been read. Here is how
the Ciardi citation would look in this alternative form:

Ciardi, John. "Robert Frost: The Way to the Poem." Saturday Review 40 (12 Apr. 1958): 15+.
        Rpt. in The Informed Argument. Ed. Robert K. Miller. San Diego: Harcourt, 1992,
        467–72.

Ciardi's essay began on page 15 and ended on page 65 in the magazine in which it first appeared,
but it was not a 50-page-long article so it would be a mistake to write 15–65. As often happens
in general circulation magazines, the article was broken up and "continued" on a number of
different pages. In a case like this in which the pages are not continuous, use the plus (+)
immediately after the page on which the material begins. Note that the abbreviation "Rpt." is
used for "reprinted."

One of the two ways of citing material in an anthology, this alternative form is the more
scholarly. Check with your instructor to find if he or she requires the additional information
that is included within this form.

A Valediction: Forbidding
Mourning

As virtuous men pass mildly away,
    And whisper to their souls to go,
While some of their sad friends do say,
    The breath goes now, and some say, no:

5   So let us melt, and make no noise,
        No tear-floods, nor sigh-tempests move;
    'Twere profanation of our joys
        To tell the laity our love.

    Moving of th' earth brings harms and fears,
10   Men reckon what it did and meant,
    But trepidation of the spheres,
        Though greater far, is innocent.

    Dull sublunary lovers' love
        (Whose soul is sense) cannot admit
15 Absence, because it doth remove
        Those things which elemented it.

    But we by a love so much refined,
        That ourselves know not what it is,
    Inter-assurèd of the mind,
20 Care less, eyes, lips, and hands to miss.

    Our two souls therefore, which are one,
        Though I must go, endure not yet
    A breach, but an expansion,
        Like gold to airy thinness beat.

25 If they be two, they are two so
        As stiff twin compasses are two;
    Thy soul the fixed foot, makes no show
        To move, but doth, if th' other do.

    And though it in the center sit,
30   Yet when the other far doth roam,
    It leans, and hearkens after it,
        And grows erect, as that comes home.

    Such wilt thou be to me, who must
        Like th' other foot, obliquely run;
35 Thy firmness makes my circle just,
        And makes me end, where I begun.

John Donne
1572–1631

The Night

Through that pure virgin shrine,
That sacred veil drawn o'er Thy glorious noon,
That men might look and live, as glowworms shine,
    And face the moon,
5   Wise Nicodemus saw such light
As made him know his God by night.

Most blest believer he!
Who in that land of darkness and blind eyes
Thy long-expected healing wings could see,
10   When Thou didst rise!
And, what can never more be done,
Did at midnight speak with the Sun!

O who will tell me where
He found Thee at that dead and silent hour?
15   What hallowed solitary ground did bear
    So rare a flower,
Within whose sacred leaves did lie
The fulness of the Deity?

No mercy-seat of gold,
20   No dead and dusty cherub, nor carved stone,
But His own living works did my Lord hold
    And lodge alone;
Where trees and herbs did watch and peep
And wonder, while the Jews did sleep.

25   Dear night! this world's defeat;
The stop to busy fools; care's check and curb;
The day of spirits; my soul's calm retreat
    Which none disturb!
Christ's progress, and His prayer time;
30   The hours to which high heaven doth chime.

God's silent, searching flight;
When my Lord's head is filled with dew, and all
His locks are wet with the clear drops of night;
    His still, soft call;
35   His knocking time; the soul's dumb watch,
When spirits their fair kindred catch.

Were all my loud, evil days
Calm and unhaunted as is thy dark tent,
Whose peace but by some angel's wing or voice
40   Is seldom rent,
Then I in heaven all the long year
Would keep, and never wander here.

But living where the sun
Doth all things wake, and where all mix and tire
45 Themselves and others, I consent and run
To every mire,
And by this world's ill-guiding light,
Err more than I can do by night.

There is in God, some say,
50 A deep but dazzling darkness, as men here
Say it is late and dusky; because they
See not all clear.
O for that night! where I in Him
Might live invisible and dim!

Henry Vaughan
1622–1695

The Sick Rose

O Rose, thou art sick.
The invisible worm
That flies in the night
In the howling storm

5   Has found out thy bed
Of crimson joy,
And his dark secret love
Does thy life destroy.

William Blake
1757–1827

Ode on a Grecian Urn

Thou still unravished bride of quietness,
Thou foster-child of silence and slow time,
Sylvan historian, who canst thus express
A flowery tale more sweetly than our rhyme:
5   What leaf-fringed legend haunts about thy shape
Of deities or mortals, or of both,
In Tempe or the dales of Arcady?
What men or gods are these? What maidens loth?
What mad pursuit? What struggle to escape?
10   What pipes and timbrels? What wild ecstasy?

Heard melodies are sweet, but those unheard
　　Are sweeter; therefore, ye soft pipes, play on;
Not to the sensual ear, but, more endeared,
　　Pipe to the spirit ditties of no tone:
15 Fair youth, beneath the trees, thou canst not leave
　　Thy song, nor ever can those trees be bare;
　　　　Bold lover, never, never canst thou kiss,
Though winning near the goal—yet, do not grieve;
　　She cannot fade, though thou hast not thy bliss,
20 For ever wilt thou love, and she be fair!

Ah, happy, happy boughs! that cannot shed
　　Your leaves, nor ever bid the spring adieu;
And, happy melodist, unwearièd,
　　For ever piping songs for ever new;
25 More happy love! more happy, happy love!
　　For ever warm and still to be enjoyed,
　　　　For ever panting and for ever young;
All breathing human passion far above,
　　That leaves a heart high-sorrowful and cloyed,
30 　　A burning forehead, and a parching tongue.

Who are these coming to the sacrifice?
　　To what green altar, O mysterious priest,
Lead'st thou that heifer lowing at the skies,
　　And all her silken flanks with garlands drest?
35 What little town by river or sea shore,
　　Or mountain-built with peaceful citadel,
　　　　Is emptied of its folk, this pious morn?
And, little town, thy streets for evermore
　　Will silent be; and not a soul to tell
40 　　Why thou art desolate, can e'er return.

O Attic shape! Fair attitude! with brede
　　Of marble men and maidens overwrought,
With forest branches and the trodden weed;
　　Thou, silent form, dost tease us out of thought
45 As doth eternity: Cold Pastoral!
　　When old age shall this generation waste,
　　　　Thou shalt remain, in midst of other woe
Than ours, a friend to man, to whom thou say'st,
Beauty is truth, truth beauty,—that is all
50 　　Ye know on earth, and all ye need to know.

John Keats
1795–1821

Brahma

If the red slayer thinks he slays,
  Or if the slain think he is slain,
They know not well the subtle ways
  I keep, and pass, and turn again.

5 Far or forgot to me is near;
  Shadow and sunlight are the same;
The vanished gods to me appear;
  And one to me are shame and fame.

They reckon ill who leave me out;
10   When me they fly, I am the wings;
I am the doubter and the doubt,
  And I the hymn the Brahmin sings.

The strong gods pine for my abode,
  And pine in vain the sacred Seven;
15 But thou, meek lover of the good!
  Find me, and turn thy back on heaven.

Ralph Waldo Emerson
1803–1882

I Saw In Louisiana a Live-Oak Growing

I saw in Louisiana a live-oak growing,
All alone stood it and the moss hung down from the branches,
Without any companion it grew there uttering joyous leaves of dark
    green,
And its look, rude, unbending, lusty, made me think of myself,
5 But I wonder'd how it could utter joyous leaves standing alone
    there without its friend near, for I knew I could not,
And I broke off a twig with a certain number of leaves upon it,
    and twined around it a little moss,
And brought it away, and I have placed it in sight in my room,
It is not needed to remind me as of my own dear friends,
(For I believe lately I think of little else than of them,)
10 Yet it remains to me a curious token, it makes me think of manly
    love;
For all that, and though the live-oak glistens there in Louisiana
    solitary in a wide flat space,
Uttering joyous leaves all its life without a friend a lover near,
I know very well I could not.

Walt Whitman
1819–1892

Dover Beach

The sea is calm tonight.
The tide is full, the moon lies fair
Upon the straits; on the French coast the light
Gleams and is gone; the cliffs of England stand,
5 Glimmering and vast, out in the tranquil bay.
Come to the window, sweet is the night-air!
Only, from the long line of spray
Where the sea meets the moon-blanched land.
Listen! you hear the grating roar
10 Of pebbles which the waves draw back, and fling,
At their return, up the high strand,
Begin, and cease, and then again begin,
With tremulous cadence slow, and bring
The eternal note of sadness in.

15 Sophocles long ago
Heard it on the Aegean, and it brought
Into his mind the turbid ebb and flow
Of human misery; we
Find also in the sound a thought,
20 Hearing it by this distant northern sea.

The Sea of Faith
Was once, too, at the full, and round earth's shore
Lay like the folds of a bright girdle furled.
But now I only hear
25 Its melancholy, long, withdrawing roar,
Retreating, to the breath
Of the night-wind, down the vast edges drear
And naked shingles of the world.

Ah, love, let us be true
30 To one another! for the world, which seems
To lie before us like a land of dreams,
So various, so beautiful, so new,
Hath really neither joy, nor love, nor light,
Nor certitude, nor peace, nor help for pain;
35 And we are here as on a darkling plain
Swept with confused alarms of struggle and flight,
Where ignorant armies clash by night.

Matthew Arnold
1822–1888

A Bird Came Down the Walk

A Bird came down the Walk—
He did not know I saw—
He bit an Angleworm in halves
And ate the fellow, raw,

5   And then he drank a Dew
From a convenient Grass—
And then hopped sidewise to the Wall
To let a Beetle pass—

He glanced with rapid eyes
10   That hurried all around—
They looked like frightened Beads, I thought—
He stirred his Velvet Head

Like one in danger, Cautious,
I offered him a Crumb
15   And he unrolled his feathers
And rowed him softer home—

Than Oars divide the Ocean,
Too silver for a seam—
Or Butterflies, off Banks of Noon
20   Leap, plashless as they swim.

Emily Dickinson
1830–1886

PART 5

SOME CLASSIC ARGUMENTS

◆ ——

PLATO
The Allegory of the Cave

One of the most important thinkers in the history of Western civilization, Plato (c. 428–348 B.C.) grew up in Athens during the difficult years of the Peloponnesian War. He was the student of Socrates, and it is through Plato that Socratic thought has been passed down to us. Socrates is the principal figure in Plato's early dialogues—discussing with the young such questions as "What should men live for?" and "What is the nature of virtue?" Plato devoted his life to answering questions of this sort and teaching others to understand them. In 387 B.C., he founded his Academy, where he taught the future rulers of numerous Greek states. The Academy survived for almost a thousand years, before closing in A.D. 529.

Plato's major works include Gorgias, Meno, Phaedo, Symposium, The Republic, *and* Phaedrus. *In each of these works, Plato insists upon two ideas that are fundamental to his philosophy. He believed that man has an immortal soul existing separately from the body both before birth and after death. Also, he believed that the physical world consists only of appearances; truth consists of ideas that can be discovered and understood only through systematic thought.*

"The Allegory of the Cave" is taken from The Republic, *which is widely considered Plato's greatest work. It is written in the form of a dialogue. The speaker is Socrates, and his "audience" is Glaucon, Plato's brother. But the dialogue should be regarded as a literary device, rather than an actual conversation. Its ultimate audience consists of everyone who wants to think seriously about the nature of truth, justice, and wisdom.*

Next, said I, here is a parable to illustrate the degrees in which our nature   1
may be enlightened or unenlightened. Imagine the condition of men living
in a sort of cavernous chamber underground, with an entrance open to the
light and a long passage all down the cave. Here they have been from childhood, chained by the leg and also by the neck, so that they cannot move and
can see only what is in front of them, because the chains will not let them
turn their heads. At some distance higher up is the light of a fire burning
behind them; and between the prisoners and the fire is a track with a parapet
built along it, like the screen at a puppet-show, which hides the performers
while they show their puppets over the top.

    I see, said he.   2

    Now behind this parapet imagine persons carrying along various arti-   3
ficial objects, including figures of men and animals in wood or stone or other
materials, which project above the parapet. Naturally, some of these persons
will be talking, others silent.

    It is a strange picture, he said, and a strange sort of prisoners.   4

    Like ourselves, I replied; for in the first place prisoners so confined   5
would have seen nothing of themselves or of one another, except the
shadows thrown by the fire-light on the wall of the Cave facing them,
would they?

    Not if all their lives they have been prevented from moving their heads.   6

    And they would have seen as little of the objects carried past.   7

    Of course.   8

    Now, if they could talk to one another, would they not suppose that   9
their words referred only to those passing shadows which they saw?

    Necessarily.   10

    And suppose their prison had an echo from the wall facing them? When   11
one of the people crossing behind them spoke, they could only suppose that
the sound came from the shadow passing before their eyes.

    No doubt.   12

    In every way, then, such prisoners would recognize as reality nothing   13
but the shadows of those artificial objects.

    Inevitably.   14

    Now consider what would happen if their release from the chains and   15
the healing of their unwisdom should come about in this way. Suppose one
of them were set free and forced suddenly to stand up, turn his head, and
walk with eyes lifted to the light; all these movements would be painful, and
he would be too dazzled to make out the objects whose shadows he had been
used to see. What do you think he would say, if someone told him that what
he had formerly seen was meaningless illusion, but now, being somewhat
nearer to reality and turned towards more real objects, he was getting a truer
view? Suppose further that he were shown the various objects being carried
by and were made to say, in reply to questions, what each of them was.
Would he not be perplexed and believe the objects now shown him to be not
so real as what he formerly saw?

    Yes, not nearly so real.   16

And if he were forced to look at the fire-light itself, would not his eyes   17
ache, so that he would try to escape and turn back to the things which he
could see distinctly, convinced that they really were clearer than these other
objects now being shown to him?

Yes.   18

And suppose someone were to drag him away forcibly up the steep and   19
rugged ascent and not let him go until he had hauled him out into the sunlight, would he not suffer pain and vexation at such treatment, and, when he
had come out into the light, find his eyes so full of its radiance that he could
not see a single one of the things that he was now told were real?

Certainly he would not see them all at once.   20

He would need, then, to grow accustomed before he could see things   21
in that upper world. At first it would be easiest to make out shadows, and
then the images of men and things reflected in water, and later on the things
themselves. After that, it would be easier to watch the heavenly bodies and
the sky itself by night, looking at the light of the moon and stars rather
than the Sun and the Sun's light in the day-time.

Yes, surely.   22

Last of all, he would be able to look at the Sun and contemplate its   23
nature, not as it appears when reflected in water or any alien medium, but as
it is in itself in its own domain.

No doubt.   24

And now he would begin to draw the conclusion that it is the Sun that   25
produces the seasons and the course of the year and controls everything in
the visible world, and moreover is in a way the cause of all that he and his
companions used to see.

Clearly he would come at last to that conclusion.   26

Then if he called to mind his fellow prisoners and what passed for wis-   27
dom in his former dwelling-place, he would surely think himself happy in
the change and be sorry for them. They may have had a practice of honour-
ing and commending one another, with prizes for the man who had the
keenest eye for the passing shadows and the best memory for the order in
which they followed or accompanied one another, so that he could make a
good guess as to which was going to come next. Would our released prisoner
be likely to covet those prizes or to envy the men exalted to honour and
power in the Cave? Would he not feel like Homer's Achilles, that he would
far sooner 'be on earth as a hired servant in the house of a landless man'
or endure anything rather than go back to his old beliefs and live in the
old way?

Yes, he would prefer any fate to such a life.   28

Now imagine what would happen if he went down again to take his   29
former seat in the Cave. Coming suddenly out of the sunlight, his eyes would
be filled with darkness. He might be required once more to deliver his opinion on those shadows, in competition with the prisoners who had never been
released, while his eyesight was still dim and unsteady; and it might take
some time to become used to the darkness. They would laugh at him and

say that he had gone up only to come back with his sight ruined; it was worth no one's while even to attempt the ascent. If they could lay hands on the man who was trying to set them free and lead them up, they would kill him.

Yes, they would.   30

Every feature in this parable, my dear Glaucon, is meant to fit our   31 earlier analysis. The prison dwelling corresponds to the region revealed to us through the sense of sight, and the fire-light within it to the power of the Sun. The ascent to see the things in the upper world you may take as standing for the upward journey of the soul into the region of the intelligible; then you will be in possession of what I surmise, since that is what you wish to be told. Heaven knows whether it is true; but this, at any rate, is how it appears to me. In the world of knowledge, the last thing to be perceived and only with great difficulty is the essential Form of Goodness. Once it is perceived, the conclusion must follow that, for all things, this is the cause of whatever is right and good; in the visible world it gives birth to light and to the lord of light, while it is itself sovereign in the intelligible world and the parent of intelligence and truth. Without having had a vision of this Form no one can act with wisdom, either in his own life or in matters of state.

So far as I can understand, I share your belief.   32

Then you may also agree that it is no wonder if those who have reached   33 this height are reluctant to manage the affairs of men. Their souls long to spend all their time in that upper world—naturally enough, if here once more our parable holds true. Nor, again, is it at all strange that one who comes from the contemplation of divine things to the miseries of human life should appear awkward and ridiculous when, with eyes still dazed and not yet accustomed to the darkness, he is compelled, in a law-court or elsewhere, to dispute about the shadows of justice or the images that cast those shadows, and to wrangle over the notions of what is right in the minds of men who have never beheld Justice itself.

It is not at all strange.   34

No; a sensible man will remember that the eyes may be confused in   35 two ways—by a change from light to darkness or from darkness to light; and he will recognize that the same thing happens to the soul. When he sees it troubled and unable to discern anything clearly, instead of laughing thoughtlessly, he will ask whether, coming from a brighter existence, its unaccustomed vision is obscured by the darkness, in which case he will think its condition enviable and its life a happy one; or whether, emerging from the depths of ignorance, it is dazzled by excess of light. If so, he will rather feel sorry for it; or, if he were inclined to laugh, that would be less ridiculous than to laugh at the soul which has come down from the light.

That is a fair statement.   36

If this is true, then, we must conclude that education is not what it is   37 said to be by some, who profess to put knowledge into a soul which does not possess it, as if they could put sight into blind eyes. On the contrary, our own account signifies that the soul of every man does possess the power of learning the truth and the organ to see it with; and that, just as one might have to turn the whole body round in order that the eye should see light instead of darkness, so the entire soul must be turned away from this changing world, until its eye can bear to contemplate reality and that supreme splendour which we have called the Good. Hence there may well be an art whose aim would be to effect this very thing, the conversion of the soul, in the readiest way; not to put the power of sight into the soul's eye, which already has it, but to ensure that, instead of looking in the wrong direction, it is turned the way it ought to be.

Yes, it may well be so.   38

It looks, then, as though wisdom were different from those ordinary   39 virtues, as they are called, which are not far removed from bodily qualities, in that they can be produced by habituation and exercise in a soul which has not possessed them from the first. Wisdom, it seems, is certainly the virtue of some diviner faculty, which never loses its power, though its use for good or harm depends on the direction towards which it is turned. You must have noticed in dishonest men with a reputation for sagacity the shrewd glance of a narrow intelligence piercing the objects to which it is directed. There is nothing wrong with their power of vision, but it has been forced into the service of evil, so that the keener its sight, the more harm it works.

Quite true.   40

And yet if the growth of a nature like this had been pruned from ear-   41 liest childhood, cleared of those clinging overgrowths which come of gluttony and all luxurious pleasure and, like leaden weights charged with affinity to this mortal world, hang upon the soul, bending its vision downwards; if, freed from these, the soul were turned round towards true reality, then this same power in these very men would see the truth as keenly as the objects it is turned to now.

Yes, very likely.   42

Is it not also likely, or indeed certain after what has been said, that a   43 state can never be properly governed either by the uneducated who know nothing of truth or by men who are allowed to spend all their days in the pursuit of culture? The ignorant have no single mark before their eyes at which they must aim in all the conduct of their own lives and of affairs of state; and the others will not engage in action if they can help it, dreaming that, while still alive, they have been translated to the Islands of the Blest.

Quite true.   44

It is for us, then, as founders of a commonwealth, to bring compulsion   45 to bear on the noblest natures. They must be made to climb the ascent to the vision of Goodness, which we called the highest object of knowledge; and, when they have looked upon it long enough, they must not be allowed, as they now are, to remain on the heights, refusing to come down again to the prisoners or to take any part in their labours and rewards, however much or little these may be worth.

Shall we not be doing them an injustice, if we force on them a worse   46 life than they might have?

You have forgotten again, my friend, that the law is not concerned to   47
make any one class specially happy, but to ensure the welfare of the commonwealth as a whole. By persuasion or constraint it will unite the citizens
in harmony, making them share whatever benefits each class can contribute
to the common good; and its purpose in forming men of that spirit was not
that each should be left to go his own way, but that they should be instrumental in binding the community into one.

True, I had forgotten.   48

You will see, then, Glaucon, that there will be no real injustice in com-   49
pelling our philosophers to watch over and care for the other citizens. We
can fairly tell them that their compeers in other states may quite reasonably
refuse to collaborate: there they have sprung up, like a self-sown plant, in
despite of their country's institutions; no one has fostered their growth, and
they cannot be expected to show gratitude for a care they have never received. 'But,' we shall say, 'it is not so with you. We have brought you into
existence for your country's sake as well as for your own, to be like leaders
and king-bees in a hive; you have been better and more thoroughly educated
than those others and hence you are more capable of playing your part both
as men of thought and as men of action. You must go down, then, each in
his turn, to live with the rest and let your eyes grow accustomed to the
darkness. You will then see a thousand times better than those who live there
always; you will recognize every image for what it is and know what it
represents, because you have seen justice, beauty, and goodness in their reality; and so you and we shall find life in our commonwealth no mere dream,
as it is in most existing states, where men live fighting one another about
shadows and quarreling for power, as if that were a great prize; whereas in
truth government can be at its best and free from dissension only where the
destined rulers are least desirous of holding office.'

Quite true.   50

Then will our pupils refuse to listen and to take their turns at sharing   51
in the work of the community, though they may live together for most of
their time in a purer air?

No; it is a fair demand, and they are fair-minded men. No doubt, un-   52
like any ruler of the present day, they will think of holding power as an
unavoidable necessity.

Yes, my friend; for the truth is that you can have a well-governed so-   53
ciety only if you can discover for your future rulers a better way of life than
being in office; then only will power be in the hands of men who are rich,
not in gold, but in the wealth that brings happiness, a good and wise life.
All goes wrong when, starved for lack of anything good in their own lives,
men turn to public affairs hoping to snatch from thence the happiness they
hunger for. They set about fighting for power, and this internecine conflict
ruins them and their country. The life of true philosophy is the only one that
looks down upon offices of state; and access to power must be confined to
men who are not in love with it; otherwise rivals will start fighting. So

whom else can you compel to undertake the guardianship of the commonwealth, if not those who, besides understanding best the principles of government, enjoy a nobler life than the politician's and look for rewards of a
different kind?

There is indeed no other choice.   54

QUESTIONS FOR MEANING

1. Describe the cave and the situation of the men who live within it. What
   must by done before anyone can leave the cave?
2. According to Plato, the men in the cave see only the moving shadows of
   artificial objects that are paraded before them. What activities do people
   pursue today that involve watching artificial images move across a screen?
   If you spent a lifetime watching such images, would you mistake the artificial for the real?
3. Having escaped from the cave, why would anyone want to return to it?
4. In paragraph 29, Plato claims that the men in the cave would kill someone
   who returned from the upper world to teach them the truth. What reason
   did Plato have for making this claim?
5. What does "The Allegory of the Cave" reveal about the importance of
   education? Why is education necessary before one can leave the cave? How
   does Plato perceive the nature of education?
6. What types of people should be excluded from government in an ideal
   republic? Why would it be necessary to force philosophers to rule, and
   why does Plato believe that making such men rule against their will is
   ethically defensible?
7. If philosophers are attuned to a higher "reality" than the men and women
   they govern, how can they understand the problems of the people
   they rule?
8. What would Plato think of American politics?
9. Vocabulary: parapet (1), perplexed (15), vexation (19), surmise (31), affinity (41), collaborate (49).

QUESTIONS ABOUT STRATEGY

1. What assumptions about human nature underlie Plato's allegory? What
   assumptions does he make about the nature of government? If you were
   to summarize Plato's argument and put it into deductive form, what would
   be your premise?
2. How effective is the use of dialogue as a method for developing an argument? Is it hard to follow?
3. What role does Glaucon serve? Why does he usually agree rather than ask
   difficult questions?
4. What is the function of paragraph 31?

NICCOLÒ MACHIAVELLI
Should Princes Tell the Truth?

Historian, playwright, poet, and political philosopher, Niccolò Machiavelli (1469–1527) lived in Florence during the turbulence of the Italian Renaissance. From 1498 to 1512, he served in the Chancellery of the Florentine Republic and held the position of secretary for the committee in charge of diplomatic relations and military operations. In fulfilling his responsibilities, Machiavelli traveled to France, Germany, and elsewhere in Italy—giving him the opportunity to observe numerous rulers and the strategies they used to maintain and extend their power. When the Florentine Republic collapsed in 1512 and the Medici returned to power, Machiavelli was dismissed from office, tortured, and temporarily exiled. He retired to an estate not far from Florence and devoted himself to writing the books for which he is now remembered: The Prince *(1513),* The Discourses *(1519),* The Art of War *(1519–1520), and the* Florentine History *(1525). Of these works the most famous is* The Prince.

In writing The Prince, *Machiavelli set out to define the rules of politics as he understood them. His work became a handbook on how to acquire and maintain power. Machiavelli's experience taught him that successful rulers are not troubled by questions of ethics. He observed that it is better to be feared than to be loved. As the following excerpt reveals, he believed that virtues such as honesty are irrelevant to the successful pursuit of power. The amorality of Machiavelli's book continues to disturb many readers, and its shrewd observations on the nature of politics have made the author's name synonymous with craftiness and intrigue.*

How laudable it is for a prince to keep good faith and live with integrity, and not with astuteness, every one knows. Still the experience of our times shows those princes to have done great things who have had little regard for good faith, and have been able by astuteness to confuse men's brains, and who have ultimately overcome those who have made loyalty their foundation. 1

You must know, then, that there are two methods of fighting, the one by law, the other by force: the first method is that of men, the second of beasts; but as the first method is often insufficient, one must have recourse to the second. It is therefore necessary for a prince to know well how to use both the beast and the man. This was covertly taught to rulers by ancient writers, who relate how Achilles and many others of those ancient princes were given to Chiron the centaur to be brought up and educated under his discipline. The parable of this semi-animal, semi-human teacher is meant to indicate that a prince must know how to use both natures, and that the one without the other is not durable. 2

A prince being thus obliged to know well how to act as a beast must imitate the fox and the lion, for the lion cannot protect himself from traps, and the fox cannot defend himself from wolves. One must therefore be a fox 3 to recognise traps, and a lion to frighten wolves. Those that wish to be only lions do not understand this. Therefore, a prudent ruler ought not to keep faith when by so doing it would be against his interest, and when the reasons which made him bind himself no longer exist. If men were all good, this precept would not be a good one; but as they are bad, and would not observe their faith with you, so you are not bound to keep faith with them. Nor have legitimate grounds ever failed a prince who wished to show colourable excuse for the non-fulfillment of his promise. Of this one could furnish an infinite number of modern examples, and show how many times peace has been broken, and how many promises rendered worthless by the faithlessness of princes, and those that have been best able to imitate the fox have succeeded best. But it is necessary to be able to disguise this character well, and to be a great feigner and dissembler; and men are so simple and so ready to obey present necessities, that one who deceives will always find those who allow themselves to be deceived.

I will only mention one modern instance. Alexander VI did nothing   4
else but deceive men, he thought of nothing else, and found the occasion for it; no man was ever more able to give assurances, or affirmed things with stronger oaths, and no man observed them less; however, he always succeeded in his deceptions, as he well knew this aspect of things.

It is not, therefore, necessary for a prince to have all the above-named   5
qualities, but it is very necessary to seem to have them. I would even be bold to say that to possess them and always to observe them is dangerous, but to appear to possess them is useful. Thus it is well to seem merciful, faithful, humane, sincere, religious, and also to be so; but you must have the mind so disposed that when it is needful to be otherwise you may be able to change to the opposite qualities. And it must be understood that a prince, and especially a new prince, cannot observe all those things which are considered good in men, being often obliged, in order to maintain the state, to act against faith, against charity, against humanity, and against religion. And, therefore, he must have a mind disposed to adapt itself according to the wind, and as the variations of fortune dictate, and, as I said before, not deviate from what is good, if possible, but be able to do evil if constrained.

A prince must take great care that nothing goes out of his mouth which   6
is not full of the above-named five qualities, and, to see and hear him, he should seem to be all mercy, faith, integrity, humanity, and religion. And nothing is more necessary than to seem to have this last quality, for men in general judge more by the eyes than by the hands, for every one can see, but very few have to feel. Everybody sees what you appear to be, few feel what you are, and those few will not dare to oppose themselves to the many, who have the majesty of the state to defend them; and in the actions of men, and especially of princes, from which there is no appeal, the end justifies the means. Let a prince therefore aim at conquering and maintaining the state, and the means will always be judged honourable and praised by every one, for the vulgar is always taken by appearances and the issue of the event; and the world consists only of the vulgar, and the few who are not vulgar are

isolated when the many have a rallying point in the prince. A certain prince of the present time, whom it is well not to name, never does anything but preach peace and good faith, but he is really a great enemy to both, and either of them, had he observed them, would have lost him state or reputation on many occasions.

QUESTIONS FOR MEANING

1. What are the two methods of fighting cited by Machiavelli? Why is it important for princes to master both?
2. Machiavelli insists that princes must be both "lions" and "foxes." Explain what he means by this.
3. Under what circumstances should princes break their word?
4. Why is it useful for princes "to seem merciful, faithful, humane, sincere, religious, and also to be so"?
5. In paragraph 6, Machiavelli observes, "men in general judge more by the eyes than by the hands, for every one can see, but very few have to feel." What does this mean? Describe Machiavelli's opinion of the average man.

QUESTIONS ABOUT STRATEGY

1. What premise underlies Machiavelli's argument, and where does he first state it?
2. Consider the tone of this work. What sort of assumptions has Machiavelli made about his audience?
3. Machiavelli mentions Alexander VI by name in paragraph 4, but refuses to identify the prince he alludes to in paragraph 6. What does this reveal?
4. How would you characterize Machiavelli's point of view? Is it cynical or realistic?

ANDREW MARVELL

To His Coy Mistress

Andrew Marvell (1621–1678) was a Puritan patriot and political writer who is now remembered for writing a book of poetry that was published after his death. He graduated from Trinity College, Cambridge, in 1639, and after the death of his father in 1641, he spent several years traveling in Europe, presumably as a tutor. Upon his return to England, he became tutor to a ward of Oliver Cromwell, the man who ruled England during the period between the execution of Charles I in 1649 and the restoration of the monarchy in 1660. Through his connection with Cromwell, Marvell became assistant Latin Secretary for the Council of State, but he was not seriously involved in government until 1658, when he was elected to

Parliament. He served in Parliament for the next twenty years, and his political experience led him to write a number of prose satires on government and religion. Claiming that Marvell owed her money at the time of his death in 1678, his housekeeper went through his private papers, gathered together the miscellaneous poems that Marvell had written for his own pleasure, and arranged for their publication in 1681.

The seventeenth century was a great age for English poetry, and although Marvell cannot be said to rank with Shakespeare, Milton, or Donne, a few of his poems are so very fine that they have won for him an honored place in the history of literature. Of these poems the most famous is "To His Coy Mistress," an argument in the form of a poem.

To His Coy Mistress

Had we but world enough, and time,
This coyness, lady, were no crime.
We would sit down, and think which way
To walk, and pass our long love's day.
5   Thou by the Indian Ganges' side
Should'st rubies find: I by the tide
Of Humber would complain. I would
Love you ten years before the Flood,
And you should, if you please, refuse
10   Till the conversion of the Jews.
My vegetable love should grow
Vaster than empires, and more slow.
An hundred years should go to praise
Thine eyes, and on thy forehead gaze.
15   Two hundred to adore each breast:
But thirty thousand to the rest.
An age at least to every part,
And the last age should show your heart.
For, lady, you deserve this state,
20   Nor would I love at lower rate.
       But at my back I always hear
Time's wingèd chariot hurrying near;
And yonder all before us lie
Deserts of vast eternity.
25   Thy beauty shall no more be found,
Nor in thy marble vault shall sound
My echoing song; then worms shall try
That long preserved virginity,
And your quaint honor turn to dust,
30   And into ashes all my lust.
The grave's a fine and private place,
But none, I think, do there embrace.
       Now therefore, while the youthful hue
Sits on thy skin like morning dew,

35   And while thy willing soul transpires
      At every pore with instant fires,
      Now let us sport us while we may;
      And now, like am'rous birds of prey,
      Rather at once our time devour,
40   Than languish in his slow-chapt power,
      Let us roll all our strength, and all
      Our sweetness, up into one ball;
      And tear our pleasures with rough strife
      Thorough the iron gates of life.
45   Thus, though we cannot make our sun
      Stand still, yet we will make him run.

QUESTIONS FOR MEANING

1. What do we learn from the title of this poem? In the seventeenth century, "mistress" was a synonym for "sweetheart." But what does Marvell mean by "coy"?
2. What kind of woman inspired this poem? Identify the lines that reveal her character as it is presented in the poem.
3. How does the poet feel about this woman? Does he love her? Is this a love poem?
4. What is the poet urging this woman to do? Under what circumstances would he be willing to spend more time pleading with her? Why is this not possible?
5. Why does the poet describe his feelings as a "vegetable love"? What are the implications of this phrase?
6. What is the "marble vault" referred to in line 26?
7. Identify the references to "Ganges" (line 5), "Humber" (line 7), and "the Flood" (line 8). What does Marvell mean by "Time's wingèd chariot" (line 22) and "the iron gates of life" (line 44)?
8. Explain the last two lines of the poem. Is the sun a figure of speech? How is it possible to make it "run" when we lack the power to make it stand still?

QUESTIONS ABOUT STRATEGY

1. This poem is divided into three sections. Consider separately the tone of each. How do they differ?
2. Summarize the argument of this poem in three sentences, one for each section. Is the conclusion valid, or does it rest upon a questionable premise?
3. What role does humor play in the poem? What serious emotions does the poet invoke in order to make his argument more persuasive?
4. How does Marvell use rhyme as a device for advancing his argument?

JONATHAN SWIFT

A Modest Proposal

For preventing the Children of Poor People in Ireland from Being a Burden to Their Parents or Country, and for Making Them Beneficial to the Public

Jonathan Swift (1667–1745) was a clergyman, poet, wit, and satirist. Born in Ireland as a member of the Protestant ruling class, Swift attended Trinity College in Dublin before settling in England in 1689. For the next ten years, he was a member of the household of Sir William Temple at Moor Park, Surrey. It was there that Swift met Esther Johnson, the "Stella" to whom he later wrote a famous series of letters known as Journal to Stella *(1710–1713). Although he was ordained a priest in the Church of Ireland in 1695, and made frequent trips to Ireland, Swift's ambition always brought him back to England. His reputation as a writer grew rapidly after the publication of his first major work,* A Tale of a Tub, *in 1704. He became a writer on behalf of the ruling Tory party, and was appointed Dean of St. Patrick's Cathedral in Dublin as a reward for his services. When the Tories fell from power in 1714, Swift retired to Ireland, where he remained for the rest of his life, except for brief visits to England in 1726 and 1727. It was in Ireland that he wrote* Gulliver's Travels *(1726), which is widely recognized as one of the masterpieces of English literature, and "A Modest Proposal"* **(1729),** *one of the greatest of all essays.*

Ruled as an English colony and subject to numerous repressive laws, Ireland in Swift's time was a desperately poor country. Swift wrote "A Modest Proposal" in order to expose the plight of Ireland and the unfair policies under which it suffered. As you read it, you will find that Swift's proposal for solving the problem of poverty is anything but "modest." Even when we know that we are reading satire, this brilliant and bitter essay retains the power to shock all but the most careless of readers.

It is a melancholy object to those who walk through this great town or travel   1
in the country, when they see the streets, the roads, and cabin doors, crowded with beggars of the female sex, followed by three, four, or six children, all in rags and importuning every passenger for an alms. These mothers, instead of being able to work for their honest livelihood, are forced to employ all their time in strolling to beg sustenance for their helpless infants, who, as they grow up, either turn thieves for want of work, or leave their dear native country to fight for the Pretender in Spain, or sell themselves to the Barbados.

I think it is agreed by all parties that this prodigious number of children   2
in the arms, or on the backs, or at the heels of their mothers, and frequently
of their fathers, is in the present deplorable state of the kingdom a very great
additional grievance; and therefore whoever could find out a fair, cheap, and
easy method of making these children sound, useful members of the commonwealth would deserve so well of the public as to have his statue set up
for a preserver of the nation.

But my intention is very far from being confined to provide only for   3
the children of professed beggars; it is of a much greater extent, and shall
take in the whole number of infants at a certain age who are born of parents
in effect as little able to support them as those who demand our charity in
the streets.

As to my own part, having turned my thoughts for many years upon   4
this important subject, and maturely weighed the several schemes of other
projectors, I have always found them grossly mistaken in their computation.
It is true, a child just dropped from its dam may be supported by her milk
for a solar year, with little other nourishment; at most not above the value
of two shillings, which the mother may certainly get, or the value in scraps,
by her lawful occupation of begging; and it is exactly at one year that I
propose to provide for them in such a manner as instead of being a charge
upon their parents or the parish, or wanting food and raiment for the rest of
their lives, they shall on the contrary contribute to the feeding, and partly to
the clothing, of many thousands.

There is likewise another great advantage in my scheme, that it will   5
prevent those voluntary abortions, and that horrid practice of women murdering their bastard children, alas, too frequent among us, sacrificing the
poor innocent babes, I doubt, more to avoid the expense than the shame,
which would move tears and pity in the most savage and inhuman breast.

The number of souls in this kingdom being usually reckoned one mil-   6
lion and a half, of these I calculate there may be about two hundred thousand
couples whose wives are breeders; from which number I subtract thirty thousand couples who are able to maintain their own children, although I apprehend there cannot be so many under the present distress of the kingdom; but
this being granted, there will remain an hundred and seventy thousand breeders.
I again subtract fifty thousand for those women who miscarry, or whose
children die by accident or disease within the year. There only remain an
hundred and twenty thousand children of poor parents annually born. The
question therefore is, how this number shall be reared and provided for,
which, as I have already said, under the present situation of affairs, is utterly
impossible by all the methods hitherto proposed. For we can neither employ
them in handicraft or agriculture; we neither build houses (I mean in the
country) nor cultivate land. They can very seldom pick up a livelihood by
stealing till they arrive at six years old, except where they are of towardly
parts; although I confess they learn the rudiments much earlier, during which
time they can however be looked upon only as probationers, as I have been
informed by a principal gentleman in the country of Cavan, who protested

to me that he never knew above one or two instances under the age of six, even in a part of the kingdom so renowned for the quickest proficiency in that art.

I am assured by our merchants that a boy or a girl before twelve years old is no salable commodity; and even when they come to this age they will not yield above three pounds, or three pounds and half a crown at most on the Exchange; which cannot turn to account either to the parents or the kingdom, the charge of nutriment and rags having been at least four times that value. 7

I shall now therefore humbly propose my own thoughts, which I hope will not be liable to the least objection. 8

I have been assured by a very knowing American of my acquaintance in London, that a young healthy child well nursed is at a year old a most delicious, nourishing, and wholesome food, whether stewed, roasted, baked, or boiled; and I make no doubt that it will equally serve in a fricassee or a ragout. 9

I do therefore humbly offer it to public consideration that of the hundred and twenty thousand children, already computed, twenty thousand may be reserved for breed, whereof only one fourth part to be males, which is more than we allow to sheep, black cattle, or swine; and my reason is that these children are seldom the fruits of marriage, a circumstance not much regarded by our savages, therefore one male will be sufficient to serve four females. That the remaining hundred thousand may at a year old be offered in sale to the persons of quality and fortune through the kingdom, always advising the mother to let them suck plentifully in the last month, so as to render them plump and fat for a good table. A child will make two dishes at an entertainment for friends; and when the family dines alone, the fore or hind quarter will make a reasonable dish, and seasoned with a little pepper or salt will be very good boiled on the fourth day, especially in winter. 10

I have reckoned upon a medium that a child just born will weigh twelve pounds, and in a solar year if tolerably nursed increaseth to twenty-eight pounds. 11

I grant this food will be somewhat dear, and therefore very proper for landlords, who, as they have already devoured most of the parents, seem to have the best title to the children. 12

Infant's flesh will be in season throughout the year, but more plentiful in March, and a little before and after. For we are told by a grave author, an eminent French physician, that fish being a prolific diet, there are more children born in Roman Catholic countries about nine months after Lent than at any other season; therefore, reckoning a year after Lent, the markets will be more glutted than usual, because the number of popish infants is at least three to one in this kingdom; and therefore it will have one other collateral advantage, by lessening the number of Papists among us. 13

I have already computed the charge of nursing a beggar's child (in which list I reckon all cottagers, laborers, and four-fifths of the farmers) to be about two shillings per annum, rags included; and I believe no gentleman would 14 repine to give ten shillings for the carcass of a good fat child, which, as I have said, will make four dishes of excellent nutritive meat, when he hath only some particular friend or his own family to dine with him. Thus the squire will learn to be a good landlord, and grow popular among the tenants; the mother will have eight shillings net profit, and be fit for work till she produces another child.

Those who are more thrifty (as I must confess the times require) may 15 flay the carcass; the skin of which artificially dressed will make admirable gloves for ladies, and summer boots for fine gentlemen.

As to our city of Dublin, shambles may be appointed for this purpose 16 in the most convenient parts of it, and butchers we may be assured will not be wanting; although I rather recommend buying the children alive, and dressing them hot from the knife as we do roasting pigs.

A very worthy person, a true lover of his country, and whose virtues I 17 highly esteem, was lately pleased in discoursing on this matter to offer a refinement upon my scheme. He said that many gentlemen of his kingdom, having of late destroyed their deer, he conceived that the want of venison might be well supplied by the bodies of young lads and maidens, not exceeding fourteen years of age nor under twelve, so great a number of both sexes in every county being now ready to starve for want of work and service; and these to be disposed of by their parents, if alive, or otherwise by their nearest relations. But with due deference to so excellent a friend and so deserving a patriot, I cannot be altogether in his sentiments; for as to the males, my American acquaintance assured me from frequent experience that their flesh was generally tough and lean, like that of our schoolboys, by continual exercise, and their taste disagreeable; and to fatten them would not answer the charge. Then as to the females, it would, I think with humble submission, be a loss to the public, because they soon would become breeders themselves; and besides, it is not improbable that some scrupulous people might be apt to censure such a practice (although indeed very unjustly) as a little bordering upon cruelty; which, I confess, hath always been with me the strongest objection against any project, how well soever intended.

But in order to justify my friend, he confessed that this expedient was 18 put into his head by the famous Psalmanazar, a native of the island Formosa, who came from thence to London about twenty years ago, and in conversation told my friend that in his country when any young person happened to be put to death, the executioner sold the carcass to persons of quality as a prime dainty; and that in his time the body of a plump girl of fifteen, who was crucified for an attempt to poison the emperor, was sold to his Imperial Majesty's prime minister of state, and other great mandarins of the court, in joints from the gibbet, at four hundred crowns. Neither indeed can I deny that if the same use were made of several plump young girls in this town, who without one single groat to their fortunes cannot stir abroad without a chair, and appear at the playhouse and assemblies in foreign fineries which they never will pay for, the kingdom would not be the worse.

Some persons of a desponding spirit are in great concern about that vast   19
number of poor people who are aged, diseased, or maimed, and I have been
desired to employ my thoughts what course may be taken to ease the nation
of so grievous an encumbrance. But I am not in the least pain upon that
matter, because it is very well known that they are every day dying and
rotting by cold and famine, and filth and vermin, as fast as can be reasonably
expected. And as to the younger laborers, they are now in almost as hopeful
a condition. They cannot get work, and consequently pine away for want of
nourishment to a degree that if any time they are accidentally hired to common labor, they have not strength to perform it; and thus the country and
themselves are happily delivered from the evils to come.

I have too long digressed, and therefore shall return to my subject. I   20
think the advantages by the proposal which I have made are obvious and
many, as well as of the highest importance.

For first, as I have already observed, it would greatly lessen the number   21
of Papists, with whom we are yearly overrun, being the principal breeders of the nation as well as our most dangerous enemies; and who stay at
home on purpose to deliver the kingdom to the Pretender, hoping to take
their advantage by the absence of so many good Protestants, who have chosen rather to leave their country than to stay at home and pay tithes against
their conscience to an Episcopal curate.

Secondly, the poorer tenants will have something valuable of their own,   22
which by law may be made liable to distress, and help to pay their landlord's
rent, their corn and cattle being already seized and money a thing unknown.

Thirdly, whereas the maintenance of an hundred thousand children, from   23
two years old and upwards, cannot be computed at less than ten shillings a
piece per annum, the nation's stock will be thereby increased fifty thousand
pounds per annum, besides the profit of a new dish introduced to the tables
of all gentlemen of fortune in the kingdom who have any refinement in taste.
And the money will circulate among ourselves, the goods being entirely of
our own growth and manufacture.

Fourthly, the constant breeders, besides the gain of eight shillings ster-   24
ling per annum by the sale of their children, will be rid of the charge of
maintaining them after the first year.

Fifthly, this food would likewise bring great custom to taverns, where   25
the vintners will certainly be so prudent as to procure the best receipts for
dressing it to perfection, and consequently have their houses frequented by
all the fine gentlemen, who justly value themselves upon their knowledge in
good eating; and a skillful cook, who understands how to oblige his guests,
will contrive to make it as expensive as they please.

Sixthly, this would be a great inducement to marriage, which all wise   26
nations have either encouraged by rewards or enforced by laws and penalties.
It would increase the care and tenderness of mothers toward their children,
when they were sure of a settlement for life to the poor babes, provided in
some sort by the public, to their annual profit instead of expense. We should

see an honest emulation among the married women, which of them could bring the fattest child to the market. Men would become as fond of their wives during the time of their pregnancy as they are now of their mares in foal, their cows in calf, or sows when they are ready to farrow; nor offer to beat or kick them (as is too frequent a practice) for fear of a miscarriage.

Many other advantages might be enumerated. For instance, the addi-   27
tion of some thousand carcasses in our exportation of barreled beef, the prop-
agation of swine's flesh, and improvements in the art of making good bacon, so much wanted among us by the great destruction of pigs, too frequent at our tables, which are no way comparable in taste or magnificence to a well-grown, fat, yearling child, which roasted whole will make a considerable figure at a lord mayor's feast or any other public entertainment. But this and many others I omit, being studious of brevity.

Supposing that one thousand families in this city would be constant   28
customers for infants' flesh, besides others who might have it at merry meet-ings, particularly weddings and christenings, I compute that Dublin would take off annually about twenty thousand carcasses, and the rest of the king-dom (where probably they will be sold somewhat cheaper) the remaining eighty thousand.

I can think of no one objection that will possibly be raised against this   29
proposal, unless it should be urged that the number of people will be thereby much lessened in the kingdom. This I freely own, and it was indeed one principal design in offering it to the world. I desire the reader will observe, that I calculate my remedy for this one individual kingdom of Ireland and for no other that ever was, is, or I think ever can be upon earth. Therefore let no man talk to me of other expedients: of taxing our absentees at five shillings a pound: of using neither clothes nor household furniture except what is of our own growth and manufacture: of utterly rejecting the mate-rials and instruments that promote foreign luxury: of curing the expensive-ness of pride, vanity, idleness, and gaming in our women: of introducing a vein of parsimony, prudence, and temperance: of learning to love our coun-try, in the want of which we differ even from Laplanders and the inhabitants of Topinamboo: of quitting our animosities and factions, nor acting any longer like the Jews, who were murdering one another at the very moment their city was taken: of being a little cautious not to sell our country and con-science for nothing: of teaching landlords to have at least one degree of mercy toward their tenants: lastly, of putting a spirit of honesty, industry, and skill into our shopkeepers; who, if a resolution could now be taken to buy only our native goods, would immediately unite to cheat and exact upon us in the price, the measure, and the goodness, nor could ever yet be brought to make one fair proposal of just dealing, though often and earnestly invited to it.

Therefore I repeat, let no man talk to me of these and the like expedi-   30
ents, till he hath at least some glimpse of hope that there will ever be some hearty and sincere attempt to put them in practice.

But as to myself, having been wearied out for many years with offering   31
vain, idle, visionary thoughts, and at length utterly despairing of success, I

fortunately fell upon this proposal, which, as it is wholly new, so it hath something solid and real, of no expense and little trouble, full in our own power, and whereby we can incur no danger in disobliging England. For this kind of commodity will not bear exportation, the flesh being of too tender a consistence to admit a long continuance in salt, although perhaps I could name a country which would be glad to eat up our whole nation without it.

After all, I am not so violently bent upon my own opinion as to reject   32 any offer proposed by wise men, which shall be found equally innocent, cheap, easy, and effectual. But before something of that kind shall be advanced in contradiction to my scheme, and offering a better, I desire the author or authors will be pleased maturely to consider two points. First, as things now stand, how they will be able to find food and raiment for an hundred thousand useless mouths and backs. And secondly, there being a round million of creatures in human figure throughout this kingdom, whose sole subsistence put into a common stock would leave them in debt two millions of pounds sterling, adding those who are beggars by profession to the bulk of farmers, cottagers, and laborers, with their wives and children who are beggars in effect; I desire those politicians who dislike my overture, and may perhaps be so bold to attempt an answer, that they will first ask the parents of these mortals whether they would not at this day think it a great happiness to have been sold for food at a year old in this manner I prescribe, and thereby have avoided such a perpetual scene of misfortunes as they have since gone through by the oppression of landlords, the impossibility of paying rent without money or trade, the want of common sustenance, with neither house nor clothes to cover them from the inclemencies of the weather, and the most inevitable prospect of entailing the like or greater miseries upon their breed forever.

I profess, in the sincerity of my heart, that I have not the least personal   33 interest in endeavoring to promote this necessary work, having no other motive than the public good of my country, by advancing our trade, providing for infants, relieving the poor, and giving some pleasure to the rich. I have no children by which I can propose to get a single penny; the youngest being nine years old, and my wife past childbearing.

QUESTIONS FOR MEANING

1. What do we learn in this essay about the condition of Ireland in Swift's time, and how Ireland was viewed by England? Does Swift provide any clue about what has caused the poverty he describes?
2. What specific "advantages" does Swift cite on behalf of his proposal?
3. Why does Swift limit his proposal to infants? On what grounds does he exclude older children from consideration as marketable commodities? Why does he claim that we need not worry about the elderly?
4. What does this essay reveal about the relations between Catholics and Protestants in the eighteenth century?

5. Where in the essay does Swift tell us what he really wants? What serious reforms does he propose to improve conditions in Ireland?
6. Vocabulary: importuning (1), sustenance (1), prodigious (2), rudiments (6), ragout (9), collateral (13), desponding (19), inducement (26), emulation (26), propagation (27), parsimony (29) incur (31).

QUESTIONS ABOUT STRATEGY

1. How does Swift present himself in this essay? Many readers have taken this essay seriously and come away convinced that Swift was heartless and cruel. Why is it possible for some readers to be deceived in this way? What devices does Swift employ to create the illusion that he is serious? How does this strategy benefit the essay?
2. Does the language of the first few paragraphs contain any hint of irony? At what point in the essay did it first become clear to you that Swift is writing tongue in cheek?
3. Where in the essay does Swift pretend to anticipate objections that might be raised against his proposal? How does he dispose of these objections?
4. How does the style of this essay contrast with its subject matter? How does this contrast contribute to the force of the essay as a whole?
5. What is the function of the concluding paragraph?
6. What is the premise of this essay if we take its argument at face value? When we realize that Swift is writing ironically, what underlying premise begins to emerge?
7. What advantage is there in writing ironically? Why do you think Swift chose to treat his subject in this manner?

THOMAS JEFFERSON
The Declaration of Independence

Thomas Jefferson (1743–1826) was the third president of the United States and one of the most talented men ever to hold that office. A farmer, architect, writer, and scientist, Jefferson entered politics in 1769 as a member of the Virginia House of Burgesses. In 1775, he was a member of Virginia's delegation to the Second Continental Congress. He was governor of Virginia from 1779 to 1781, represented the United States in Europe from 1784 to 1789, and was elected to the first of two terms as president in 1801. Of all his many accomplishments, Jefferson himself was most proud of having founded the University of Virginia in 1819.

Although the Continental Congress had delegated the responsibility for writing a declaration of independence to a committee that included Benjamin Franklin and John Adams as well as Jefferson, it was Jefferson who undertook the actual composition. His colleagues respected him as the best writer among them. Jefferson wrote at least two, and possibly three, drafts during the seventeen days allowed for the assignment. His work was reviewed by the other members of the committee, but they made only minor revisions—mainly in the first two paragraphs. When it came to adopting the declaration, Congress was harder to please. After lengthy and spirited debate, Congress made twenty-four changes and deleted over three hundred words. Nevertheless, "The Declaration of Independence," as approved by Congress on July 4, 1776, is almost entirely the work of Jefferson. In addition to being an eloquent example of eighteenth-century prose, it is a clear example of deductive reasoning.

When in the Course of human events, it becomes necessary for one people   1
to dissolve the political bands which have connected them with another, and to assume among the powers of the earth, the separate and equal station to which the Laws of Nature and of Nature's God entitle them, a decent respect to the opinions of mankind requires that they should declare the causes which impel them to the separation.

We hold these truths to be self-evident, that all men are created equal,   2
that they are endowed by their Creator with certain unalienable Rights, that among these are Life, Liberty and the pursuit of Happiness. That to secure these rights, Governments are instituted among Men, deriving their just powers from the consent of the governed. That whenever any Form of Government becomes destructive of these ends it is the Right of the People to alter or to abolish it, and to institute new Government, laying its foundation on such principles and organizing its powers in such form, as to them shall seem most likely to effect their Safety and Happiness. Prudence, indeed, will dictate that Governments long established should not be changed for light and transient causes; and accordingly all experience has shewn, that mankind are more disposed to suffer, while evils are sufferable, than to right themselves by abolishing the forms to which they are accustomed. But when a long train of abuses and usurpations, pursuing invariably the same Object evinces a design to reduce them under absolute Despotism, it is their right, it is their duty, to throw off such Government, and to provide new Guards for their future security. Such has been the patient sufferance of these Colonies; and such is now the necessity which constrains them to alter their former Systems of Government. The history of the present King of Great Britain is a history of repeated injuries and usurpations, all having in direct object the establishment of an absolute Tyranny over these States. To prove this, let Facts be submitted to a candid world.

He has refused his Assent to Laws, the most wholesome and necessary   3
for the public good.

He has forbidden his Governors to pass Laws of immediate and press-   4
ing importance, unless suspended in their operation till his Assent should be obtained; and when so suspended, he has utterly neglected to attend to them. He has refused to pass other Laws for the accommodation of large districts

of people, unless those people would relinquish the right of Representation in the Legislature, a right inestimable to them and formidable to tyrants only.

He has called together legislative bodies at places unusual, uncomfort- 5
able, and distant from the depository of their public Records, for the sole purpose of fatiguing them into compliance with his measures.

He has dissolved Representative Houses repeatedly, for opposing with 6
manly firmness his invasions on the rights of the people.

He has refused for a long time, after such dissolutions, to cause others 7
to be elected; whereby the Legislative powers, incapable of Annihilation, have returned to the People at large for their exercise; the State remaining in the mean time exposed to all the dangers of invasion from without, and convulsions within.

He has endeavoured to prevent the population of these States; for that 8
purpose obstructing the Laws for Naturalization of Foreigners; refusing to pass others to encourage their migrations hither, and raising the conditions of new Appropriations of Lands.

He has obstructed the Administration of Justice, by refusing his assent 9
to Laws for establishing Judiciary powers.

He has made Judges dependent on his Will alone, for the tenure of their 10
offices, and the amount and payment of their salaries.

He has erected a multitude of New Offices, and sent hither swarms of 11
Officers to harass our People, and eat out their substance.

He has kept among us, in times of peace, standing Armies without the 12
Consent of our legislatures.

He has affected to render the Military independent of and superior to 13
the Civil power.

He has combined with others to subject us to a jurisdiction foreign to 14
our constitution, and unacknowledged by our laws; giving his Assent to their Acts of pretended Legislation:

For Quartering large bodies of armed troops among us: 15

For protecting them, by a mock Trial, from punishment for any Mur- 16
ders which they should commit on the Inhabitants of these States:

For cutting off our Trade with all parts of the world: 17

For imposing Taxes on us without our Consent: 18

For depriving us in many cases of the benefits of Trial by Jury: 19

For transporting us beyond Seas to be tried for pretended offences: 20

For abolishing the free System of English Laws in a neighbouring Prov- 21
ince, establishing therein an Arbitrary government, and enlarging its Boundaries so as to render it at once an example and fit instrument for introducing the same absolute rule into these Colonies:

For taking away our Charters, abolishing our most valuable Laws, and 22
altering fundamentally the Forms of our Governments:

For suspending our own Legislatures, and declaring themselves in- 23
vested with power to legislate for us in all cases whatsoever.

He has abdicated Government here, by declaring us out of his Protec- 24
tion and waging War against us.

He has plundered our seas, ravaged our Coasts, burnt our towns, and   25
destroyed the Lives of our people.

He is at this time transporting large Armies of foreign Mercenaries to   26
compleat the works of death, desolation and tyranny, already begun with
circumstances of Cruelty & perfidy scarcely paralleled in the most barbarous
ages, and totally unworthy the Head of a civilized nation.

He has constrained our fellow Citizens taken Captive on the high Seas   27
to bear Arms against their Country, to become the executioners of their friends
and Brethren, or to fall themselves by their Hands.

He has excited domestic insurrections amongst us, and has endeavoured   28
to bring on the inhabitants of our frontiers, the merciless Indian Savages,
whose known rule of warfare, is an undistinguished destruction of all ages,
sexes and conditions.

In every stage of these Oppressions We have Petitioned for Redress in   29
the most humble terms: Our repeated Petitions have been answered only by
repeated injury. A Prince, whose character is thus marked by every act which
may define a Tyrant, is unfit to be the ruler of a free people.

Nor have We been wanting in attentions to our British brethren. We   30
have warned them from time to time of attempts by their legislature to extend an unwarrantable jurisdiction over us. We have reminded them of the
circumstances of our emigration and settlement here. We have appealed to
their native justice and magnanimity, and we have conjured them by the ties
of our common kindred to disavow these usurpations, which, would inevitably interrupt our connections and correspondence. They too have been deaf
to the voice of Justice and of consanguinity. We must, therefore, acquiesce
in the necessity, which denounces our Separation, and hold them, as we hold
the rest of mankind, Enemies in War, in Peace Friends.

We, therefore, the Representatives of the United States of America, in   31
General Congress, Assembled, appealing to the Supreme Judge of the world
for the rectitude of our intentions, do, in the Name, and by Authority of the
good People of these Colonies, solemnly publish and declare, That these United
Colonies are, and of Right ought to be Free and Independent States; that they
are Absolved from all Allegiance to the British Crown, and that all political
connection between them and the State of Great Britain, is and ought to be
totally dissolved; and that as Free and Independent States, they have full Power
to levy War, conclude Peace, contract Alliances, establish Commerce, and to
do all other Acts and Things which Independent States may of right do. And
for the support of this Declaration, with a firm reliance on the protection of
divine Providence, we mutually pledge to each other our Lives, our Fortunes
and our sacred Honor.

John Hancock	Joseph Hewes,
Button Gwinnett	John Penn
Lyman Hall	Edward Rutledge.
Geo Walton.	Thos. Heyward Junr.
Wm. Hooper	Thomas Lynch Junr.

Arthur Middleton	Tho M:Kean
Samuel Chase	Wm. Floyd
Wm. Paca	Phil. Livingston
Thos. Stone	Frans. Lewis
Charles Carroll of Carrollton	Lewis Morris
George Wythe	Richd. Stockton
Richard Henry Lee	Jno Witherspoon
Th: Jefferson	Fras. Hopkinson
Benja. Harrison	John Hart
Thos. Nelson jr.	Abra Clark
Francis Lightfoot Lee	Josiah Bartlett
Carter Braxton	Wm: Whipple
Robt. Morris	Saml. Adams
Benjamin Rush	John Adams
Benja. Franklin	Robt. Treat Paine
John Morton	Elbridge Gerry
Geo Clymer	Step. Hopkins
Jas. Smith	William Ellery
Geo. Taylor	Roger Sherman
James Wilson	Saml. Huntington
Geo. Ross	Wm. Williams
Caesar Rodney	Oliver Wolcott
Geo Read	Matthew Thornton

QUESTIONS FOR MEANING

1. What was the purpose of "The Declaration of Independence"? What reason does Jefferson himself give for writing it?
2. In paragraph 1, what does Jefferson mean by "the Laws of Nature and of Nature's God"?
3. Paragraphs 3–28 are devoted to enumerating a list of grievances against King George III. Which of these are the most important? Are any of them relatively trivial? Taken together do they justify Jefferson's description of George III as "A Prince, whose character is thus marked by every act which may define a Tyrant"?
4. How would you summarize Jefferson's conception of the relationship between people and government?
5. How does Jefferson characterize his fellow Americans? At what points does he put the colonists in a favorable light?
6. What does Jefferson mean by "the Supreme Judge of the world"? Why does he express "a firm reliance on the protection of a divine Providence"?
7. Vocabulary: transient (2), evinces (2), usurpations (2), candid (2), annihilation (7), render (13), perfidy (26), unwarrantable (30), consanguinity (30), acquiesce (30), rectitude (31).

QUESTIONS ABOUT STRATEGY

1. In paragraph 2, why does Jefferson declare certain truths to be "self-evident"? Paraphrase this paragraph and explain the purpose it serves in Jefferson's argument.
2. In evaluating "The Declaration of Independence" as an argument, what is more important: the general "truths" outlined in the second paragraph, or the specific accusations listed in the paragraphs that follow? If you were to write a counterargument to "The Declaration of Independence," on what points would you concentrate? Where is it most vulnerable?
3. Jefferson is often cited as a man of great culture and liberal values. Are there any points of "The Declaration of Independence" that now seem illiberal?
4. Does Jefferson use any loaded terms? He was forced to delete exaggerated language from his first two drafts of "The Declaration." Do you see any exaggerations that Congress failed to catch?
5. For what sort of audience did Jefferson write "The Declaration of Independence"? Is it directed primarily to the American people, the British government, or the world in general?

MARY WOLLSTONECRAFT
The Playthings of Tyrants

An English writer of Irish extraction, Mary Wollstonecraft (1759–1797) was an early advocate of women's rights. After working as a governess and a publisher's assistant, she went to France in 1792 in order to witness the French Revolution. She lived there with an American, Captain Gilbert Imlay, and had a child by him in 1794. Her relationship with Imlay broke down soon afterwards, and, in 1795, Wollstonecraft tried to commit suicide by drowning herself. She was rescued, however, and returned to London, where she became a member of a group of radical writers that included Thomas Paine, William Blake, and William Godwin. Wollstonecraft became pregnant by Godwin in 1796, and they were married the following year. Their child, Mary (1797–1851), would eventually win fame as the author of Frankenstein. *Wollstonecraft died only eleven days after Mary's birth.*

Wollstonecraft's fame rests upon one work, A Vindication of the Rights of Women *(1792). Although she had written about the need for educated women several years earlier in* Thoughts on the Education of Daughters *(1787), she makes a stronger and better-reasoned argument in her* Vindication. *"The Playthings of Tyrants" is an editor's title for an excerpt from the second chapter, "The Prevailing Opinion of a Sexual Character Discussed." As the excerpt suggests, Wollstonecraft was not especially interested in securing political rights for women.*

Her object was to emancipate women from the roles imposed upon them by men and to urge women to think for themselves.

To account for, and excuse the tyranny of man, many ingenious arguments   1
have been brought forward to prove, that the two sexes, in the acquirement
of virtue, ought to aim at attaining a very different character: or, to speak
explicitly, women are not allowed to have sufficient strength of mind to
acquire what really deserves the name of virtue. Yet it should seem, allowing
them to have souls, that there is but one way appointed by Providence to
lead *mankind* to either virtue or happiness.

If then women are not a swarm of ephemeron triflers, why should they   2
be kept in ignorance under the specious name of innocence? Men complain,
and with reason, of the follies and caprices of our sex, when they do not
keenly satirize our headstrong passions and groveling vices.—Behold, I should
answer, the natural effect of ignorance! The mind will ever be unstable that
has only prejudices to rest on, and the current will run with destructive fury
when there are no barriers to break its force. Women are told from their
infancy, and taught by the example of their mothers, that a little knowledge
of human weakness, justly termed cunning, softness of temper, *outward* obedience, and a scrupulous attention to a puerile kind of propriety, will obtain
for them the protection of man; and should they be beautiful, every thing
else is needless, for, at least, twenty years of their lives.

Thus Milton describes our first frail mother; though when he tells us   3
that women are formed for softness and sweet attractive grace, I cannot comprehend his meaning, unless, in the true Mahometan strain, he meant to
deprive us of souls, and insinuate that we were beings only designed by
sweet attractive grace, and docile blind obedience, to gratify the senses of
man when he can no longer soar on the wing of contemplation.

How grossly do they insult us who thus advise us only to render our-   4
selves gentle, domestic brutes! For instance, the winning softness so warmly,
and frequently, recommended, that governs by obeying. What childish
expressions, and how insignificant is the being—can it be an immortal one?
who will condescend to govern by such sinister methods! 'Certainly,' says
Lord Bacon, 'man is of kin to the beasts by his body; and if he be not of kin
to God by his spirit, he is a base and ignoble creature!' Men, indeed, appear
to me to act in a very unphilosophical manner when they try to secure the
good conduct of women by attempting to keep them always in a state of
childhood. Rousseau was more consistent when he wished to stop the progress of reason in both sexes, for if men eat of the tree of knowledge, women
will come in for a taste; but, from the imperfect cultivation which their understandings now receive, they only attain a knowledge of evil.

Children, I grant, should be innocent; but when the epithet is applied   5
to men, or women, it is but a civil term for weakness. For if it be allowed
that women were destined by Providence to acquire human virtues, and by
the exercise of their understandings, that stability of character which is the

firmest ground to rest our future hopes upon, they must be permitted to turn to the fountain of light, and not forced to shape their course by the twinkling of a mere satellite. Milton, I grant, was of a very different opinion; for he only bends to the indefeasible right of beauty, though it would be difficult to render two passages which I now mean to contrast, consistent. But into similar inconsistencies are great men often led by their senses.

'To whom thus Eve with *perfect beauty* adorn'd.
'My Author and Disposer, what thou bidst
'*Unargued* I obey; So God ordains;
'God is *thy law*; *thou mine*: to know no more
'Is Woman's *happiest* knowledge and her *praise.*'

These are exactly the arguments that I have used to children; but I have   6
added, your reason is now gaining strength, and, till it arrives at some degree of maturity, you must look up to me for advice—then you ought to *think*, and only rely on God.

Yet in the following lines Milton seems to coincide with me; when he   7
makes Adam thus expostulate with his Maker.

'Hast thou not made me here thy substitute,
'And these inferior far beneath me set?
'Among *unequals* what society
'Can sort, what harmony or true delight?
'Which must be mutual, in proportion due
'Giv'n and receiv'd; but in *disparity*
'The one intense, the other still remiss
'Cannot well suit with either, but soon prove
'Tedious alike: of *fellowship* I speak
'Such as I seek, fit to participate
'All rational delight—'

In treating, therefore, of the manners of women, let us, disregarding   8
sensual arguments, trace what we should endeavour to make them in order to cooperate, if the expression be not too bold, with the supreme Being.

By individual education, I mean, for the sense of the word is not pre-   9
cisely defined, such an attention to a child as will slowly sharpen the senses, form the temper, regulate the passions as they begin to ferment, and set the understanding to work before the body arrives at maturity; so that the man may only have to proceed, not to begin, the important task of learning to think and reason.

To prevent any misconstruction, I must add, that I do not believe that   10
a private education can work the wonders which some sanguine writers have attributed to it. Men and women must be educated, in a great degree, by the opinions and manners of the society they live in. In every age there has been a stream of popular opinion that has carried all before it, and given a family character, as it were, to the century. It may then fairly be inferred, that, till

society be differently constituted, much cannot be expected from education. It is, however, sufficient for my present purpose to assert, that, whatever effect circumstances have on the abilities, every being may become virtuous by the exercise of its own reason; for if but one being was created with vicious inclinations, that is positively bad, what can save us from atheism? or if we worship a God, is not that God a devil?

Consequently, the most perfect education, in my opinion, is such an   11
exercise of the understanding as is best calculated to strengthen the body and form the heart. Or, in other words, to enable the individual to attain such habits of virtue as will render it independent. In fact, it is a farce to call any being virtuous whose virtues do not result from the exercise of its own reason. This was Rousseau's opinion respecting men: I extend it to women, and confidently assert that they have been drawn out of their sphere by false refinement, and not by an endeavour to acquire masculine qualities. Still the regal homage which they receive is so intoxicating, that till the manners of the times are changed, and formed on more reasonable principles, it may be impossible to convince them that the illegitimate power, which they obtain, by degrading themselves, is a curse, and that they must return to nature and equality, if they wish to secure the placid satisfaction that unsophisticated affections impart. But for this epoch we must wait—wait, perhaps, till kings and nobles, enlightened by reason, and, preferring the real dignity of man to childish state, throw off their gaudy hereditary trappings: and if then women do not resign the arbitrary power of beauty—they will prove that they have *less* mind than man. . . .

Many are the causes that, in the present corrupt state of society, con-   12
tribute to enslave women by cramping their understandings and sharpening their senses. One, perhaps, that silently does more mischief than all the rest, is their disregard of order.

To do every thing in an orderly manner, is a most important precept,   13
which women, who, generally speaking, receive only a disorderly kind of education, seldom attend to with that degree of exactness that men, who from their infancy are broken into method, observe. This negligent kind of guess-work, for what other epithet can be used to point out the random exertions of a sort of instinctive common sense, never brought to the test of reason? prevents their generalizing matters of fact—so they do to-day, what they did yesterday, merely because they did it yesterday.

This contempt of the understanding in early life has more baneful con-   14
sequences than is commonly supposed; for the little knowledge which women of strong minds attain, is, from various circumstances, of a more desultory kind than the knowledge of men, and it is acquired more by sheer observations on real life, than from comparing what has been individually observed with the results of experience generalized by speculation. Led by their dependent situation and domestic employments more into society, what they learn is rather by snatches; and as learning is with them, in general, only a secondary thing, they do not pursue any one branch with that persevering ardour

necessary to give vigour to the faculties, and clearness to the judgment. In the present state of society, a little learning is required to support the character of a gentleman; and boys are obliged to submit to a few years of discipline. But in the education of women, the cultivation of the understanding is always subordinate to the acquirement of some corporeal accomplishment; even while enervated by confinement and false notions of modesty, the body is prevented from attaining that grace and beauty which relaxed half-formed limbs never exhibit. Besides, in youth their faculties are not brought forward by emulation; and having no serious scientific study, if they have natural sagacity it is turned too soon on life and manners. They dwell on effects, and modifications, without tracing them back to causes; and complicated rules to adjust behaviour are a weak substitute for simple principles.

As a proof that education gives this appearance of weakness to females,   15
we may instance the example of military men, who are, like them, sent into the world before their minds have been stored with knowledge or fortified by principles. The consequences are similar; soldiers acquire a little superficial knowledge, snatched from the muddy current of conversation, and, from continually mixing with society, they gain, what is termed a knowledge of the world; and this acquaintance with manners and customs has frequently been confounded with a knowledge of the human heart. But can the crude fruit of casual observation, never brought to the test of judgment, formed by comparing speculation and experience, deserve such a distinction? Soldiers, as well as women, practice the minor virtues with punctilious politeness. Where is then the sexual difference, when the education has been the same? All the difference that I can discern, arises from the superior advantage of liberty, which enables the former to see more of life.

It is wandering from my present subject, perhaps, to make a political   16
remark; but, as it was produced naturally by the train of my reflections, I shall not pass it silently over.

Standing armies can never consist of resolute, robust men; they may be   17
well disciplined machines, but they will seldom contain men under the influence of strong passions, or with very vigorous faculties. And as for any depth of understanding, I will venture to affirm, that it is as rarely to be found in the army as amongst women; and the cause, I maintain, is the same. It may be further observed, that officers are also particularly attentive to their persons, fond of dancing, crowded rooms, adventures, and ridicule. Like the *fair* sex, the business of their lives is gallantry.—They were taught to please, and they only live to please. Yet they do not lose their rank in the distinction of sexes, for they are still reckoned superior to women, though in what their superiority consists, beyond what I have just mentioned, it is difficult to discover.

The great misfortune is this, that they both acquire manners before   18
morals, and a knowledge of life before they have, from reflections, any acquaintance with the grand ideal outline of human nature. The consequence is natural; satisfied with common nature, they become a prey to prejudices, and

taking all their opinions on credit, they blindly submit to authority. So that, if they have any sense, it is a kind of instinctive glance, that catches proportions, and decides with respect to manners; but fails when arguments are to be pursued below the surface, or opinions analyzed.

May not the same remark be applied to women? Nay, the argument 19 may be carried still further, for they are both thrown out of a useful station by the unnatural distinctions established in civilized life. Riches and hereditary honours have made cyphers of women to give consequence to the numerical figure; and idleness has produced a mixture of gallantry and despotism into society, which leads the very men who are the slaves of their mistresses to tyrannize over their sisters, wives, and daughters. This is only keeping them in rank and file, it is true. Strengthen the female mind by enlarging it, and there will be an end to blind obedience; but, as blind obedience is ever sought for by power, tyrants and sensualists are in the right when they endeavor to keep women in the dark, because the former only wants slaves, and the latter a play-thing. The sensualist, indeed, has been the most dangerous of tyrants, and women have been duped by their lovers, as princes by their ministers, whilst dreaming that they reigned over them.

QUESTIONS FOR MEANING

1. What's wrong with treating women as children and expecting "blind obedience"?
2. What causes does Wollstonecraft cite for the degradation of women? On what grounds does she defend their "follies" and "vices"?
3. What does Wollstonecraft mean by "false refinement" in paragraph 11? Explain why she believes it is dangerous to acquire "manners before morals."
4. Where in her essay does Wollstonecraft define the sort of education she believes women should receive? Why does she object to educating women privately in their homes?
5. Wollstonecraft was perceived as a radical by her contemporaries, and relatively few people took her ideas seriously. Looking back upon her work after two hundred years, can you find any traditional values that Wollstonecraft accepted without question? Could you argue that she was conservative in some ways?
6. Explain why "the sensualist" has been "the most dangerous of tyrants."
7. Vocabulary: ephemeron (2), specious (2), caprices (2), puerile (2), propriety (2), insinuate (3), docile (3), sanguine (10), desultory (14), corporeal (14), enervated (14), sagacity (14), punctilious (15) cyphers (19).

QUESTIONS ABOUT STRATEGY

1. What is the premise of this argument? Where does Wollstonecraft first state it, and where is it restated?
2. What is the function of the last sentence in the second paragraph?

3. Why does Wollstonecraft quote John Milton and Francis Bacon? What do these quotations contribute to her argument?

4. Comment on the analogy Wollstonecraft makes between women and soldiers. What type of soldiers did she have in mind? Is her analogy valid?

5. Do you think Wollstonecraft wrote this argument primarily for men or for women? What kind of an audience could she have expected in the eighteenth century?

KARL MARX AND FRIEDRICH ENGELS
The Communist Manifesto

Karl Marx (1818–1883) was a German social scientist and political philosopher who believed that history is determined by economics. Originally intending to teach, Marx studied at the University of Berlin, receiving his Ph.D. in 1841. But, in 1842, he abandoned academics to become editor of the Rheinische Zeitung, *an influential newspaper published in Cologne. His editorials led the government to close the paper within a year, and Marx went into exile—first in France and Belgium, and eventually in England, where he spent the last thirty-three years of his life.*

It was in 1843 that Marx met Friedrich Engels (1820–1895), the son of a wealthy German industrialist with business interests in England. The two men discovered that they shared the same political beliefs, and they worked together closely for the next forty years. It was not until 1867 that Marx was able to publish the first volume of Das Kapital, *his most important work. The second and third volumes were published after his death, completed by Engels, who worked from the extensive notes that Marx left behind him.* Das Kapital, *or* Capital, *provided the theoretical basis for what is variously known as "Marxism" or "Communism." It is an indictment of nineteenth-century capitalism that predicts a proletarian revolution in which the workers would take over the means of production and distribute goods according to needs, creating an ideal society in which the state would wither away.*

But Marx and Engels had outlined their views long before the publication of Das Kapital. *In **1848,** they published a pamphlet called* The Communist Manifesto. *It was written during a period of great political unrest. Within months of its publication, revolutions broke out in several European countries. Most of the revolutions of 1848 were quickly aborted, but "the specter of Communism" continued to haunt the world. Here are the first few pages of this classic argument.*

A specter is haunting Europe—the specter of Communism. All the Powers   1
of old Europe have entered into a holy alliance to exorcise this specter; Pope and Czar, Metternich and Guizot, French Radicals and German police-spies.

Where is the party in opposition that has not been decried as commu-   2
nistic by its opponents in power? Where the Opposition that has not hurled
back the branding reproach of Communism against the more advanced opposition parties, as well as against its reactionary adversaries?

Two things result from this fact.   3

   I. Communism is already acknowledged by all European Powers to be   4
     itself a Power.
  II. It is high time that Communists should openly, in the face of the   5
     whole world, publish their views, their aims, their tendencies, and
     meet this nursery tale of the specter of Communism with a Manifesto
     of the party itself.

To this end, Communists of various nationalities have assembled in   6
London and sketched the following Manifesto, to be published in the English, French, German, Italian, Flemish and Danish languages.

Bourgeois and Proletarians*

The history of all hitherto existing society is the history of class struggles.   7

Freeman and slave, patrician and plebian, lord and serf, guild-master   8
and journeyman, in a word, oppressor and oppressed, stood in constant opposition to one another, carried on uninterrupted, now hidden, now open
fight, a fight that each time ended, either in a revolutionary re-constitution
of society at large, or in the common ruin of the contending classes.

In the earlier epochs of history we find almost everywhere a compli-   9
cated arrangement of society into various orders, a manifold gradation of
social rank. In ancient Rome we have patricians, knights, plebians, slaves; in
the Middle Ages, feudal lords, vassals, guild-masters, journeymen, appren-
tices, serfs; in almost all of these classes, again, subordinate gradations.

The modern bourgeois society that has sprouted from the ruins of feu-   10
dal society, has not done away with class antagonisms. It has but established
new classes, new conditions of oppression, new forms of struggle in place of
the old ones.

Our epoch, the epoch of the bourgeoisie, possesses, however, this dis-   11
tinctive feature; it has simplified the class antagonisms. Society as a whole is
more and more splitting up into two great hostile camps, into two great
classes directly facing each other: Bourgeoisie and Proletariat.

From the serfs of the Middle Ages sprang the chartered burghers of the   12
earliest towns. From these burgesses the first elements of the bourgeoisie
were developed.

*By bourgeoisie is meant the class of modern Capitalists, owners of the means of social pro-
duction and employers of wage labor. By proletariat, the class of modern wage laborers who,
having no means of production of their own, are reduced to selling their labor-power in order
to live. [Marx's note]

The discovery of America, the rounding of the Cape, opened up fresh   13
ground for the rising bourgeoisie. The East Indian and Chinese markets, the
colonization of America, trade with the colonies, the increase in the means
of exchange and in commodities generally, gave to commerce, to navigation,
to industry, an impulse never before known, and thereby, to the revolutionary element in the tottering feudal society, a rapid development.

The feudal system of industry, under which industrial production was   14
monopolized by closed guilds, now no longer sufficed for the growing wants
of the new market. The manufacturing system took its place. The guild-
masters were pushed on one side by the manufacturing middle-class: division
of labor between the different corporate guilds vanished in the face of division of labor in each single workshop.

Meantime the markets kept ever growing, the demand ever rising. Even   15
manufacture no longer sufficed. Thereupon, steam and machinery revolu-
tionized industrial production. The place of manufacture was taken by the
giant, Modern Industry, the place of the industrial middle-class, by industrial
millionaires, the leaders of whole industrial armies, the modern bourgeois.

Modern industry has established the world market, for which the dis-   16
covery of America paved the way. This market has given an immense development to commerce, to navigation, to communication by land. This
development has, in its turn, reacted on the extension of industry; and in proportion as industry, commerce, navigation, railways extended, in the same
proportion the bourgeoisie developed, increased its capital, and pushed into
the background every class handed down from the Middle Ages.

We see, therefore, how the modern bourgeoisie is itself the product of   17
a long course of development, a series of revolutions in the modes of production and of exchange.

Each step in the development of the bourgeoisie was accompanied by a   18
corresponding political advance of that class. An oppressed class under the
sway of the feudal nobility, an armed and self-governing association in the
medieval commune, here independent urban republic (as in Italy and Germany), there taxable "third estate" of the monarchy (as in France), afterwards, in the period of manufacture proper, serving either the semi-feudal or
the absolute monarchy as a counterpoise against nobility, and, in fact, corner-
stone of the great monarchies in general, the bourgeoisie has at last, since the
establishment of Modern Industry and of the world-market, conquered for
itself, in the modern representative State, exclusive political sway. The executive of the modern State is but a committee for managing the common
affairs of the whole bourgeoisie.

The bourgeoisie, historically, has played a most revolutionary part.   19

The bourgeoisie, wherever it has got the upper hand, has put an end to   20
all feudal, patriarchal, idyllic relations. It has pitilessly torn asunder the mot-
ley feudal ties that bound man to his "natural superiors," and has left no
other nexus between man and man than naked self-interest, than callous "cash
payment." It has drowned the most heavenly ecstasies of religious fervor, of

chivalrous enthusiasm, of Philistine sentimentalism, in the icy water of ego-
tistical calculation. It has resolved personal worth into exchange value, and
in place of the numberless indefeasible chartered freedoms, has set up that
single, unconscionable freedom—Free Trade. In one word, for exploitation,
veiled by religious and political illusions, it has submitted naked, shameless,
direct, brutal exploitation.

The bourgeoisie has stripped of its halo every occupation hitherto hon-   21
ored and looked up to with reverent awe. It has converted the physician, the
lawyer, the priest, the poet, the man of science, into its paid wage laborers.

The bourgeoisie has torn away from the family its sentimental veil, and   22
has reduced the family relation to a mere money relation.

The bourgeoisie has disclosed how it came to pass that the brutal dis-   23
play of vigor in the Middle Ages, which reactionists so much admire, found
its fitting complement in the most slothful indolence. It has been the first to
show what man's activity can bring about. It has accomplished wonders far
surpassing Egyptian pyramids, Roman aqueducts and Gothic cathedrals; it
has conducted expeditions that put in the shade all former Exoduses of nations and crusades.

The bourgeoisie cannot exist without constantly revolutionizing the in-   24
strument of production, and thereby the relations of production, and with
them the whole relations of society. Conservation of the old modes of production in unaltered form was, on the contrary, the first condition of existence for all earlier industrial classes. Constant revolutionizing of production,
uninterrupted disturbance of all social conditions, everlasting uncertainty and
agitation distinguish the bourgeois epoch from all earlier ones. All fixed, fast
frozen relations, with their train of ancient and venerable prejudices and
opinions, are swept away, all new formed ones become antiquated before
they can ossify. All that is solid melts into the air, all that is holy is profaned,
and man is at last compelled to face with sober senses, his real conditions of
life, and his relations with his kind.

The need of a constantly expanding market for its products chases the   25
bourgeoisie over the whole surface of the globe. It must nestle everywhere,
settle everywhere, establish connections everywhere.

The bourgeoisie has through its exploitation of the world-market given   26
a cosmopolitan character to production and consumption in every country.
To the great chagrin of reactionists, it has drawn from under the feet of
industry the national ground on which it stood. All old-established national
industries have been destroyed or are daily being destroyed. They are dis-
lodged by new industries, whose introduction becomes a life and death question for all civilized nations, by industries that no longer work up indigenous
raw material, but raw material drawn from the remotest zones; industries
whose products are consumed, not only at home, but in every quarter of the
globe. In place of the old wants, satisfied by the productions of the country,
we find new wants, requiring for their satisfaction the products of distant
lands and climes. In place of the old local and national seclusion and

self-sufficiency, we have intercourse in every direction, universal interdependence of nations. And as in material, so also in intellectual production. The intellectual creations of individual nations become common property. National onesidedness and narrowmindedness become more and more possible, and from the numerous national and local literatures there arises a world-literature.

The bourgeoisie, by the rapid improvement of all instruments of production, by the immensely facilitated means of communication, draws all, even the most barbarian nations into civilization. The cheap prices of its commodities are the heavy artillery with which it batters down all Chinese walls, with which it forces the barbarians' intensely obstinate hatred of foreigners to capitulate. It compels all nations, on pain of extinction, to adopt the bourgeois mode of production; it compels them to introduce what it calls civilization into their midst, i.e., to become bourgeois themselves. In a word, it creates a world after its own image.   27

The bourgeoisie has subjected the country to the rule of the towns. It has created enormous cities, has greatly increased the urban population as compared with the rural and has thus rescued a considerable part of the population from the idiocy of rural life. Just as it has made the country dependent on the towns, so it has made barbarian and semi-barbarian countries dependent on civilized ones, nations of peasants on nations of bourgeois, the East on the West.   28

The bourgeoisie keeps more and more doing away with the scattered state of the population, of the means of production, and of property. It has agglomerated population, centralized means of production, and has concentrated property in a few hands. The necessary consequence of this was political centralization. Independent, or but loosely connected provinces, with separate interests, laws, governments, and systems of taxation, become lumped together in one nation, with one government, one code of laws, one national class interest, one frontier and one customs tariff.   29

The bourgeoisie, during its rule of scarce one hundred years, has created more massive and more colossal productive forces than have all preceding generations together. Subjection of Nature's forces to man, machinery, application of chemistry to industry and agriculture, steam-navigation, railways, electric telegraphs, clearing of whole continents for cultivation, canalization of rivers, whole populations conjured out of the ground—what earlier century had even a presentiment that such productive forces slumbered in the lap of social labor?   30

We see then: the means of production and of exchange on whose foundation the bourgeoisie built itself up, were generated in feudal society. At a certain stage in the development of these means of production and of exchange, the conditions under which feudal society produced and exchanged, the feudal organization of agriculture and manufacturing industry, in one word, the feudal relations of property became no longer compatible with the already developed productive forces; they became so many fetters. They had to burst asunder; they were burst asunder.   31

Into their places stepped free competition, accompanied by social and   32
political constitution adapted to it, and by economical and political sway of
the bourgeois class.

A similar movement is going on before our own eyes. Modern bour-   33
geois society with its relations of production, of exchange and of property, a
society that has conjured up such gigantic means of production and of exchange, is like the sorcerer, who is no longer able to control the powers of
the nether world whom he has called up by his spells. For many a decade
past, the history of industry and commerce is but the history of the revolt of
modern productive forces against modern conditions of production, against
the property relations that are the conditions for the existence of the bourgeoisie and of its rule. It is enough to mention the commercial crises that by
their periodical return put on its trial, each time more threateningly, the existence of the entire bourgeois society. In these crises a great part not only of
the existing products, but also of the previously created productive forces,
are periodically destroyed. In these crises there breaks out an epidemic that,
in all earlier epochs, would have seemed an absurdity—the epidemic of over-
production. Society suddenly finds itself put back into a state of momentary
barbarism; it appears as if a famine, a universal war of devastation, had cut
off the supply of every means of subsistence; industry and commerce seem
to be destroyed; and why? Because there is too much civilization, too much
means of subsistence, too much industry, too much commerce. The productive forces at the disposal of society no longer tend to further the development of the conditions of the bourgeois property; on the contrary, they have
become too powerful for these conditions by which they are fettered, and as
soon as they overcome these fetters they bring disorder into the whole of
bourgeois society, endanger the existence of bourgeois property. The conditions of bourgeois society are too narrow to comprise the wealth created by
them. And how does the bourgeoisie get over these crises? On the one hand
by enforced destruction of a mass of productive forces; on the other, by the
conquest of new markets, and by the more thorough exploitation of the old
ones. That is to say, by paving the way for more extensive and more destructive crises, and by diminishing the means whereby crises are prevented.

The weapons with which the bourgeoisie felled feudalism to the ground   34
are now turned against the bourgeoisie itself.

But not only has the bourgeoisie forged the weapons that bring death   35
to itself; it has also called into existence the men who are to wield those
weapons—the modern working class—the proletarians.

In proportion as the bourgeoisie, i.e., capital, is developed, in the same   36
proportion is the proletariat, the modern working class, developed, a class of
laborers who live only so long as they find work, and who find work only
so long as their labor increases capital. These laborers, who must sell themselves piecemeal, are a commodity, like every other article of commerce, and
are consequently exposed to all the vicissitudes of competition, to all the
fluctuations of the market.

Owing to the extensive use of machinery and to division of labor, the   37
work of the proletarians has lost all individual character, and, consequently,
all charm for the workman. He becomes an appendage of the machine, and
it is only the most simple, most monotonous and most easily acquired knack
that is required of him. Hence, the cost of production of a workman is restricted almost entirely to the means of subsistence that he requires for his
maintenance, and for the propagation of his race. But the price of a commodity, and also of labor, is equal to its cost of production. In production,
therefore, as the repulsiveness of the work increases the wage decreases. Nay
more, in proportion as the use of machinery and division of labor increases,
in the same proportion the burden of toil increases, whether by prolongation
of the working hours, by increase of the work enacted in a given time, or by
increased speed of the machinery, etc.

Modern industry has converted the little workshop of the patriarchal   38
master into the great factory of the industrial capitalist. Masses of laborers,
crowded into factories, are organized like soldiers. As privates of the industrial army they are placed under the command of a perfect hierarchy of officers and sergeants. Not only are they the slaves of the bourgeois class and of
the bourgeois state, they are daily and hourly enslaved by the machine, by
the overlooker, and above all, by the individual bourgeois manufacturer himself. The more openly this despotism proclaims gain to be its end and aim,
the more petty, the more hateful and the more embittering it is.

The less the skill and exertion or strength implied in manual labor, in   39
other words, the more modern industry becomes developed, the more is the
labor of men superseded by that of women. Differences of age and sex have
no longer any distinctive social validity for the working class. All are instruments of labor, more or less expensive to use, according to their age and sex.

No sooner is the exploitation of the laborer by the manufacturer, so far   40
at an end, that he receives his wages in cash, than he is set upon by the other
portions of the bourgeoisie, the landlord, the shopkeeper, the pawn-
broker, etc.

The lower strata of the middle class—the small trades-people, shop-   41
keepers and retired tradesmen generally, the handicraftsmen and peasants—
all these sink gradually into the proletariat, partly because their diminutive
capital does not suffice for the scale on which Modern Industry is carried on,
and is swamped in the competition with the large capitalists, partly because
their specialized skill is rendered worthless by new methods of production.
Thus the proletariat is recruited from all classes of the population.

The proletariat goes through various stages of development. With its   42
birth begins its struggle with the bourgeoisie. At first the contest is carried
on by individual laborers, then by the workpeople of a factory, then by the
operatives of one trade, in one locality, against the individual bourgeois who
directly exploits them. They direct their attacks not against the bourgeois
conditions of production, but against the instruments of production themselves; they destroy imported wares that compete with their labor, they smash

to pieces machinery, they set factories ablaze, they seek to restore by force the vanished status of the workman of the Middle Ages.

At this stage the laborers still form an incoherent mass scattered over   43 the whole country, and broken up by their mutual competition. If anywhere they unite to form more compact bodies, this is not yet the consequence of their own active union, but of the union of the bourgeoisie, which class, in order to attain its own political ends, is compelled to set the whole proletariat in motion, and is moreover yet, for a time, able to do so. At this stage, therefore, the proletarians do not fight their enemies, but the enemies of their enemies, the remnants of absolute monarchy, the landowners, the non-industrial bourgeois, the petty bourgeoisie. Thus the whole historical movement is concentrated in the hands of the bourgeoisie, every victory so obtained is a victory for the bourgeoisie.

But with the development of industry the proletariat not only increases   44 in number; it becomes concentrated in greater masses, its strength grows and it feels that strength more. The various interests and conditions of life within the ranks of the proletariat are more and more equalized, in proportion as machinery obliterates all distinctions of labor, and nearly everywhere reduces wages to the same low level. The growing competition among the bourgeois, and the resulting commercial crisis, makes the wages of the workers even more fluctuating. The unceasing improvement of machinery, ever more rapidly developing, makes their livelihood more and more precarious; the collisions between individual workmen and individual bourgeois take more and more the character of collisions between two classes. Thereupon the workers begin to form combinations (Trades' Unions) against the bourgeois; they club together in order to make provision beforehand for these occasional revolts. Here and there the contest breaks out into riots.

Now and then the workers are victorious, but only for a time. The real   45 fruit of their battle lies not in the immediate result but in the ever-expanding union of workers. This union is helped on by the improved means of communication that are created by modern industry, and that places the workers of different localities in contact with one another. It was just this contact that was needed to centralize the numerous local struggles, all of the same character, into one national struggle between classes. But every class struggle is a political struggle. And that union, to attain which the burghers of the Middle Ages with their miserable highways, required centuries, the modern proletarians, thanks to railways, achieve in a few years.

This organization of the proletarians into a class, and consequently into   46 a political party, is continually being upset again by the competition between the workers themselves. But it ever rises up again, stronger, firmer, mightier. It compels legislative recognition of particular interests of the workers by taking advantage of the divisions among the bourgeoisie itself. Thus the ten hours' bill in England was carried.

Altogether collisions between the classes of the old society further, in   47 many ways, the course of development of the proletariat. The bourgeoisie finds itself involved in a constant battle. At first with the aristocracy; later on, with those portions of the bourgeoisie itself whose interests have become antagonistic to the progress of industry; at all times, with the bourgeoisie of foreign countries. In all these battles it sees itself compelled to appeal to the proletariat, to ask for its help, and thus, to drag it into the political arena. The bourgeoisie itself, therefore, supplies the proletariat with its own elements of political and general education; in other words, it furnishes the proletariat with weapons for fighting the bourgeoisie.

Further, as we have already seen, entire sections of the ruling classes   48
are, by the advance of industry, precipitated into the proletariat, or are at least threatened in their conditions of existence. These also supply the proletariat with fresh elements of enlightenment and progress.

Finally, in times when the class-struggle nears the decisive hour, the   49
process of dissolution going on within the ruling class—in fact, within the whole range of an old society—assumes such a violent, glaring character that a small section of the ruling class cuts itself adrift and joins the revolutionary class, the class that holds the future in its hands. Just as, therefore, at an earlier period, a section of the nobility went over to the bourgeoisie, so now a portion of the bourgeoisie goes over to the proletariat, and in particular, a portion of the bourgeois ideologists, who have raised themselves to the level of comprehending theoretically the historical movements as a whole.

Of all the classes that stand face to face with the bourgeoisie today the   50
proletariat alone is a really revolutionary class. The other classes decay and finally disappear in the face of modern industry; the proletariat is its special and essential product.

The lower middle class, the small manufacturer, the shopkeeper, the   51
artisan, the peasant, all these fight against the bourgeoisie, to save from extinction their existence as fractions of the middle class. They are therefore not revolutionary, but conservative. Nay, more; they are reactionary, for they try to roll back the wheel of history. If by chance they are revolutionary, they are so only in view of their impending transfer into the proletariat; they thus defend not their present, but their future interests; they desert their own standpoint to place themselves at that of the proletariat.

The "dangerous class," the social scum, that passively rotting mass   52
thrown off by the lowest layers of old society, may, here and there, be swept into the movement by a proletarian revolution; its conditions of life, however, prepare it far more for the part of a bribed tool of reactionary intrigue.

In the conditions of the proletariat, those of the old society at large are   53
already virtually swamped. The proletarian is without property; his relation to his wife and children has no longer anything in common with the bourgeois family relations; modern industrial labor, modern subjection to capital, the same in England as in France, in America as in Germany, has stripped him of every trace of national character. Law, morality, religion, are to him so many bourgeois prejudices, behind which lurk in ambush just as many bourgeois interests.

All the preceding classes that got the upper hand sought to fortify their   54
already acquired status by subjecting society at large to their conditions of

appropriation. The proletarians cannot become masters of the productive forces of society, except by abolishing their own previous mode of appropriation, and thereby also every other previous mode of appropriation. They have nothing of their own to secure and to fortify; their mission is to destroy all previous securities for and insurances of individual property.

All previous historical movements were movements of minorities, or   55
in the interest of minorities. The proletarian movement is the self-conscious, independent movement of the immense majority. The proletariat, the lowest stratum of our present society, cannot stir, cannot raise itself up without the whole superincumbent strata of official society being sprung into the air.

Though not in substance, yet in form, the struggle of the proletariat   56
with the bourgeoisie is at first a national struggle. The proletariat of each country must, of course, first of all settle matters with its own bourgeoisie.

In depicting the most general phases of the development of the prole-   57
tariat, we traced the more or less veiled civil war, raging within existing society, up to the point where that war breaks out into open revolution, and where the violent overthrow of the bourgeoisie, lays the foundations for the sway of the proletariat.

Hitherto every form of society has been based, as we have already seen,   58
on the antagonism of oppressing and oppressed classes. But in order to oppress a class, certain conditions must be assured to it under which it can, at least, continue its slavish existence. The serf, in the period of serfdom, raised himself to membership in the commune, just as the petty bourgeois, under the yoke of feudal absolutism managed to develop into a bourgeois. The modern laborer, on the contrary, instead of rising with the progress of industry, sinks deeper and deeper below the conditions of existence of his own class. He becomes a pauper, and pauperism develops more rapidly than population and wealth. And here it becomes evident that the bourgeoisie is unfit any longer to be the ruling class in society, and impose its conditions of existence upon society as an over-riding law. It is unfit to rule, because it is incompetent to assure an existence to its slave within his slavery, because it cannot help letting him sink into such a state that it has to feed him, instead of being fed by him. Society can no longer live under this bourgeoisie; in other words, its existence is no longer compatible with society.

The essential condition for the existence, and for the sway of the bour-   59
geois class, is the formation and augmentation of capital; the condition for capital is wage labor. Wage labor rests exclusively on competition between the laborers. The advance of industry, whose involuntary promoter is the bourgeoisie, replaces the isolation of the laborers, due to competition, by their involuntary combination, due to association. The development of Modern Industry, therefore, cuts from under its feet the very foundation on which the bourgeoisie produces and appropriates products. What the bourgeoisie therefore produces, above all, are its own grave diggers. Its fall and the victory of the proletariat are equally inevitable.

QUESTIONS FOR MEANING

1. Comment on the authors' claim in paragraph 7 that the "history of all hitherto existing society is the history of class struggles." What does this mean?
2. In paragraph 11, the authors write: "Society as a whole is more and more splitting up into two great hostile camps, into two great classes directly facing each other: Bourgeoisie and Proletariat." Has history proven them right? How would you describe class relations within the United States? Can American history be seen in Marxist terms?
3. Explain the distinction in paragraph 14 between the feudal and manufacturing systems of industry.
4. Do Marx and Engels concede that modern history has accomplished anything admirable? Do they credit the bourgeoisie with any virtues?
5. Why do Marx and Engels believe that the bourgeoisie is unfit to rule? Why do they believe that the rise of the proletariat is inevitable?
6. What do Marx and Engels mean when they claim "there is too much civilization, too much means of subsistence, too much industry, too much commerce"? Paraphrase paragraph 33.
7. What is "the social scum" that Marx and Engels dismiss in paragraph 52? Why do they believe this class is dangerous?
8. Vocabulary: exorcise (1), patrician (8), plebeian (8), vassals (9), patriarchal (20), nexus (20), slothful (23), indigenous (26), agglomerated (29), presentiment (30), vicissitudes (36), diminutive (41), obliterates (44), precarious (44), augmentation (59).

QUESTIONS ABOUT STRATEGY

1. Why do Marx and Engels open their manifesto by describing Communism as "a specter"? Explain what they mean by this and how it serves as an introduction to the political analysis that follows.
2. In interpreting history entirely in economic terms, are there any major conflicts that Marx and Engels overlook?
3. What is the function of paragraphs 31 and 32?
4. Can you point to anything in this work that reveals that Marx and Engels were writing for an international audience?
5. What parts of this essay are the strongest? Where do Marx and Engels make the most sense?
6. Can you identify any exaggerations in *The Communist Manifesto*? If you were to write a rebuttal, are there any claims that you could prove to be oversimplified?
7. Is this "manifesto" an argument or an exhortation? Is it designed to convince readers who have no political opinions, or to rally the men and women who are already committed to revolution? What is its purpose?

HENRY DAVID THOREAU
Resistance to Civil Government

Henry David Thoreau (1817–1862) was one of the most important American writers of the nineteenth century. A graduate of Harvard, Thoreau chose to live alone in a hut of his own making from 1845 to 1847 near Walden Pond outside of Concord, Massachusetts. He devoted himself there to living simply and striving to be self-sufficient—spending much of his time reading, thinking, and studying nature. The record of this experience can be found in Walden *(1854), Thoreau's most influential and widely read book. His other books include* A Week on the Concord and Merrimack River *(1849),* The Main Woods *(1864), and* Cape Cod *(1865). He was also the author of several important essays, foremost among which is the following selection—popularly known as "Civil Disobedience." It was first published in* **1849,** *shortly after the conclusion of the Mexican War.*

I heartily accept the motto,—"That government is best which governs least;"   1
and I should like to see it acted up to more rapidly and systematically. Carried out, it finally amounts to this, which also I believe,—"That government is best which governs not at all;" and when men are prepared for it, that will be the kind of government which they will have. Government is at best but an expedient; but most governments are usually, and all governments are sometimes, inexpedient. The objections which have been brought against a standing army, and they are many and weighty, and deserve to prevail, may also at last be brought against a standing government. The standing army is only an arm of the standing government. The government itself, which is only the mode which the people have chosen to execute their will, is equally liable to be abused and perverted before the people can act through it. Witness the present Mexican war, the work of comparatively a few individuals using the standing government as their tool; for, in the outset, the people would not have consented to this measure.

This American government,—what is it but a tradition, though a recent   2
one, endeavoring to transmit itself unimpaired to posterity, but each instant losing some of its integrity? It has not the vitality and force of a single living man; for a single man can bend it to his will. It is a sort of wooden gun to the people themselves; and, if ever they should use it in earnest as a real one against each other, it will surely split. But it is not the less necessary for this; for the people must have some complicated machinery or other, and hear its din, to satisfy that idea of government which they have. Governments show thus how successfully men can be imposed on, even impose on themselves, for their own advantage. It is excellent, we must all allow; yet this government never of itself furthered any enterprise, but by the alacrity with which it got out of its way. *It* does not keep the country free. *It* does not settle the West. *It* does not educate. The character inherent in the American people has done all that has been accomplished; and it would have done somewhat more,

if the government had not sometimes got in its way. For government is an expedient by which men would fain succeed in letting one another alone; and, as has been said, when it is most expedient, the governed are most let alone by it. Trade and commerce, if they were not made of India rubber, would never manage to bounce over the obstacles which legislators are continually putting in their way; and, if one were to judge these men wholly by the effects of their actions, and not partly by their intentions, they would deserve to be classed and punished with those mischievous persons who put obstructions on the railroads.

But, to speak practically and as a citizen, unlike those who call themselves no-government men, I ask for, not at once no government, but at *once* a better government. Let every man make known what kind of government would command his respect, and that will be one step toward obtaining it. 3

After all, the practical reason why, when the power is once in the hands of the people, a majority are permitted, and for a long period continue, to rule, is not because they are most likely to be in the right, nor because this seems fairest to the minority, but because they are physically the strongest. But a government in which the majority rule in all cases cannot be based on justice, even as far as men understand it. Can there not be a government in which majorities do not virtually decide right and wrong, but conscience?— in which majorities decide only those questions to which the rule of expediency is applicable? Must the citizen ever for a moment, or in the last degree, resign his conscience to the legislator? Why has every man a conscience, then? I think that we should be men first, and subjects afterward. It is not desirable to cultivate a respect for the law, so much as for the right. The only obligation which I have a right to assume, is to do at any time what I think right. It is truly enough said, that a corporation has no conscience; but a corporation of conscientious men is a corporation *with* a conscience. Law never made men a whit more just; and, by means of their respect for it, even the well-disposed are daily made the agents of injustice. A common and natural result of an undue respect for law is, that you may see a file of soldiers, colonel, captain, corporal, privates, powder-monkeys and all, marching in admirable order over hill and dale to the wars, against their wills, aye, against their common sense and consciences, which makes it very steep marching indeed, and produces a palpitation of the heart. They have no doubt that it is a damnable business in which they are concerned; they are all peaceably inclined. Now, what are they? Men at all? or small moveable forts and magazines, at the service of some unscrupulous man in power? Visit the Navy Yard, and behold a marine, such a man as an American government can make, or such as it can make a man with its black arts, a mere shadow and reminiscence of humanity, a man laid out alive and standing, and already, as one may say, buried under arms with funeral accompaniments, though it may be 4

> "Not a drum was heard, not a funeral note,
>   As his corse to the rampart we hurried;

> Not a soldier discharged his farewell shot
> O'er the grave where our hero we buried."

The mass of men serve the State thus, not as men mainly, but as ma-   5
chines, with their bodies. They are the standing army, and the militia, jailers,
constables, *posse comitatus,* &c. In most cases there is no free exercise whatever of the judgment or of the moral sense; but they put themselves on a
level with wood and earth and stones, and wooden men can perhaps be manufactured that will serve the purpose as well. Such command no more respect
than men of straw, or a lump of dirt. They have the same sort of worth only
as horses and dogs. Yet such as these even are commonly esteemed good
citizens. Others, as most legislators, politicians, lawyers, ministers, and of-
ficeholders, serve the State chiefly with their heads; and, as they rarely make
any moral distinctions, they are as likely to serve the devil, without intending
it, as God. A very few, as heroes, patriots, martyrs, reformers in the great
sense, and *men,* serve the State with their consciences also, and so necessarily
resist it for the most part; and they are commonly treated by it as enemies.
A wise man will only be useful as a man, and will not submit to be "clay,"
and "stop a hole to keep the wind away," but leave that office to his dust at
least:—

> "I am too high-born to be propertied,
> To be a secondary at control,
> Or useful serving-man and instrument
> To any sovereign state throughout the world."

He who gives himself entirely to his fellow-men appears to them use-   6
less and selfish; but he who gives himself partially to them is pronounced a
benefactor and philanthropist.

How does it become a man to behave toward this American govern-   7
ment to-day? I answer that he cannot without disgrace be associated with it.
I cannot for an instant recognize that political organization as *my* government
which is the *slave's* government also.

All men recognize the right of revolution; that is, the right to refuse   8
allegiance to and to resist the government, when its tyranny or its ineffi-
ciency are great and unendurable. But almost all say that such is not the case
now. But such was the case, they think, in the Revolution of '75. If one were
to tell me that this was a bad government because it taxed certain foreign
commodities brought to its ports, it is most probable that I should not make
an ado about it, for I can do without them: all machines have their friction;
and possibly this does enough good to counterbalance the evil. At any rate,
it is a great evil to make a stir about it. But when the friction comes to have
its machine, and oppression and robbery are organized, I say, let us not have
such a machine any longer. In other words, when a sixth of the population
of a nation which has undertaken to be the refuge of liberty are slaves, and a
whole country is unjustly overrun and conquered by a foreign army, and

subjected to military law, I think that it is not too soon for honest men to rebel and revolutionize. What makes this duty the more urgent is the fact, that the country so overrun is not our own, but ours is the invading army.

Paley, a common authority with many on moral questions, in his chap-   9
ter on the "Duty of Submission to Civil Government," resolves all civil ob-
ligation into expediency; and he proceeds to say, "that so long as the interest of the whole society requires it, that is, so long as the established government cannot be resisted or changed without public inconveniency, it is the will of God that the established government be obeyed, and no longer." . . . "This principle being admitted, the justice of every particular case of resistance is reduced to a computation of the quantity of the danger and grievance on the one side, and of the probability and expense of redressing it on the other." Of this, he says, every man shall judge for himself. But Paley appears never to have contemplated those cases to which the rule of expediency does not apply, in which a people, as well as an individual, must do justice, cost what it may. If I have unjustly wrested a plank from a drowning man, I must restore it to him though I drown myself. This, according to Paley, would be inconvenient. But he that would save his life, in such a case, shall lose it. This people must cease to hold slaves, and to make war on Mexico, though it cost them their existence as a people.

In their practice, nations agree with Paley; but does any one think that   10
Massachusetts does exactly what is right at the present crisis?

> "A drab of state, a cloth-o'-silver slut,
> To have her train borne up, and her soul trail in the dirt."

Practically speaking, the opponents to a reform in Massachusetts are   11
not a hundred thousand politicians at the South, but a hundred thousand merchants and farmers here, who are more interested in commerce and ag-
riculture than they are in humanity, and are not prepared to do justice to the slave and to Mexico, *cost what it may*. I quarrel not with far-off foes, but with those who, near at home, co-operate with, and do the bidding of those far away, and without whom the latter would be harmless. We are accustomed to say, that the mass of men are unprepared; but improvement is slow, because the few are not materially wiser or better than the many. It is not so important that many should be as good as you, as that there be some abso-
lute goodness somewhere; for that will leaven the whole lump. There are thousands who are *in opinion* opposed to slavery and to the war, who yet in effect do nothing to put an end to them; who, esteeming themselves children of Washington and Franklin, sit down with their hands in their pockets, and say that they know not what to do, and do nothing; who even postpone the question of freedom to the question of free-trade, and quietly read the prices-
current along with the latest advices from Mexico, after dinner, and, it may be, fall asleep over them both. What is the price-current of an honest man and patriot to-day? They hesitate, and they regret, and sometimes they petition; but they do nothing in earnest and with effect. They will wait,

well-disposed, for others to remedy the evil, that they may no longer have it to regret. At most, they give only a cheap vote, and a feeble countenance and God-speed, to the right, as it goes by them. There are nine hundred and ninety-nine patrons of virtue to one virtuous man; but it is easier to deal with the real possessor of a thing than with the temporary guardian of it.

All voting is a sort of gaming, like chequers or backgammon, with a   12
slight moral tinge to it, a playing with right and wrong, with moral questions; and betting naturally accompanies it. The character of the voters is not staked. I cast my vote, perchance, as I think right; but I am not vitally concerned that that right should prevail. I am willing to leave it to the majority. Its obligation, therefore, never exceeds that of expediency. Even voting *for the right* is *doing* nothing for it. It is only expressing to men feebly your desire that it should prevail. A wise man will not leave it to the majority. There is but little virtue in the action of masses of men. When the majority shall at length vote for the abolition of slavery, it will be because they are indifferent to slavery, or because there is but little slavery left to be abolished by their vote. *They* will then be the only slaves. Only *his* vote can hasten the abolition of slavery who asserts his own freedom by his vote.

I hear of a convention to be held at Baltimore, or elsewhere, for the   13
selection of a candidate for the Presidency, made up chiefly of editors, and men who are politicians by profession; but I think, what is it to any independent, intelligent, and respectable man what decision they may come to, shall we not have the advantage of his wisdom and honesty, nevertheless? Can we not count upon some independent votes? Are there not many individuals in the country who do not attend conventions? But no: I find that the respectable man, so called, has immediately drifted from his position, and despairs of his country, when his country has more reason to despair of him. He forthwith adopts one of the candidates thus selected as the only *available* one, thus proving that he is himself *available* for any purposes of the demagogue. His vote is of no more worth than that of any unprincipled foreigner or hireling native, who may have been bought. Oh for a man who is a *man,* and, as my neighbor says, has a bone in his back which you cannot pass your hand through! Our statistics are at fault: the population has been returned too large. How many *men* are there to a square thousand miles in this country? Hardly one. Does not America offer any inducement for men to settle here? The American has dwindled into an Odd Fellow,—one who may be known by the development of his organ of gregariousness, and a manifest lack of intellect and cheerful self-reliance; whose first and chief concern, on coming into the world, is to see that the alms-houses are in good repair; and, before yet he lawfully donned the virile garb, to collect a fund for the support of the widows and orphans that may be; who, in short, ventures to live only by the aid of the mutual insurance company, which has promised to bury him decently.

It is not a man's duty, as a matter of course, to devote himself to the   14
eradication of any, even the most enormous wrong; he may still properly have other concerns to engage him; but it is his duty, at least, to wash his hands

of it, and, if he gives it no thought longer, not to give it practically his support. If I devote myself to other pursuits and contemplations, I must first see, at least, that I do not pursue them sitting upon another man's shoulders. I must get off him first, that he may pursue his contemplations too. See what gross inconsistency is tolerated. I have heard some of my townsmen say, "I should like to have them order me out to help put down an insurrection of the slaves, or to march to Mexico,—see if I would go;" and yet these very men have each, directly by their allegiance, and so indirectly, at least, by their money, furnished a substitute. The soldier is applauded who refuses to serve in an unjust war by those who do not refuse to sustain the unjust government which makes the war; is applauded by those whose own act and authority he disregards and sets at nought; as if the State were penitent to that degree that it hired one to scourge it while it sinned, but not to that degree that it left off sinning for a moment. Thus, under the name of order and civil government, we are all made at least to pay homage to and support our own meanness. After the first blush of sin, comes its indifference and from immoral it becomes, as it were, *un*moral, and not quite unnecessary to that life which we have made.

The broadest and most prevalent error requires the most disinterested   15
virtue to sustain it. The slight reproach to which the virtue of patriotism is commonly liable, the noble are most likely to incur. Those who, while they disapprove of the character and measures of a government, yield to it their allegiance and support, are undoubtedly its most conscientious supporters, and so frequently the most serious obstacles to reform. Some are petitioning the State to dissolve the Union, to disregard the requisitions of the President. Why do they not dissolve it themselves,—the union between themselves and the State,—and refuse to pay their quota into its treasury? Do not they stand in the same relation to the State, that the State does to the Union? And have not the same reasons prevented the State from resisting the Union, which have prevented them from resisting the State?

How can a man be satisfied to entertain an opinion merely, and enjoy   16
it? Is there any enjoyment in it, if his opinion is that he is aggrieved? If you are cheated out of a single dollar by your neighbor, you do not rest satisfied with knowing that you are cheated, or with saying that you are cheated, or even with petitioning him to pay you your due; but you take effectual steps at once to obtain the full amount, and see that you are never cheated again. Action from principle,—the perception and the performance of right,—changes things and relations; it is essentially revolutionary, and does not consist wholly with any thing which was. It not only divides states and churches, it divides families; aye, it divides the *individual,* separating the diabolical in him from the divine.

Unjust laws exist: shall we be content to obey them, or shall we en-   17
deavor to amend them, and obey them until we have succeeded, or shall we transgress them at once? Men generally, under such a government as this, think that they ought to wait until they have persuaded the majority to alter them. They think that, if they should resist, the remedy would be worse

than the evil. But it is the fault of the government itself that the remedy *is* worse than the evil. *It* makes it worse. Why is it not more apt to anticipate and provide for reform? Why does it not cherish its wise minority? Why does it cry and resist before it is hurt? Why does it not encourage its citizens to be on the alert to point out its faults, and *do* better than it would have them? Why does it always crucify Christ, and excommunicate Copernicus and Luther, and pronounce Washington and Franklin rebels?

One would think, that a deliberate and practical denial of its authority   18
was the only offence never contemplated by government; else, why has it not assigned its definite, its suitable and proportionate penalty? If a man who has no property refuses but once to earn nine shillings for the State, he is put in prison for a period unlimited by any law that I know, and determined only by the discretion of those who placed him there; but if he should steal ninety times nine shillings from the State, he is soon permitted to go at large again.

If the injustice is part of the necessary friction of the machine of gov-   19
ernment, let it go, let it go: perchance it will wear smooth,—certainly the machine will wear out. If the injustice has a spring, or a pulley, or a rope, or a crank, exclusively for itself, then perhaps you may consider whether the remedy will not be worse than the evil; but if it is of such a nature that it requires you to be the agent of injustice to another, then, I say, break the law. Let your life be a counter friction to stop the machine. What I have to do is to see, at any rate, that I do not lend myself to the wrong which I condemn.

As for adopting the ways which the State has provided for remedying   20
the evil, I know not of such ways. They take too much time, and a man's life will be gone. I have other affairs to attend to. I came into this world, not chiefly to make this a good place to live in, but to live in it, be it good or bad. A man has not every thing to do, but something; and because he cannot do *every thing,* it is not necessary that he should do *something* wrong. It is not my business to be petitioning the governor or the legislature any more than it is theirs to petition me; and, if they should not hear my petition, what should I do then? But in this case the State has provided no way: its very Constitution is the evil. This may seem to be harsh and stubborn and unconciliatory; but it is to treat with the utmost kindness and consideration the only spirit that can appreciate or deserves it. So is all change for the better, like birth and death which convulse the body.

I do not hesitate to say, that those who call themselves abolitionists   21
should at once effectually withdraw their support, both in person and property, from the government of Massachusetts, and not wait till they constitute a majority of one, before they suffer the right to prevail through them. I think that it is enough if they have God on their side, without waiting for that other one. Moreover, any man more right than his neighbors, constitutes a majority of one already.

I meet this American government, or its representative the State gov-   22
ernment, directly, and face to face, once a year, no more, in the person of its

tax-gatherer; this is the only mode in which a man situated as I am necessarily meets it; and it then says distinctly, Recognize me; and the simplest, the most effectual, and, in the present posture of affairs, the indispensablest mode of treating with it on this head, of expressing your little satisfaction with and love for it, is to deny it then. My civil neighbor, the tax-gatherer, is the very man I have to deal with,—for it is, after all, with men and not with parchment that I quarrel,—and he has voluntarily chosen to be an agent of the government. How shall he ever know well what he is and does as an officer of the government, or as a man, until he is obliged to consider whether he shall treat me, his neighbor, for whom he has respect, as a neighbor and well-disposed man, or as a maniac and disturber of the peace, and see if he can get over this obstruction to his neighborliness without a ruder and more impetuous thought or speech corresponding with his action? I know this well, that if one thousand, if one hundred, if ten men whom I could name,— if ten *honest* men only,—aye, if *one* HONEST man, in the State of Massachusetts, *ceasing to hold slaves*, were actually to withdraw from this copartnership, and be locked up in the county jail therefor, it would be the abolition of slavery in America. For it matters not how small the beginning may seem to be: what is once well done is done for ever. But we love better to talk about it: that we say is our mission. Reform keeps many scores of newspapers in its service, but not one man. If my esteemed neighbor, the State's ambassador, who will devote his days to the settlement of the question of human rights in the Council Chamber, instead of being threatened with the prisons of Carolina, were to sit down the prisoner of Massachusetts, that State which is so anxious to foist the sin of slavery upon her sister,—though at present she can discover only an act of inhospitality to be the ground of a quarrel with her,—the Legislature would not wholly waive the subject the following winter.

Under a government which imprisons any unjustly, the true place for   23
a just man is also a prison. The proper place to-day, the only place which Massachusetts has provided for her freer and less desponding spirits, is in her prisons, to be put out and locked out of the State by her own act, as they have already put themselves out by their principles. It is there that the fugitive slave, and the Mexican prisoner on parole, and the Indian come to plead the wrongs of his race, should find them; on that separate, but more free and honorable ground, where the State places those who are not *with* her but *against* her,—the only house in a slave-state in which a free man can abide with honor. If any think that their influence would be lost there, and their voices no longer afflict the ear of the State, that they would not be as an enemy within its walls, they do not know by how much truth is stronger than error, nor how much more eloquently and effectively he can combat injustice who has experienced a little in his own person. Cast your whole vote, not a strip of paper merely, but your whole influence. A minority is powerless while it conforms to the majority; it is not even a minority then; but it is irresistible when it clogs by its whole weight. If the alternative is to keep all just men in prison, or give up war and slavery, the State will not

hesitate which to choose. If a thousand men were not to pay their tax-bills this year, that would not be a violent and bloody measure, as it would be to pay them, and enable the State to commit violence and shed innocent blood. This is, in fact, the definition of a peaceable revolution, if any such is possible. If the tax-gatherer, or any other public officer, asks me, as one has done, "But what shall I do?" my answer is, "If you really wish to do any thing, resign your office." When the subject has refused allegiance, and the officer has resigned his office, then the revolution is accomplished. But even suppose blood should flow. Is there not a sort of blood shed when the conscience is wounded? Through this wound a man's real manhood and immortality flow out, and he bleeds to an everlasting death. I see this blood flowing now.

I have contemplated the imprisonment of the offender, rather than the seizure of his goods,—though both will serve the same purpose,—because they who assert the purest right, and consequently are most dangerous to a corrupt State, commonly have not spent much time in accumulating property. To such the State renders comparatively small service, and a slight tax is wont to appear exorbitant, particularly if they are obliged to earn it by special labor with their hands. If there were one who lived wholly without the use of money, the State itself would hesitate to demand it of him. But the rich man—not to make any invidious comparison—is always sold to the institution which makes him rich. Absolutely speaking, the more money, the less virtue; for money comes between a man and his objects, and obtains them for him; and it was certainly no great virtue to obtain it. It puts to rest many questions which he would otherwise be taxed to answer; while the only new question which it puts is the hard but superfluous one, how to spend it. Thus his moral ground is taken from under his feet. The opportunities of living are diminished in proportion as what are called the "means" are increased. The best thing a man can do for his culture when he is rich is to endeavour to carry out those schemes which he entertained when he was poor. Christ answered the Herodians according to their condition. "Show me the tribute-money," said he;—and one took a penny out of his pocket;—If you use money which has the image of Cæsar on it, and which he has made current and valuable, that is, *if you are men of the State,* and gladly enjoy the advantages of Cæsar's government, then pay him back some of his own when he demands it; "Render therefore to Cæsar that which is Cæsar's, and to God those things which are God's,"—leaving them no wiser than before as to which was which; for they did not wish to know.   24

When I converse with the freest of my neighbors, I perceive that, whatever they may say about the magnitude and seriousness of the question, and their regard for the public tranquillity, the long and short of the matter is, that they cannot spare the protection of the existing government, and they dread the consequences of disobedience to it to their property and families. For my own part, I should not like to think that I ever rely on the protection of the State. But, if I deny the authority of the State when it presents its tax-bill, it will soon take and waste all my property, and so harass me and my   25 children without end. This is hard. This makes it impossible for a man to live honestly and at the same time comfortably in outward respects. It will not be worth the while to accumulate property; that would be sure to go again. You must hire or squat somewhere, and raise but a small crop, and eat that soon. You must live within yourself, and depend upon yourself, always tucked up and ready for a start, and not have many affairs. A man may grow rich in Turkey even, if he will be in all respects a good subject of the Turkish government. Confucius said,—"If a State is governed by the principles of reason, poverty and misery are subjects of shame; if a State is not governed by the principles of reason, riches and honors are the subjects of shame." No: until I want the protection of Massachusetts to be extended to me in some distant southern port, where my liberty is endangered, or until I am bent solely on building up an estate at home by peaceful enterprise, I can afford to refuse allegiance to Massachusetts, and her right to my property and life. It costs me less in every sense to incur the penalty of disobedience to the State, than it would to obey. I should feel as if I were worth less in that case.

Some years ago, the State met me in behalf of the church, and commanded me to pay a certain sum toward the support of a clergyman whose preaching my father attended, but never I myself. "Pay it," it said, "or be locked up in the jail." I declined to pay. But, unfortunately, another man saw fit to pay it. I did not see why the schoolmaster should be taxed to support the priest, and not the priest the schoolmaster; for I was not the State's schoolmaster, but I supported myself by voluntary subscription. I did not see why the lyceum should not present its tax-bill, and have the State to back its demand, as well as the church. However, at the request of the selectmen, I condescended to make some such statement as this in writing:— "Know all men by these presents, that I, Henry Thoreau, do not wish to be regarded as a member of an incorporated society which I have not joined." This I gave to the town-clerk; and he has it. The State, having thus learned that I did not wish to be regarded as a member of that church, has never made a like demand on me since; though it said that it must adhere to its original presumption that time. If I had known how to name them, I should then have signed off in detail from all the societies which I never signed on to; but I did not know where to find a complete list. 26

I have paid no poll-tax for six years. I was put into jail once on this account, for one night; and, as I stood considering the walls of solid stone, two or three feet thick, the door of wood and iron, a foot thick, and the iron grating which strained the light, I could not help being struck with the foolishness of that institution which treated me as if I were mere flesh and blood and bones, to be locked up. I wondered that it should have concluded at length that this was the best use it could put me to, and had never thought to avail itself of my services in some way. I saw that, if there was a wall of stone between me and my townsmen, there was a still more difficult one to climb or break through, before they could get to be as free as I was. I did not for a moment feel confined, and the walls seemed a great waste of stone 27 and mortar. I felt as if I alone of all my townsmen had paid my tax. They plainly did not know how to treat me, but behaved like persons who are underbred. In every threat and in every compliment there was a blunder; for they thought that my chief desire was to stand the other side of that stone wall. I could not but smile to see how industriously they locked the door on my meditations, which followed them out again without let or hinderance, and *they* were really all that was dangerous. As they could not reach me, they had resolved to punish my body; just as boys, if they cannot come at some person against whom they have a spite, will abuse his dog. I saw that the State was half-witted, that it was timid as a lone woman with her silver spoons, and that it did not know its friends from its foes, and I lost all my remaining respect for it, and pitied it.

Thus the State never intentionally confronts a man's sense, intellectual   28 or moral, but only his body, his senses. It is not armed with superior wit or honesty, but with superior physical strength. I was not born to be forced. I will breathe after my own fashion. Let us see who is the strongest. What force has a multitude? They only can force me who obey a higher law than I. They force me to become like themselves. I do not hear of *men* being *forced* to live this way or that by masses of men. What sort of life were that to live? When I meet a government which says to me, "Your money or your life," why should I be in haste to give it my money? It may be in a great strait, and not know what to do: I cannot help that. It must help itself; do as I do. It is not worth the while to snivel about it. I am not responsible for the successful working of the machinery of society. I am not the son of the engineer. I perceive that, when an acorn and a chestnut fall side by side, the one does not remain inert to make way for the other, but both obey their own laws, and spring and grow and flourish as best they can, till one, perchance, overshadows and destroys the other. If a plant cannot live according to its nature, it dies; and so a man.

The night in prison was novel and interesting enough. The prisoners in   29 their shirt-sleeves were enjoying a chat and the evening air in the door-way, when I entered. But the jailer said, "Come, boys, it is time to lock up;" and so they dispersed, and I heard the sound of their steps returning into the hollow apartments. My roommate was introduced to me by the jailer, as "a first-rate fellow and a clever man." When the door was locked, he showed me where to hang my hat, and how he managed matters there. The rooms were white-washed once a month; and this one, at least, was the whitest, most simply furnished, and probably the neatest apartment in the town. He naturally wanted to know where I came from, and what brought me there; and, when I had told him, I asked him in my turn how he came there, presuming him to be an honest man, of course; and, as the world goes, I believe he was. "Why," said he, "they accuse me of burning a barn; but I never did it." As near as I could discover, he had probably gone to bed in a barn when drunk, and smoked his pipe there; and so a barn was burnt. He had the reputation of being a clever man, had been there some three months waiting for his trial to come on, and would have to wait as much longer; but he was quite domesticated and con-tented, since he got his board for nothing, and thought that he was well treated.

He occupied one window, and I the other; and I saw, that, if one stayed   30
there long, his principal business would be to look out the window. I had soon
read all the tracts that were left there, and examined where former prisoners
had broken out, and where a grate had been sawed off, and heard the history
of the various occupants of that room; for I found that even here there was a
history and a gossip which never circulated beyond the walls of the jail. Probably this is the only house in the town where verses are composed, which are
afterward printed in a circular form, but not published. I was shown quite a
long list of verses which were composed by some young men who had been
detected in an attempt to escape, who avenged themselves by singing them.

I pumped my fellow-prisoner as dry as I could, for fear I should never   31
see him again; but at length he showed me which was my bed, and left me to
blow out the lamp.

It was like travelling into a far country, such as I had never expected to   32
behold, to lie there for one night. It seemed to me that I never had heard the
town-clock strike before, nor the evening sounds of the village; for we slept
with the windows open, which were inside the grating. It was to see my native
village in the light of the middle ages, and our Concord was turned into a Rhine
stream, and visions of knights and castles passed before me. They were the
voices of old burghers that I heard in the streets. I was an involuntary spectator
and auditor of whatever was done and said in the kitchen of the adjacent village-
inn,—a wholly new and rare experience to me. It was a closer view of my
native town. I was fairly inside of it. I never had seen its institutions before.
This is one of its peculiar institutions; for it is a shire town. I began to comprehend what its inhabitants were about.

In the morning, our breakfasts were put through the hole in the door, in   33
small oblong-square tin pans, made to fit, and holding a pint of chocolate, with
brown bread, and an iron spoon. When they called for the vessels again, I was
green enough to return what bread I had left; but my comrade seized it, and
said that I should lay that up for lunch or dinner. Soon after, he was let out to
work at haying in a neighboring field, whither he went every day, and would
not be back till noon; so he bade me good-day, saying that he doubted if he
should see me again.

When I came out of prison,—for some one interfered, and paid the tax,—   34
I did not perceive that great changes had taken place on the common, such as
he observed who went in a youth, and emerged a tottering and grayheaded
man; and yet a change had to my eyes come over the scene,—the town, and
State, and country,—greater than any that mere time could effect. I saw yet
more distinctly the State in which I lived. I saw to what extent the people
among whom I lived could be trusted as good neighbors and friends; that their
friendship was for summer weather only; that they did not greatly purpose to
do right; that they were a distinct race from me by their prejudices and superstitions, as the Chinamen and Malays are; that, in their sacrifices to humanity,
they ran no risks, not even to their property; that, after all, they were not so
noble but they treated the thief as he had treated them, and hoped, by a certain
outward observance and a few prayers, and by walking in a particular straight
though useless path from time to time, to save their souls. This may be to judge
my neighbors harshly; for I believe that most of them are not aware that they
have such an institution as the jail in their village.

It was formerly the custom in our village, when a poor debtor came out   35
of jail, for his acquaintances to salute him, looking through their fingers, which

were crossed to represent the grating of a jail window. "How do ye do?" My neighbors did not thus salute me, but first looked at me, and then at one another, as if I had returned from a long journey. I was put into jail as I was going to the shoemaker's to get a shoe which was mended. When I was let out the next morning, I proceeded to finish my errand, and having put on my mended shoe, joined a huckleberry party, who were impatient to put themselves under my conduct; and in half an hour,—for the horse was soon tackled,—was in the midst of a huckleberry field, on one of our highest hills, two miles off; and then the State was nowhere to be seen.

This is the whole history of "My Prisons." 3(

I have never declined paying the highway tax, because I am as desirous 37 of being a good neighbor as I am of being a bad subject; and, as for supporting schools, I am doing my part to educate my fellow-countrymen now. It is for no particular item in the tax-bill that I refuse to pay it. I simply wish to refuse allegiance to the State, to withdraw and stand aloof from it effectually. I do not care to trace the course of my dollar, if I could, till it buys a man, or a musket to shoot one with,—the dollar is innocent,—but I am concerned to trace the effects of my allegiance. In fact, I quietly declare war with the State, after my fashion, though I will still make what use and get what advantage of her I can, as is usual in such cases.

If others pay the tax which is demanded of me, from a sympathy with 38 the State, they do but what they have already done in their own case, or rather they abet injustice to a greater extent than the State requires. If they pay the tax from a mistaken interest in the individual taxed, to save his property or prevent his going to jail, it is because they have not considered wisely how far they let their private feelings interfere with the public good.

This, then, is my position at present. But one cannot be too much on 39 his guard in such a case, lest his action be biassed by obstinacy, or an undue regard for the opinions of men. Let him see that he does only what belongs to himself and to the hour.

I think sometimes, Why, this people mean well; they are only ignorant; 40 they would do better if they knew how: why give your neighbors this pain to treat you as they are not inclined to? But I think, again, this is no reason why I should do as they do, or permit others to suffer much greater pain of a different kind. Again, I sometimes say to myself, When many millions of men, without heat, without ill-will, without personal feeling of any kind, demand of you a few shillings only, without the possibility, such is their constitution, of retracting or altering their present demand, and without the possibility, on your side, of appeal to any other millions, why expose yourself to this overwhelming brute force? You do not resist cold and hunger, the winds and the waves, thus obstinately; you quietly submit to a thousand similar necessities. You do not put your head into the fire. But just in proportion as I regard this as not wholly a brute force, but partly a human force, and consider that I have relations to those millions as to so many millions of men, and not of mere brute or inanimate things, I see that appeal is possible, first and instantaneously, from them to the Maker of them, and, secondly, from them to themselves. But, if I put my head deliberately into the fire, there is no appeal to fire or to the Maker of fire, and I have only myself to blame. If I could convince myself that I have any right to be satisfied with men as they are, and to treat them accordingly, and not according, in some respects, to my requisitions and expectations of what they and I ought to be, then, like a good Mussulman and fatalist, I should endeavor to be satisfied with things as they are, and say it is the will of God. And, above all, there is this difference between resisting this and a purely brute or natural force, that I can resist this with some effect, but I cannot expect, like Orpheus, to change the nature of the rocks and trees and beasts.

I do not wish to quarrel with any man or nation. I do not wish to split   41
hairs, to make fine distinctions, or set myself up as better than my neighbors. I seek rather, I may say, even an excuse for conforming to the laws of the land. I am but too ready to conform to them. Indeed I have reason to suspect myself on this head; and each year, as the tax-gatherer comes round, I find myself disposed to review the acts and position of the general and state governments, and the spirit of the people, to discover a pretext for conformity. I believe that the State will soon be able to take all my work of this sort out of my hands, and then I shall be no better a patriot than my fellow-countrymen. Seen from a lower point of view, the Constitution, with all its faults, is very good; the law and the courts are very respectable; even this State and this American government are, in many respects, very admirable and rare things, to be thankful for, such as a great many have described them; but seen from a point of view a little higher, they are what I have described them; seen from a higher still, and the highest, who shall say what they are, or that they are worth looking at or thinking of at all?

However, the government does not concern me much, and I shall be-   42
stow the fewest possible thoughts on it. It is not many moments that I live under a government, even in this world. If a man is thought-free, fancy-free, imagination-free, that which is *not* never for a long time appearing *to be* to him, unwise rulers or reformers cannot fatally interrupt him.

I know that most men think differently from myself; but those whose   43
lives are by profession devoted to the study of these or kindred subjects, content me as little as any. Statesmen and legislators, standing so completely within the institution, never distinctly and nakedly behold it. They speak of moving society; but have no resting-place without it. They may be men of a certain experience and discrimination, and have no doubt invented ingenious and even useful systems, for which we sincerely thank them; but all their wit and usefulness lie within certain not very wide limits. They are wont to forget that the world is not governed by policy and expediency. Webster never goes behind government, and so cannot speak with authority about it. His words are wisdom to those legislators who contemplate no essential reform in the existing government; but for thinkers, and those who legislate for all time, he never once glances at the subject. I know of those whose serene and wise speculations on this theme would soon reveal the limits of his mind's range and hospitality. Yet, compared with the cheap

professions of most reformers, and the still cheaper wisdom and eloquence of politicians in general, his are almost the only sensible and valuable words, and we thank Heaven for him. Comparatively, he is always strong, original, and, above all, practical. Still his quality is not wisdom, but prudence. The lawyer's truth is not Truth, but consistency, or a consistent expediency. Truth is always in harmony with herself, and is not concerned chiefly to reveal the justice that may consist with wrong-doing. He well deserves to be called, as he has been called, the Defender of the Constitution. There are really no blows to be given by him but defensive ones. He is not a leader, but a follower. His leaders are the men of '87. "I have never made an effort," he says, "and never propose to make an effort; I have never countenanced an effort, and never mean to countenance an effort, to disturb the arrangement as originally made, by which the various States came into the Union." Still thinking of the sanction which the Constitution gives to slavery, he says, "Because it was a part of the original compact,—let it stand." Notwithstanding his special acuteness and ability, he is unable to take a fact out of its merely political relations, and behold it as it lies absolutely to be disposed of by the intellect,—what, for instance, it behoves a man to do here in America to-day with regard to slavery,—but ventures, or is driven, to make some such desperate answer as the following, while professing to speak absolutely, and as a private man,—from which what new and singular code of social duties might be inferred?—"The manner," says he, "in which the governments of those States where slavery exists are to regulate it, is for their own consideration, under their responsibility to their constituents, to the general laws of propriety, humanity, and justice, and to God. Associations formed elsewhere, springing from a feeling of humanity, or any other cause, have nothing whatever to do with it. They have never received any encouragement from me, and they never will."

They who know of no purer sources of truth, who have traced up its   44
stream no higher, stand, and wisely stand, by the Bible and the Constitution, and drink at it there with reverence and humility; but they who behold where it comes trickling into this lake or that pool, gird up their loins once more, and continue their pilgrimage toward its fountain-head.

No man with a genius for legislation has appeared in America. They   45
are rare in the history of the world. There are orators, politicians, and eloquent men, by the thousand; but the speaker has not yet opened his mouth to speak, who is capable of settling the much-vexed questions of the day. We love eloquence for its own sake, and not for any truth which it may utter, or any heroism it may inspire. Our legislators have not yet learned the comparative value of free-trade and of freedom, of union, and of rectitude, to a nation. They have no genius or talent for comparatively humble questions of taxation and finance, commerce and manufactures and agriculture. If we were left solely to the wordy wit of legislators in Congress for our guidance, uncorrected by the seasonable experience and the effectual complaints of the people, America would not long retain her rank among the nations. For eighteen hundred years, though perchance I have no right to say it, the

New Testament has been written, yet where is the legislator who has wisdom and practical talent enough to avail himself of the light which it sheds on the science of legislation?

The authority of government, even such as I am willing to submit to,— for I will cheerfully obey those who know and can do better than I, and in many things even those who neither know nor can do so well,—is still an impure one: to be strictly just, it must have the sanction and consent of the governed. It can have no pure right over my person and property but what I concede to it. The progress from an absolute to a limited monarchy, from a limited monarchy to a democracy, is a progress toward a true respect for the individual. Is a democracy, such as we know it, the last improvement possible in government? Is it not possible to take a step further towards recognizing and organizing the rights of man? There will never be a really free and enlightened State, until the State comes to recognize the individual as a higher and independent power, from which all its own power and authority are derived, and treats him accordingly. I please myself with imagining a State at last which can afford to be just to all men, and to treat the individual with respect as a neighbor; which even would not think it inconsistent with its own repose, if a few were to live aloof from it, not meddling with it, nor embraced by it, who fulfilled all the duties of neighbors and fellow-men. A State which bore this kind of fruit, and suffered it to drop off as fast as it ripened, would prepare the way for a still more perfect and glorious State, which also I have imagined, but not yet anywhere seen.

46

QUESTIONS FOR MEANING

1. What is the only obligation that Thoreau recognizes?
2. What is Thoreau's opinion of the average man and woman?
3. Why is Thoreau unwilling to vote?
4. Under what circumstances did Thoreau believe that it was right to break the law? How can prison be "the true place for a just man"? Why was Thoreau imprisoned?
5. What does Thoreau mean when he declares, "the more money, the less virtue"? Why was he critical of the rich?
6. Would Thoreau approve of Social Security?
8. Vocabulary: endeavoring (2), expediency (4), redressing (9), gregariousness (13), eradication (14), discretion (18), impetuous (22), exorbitant (24), snivel (28), fatalist (40), sanction (43).

QUESTIONS ABOUT STRATEGY

1. Consider the opening of paragraph 3. What advantage is there for Thoreau to declare that he intends to speak "practically and as a citizen"? Where else does he try to put himself in a favorable light? Does he ever put himself in a bad light?

2. Where does Thoreau first reveal his concern about slavery? Should he have said more about this issue?

3. Why do you think Thoreau chose to "quarrel not with far-off foes, but with those who, near at home, co-operate with, and do the bidding of those far away"?

4. Could Thoreau's argument be used for selfish purposes?

5. How does Thoreau respond to the argument that revolution often involves bloodshed? Where does he anticipate and respond to the argument that he enjoys the protection of the state he is unwilling to support?

6. What are the implications of the analogy Thoreau draws in paragraph 28 between the life of a man and the life of a plant?

7. What is the function of the eight-paragraph-long narration of Thoreau's one night in jail? What is it meant to illustrate? Does it reveal anything about Thoreau that he may not have intended to reveal?

8. This essay has been often reprinted as "Civil Disobedience." Which is the better title?

JOHN HENRY NEWMAN
Knowledge as Its Own End

One of the most influential religious thinkers of the nineteenth century, John Henry Newman (1801–1890) attended Trinity College, Oxford, before becoming a Fellow of Oriel College in 1822. In 1824 he became a minister in the Church of England, and four years later he became vicar of St. Mary's Church in Oxford where his sermons drew a large audience. During the second half of the 1830s, he was one of the principal figures of "The Oxford Movement," a movement which began as a protest against the right of the British government to regulate the Anglican Church and which became increasingly controversial as the decade progressed. Newman published the "Tracts for the Times," a series of arguments through which the movement sought to advance its views. The most controversial of these tracts was number 90 (1841) which argued that the doctrines of the Church of England were compatible with Roman Catholicism on almost all points. Newman gave his last sermon as an Anglican in 1843; two years later, he converted to Catholicism—a decision for which he was much criticized in England. In 1847 he became a Catholic priest. Upon the petition of Catholic laymen, he was made a Cardinal by Pope Leo XIII in 1879.

Newman's greatest influence has been through his writing. His most important works include Apologia pro Vita Sua *(1864),* An Essay in Aid of a Grammar of Assent *(1870), and* The Idea of a University *(1873), from which the following selection is taken. It originated in a series of lectures Newman gave in 1852 in Dublin, where he was instrumental in founding the Catholic University of Ireland.*

Things, which can bear to be cut off from everything else and yet persist in   1
living, must have life in themselves; pursuits, which issue in nothing, and
still maintain their ground for ages, which are regarded as admirable, though
they have not as yet proved themselves to be useful, must have their sufficient end in themselves, whatever it turn out to be. And we are brought to
the same conclusion by considering the force of the epithet, by which the
knowledge under consideration is popularly designated. It is common to speak
of *"liberal* knowledge," of the *"liberal* arts and studies," and of a *"liberal*
education," as the especial characteristic or property of a University and of a
gentleman; what is really meant by the word? Now, first, in its grammatical
sense it is opposed to *servile;* and by "servile work" is understood, as our
catechisms inform us, bodily labour, mechanical employment, and the like,
in which the mind has little or no part. Parallel to such servile works are
those arts, if they deserve the name, of which the poet speaks, which owe
their origin and their method to hazard, not to skill; as, for instance, the
practice and operations of an empire. As far as this contrast may be considered as a guide into the meaning of the word, liberal education and liberal
pursuits are exercises of mind, of reason, of reflection.

But we want something more for its explanation, for there are bodily   2
exercises which are liberal, and mental exercises which are not so. For instance, in ancient times the practitioners in medicine were commonly slaves;
yet it was an art as intellectual in its nature, in spite of the pretence, fraud
and quackery with which it might then, as now, be debased, as it was heavenly in its aim. And so in like manner, we contrast a liberal education with
a commercial education or a professional; yet no one can deny that commerce
and the professions afford scope for the highest and most diversified powers
of mind. There is then a great variety of intellectual exercises, which are not
technically called "liberal"; on the other hand, I say, there are exercises of
the body which do receive that appellation. Such, for instance, was the palæstra,
in ancient times; such the Olympic games, in which strength and dexterity
of body as well as of mind gained the prize. In Xenophon we read of the
young Persian nobility being taught to ride on horseback and to speak the
truth; both being among the accomplishments of a gentleman. War, too,
however rough a profession, has ever been accounted liberal, unless in cases
when it becomes heroic, which would introduce us to another subject.

Now comparing these instances together, we shall have no difficulty in   3
determining the principle of this apparent variation in the application of the
term which I am examining. Manly games, or games of skill, or military
prowess, though bodily, are, it seems, accounted liberal; on the other hand,
what is merely professional, though highly intellectual, nay, though liberal
in comparison of trade and manual labour, is not simply called liberal, and
mercantile occupations are not liberal at all. Why this distinction? because
that alone is liberal knowledge, which stands on its own pretensions, which
is independent of sequel, expects no complement, refuses to be *informed* (as it
is called) by any end, or absorbed into any art, in order duly to present itself

to our contemplation. The most ordinary pursuits have this specific character, if they are self-sufficient and complete; the highest lose it, when they minister to something beyond them. It is absurd to balance, in point of worth and importance, a treatise on reducing fractures with a game of cricket or a fox-chase; yet of the two the bodily exercise has that quality which we call "liberal," and the intellectual has not. And so of the learned professions altogether, considered merely as professions; although one of them be the most popularly beneficial, and another the most politically important, and the third the most intimately divine of all human pursuits, yet the very greatness of their end, the health of the body, or of the commonwealth, or of the soul, diminishes, not increases, their claim to the appellation "liberal," and that still more, if they are cut down to the strict exigencies of that end. If, for instance, Theology instead of being cultivated as a contemplation, be limited to the purposes of the pulpit or be represented by the catechism, it loses—not its usefulness, not its divine character, not its meritoriousness, (rather it gains a claim upon these titles by such charitable condescension),—but it does lose the particular attribute which I am illustrating; just as a face worn by tears and fasting loses its beauty, or a labourer's hand loses its delicateness;—for Theology thus exercised is not simple knowledge, but rather is an art or a business making use of Theology. And thus it appears that even what is supernatural need not be liberal, nor need a hero be a gentleman, for the plain reason that one idea is not another idea. And in like manner the Baconian Philosophy, by using its physical sciences in the service of man, does thereby transfer them from the order of Liberal Pursuits to, I do not say the inferior, but the distinct class of the Useful. And, to take a different instance, hence again, as is evident, whenever personal gain is the motive, still more distinctive an effect has it upon the character of a given pursuit; thus racing, which was a liberal exercise in Greece, forfeits its rank in times like these, so far as it is made the occasion of gambling.

All that I have been now saying is summed up in a few characteristic   4
words of the great Philosopher [Aristotle]. "Of possessions," he says, "those rather are useful, which bear fruit; those *liberal, which tend to enjoyment.* By fruitful, I mean, which yield revenue; by enjoyable, where *nothing accrues of consequence beyond the using.*"

QUESTIONS FOR MEANING

1. How does Newman define the liberal arts? Why is it that the study of medicine, law, or engineering is not "liberal" in Newman's sense of the term?
2. Who was Xenophon? If you've never heard of him, what can you conclude about him from the context in which he is mentioned (paragraph 2)? How could you learn more about him?
3. Does Newman believe that liberal knowledge is superior to other forms of knowledge?
4. What does Newman mean by "Baconian Philosophy" in paragraph 3?

5. Vocabulary: epithet (1), servile (1), empiric (1), dexterity (2), treatise (3), exigencies (3), accrues (4).

QUESTIONS ABOUT STRATEGY

1. How would you describe Newman's sentence structure? Is his style appropriate for his topic?
2. Like many other nineteenth-century prose writers, Newman tended to write long paragraphs. Could any of the paragraphs in this selection be broken up?
3. Consider the analogy that Newman makes in paragraph 3 between a "business making use of Theology" and a face "worn by tears and fasting" that has lost its beauty or "a labourer's hand" that has lost its "delicateness." What do these lines reveal about Newman's values?

MARK TWAIN
Fenimore Cooper's Literary Offenses

Mark Twain is the name Samuel Clemens (1835–1910) assumed in 1863 at the beginning of what would be a long, successful career as a writer. Once called "the Lincoln of our literature," he has remained one of the most widely read of major American writers—admired for his distinctive humor and also for the skill with which he captured the varied forms of American dialect. His best known works include The Adventures of Tom Sawyer *(1876),* The Prince and the Pauper *(1877),* Life on the Mississippi *(1883),* The Adventures of Huckleberry Finn *(1885), and* A Connecticut Yankee in King Arthur's Court *(1889).*

In addition to his achievement as a writer of fiction, Twain is also valued for the penetrating social and literary criticism that can be found in his many essays. "Fenimore Cooper's Literary Offenses," written in **1895,** *is one of two essays Twain wrote to explain why he objected to James Fenimore Cooper (1789–1851)—an important American novelist whose reputation has never altogether recovered from Twain's charges. But you should try to read the following essay as an argument on how fiction should be written and not simply as an attack on Cooper.*

The Pathfinder *and* The Deerslayer stand at the head of Cooper's novels as artistic creations. There are others of his works which contain parts as perfect as are to be found in these, and scenes even more thrilling. Not one can be compared with either of them as a finished whole.

The defects in both of these tales are comparatively slight. They were pure works of art.—*Prof Lounsbury.*

The five tales reveal an extraordinary fulness of invention.
. . . One of the very greatest characters in fiction, Natty Bumppo. . . .
The craft of the woodsman, the tricks of the trapper, all the delicate art of the forest, were familiar to Cooper from his youth up.—*Prof. Brander Matthews.*

Cooper is the greatest artist in the domain of romantic fiction yet produced by America.—*Wilkie Collins.*

It seems to me that it was far from right for the Professor of English Literature in Yale, the Professor of English Literature in Columbia, and Wilkie Collins to deliver opinions on Cooper's literature without having read some of it. It would have been much more decorous to keep silent and let persons talk who have read Cooper.   1

Cooper's art has some defects. In one place in *Deerslayer,* and in the restricted space of two-thirds of a page, Cooper has scored 114 offenses against literary art out of a possible 115. It breaks the record.   2

There are nineteen rules governing literary art in the domain of romantic fiction—some say twenty-two. In *Deerslayer* Cooper violated eighteen of them. These eighteen require: 3

1. That a tale shall accomplish something and arrive somewhere. But the *Deerslayer* tale accomplishes nothing and arrives in the air.
2. They require that the episodes of a tale shall be necessary parts of the tale, and shall help to develop it. But as the *Deerslayer* tale is not a tale, and accomplishes nothing and arrives nowhere, the episodes have no rightful place in the work, since there was nothing for them to develop.
3. They require that the personages in a tale shall be alive, except in the cases of corpses, and that always the reader shall be able to tell the corpses from the others. But this detail has often been overlooked in the *Deerslayer* tale.
4. They require that the personages in a tale, both dead and alive, shall exhibit a sufficient excuse for being there. But this detail also has been overlooked in the *Deerslayer* tale.
5. They require that when the personages of a tale deal in conversation, the talk shall sound like human talk, and be talk such as human beings would be likely to talk in the given circumstances, and have a discoverable meaning, also a discoverable purpose, and a show of relevancy, and remain in the neighborhood of the subject in hand, and be interesting to the reader, and help out the tale, and stop when the people cannot think of anything more to say. But this requirement has been ignored from the beginning of the *Deerslayer* tale to the end of it.
6. They require that when the author describes the character of a personage in his tale, the conduct and conversation of that personage

shall justify said description. But this law gets little or no attention in the *Deerslayer* tale, as Natty Bumppo's case will amply prove.

7. They require that when a personage talks like an illustrated, gilt-edged, tree-calf, hand-tooled, seven-dollar Friendship's Offering in the beginning of a paragraph, he shall not talk like a negro minstrel in the end of it. But this rule is flung down and danced upon in the *Deerslayer* tale.

8. They require that crass stupidities shall not be played upon the reader as "the craft of the woodsman, the delicate art of the forest," by either the author or the people in the tale. But this rule is persistently violated in the *Deerslayer* tale.

9. They require that the personages of a tale shall confine themselves to possibilities and let miracles alone; or, if they venture a miracle, the author must so plausibly set it forth as to make it look possible and reasonable. But these rules are not respected in the *Deerslayer* tale.

10. They require that the author shall make the reader feel a deep interest in the personages of his tale and in their fate; and that he shall make the reader love the good people in the tale and hate the bad ones. But the reader of the *Deerslayer* tale dislikes the good people in it, is indifferent to the others, and wishes they would all get drowned together.

11. They require that the characters in a tale shall be so clearly defined that the reader can tell beforehand what each will do in a given emergency. But in the *Deerslayer* tale this rule is vacated.

In addition to these large rules there are some little ones. These require that the author shall

12. *Say* what he is proposing to say, not merely come near it.
13. Use the right word, not its second cousin.
14. Eschew surplusage.
15. Not omit necessary details.
16. Avoid slovenliness of form.
17. Use good grammar.
18. Employ a simple and straightforward style.

Even these seven are coldly and persistently violated in the *Deerslayer* tale.

Cooper's gift in the way of invention was not a rich endowment; but such as it was he liked to work it, he was pleased with the effects, and indeed he did some quite sweet things with it. In his little box of stage-properties he kept six or eight cunning devices, tricks, artifices for his savages and woodsmen to deceive and circumvent each other with, and he was never so happy as when he was working these innocent things and seeing them go. A favorite one was to make a moccasined person tread in the tracks of the moccasined enemy, and thus hide his own trail. Cooper wore out barrels and barrels of moccasins in working that trick. Another stage-property that he pulled out of his box pretty frequently was his broken twig. He prized his broken twig above all the rest of his effects, and worked it the hardest. It is a restful chapter in any book of his when somebody doesn't step on a dry twig and alarm all the reds and whites for two hundred yards around. Every time a Cooper person is in peril, and absolute silence is worth four dollars a minute, he is sure to step on a dry twig. There may be a hundred handier things to step on, but that wouldn't satisfy Cooper. Cooper requires him to turn out and find a dry twig; and if he can't do it, go and borrow one. In fact, the Leather Stocking Series ought to have been called the Broken Twig Series.

I am sorry there is not room to put in a few dozen instances of the   5
delicate art of the forest, as practiced by Natty Bumppo and some of the other Cooperian experts. Perhaps we may venture two or three samples. Cooper was a sailor—a naval officer; yet he gravely tells us how a vessel, driving toward a lee shore in a gale, is steered for a particular spot by her skipper because he knows of an *undertow* there which will hold her back against the gale and save her. For just pure woodcraft, or sailorcraft, or whatever it is, isn't that neat? For several years Cooper was daily in the society of artillery, and he ought to have noticed that when a cannon-ball strikes the ground it either buries itself or skips a hundred feet or so; skips again a hundred feet or so—and so on, till finally it gets tired and rolls. Now in one place he loses some "females"—as he always calls women—in the edge of a wood near a plain at night in a fog, on purpose to give Bumppo a chance to show off the delicate art of the forest before the reader. These mislaid people are hunting for a fort. They hear a cannon-blast, and a cannon-ball presently comes rolling into the wood and stops at their feet. To the females this suggests nothing. The case is very different with the admirable Bumppo. I wish I may never know peace again if he doesn't strike out promptly and *follow the track* of that cannon-ball across the plain through the dense fog and find the fort. Isn't it a daisy? If Cooper had any real knowledge of Nature's ways of doing things, he had a most delicate art in concealing the fact. For instance: one of his acute Indian experts, Chingachgook (pronounced Chicago, I think), has lost the trail of a person he is tracking through the forest. Apparently that trail is hopelessly lost. Neither you nor I could have guessed out the way to find it. It was very different with Chicago. Chicago was not stumped for long. He turned a running stream out of its course, and there, in the slush in its old bed, were that person's moccasin-tracks. The current did not wash them away, as it would have done in all other cases—no, even the eternal laws of Nature have to vacate when Cooper wants to put up a delicate job of woodcraft on the reader.

We must be a little wary when Brander Matthews tells us that Cooper's   6
books "reveal an extraordinary fulness of invention." As a rule, I am quite willing to accept Brander Matthews's literary judgments and applaud his lucid and graceful phrasing of them; but that particular statement needs to be taken with a few tons of salt. Bless your heart, Cooper hadn't any more

invention than a horse; and I don't mean a high-class horse, either; I mean a clothes-horse. It would be very difficult to find a really clever "situation" in Cooper's books, and still more difficult to find one of any kind which he has failed to render absurd by his handling of it. Look at the episodes of "the caves"; and at the celebrated scuffle between Maqua and those others on the table-land a few days later; and at Hurry Harry's queer water-transit from the castle to the ark; and at Deerslayer's half-hour with his first corpse; and at the quarrel between Hurry Harry and Deerslayer later; and at—but choose for yourself; you can't go amiss.

If Cooper had been an observer his inventive faculty would have worked   7
better; not more interestingly, but more rationally, more plausibly. Cooper's proudest creations in the way of "situations" suffer noticeably from the absence of the observer's protecting gift. Cooper's eye was splendidly inaccurate. Cooper seldom saw anything correctly. He saw nearly all things as through a glass eye, darkly. Of course a man who cannot see the commonest little every-day matters accurately is working at a disadvantage when he is constructing a "situation." In the *Deerslayer* tale Cooper has a stream which is fifty feet wide where it flows out of a lake; it presently narrows to twenty as it meanders along for no given reason, and yet when a stream acts like that it ought to be required to explain itself. Fourteen pages later the width of the brook's outlet from the lake has suddenly shrunk thirty feet, and become "the narrowest part of the stream." This shrinkage is not accounted for. The stream has bends in it, a sure indication that it has alluvial banks and cuts them; yet these bends are only thirty and fifty feet long. If Cooper had been a nice and punctilious observer he would have noticed that the bends were oftener nine hundred feet long than short of it.

Cooper made the exit of that stream fifty feet wide, in the first place,   8
for no particular reason; in the second place, he narrowed it to less than twenty to accommodate some Indians. He bends a "sapling" to the form of an arch over this narrow passage, and conceals six Indians in its foliage. They are "laying" for a settler's scow or ark which is coming up the stream on its way to the lake; it is being hauled against the stiff current by a rope whose stationary end is anchored in the lake; its rate of progress cannot be more than a mile an hour. Cooper describes the ark, but pretty obscurely. In the matter of dimensions "it was little more than a modern canal-boat." Let us guess, then, that it was about one hundred and forty feet long. It was of "greater breadth than common." Let us guess, then, that it was about sixteen feet wide. This leviathan had been prowling down bends which were but a third as long as itself, and scraping between banks where it had only two feet of space to spare on each side. We cannot too much admire this miracle. A low-roofed log dwelling occupies "two-thirds of the ark's length"—a dwelling ninety feet long and sixteen feet wide, let us say—a kind of vestibule train. The dwelling has two rooms—each forty-five feet long and sixteen feet wide, let us guess. One of them is the bedroom of the Hutter girls, Judith and Hetty; the other is the parlor in the daytime, at night it is papa's bedchamber. The ark is arriving at the stream's exit now, whose width has been

reduced to less than twenty feet to accommodate the Indians—say to eighteen. There is a foot to spare on each side of the boat. Did the Indians notice that there was going to be a tight squeeze there? Did they notice that they could make money by climbing down out of that arched sapling and just stepping aboard when the ark scraped by? No, other Indians would have noticed these things, but Cooper's Indians never notice anything. Cooper thinks they are marvelous creatures for noticing, but he was almost always in error about his Indians. There was seldom a sane one among them.

The ark is one hundred and forty feet long; the dwelling is ninety feet long. The idea of the Indians is to drop softly and secretly from the arched sapling to the dwelling as the ark creeps along under it at the rate of a mile an hour, and butcher the family. It will take the ark a minute and a half to pass under. It will take the ninety-foot dwelling a minute to pass under. Now, then, what did the six Indians do? It would take you thirty years to guess, and even then you would have to give it up, I believe. Therefore, I will tell you what the Indians did. Their chief, a person of quite extraordinary intellect for a Cooper Indian, warily watched the canal-boat as it squeezed along under him, and when he had got his calculations fined down to exactly the right shade, as he judged, he let go and dropped. And *missed the house!* That is actually what he did. He missed the house, and landed in the stern of the scow. It was not much of a fall, yet it knocked him silly. He lay there unconscious. If the house had been ninety-seven feet long he would have made the trip. The fault was Cooper's, not his. The error lay in the construction of the house. Cooper was no architect.   9

There still remained in the roost five Indians. The boat has passed under and is now out of their reach. Let me explain what the five did—you would not be able to reason it out for yourself. No. 1 jumped for the boat, but fell in the water astern of it. Then No. 2 jumped for the boat, but fell in the water still farther astern of it. Then No. 3 jumped for the boat, and fell a good way astern of it. Then No. 4 jumped for the boat, and fell in the water *away* astern. Then even No. 5 made a jump for the boat—for he was a Cooper Indian. In the matter of intellect, the difference between a Cooper Indian and the Indian that stands in front of the cigarshop is not spacious. The scow episode is really a sublime burst of invention; but it does not thrill, because the inaccuracy of the detail throws a sort of air of fictitiousness and general improbability over it. This comes of Cooper's inadequacy as an observer.   10

The reader will find some examples of Cooper's high talent for inaccurate observation in the account of the shooting-match in *The Pathfinder*.   11

> A common wrought nail was driven lightly into the target, its head having been first touched with paint.

The color of the paint is not stated—an important omission, but Cooper deals freely in important omissions. No, after all, it was not an important omission; for this nailhead is *a hundred yards from* the marksmen, and could not be seen by them at that distance, no matter what its color might be.   12

How far can the best eyes see a common house-fly? A hundred yards? It is quite impossible. Very well; eyes that cannot see a house-fly that is a hundred yards away cannot see an ordinary nail head at that distance, for the size of the two objects is the same. It takes a keen eye to see a fly or a nail-head at fifty yards—one hundred and fifty feet. Can the reader do it?

The nail was lightly driven, its head painted, and game called. Then the   13
Cooper miracles begin. The bullet of the first marksman chipped an edge of the nail-head; the next man's bullet drove the nail a little way into the target—and removed all the paint. Haven't the miracles gone far enough now? Not to suit Cooper; for the purpose of this whole scheme is to show off his prodigy, Deerslayer-Hawkeye-Long-Rifle-Leather-Stocking-Pathfinder-Bumppo before the ladies.

> "Be all ready to clench it, boys!" cried out Pathfinder, stepping into his friend's tracks the instant they were vacant. "Never mind a new nail; I can see that, though the paint is gone, and what I can see I can hit at a hundred yards, though it were only a mosquito's eye. Be ready to clench!"
> The rifle cracked, the bullet sped its way, and the head of the nail was buried in the wood, covered by the piece of flattened lead.

There, you see, is a man who could hunt flies with a rifle, and com-   14
mand a ducal salary in a Wild West show today if we had him back with us.

The recorded feat is certainly surprising just as it stands; but it is not   15
surprising enough for Cooper. Cooper adds a touch. He has made Pathfinder do this miracle with another man's rifle; and not only that, but Pathfinder did not have even the advantage of loading it himself. He had everything against him, and yet he made that impossible shot; and not only made it, but did it with absolute confidence, saying, "Be ready to clench." Now a person like that would have undertaken that same feat with a brick-bat, and with Cooper to help he would have achieved it, too.

Pathfinder showed off handsomely that day before the ladies. His very   16
first feat was a thing which no Wild West show can touch. He was standing with the group of marksmen, observing—a hundred yards from the target, mind; one Jasper raised his rifle and drove the center off the bull's-eye. Then the Quartermaster fired. The target exhibited no result this time. There was a laugh. "It's a dead miss," said Major Lundie. Pathfinder waited an impressive moment or two; then said, in that calm, indifferent, know-it-all way of his, "No, Major, he has covered Jasper's bullet, as will be seen if anyone will take the trouble to examine the target."

Wasn't it remarkable! How *could* he see that little pellet fly through the   17
air and enter that distant bullet-hole? Yet that is what he did; for nothing is impossible to a Cooper person. Did any of those people have any deep-seated doubts about this thing? No; for that would imply sanity, and these were all Cooper people.

> The respect for Pathfinder's skill and for his *quickness and accuracy of sight*
> [the italics are mine] was so profound and general, that the instant he made this

declaration the spectators began to distrust their own opinions, and a dozen rushed to the target in order to ascertain the fact. There, sure enough, it was found that the Quartermaster's bullet had gone through the hole made by Jasper's, and that, too, so accurately as to require a minute examination to be certain of the circumstance, which, however, was soon clearly established by discovering one bullet over the other in the stump against which the target was placed.

They made a "minute" examination; but never mind, how could they 18 know that there were two bullets in that hole without digging the latest one out? for neither probe nor eyesight could prove the presence of any more than one bullet. Did they dig? No; as we shall see. It is the Pathfinder's turn now; he steps out before the ladies, takes aim, and fires.

But, alas! here is a disappointment; an incredible, an unimaginable dis- 19 appointment—for the target's aspect is unchanged; there is nothing there but that same old bullet-hole!

> "If one dared to hint at such a thing," cried Major Duncan, "I should say that the Pathfinder has also missed the target!"

As nobody had missed it yet, the "also" was not necessary; but never 20 mind about that, for the Pathfinder is going to speak.

> "No, no, Major," said he, confidently, "that *would* be a risky declaration. I didn't load the piece, and can't say what was in it; but if it was lead, you will find the bullet driving down those of the Quartermaster and Jasper, else is not my name Pathfinder."
> A shout from the target announced the truth of this assertion.

Is the miracle sufficient as it stands? Not for Cooper. The Pathfinder 21 speaks again, as he "now slowly advances towards the stage occupied by the females":

> "That's not all, boys, that's not all; if you find the target touched at all, I'll own to a miss. The Quartermaster cut the wood, but you'll find no wood cut by that last messenger."

The miracle is at last complete. He knew—doubtless *saw*—at the dis- 22 tance of a hundred yards—that his bullet had passed into the hole *without fraying the edges*. There were now three bullets in that one hole—three bullets embedded processionally in the body of the stump back of the target. Everybody knew this—somehow or other—and yet nobody had dug any of them out to make sure. Cooper is not a close observer, but he is interesting. He is certainly always that, no matter what happens. And he is more interesting when he is not noticing what he is about than when he is. This is a considerable merit.

The conversations in the Cooper books have a curious sound in our   23
modern ears. To believe that such talk really ever came out of people's mouths
would be to believe that there was a time when time was of no value to a
person who thought he had something to say; when it was the custom to
spread a two-minute remark out to ten; when a man's mouth was a rolling-
mill, and busied itself all day long in turning four-foot pigs of thought into
thirty-foot bars of conversational railroad iron by attenuation; when subjects
were seldom faithfully stuck to, but the talk wandered all around and arrived
nowhere; when conversations consisted mainly of irrelevancies, with here
and there a relevancy, a relevancy with an embarrassed look, as not being
able to explain how it got there.

Cooper was certainly not a master in the construction of dialogue. In-   24
accurate observation defeated him here as it defeated him in so many other
enterprises of his. He even failed to notice that the man who talks corrupt
English six days in the week must and will talk it on the seventh, and can't
help himself. In the *Deerslayer* story he lets Deerslayer talk the showiest kind
of book-talk sometimes, and at other times the basest of base dialects. For
instance, when someone asks him if he has a sweetheart, and if so, where she
abides, this is his majestic answer:

> "She's in the forest—hanging from the boughs of the trees, in a soft
> rain—in the dew on the open grass—the clouds that float about in the blue
> heavens—the birds that sing in the woods—the sweet springs where I slake my
> thirst—and in all the other glorious gifts that come from God's Providence!"

And he preceded that, a little before, with this: 25

> "It consarns me as all things that touches a fri'nd consarns a fri'nd."

And this is another of his remarks: 26

> "If I was Injin born, now, I might tell of this, or carry in the scalp and
> boast of the expl'ite afore the whole tribe; or if my inimy had only been a bear"

—and so on.

We cannot imagine such a thing as a veteran Scotch Commander-in-   27
Chief comporting himself in the field like a windy melodramatic actor, but
Cooper could. On one occasion Alice and Cora were being chased by the
French through a fog in the neighborhood of their father's fort:

> "*Point de quartier aux coquins!*" cried an eager pursuer, who seemed to
> direct the operations of the enemy.
> "Stand firm and be ready. my gallant 60ths!" suddenly exclaimed a voice
> above them; "wait to see the enemy; fire low, and sweep the glacis."
> "Father! father!" exclaimed a piercing cry from out the mist; "it is I!
> Alice! thy own Elsie! spare, O! save your daughters!"

"Hold!" shouted the former speaker, in the awful tones of parental agony, the sound reaching even to the woods, and rolling back in solemn echo.
" 'Tis she! God has restored me my children! Throw open the sally-port; to the
field, 60ths, to the field! pull not a trigger, lest ye kill my lambs! Drive off
these dogs of France with your steel!"

Cooper's word-sense was singularly dull. When a person has a poor ear   28
for music he will flat and sharp right along without knowing it. He keeps
near the tune, but it is *not* the tune. When a person has a poor ear for words,
the result is a literary flatting and sharping; you perceive what he is intending
to say, but you also perceive that he doesn't *say* it. This is Cooper. He was
not a word-musician. His ear was satisfied with the *approximate* word. I will
furnish some circumstantial evidence in support of this charge. My instances
are gathered from half a dozen pages of the tale called *Deerslayer*. He uses
"verbal," for "oral"; "precision," for "facility"; "phenomena," for "marvels"; "necessary," for "predetermined"; "unsophisticated," for "primitive";
"preparation," for "expectancy"; "rebuked," for "subdued"; "dependent on,"
for "resulting from"; "fact," for "condition"; "fact," for "conjecture"; "pre-
caution," for "caution"; "explain," for "determine"; "mortified," for "disappointed"; "meretricious," for "factitious"; "materially," for "considerably";
"decreasing," for "deepening"; "increasing," for "disappearing"; "embedded," for "enclosed"; "treacherous," for "hostile"; "stood," for "stooped";
"softened," for "replaced"; "rejoined," for "remarked"; "situation," for
"condition"; "different," for "differing"; "insensible," for "unsentient";
"brevity," for "celerity"; "distrusted," for "suspicious"; "mental imbecility," for "imbecility"; "eyes," for "sight"; "counteracting," for "opposing";
"funeral obsequies," for "obsequies."

There have been daring people in the world who claimed that Cooper   29
could write English, but they are all dead now—all dead but Lounsbury. I
don't remember that Lounsbury makes the claim in so many words, still he
makes it, for he says that *Deerslayer* is a "pure work of art." Pure, in that
connection, means faultless—faultless in all details—and language is a detail.
If Mr. Lounsbury had only compared Cooper's English with the English
which he writes himself—but it is plain that he didn't; and so it is likely that
he imagines until this day that Cooper's is as clean and compact as his own.
Now I feel sure, deep down in my heart, that Cooper wrote about the poorest English that exists in our language, and that the English of *Deerslayer* is
the very worst that even Cooper ever wrote.

I may be mistaken, but it does seem to me that *Deerslayer* is not a work   30
of art in any sense; it does seem to me that it is destitute of every detail that
goes to the making of a work of art; in truth, it seems to me that *Deerslayer*
is just simply a literary *delirium tremens*.

A work of art? It has no invention; it has no order, system, sequence,   31
or result; it has no lifelikeness, no thrill, no stir, no seeming of reality; its
characters are confusedly drawn, and by their acts and words they prove that
they are not the sort of people the author claims that they are; its humor is

pathetic; its pathos is funny; its conversations are—oh! indescribable; its love-scenes odious; its English a crime against the language.

Counting these out, what is left is Art. I think we must all admit that.   32

QUESTIONS FOR MEANING

1. What do Wilkie Collins and Twain mean by "romantic fiction"?
2. Demonstrate that you have understood Twain's first eleven rules for literature by paraphrasing them.
3. Why does Twain object to Cooper's use of the device of having a character cause alarm by stepping on a dry twig?
4. Why does Twain believe that Cooper was not observant?
5. What is wrong with Cooper's characterization of the Indians discussed in paragraph 10?
6. Why does Twain object to Cooper's dialogue?
7. Vocabulary: decorous (1), eschew (3), lucid (6), plausibly (7), leviathan (8), ducal (14), attenuation (23), obsequies (28).

QUESTIONS ABOUT STRATEGY

1. How important are the quotations that preface this essay?
2. Twain has been much praised for his humor. How does he use humor in this essay to make his point?
3. Did Twain persuade you that he has read Cooper carefully? If so, how? If not, why not?
4. Has Twain assumed that his audience is familiar with Cooper? Could someone who has not read Cooper understand this essay?

ÉMILE ZOLA
"J'Accuse"

Letter to M. Félix Faure, President of the Republic

The author of twenty novels, Émile Zola (1840–1902) is considered one of the most important French writers of the nineteenth century. Much of his work was devoted to subjects that were considered shocking by many of the author's contemporaries. Nana (1880) is the story of a courtesan; Germinal (1885) exposes the brutal lives of miners. As titles like The Drunkard (1877) and The Beast in Man (1890) suggest, Zola used fiction to show people who have little control over their own lives—one of the main themes of naturalism, a literary movement that quickly spread beyond France as the result of Zola's influence.

Unafraid of controversy, Zola was one of the first to defend the Impression-ists, publishing a biography and critical study of Manet in 1867. But of all the controversies in which he became involved, none was so bitter as the Dreyfus Affair. As the result of publishing the argument reprinted here, Zola was sentenced to a year in prison and ordered to pay a fine of three thousand francs.

Alfred Dreyfus (1859–1935) was an army captain working in the French War Ministry when, in 1894, he was accused of selling secrets to the German mili-tary attaché. He was courtmartialed and sentenced to Devil's Island for life. But many people believed that Dreyfus was the innocent victim of anti-Semitism. Evi-dence supporting his innocence emerged during the next several years, but the army attempted to suppress it. One discovery was especially significant: an incriminating document (the bordereau *about which Zola writes) was shown to be in the hand-writing of Major C. F. Esterhazy, but the Army refused to admit this for it would have involved admitting to both a judicial error and a coverup. France was bitterly divided by the Dreyfus Affair, and in response to public pressure—most notably the* **1898** *publication of "J'Accuse" in a Paris newspaper—Dreyfus was brought back to France for a second courtmartial. The Army declared him guilty but pardoned him. Rather than return to Devil's Island, Dreyfus accepted the pardon but declared that he would continue to try to prove his innocence. In 1906, a civilian court found Dreyfus innocent of all charges that had been brought against him. He was rein-stated in the Army, decorated with the Legion of Honor, and subsequently served as a Lieutenant Colonel in World War I.*

Monsieur le Président:

Will you permit me, in my gratitude for the kindly welcome that you once extended to me, to have a care for the glory that belongs to you, and to say to you that your star, so lucky hitherto, is threatened with the most shameful, the most ineffaceable, of stains?   1

You have emerged from base calumnies safe and sound; you have con-quered hearts. You seem radiant in the apotheosis of that patriotic *fête* which the Russian alliance has been for France, and you are preparing to preside at the solemn triumph of our Universal Exposition, which will crown our great century of labor, truth, and liberty. But what a mud stain on your name—I was going to say on your reign—is this abominable Dreyfus affair! A council of war has just dared to acquit an Esterhazy in obedience to orders, a final blow at all truth, at all justice. And now it is done! France has this stain upon her cheek; it will be written in history that under your presidency it was possible for this social crime to be committed.   2

Since they have dared, I too will dare. I will tell the truth, for I have promised to tell it, if the courts, once regularly appealed to, did not bring it out fully and entirely. It is my duty to speak; I will not be an accomplice. My nights would be haunted by the specter of the innocent man who is   3 atoning, in a far-away country, by the most frightful of tortures, for a crime that he did not commit.

And to you, *Monsieur le Président,* will I cry this truth, with all the force   4 of an honest man's revolt. Because of your honor I am convinced that you are ignorant of it. And to whom then shall I denounce the malevolent gang of the really guilty, if not to you, the first magistrate of the country?

First, the truth as to the trial and conviction of Dreyfus.   5

A calamitous man has managed it all, has done it all—Colonel du Paty   6 de Clam, then a simple major. He is the entire Dreyfus case; it will be fully known only when a sincere investigation shall have clearly established his acts and his responsibilities. He appears as the most heady, the most intricate, of minds, haunted with romantic intrigues, delighting in the methods of the newspaper novel, stolen papers, anonymous letters, meetings in deserted spots, mysterious women who peddle overwhelming proofs by night. It is he who conceived the idea of dictating the *bordereau* [memo] to Dreyfus; it is he who dreamed of studying it in a room completely lined with mirrors; it is he whom Major Forzinetti represents to us armed with a dark lantern, trying to gain access to the accused when asleep, in order to throw upon his face a sudden flood of light, and thus surprise a confession of his crime in the confusion of his awakening. And I have not to tell the whole; let them look, they will find. I declare simply that Major du Paty de Clam, entrusted as a judicial officer with the duty of preparing the Dreyfus case, is, in the order of dates and responsibilities, the first person guilty of the fearful judicial error that has been committed.

The *bordereau* already had been for some time in the hands of Colonel   7 Sandherr, director of the Bureau of Information, who since then has died of general paralysis. "Flights" have taken place; papers have disappeared, as they continue to disappear even today; and the authorship of the *bordereau* was an object of inquiry, when little by little an *a priori* conclusion was arrived at that the author must be a staff officer and an officer of artillery,—clearly a double error, which shows how superficially this *bordereau* had been studied, for a systematic examination proves that it could have been written only by an officer of troops. So they searched their own house; they examined writings; it was a sort of family affair,—a traitor to be surprised in the war offices themselves, that he might be expelled therefrom. I need not again go over a story already known in part. It is sufficient to say that Major du Paty de Clam enters upon the scene as soon as the first breath of suspicion falls upon Dreyfus. Starting from that moment, it is he who invented Dreyfus; the case becomes his case; he undertakes to confound the traitor, and induce him to make a complete confession. There is also, to be sure, the minister of war, General Mercier, whose intelligence seems rather inferior; there is also the Chief of Staff, General de Boisdeffre, who seems to have yielded to his clerical passion, and the sub-Chief of Staff, General Gonse, whose conscience has succeeded in accommodating itself to many things. But at bottom there was at first only Major du Paty de Clam, who leads them all, who hypnotizes them,—for he concerns himself also with spiritualism, with occultism, holding converse with spirits. Incredible are the experiences to which he submitted the unfortunate Dreyfus, the traps into which he tried to lead him, the mad inquiries, the monstrous fancies, a complete and torturing madness.

Ah! this first affair is a nightmare to one who knows it in its real details. 8 Major du Paty de Clam arrests Dreyfus, puts him in close confinement; he runs to Mme. Dreyfus, terrorizes her, tells her that, if she speaks, her husband is lost. Meantime the unfortunate was tearing his flesh, screaming his innocence. And thus the examination went on, as in a fifteenth-century chronicle, amid mystery, with a complication of savage expedients, all based on a single childish charge, this imbecile *bordereau,* which was not simply a vulgar treason, but also the most shameless of swindles, for the famous secrets delivered proved, almost all of them, valueless. If I insist, it is because here lies the egg from which later was to be hatched the real crime, the frightful denial of justice, of which France lies ill. I should like to show in detail how the judicial error was possible; how it was born of the machinations of Major du Paty de Clam; how General Mercier and Generals de Boisdeffre and Gonse were led into it, gradually assuming responsibility for this error, which afterward they believed it their duty to impose as sacred truth, truth beyond discussion. At the start there was, on their part, only carelessness and lack of understanding. At worst we see them yielding to the religious passions of their surroundings, and to the prejudices of the *esprit de corps.* They have suffered folly to do its work.

But here is Dreyfus before the council of war. The most absolute secrecy is demanded. Had a traitor opened the frontier to the enemy in order to lead the German emperor to Notre Dame, they would not have taken stricter measures of silence and mystery. The nation is awe-struck; there are whisperings of terrible doings, of those monstrous treasons that excite the indignation of History, and naturally the nation bows. There is no punishment severe enough; it will applaud even public degradation; it will wish the guilty man to remain upon his rock of infamy, eaten by remorse. Are they real then,—these unspeakable things, these dangerous things, capable of setting Europe aflame, which they have had to bury carefully behind closed doors? No, there was nothing behind them save the romantic and mad fancies of Major du Paty de Clam. All this was done only to conceal the most ridiculous of newspaper novels. And, to assure one's self of it, one need only study attentively the indictment read before the council of war.

Ah! the emptiness of this indictment! That a man could have been condemned on this document is a prodigy of iniquity. I defy honest people to read it without feeling their hearts leap with indignation and crying out their revolt at the thought of the unlimited atonement yonder, on Devil's Island. Dreyfus knows several languages—a crime; no compromising document was found on his premises—a crime; he sometimes visits the neighborhood of his birth—a crime; he is industrious, he is desirous of knowing everything—a crime; he does not get confused—a crime; he gets confused—a crime. And the simplicities of this document, the formal assertions in the void! We were told of fourteen counts, but we find, after all, only one,—that of the *bordereau.* And even as to this we learn that the experts were not in agreement;

that one of them, M. Gobert, was hustled out in military fashion, because he permitted himself to arrive at another than the desired opinion. We were told also of twenty-three officers who came to overwhelm Dreyfus with their testimony. We are still in ignorance of their examination, but it is certain that all of them did not attack him, and it is to be remarked, furthermore, that all of them belonged to the war offices. It is a family trial; there they are all at home; and it must be remembered that the staff wanted the trial, sat in judgment at it, and has just passed judgment a second time.

So there remained only the *bordereau,* concerning which the experts were   11 not in agreement. It is said that in the council chamber the judges naturally were going to acquit. And, after that, how easy to understand the desperate obstinacy with which, in order to justify the conviction, they affirm today the existence of a secret overwhelming document, a document that cannot be shown, that legitimates everything, before which we must bow, an invisible and unknowable god. I deny this document; I deny it with all my might. A ridiculous document, yes, perhaps a document concerning little women, in which there is mention of a certain D——— who becomes too exacting; some husband doubtless, who thinks that they pay him too low a price for his wife. But a document of interest to the national defense the production of which would lead to a declaration of war tomorrow! No, no; it is a lie; and a lie the more odious and cynical because they lie with impunity, in such a way that no one can convict them of it. They stir up France; they hide themselves behind her legitimate emotion; they close mouths by disturbing hearts, by perverting minds. I know no greater civic crime.

These, then, *Monsieur le Président*, are the facts which explain how it   12 was possible to commit a judicial error; and the moral proofs, the position of Dreyfus as a man of wealth, the absence of motive, this continual cry of innocence, complete the demonstration that he is a victim of the extraordinary fancies of Major du Paty de Clam, of his clerical surroundings, of that hunting down of the "dirty Jews" which disgraces our epoch.

And we come to the Esterhazy case. Three years have passed; many   13 consciences remain profoundly disturbed, are anxiously seeking, and finally become convinced of the innocence of Dreyfus.

I shall not give the history of M. Scheurer-Kestner's doubts, which   14 later became convictions. But, while he was investigating for himself, serious things were happening to the staff. Colonel Sandherr was dead, and Lieutenant-Colonel Picquart had succeeded him as Chief of the Bureau of Information. And it is in this capacity that the latter, in the exercise of his functions, came one day into possession of a letter-telegram addressed to Major Esterhazy by an agent of a foreign power. His plain duty was to open an investigation. It is certain that he never acted except at the command of his superiors. So he submitted his suspicions to his hierarchical superiors, first to General Gonse, then to General de Boisdeffre, then to General Billot, who had succeeded General Mercier as Minister of War. The famous Picquart documents, of which we have heard so much, were never anything but the Billot documents,—I mean, the documents collected by a subordinate for his minister, the documents which must be still in existence in the war department. The inquiries lasted from May to September, 1896, and here it must be squarely affirmed that General Gonse was convinced of Esterhazy's guilt, and that General de Boisdeffre and General Billot had no doubt that the famous *bordereau* was in Esterhazy's handwriting. Lieutenant-Colonel Picquart's investigation had ended in the certain establishment of this fact. But the emotion thereat was great, for Esterhazy's conviction inevitably involved a revision of the Dreyfus trial; and this the staff was determined to avoid at any cost.

Then there must have been a psychological moment, full of anguish. Note that General Billot was in no way compromised; he came freshly to the matter; he could bring out the truth. He did not dare, in terror, undoubtedly, of public opinion, and certainly fearful also of betraying the entire staff, General de Boisdeffre, General Gonse, to say nothing of their subordinates. Then there was but a minute of struggle between his conscience and what he believed to be the military interest. When this minute had passed, it was already too late. He was involved himself; he was compromised. And since then his responsibility has only grown; he has taken upon his shoulders the crime of others, he is as guilty as the others, he is more guilty than they, for it was in his power to do justice, and he did nothing. Understand this; for a year General Billot, Generals de Boisdeffre and Gonse have known that Dreyfus is innocent, and they have kept this dreadful thing to themselves. And these people sleep, and they have wives and children whom they love!

Colonel Picquart had done his duty as an honest man. He insisted in the presence of his superiors, in the name of justice; he even begged of them; he told them how impolitic were their delays, in view of the terrible storm which was gathering, and which would surely burst as soon as the truth should be known. Later there was the language that M. Scheurer-Kestner held likewise to General Billot, adjuring him in the name of patriotism to take the matter in hand, and not to allow it to be aggravated till it should become a public disaster. No, the crime had been committed; now the staff could not confess it. And Lieutenant-Colonel Picquart was sent on a mission; he was farther and farther removed, even to Tunis, where one day they even wanted to honor his bravery by charging him with a mission which would surely have led to his massacre in the district where the Marquis de Morès met his death. He was not in disgrace; Gen. Gonse was in friendly correspondence with him; but there are secrets which it does one no good to find out.

At Paris the truth went on, irresistibly, and we know in what way the expected storm broke out. M. Mathieu Dreyfus denounced Major Esterhazy as the real author of the *bordereau,* at the moment when M. Scheurer-Kestner was about to lodge a demand for a revision of the trial with the keeper of the seals. And it is here that Major Esterhazy appears. The evidence shows that at first he was dazed, ready for suicide or flight. Then suddenly he determines to brazen it out; he astonishes Paris by the violence of his attitude. The fact was that aid had come to him; he had received an anonymous letter warning him of the intrigues of his enemies; a mysterious woman had even disturbed herself at night to hand to him a document stolen from the staff, which would save him. And I cannot help seeing here again the hand of Lieutenant-Colonel du Paty de Clam, recognizing the expedients of his fertile imagination. His work, the guilt of Dreyfus, was in danger, and he was determined to defend it. A revision of the trial,—why, that meant the downfall of the newspaper novel, so extravagant, so tragic, with its abominable *dénouement* on Devil's Island. That would never do. Thenceforth there was to be a duel between Lieutenant-Colonel Picquart and Lieutenant-Colonel du Paty de Clam, the one with face uncovered, the other masked. Presently we shall meet them both in the presence of civil justice. At bottom it is always the staff defending itself, unwilling to confess its crime, the abomination of which is growing from hour to hour.

It has been wonderingly asked who were the protectors of Major Esterhazy. First, in the shadow, Lieutenant-Colonel du Paty de Clam, who devised everything, managed everything; his hand betrays itself in the ridiculous methods. Then there is General de Boisdeffre, General Gonse, General Billot himself, who are obliged to acquit the major, since they cannot permit the innocence of Dreyfus to be recognized, for, if they should, the war offices would fall under the weight of public contempt. And the beautiful result of this prodigious situation is that the one honest man in the case, Lieutenant-Colonel Picquart, who alone has done his duty, is to be the victim, the man to be derided and punished. O justice, what frightful despair grips the heart! They go so far as to say that he is a forger; that he manufactured the telegram, to ruin Esterhazy. But, in heaven's name, why? For what purpose? Show a motive. Is he, too, paid by the Jews? The pretty part of the story is that he himself was an anti-Semite. Yes, we are witnesses of this infamous spectacle,—the proclamation of the innocence of men ruined with debts and crimes, while honor itself, a man of stainless life, is stricken down. When a society reaches that point, it is beginning to rot.   18

There you have, then, *Monsieur le Président,* the Esterhazy case,—a guilty man to be declared innocent. We can follow the beautiful business, hour by hour, for the last two months. I abridge, for this is but the *résumé* of a story whose burning pages will some day be written at length. So we have seen General de Pellieux, and then Major Ravary, carrying on a rascally investigation whence knaves come transfigured and honest people sullied. Then they convened the council of war.   19

How could it have been expected that a council of war would undo what a council of war had done?   20

I say nothing of the choice, always possible, of the judges. Is not the superior idea of discipline, which is in the very blood of these soldiers, enough to destroy their power to do justice? Who says discipline says obedience. When the Minister of War, the great chief, has publicly established, amid the applause of the nation's representatives, the absolute authority of the thing judged, do you expect a council of war formally to contradict him? Hierarchically that is impossible. General Billot conveyed a suggestion to the judges by his declaration, and they passed judgment as they must face the cannon's mouth, without reasoning. The preconceived opinion that they took with   21 them to their bench is evidently this: "Dreyfus has been condemned for the crime of treason by a council of war; then he is guilty, and we, a council of war, cannot declare him innocent. Now, we know that to recognize Ester-hazy's guilt would be to proclaim the innocence of Dreyfus." Nothing could turn them from that course of reasoning.

They have rendered an iniquitous verdict which will weigh forever upon   22 our councils of war, which will henceforth tinge with suspicion all their de-crees. The first council of war may have been lacking in comprehension; the second is necessarily criminal. Its excuse, I repeat, is that the supreme chief had spoken, declaring the thing judged unassailable, sacred and superior to men, so that inferiors could say naught to the contrary. They talk to us of the honor of the Army; they want us to love it, to respect it. Ah! certainly, yes, the Army which would rise at the first threat, which would defend French soil; that Army is the whole people, and we have for it nothing but tenderness and respect. But it is not a question of that Army, whose dignity is our special desire, in our need of justice. It is the sword that is in question; the master that they may give us tomorrow. And piously kiss the sword hilt, the god? No!

I have proved it, moreover; the Dreyfus case was the case of the war   23 offices, a staff officer, accused by his staff comrades, convicted under the pressure of the Chiefs of Staff. Again I say, he cannot come back innocent, unless all the staff is guilty. Consequently the war offices, by all imaginable means, by press campaigns, by communications, by influences, have covered Esterhazy only to ruin Dreyfus a second time. Ah! with what a sweep the Republican Government should clear away this band of Jesuits, as General Billot himself calls them! Where is the truly strong and wisely patriotic min-ister who will dare to reshape and renew all? How many of the people I know are trembling with anguish in view of a possible war, knowing in what hands lies the national defense! And what a nest of base intrigues, gos-sip, and dilapidation has this sacred asylum, entrusted with the fate of the country, become! We are frightened by the terrible light thrown upon it by the Dreyfus case, this human sacrifice of an unfortunate, of a "dirty Jew." Ah! what a mixture of madness and folly, of crazy fancies, of low police practices, of inquisitorial and tyrannical customs, the good pleasure of a few persons in gold lace, with their boots on the neck of the nation, cramming back into its throat its cry of truth and justice, under the lying and sacrile-gious pretext of the *raison d'État!*

And another of their crimes is that they have accepted the support of   24 the unclean press, have suffered themselves to be championed by all the knavery of Paris, so that now we witness knavery's insolent triumph in the downfall of right and of simple probity. It is a crime to have accused of troubling France those who wish to see her generous, at the head of the free and just nations, when they themselves are hatching the impudent conspiracy to im-pose error, in the face of the entire world. It is a crime to mislead opinion, to utilize for a task of death this opinion that they have perverted to the point of delirium. It is a crime to poison the minds of the little and the humble, to exasperate the passions of reaction and intolerance, while seeking shelter behind odious anti-Semitism, of which the great liberal France of the rights of man will die, if she is not cured. It is a crime to exploit patriotism for works of hatred, and, finally, it is a crime to make the sword the modern god, when all human science is at work on the coming temple of truth and justice.

This truth, this justice, for which we have so ardently longed,—how distressing it is to see them thus buffeted, more neglected and more obscured. I have a suspicion of the fall that must have occurred in the soul of M. Scheurer-Kestner, and I really believe that he will finally feel remorse that he did not act in a revolutionary fashion, on the day of interpellation in the Senate, by thoroughly ventilating the whole matter, to topple everything over. He has been the highly honest man, the man of loyal life, and he thought that the truth was sufficient unto itself, especially when it should appear as dazzling as the open day. Of what use to overturn everything, since soon the sun would shine? And it is for this confident serenity that he is now so cruelly punished. And the same is the case of Lieutenant-Colonel Picquart, who, moved by a feeling of lofty dignity, has been unwilling to publish General Gonse's letters. These scruples honor him the more because, while he remained respectful of discipline, his superiors heaped mud upon him, working up the case against him themselves, in the most unexpected and most outrageous fashion. Here are two victims, two worthy people, two simple hearts, who have trusted God, while the devil was at work. And in the case of Lieutenant-Colonel Picquart we have seen even this ignoble thing,—a French tribunal, after suffering the reporter in the case to arraign publicly a witness and accuse him of every crime, closing its doors as soon as this witness had been introduced to explain and defend himself. I say that is one crime more, and that this crime will awaken the universal conscience. Decidedly, military tribunals have a singular idea of justice. 25

Such, then, is the simple truth, *Monsieur le Président,* and it is frightful. It will remain a stain upon your presidency. I suspect that you are powerless in this matter,—that you are the prisoner of the constitution and of your environment. You have nonetheless a man's duty, upon which you will reflect, and which you will fulfill. Not indeed that I despair, the least in the world, of triumph. I repeat with more vehement certainty; truth is on the march, and nothing can stop it. Today sees the real beginning of the Affair, since not until today have the positions been clear: on one hand, the guilty, who do not want the light; on the other, the doers of justice, who will give their lives to get it. When truth is buried in the earth, it accumulates there, and assumes so mighty an explosive power that, on the day when it bursts forth, it hurls everything into the air. We shall see if they have not just made preparations for the most resounding of disasters, yet to come. 26

But this letter is long, *Monsieur le Président,* and it is time to finish. 27

I accuse Lieutenant-Colonel du Paty de Clam of having been the diabolical workman of judicial error,—unconsciously, I am willing to believe,—and of having then defended his calamitous work, for three years, by the most guilty machinations. 28

I accuse General Mercier of having made himself an accomplice, at least through weakness of mind, in one of the greatest iniquities of the century.

I accuse General Billot of having had in his hands certain proofs of the innocence of Dreyfus, and of having stifled them; of having rendered himself guilty of this crime of *lèse-humanité* and *lèse-justice* for a political purpose, and to save the compromised staff.

I accuse General de Boisdeffre and General Gonse of having made themselves accomplices in the same crime, one undoubtedly through clerical passion, the other perhaps through that *esprit de corps* which makes the war offices the Holy Ark, unassailable.

I accuse General de Pellieux and Major Ravary of having conducted a rascally inquiry,—I mean by that a monstrously partial inquiry, of which we have, in the report of the latter, an imperishable monument of naïve audacity.

I accuse the three experts in handwriting, Belhomme, Varinard, and Couard, of having made lying and fraudulent reports, unless a medical examination should declare them afflicted with diseases of the eye and of the mind.

I accuse the war offices of having carried on in the press, particularly in *L'Éclair* and in *L'Écho de Paris,* an abominable campaign, to mislead opinion and cover up their faults.

I accuse, finally, the first council of war of having violated the law by condemning an accused person on the strength of a secret document, and I accuse the second council of war of having covered this illegality, in obedience to orders, in committing in its turn the judicial crime of knowingly acquitting a guilty man.

In preferring these charges, I am not unaware that I lay myself liable under Articles 30 and 31 of the press law of July 29, 1881, which punishes defamation. And it is wilfully that I expose myself thereto.

As for the people whom I accuse, I do not know them, I have never seen them, I entertain against them no feeling of revenge or hatred. They are to me simple entities, spirits of social ill-doing. And the act that I perform here is nothing but a revolutionary measure to hasten the explosion of truth and justice.

I have but one passion, the passion for the light, in the name of humanity which has suffered so much, and which is entitled to happiness. My fiery protest is simply the cry of my soul. Let them dare, then, to bring me into the Assize Court, and let the investigation take place in the open day.

I await it.

Accept, *Monsieur le Président,* the assurance of my profound respect.

Émile Zola

QUESTIONS FOR MEANING

1. How does Zola account for an innocent man being sent to Devil's Island? Explain how Dreyfus was framed according to Zola.

2. Where does Zola lay the blame for the Dreyfus Affair? Who was almost certainly guilty of treason, and who was most responsible for the cover up?
3. How does Zola characterize Dreyfus?
4. According to Zola, did any officials behave honorably during the Dreyfus Affair?

QUESTIONS ABOUT STRATEGY

1. Although published in a widely circulated newspaper, "J'Accuse" takes the form of a letter to the president of France. How does Zola appeal specifically to him?
2. Consider the last sentence in paragraph 15. What does it imply?
3. In paragraph 27, Zola admits that this is a long letter, but in paragraph 19 he claims that he has abridged the case. Could he have abridged it further? Does he tell you more than you need to know?
4. Does Zola suggest anywhere that Dreyfus was the victim of religious prejudice?
5. How effective is the use of repetition in paragraphs 28–35? Does Zola use repetition elsewhere in his argument?
6. Why does Zola report, in paragraph 37, that he has never met the people he accuses? Would his argument be more effective or less if he claimed personal acquaintance with the men involved?
7. Zola concludes his argument by claiming to be ready to face prosecution because of what he has written. What effect does this have upon you?

MARGARET SANGER

The Cause of War

A pioneering advocate of birth control, Margaret Sanger (1883–1966) was one of eleven children. She studied nursing and worked as an obstetrical nurse in the tenements of Manhattan's Lower East Side. She became convinced of the importance of birth control in 1912 when a young woman died in her arms after a self-induced abortion. Sanger went to Europe in 1913 to study contraception, and she is credited with having coined the phrase "birth control." Upon her return to the United States, she founded a magazine, Woman Rebel, *in which she could publish her views. In 1916, she was jailed for opening a birth control clinic in New York, the first of many times she would be imprisoned for her work. She founded the National Birth Control League in 1917, an organization that eventually became the Planned Parenthood Federation of America. By the time Sanger was elected the first president of the International Planned Parenthood Federation in 1952, her views had come to be widely accepted.*

A lecturer and a writer, Sanger published several books. The following essay is drawn from Woman and the New Race *(1920). Writing at a time when Europe had not yet recovered from the horrors of World War I, Sanger argued that the underlying cause of the war was excessive population growth. Although most historians would argue that the war had multiple causes, Sanger makes a strong case on behalf of her view.*

In every nation of militaristic tendencies we find the reactionaries demanding a higher and still higher birth rate. Their plea is, first, that great armies are needed to *defend* the country from its possible enemies; second, that a huge population is required to assure the country its proper place among the powers of the world. At bottom the two pleas are the same. 1

As soon as the country becomes overpopulated, these reactionaries proclaim loudly its moral right to expand. They point to the huge population, which in the name of patriotism they have previously demanded should be brought into being. Again pleading patriotism, they declare that it is the moral right of the nation to take by force such room as it needs. Then comes war—usually against some nation supposed to be less well prepared than the aggressor. 2

Diplomats make it their business to conceal the facts, and politicians violently denounce the politicians of other countries. There is a long beating of tom-toms by the press and all other agencies for influencing public opinion. Facts are distorted and lies invented until the common people cannot get at the truth. Yet, when the war is over, if not before, we always find that "a place in the sun," "a path to the sea," "a route to India" or something of the sort is at the bottom of the trouble. These are merely other names for expansion. 3

The "need of expansion" is only another name for overpopulation. One supreme example is sufficient to drive home this truth. That the Great War, from the horror of which we are just beginning to emerge, had its source in overpopulation is too evident to be denied by any serious student of current history. 4

For the past one hundred years most of the nations of Europe have been piling up terrific debts to humanity by the encouragement of unlimited numbers. The rulers of these nations and their militarists have constantly called upon the people to breed, breed, breed! Large populations meant more people to produce wealth, more people to pay taxes, more trade for the merchants, more soldiers to protect the wealth. But more people also meant need of greater food supplies, an urgent and natural need for expansion. 5

As shown by C. V. Drysdale's famous "War Map of Europe," the great conflict began among the high birth rate countries—Germany, with its rate of 31.7, Austria-Hungary with 33.7 and 36.7, respectively, Russia with 45.4, Serbia with 38.6. Italy with her 38.7 came in, as the world is now well informed through the publication of secret treaties by the Soviet government of Russia, upon the promise of territory held by Austria. England, owing to 6 her small home area, is cramped with her comparatively low birth rate of 26.3. France, among the belligerents, is conspicuous for her low birth rate of 19.9, but stood in the way of expansion of high birth rate Germany. Nearly all of the persistently neutral countries—Holland, Denmark, Norway, Sweden and Switzerland have low birth rates, the average being a little over 26.

Owing to the part Germany played in the war, a survey of her birth   7
statistics is decidedly illuminating. The increase in the German birth rate up to 1876 was great. Though it began to decline then, the decline was not sufficient to offset the tremendous increase of the previous years. There were more millions to produce children, so while the average number of births per thousand was somewhat smaller, the net increase in population was still huge. From 41,000,000 in 1871, the year the Empire was founded, the German population grew to approximately 67,000,000 in 1918. Meanwhile her food supply increased only a very small percent. In 1910, Russia had a birth rate even higher than Germany's had ever been—a little less than 48 per thousand. When czarist Russia wanted an outlet to the Mediterranean by way of Constantinople, she was thinking of her increasing population. Germany was thinking of her increasing population when she spoke as with one voice of a "place in the sun." . . .

The militaristic claim for Germany's right to new territory was simply   8
a claim to the right of life and food for the German babies—the same right that a chick claims to burst its shell. If there had not been other millions of people claiming the same right, there would have been no war. But there *were* other millions.

The German rulers and leaders pointed out the fact that expansion meant   9
more business for German merchants, more work for German workmen at better wages, and more opportunities for Germans abroad. They also pointed out that lack of expansion meant crowding and crushing at home, hard times, heavy burdens, lack of opportunity for Germans, and what not. In this way, they gave the people of the Empire a startling and true picture of what would happen from overcrowding. Once they realized the facts, the majority of Germans naturally welcomed the so-called war of defense.

The argument was sound. Once the German mothers had submitted to   10
the plea for overbreeding, it was inevitable that imperialistic Germany should make war. Once the battalions of unwanted babies came into existence— babies whom the mothers did not want but which they bore as a "patriotic duty"—it was too late to avoid international conflict. The great crime of imperialistic Germany was its high birth rate.

It has always been so. Behind all war has been the pressure of popula-   11
tion. "Historians," says Huxley, "point to the greed and ambition of rulers, the reckless turbulence of the ruled, to the debasing effects of wealth and luxury, and to the devastating wars which have formed a great part of the occupation of mankind, as the causes of the decay of states and the foundering of old civilizations, and thereby point their story with a moral. But beneath all this superficial turmoil lay the deep-seated impulse given by unlimited multiplication."

Robert Thomas Malthus, formulator of the doctrine which bears his
name, pointed out, in the closing years of the eighteenth century, the relation
of overpopulation to war. He showed that mankind tends to increase faster
than the food supply. He demonstrated that were it not for the more common diseases, for plague, famine, floods and wars, human beings would crowd
each other to such an extent that the misery would be even greater than it
now is. These he described as "natural checks," pointing out that as long as
no other checks are employed, such disasters are unavoidable. If we do not
exercise sufficient judgment to regulate the birth rate, we encounter disease,
starvation and war.

Both Darwin and John Stuart Mill recognized, by inference at least, the
fact that so-called "natural checks"—and among them war—will operate if
some sort of limitation is not employed. In his *Origin of Species,* Darwin says:
"There is no exception to the rule that every organic being naturally increases
at so high a rate, if not destroyed, that the earth would soon be covered by
the progeny of a single pair." Elsewhere he observes that we do not permit
helpless human beings to die off, but we create philanthropies and charities,
build asylums and hospitals and keep the medical profession busy preserving
those who could not otherwise survive. John Stuart Mill, supporting the
views of Malthus, speaks to exactly the same effect in regard to the multiplying power of organic beings, among them humanity. In other words, let
countries become overpopulated and war is inevitable. It follows as daylight
follows the sunrise.

When Charles Bradlaugh and Mrs. Annie Besant were on trial in England in 1877 for publishing information concerning contraceptives, Mrs. Besant put the case bluntly to the court and the jury:

"I have no doubt that if natural checks were allowed to operate right
through the human as they do in the animal world, a better result would
follow. Among the brutes, the weaker are driven to the wall, the diseased
fall out in the race of life. The old brutes, when feeble or sickly, are killed.
If men insisted that those who were sickly should be allowed to die without
help of medicine or science, if those who are weak were put upon one side
and crushed, if those who were old and useless were killed, if those who
were not capable of providing food for themselves were allowed to starve, if
all this were done, the struggle for existence among men would be as real as
it is among brutes and would doubtless result in the production of a higher
race of men.

"But are you willing to do that or to allow it to be done?"

We are not willing to let it be done. Mother hearts cling to children,
no matter how diseased, misshapen and miserable. Sons and daughters hold
fast to parents, no matter how helpless. We do not allow the weak to depart;
neither do we cease to bring more weak and helpless beings into the world.
Among the dire results is war, which kills off, not the weak and the helpless,
but the strong and the fit.

What shall be done? We have our choice of one of three policies. We
may abandon our science and leave the weak and diseased to die, or kill

them, as the brutes do. Or we may go on overpopulating the earth and have our famines and our wars while the earth exists. Or we can accept the third, sane, sensible, moral and practicable plan of birth control. We can refuse to bring the weak, the helpless and the unwanted children into the world. We can refuse to overcrowd families, nations and the earth. There are these ways to meet the situation, and only these three ways.

The world will never abandon its preventive and curative science; it   19
may be expected to elevate and extend it beyond our present imagination. The efforts to do away with famine and the opposition to war are growing by leaps and bounds. Upon these efforts are largely based our modern social revolutions.

There remains only the third expedient—birth control, the real cure for   20
war. This fact was called to the attention of the Peace Conference in Paris, in 1919, by the Malthusian League, which adopted the following resolution at its annual general meeting in London in June of that year:

"The Malthusian League desires to point out that the proposed scheme   21
for the League of Nations has neglected to take account of the important questions of *the pressure of population*, which *causes the great international economic competition* and rivalry, and of the *increase of population*, which is put forward as a justification for *claiming increase of territory*. It, therefore, wishes to put on record its belief that the League of Nations will only be able to fulfill its aim *when it adds a clause* to the following effect:

" 'That each Nation desiring to enter into the League of Nations shall   22
pledge itself *so to restrict its birth rate* that its people shall be able to live in comfort *in their own dominions without need* for territorial expansion, and that it shall recognize that *increase of population shall not justify* a demand either for increase of territory or for the compulsion of other Nations to admit its emigrants; so that when all Nations in the League have shown their ability to live on their own resources without international rivalry, they will be in a position to fuse into an international federation, and territorial boundaries will then have little significance.' "

As a matter of course, the Peace Conference paid no attention to the   23
resolution, for, as pointed out by Frank A. Vanderlip, the American financier, that conference not only ignored the economic factors of the world situation, but seemed unaware that Europe had produced more people than its fields could feed. So the resolution amounted to so much propaganda and nothing more.

This remedy can be applied only by woman and she will apply it. She   24
must and will see past the call of pretended patriotism and of glory of empire and perceive what is true and what is false in these things. She will discover what base uses the militarist and the exploiter made of the idealism of peoples. Under the clamor of the press, permeating the ravings of the jingoes, she will hear the voice of Napoleon, the archetype of the militarists of all nations, calling for "fodder for cannon."

"Woman is given to us that she may bear children," said he. "Woman   25
is our property, we are not hers, because she produced children for us—we

do not yield any to her. She is, therefore, our possession as the fruit tree is that of the gardener."

That is what the imperialist is *thinking* when he speaks of the glory of the empire and the prestige of the nation. Every country has its appeal—its shibboleth—ready for the lips of the imperialist. German rulers pointed to the comfort of the workers, to old-age pensions, maternal benefits and minimum wage regulations, and other material benefits, when they wished to inspire soldiers for the Fatherland. England's strongest argument, perhaps, was a certain phase of liberty which she guarantees her subjects, and the protection afforded them wherever they may go. France and the United States, too, have their appeals to the idealism of democracy—appeals which the politicians of both countries know well how to use, though the peoples of both lands are beginning to awake to the fact that their countries have been living on the glories of their revolutions and traditions, rather than the substance of freedom. Behind the boast of old-age pensions, material benefits and wage regulations, behind the bombast concerning liberty in this country and tyranny in that, behind all the slogans and shibboleths coined out of the ideals of the peoples for the uses of imperialism, woman must and will see the iron hand of that same imperialism, condemning women to breed and men to die for the will of the rulers.

Upon woman the burden and the horrors of war are heaviest. Her heart is the hardest wrung when the husband or the son comes home to be buried or to live a shattered wreck. Upon her devolve the extra tasks of filling out the ranks of workers in the war industries, in addition to caring for the children and replenishing the war-diminished population. Hers is the crushing weight and the sickening of soul. And it is out of her womb that those things proceed. When she sees what lies behind the glory and the horror, the boasting and the burden, and gets the vision, the human perspective, she will end war. She will kill war by the simple process of starving it to death. For she will refuse longer to produce the human food upon which the monster feeds.

QUESTIONS FOR MEANING

1. According to Sanger, what motives have led governments to encourage population growth?
2. From an evolutionary point of view, why is war unacceptable as a "natural check" upon population growth?
3. What are the three policies that Sanger believes nations must inevitably choose among? Are there any alternatives that she overlooks?
4. World War II began less than twenty years after the publication of this essay. Do you know anything about the conditions under which that war began that could be used as evidence to support Sanger's thesis that "militarists" and "reactionaries" favor high birth rates?
5. Vocabulary: belligerents (6), conspicuous (6), turbulence (11), debasing (11), foundering (11), inference (13), base (24), jingoes (24), bombast (26), shibboleth (26).

QUESTIONS ABOUT STRATEGY

1. Is Sanger ever guilty of oversimplification? Can you think of any causes of war that have nothing to do with population?
2. How useful are the statistics cited in paragraphs 6 and 7?
3. Of the various quotations that Sanger includes in her essay, which is the most effective?
4. How would you describe the tone of this essay? Is it suitable for the subject?
5. Do you detect any bias in this essay? Does Sanger ever seem to suggest that World War I was caused by one country in particular? Is such an implication historically valid?

ADOLF HITLER

The Purpose of Propaganda

A frustrated artist, Adolf Hitler (1889–1945) served in the German Army during World War I, and became the leader of the National Socialist Party in 1920, during the turbulent period that followed the German defeat. In 1923, Hitler led a revolt in Munich, for which he subsequently served nine months in prison, using this time to write Mein Kampf *[My Struggle]. Under his direction, the Nazis gained political influence throughout the 1920s, and, in 1933, Hitler became Chancellor of Germany. Upon the death of President Paul von Hindenburg in 1934, Hitler assumed dictatorial powers and ruled Germany as* Der Führer *[The Leader]. More than any other individual, he is responsible for World War II and the deliberate murder of millions of people during that war.*

*There are many factors that contributed to Hitler's rise to power, but one of them was the skill with which the Nazis used propaganda. The **1925** publication of* Mein Kampf, *from which the following excerpt is taken, outlined Hitler's views. But at the time, many people did not take them seriously.*

Ever since I have been scrutinizing political events, I have taken a tremendous interest in propagandist activity. I saw that the Socialist-Marxist organizations mastered and applied this instrument with astounding skill. And I soon realized that the correct use of propaganda is a true art which has remained practically unknown to the bourgeois parties. Only the Christian-Social movement, especially in Lueger's time, achieved a certain virtuosity on this instrument, to which it owed many of its successes.

But it was not until the War that it became evident what immense results could be obtained by a correct application of propaganda. Here again, unfortunately, all our studying had to be done on the enemy side, for the activity on our side was modest, to say the least. The total miscarriage of the

German 'enlightenment' service stared every soldier in the face, and this spurred me to take up the question of propaganda even more deeply than before.

There was often more than enough time for thinking, and the enemy offered practical instruction which, to our sorrow, was only too good.

For what we failed to do, the enemy did, with amazing skill and really brilliant calculation. [See illustration on page 644.] I, myself, learned enormously from this enemy war propaganda. But time passed and left no trace in the minds of all those who should have benefited; partly because they considered themselves too clever to learn from the enemy, partly owing to lack of good will.

Did we have anything you could call propaganda?

I regret that I must answer in the negative. Everything that actually was done in this field was so inadequate and wrong from the very start that it certainly did no good and sometimes did actual harm.

The form was inadequate, the substance was psychologically wrong: a careful examination of German war propaganda can lead to no other diagnosis.

There seems to have been no clarity on the very first question: Is propaganda a means or an end?

It is a means and must therefore be judged with regard to its end. It must consequently take a form calculated to support the aim which it serves. It is also obvious that its aim can vary in importance from the standpoint of general need, and that the inner value of the propaganda will vary accordingly. The aim for which we were fighting the War was the loftiest, the most overpowering, that man can conceive: it was the freedom and independence of our nation, the security of our future food supply, and—our national honor; a thing which, despite all contrary opinions prevailing today, nevertheless exists, or rather should exist, since peoples without honor have sooner or later lost their freedom and independence, which in turn is only the result of a higher justice, since generations of rabble without honor deserve no freedom. Any man who wants to be a cowardly slave can have no honor, or honor itself would soon fall into general contempt.

The German nation was engaged in a struggle for a human existence, and the purpose of war propaganda should have been to support this struggle; its aim to help bring about victory.

When the nations on this planet fight for existence—when the question of destiny, 'to be or not to be,' cries out for a solution—then all considerations of humanitarianism or aesthetics crumble into nothingness; for all these concepts do not float about in the ether, they arise from man's imagination and are bound up with man. When he departs from this world, these concepts are again dissolved into nothingness, for Nature does not know them. And even among mankind, they belong only to a few nations or rather races, and this in proportion as they emanate from the feeling of the nation or race in question. Humanitarianism and aesthetics would vanish even from a world inhabited by man if this world were to lose the races that have created and upheld these concepts.

But all such concepts become secondary when a nation is fighting for   12
its existence; in fact, they become totally irrelevant to the forms of the struggle as soon as a situation arises where they might paralyze a struggling nation's power of self-preservation. And that has always been their only visible
result.

As for humanitarianism, Moltke said years ago that in war it lies in the   13
brevity of the operation, and that means that the most aggressive fighting
technique is the most humane.

But when people try to approach these questions with drivel about   14
aesthetics, etc., really only one answer is possible: where the destiny and
existence of a people are at stake, all obligation toward beauty ceases. The
most unbeautiful thing there can be in human life is and remains the yoke
of slavery. Or do these Schwabing decadents view the present lot of the
German people as 'aesthetic'? Certainly we don't have to discuss these matters with the Jews, the most modern inventors of this cultural perfume.
Their whole existence is an embodied protest against the aesthetics of the
Lord's image.

And since these criteria of humanitarianism and beauty must be elimi-   15
nated from the struggle, they are also inapplicable to propaganda.

Propaganda in the War was a means to an end, and the end was the   16
struggle for the existence of the German people; consequently, propaganda
could only be considered in accordance with the principles that were valid
for this struggle. In this case the most cruel weapons were humane if they
brought about a quicker victory; and only those methods were beautiful which
helped the nation to safeguard the dignity of its freedom.

This was the only possible attitude toward war propaganda in a life-   17
and-death struggle like ours.

If the so-called responsible authorities had been clear on this point, they   18
would never have fallen into such uncertainty over the form and application
of this weapon: for even propaganda is no more than a weapon, though a
frightful one in the hand of an expert.

The second really decisive question was this: To whom should propa-   19
ganda be addressed? To the scientifically trained intelligentsia or to the less
educated masses?

It must be addressed always and exclusively to the masses.   20

What the intelligentsia—or those who today unfortunately often go by   21
that name—what they need is not propaganda but scientific instruction. The
content of propaganda is not science any more than the object represented in
a poster is art. The art of the poster lies in the designer's ability to attract the
attention of the crowd by form and color. A poster advertising an art exhibit
must direct the attention of the public to the art being exhibited; the better it
succeeds in this, the greater is the art of the poster itself. The poster should
give the masses an idea of the significance of the exhibition, it should not be
a substitute for the art on display. Anyone who wants to concern himself
with the art itself must do more than study the poster; and it will not be
enough for him just to saunter through the exhibition. We may expect him

to examine and immerse himself in the individual works, and thus little by little form a fair opinion.

A similar situation prevails with what we today call propaganda.   22

The function of propaganda does not lie in the scientific training of the   23 individual, but in calling the masses' attention to certain facts, processes, necessities, etc., whose significance is thus for the first time placed within their field of vision.

The whole art consists in doing this so skillfully that everyone will be   24 convinced that the fact is real, the process necessary, the necessity correct, etc. But since propaganda is not and cannot be the necessity in itself, since its function, like the poster, consists in attracting the attention of the crowd, and not in educating those who are already educated or who are striving after education and knowledge, its effect for the most part must be aimed at the emotions and only to a very limited degree at the so-called intellect.

All propaganda must be popular and its intellectual level must be ad-   25 justed to the most limited intelligence among those it is addressed to. Consequently, the greater the mass it is intended to reach, the lower its purely intellectual level will have to be. But if, as in propaganda for sticking out a war, the aim is to influence a whole people, we must avoid excessive intellectual demands on our public, and too much caution cannot be exerted in this direction.

The more modest its intellectual ballast, the more exclusively it takes   26 into consideration the emotions of the masses, the more effective it will be. And this is the best proof of the soundness or unsoundness of a propaganda campaign, and not success in pleasing a few scholars or young aesthetes.

The art of propaganda lies in understanding the emotional ideas of the   27 great masses and finding, through a psychologically correct form, the way to the attention and thence to the heart of the broad masses. The fact that our bright boys do not understand this merely shows how mentally lazy and conceited they are.

Once we understand how necessary it is for propaganda to be adjusted   28 to the broad mass, the following rule results:

It is a mistake to make propaganda many-sided, like scientific instruc-   29 tion, for instance.

The receptivity of the great masses is very limited, their intelligence is   30 small, but their power of forgetting is enormous. In consequence of these facts, all effective propaganda must be limited to a very few points and must harp on these in slogans until the last member of the public understands what you want him to understand by your slogan. As soon as you sacrifice this slogan and try to be many-sided, the effect will piddle away, for the crowd can neither digest nor retain the material offered. In this way the result is weakened and in the end entirely cancelled out.

Thus we see that propaganda must follow a simple line and correspond-   31 ingly the basic tactics must be psychologically sound.

For instance, it was absolutely wrong to make the enemy ridiculous, as   32
the Austrian and German comic papers did. It was absolutely wrong because
actual contact with an enemy soldier was bound to arouse an entirely different conviction, and the results were devastating; for now the German soldier,
under the direct impression of the enemy's resistance, felt himself swindled
by his propaganda service. His desire to fight, or even to stand firm, was not
strengthened, but the opposite occurred. His courage flagged.

By contrast, the war propaganda of the English and Americans was   33
psychologically sound. By representing the Germans to their own people as
barbarians and Huns, they prepared the individual soldier for the terrors of
war, and thus helped to preserve him from disappointments. After this, the
most terrible weapon that was used against him seemed only to confirm
what his propagandists had told him; it likewise reinforced his faith in the
truth of his government's assertions, while on the other hand it increased his
rage and hatred against the vile enemy. For the cruel effects of the weapon,
whose use by the enemy he now came to know, gradually came to confirm
for him the 'Hunnish' brutality of the barbarous enemy, which he had heard
all about; and it never dawned on him for a moment that his own weapons
possibly, if not probably, might be even more terrible in their effects.

And so the English soldier could never feel that he had been misin-   34
formed by his own countrymen, as unhappily was so much the case with the
German soldier that in the end he rejected everything coming from this source
as 'swindles' and 'bunk.' All this resulted from the idea that any old simpleton (or even somebody who was intelligent 'in other things') could be assigned to propaganda work, and the failure to realize that the most brilliant
psychologists would have been none too good.

And so the German war propaganda offered an unparalleled example of   35
an 'enlightenment' service working in reverse, since any correct psychology
was totally lacking.

There was no end to what could be learned from the enemy by a man   36
who kept his eyes open, refused to let his perceptions be classified, and for
four and a half years privately turned the storm-flood of enemy propaganda
over in his brain.

What our authorities least of all understood was the very first axiom of   37
all propagandist activity: to wit, the basically subjective and one-sided attitude it must take toward every question it deals with. In this connection,
from the very beginning of the War and from top to bottom, such sins were
committed that we were entitled to doubt whether so much absurdity could
really be attributed to pure stupidity alone.

What, for example, would we say about a poster that was supposed to   38
advertise a new soap and that described other soaps as 'good'?

We would only shake our heads.   39

Exactly the same applies to political advertising.   40

The function of propaganda is, for example, not to weigh and ponder   41
the rights of different people, but exclusively to emphasize the one right

which it has set out to argue for. Its task is not to make an objective study of the truth, in so far as it favors the enemy, and then set it before the masses with academic fairness; its task is to serve our own right, always and un-flinchingly.

It was absolutely wrong to discuss war-guilt from the standpoint that   42
Germany alone could not be held responsible for the outbreak of the catas-trophe; it would have been correct to load every bit of the blame on the shoulders of the enemy, even if this had not really corresponded to the true facts, as it actually did.

And what was the consequence of this half-heartedness?   43

The broad mass of a nation does not consist of diplomats, or even pro-   44
fessors of political law, or even individuals capable of forming a rational opinion; it consists of plain mortals, wavering and inclined to doubt and uncertainty. As soon as our own propaganda admits so much as a glimmer of right on the other side, the foundation for doubt in our own right has been laid. The masses are then in no position to distinguish where foreign injustice ends and our own begins. In such a case they become uncertain and suspicious, especially if the enemy refrains from going in for the same non-sense, but unloads every bit of blame on his adversary. Isn't it perfectly un-derstandable that the whole country ends up by lending more credence to enemy propaganda, which is more unified and coherent, than to its own? And particularly a people that suffers from the mania of objectivity as much as the Germans. For, after all this, everyone will take the greatest pains to avoid doing the enemy any injustice, even at the peril of seriously besmirch-ing and even destroying his own people and country.

Of course, this was not the intent of the responsible authorities, but the   45
people never realize that.

The people in their overwhelming majority are so feminine by nature   46
and attitude that sober reasoning determines their thoughts and actions far less than emotion and feeling.

And this sentiment is not complicated, but very simple and all of a   47
piece. It does not have multiple shadings; it has a positive and a negative; love or hate, right or wrong, truth or lie, never half this way and half that way, never partially, or that kind of thing.

English propagandists understood all this most brilliantly—and acted   48
accordingly. They made no half statements that might have given rise to doubts.

Their brilliant knowledge of the primitive sentiments of the broad masses   49
is shown by their atrocity propaganda, which was adapted to this condition. As ruthless as it was brilliant, it created the preconditions for moral stead-fastness at the front, even in the face of the greatest actual defeats, and just as strikingly it pilloried the German enemy as the sole guilty party for the outbreak of the War: the rabid, impudent bias and persistence with which this lie was expressed took into account the emotional, always extreme, at-titude of the great masses and for this reason was believed.

How effective this type of propaganda was is most strikingly shown by   50
the fact that after four years of war it not only enabled the enemy to stick to
its guns, but even began to nibble at our own people.

It need not surprise us that our propaganda did not enjoy this success.   51
In its inner ambiguity alone, it bore the germ of ineffectualness. And finally
its content was such that it was very unlikely to make the necessary impression on the masses. Only our feather-brained 'statesmen' could have dared to
hope that this insipid pacifistic bilge could fire men's spirits till they were
willing to die.

As a result, their miserable stuff was useless, even harmful in fact.   52

But the most brilliant propagandist technique will yield no success un-   53
less one fundamental principle is borne in mind constantly and with unflag-
ging attention. It must confine itself to a few points and repeat them over
and over. Here, as so often in this world, persistence is the first and most
important requirement for success.

Particularly in the field of propaganda, we must never let ourselves be   54
led by aesthetes or people who have grown blasé: not by the former, because
the form and expression of our propaganda would soon, instead of being
suitable for the masses, have drawing power only for literary teas; and of the
second we must beware, because, lacking in any fresh emotion of their own,
they are always on the lookout for new stimulation. These people are quick
to weary of everything; they want variety, and they are never able to feel or
understand the needs of their fellow men who are not yet so callous. They
are always the first to criticize a propaganda campaign, or rather its content,
which seems to them too old-fashioned, too hackneyed, too out-of-date, etc.
They are always after novelty, in search of a change, and this makes them
mortal enemies of any effective political propaganda. For as soon as the organization and the content of propaganda begin to suit their tastes, it loses
all cohesion and evaporates completely.

The purpose of propaganda is not to provide interesting distraction for   55
blasé young gentlemen, but to convince, and what I mean is to convince the
masses. But the masses are slow-moving, and they always require a certain
time before they are ready even to notice a thing, and only after the simplest
ideas are repeated thousands of times will the masses finally remember them.

When there is a change, it must not alter the content of what the pro-   56
paganda is driving at, but in the end must always say the same thing. For
instance, a slogan must be presented from different angles, but the end of all
remarks must always and immutably be the slogan itself. Only in this way
can the propaganda have a unified and complete effect.

This broadness of outline from which we must never depart, in com-   57
bination with steady, consistent emphasis, allows our final success to mature.
And then, to our amazement, we shall see what tremendous results such
perseverance leads to—to results that are almost beyond our understanding.

All advertising, whether in the field of business or politics, achieves   58
success through the continuity and sustained uniformity of its application.

Here, too, the example of enemy war propaganda was typical; limited   59
to a few points, devised exclusively for the masses, carried on with indefati-
gable persistence. Once the basic ideas and methods of execution were recognized as correct, they were applied throughout the whole War without the
slightest change. At first the claims of the propaganda were so impudent that
people thought it insane; later, it got on people's nerves; and in the end, it
was believed. After four and a half years, a revolution broke out in Germany;
and its slogans originated in the enemy's war propaganda.

And in England they understood one more thing: that this spiritual   60
weapon can succeed only if it is applied on a tremendous scale, but that
success amply covers all costs.

There, propaganda was regarded as a weapon of the first order, while   61
in our country it was the last resort of unemployed politicians and a comfortable haven for slackers.

And, as was to be expected, its results all in all were zero.   62

QUESTIONS FOR MEANING

1. Why did Hitler's interest in propaganda increase after World War I? How
   important is propaganda in his view?
2. According to Hitler, how did English and American propaganda differ
   from German propaganda in World War I?
3. Why did Hitler believe that some people do not deserve freedom?
4. How important are truth and aesthetics in propaganda?
5. According to Hitler, what is the key to success in propaganda?
6. How does Hitler characterize the average person?

QUESTIONS ABOUT STRATEGY

1. Throughout this argument, Hitler emphasizes that Germany's opponents
   in World War I used propaganda "with amazing skill and really brilliant
   calculation." What advantage does he gain from making this point?
2. This argument was first published twenty years before the Allied liberation of Nazi concentration camps. Can you detect any signs of racism
   within it? Judging from this excerpt, how honest was Hitler in revealing
   his values before he came to power?
3. In paragraphs 38–40 and 58, Hitler compares propaganda to advertising.
   Is this a fair comparison? Why is it worth making?
4. Would this argument appeal to the average person? Would it appeal to
   intellectuals? What sort of audience was most likely to respond favorably
   to Hitler?

CLARENCE DARROW
The Futility of the Death Penalty

Specializing in labor and political cases, Clarence Darrow (1857–1938) was one of the most famous lawyers in American history. He was especially prominent in the 1920s, a decade that witnessed his two most celebrated cases. In 1925, he was the defense attorney for John T. Scopes, a high school biology teacher who was charged with violating a Tennessee law that prohibited teaching any theory that suggested man may have evolved from a lower species. Although Charles Darwin had published The Origin of Species *more than a half century earlier, evolution was still regarded as a dangerous doctrine that would undermine the moral authority of the Bible. The Scopes trial attracted worldwide attention as a major test of civil liberties, especially freedom of thought. Darrow lost the case, but his forceful defense of Scopes almost certainly saved teachers in other states from being prosecuted under similar laws.*

A year earlier, Darrow had undertaken an even more difficult case when he defended Nathan Leopold and Richard Loeb in a notorious murder case. Although his clients had confessed to an unusually cold-blooded murder and popular feeling demanded that they be executed, Darrow managed to win prison terms for them by arguing persuasively against the death penalty. His objections to capital punishment are best summarized in the following essay, first published in **1928.**

1   Little more than a century ago, in England, there were over two hundred offenses that were punishable with death. The death sentence was passed upon children under ten years old. And every time the sentimentalist sought to lessen the number of crimes punishable by death, the self-righteous said no, that it would be the destruction of the state; that it would be better to kill for more transgressions rather than for less.

2   Today, both in England and America, the number of capital offenses has been reduced to a very few, and capital punishment would doubtless be abolished altogether were it not for the self-righteous, who still defend it with the same old arguments. Their major claim is that capital punishment decreases the number of murders, and hence, that the state must retain the institution as its last defense against the criminal.

3   It is my purpose in this article to prove, first, that capital punishment is no deterrent to crime; and second, that the state continues to kill its victims, not so much to defend society against them—for it could do that equally well by imprisonment—but to appease the mob's emotions of hatred and revenge.

4   Behind the idea of capital punishment lie false training and crude views of human conduct. People do evil things, say the judges, lawyers, and preachers, because of depraved hearts. Human conduct is not determined by the causes which determine the conduct of other animal and plant life in the universe. For some mysterious reason human beings act as they please; and

if they do not please to act in a certain way, it is because, having the power of choice, they deliberately choose to act wrongly. The world once applied this doctrine to disease and insanity in men. It was also applied to animals, and even inanimate things were once tried and condemned to destruction. The world knows better now, but the rule has not yet been extended to human beings.

The simple fact is that every person starts life with a certain physical   5
structure, more or less sensitive, stronger or weaker. He is played upon by everything that reaches him from without, and in this he is like everything else in the universe, inorganic matter as well as organic. How a man will act depends upon the character of his human machine, and the strength of the various stimuli that affect it. Everyone knows that this is so in disease and insanity. Most investigators know that it applies to crime. But the great mass of people still sit in judgment, robed with self-righteousness, and determine the fate of their less fortunate fellows. When this question is studied like any other, we shall then know how to get rid of most of the conduct that we call "criminal," just as we are now getting rid of much of the disease that once afflicted mankind.

If crime were really the result of wilful depravity, we should be ready   6
to concede that capital punishment may serve as a deterrent to the criminally inclined. But it is hardly probable that the great majority of people refrain from killing their neighbors because they are afraid; they refrain because they never had the inclination. Human beings are creatures of habit; and, as a rule, they are not in the habit of killing. The circumstances that lead to killings are manifold, but in a particular individual the inducing cause is not easily found. In one case, homicide may have been induced by indigestion in the killer; in another, it may be traceable to some weakness inherited from a remote ancestor; but that it results from *something* tangible and understandable, if all the facts were known, must be plain to everyone who believes in cause and effect.

Of course, no one will be converted to this point of view by statistics   7
of crime. In the first place, it is impossible to obtain reliable ones; and in the second place, the conditions to which they apply are never the same. But if one cares to analyze the figures, such as we have, it is easy to trace the more frequent causes of homicide. The greatest number of killings occur during attempted burglaries and robberies. The robber knows that penalties for burglary do not average more than five years in prison. He also knows that the penalty for murder is death or life imprisonment. Faced with this alternative, what does the burglar do when he is detected and threatened with arrest? He shoots to kill. He deliberately takes the chance of death to save himself from a five-year term in prison. It is therefore as obvious as anything can be that fear of death has no effect in diminishing homicides of this kind, which are more numerous than any other type.

The next largest number of homicides may be classed as "sex mur-   8
ders." Quarrels between husbands and wives, disappointed love, or love too

much requited cause many killings. They are the result of primal emotions so deep that the fear of death has not the slightest effect in preventing them. Spontaneous feelings overflow in criminal acts, and consequences do not count.

Then there are cases of sudden anger, uncontrollable rage. The fear of death never enters into such cases; if the anger is strong enough, consequences are not considered until too late. The old-fashioned stories of men deliberately plotting and committing murder in cold blood have little foundation in real life. Such killings are so rare that they need not concern us here. The point to be emphasized is that practically all homicides are manifestations of well-recognized human emotions, and it is perfectly plain that the fear of excessive punishment does not enter into them.   9

In addition to these personal forces which overwhelm weak men and lead them to commit murder, there are also many social and economic forces which must be listed among the causes of homicides, and human beings have even less control over these than over their own emotions. It is often said that in America there are more homicides in proportion to population than in England. This is true. There are likewise more in the United States than in Canada. But such comparisons are meaningless until one takes into consideration the social and economic differences in the countries compared. Then it becomes apparent why the homicide rate in the United States is higher. Canada's population is largely rural; that of the United States is crowded into cities whose slums are the natural breeding places of crime. Moreover, the population of England and Canada is homogeneous, while the United States has gathered together people of every color from every nation in the world. Racial differences intensify social, religious, and industrial problems, and the confusion which attends this indiscriminate mixing of races and nationalities is one of the most fertile sources of crime.   10

Will capital punishment remedy these conditions? Of course it won't; but its advocates argue that the fear of this extreme penalty will hold the victims of adverse conditions in check. To this piece of sophistry the continuance and increase of crime in our large cities is a sufficient answer. No, the plea that capital punishment acts as a deterrent to crime will not stand. The real reason why this barbarous practice persists in a so-called civilized world is that people still hold the primitive belief that the taking of one human life can be atoned for by taking another. It is the age-old obsession with punishment that keeps the official headsman busy plying his trade.   11

And it is precisely upon this point that I would build my case against capital punishment. Even if one grants that the idea of punishment is sound, crime calls for something more—for careful study, for an understanding of causes, for proper remedies. To attempt to abolish crime by killing the criminal is the easy and foolish way out of a serious situation. Unless a remedy deals with the conditions which foster crime, criminals will breed faster than the hangman can spring his trap. Capital punishment ignores the causes of crime just as completely as the primitive witch doctor ignored the causes of disease; and, like the methods of the witch doctor, it is not only ineffective   12 as a remedy, but is positively vicious in at least two ways. In the first place, the spectacle of state executions feeds the basest passions of the mob. And in the second place, so long as the state rests content to deal with crime in this barbaric and futile manner, society will be lulled by a false sense of security, and effective methods of dealing with crime will be discouraged.

It seems to be a general impression that there are fewer homicides in   13
Great Britain than in America because in England punishment is more certain, more prompt, and more severe. As a matter of fact, the reverse is true. In England the average term for burglary is eighteen months; with us it is probably four or five years. In England, imprisonment for life means twenty years. Prison sentences in the United States are harder than in any country in the world that could be classed as civilized. This is true largely because, with us, practically no official dares to act on his own judgment. The mob is all-powerful and demands blood for blood. That intangible body of people called "the public" vents its hatred upon the criminal and enjoys the sensation of having him put to death by the state—this without any definite idea that it is really necessary.

For the last five or six years, in England and Wales, the homicide re-   14
ported by the police range from sixty-five to seventy a year. Death sentences meted out by jurors have averaged about thirty-five, and hangings, fifteen. More than half of those convicted by juries were saved by appeals to the Home Office. But in America there is no such percentage of lives saved after conviction. Governors are afraid to grant clemency. If they did, the newspapers and the populace would refuse to re-elect them.

It is true that trials are somewhat prompter in England than America,   15
but there no newspaper dares publish the details of any case until after the trial. In America the accused is often convicted by the public within twenty-four hours of the time a homicide occurs. The courts sidetrack all other business so that a homicide that is widely discussed may receive prompt attention. The road to the gallows is not only opened but greased for the opportunity of killing another victim.

Thus, while capital punishment panders to the passions of the mob, no   16
one takes the pains to understand the meaning of crime. People speak of crime or criminals as if the world were divided into the good and the bad. This is not true. All of us have the same emotions, but since the balance of emotions is never the same, nor the inducing causes identical, human conduct presents a wide range of differences, shading by almost imperceptible degrees from that of the saint to that of the murderer. Of those kinds of conduct which are classed as dangerous, by no means all are made criminal offenses. Who can clearly define the difference between certain legal offenses and many kinds of dangerous conduct not singled out by criminal statute? Why are many cases of cheating entirely omitted from the criminal code, such as false and misleading advertisements, selling watered stock, forestalling the market, and all the different ways in which great fortunes are accumulated to the envy and despair of those who would like to have money but do not know how to get it? Why do we kill people for the crime of homicide

and administer a lesser penalty for burglary, robbery, and cheating? Can anyone tell which is the greater crime and which is the lesser?

Human conduct is by no means so simple as our moralists have led us   17
to believe. There is no sharp line separating good actions from bad. The greed for money, the display of wealth, the despair of those who witness the display, the poverty, oppression, and hopelessness of the unfortunate—all these are factors which enter into human conduct and of which the world takes no account. Many people have learned no other profession but robbery and burglary. The processions moving steadily through our prisons to the gallows are in the main made up of these unfortunates. And how do we dare to consider ourselves civilized creatures when, ignoring the causes of crime, we rest content to mete out harsh punishments to the victims of conditions over which they have no control?

Even now, are not all imaginative and humane people shocked at the   18
spectacle of a killing by the state? How many men and women would be willing to act as executioners? How many fathers and mothers would want their children to witness an official killing? What kind of people read the sensational reports of an execution? If all right-thinking men and women were not ashamed of it, why would it be needful that judges and lawyers and preachers apologize for the barbarity? How can the state censure the cruelty of the man who—moved by strong passions, or acting to save his freedom, or influenced by weakness or fear—takes human life, when everyone knows that the state itself, after long premeditation and settled hatred, not only kills, but first tortures and bedevils its victims for weeks with the impending doom?

For the last hundred years the world has shown a gradual tendency to   19
mitigate punishment. We are slowly learning that this way of controlling human beings is both cruel and ineffective. In England the criminal code has consistently grown more humane, until now the offenses punishable by death are reduced to practically one. There is no doubt whatever that the world is growing more humane and more sensitive and more understanding. The time will come when all people will view with horror the light way in which society and its courts of law now take human life; and when that time comes, the way will be clear to devise some better method of dealing with poverty and ignorance and their frequent byproducts, which we call crime.

QUESTIONS FOR MEANING

1. In his opening paragraphs, Darrow claims that capital punishment is supported by "the self-righteous." What kind of people is he referring to? Do you agree with him?
2. Why does Darrow believe that capital punishment does not deter crime? Why does he believe it is still carried out?
3. Darrow argues that "Capital punishment ignores the causes of crime." At what points in his essay does he try to reveal what these causes are?
4. How would you describe Darrow's opinion of human nature?

5. Toward the end of his essay Darrow asks, "Why do we kill people for the crime of homicide and administer a lesser penalty for burglary, robbery, and cheating? Can anyone tell which is the greater crime and which is the lesser?" Can you?

QUESTIONS ABOUT STRATEGY

1. For what sort of audience do you think this essay was originally written? Is there any evidence in it that Darrow was not addressing "the great mass of people" or the "mob" to which he refers in paragraphs 5 and 13?
2. In paragraph 9, Darrow argues, "The old fashioned stories of men deliberately plotting and committing murder in cold blood have little foundation in real life." Consider whether you agree with him. What is his purpose in making this claim?
3. How useful is the comparison between England and the United States?
4. Why does Darrow introduce "fathers," "mothers," and "children" into his second to last paragraph?
5. This essay was written more than sixty years ago. Do you think its argument is still valid, or does it seem out of date?

MAHATMA GANDHI

Brahmacharya

The single most important figure in the struggle for Indian independence from British rule, Mohandas Karamchand Gandhi (1869–1948) earned the title "Mahatma," or "Great-Souled" by virtue of an almost saint-like commitment to nonviolence, coupled with a deep belief in the sanctity of all life and an almost complete disregard for his own physical comfort.

Raised in a strict, religious environment, Gandhi traveled to England in 1888 to study law. While there, he met George Bernard Shaw and other British intellectuals concerned with the need for social change. From 1893 to 1914, he lived and worked in South Africa—an experience that had a profound effect upon his political development. Shortly after his arrival in South Africa, Gandhi experienced humiliations such as being thrown off of a train because of the color of his skin. After leading the campaign for improving the conditions under which the large Indian population in South Africa lived, Gandhi entered Indian politics in 1919. Throughout the 1920s and 30s he used nonviolent methods to protest British rule. Gandhi's greatest disappointment was that when independence from Britain was finally secured in 1947, India was partitioned into the separate countries of India and Pakistan (now India, Pakistan, and Bangladesh). When riots broke out that year between Hindus and Moslems, he traveled around the country to bring an end to violence. By fasting in Calcutta in 1947, he managed to end a period of prolonged

*violence in that city; a subsequent fast in Delhi was also successful. But within a
few days of ending the riots in Delhi, Gandhi was shot and killed while on his way
to prayer.*

Before you read the following selection from 1947, you might note that Gandhi was married at the age of thirteen.

If it is contended that birth control is necessary for the nation because of over-population, I dispute the proposition. It has never been proved. In my opinion by a proper land system, better agriculture and a supplementary industry, this country is capable of supporting twice as many people as there are in it to-day.

What, then, is Brahmacharya? It means that men and women should refrain from carnal knowledge of each other. That is to say, they should not touch each other with a carnal thought, they should not think of it even in their dreams. Their mutual glances should be free from all suggestion of carnality. The hidden strength that God has given us should be conserved by rigid self-discipline, and transmitted into energy and power—not merely of body, but also of mind and soul.

But what is the spectacle that we actually see around us? Men and women, old and young, without exception, are caught in the meshes of sensuality. Blinded for the most part by lust, they lose all sense of right and wrong. I have myself seen even boys and girls behaving as if they were mad under its fatal influence. I too have behaved likewise under similar influences, and it could not well be otherwise. For the sake of a momentary pleasure, we sacrifice in an instant all the stock of vital energy that we have laboriously accumulated. The infatuation over, we find ourselves in a miserable condition. The next morning we feel hopelessly weak and tired, and the mind refuses to do its work. Then in order to remedy the mischief, we consume large quantities of milk, bhasmas, yakutis and what not. We take all sorts of 'nervine tonics' and place ourselves at the doctor's mercy for repairing the waste, and for recovering the capacity for enjoyment. So the days pass and years, until at length old age comes upon us, and finds us utterly emasculated in body and in mind.

But the law of Nature is just the reverse of this. The older we grow the keener should our intellect be; the longer we live the greater should be our capacity to communicate the benefit of our accumulated experience to our fellow men. And such is indeed the case with those who have been true Brahmacharis. They know no fear of death, and they do not forget God even in the hour of death; nor do they indulge in vain desires. They die with a smile on their lips, and boldly face the day of judgment. They are true men and women; and of them alone can it be said that they have conserved their health.

We hardly realize the fact that incontinence is the root cause of most vanity, anger, fear and jealousy in the world. If our mind is not under our control, if we behave once or oftener every day more foolishly than even little children, what sins may we not commit consciously or unconsciously? How can we pause to think of the consequences of our actions, however vile or sinful they may be?

But you may ask, 'Who has ever seen a true Brahmachari in this sense?   6 If all men should turn Brahmacharis, would not humanity be extinct and the whole world go to rack and ruin?' We will leave aside the religious aspect of this question and discuss it simply from the secular point of view. To my mind, these questions only betray our timidity and worse. We have not the strength of will to observe Brahmacharya and therefore set about finding pretexts for evading our duty. The race of true Brahmacharis is by no means extinct; but if they were commonly to be met with, of what value would Brahmacharya be? Thousands of hardy labourers have to go and dig deep into the bowels of the earth in search for diamonds, and at length they get perhaps merely a handful of them out of heaps and heaps of rock. How much greater, then, should be the labour involved in the discovery of the infinitely more precious diamond of a Brahmachari? If the observance of Brahmacharya should mean the end of the world, that is none of our business. Are we God that we should be so anxious about its future? He who created it will surely see to its preservation. We need not trouble to inquire whether other people practise Brahmacharya or not. When we enter a trade or profession, do we ever pause to consider what the fate of the world would be if all men were to do likewise? The true Brahmachari will, in the long run, discover for himself answers to such questions.

But how can men engrossed in the cares of the material world put these   7 ideas into practice? What about those who are married? What shall they do who have children? And what shall be done by those people who cannot control themselves? We have already seen what is the highest state for us to attain. We should keep this ideal constantly before us, and try to approach it to the utmost of our capacity. When little children are taught to write the letters of the alphabet, we show them the perfect shapes of the letters, and they try to reproduce them as best they can. In the same way, if we steadily work up to the ideal of Brahmacharya we may ultimately succeed in realizing it. What if we have married already? The law of Nature is that Brahmacharya may be broken only when the husband and wife feel a desire for progeny. Those, who, remembering this law, violate Brahmacharya once in four or five years, will not become slaves to lust, nor lose much of their stock of vital energy. But, alas! How rare are those men and women who yield to the sexual craving merely for the sake of offspring! The vast majority turn to sexual enjoyment merely to satisfy their carnal passion, with the result that children are born to them quite against their will. In the madness of sexual passion, they give no thought to the consequences of their acts. In this respect, men are even more to blame than women. The man is blinded so much by his lust that he never cares to remember that his wife is weak and unable to bear or rear up a child. In the West, indeed, people have transgressed all bounds. They indulge in sexual pleasures and devise measures in order to evade the responsibilities of parenthood. Many books have been written on this subject and a regular trade is being carried on in contraceptives. We are as yet free from this sin, but we do not shrink from imposing heavy burden of maternity on our women, and we are not concerned even to find that our children are weak, impotent and imbecile.

We are, in this respect, far worse than even the lower animals; for in their case the male and the female are brought together solely with the object of breeding from them. Man and woman should regard it a sacred duty to keep apart from the moment of conception up to the time when the child is weaned. But we go on with our fatal merry-making blissfully forgetful of that sacred obligation. This almost incurable disease enfeebles our mind and leads us to an early grave, after making us drag a miserable existence for a short while. Married people should understand the true function of marriage, and should not violate Brahmacharya except with a view to progeny. 8

But this is so difficult under present conditions of life. Our diet, our ways of life, our common talk, and our environments are all equally calculated to rouse animal passions; and sensuality is like a poison eating into our vitals. Some people may doubt the possibility of our being able to free ourselves from this bondage. This book is written not for those who go about with such doubting of heart, but only for those who are really in earnest, and who have the courage to take active steps for self-improvement. Those who are quite content with their present abject condition will find this tedious even to read; but I hope it will be of some service to those who have realized and are disgusted with their own miserable plight. 9

From all that has been said it follows that those who are still unmarried should try to remain so; but if they cannot help marrying, they should defer it as long as possible. Young men, for instance, should take a vow to remain unmarried till the age of twenty-five or thirty. We cannot consider here all the advantages other than physical which they will reap and which are as it were added unto the rest. 10

My request to those parents who read this chapter is that they should not tie a millstone round the necks of their children by marrying them young. They should look to the welfare of the rising generation, and not merely seek to pamper their own vanity. They should cast aside all silly notions of family pride or respectability, and cease to indulge in such heartless practices. Let them rather, if they are true well-wishers of their children, look to their physical, mental and moral improvement. What greater disservice can they do to their progeny than compel them to enter upon married life, with all its tremendous responsibilities and cares, while they are mere children? 11

Then again the true laws of health demand that the man who loses his wife, as well as the woman that loses her husband, should remain single ever after. There is a difference of opinion among medical men as to whether young men and women need ever let their vital energy escape, some answering the question in the affirmative, others in the negative. But while doctors thus disagree we must not give way to over-indulgence from an idea that we are supported by medical authority. I can affirm, without the slightest hesitation, from my own experience as well as that of others, that sexual 12 enjoyment is not only not necessary for, but is positively injurious to health. All the strength of body and mind that has taken long to acquire is lost all at once by a single dissipation of the vital energy. It takes a long time to regain this lost vitality, and even then there is no saying that it can be thoroughly recovered. A broken mirror may be mended and made to do its work, but it can never be anything but a broken mirror.

As has already been pointed out, the preservation of our vitality is impossible without pure air, pure water, pure and wholesome food, as well as pure thoughts. So vital indeed is the relation between health and morals that we can never be perfectly healthy unless we lead a clean life. The earnest man, who, forgetting the errors of the past, begins to live a life of purity, will be able to reap the fruit of it straightaway. Those who practise true Brahmacharya even for a short period will see how their body and mind improve steadily in strength and power, and they will not at any cost be willing to part with this treasure. I have myself been guilty of lapses even after having fully understood the value of Brahmacharya, and have of course paid dearly for it. I am filled with shame and remorse when I think of the terrible contrast between my condition before and after these lapses. But from the errors of the past I have now learnt to preserve this treasure intact, and I fully hope, with God's grace to continue to preserve it in the future; for I have, in my own person, experienced the inestimable benefits of Brahmacharya. I was married early, and had become the father of children as a mere youth. When at length, I awoke to the reality of my situation, I found that I was steeped in ignorance about the fundamental laws of our being. I shall consider myself amply rewarded for writing this chapter if at least a single reader takes a warning from my failings and experiences, and profits thereby. Many people have told—and I also believe it—that I am full of energy and enthusiasm, and that I am by no means weak in mind; some even accuse me of strength bordering on obstinacy. Nevertheless there is still bodily and mental ill-health as a legacy of the past. And yet when compared with my friends, I may call myself healthy and strong. If even after twenty years of sensual enjoyment, I have been able to reach this state, how much better off should I have been if I had kept myself pure during those twenty years as well? It is my full conviction, that if only I had lived a life of unbroken Brahmacharya all through, my energy and enthusiasm would have been a thousandfold greater and I should have been able to devote them all to the furtherance of my country's cause as my own. If an imperfect Brahmachari like myself can reap such benefit, how much more wonderful must be the gain in power—physical, mental, as well as moral—that unbroken Brahmacharya can bring to us. 13

When so strict is the law of Brahmacharya what shall we say of those guilty of the unpardonable sin of illegitimate sexual enjoyment? The evil arising from adultery and prostitution is a vital question of religion and morality and cannot be fully dealt with in a treatise on health. Here we are only concerned to point out how thousands who are guilty of these sins are afflicted by venereal diseases. God is merciful in this that the punishment swiftly overtakes sinners. Their short span of life is spent in object bondage to quacks 14 in a futile quest after a remedy for their ills. If adultery and prostitution disappeared, at least half the present number of doctors would find their occupation gone. So inextricably indeed has venereal disease caught mankind in its clutches that thoughtful medical men have been forced to admit, that so long as adultery and prostitution continue, there is no hope for the human race, all the discoveries of curative medicine notwithstanding. The medicines for these diseases are so poisonous that although they may appear to have done some good for the time being, they give rise to other and still more terrible diseases which are transmitted from generation to generation.

No one need therefore despair. My Mahatmaship is worthless. It is due   15
to my outward activities, due to my politics which is the least part of me and is therefore evanescent. What is of abiding worth is my insistence on truth, non-violence and Brahmacharya, which is the real part of me. That permanent part of me, however small, is not to be despised. It is my all. I prize even the failures and disillusionments which are but steps towards success.

QUESTIONS FOR MEANING

1. How does Gandhi define *Brahmacharya*?
2. According to Gandhi, what are the advantages of abstaining from sex?
3. What advice does Gandhi offer on the subject of marriage?
4. Does Gandhi believe that men and women experience sexual desire to the same degree?
5. Vocabulary: carnal (2), emasculated (3), incontinence (5), impotent (7), progeny (8).

QUESTIONS ABOUT STRATEGY

1. Why do you think Gandhi begins his case by dismissing an argument that he could have used when arguing on behalf of celibacy?
2. Where does Gandhi admit to having experienced sexual activity? What does he gain from making this admission?
3. How does Gandhi respond to opponents who might argue that there would be no future for humanity if everyone practiced Brahmacharya?
4. Does Gandhi make any claims that leave him open to counterargument?

NELSON MANDELA
The Struggle Is My Life

Educated at the University College of Fort Hare and the University of Wintwaters-rand, Nelson Mandela is a South African lawyer who led the struggle for black rights in a country long ruled by a white minority. He joined the African National Congress in 1944 and was first tried for treason in a case that lasted from 1956 to

1961, when he was acquitted. In 1964, he was charged with attempting to over-
throw the government and sentenced to life imprisonment. He would not be released
until 1990, but his influence remained strong during the long, difficult years of his
confinement. He received the Jawaharlal Nehru Award in 1979 and the Bruno
Kreisky Prize for Human Rights in 1981. He has also been awarded many honor-
ary degrees. His books include No Easy Walk to Freedom *(1965),* I Am Prepared to Die *(1979), and* The Struggle Is My Life *(1978), from which the*
following press statement is reprinted. It was originally issued by Mandela on June
26, **1961.**

The magnificent response to the call of the National Action Council for a   1
three-day strike and the wonderful work done by our organisers and field
workers throughout the country proves once again that no power on earth
can stop an oppressed people determined to win their freedom. In the face of
unprecedented intimidation by the government and employers and of blatant
falsehoods and distortions by the press, immediately before and during the
strike, the freedom-loving people of South Africa gave massive and solid
support to the historic and challenging resolutions of the Pietermaritzburg
Conference. Factory and office workers, businessmen in town and country,
students in university colleges, in primary and secondary schools, inspired
by genuine patriotism and threatened with loss of employment, cancellation
of business licences and the ruin of school careers, rose to the occasion and
recorded in emphatic tones their opposition to a White republic forcibly imposed on us by a minority. In the light of the formidable array of hostile
forces that stood against us, and the difficult and dangerous conditions under
which we worked, the results were most inspiring. I am confident that if we
work harder and more systematically, the Nationalist government will not
survive for long. No organization in the world could have withstood and
survived the full-scale and massive bombardment directed against us by the
government during the last month.

In the history of our country no political campaign has ever merited   2
the serious attention and respect which the Nationalist government gave us.
When a government seeks to suppress a peaceful demonstration of an unarmed people by mobilising the entire resources of the State, military and
otherwise, it concedes powerful mass support for such a demonstration. Could
there be any other evidence to prove that we have become a power to be
reckoned with and the strongest opposition to the government? Who can
deny the plain fact that ever since the end of last month the issue that dominated South African politics was not the republican celebrations, but our plans
for a general strike?

Today is 26 June, a day known throughout the length and breadth of   3
our country as Freedom Day. On this memorable day, nine years ago, eight
thousand five hundred of our dedicated freedom fighters struck a mighty
blow against the repressive colour policies of the government. Their match-
less courage won them the praise and affection of millions of people here and

abroad. Since then we have had many stirring campaigns on this date and it has been observed by hundreds of thousands of our people as a day of dedication. It is fit and proper that on this historic day I should speak to you and announce fresh plans for the opening of the second phase in the fight against the Verwoerd republic, and for a National Convention.

You will remember that the Pietermaritzburg Resolutions warned that   4 if the government did not call a National Convention before the end of May, 1961, Africans, Coloureds, Indians and European democrats would be asked not to collaborate with the republic or any government based on force. On several occasions since then the National Action Council explained that the last strike marked the beginning of a relentless mass struggle for the defeat of the Nationalist government, and for a sovereign multi-racial convention. We stressed that the strike would be followed by other forms of mass pressure to force the race maniacs who govern our beloved country to make way for a democratic government of the people, by the people and for the people. A full-scale and country-wide campaign of non-co-operation with the government will be launched immediately. The precise form of the contemplated action, its scope and dimensions and duration will be announced to you at the appropriate time.

At the present moment it is sufficient to say that we plan to make   5 government impossible. Those who are voteless cannot be expected to continue paying taxes to a government which is not responsible to them. People who live in poverty and starvation cannot be expected to pay exorbitant house rents to the government and local authorities. We furnish the sinews of agriculture and industry. We produce the work of the gold mines, the diamonds and the coal, of the farms and industry, in return for miserable wages. Why should we continue enriching those who steal the products of our sweat and blood? Those who exploit us and refuse us the right to organise trade unions? Those who side with the government when we stage peaceful demonstrations to assert our claims and aspirations? How can Africans serve on School Boards and Committees which are part of Bantu Education, a sinister scheme of the Nationalist government to deprive the African people of real education in return for tribal education? Can Africans be expected to be content with serving on Advisory Boards and Bantu Authorities when the demand all over the continent of Africa is for national independence and self-government? Is it not an affront to the African people that the government should now seek to extend Bantu Authorities to the cities, when people in the rural areas have refused to accept the same system and fought against it tooth and nail? Which African does not burn with indignation when thousands of our people are sent to gaol every month under the cruel pass laws? Why should we continue carrying these badges of slavery? Non-collaboration is a dynamic weapon. We must refuse. We must use it to send this government to the grave. It must be used vigorously and without delay. The entire resources of the Black people must be mobilised to withdraw all co-operation with the Nationalist government. Various forms of industrial and economic action will be employed to undermine the already tottering economy of the country. We will call upon the international bodies to expel South

Africa and upon nations of the world to sever economic and diplomatic relations with the country.

I am informed that a warrant for my arrest has been issued, and that   6
the police are looking for me. The National Action Council has given full
and serious consideration to this question, and has sought the advice of many
trusted friends and bodies and they have advised me not to surrender myself.
I have accepted this advice, and will not give myself up to a government I
do not recognise. Any serious politician will realize that under present-day
conditions in this country, to seek for cheap martyrdom by handing myself
to the police is naive and criminal. We have an important programme before
us and it is important to carry it out very seriously and without delay.

I have chosen this latter course, which is more difficult and which en-   7
tails more risk and hardship than sitting in gaol. I have had to separate myself
from my dear wife and children, from my mother and sisters, to live as an
outlaw in my own land. I have had to close my business, to abandon my
profession, and live in poverty and misery, as many of my people are doing.
I will continue to act as the spokesman of the National Action Council during the phase that is unfolding and in the tough struggles that lie ahead. I
shall fight the government side by side with you, inch by inch, and mile by
mile, until victory is won. What are you going to do? Will you come along
with us, or are you going to co-operate with the government in its efforts to
suppress the claims and aspirations of your own people? Or are you going
to remain silent and neutral in a matter of life and death to my people, to
our people? For my own part I have made my choice. I will not leave South
Africa, nor will I surrender. Only through hardship, sacrifice and militant
action can freedom be won. The struggle is my life. I will continue fighting
for freedom until the end of my days.

QUESTIONS FOR MEANING

1. What evidence of oppression does Mandela cite?
2. On what grounds does Mandela claim that the South African government
   had come to take the National Action Council seriously?
3. Why did Mandela seek to avoid arrest by going underground? What did
   this decision cost him?
4. Does Mandela give any idea of what types of action he envisioned in the
   continuing struggle against the government of South Africa?

QUESTIONS ABOUT STRATEGY

1. Why did Mandela issue this press statement on the 26th of June?
2. Does Mandela cast his struggle as a conflict between whites and blacks,
   or does he put it in broader terms?
3. To whom is this statement addressed?
4. How does Mandela characterize the South African government? Does his
   statement as a whole make this characterization credible?

MARTIN LUTHER KING, JR.
Letter from Birmingham Jail

Martin Luther King, Jr. (1929–1968) was the most important leader of the move-
ment to secure civil rights for black Americans during the mid-twentieth century.
Ordained a Baptist minister in his father's church in Atlanta, King went on to re-
ceive a Ph.D. from Boston University in 1955. Two years later, he became the
founder and director of the Southern Christian Leadership Conference, an organiza-
tion he continued to lead until his assassination in 1968. He first came to national
attention by organizing a boycott of the buses in Montgomery, Alabama (1955–
1956)—a campaign that he recounts in Stride Toward Freedom: The Montgomery Story *(1958). His other books include* The Measure of a Man *(1959),*
Why We Can't Wait *(1963), and* Where Do We Go from Here: Chaos or
Community? *(1967). An advocate of nonviolence, King was jailed fourteen times*
in the course of his work for civil rights. His efforts helped secure the passage of the
Civil Rights Bill in 1963, and, during the last years of his life, he was the recipient
of many awards, most notably the Nobel Peace Prize in 1964.

"Letter from Birmingham Jail" was written in **1963,** *when King was jailed*
for eight days as the result of his campaign against segregation in Birmingham, Ala-
bama. In it, King responds to white clergymen who had criticized his work and
blamed him for breaking the law. But "Letter from Birmingham Jail" is much more
than a rebuttal of criticism. It is a well-reasoned and carefully argued defense of civil
disobedience as a means of securing civil liberties.

April 16, 1963

My Dear Fellow Clergymen:

While confined here in the Birmingham city jail, I came across your   1
recent statement calling my present activities "unwise and untimely." Seldom do I pause to answer criticism of my work and ideas. If I sought to
answer all the criticisms that cross my desk, my secretaries would have little
time for anything other than such correspondence in the course of the day,
and I would have no time for constructive work. But since I feel that you
are men of genuine good will and that your criticisms are sincerely put forth,
I want to try to answer your statement in what I hope will be patient and
reasonable terms.

I think I should indicate why I am here in Birmingham, since you have   2
been influenced by the view which argues against "outsiders coming in." I
have the honor of serving as president of the Southern Christian Leadership
Conference, an organization operating in every southern state, with headquarters in Atlanta, Georgia. We have some eighty-five affiliated organizations across the South, and one of them is the Alabama Christian Movement
for Human Rights. Frequently we share staff, educational, and financial resources with our affiliates. Several months ago the affiliate here in Birmingham asked us to be on call to engage in a nonviolent direct-action program

if such were deemed necessary. We readily consented, and when the hour came we lived up to our promise. So I, along with several members of my staff, am here because I was invited here. I am here because I have organizational ties here.

But more basically, I am in Birmingham because injustice is here. Just   3
as the prophets of the eighth century B.C. left their villages and carried their "thus saith the Lord" far beyond the boundaries of their home towns, and just as the Apostle Paul left his village of Tarsus and carried the gospel of Jesus Christ to the far corners of the Greco-Roman world, so am I compelled to carry the gospel of freedom beyond my own home town. Like Paul, I must constantly respond to the Macedonian call for aid.

Moreover, I am cognizant of the interrelatedness of all communities   4
and states. I cannot sit idly by in Atlanta and not be concerned about what happens in Birmingham. Injustice anywhere is a threat to justice everywhere. We are caught in an inescapable network of mutuality, tied in a single garment of destiny. Whatever affects one directly, affects all indirectly. Never again can we afford to live with the narrow, provincial, "outside agitator" idea. Anyone who lives inside the United States can never be considered an outsider anywhere within its bounds.

You deplore the demonstrations taking place in Birmingham. But your   5
statement, I am sorry to say, fails to express a similar concern for the conditions that brought about the demonstrations. I am sure that none of you would want to rest content with the superficial kind of social analysis that deals merely with effects and does not grapple with underlying causes. It is unfortunate that demonstrations are taking place in Birmingham, but it is even more unfortunate that the city's white power structure left the Negro community with no alternative.

In any nonviolent campaign there are four basic steps: collection of the   6
facts to determine whether injustices exist; negotiation; self-purification; and direct action. We have gone through all these steps in Birmingham. There can be no gainsaying the fact that racial injustice engulfs this community. Birmingham is probably the most thoroughly segregated city in the United States. Its ugly record of brutality is widely known. Negroes have experienced grossly unjust treatment in courts. There have been more unsolved bombings of Negro homes and churches in Birmingham than in any other city in the nation. These are the hard, brutal facts of the case. On the basis of these conditions, Negro leaders sought to negotiate with the city fathers. But the latter consistently refused to engage in good-faith negotiation.

Then, last September, came the opportunity to talk with leaders of Bir-   7
mingham's economic community. In the course of the negotiations, certain promises were made by the merchants—for example, to remove the stores' humiliating racial signs. On the basis of these promises, the Reverend Fred Shuttlesworth and the leaders of the Alabama Christian Movement for Human Rights agreed to a moratorium on all demonstrations. As the weeks and months went by, we realized that we were the victims of a broken promise. A few signs, briefly removed, returned; the others remained.

As in so many past experiences, our hopes had been blasted, and the   8
shadow of deep disappointment settled upon us. We had no alternative except to prepare for direct action, whereby we would present our very bodies
as means of laying our case before the conscience of the local and the national
community. Mindful of the difficulties involved, we decided to undertake a
process of self-purification. We began a series of workshops on nonviolence,
and we repeatedly asked ourselves: "Are you able to accept blows without
retaliating?" "Are you able to endure the ordeal of jail?" We decided to schedule
our direct-action program for the Easter season, realizing that except for
Christmas, this is the main shopping period of the year. Knowing that a
strong economic-withdrawal program would be the by-product of direct action, we felt that this would be the best time to bring pressure to bear on the
merchants for the needed change.

Then it occurred to us that Birmingham's mayoral election was coming   9
up in March, and we speedily decided to postpone action until after election
day. When we discovered that the Commissioner of Public Safety, Eugene
"Bull" Connor, had piled up enough votes to be in the run-off, we decided
again to postpone action until the day after the run-off so that the demonstrations could not be used to cloud the issues. Like many others, we waited
to see Mr. Connor defeated, and to this end we endured postponement after
postponement. Having aided in this community need, we felt that our direct-
action program could be delayed no longer.

You may well ask, "Why direct action? Why sit-ins, marches, and so   10
forth? Isn't negotiation a better path?" You are quite right in calling for
negotiation. Indeed, this is the very purpose of direct action. Nonviolent
direct action seeks to create such a crisis and foster such a tension that a community which has constantly refused to negotiate is forced to confront
the issue. It seeks so to dramatize the issue that it can no longer be ignored.
My citing the creation of tension as part of the work of the nonviolent-
resister may sound rather shocking. But I must confess that I am not afraid
of the word "tension." I have earnestly opposed violent tension, but
there is a type of constructive, nonviolent tension which is necessary for
growth. Just as Socrates felt that it was necessary to create a tension in
the mind so that individuals could rise from the bondage of myths and
half-truths to the unfettered realm of creative analysis and objective appraisal, so must we see the need for nonviolent gadflies to create the
kind of tension in society that will help men rise from the dark depths of
prejudice and racism to the majestic heights of understanding and brotherhood.

The purpose of our direct-action program is to create a situation so   11
crisis-packed that it will inevitably open the door to negotiation. I therefore
concur with you in your call for negotiation. Too long has our beloved
Southland been bogged down in a tragic effort to live in monologue rather
than dialogue.

One of the basic points in your statement is that the action that I and   12
my associates have taken in Birmingham is untimely. Some have asked: "Why

didn't you give the new city administration time to act?" The only answer that I can give to this query is that the new Birmingham administration must be prodded about as much as the outgoing one, before it will act. We are sadly mistaken if we feel that the election of Albert Boutwell as mayor will bring the millennium to Birmingham. While Mr. Boutwell is a much more gentle person than Mr. Connor, they are both segregationists, dedicated to maintenance of the status quo. I have hoped that Mr. Boutwell will be reasonable enough to see the futility of massive resistance to desegregation. But he will not see this without pressure from devotees of civil rights. My friends, I must say to you that we have not made a single gain in civil rights without determined legal and nonviolent pressure. Lamentably, it is an historical fact that privileged groups seldom give up their privileges voluntarily. Individuals may see the moral light and voluntarily give up their unjust posture; but, as Reinhold Niebuhr has reminded us, groups tend to be more immoral than individuals.

We know through painful experience that freedom is never voluntarily   13
given by the oppressor; it must be demanded by the oppressed. Frankly, I have yet to engage in a direct-action campaign that was "well timed" in the view of those who have not suffered unduly from the disease of segregation. For years now I have heard the word "Wait!" It rings in the ear of every Negro with piercing familiarity. This "Wait" has almost always meant "Never." We must come to see, with one of our distinguished jurists, that "justice too long delayed is justice denied."

We have waited for more than 340 years for our constitutional and   14
God-given rights. The nations of Asia and Africa are moving with jetlike speed toward gaining political independence, but we still creep at horse-and-buggy pace toward gaining a cup of coffee at a lunch counter. Perhaps it is easy for those who have never felt the stinging darts of segregation to say, "Wait." But when you have seen vicious mobs lynch your mothers and fathers at will and drown your sisters and brothers at whim; when you have seen hate-filled policemen curse, kick, and even kill your black brothers and sisters; when you see the vast majority of your twenty million Negro brothers smothering in an airtight cage of poverty in the midst of an affluent society; when you suddenly find your tongue twisted and your speech stammering as you seek to explain to your six-year-old daughter why she can't go to the public amusement park that has just been advertised on television, and see tears welling up in her eyes when she is told that Funtown is closed to colored children, and see ominous clouds of inferiority beginning to form in her little mental sky, and see her beginning to distort her personality by developing an unconscious bitternsss toward white people; when you have to concoct an answer for a five-year-old son who is asking, "Daddy, why do white people treat colored people so mean?"; when you take a cross-country drive and find it necessary to sleep night after night in the uncomfortable corners of your automobile because no motel will accept you; when you are humiliated day in and day out by nagging signs reading "white" and

"colored"; when your first name becomes "nigger," your middle name becomes "boy" (however old you are) and your last name becomes "John," and your wife and mother are never given the respected title "Mrs."; when you are harried by day and haunted by night by the fact that you are a Negro, living constantly at tiptoe stance, never quite knowing what to expect next, and are plagued with inner fears and outer resentments; when you are forever fighting a degenerating sense of "nobodiness"—then you will understand why we find it difficult to wait. There comes a time when the cup of endurance runs over, and men are no longer willing to be plunged into the abyss of despair. I hope, sirs, you can understand our legitimate and unavoidable impatience.

You express a great deal of anxiety over our willingness to break laws.   15 This is certainly a legitimate concern. Since we so diligently urge people to obey the Supreme Court's decision of 1954 outlawing segregation in the public schools, at first glance it may seem rather paradoxical for us consciously to break laws. One may well ask: "How can you advocate breaking some laws and obeying others?" The answer lies in the fact that there are two types of laws; just and unjust. I would be the first to advocate obeying just laws. One has not only a legal but a moral responsibility to obey just laws. Conversely, one has a moral responsibility to disobey unjust laws. I would agree with St. Augustine that "an unjust law is no law at all."

Now, what is the difference between the two? How does one determine   16 whether a law is just or unjust? A just law is a man-made code that squares with the moral law or the law of God. An unjust law is a code that is out of harmony with the moral law. To put it in the terms of St. Thomas Aquinas: An unjust law is a human law that is not rooted in eternal law and natural law. Any law that uplifts human personality is just. Any law that degrades human personality is unjust. All segregation statutes are unjust because segregation distorts the soul and damages the personality. It gives the segregator a false sense of superiority and the segregated a false sense of inferiority. Segregation, to use the terminology of the Jewish philosopher Martin Buber, substitutes an "I-it" relationship for an "I-thou" relationship and ends up relegating persons to the status of things. Hence segregation is not only politically, economically, and sociologically unsound, it is morally wrong and sinful. Paul Tillich has said that sin is segregation. Is not segregation an existential expression of man's tragic separation, his awful estrangement, his terrible sinfulness? Thus it is that I can urge men to obey the 1954 decision of the Supreme Court, for it is morally right; and I can urge them to disobey segregation ordinances, for they are morally wrong.

Let us consider a more concrete example of just and unjust laws. An   17 unjust law is a code that a numerical or power majority group compels a minority group to obey but does not make binding on itself. This is *difference* made legal. By the same token, a just law is a code that a majority compels a minority to follow and that it is willing to follow itself. This is *sameness* made legal.

Let me give another explanation. A law is unjust if it is inflicted on a   18
minority that, as a result of being denied the right to vote, had no part in
enacting or devising the law. Who can say that the legislature of Alabama
which set up that state's segregation laws was democratically elected?
Throughout Alabama all sorts of devious methods are used to prevent Negroes from becoming registered voters, and there are some counties in which,
even though Negroes constitute a majority of the population, not a single
Negro is registered. Can any law enacted under such circumstances be considered democratically structured?

Sometimes a law is just on its face and unjust in its application. For   19
instance, I have been arrested on a charge of parading without a permit.
Now, there is nothing wrong in having an ordinance which requires a permit
for a parade. But such an ordinance becomes unjust when it is used to maintain segregation and to deny citizens the First-Amendment privilege of peaceful assembly and protest.

I hope you are able to see the distinction I am trying to point out. In   20
no sense do I advocate evading or defying the law, as would the rabid segregationist. That would lead to anarchy. One who breaks an unjust law must
do so openly, lovingly, and with a willingness to accept the penalty. I submit
that an individual who breaks a law that conscience tells him is unjust, and
who willingly accepts the penalty of imprisonment in order to arouse the
conscience of the community over its injustice, is in reality expressing the
highest respect for law.

Of course, there is nothing new about this kind of civil disobedience.   21
It was evidenced sublimely in the refusal of Shadrach, Meshach, and Abed-
nego to obey the laws of Nebuchadnezzar, on the ground that a higher moral
law was at stake. It was practiced superbly by the early Christians, who were
willing to face hungry lions and the excruciating pain of chopping blocks
rather than submit to certain unjust laws of the Roman Empire. To a degree,
academic freedom is a reality today because Socrates practiced civil disobedience. In our own nation, the Boston Tea Party represented a massive act
of civil disobedience.

We should never forget that everything Adolf Hitler did in Germany   22
was "legal" and everything the Hungarian freedom fighters did in Hungary was "illegal." It was "illegal" to aid and comfort a Jew in Hitler's Germany. Even so, I am sure that, had I lived in Germany at the time, I would
have aided and comforted my Jewish brothers. If today I lived in a Communist country where certain principles dear to the Christian faith are suppressed, I would openly advocate disobeying that country's anti-religious laws.

I must make two honest confessions to you, my Christian and Jewish   23
brothers. First, I must confess that over the past few years I have been gravely
disappointed with the white moderate. I have almost reached the regrettable
conclusion that the Negro's great stumbling block in his stride toward freedom is not the White Citizen's Counciler or the Ku Klux Klanner, but the
white moderate, who is more devoted to "order" than to justice; who prefers
a negative peace which is the absence of tension to a positive peace which is

the presence of justice; who constantly says, "I agree with you in the goal you seek, but I cannot agree with your methods of direct action"; who paternalistically believes he can set the timetable for another man's freedom; who lives by a mythical concept of time and who constantly advises the Negro to wait for a "more convenient season." Shallow understanding from people of good will is more frustrating than absolute misunderstanding from people of ill will. Lukewarm acceptance is much more bewildering than outright rejection.

I had hoped that the white moderate would understand that law and   24
order exist for the purpose of establishing justice and that when they fail in this purpose they become the dangerously structured dams that block the flow of social progress. I had hoped that the white moderate would understand that the present tension in the South is a necessary phase of the transition from an obnoxious negative peace, in which the Negro passively accepted his unjust plight, to a substantive and positive peace, in which all men will respect the dignity and worth of human personality. Actually, we who engage in nonviolent direct action are not the creators of tension. We merely bring to the surface the hidden tension that is already alive. We bring it out in the open, where it can be seen and dealt with. Like a boil that can never be cured so long as it is covered up but must be opened with all its ugliness to the natural medicines of air and light, injustice must be exposed, with all the tension its exposure creates, to the light of human conscience and the air of national opinion, before it can be cured.

In your statement you assert that our actions, even though peaceful,   25
must be condemned because they precipitate violence. But is this a logical assertion? Isn't this like condemning a robbed man because his possession of money precipitated the evil act of robbery? Isn't this like condemning Socrates because his unswerving commitment to truth and his philosophical inquiries precipitated the act by the misguided populace in which they made him drink hemlock? Isn't this like condemning Jesus because his unique God-consciousness and never-ceasing devotion to God's will precipitated the evil act of crucifixion? We must come to see that, as the federal courts have consistently affirmed, it is wrong to urge an individual to cease his efforts to gain his basic constitutional rights because the quest may precipitate violence. Society must protect the robbed and punish the robber.

I had also hoped that the white moderate would reject the myth con-   26
cerning time in relation to the struggle for freedom. I have just received a letter from a white brother in Texas. He writes: "All Christians know that the colored people will receive equal rights eventually, but it is possible that you are in too great a religious hurry. It has taken Christianity almost two thousand years to accomplish what it has. The teachings of Christ take time to come to earth." Such an attitude stems from a tragic misconception of time, from the strangely irrational notion that there is something in the very flow of time that will inevitably cure all ills. Actually, time itself is neutral; it can be used either destructively or constructively. More and more I feel that the people of ill will have used time much more effectively than have

the people of good will. We will have to repent in this generation not merely for the hateful words and actions of the bad people, but for the appalling silence of the good people. Human progress never rolls in on wheels of inevitability; it comes through the tireless efforts of men willing to be coworkers with God, and without this hard work, time itself becomes an ally of the forces of social stagnation. We must use time creatively, in the knowledge that the time is always ripe to do right. Now is the time to make real the promise of democracy and transform our pending national elegy into a creative psalm of brotherhood. Now is the time to lift our national policy from the quicksand of racial injustice to the solid rock of human dignity.

You speak of our activity in Birmingham as extreme. At first I was 27 rather disappointed that fellow clergymen would see my nonviolent efforts as those of an extremist. I began thinking about the fact that I stand in the middle of two opposing forces in the Negro community. One is a force of complacency, made up in part of Negroes who, as a result of long years of oppression, are so drained of self-respect and a sense of "somebodiness" that they have adjusted to segregation; and in part of a few middle-class Negroes who, because of a degree of academic and economic security and because in some ways they profit by segregation, have become insensitive to the problems of the masses. The other force is one of bitterness and hatred, and it comes perilously close to advocating violence. It is expressed in the various black nationalist groups that are springing up across the nation, the largest and best-known being Elijah Muhammad's Muslim movement. Nourished by the Negro's frustration over the continued existence of racial discrimination, this movement is made up of people who have lost faith in America, who have absolutely repudiated Christianity, and who have concluded that the white man is an incorrigible "devil."

I have tried to stand between these two forces, saying that we need 28 emulate neither the "do-nothingism" of the complacent nor the hatred and despair of the black nationalist. For there is the more excellent way of love and nonviolent protest. I am grateful to God that, through the influence of the Negro church, the way of nonviolence became an integral part of our struggle.

If this philosophy had not emerged, by now many streets of the South 29 would, I am convinced, be flowing with blood. And I am further convinced that if our white brothers dismiss as "rabble-rousers" and "outside agitators" those of us who employ nonviolent direct action, and if they refuse to support our nonviolent efforts, millions of Negroes will, out of frustration and despair, seek solace and security in black-nationalist ideologies—a development that would inevitably lead to a frightening racial nightmare.

Oppressed people cannot remain oppressed forever. The yearning for 30 freedom eventually manifests itself, and that is what has happened to the American Negro. Something within has reminded him of his birthright of freedom, and something without has reminded him that it can be gained. Consciously or unconsciously, he has been caught up by the *Zeitgeist,* and with his black brothers of Africa and his brown and yellow brothers of Asia,

South America, and the Caribbean, the United States Negro is moving with a sense of great urgency toward the promised land of racial justice. If one recognizes this vital urge that has engulfed the Negro community, one should readily understand why public demonstrations are taking place. The Negro has many pent-up resentments and latent frustrations, and he must release them. So let him march; let him make prayer pilgrimages to the city hall; let him go on freedom rides—and try to understand why he must do so. If his repressed emotions are not released in nonviolent ways, they will seek expression through violence; this is not a threat but a fact of history. So I have not said to my people, "Get rid of your discontent." Rather, I have tried to say that this normal and healthy discontent can be channeled into the creative outlet of nonviolent direct action. And now this approach is being termed extremist.

But though I was initially disappointed at being categorized as an ex-   31
tremist, as I continued to think about the matter I gradually gained a measure of satisfaction from the label. Was not Jesus an extremist for love: "Love your enemies, bless them that curse you, do good to them that hate you, and pray for them which despitefully use you, and persecute you." Was not Amos an extremist for justice: "Let justice roll down like waters and righteousness like an everflowing stream." Was not Paul an extremist for the Christian gospel: "I bear in my body the marks of the Lord Jesus." Was not Martin Luther an extremist: "Here I stand; I cannot do otherwise, so help me God." And John Bunyan: "I will stay in jail to the end of my days before I make a butchery of my conscience." And Abraham Lincoln: "This nation cannot survive half slave and half free." And Thomas Jefferson: "We hold these truths to be self-evident, that all men are created equal. . . ." So the question is not whether we will be extremists, but what kind of extremists we will be. Will we be extremists for hate or for love? Will we be extremists for the preservation of injustice or for the extension of justice? In that dramatic scene on Calvary's hill three men were crucified. We must never forget that all three were crucified for the same crime—the crime of extremism. Two were extremists for immorality, and thus fell below their environment. The other, Jesus Christ, was an extremist for love, truth, and goodness, and thereby rose above his environment. Perhaps the South, the nation, and the world are in dire need of creative extremists.

I had hoped that the white moderate would see this need. Perhaps I was   32
too optimistic; perhaps I expected too much. I suppose I should have realized that few members of the oppressor race can understand the deep groans and passionate yearnings of the oppressed race, and still fewer have the vision to see that injustice must be rooted out by strong, persistent, and determined action. I am thankful, however, that some of our white brothers in the South have grasped the meaning of this social revolution and committed themselves to it. They are still all too few in quantity, but they are big in quality. Some—such as Ralph McGill, Lillian Smith, Harry Golden, James McBride Dabbs, Ann Braden, and Sarah Patton Boyle—have written about our struggle in eloquent and prophetic terms. Others have marched with us down nameless

streets of the South. They have languished in filthy, roach-infested jails, suffering the abuse and brutality of policemen who view them as "dirty niggerlovers." Unlike so many of their moderate brothers and sisters, they have recognized the urgency of the moment and sensed the need for powerful "action" antidotes to combat the disease of segregation.

Let me take note of my other major disappointment. I have been so greatly disappointed with the white church and its leadership. Of course, there are some notable exceptions. I am not unmindful of the fact that each of you has taken some significant stands on this issue. I commend you, Reverend Stallings, for your Christian stand on this past Sunday, in welcoming Negroes to your worship service on a nonsegregated basis. I commend the Catholic leaders of this state for integrating Spring Hill College several years ago.   33

But despite these notable exceptions, I must honestly reiterate that I have been disappointed with the church. I do not say this as one of those negative critics who can always find something wrong with the church. I say this as a minister of the gospel, who loves the church; who was nurtured in its bosom; who has been sustained by its spiritual blessings and who will remain true to it as long as the cord of life shall lengthen.   34

When I was suddenly catapulted into the leadership of the bus protest in Montgomery, Alabama, a few years ago, I felt we would be supported by the white church. I felt that the white ministers, priests, and rabbis of the South would be among our strongest allies. Instead, some have been outright opponents, refusing to understand the freedom movement and misrepresenting its leaders; all too many others have been more cautious than courageous and have remained silent behind the anesthetizing security of stained-glass windows.   35

In spite of my shattered dreams, I came to Birmingham with the hope that the white religious leadership of this community would see the justice of our cause and, with deep moral concern, would serve as the channel through which our just grievances could reach the power structure. I had hoped that each of you would understand. But again I have been disappointed.   36

There was a time when the church was very powerful—in the time when the early Christians rejoiced at being deemed worthy to suffer for what they believed. In those days the church was not merely a thermometer that recorded the ideas and principles of popular opinion; it was a thermostat that transformed the mores of society. Whenever the early Christians entered a town, the people in power became disturbed and immediately sought to convict the Christians for being "disturbers of the peace" and "outside agitators." But the Christians pressed on, in the conviction that they were "a colony of heaven," called to obey God rather than man. Small in number, they were big in commitment. They were too God-intoxicated to be "astronomically intimidated." By their effort and example they brought an end to such ancient evils as infanticide and gladiatorial contests.   37

Things are different now. So often the contemporary church is a weak, ineffectual voice with an uncertain sound. So often it is an archdefender of   38 the status quo. Far from being disturbed by the presence of the church, the power structure of the average community is consoled by the church's silent—and often even vocal—sanction of things as they are.

But the judgment of God is upon the church as never before. If today's   39 church does not recapture the sacrificial spirit of the early church, it will lose its authenticity, forfeit the loyalty of millions, and be dismissed as an irrelevant social club with no meaning for the twentieth century. Every day I meet young people whose disappointment with the church has turned into outright disgust.

Perhaps I have once again been too optimistic. Is organized religion too   40 inextricably bound to the status quo to save our nation and the world? Perhaps I must turn my faith to the inner spiritual church, the church within the church, as the true *ekklesia* and the hope of the world. But again I am thankful to God that some noble souls from the ranks of organized religion have broken loose from the paralyzing chains of conformity and joined us as active partners in the struggle for freedom. They have left their secure congregations and walked the streets of Albany, Georgia, with us. They have gone down the highways of the South on torturous rides for freedom. Yes, they have gone to jail with us. Some have been dismissed from their churches, have lost the support of their bishops and fellow ministers. But they have acted in the faith that right defeated is stronger than evil triumphant. Their witness has been the spiritual salt that has preserved the true meaning of the gospel in these troubled times. They have carved a tunnel of hope through the dark mountain of disappointment.

I hope the church as a whole will meet the challenge of this decisive   41 hour. But even if the church does not come to the aid of justice, I have no despair about the future. I have no fear about the outcome of our struggle in Birmingham, even if our motives are at present misunderstood. We will reach the goal of freedom in Birmingham and all over the nation, because the goal of America is freedom. Abused and scorned though we may be, our destiny is tied up with America's destiny. Before the pilgrims landed at Plymouth, we were here. Before the pen of Jefferson etched the majestic words of the Declaration of Independence across the pages of history, we were here. For more than two centuries our forebears labored in this country without wages; they made cotton king; they built the homes of their masters while suffering gross injustice and shameful humiliation—and yet out of a bottomless vitality they continued to thrive and develop. If the inexpressible cruelties of slavery could not stop us, the opposition we now face will surely fail. We will win our freedom because the sacred heritage of our nation and the eternal will of God are embodied in our echoing demands.

Before closing I feel impelled to mention one other point in your state-   42 ment that has troubled me profoundly. You warmly commended the Birmingham police force for keeping "order" and "preventing violence." I doubt that you would have so warmly commended the police force if you had seen its dogs sinking their teeth into unarmed, nonviolent Negroes. I doubt that you would so quickly commend the policemen if you were to observe their ugly and inhumane treatment of Negroes here in the city jail; if you were to watch them push and curse old Negro women and young Negro girls; if you were to see them slap and kick old Negro men and young boys; if you were to observe them, as they did on two occasions, refuse to give us food because we wanted to sing our grace together. I cannot join you in your praise of the Birmingham police department.

It is true that the police have exercised a degree of discipline in handling the demonstrators. In this sense they have conducted themselves rather "non-violently" in public. But for what purpose? To preserve the evil system of segregation. Over the past few years I have consistently preached that non-violence demands that the means we use must be as pure as the ends we seek. I have tried to make clear that it is wrong to use immoral means to attain moral ends. But now I must affirm that it is just as wrong, or perhaps even more so, to use moral means to preserve immoral ends. Perhaps Mr. Connor and his policemen have been rather nonviolent in public, as was Chief Pritchett in Albany, Georgia, but they have used the moral means of nonviolence to maintain the immoral end of racial injustice. As T. S. Eliot has said, "The last temptation is the greatest treason: To do the right deed for the wrong reason."   43

I wish you had commended the Negro sit-inners and demonstrators of Birmingham for their sublime courage, their willingness to suffer, and their amazing discipline in the midst of great provocation. One day the South will recognize its real heroes. They will be the James Merediths, with the noble sense of purpose that enables them to face jeering and hostile mobs, and with the agonizing loneliness that characterizes the life of the pioneer. They will be old, oppressed, battered Negro women, symbolized in a seventy-two-year-old woman in Montgomery, Alabama, who rose up with a sense of dignity and with her people decided not to ride segregated buses, and who responded with ungrammatical profundity to one who inquired about her weariness: "My feets is tired, but my soul is at rest." They will be the young high school and college students, the young ministers of the gospel and a host of their elders, courageously and nonviolently sitting in at lunch counters and willingly going to jail for conscience's sake. One day the South will know that when these disinherited children of God sat down at lunch counters, they were in reality standing up for what is best in the American dream and for the most sacred values in our Judeo-Christian heritage, thereby bringing our nation back to those great wells of democracy which were dug deep by the founding fathers in their formulation of the Constitution and the Declaration of Independence.   44

Never before have I written so long a letter. I'm afraid it is much too long to take your precious time. I can assure you that it would have been much shorter if I had been writing from a comfortable desk, but what else can one do when he is alone in a narrow jail cell, other than write long letters, think long thoughts, and pray long prayers?   45

If I have said anything in this letter that overstates the truth and indicates an unreasonable impatience, I beg you to forgive me. If I have said   46 anything that understates the truth and indicates my having a patience that allows me to settle for anything less than brotherhood, I beg God to forgive me.

I hope this letter finds you strong in the faith. I also hope that circumstances will soon make it possible for me to meet each of you, not as an integrationist or a civil-rights leader but as a fellow clergyman and a Christian brother. Let us all hope that the dark clouds of racial prejudice will soon pass away and the deep fog of misunderstanding will be lifted from our fear-drenched communities, and in some not too distant tomorrow the radiant stars of love and brotherhood will shine over our great nation with all their scintillating beauty.

47

Yours for the cause of Peace and Brotherhood,
Martin Luther King, Jr.

QUESTIONS FOR MEANING

1. What reason does King give for writing this letter? What justification does he provide for its length? How do these explanations work to his advantage?
2. One of the many charges brought against King at the time of his arrest was that he was an "outsider" who had no business in Birmingham. How does King defend himself? What three reasons does he cite to justify his presence in Birmingham?
3. King also responds to the criticism that his campaign for civil rights was "untimely." What is his defense against this charge?
4. What does King mean by nonviolent "direct action"? What sort of activities did he lead people to pursue? Identify the four basic steps to a direct-action campaign and explain what such campaigns were meant to accomplish.
5. Why did King believe that a direct-action campaign was necessary in Birmingham? Why did the black community in Birmingham turn to King? What problems were they facing, and what methods had they already tried before deciding upon direct action?
6. What was the 1954 Supreme Court decision that King refers to in paragraph 16? Why was King able to charge that the "rabid segregationist" breaks the law?
7. King's critics charged that he obeyed the law selectively. He answers by arguing there is a difference between just and unjust laws, and that moral law requires men and women to break unjust laws that are imposed upon them. How can you tell the difference between laws that you should honor and laws that you should break? What is King's definition of an unjust law, and what historical examples does he give to illustrate situations in which unjust laws have to be broken?
8. What does King mean when he complains of the "anesthetizing security of stained-glass windows"? How can churches make men and women feel falsely secure?

QUESTIONS ABOUT STRATEGY

1. Why did King address his letter to fellow clergymen? Why was he disappointed in them, and what did he expect his letter to accomplish?
2. Is there anything in the substance of this letter that reveals it was written for an audience familiar with the Bible and modern theology? Do you think King intended this letter to be read only by clergymen? Can you point to anything that suggests King may have really written for a larger, more general audience?
3. How does King characterize himself in this letter? What sort of a man does he seem to be, and what role does his presentation of himself play in his argument? How does he establish that he is someone worth listening to—and that it is important to listen to what he has to say?
4. *Ekklesia* is Greek for assembly, congregation, or church. Why does King use this word in paragraph 40 instead of simply saying "the church"?
5. Martin Luther King had much experience as a preacher when he wrote this famous letter. Is there anything about its style that reminds you of oratory? How effective would this letter be if delivered as a speech?

BETTY FRIEDAN

The Importance of Work

Betty Friedan was one of the founders of the National Organization for Women, serving as NOW's first president between 1966 and 1970. Born in Peoria, Illinois, and educated at Smith College, the University of California, and the University of Iowa, Friedan has lectured at more than fifty universities and institutes. Her essays have appeared in numerous periodicals, including the Saturday Review, Harper's, McCall's, Redbook, Good Housekeeping, *and the* Ladies' Home Journal. *Her books include* It Changed My Life *(1976) and* The Second Stage *(1981). The following essay is drawn from the book that made her famous,* The Feminine Mystique *(1963).*

    More than a quarter of a century has now passed since Friedan published this book, and the leadership of the women's movement has passed to a younger generation. But if the development of that movement could be traced back to the publication of a single work, it would have to be The Feminine Mystique. *Friedan believed that women needed to escape from the roles they had assumed as wives and mothers, and if her ideas no longer seem as bold as they once were, it is because she anticipated most of the concerns that would dominate the analysis of male/female relations during the 1970s and 1980s. "The Importance of Work" is an editor's title for the concluding pages of Friedan's book, an excerpt that reveals Friedan's conviction that women need to enter the mainstream of the American workforce—not simply as typists and file clerks, but as the full equals of men.*

The question of how a person can most fully realize his own capacities and   1
thus achieve identity has become an important concern of the philosophers
and the social and psychological thinkers of our time—and for good reason.
Thinkers of other times put forth the idea that people were, to a great extent,
defined by the work they did. The work that a man had to do to eat, to stay
alive, to meet the physical necessities of his environment, dictated his identity. And in this sense, when work was seen merely as a means of survival,
human identity was dictated by biology.

But today the problem of human identity has changed. For the work   2
that defined man's place in society and his sense of himself has also changed
man's world. Work, and the advance of knowledge, has lessened man's dependence on his environment; his biology and the work he must do for biological survival are no longer sufficient to define his identity. This can be
most clearly seen in our own abundant society; men no longer need to work
all day to eat. They have an unprecedented freedom to choose the kind of
work they will do; they also have an unprecedented amount of time apart
from the hours and days that must actually be spent in making a living. And
suddenly one realizes the significance of today's identity crisis—for women,
and increasingly, for men. One sees the human significance of work—not
merely as the means of biological survival, but as the giver of self and the
transcender of self, as the creator of human identity and human evolution.

For "self-realization" or "self-fulfillment" or "identity" does not come   3
from looking into a mirror in rapt contemplation of one's own image. Those
who have most fully realized themselves, in a sense that can be recognized
by the human mind even though it cannot be clearly defined, have done so
in the service of a human purpose larger than themselves. Men from varying
disciplines have used different words for this mysterious process from which
comes the sense of self. The religious mystics, the philosophers, Marx, Freud—
all had different names for it: man finds himself by losing himself; man is
defined by his relation to the means of production; the ego, the self, grows
through understanding and mastering reality—through work and love.

The identity crisis, which has been noted by Erik Erikson and others in   4
recent years in the American man, seems to occur for lack of, and be cured
by finding, the work, or cause, or purpose that evokes his own creativity.
Some never find it, for it does not come from busy-work or punching a time
clock. It does not come from just making a living, working by formula,
finding a secure spot as an organization man. The very argument, by Ries-
man and others, that man no longer finds identity in the work defined as a
paycheck job, assumes that identity for man comes through creative work of
his own that contributes to the human community: the core of the self becomes aware, becomes real, and grows through work that carries forward
human society.

Work, the shopworn staple of the economists, has become the new   5
frontier of psychology. Psychiatrists have long used "occupational therapy"
with patients in mental hospitals; they have recently discovered that to be of

real psychological value, it must be not just "therapy," but real work, serving a real purpose in the community. And work can now be seen as the key to the problem that has no name. The identity crisis of American women began a century ago, as more and more of the work important to the world, more and more of the work that used their human abilities and through which they were able to find self-realization, was taken from them.

Until, and even into, the last century, strong, capable women were   6
needed to pioneer our new land; with their husbands, they ran the farms and plantations and Western homesteads. These women were respected and self-respecting members of a society whose pioneering purpose centered in the home. Strength and independence, responsibility and self-confidence, self-discipline and courage, freedom and equality were part of the American character for both men and women, in all the first generations. The women who came by steerage from Ireland, Italy, Russia, and Poland worked beside their husbands in the sweatshops and the laundries, learned the new language, and saved to send their sons and daughters to college. Women were never quite as "feminine," or held in as much contempt, in America as they were in Europe. American women seemed to European travelers, long before our time, less passive, childlike, and feminine than their own wives in France or Germany or England. By an accident of history, American women shared in the work of society longer, and grew with the men. Grade- and high-school education for boys and girls alike was almost always the rule; and in the West, where women shared the pioneering work the longest, even the universities were coeducational from the beginning.

The identity crisis for women did not begin in America until the fire   7
and strength and ability of the pioneer women were no longer needed, no longer used, in the middle-class homes of the Eastern and Midwestern cities, when the pioneering was done and men began to build the new society in industries and professions outside the home. But the daughters of the pioneer women had grown too used to freedom and work to be content with leisure and passive femininity.

It was not an American, but a South African woman, Mrs. Olive   8
Schreiner, who warned at the turn of the century that the quality and quantity of women's functions in the social universe was decreasing as fast as civilization was advancing; that if women did not win back their right to a full share of honored and useful work, woman's mind and muscle would weaken in a parasitic state; her offspring, male and female, would weaken progressively, and civilization itself would deteriorate.

The feminists saw clearly that education and the right to participate in   9
the more advanced work of society were women's greatest needs. They fought for and won the rights to new, fully human identity for women. But how very few of their daughters and granddaughters have chosen to use their education and their abilities for any large creative purpose, for responsible work in society? How many of them have been deceived, or have deceived themselves, into clinging to the outgrown, childlike femininity of "Occupation: housewife"?

It was not a minor matter, their mistaken choice. We now know that   10
the same range of potential ability exists for women as for men. Women, as
well as men, can only find their identity in work that uses their full capacities. A woman cannot find her identity through others—her husband, her
children. She cannot find it in the dull routine of housework. As thinkers of
every age have said, it is only when a human being faces squarely the fact
that he can forfeit his own life, that he becomes truly aware of himself, and
begins to take his existence seriously. Sometimes this awareness comes only
at the moment of death. Sometimes it comes from a more subtle facing of
death: the death of self in passive conformity, in meaningless work. The
feminine mystique prescribes just such a living death for women. Faced with
the slow death of self, the American woman must begin to take her life
seriously.

"We measure ourselves by many standards," said the great American   11
psychologist William James, nearly a century ago. "Our strength and our
intelligence, our wealth and even our good luck, are things which warm our
heart and make us feel ourselves a match for life. But deeper than all such
things, and able to suffice unto itself without them, is the sense of the amount
of effort which we can put forth."

If women do not put forth, finally, that effort to become all that they   12
have it in them to become, they will forfeit their own humanity. A woman
today who has no goal, no purpose, no ambition patterning her days into
the future, making her stretch and grow beyond that small score of years in
which her body can fill its biological function, is committing a kind of suicide. For that future half a century after the child-bearing years are over is a
fact that an American woman cannot deny. Nor can she deny that as a
housewife, the world is indeed rushing past her door while she just sits and
watches. The terror she feels is real, if she has no place in that world.

The feminine mystique has succeeded in burying millions of American   13
women alive. There is no way for these women to break out of their comfortable concentration camps except by finally putting forth an effort—that
human effort which reaches beyond biology, beyond the narrow walls of
home, to help shape the future. Only by such a personal commitment to the
future can American women break out of the housewife trap and truly find
fulfillment as wives and mothers—by fulfilling their own unique possibilities
as separate human beings.

QUESTIONS FOR MEANING

1. In her opening paragraph, Friedan writes, "when work was seen merely
   as a means of survival, human identity was dictated by biology." What
   does this mean?
2. Does Friedan believe that all types of work are equally satisfying? Where
   does she define the type of work that has "human significance"?
3. According to Friedan, what is the historical explanation for the identity
   crisis many American women suffered during the twentieth century?

4. What's wrong with "Occupation: housewife"? Why does Friedan believe that women cannot find fulfillment simply by being wives and mothers?
5. Explain Friedan's allusion to "feminists" in paragraph 9. Who were the early feminists, and what did they accomplish?
6. Although you have been given only the last few pages of Friedan's book, can you construct a definition for what she means by "the feminine mystique"?
7. Vocabulary: transcender (2), rapt (3), mystics (3), parasitic (8), deteriorate (8), forfeit (10).

QUESTIONS ABOUT STRATEGY

1. What is the premise that underlies Friedan's argument on behalf of meaningful careers for women?
2. Why does Friedan discuss women within the context of psychological "identity"? Why is it important for her to link the needs of women with the needs of men?
3. Comment on Friedan's use of quotation. She refers, for support, to four men (Marx, Freud, Erik Erikson, and William James) and to only one woman, Olive Schreiner. Does her reliance upon male authorities help or hurt her argument?
4. When Friedan declares that housewives are "committing a kind of suicide" trapped within homes that are "comfortable concentration camps," is she drawing her work together with a forceful conclusion or weakening it through exaggeration?

CAROLINE BIRD
Where College Fails Us

After working as a researcher for Newsweek *and* Fortune *magazines in the mid-1940s, Caroline Bird went on to a successful career in public relations. Her many books reflect her interest in business and, in particular, the position of women in the business world. These books include* Born Female: The High Cost of Keeping Women Down *(1968),* Everything a Woman Needs to Know to Get Paid What She's Worth *(1973),* What Women Want *(1978), and* The Two Paycheck Marriage *(1979). The following essay, which has appeared in many anthologies since its first publication in* **1975,** *is one of Bird's best-known works. Drawing upon her knowledge of the economy and her skills as a researcher, Bird makes a detailed attack upon the much cherished notion that going to college leads to a good paying job.*

The case *for* college has been accepted without question for more than a gen-   1
eration. All high school graduates ought to go, says Conventional Wisdom
and statistical evidence, because college will help them earn more money,
become "better" people, and learn to be more responsible citizens than those
who don't go.

But college has never been able to work its magic for everyone. And   2
now that close to half our high school graduates are attending, those who
don't fit the pattern are becoming more numerous, and more obvious. College graduates are selling shoes and driving taxis; college students sabotage
each other's experiments and forge letters of recommendation in the intense
competition for admission to graduate school. Others find no stimulation in
their studies, and drop out—often encouraged by college administrators.

Some observers say the fault is with the young people themselves—   3
they are spoiled, stoned, overindulged, and expecting too much. But that's
mass character assassination, and doesn't explain all campus unhappiness.
Others blame the state of the world, and they are partly right. We've been
told that young people have to go to college because our economy can't
absorb an army of untrained eighteen-year-olds. But disillusioned graduates
are learning that it can no longer absorb an army of trained twenty-two-
year-olds, either.

Some adventuresome educators and campus watchers have openly be-   4
gun to suggest that college may not be the best, the proper, the only place
for every young person after the completion of high school. We may have
been looking at all those surveys and statistics upside down, it seems, and
through the rosy glow of our own remembered college experiences. Perhaps
college doesn't make people intelligent, ambitious, happy, liberal, or quick
to learn new things—maybe it's just the other way around, and intelligent,
ambitious, happy, liberal, and quick-learning people are merely the ones who
have been attracted to college in the first place. And perhaps all those successful college graduates would have been successful whether they had gone
to college or not. This is heresy to those of us who have been brought up to
believe that if a little schooling is good, more has to be much better. But
contrary evidence is beginning to mount up.

The unhappiness and discontent of young people is nothing new, and   5
problems of adolescence are always painfully intense. But while traveling
around the country, speaking at colleges, and interviewing students at all
kinds of schools—large and small, public and private—I was overwhelmed
by the prevailing sadness. It was as visible on campuses in California as in
Nebraska and Massachusetts. Too many young people are in college reluctantly, because everyone told them they ought to go, and there didn't seem
to be anything better to do. Their elders sell them college because it's good
for them. Some never learn to like it, and talk about their time in school as
if it were a sentence to be served.

Students tell us the same thing college couselors tell us—they go be-   6
cause of pressure from parents and teachers, and stay because it seems to be

an alternative to a far worse fate. It's "better" than the Army or a dead-end job, and it has to be pretty bad before it's any worse than staying at home.

College graduates say that they don't want to work "just" for money: 7
They want work that matters. They want to help people and save the world. But the numbers are stacked against them. Not only are there not enough jobs in world-saving fields, but in the current slowdown it has become evident that there never were, and probably never will be, enough jobs requiring higher education to go around.

Students who tell their advisers they want to help people, for example,   8
are often directed to psychology. This year the Department of Labor estimates that there will be 4,300 new jobs for psychologists, while colleges will award 58,430 bachelor's degree in psychology.

Sociology has become a favorite major on socially conscious campuses,   9
but graduates find that social reform is hardly a paying occupation. Male sociologists from the University of Wisconsin reported as gainfully employed a year after graduation included a legal assistant, sports editor, truck unloader, Peace Corps worker, publications director, and a stockboy—but no sociologist per se. The highest paid worked for the post office.

Publishing, writing, and journalism are presumably the vocational goal   10
of a large proportion of the 104,000 majors in Communications and Letters expected to graduate in 1975. The outlook for them is grim. All of the daily newspapers in the country combined are expected to hire a total of 2,600 reporters this year. Radio and television stations may hire a total of 500 announcers, most of them in local radio stations. Nonpublishing organizations will need 1,100 technical writers, and public-relations activities another 4,400. Even if new graduates could get all these jobs (they can't, of course), over 90,000 of them will have to find something less glamorous to do.

Other fields most popular with college graduates are also pathetically   11
small. Only 1,900 foresters a year will be needed during this decade, although schools of forestry are expected to continue graduating twice as many. Some will get sub-professional jobs as forestry aides. Schools of architecture are expected to turn out twice as many as will be needed, and while all sorts of people want to design things, the Department of Labor forecasts that there will be jobs for only 400 new industrial designers a year. As for anthropologists, only 400 will be needed every year in the 1970s to take care of all the college courses, public-health research, community surveys, museums, and all the archaeological digs on every continent. (For these jobs graduate work in anthropology is required.)

Many popular occupations may seem to be growing fast without necessarily offering employment to very many. "Recreation work" is always   12
cited as an expanding field, but it will need relatively few workers who require more special training than life guards. "Urban planning" has exploded in the media, so the U.S. Department of Labor doubled its estimate of the number of jobs to be filled every year in the 1970s—to a big, fat 800. A mere 200 oceanographers a year will be able to do all the exploring of "inner space"—

and all that exciting underwater diving you see demonstrated on television—
for the entire decade of the 1970s.

Whatever college graduates *want* to do, most of them are going to wind   13
up doing what *there is* to do. During the next few years, according to the
Labor Department, the biggest demand will be for stenographers and secretaries, followed by retail-trade salesworkers, hospital attendants, book-
keepers, building custodians, registered nurses, foremen, kindergarten and
elementary school teachers, receptionists, cooks, cosmetologists, private-
household workers, manufacturing inspectors, and industrial machinery re-
pairmen. These are the jobs which will eventually absorb the surplus ar-
chaeologists, urban planners, oceanographers, sociologists, editors, and college
professors.

Vocationalism is the new look on campus because of the discouraging   14
job market faced by the generalists. Students have been opting for medicine
and law in droves. If all those who check "doctor" as their career goal succeed in getting their MDs, we'll immediately have ten times the target ratio
of doctors for the population of the United States. Law schools are already
graduating twice as many new lawyers every year as the Department of Labor thinks we will need, and the oversupply grows annually.

Specialists often find themselves at the mercy of shifts in demand, and   15
the narrower the vocational training, the more risky the long-term prospects.
Engineers are the classic example of the "Yo-Yo" effect in supply and demand. Today's shortage is apt to produce a big crop of engineering graduates
after the need has crested, and teachers face the same squeeze.

Worse than that, when the specialists turn up for work, they often find   16
that they have learned a lot of things in classrooms that they will never use,
that they will have to learn a lot of things on the job that they were never
taught, and that most of what they have learned is less likely to "come in
handy later" than to fade from memory. One disillusioned architecture student, who had already designed and built houses, said, "It's the degree you
need, not everything you learn getting it."

A diploma saves the employer the cost of screening candidates and gives   17
him a predictable product: He can assume that those who have survived the
four-year ordeal have learned how to manage themselves. They have learned
how to budget their time, meet deadlines, set priorities, cope with impersonal authority, follow instructions, and stick with a task that may be tire-
some without direct supervision.

The employer is also betting that it will be cheaper and easier to train   18
the college graduate because he has demonstrated his ability to learn. But if
the diploma serves only to identify those who are talented in the art of
schoolwork, it becomes, in the words of Harvard's Christopher Jencks, "a
hell of an expensive aptitude test." It is unfair to the candidates because they
themselves must bear the cost of the screening—the cost of college. Candidates without the funds, the academic temperament, or the patience for the
four-year obstacle race are ruled out, no matter how well they may perform

on the job. But if "everyone" has a diploma, employers will have to find another way to choose employees, and it will become an empty credential.

(Screening by diploma may in fact already be illegal. The 1971 ruling 19 of the Supreme Court in *Griggs* v. *Duke Power Co.* contended that an employer cannot demand a qualification which systematically excludes an entire class of applicants, unless that qualification reliably predicts success on the job. The requiring of a high school diploma was outlawed in the *Griggs* case, and this could extend to a college diploma.)

The bill for four years at an Ivy League college is currently climbing 20 toward $25,000; at a state university, a degree will cost the student and his family about $10,000 (with taxpayers making up the difference).

Not many families can afford these sums, and when they look for fi- 21 nancial aid, they discover that someone else will decide how much they will actually have to pay. The College Scholarship Service, which establishes a family's degree of need for most colleges, is guided by noble principles: uniformity of sacrifice, need rather than merit. But families vary in their willingness to "sacrifice" as much as the bureaucracy of the CSS thinks they ought to. This is particularly true of middle-income parents, whose children account for the bulk of the country's college students. Some have begun to rebel against this attempt to enforce the same values and priorities on all. "In some families, a college education competes with a second car, a color television, or a trip to Europe—and it's possible that college may lose," one financial-aid officer recently told me.

Quite so. College is worth more to some middle-income families than 22 to others. It is chilling to consider the undercurrent of resentment that families who "give up everything" must feel toward their college-age children, or the burden of guilt children must bear every time they goof off or receive less than top grades in their courses.

The decline in return for a college degree within the last generation has 23 been substantial. In the 1950s, a Princeton student could pay his expenses for the school year—eating club and all—on less than $3,000. When he graduated, he entered a job market which provided a comfortable margin over the earnings of his agemates who had not been to college. To be precise, a freshman entering Princeton in 1956, the earliest year for which the Census has attempted to project lifetime earnings, could expect to realize a 12.5 percent return on his investment. A freshman entering in 1972, with the cost nearing $6,000 annually, could expect to realize only 9.3 percent, less than might be available in the money market. This calculation was made with the help of a banker and his computer, comparing college as an investment in future earnings with other investments available in the booming money market of 1974, and concluded that in strictly financial terms, college is not always the best investment a young person can make.

I postulated a young man (the figures are different with a young woman, 24 but the principle is the same) whose rich uncle would give him, in cash, the total cost of four years at Princeton—$34,181. (The total includes what the young man would earn if he went to work instead of to college right after high school.) If he did not spend the money on Princeton, but put it in the savings bank at 7.5 percent interest compounded daily, he would have, at retirement age sixty-four, more than five times as much as the $199,000 extra he could expect to earn between twenty-two and sixty as a college man rather than a mere high school graduate. And with all that money accumulating in the bank, he could invest in something with a higher return than a diploma. At age twenty-eight, when his nest egg had reached $73,113, he could buy a liquor store, which would return him well over 20 percent on his investment, as long as he was willing to mind the store. He might get a bit fidgety sitting there, but he'd have to be dim-witted to lose money on a liquor store, and right now we're talking only about dollars.

If the young man went to a public college rather than Princeton, the investment would be lower, and the payoff higher, of course, because other people—the taxpayers—put up part of the capital for him. But the difference in return between an investment in public and private colleges is minimized because the biggest part of the investment in either case is the money a student might earn if he went to work, not to college—in economic terms, his "foregone income." That he bears himself.

Rates of return and dollar signs on education are a fascinating brain teaser, and, obviously, there is a certain unreality to the game. But the same unreality extends to the traditional calculations that have always been used to convince taxpayers that college is a worthwhile investment.

The ultimate defense of college has always been that while it may not teach you anything vocationally useful, it will somehow make you a better person, able to do anything better, and those who make it through the process are initiated into the "fellowship of educated men and women." In a study intended to probe what graduates seven years out of college thought their colleges should have done for them, the Carnegie Commission found that most alumni expected the "development of my abilities to think and express myself." But if such respected educational psychologists as Bruner and Piaget are right, specific learning skills have to be acquired very early in life, perhaps even before formal schooling begins.

So, when pressed, liberal-arts defenders speak instead about something more encompassing, and more elusive. "College changed me inside," one graduate told us fervently. The authors of a Carnegie Commission report, who obviously struggled for a definition, concluded that one of the common threads in the perceptions of a liberal education is that it provides "an integrated view of the world which can serve as an inner guide." More simply, alumni say that college should have "helped me to formulate the values and goals of my life."

In theory, a student is taught to develop these values and goals himself, but in practice, it doesn't work quite that way. All but the wayward and the saintly take their sense of the good, the true, and the beautiful from the people around them. When we speak of students acquiring "values" in college, we often mean that they will acquire the values—and sometimes that means only the tastes—of their professors. The values of professors may be "higher" than many students will encounter elsewhere, but they may not be relevant to situations in which students find themselves in college and later.

Of all the forms in which ideas are disseminated, the college professor   30 lecturing a class is the slowest and most expensive. You don't have to go to college to read the great books or learn about the great ideas of Western Man. Today you can find them everywhere—in paperbacks, in the public libraries, in museums, in public lectures, in adult-education courses, in abridged, summarized, or adapted form in magazines, films, and television. The problem is no longer one of access to broadening ideas; the problem is the other way around: how to choose among the many courses of action proposed to us, how to edit the stimulations that pour into our eyes and ears every waking hour. A college experience that piles option on option and stimulation on stimulation merely adds to the contemporary nightmare.

What students and graduates say that they did learn on campus comes   31 under the heading of personal, rather than intellectual, development. Again and again I was told that the real value of college is learning to get along with others, to practice social skills, to "sort out my head," and these have nothing to do with curriculum.

For whatever impact the academic experience used to have on college   32 students, the sheer size of many undergraduate classes in the 1970s dilutes faculty-student dialogue, and, more often than not, they are taught by teachers who were hired when colleges were faced with a shortage of qualified instructors, during their years of expansion and when the big rise in academic pay attracted the mediocre and the less than dedicated.

On the social side, colleges are withdrawing from responsibility for   33 feeding, housing, policing, and protecting students at a time when the environment of college may be the most important service it could render. College officials are reluctant to "intervene" in the personal lives of the students. They no longer expect to take over from parents, but often insist that students—who have, most often, never lived away from home before—take full adult responsibility for their plans, achievements, and behavior.

Most college students do not live in the plush, comfortable country-   34 clublike surroundings their parents envisage, or, in some cases, remember. Open dorms, particularly when they are coeducational, are noisy, usually over-crowded, and often messy. Some students desert the institutional "zoos" (their own word for dorms) and move into run-down, overpriced apartments. Bulletin boards in student centers are littered with notices of apartments to share and the drift of conversation suggests that a lot of money is dissipated in scrounging for food and shelter.

Taxpayers now provide more than half of the astronomical sums that   35 are spent on higher education. But less than half of today's high school graduates go on, raising a new question of equity: Is it fair to make all the taxpayers pay for the minority who actually go to college? We decided long ago that it is fair for childless adults to pay school taxes because everyone, parents and nonparents alike, profits by a literate population. Does the same reasoning hold true for state-supported higher education? There is no conclusive evidence on either side.

Young people cannot be expected to go to college for the general good   36
of mankind. They may be more altruistic than their elders, but no great
numbers are going to spend four years at hard intellectual labor, let alone
tens of thousands of family dollars, for "the advancement of human capability in society at large," one of the many purposes invoked by the Carnegie
Commission report. Nor do any considerable number of them want to go
to college to beat the Russians to Jupiter, improve the national defense, increase the Gross National Product, lower the crime rate, improve automobile
safety, or create a market for the arts—all of which have been suggested at
one time or other as benefits taxpayers get for supporting higher education.

One sociologist said that you don't have to have a reason for going to   37
college because it's an institution. His definition of an institution is something everyone subscribed to without question. The burden of proof is not
on why you should go to college, but why anyone thinks there might be a
reason for not going. The implication—and some educators express it quite
frankly—is that an eighteen-year-old high school graduate is still too young
and confused to know what he wants to do, let alone what is good for him.

Mother knows best, in other words.   38

It had always been comfortable for students to believe that authorities,   39
like Mother, or outside specialists, like educators, could determine what was
best for them. However, specialists and authorities no longer enjoy the credibility former generations accorded them. Patients talk back to doctors and
are not struck suddenly dead. Clients question the lawyer's bills and sometimes get them reduced. It is no longer self-evident that all adolescents must
study a fixed curriculum that was constructed at a time when all educated
men could agree on precisely what it was that made them educated.

The same with college. If high school graduates don't want to continue   40
their education, or don't want to continue it right away, they may perceive
more clearly than their elders that college is not for them.

College is an ideal place for those young adults who love learning for   41
its own sake, who would rather read than eat, and who like nothing better
than writing research papers. But they are a minority, even at the prestigious
colleges, which recruit and attract the intellectually oriented.

The rest of our high school graduates need to look at college more   42
closely and critically, to examine it as a consumer product, and decide if the
cost in dollars, in time, in continued dependency, and in future returns, is
worth the very large investment each student—and his family—must make.

QUESTIONS FOR MEANING

1. What does Bird see as the principal failure of college education? Why is
   college a "four year ordeal," and a "four year obstacle race"? Who should
   go to college, and who should not?
2. What risks does Bird concede to be in choosing a vocational education?
3. How do values differ from taste (paragraph 29)?
4. What does Bird mean when she demands that college should be examined
   as "a consumer product"?

5. How does Bird characterize the average college teacher? Is her appraisal justified by your own experience, or does it seem unfair?

6. Bird argues that college dorms are "noisy, usually overcrowded, and often messy," a far cry from the "country-clublike surroundings" many parents imagine. Is she right? If your school has dorms, are they attractive places to live? Does Bird overlook any advantages to living in a dorm?

7. Have colleges changed in the years since this essay was written? Has the economy become more receptive to college graduates?

8. Does Bird ever reveal what will happen to the thousands of high school graduates she would discourage from going to college? What do you think would happen if college attendance was suddenly reduced by half?

9. Vocabulary: pathetically (11), postulated (24), integrated (28), abridged (30), envisage (34), dissipated (34), altruistic (36), credibility (39).

QUESTIONS ABOUT STRATEGY

1. In her opening paragraph, Bird introduces the three main arguments that people usually advance on behalf of going to college. If you study her essay, you will find that she responds to each of these arguments in the order in which she introduces them. This helps make her argument seem well-organized. But are there any arguments for college education that she overlooks?

2. Why does Bird put quotation marks around "better" in paragraph 1?

3. Was this essay originally intended for an audience of students or an audience of college graduates? Could someone understand Bird's argument before going to college, or is a college education necessary to understand what Bird is saying? If the latter is true, how does this affect the credibility of the argument? Define Bird's audience. Then explain what you think she was trying to accomplish with this essay.

4. Bird uses many statistics to strengthen her argument. Does she reveal where she got them? Are you impressed by the various numbers she cites concerning job placement and the value of a college education as an investment? How vital are these numbers to the argument as a whole? How relevant are they to higher education in the 1990s?

5. What is the function of paragraphs 24–25? How useful is this example?

6. In paragraphs 38–40, Bird rejects the argument that many high school graduates are too young and confused to know what to do with their lives—and the implied argument that college gives them the time to "grow up." When you graduated from high school, how many of your friends had clear career goals? Now that you are in college, do your fellow students seem more mature? Do you agree with this aspect of Bird's argument?

SUGGESTIONS FOR WRITING

1. Defend or attack Plato's claim that "government can be at its best and free from dissension only where the destined rulers are least desirous of holding office."
2. Identify a modern politician who governs according to Machiavellian principles. Be careful not to make groundless accusations. Do research if necessary to write an argument that will include specific evidence.
3. Write a dialogue between Plato and Machiavelli on the question of how a republic should be ruled.
4. Respond to Marvell by writing an argument from a woman's point of view.
5. Using "A Modest Proposal" as your model, write a satirical essay proposing a "solution" to a contemporary social problem other than poverty.
6. Write a counterargument to Jefferson, a "Declaration of Continued Dependence" from the point of view of George III.
7. Drawing upon the work of Mary Wollstonecraft, Margaret Sanger, and Betty Friedan, write a "Declaration of Independence for Women."
8. Marx and Engels predicted that communism would triumph in advanced industrialized nations with large proletariats. But Russia was primarily an agricultural country at the time of the Russian Revolution, and Marxism now seems to have lost most of the appeal it once enjoyed. Defend or attack *The Communist Manifesto* in the light of twentieth-century history.
9. Do a research paper on the Dreyfus Affair. Include an evaluation of how accurately Émile Zola presents the case in "J'Accuse."
10. Do a research paper on birth control in Mexico, India, or China.
11. Clarence Darrow argues that capital punishment does nothing to resolve the causes of violent crime. Identify a social problem which you believe to be a cause of violence and argue on behalf of a specific reform.
12. Compare the propaganda posters reprinted on pages 644–45. How do they reflect the principles outlined by Adolf Hitler in "The Purpose of Propaganda"? Explain the strategy behind each of these posters and determine their relative effectiveness.
13. Summarize what Mark Twain taught about good writing style, and apply his criteria to a novel of your own choice.
14. Drawing upon "Resistance to Civil Government," "The Struggle Is My Life," and "Letter from Birmingham Jail," defend an illegal act that you would be willing to commit in order to fight for something in which you strongly believe.
15. How would John Henry Newman respond to Caroline Bird's "Where College Fails Us"? Write a counterargument to Bird that justifies the value of higher education.

Figure 1 is an example of an English poster from the First World War (1914–1919). Figure 2 is a Nazi election poster from the early 1930s. It reads, "Work and Bread through List One." (List One refers to the position of Nazi candidates on the ballot before Hitler seized power.) Figure 3 is a Nazi propaganda poster used in Poland after the German invasion of that country in 1939. The caption, in Polish, reads: "England! This is your work!" The picture shows a wounded Polish soldier pointing to the ruins of Warsaw and addressing Neville Chamberlain, the British Prime Minister at the beginning of the war.

FIGURE 1

FIGURE 2

FIGURE 3

PART 6

A GUIDE TO
RESEARCH

◆

If forced to write about an unfamiliar subject, even the best writers can find themselves drifting into wordiness, repetition, and vague generalizations. One of the great advantages of research is that it gives you material for writing. You need to organize this material and determine its worth before you can write a good research paper. You also need to know how to handle the mechanics of a research paper, since this is the most formal type of writing that most students are expected to do. But there is nothing especially difficult about writing a research paper if you approach it as a process that begins long before the assignment is due.

Your instructor may allow you to choose your own subject for research. Or you may be required to work on a subject that has been assigned to you. But in either case, there are two basic points that you need to remember when undertaking a research paper: (1) A graceful style cannot compensate for a failure to do thorough research. Even if you are an excellent writer, your paper will be superficial if your research has been superficial. (2) Although research is essential to the process of writing a research paper, there is more to the research paper than research alone. You can spend months investigating your subject, but your essay will be a failure if it consists of nothing more than one quotation after another. You should remember that you are a writer as well as an investigator, and your own thoughts and interpretations are ultimately as important as the research itself. You may occasionally have an assignment that requires nothing more than reporting on a technical question such as "How is gasoline refined?" or "How do eagles mate?" But most research papers require that the writer have a thesis and a point of view about the subject under consideration. Unless specifically instructed otherwise, you should think of the research paper as an extended form of argument—an argument which is supported by evidence you have discovered through research.

There are two types of research: primary and secondary. *Primary research* requires firsthand experimentation or analysis. This is the sort of research that is done in scientific laboratories and scholarly archives. Research of this sort is seldom expected of college students, although, if you interview someone, you are doing a type of primary research. An undergraduate research paper is usually based upon *secondary research*, which means the examination of what other people have already published on a given subject. In order to do this type of research efficiently, you must know where to look. And this means that you must be familiar with the resources that are available to you in your library and develop a strategy for using these resources effectively.

GETTING STARTED

Your primary goal in preliminary research is to get your subject in focus. This usually means narrowing your subject to a specific topic. A clear focus is essential if your paper is to have depth and coherence. A ten-page paper on "The Question of Race in *Huckleberry Finn*" is likely to be much more thoughtful than one of that length on "Mark Twain: America's Favorite Writer." Moreover, the clearer your focus, the easier your research will be. When you know what you are looking for, you know what you need to read and what you can afford to pass over. This will keep you from feeling overwhelmed as your research progresses.

Different instructors make different assignments, and you should always be certain that you have understood what your instructor expects of you. But if you have been asked to write a fixed number of pages on a subject of your own choice, a good rule to follow is to narrow your subject as much as possible without narrowing yourself out of the library. Don't put yourself in the position of aimlessly reading dozens of books on an unnecessarily broad subject. On the other hand, don't make your subject so obscure that you will be unable to find enough material to write a paper of the length required.

If you know very little about your subject, you may want to begin your research by reading whatever can be found in a general encyclopedia, such as the *Encyclopedia Britannica* or the *Encyclopedia Americana*. Encyclopedias contain the basic background information that other works may assume you already possess. Within the reference rooms of most libraries, you can also find special encyclopedias and dictionaries for major fields such as art, biography, economics, education, history, law, literature, medicine, music, philosophy, and psychology. Do some preliminary reading in an encyclopedia if doing so will make you feel more comfortable with your subject, but do not spend a lot of time reading in the library at this early stage of your research. Although the reference room may be a good place to begin your work, it has a great disadvantage: The books in this room are seldom allowed to circulate. Your first day in the library should be devoted primarily to finding out what types of material are going to be available to you in the days ahead.

LOOKING FOR BOOKS

When doing research, it is usually wise to look for books that have been published on your subject. Never assume that your topic is so new, or so specialized, that the library will not have books on it. A subject that seems new to you may not necessarily be new to others. By looking for books, you will often find sources of great value. And while there are some topics on which you may not be able to find a book, you will have more confidence in your research if you have taken the trouble to check.

Using the Main Catalog

One of the first steps in your search strategy should be to consult your library's *main catalog*, which lists all of the books in its collection. Some libraries use a card catalog in which cards for each book in the collection are arranged alphabetically in drawers. Other libraries have computerized their catalogs, providing work stations at which users can search for books by pressing a few keys at typewriter-like terminals. Still other libraries may have both a card catalog and a computerized catalog, in which case you should consult a librarian to see if they are both current: A library that has computerized its holdings may have stopped adding new acquisitions to the card catalog several years ago, and a library that has only recently acquired computers may have only part of its collection on-line.

Card catalogs usually include two or three cards for every book the library owns. This allows you to locate books in a variety of ways, depending upon how much you already know. You may be looking for books by a particular author, so libraries provide *author cards*. You may know the title of a book but not who wrote it, so libraries also provide *title cards*. In many libraries, these two types of cards are filed together in one catalog known as the author/title catalog. But when doing research, you may not know the names of authors or titles of works on your subject. For this reason, books are also filed under subject headings.

When the main catalog is recorded on cards, the *subject catalog* is usually separate from the author/title catalog. Large subjects, such as American history, are broken down into numerous subcategories. If you have chosen a large subject and are unsure about how to narrow it down, it is often useful to consult a subject catalog. Not only will you be able to see how professional indexers have divided the subject into manageable components, but you will see how many books are available within each subdivision. If you are unable to find material under the heading you have consulted, you should explore alternative headings. Books on the Civil War, for example, might be

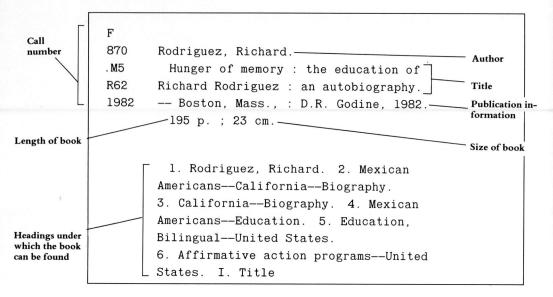

FIGURE 1
An Author card from a card catalog

listed under "War Between the States." The subject catalog may include references directing you to the appropriate heading, but you may also need to draw upon your own ingenuity. If you are sure that the library must have books on your subject and that you are simply unable to find the correct subject heading, ask a librarian for help.

Like the card catalogs they are gradually replacing, computerized catalogs enable users to search for books by author, title, or subject. Many of these catalogs also enable users to search for material by providing a call number or a key word that may appear somewhere in the title or description. The most commonly used programs are easy to use, and librarians can help you if you encounter any problems. Although they provide access to essentially the same information as card catalogs, computerized catalogs can often make research more efficient by providing instant access to information that might otherwise be recorded in the different drawers of a card catalog. Also, computerized catalogs are often designed to report whether or not the book is currently available.

Figures 1 and 2 show how a catalog card compares to an entry on a computer screen. The two entries are very similar despite some minor differences in format. As you do research, you should expect to find variations on these examples. Author cards, title cards, and subject cards will each have slightly different headings so that they can be filed in different places. And the precise format of a computerized entry depends upon the program employed by the library you are using.

```
PUBLIC CATALOG                              Searching:UWSP

Rodriguez, Richard.
    Hunger of memory : the education of Richard Rodriguez : an
        autobiography.
Boston, Mass. : D.R. Godine, 1982.
    195 p. ; 23 cm.


    Rodriguez, Richard.
    Mexican Americans_California_Biography.
    Mexican Americans_Education.
    Education, Bilingual_United States.
    Affirmative action programs_United States.
    California_Biography.



    LOCATION       CALL #/VOL/NO/COPY              STATUS

    STACKS             F870.M5 R62 1982          Available



    (END) Press RETURN to continue or /ES to start a new search:
```

FIGURE 2
An entry from a computer catalog

There is no foolproof method for determining the quality or usefulness of a book from a catalog entry. The best way to judge a book is always to read it. But a catalog listing can reveal some useful clues if you know how to find them. Consider, for example, the date of publication. There is no reason to assume that new books are always better than old books, but unless you are researching an historical or literary topic you should be careful not to rely heavily upon material that may be out of date. Consider also the length of the book. A book with 300 pages is likely to provide more information than a book half that size. A book with a bibliography may help you to find more material. Finally, you might also consider the reputation of the publisher. Any conclusion that you draw at this point should be tentative. But some books are better than others, and it is your responsibility as a researcher to evaluate the material that you use. (For additional information on evaluating sources, see pp. 54–56.) If you are fortunate enough to find several books on your subject, select the books that seem the best.

Understanding Classification Systems

Most American libraries use one of two systems for classifying the books in their collections: the Dewey Decimal system or the Library of Congress system. If you understand how these systems work, you can save valuable time in the library by knowing where to look for material when you are already working in the stacks.

The Dewey Decimal system classifies books numerically:

000–099	General Works
100–199	Philosophy
200–299	Religion
300–399	Social Sciences
400–499	Language
500–599	Natural Sciences
600–699	Technology
700–799	Fine Arts
800–899	Literature
900–999	History and Geography

These major divisions are subdivided by ten to identify specializations within each general field. For example, within the 800–899 category for literature, American literature is found between 810 and 819, English literature between 820 and 829, German literature between 830 and 839—and so forth. Specific numbers narrow these areas further, so that 811 represents American poetry, for example, and 812 American drama. Additional numbers after the decimal point enable catalogers to classify books more precisely: 812.54 would indicate an American play written since 1945. In order to distinguish individual books from others that are similar, an additional number is usually placed beneath the Dewey number.

Most libraries that use the Dewey Decimal system combine it with one of three systems for providing what is called an "author mark." These systems (Cutter two-figure, Cutter three-figure, and Cutter-Sanborn) all work according to the same principle. Librarians consult a reference table which provides a numerical representation for the first four to six letters of every conceivable last name. The first letter of the author's last name is placed immediately before this number, and the first letter of the first significant word in the title is placed after the number. Here is a complete call number for *Cat on a Hot Tin Roof,* by the American playwright Tennessee Williams:

812.54
W675c

Although the Dewey Decimal system remains the most widely used system for the classification of books in American libraries, many university libraries prefer to use the Library of Congress system, which uses the alphabet to distinguish twenty-one major categories as opposed to Dewey's ten:

A	General Works
B	Philosophy, Psychology, and Religion
C	General History
D	Foreign History
E–F	American History (North and South)
G	Geography and Anthropology
H	Social Sciences
J	Political Science
K	Law
L	Education
M	Music
N	Fine Arts
P	Language and Literature
Q	Science
R	Medicine
S	Agriculture
T	Technology
U	Military Science
V	Naval Science
Z	Bibliography and Library Science

Each of these categories can be subdivided through additional letters and numbers. PR, for example, indicates English literature, and PS indicates American. The complete entry will usually involve three lines. Unless you are planning to become a librarian, you will not find it necessary to memorize the complete code. But whether you are using Dewey or the Library of Congress, always be sure to copy down the complete call number for any book you wish to find. If you leave out part of the number you may find yourself wandering in the stacks and unable to find the book you want.

USING PERIODICAL INDEXES

A good researcher wants to be aware of the latest developments in his or her field. A scholarly book may be several years in the making; publication may be delayed, and another year or two may pass before the book is purchased and cataloged by your library. You may also need to obtain detailed information on a particular subtopic that is discussed only briefly in the books that are available to you. Therefore, you will often need to turn to periodicals after searching for books. "Periodicals" means magazines, newspapers, and scholarly journals: Material that is published at periodic intervals. And there are numerous indexes to help you find literature of this sort.

The best known of these indexes is the *Readers' Guide to Periodical Literature,* which is now available not only in the green, bound volumes in which it has been published for several decades but also on a CD-ROM disk for use with a computer. The *Readers' Guide* covers 150 magazines and journals, indexing material by subject and by author. Because it indexes popular, mass-circulation periodicals, it will lead you to articles that are often relatively short and general.

Most college libraries have a variety of other indexes that will lead you to more substantial material. Almost every field has its own index, which you should be able to use with little difficulty once you are familiar with the *Readers' Guide.* Detailed lists of such indexes and other reference books can be found in *Guide to Reference Books,* by Eugene P. Sheehy and *American Reference Books Annual,* edited by Boydan S. Wynar. Among the specialized indexes most frequently used are:

Applied Science and Technology Index	*Index to Legal Periodicals*
	Index Medicus (for medicine)
Art Index	*Music Index*
Biological and Agricultural Index	*Philosopher's Index*
Business Periodicals Index	*Science Citation Index*
Education Index	*Social Sciences Index*
Humanities Index	

Like the *Readers' Guide,* many specialized indexes are now available on CD-ROM disks that cover several years—a great advantage over bound volumes which cover only a single year. Anyone doing research in literature should also be familiar with the *MLA International Bibliography* (which includes both books and articles written about English, American, and foreign language literature) and also with the *Essay and General Literature Index,* which indexes essays and articles which have appeared in books rather than in journals.

Although there is occasionally some overlapping from one index to another, you need to realize that each of these indexes covers different periodicals. The references that you find in one will usually be entirely different from the references you find in another. This is worth remembering for two reasons: (1) You should not get easily discouraged when searching for periodical literature. If you cannot locate any material in the last few years of one index, then you should try another index that sounds as if it might include

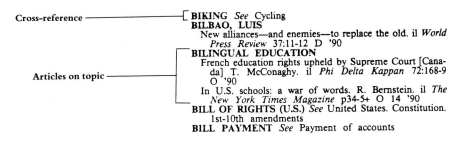

Cross-reference ——————— BIKING *See* Cycling
BILBAO, LUIS
  New alliances—and enemies—to replace the old. il *World Press Review* 37:11-12 D '90
BILINGUAL EDUCATION
  French education rights upheld by Supreme Court [Canada] T. McConaghy. il *Phi Delta Kappan* 72:168-9 O '90
Articles on topic ———————
  In U.S. schools: a war of words. R. Bernstein. il *The New York Times Magazine* p34-5+ O 14 '90
BILL OF RIGHTS (U.S.) *See* United States. Constitution. 1st-10th amendments
BILL PAYMENT *See* Payment of accounts

FIGURE 3
An excerpt from the *Readers' Guide*

references to your subject. (2) Many subjects of general interest will be found in more than one index, and if you consult more than one index, you are increasing the likelihood of being exposed to different points of view.

You may choose to do a research paper on one of the subjects discussed in Parts 3, 4, and 5 of this book. But in order for you to see how different indexes lead to different types of material, let us take an example from outside the book—following the search strategy for a paper on bilingual education.

The search for periodical literature on this subject began with the *Readers' Guide*. Figure 3 shows an excerpt from the February 1991 volume. The most recent volume available when this research was conducted, it identified two articles on bilingual education, one of which proved to be a useful source for the paper reprinted on pp. 671–80. To locate additional sources through the bound volumes of the *Readers' Guide,* you would need to consult volumes covering other periods. (Bound volumes are usually printed annually, although the current year is published in installments.)

If you consulted the *Readers' Guide* on a CD-ROM disk, you would find the same sources, but you would find them a little more quickly. The disk covering the period between January 1, 1983, and December 28, 1990, included fifty-one citations on bilingual education. Figure 4 shows an excerpt from the printout obtained after consulting the *Readers' Guide* at a computer workstation equipped with a CD-ROM disk. Note that the computer identifies the most recently indexed source first and then works backwards from it. The information is essentially the same as the information in the bound volumes, but the disk also provides a list of the subjects covered in each article—a feature that can help you to evaluate the potential usefulness of sources.

Of the various specialized indexes that can lead you to material in professional journals, *The Education Index* is the most useful to consult for a paper on bilingual education. Figure 5 shows a partial listing of sources obtained through this index. Note that journals such as *Topics in Language Disorders* or *Journal of Instructional Psychology* are not indexed in the *Readers' Guide,* so you would not have located these sources if you had limited your search to the *Readers' Guide*. Note also that three of the four sources in this excerpt

Readers' Guide ⎯ 1 RDG
McConaghy, Tom
French education rights upheld by Supreme Court
Phi Delta Kappan v72 p168=9 October '90

Illustrated ⎯ i l

SUBJECTS COVERED:
Canada/Languages
Bilingual education
Educational laws and regulations/Canada
Canada/Supreme Court/Decisions

2 RDG
Book Review
Porter, Rosalie Pedalino
Forked tongue ; the politics of bilingual education
reviewed by Randolph, Allen
National Review v42 p52 November 19 '90

**This feature
found in printout
but not in bound
version (see Fig.3).**
SUBJECTS COVERED:
Education, Bilingual/United States
Linguistic minorities/Education/United States

3 RDG
Bernstein, Richard
In U.S. schools: a war of words
The New York Times Magazine p34=5+ October 14 '90
i l

SUBJECTS COVERED:
Bilingual education

4 RDG
The new apartheid
National Review v42 p14=16 July 23 '90

SUBJECTS COVERED:
Bilingual education/Federal aid

5 RDG
**Printout
provides
author's full
name**
Banks, Howard
Do we want Quebec here?
Forbes v145 p62+ June 11 '90
i l

SUBJECTS COVERED:
Hispanic Americans/Education
Bilingual education
Spanish language in the United States

FIGURE 4
A sample printout from the *Readers' Guide* on CD-ROM disk

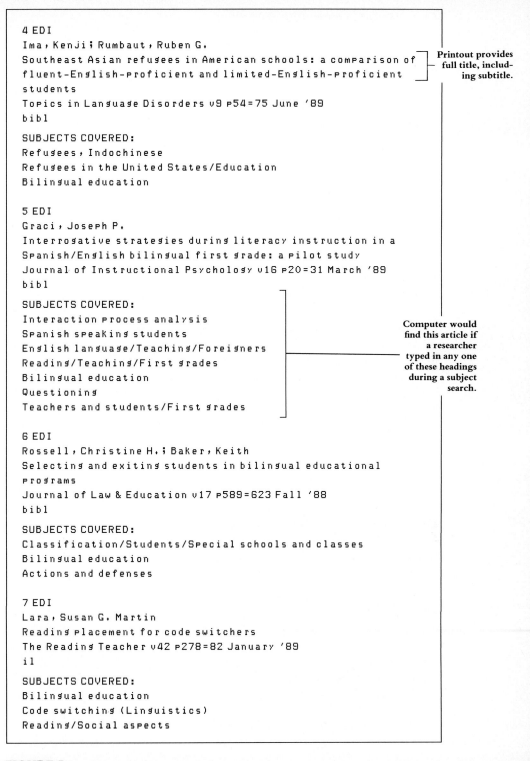

4 EDI
Ima, Kenji; Rumbaut, Ruben G.
Southeast Asian refugees in American schools: a comparison of
fluent-English-proficient and limited-English-proficient
students
Topics in Language Disorders v9 p54=75 June '89
bibl

SUBJECTS COVERED:
Refugees, Indochinese
Refugees in the United States/Education
Bilingual education

Printout provides full title, including subtitle.

5 EDI
Graci, Joseph P.
Interrogative strategies during literacy instruction in a
Spanish/English bilingual first grade: a pilot study
Journal of Instructional Psychology v16 p20=31 March '89
bibl

SUBJECTS COVERED:
Interaction process analysis
Spanish speaking students
English language/Teaching/Foreigners
Reading/Teaching/First grades
Bilingual education
Questioning
Teachers and students/First grades

Computer would find this article if a researcher typed in any one of these headings during a subject search.

6 EDI
Rossell, Christine H.; Baker, Keith
Selecting and exiting students in bilingual educational
programs
Journal of Law & Education v17 p589=623 Fall '88
bibl

SUBJECTS COVERED:
Classification/Students/Special schools and classes
Bilingual education
Actions and defenses

7 EDI
Lara, Susan G. Martin
Reading placement for code switchers
The Reading Teacher v42 p278=82 January '89
il

SUBJECTS COVERED:
Bilingual education
Code switching (Linguistics)
Reading/Social aspects

FIGURE 5
A sample printout from *The Education Index*

include bibliographies; one of the sources is twenty-one pages long, another is eleven, and a third is thirty-four. These articles are going to be more difficult to read than articles in popular magazines. But you can overcome this difficulty through proper preparation: Do not try to read articles in scholarly journals until you have completed some preliminary reading in encyclopedias, books, and magazines.

Continuing your search, you might find additional material on bilingual education through *The Social Sciences Index,* which covers sociology, psychology, and other related fields. And the *Index to Legal Periodicals* might lead to a source discussing laws that help shape the nature of public education. The articles would be different, but the form of the citations would be similar, just as the citations in the *Education Index* are similar to those in the *Readers' Guide.*

USING A NEWSPAPER INDEX

Newspapers are often an excellent source of information, and there are indexes available to help you locate articles in such newspapers as *The Wall Street Journal* and the *Christian Science Monitor.* In addition to bound volumes for specific newspapers, some libraries have CD-ROM disks that can cover a number of newspapers within a single search. But if your library has only one index, it is most likely to be the *New York Times Index,* which has been published since 1913. Figure 6 is an example of what you would find if you

EDUCATION AND SCHOOLS – Cont

Two Houston, Tex, schools turn gymnasiums into shelters for schoolchildren who have no other place to sleep; eight children, aged 5 to 18, show up first night, leading school officials to believe there are many more who will show up in future; photo (M), Ja 14,1,6:1

Gov Thomas H Kean's call for end to mandatory daily gym classes in New Jersey high schools is attacked by politicians, principals, gym teachers, pediatricians and legislators; many students are with Kean; photo (M), Ja 14, 1,27:2

Anthony Reyes, 16, is arrested on charge of bringing unloaded revolver to Immaculata High School in Manhattan and hiding it in his locker (S), Ja 14,1,30:6

New York State Comr of Educaiton, Thomas Sobol, announces broadened policy of bilingual education in state's public schools to meet anticipated needs of growing population of students with limited skills in English (M), Ja 15,1,22:6

Standardized college admission testing is seen as growth industry, one that provided $226 million last year to Education Testing Service, which administers Scholastic Aptitude Test and many others, and $50 million to American College Testing Program, which administers ACT; success continues despite criticism that tests are inaccurate and biased against women and members of minority groups; tests are also being increasingly used for purposes that go well beyond admissions decisions; photo (M), Ja 15,IV,28:4

(M) means that this is of medium length. The date of issue is January 15 (of 1989, the year of the volume consulted). "I" means that the article is in section one—on page 22, column 6, in this case.

FIGURE 6

Excerpt from the *New York Times Index*

consulted this index for a paper on bilingual education. Note that the *New York Times Index* gives you a one-sentence summary of each article, rather than article titles.

Although the *New York Times* was not essential to research on bilingual education, the index did lead to a potentially useful article. Bear in mind that the *New York Times* is especially useful when researching historical events or topics that have only recently made news. When using a newspaper index— or any other index—you should always consider whether it is appropriate for the topic you are researching. An index that did not lead to any articles for your last research paper may yield several dozen for your next.

USING ABSTRACTING SERVICES

There is another type of print resource usually available in a college library and that is an *abstract*, which means a summary of an article or book (see p. 388 for an example). Among the most important abstracting services are:

Abstracts in Anthropology

Biological Abstracts

Chemical Abstracts

Historical Abstracts

Physics Abstracts

Psychological Abstracts

Sociological Abstracts

Women Studies Abstracts

These abstracts are organized in different ways. If you are searching for abstracts through a computer, you will usually follow a procedure that is similar to a search for periodical literature. When consulting bound volumes of abstracts, you may need to consult the instructions that can be found in the front of most volumes. But here is an example of what you would find if you looked up "bilingual education" in *Psychological Abstracts*—which requires that you consult an index before you locate any specific summary. Figure 7 (p. 660) shows an excerpt from the subject index for 1989. Reading through the entries in the subject index should help you to identify citations that seem promising. The number that appears at the end of each citation is not a page number. It is the number of the article being summarized. Article summaries can be found in numerical order, either at the front of the volume containing the subject index or in a separate volume (which will be shelved beside it) depending upon how your library decides to bind them. Figure 8 (p. 661) shows a partial page of summaries, including one for an article on bilingual education located through the subject index illustrated in Figure 7. Note that it is only at this point that you learn the author(s) of the article,

Bilingual Education

cognition & learning mathematics in 2nd language, Black secondary school students, South Africa, 38140

culture specific bilingual career awareness program, Chinese & Korean American parents, 27836

early vs late immersion, attitudes & French language skills, 7th graders, Canada, 31038

French language immersion & linguistic skills & bilingualism, bilingual education students, Canada, literature review, 31077

French vs English passages, oral reading, 1st & 2nd graders in French immersion program, Canada, 31062

Brief description ──── issues in bilingualism & bilingual education, children, 27561
of article (not a
title)

limited English proficiency, individualized education plans & use of native language or ESL instruction, Hispanic 2nd–5th graders with learning disabilities, 34766

meaning of alternating languages in ongoing bilingual discourse in classroom & communicative competence, bilingual students, implications for bilingual teachers, 10139

need for bilingual education, limited English proficiency students with communication disorders, 10225

prediction in teaching strategies & materials in Chinese-English bilingual classroom, ethnic Chinese kindergartners, 20457

questions & responses during Spanish & English reading lesson, Spanish dominant bilingual 1st graders & their teacher, 38087

Quranic preschool & reading education in Arabic & French, Arabic reading achievement, Arabic vs Berber speaking 1st graders, Morocco, 5 yr study, implications for bilingual education, 31096

Bilingualism

abstract vs concrete paragraphs & task context & comprehension instructions, prose recall, monolingual vs bilingual college students, 38919

anxiety producing conditions, language shift & coping behavior & treatment, bilingual patients in psychotherapy, 23193

assessment of 1st or 2nd language proficiency, bilingual 6–7 yr olds, England, 13718

auditory reception of second language, cerebral lateralization in simultaneous tasks requiring time sharing, Chinese-English bilingual college students, 35602

> The entry number under which you can find the article abstract

FIGURE 7
Excerpt from subject index for *Psychological Abstracts*

the title of the article, and the journal, volume, date, and pages where it can be found.

Abstracts can be difficult to use, especially at first. But they offer a great advantage. Sometimes it is hard to tell from the title alone if an article will be useful, and a summary can help you to decide whether or not you want to read the entire article. A good rule to follow with abstracts is that if you can't understand the summary, you probably won't understand the article. And there is one other point to remember when using abstracting services. Many of them are international in scope. Just because the article summary

Corresponding entry number (from subject index)

Journal title

27560. **Griffiths, Alan K.; Thomey, Kevin; Cooke, Bren & Normore, Glen.** (Memorial U of Newfoundland, St John's, Canada) **Remediation of student-specific misconceptions relating to three science concepts.** *Journal of Research in Science Teaching,* 1988(Dec), Vol 25(9), 709–719. —Investigated whether misconceptions are more amenable to change because they are likely to be less firmly rooted. R. M. Gagné's (1977) theory of hierarchical learning of intellectual skills was applied to the remediation of misconceptions relating to 3 science concepts: the performance of stoichiometric calculations, food web problems, and problems requiring correct understanding of the conservation of mechanical energy. 723 high school students were placed in 3 levels of remediation using (1) a hierarchy with reference to skills missed and to specific misconceptions, (2) a hierarchy with reference to skills missed but without reference to misconceptions, and (3) no reference to hierarchy or individual misconceptions. No significant differences were found between treatments.

27561. **Hakuta, Kenji & Garcia, Eugene E.** (U California, Board of Studies in Education, Santa Cruz) **Bilingualism and education.** Special Issue: Children and their development: Knowledge base, research agenda, and social policy application. *American Psychologist,* 1989(Feb), Vol 44(2), 374–379. —The concept of bilingualism as applied to individual children and to educational programs is discussed, and the history of research on bilingual children and bilingual education programs in the United States is reviewed. Bilingualism has been defined predominantly in linguistic dimensions despite the fact that bilingualism is correlated with a number of nonlinguistic social parameters. The linguistic handle has served policymakers well in focusing on an educationally vulnerable population of students, but the handle is inadequate as the single focus of educational intervention. Future research will have to be directed toward a multifaceted perspective of bilingualism as a phenomenon embedded in society. —*Journal abstract.*

27562. **Hansen, C. Bobbi.** (United States International U, San Diego, CA) **Cooperative learning: A person-centered approach to instruction.** Special Issue: The person-centered approach in education. *Person-Centered Review,* 1988(Feb), Vol 3(1), 86–95. —Notes that C. Rogers (1983) thought that the act of teaching should become less directive and more facilitative in nature. The author discusses the cooperative learning teaching approach and argues that this approach is person-centered, as it is by nature more facilitative than directive.

Date of issue

Volume and issue number

Authors' institutional affiliation

Article title

Page reference

FIGURE 8
Sample summaries from *Psychological Abstracts*

is written in English does not mean that this is true of the article itself. But if an article is written in a foreign language, that will usually be indicated.

USING OTHER SOURCES

Because of the great amount of material being published, many libraries are now using devices that allow for material to be stored in less space than would be required by its original form. When looking for books or articles, you may need to use some type of microform—which means printed material which has been reduced in size through microphotography. Libraries that use microform provide users with special readers that magnify the material in question—whether it is available on microfilm or microfiche, which means a flat sheet of microfilm.

But even when space is not an issue, most libraries can afford to purchase only a fraction of the material that is published each year. Although a good college library should give you all the sources you need for most research papers, you may occasionally find it necessary to look beyond the library where you normally work. If you live in or near a city, there may be several other libraries that you can use. If this is not the case, remember that most libraries also provide an interlibrary loan service which allows you to request a book or journal article that your own library does not possess. When a library offers interlibrary loan, you will be asked to provide bibliographical information about the material you are requesting. Librarians will then do the work of locating and securing a copy of the book or article for you. You should ask for material only if you are reasonably certain that it would be an important asset for you, and that an equivalent resource is not already available in your own library. You should also recognize that obtaining a source through interlibrary loan can take two weeks or longer, so it will be of no use if you defer your research until a few days before your paper is due.

In addition to interlibrary loan, many libraries subscribe to one or more data-base services which link individual libraries with computerized lists of material available throughout the United States and Canada. The most commonly used bibliographic networks are BRS (Bibliographic Retrieval Services), DIALOG (operated by Knight-Ridder), RLIN (Research Libraries Information Network), and OCLC (Online Computer Library Center). A data-base search usually identifies sources that you must then proceed to locate on your own, but there are some programs that also allow for the full retrieval of a short text. Policies regarding data-base searches vary from library to library, and some libraries charge a fee for this service. Inquire about the policy at your own library before requesting a data-base search.

For some topics, you may want to use a nonprint source, such as the personal interview. Although interviews are usually inappropriate for literary and scientific papers, they can be helpful in many other fields. If you are writing a paper on bilingual education, you might decide to interview teachers, children, and members of a local school board. But unless your instructor has encouraged you to do some interviews, you should check to make sure that interviews are acceptable for your assignment. Remember also that interviews need to be planned ahead, and you should have a list of questions before you go. But don't feel compelled to adhere rigidly to the questions you prepared in advance. A good interviewer knows how to ask a follow-up question that is inspired by a provocative response to an earlier question. Do not get so caught up in an interview, however, that you forget to take careful notes. (If you want to use a tape recorder, courtesy demands that you ask permission to do so when you arrange for the interview.) Since you will need to include the interview in your bibliography, record the date of the interview and the full name of the person you have interviewed.

COMPILING A PRELIMINARY BIBLIOGRAPHY

As you begin locating sources of possible value for your paper, you should be careful to record certain essential information about the books and articles you have discovered. You will need this information in order to compose a preliminary bibliography. For books, you need to record the full title, the full name of the author or authors, the city of publication, the publisher, and the date of publication. If you are using a particular part of a book, be sure to record the pages in question. And if you are using an article or a story included in an anthology edited by someone other than the author of the material you are using, make the distinction between the author and the title of the selection and the editor and title of the book as a whole. When you have located articles in periodicals, record the author(s) of the article, the title of the article, the title of the journal in which it was published, the volume number, the issue number (if there is one), the date of the issue, and the pages between which the article can be found.

The easiest way to compile a preliminary bibliography is to use a set of 3×5 note cards, recording separate sources on separate cards. This involves a little more trouble than jotting references down on whatever paper you have at hand, but it will be to your ultimate advantage. As your research progresses, you can easily eliminate any sources that you were unable to obtain—or that you have rejected as inappropriate for one reason or another. And by using this method, you will later find it easier to arrange your sources in the order in which they should appear in the formal bibliography which will be included at the end of your finished paper. But whatever method you use, be sure to keep accurate notes. No one enjoys discovering a failure to record an important reference—especially if this discovery comes after the paper is written and shortly before it must be handed in.

TAKING NOTES

If you have never done a research paper before, you would be wise to take notes on 3×5 note cards. Note-taking is essential to research. Unfortunately, few researchers can tell in advance exactly what material they will want to include in their final paper. Especially during the early stages of your research, you may record information that will later seem unnecessary when you have become more expert on your subject and have a clear thesis. So you will probably have to discard some of your notes when you are ready to write your paper.

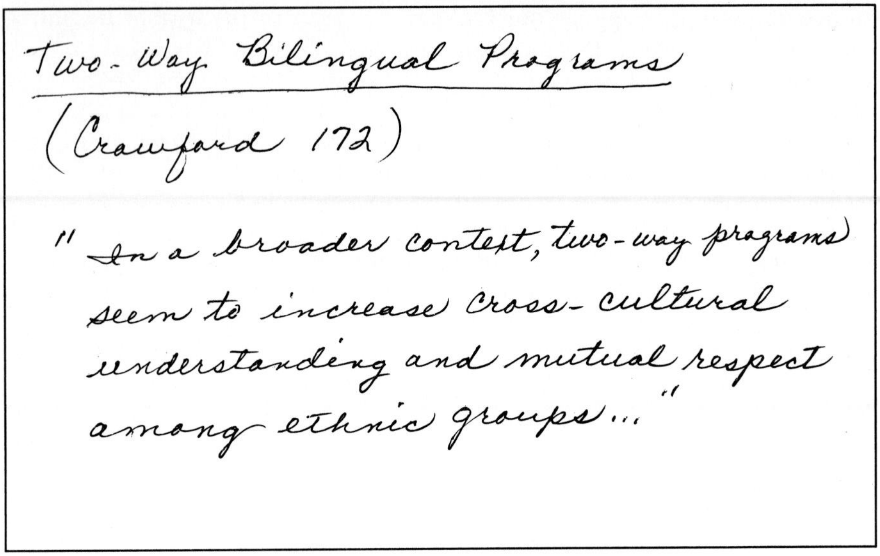

Two - Way Bilingual Programs

(Crawford 172)

" In a broader context, two-way programs
seem to increase cross-cultural
understanding and mutual respect
among ethnic groups ... "

FIGURE 9
Sample note card

The advantage of the note card system is that it allows for flexibility when you are ready to move from research to composition. The odds are against discovering material in the exact order in which you will want to use it. By spreading your note cards out on a desk or table, you can study how they best fit together. You can arrange and rearrange note cards until you have them in a meaningful sequence. This system only works, however, when you have the self-restraint to limit yourself to recording one fact, one idea, or one quotation to a card, as shown in Figure 9. This means that many of your cards will have a lot of empty space that you may be tempted to fill. Don't. As soon as you decide to put two ideas on the same card, you have made an editorial decision that you may later regret. The cost of a set of note cards is minimal compared to the amount of time you must invest in doing a good research paper.

Sorting your note cards is also one of the easiest ways to determine if you have enough material to write a good paper. If your notes fall into a half-dozen different categories, your research might lack focus. In this case you should do some more research, concentrating on the category that interests you the most. If, on the other hand, your notes fall into a clear pattern, you may be ready to start writing. Of course, the point at which you move from research into writing will depend not only on your notes but also on the length of the paper you have in mind: Long papers usually involve more research than short papers. But if you classify your notes every few days during the process of doing your research, you will be in a position to judge when you have taken as many notes as you will need.

AVOIDING SELECTIVE RESEARCH

Although your research should have a clear focus, and you may have a tentative thesis in mind, you should formulate your final thesis only after your research is complete. Your research strategy should be designed to answer a question that you have posed to yourself, such as "Under what circumstances can bilingual education be most effective?" This is very different from starting your research with your thesis predetermined. A student who is convinced that all Americans should speak English, and nothing but English, may be tempted to take notes only from sources that report problems with bilingual education—rejecting as irrelevant any source that describes a successful program. Research, in this case, is not leading to greater knowledge or understanding. On the contrary, it is being used to reinforce personal beliefs that may border on prejudice.

We have seen that "anticipating the opposition" is important even in short essays of opinion. It is no less important in the research paper. Almost any topic worth investigating will yield facts and ideas that could support different conclusions. The readings assembled in this book have demonstrated that it is possible to defend or attack mandatory drug testing, gun control, animal experimentation, and censorship—among other issues. As you may have already observed, some of the most opinionated people are also the most ignorant. Well-educated men and women are usually aware of how most problems are complex, and this is because they have been exposed to different points of view during their education. Good students remember this when they are doing research. They allow their reading to influence their thought, and not their thoughts to determine their reading. Your own research may ultimately support a belief that you already hold, but it could just as easily lead you to realize that you were misinformed. When taking notes, you should remember the question that you have posed for yourself so that you do not waste time recording information that is not relevant to the question. But you should not be tempted to overlook material that directly concerns your question just because you don't agree with what this material says. If you have a good reason to reject the conclusion of someone else's work, your paper will be stronger if you recognize that this disagreement exists and then demonstrate why you favor one position over another.

ORGANIZING YOUR PAPER

If you have used the note card system, you may be able to dispense with an outline and compose your first draft by working directly from your notes—assuming that you have sorted them carefully and arranged them into an easily understandable sequence. But many writers find it useful to outline the ideas they plan to cover. Anyone who lacks experience in writing long papers is especially likely to benefit from taking the trouble to prepare an outline before attempting to write.

If you decide to outline your paper, you should use the standard format for a formal outline:

I. Major idea
   A. Supporting idea
      1. Minor idea
         a. Supporting detail
         b. Supporting detail
      2. Minor idea
   B. Supporting idea
II. Major idea

And so forth. Subdivisions only make sense when there are at least two categories—otherwise there would be no need to subdivide. So Roman numeral I usually implies the existence of Roman numeral II, and supporting idea "A" implies the existence of supporting idea "B." A good outline is usually parallel, with each part in balance with the others.

An outline may consist of complete sentences or simply of topics, but follow consistently whichever system you choose. (For an example of a topic outline, see page 670.) The extent to which you benefit from an outline is usually determined by the amount of effort you devote to preparing it. The more developed your outline, the more likely you are to have thought your essay through and considered how it can be best organized. Your outline may show you that you have much to say about one part of your paper and little about another. This could result in a lopsided paper if the parts should be of equal importance. In this case, your outline may lead you to do some additional research in order to obtain more information for the part of the paper that looks as if it is going to be weak. Or you may decide to rethink your essay and draft another outline, narrowing your paper to the discussion of the part that had most interested you. Either of these decisions would make it easier for you to write a well-organized paper by reducing the risk of introducing ideas you could not pursue.

You should remember that an outline is not an end in itself; it is only a device to help you write a good paper. You can rewrite an outline much more easily than you can rewrite a paper, so do not think of an outline as some sort of fixed contract which you must honor at all cost. Be prepared to rework any outline that does not help you to write better.

WRITING YOUR PAPER

When writing a research paper, you should allow ample time for drafting and revision. Even if you have extensive notes, you may discover that you lack information to support a claim that occurred to you when you sat down to write—for ideas often evolve during the writing process. You would then need to do some more research or modify your claim. The first draft may also include paragraphs that do not relate to the focus of your paper, and these will need to be removed once you realize that they do not fit.

One of the challenges involved in writing a research paper is the need to integrate source material into a work that remains distinctively your own. Many research papers suffer because they include too many long quotations or because quotations (be they long or short) seem arbitrarily placed. Make sure that any quotations in your paper fit smoothly within the essay as a whole by providing transitions that link quotations to whatever has come before them. And, as a general rule, anything worth quoting at length requires some discussion. After you have quoted someone, you should usually include some analysis or commentary that will make the significance of the quotation clear. Let your readers know how you would like them to respond to the material that you are citing. Identify what you agree with and what you question.

To help keep your paper your own, you should try to avoid using long quotations. Quote only what you need most and edit long quotations whenever possible. Use the ellipsis (. . .) to indicate that you have omitted a word or phrase within a sentence, leaving a space before and after each period and including a fourth period with no space before it when the ellipsis comes at the end of the sentence(. . . .). But when editing quotations in this way, make sure that they remain clear and grammatical. If the addition of an extra word or two would help make the quotation more easily understandable, you can make an editorial interpolation by enclosing the inserted material within square brackets [   ]. If your typewriter does not have brackets, you can draw them in by hand.

Remember also that sources do not need to be quoted in order to be cited. As noted in Part 2 (61–63), paraphrasing and summarizing are important writing skills. When revising your paper, use these skills whenever possible. They can help you to avoid writing a paper that sounds like nothing more than one quotation after another, or using quotations that are so heavily edited that readers start wondering about what you have cut out. When you put another writer's ideas into your own words (being careful, of course, to provide proper documentation), you are demonstrating that you have control over your material. And by doing so, you can often make your paper flow more smoothly.

PREPARING YOUR FINAL DRAFT

After investing considerable time in researching and writing your paper, be sure to allow sufficient time for editing your final draft. If you rush this stage of the process, the work you submit for evaluation may not adequately reflect the investment of time you gave to the project as a whole. Unless instructed otherwise, you should be guided by the rules in the following checklist.

A CHECKLIST FOR MANUSCRIPT FORM

1. Research papers should be typed or word-processed. Use nonerasable 8-½ by 11-inch white, 20-pound paper. Type on one side of each page only. Doublespace all lines, leaving a margin of one inch on all sides. If word-processing, use a printer that will produce well-defined letters.
2. In the upper left corner of page 1, or on a separate title page, include the following information: your name, your instructor's name, the course and section number, and the date the essay is submitted.
3. Number each page in the upper right corner, ½-inch from the top. If using MLA-style documentation, type your last name immediately before the number. If using APA-style documentation, type a shortened version of the title (one or two words) before the number.
4. Make sure that you consistently follow a documentation style acceptable to your instructor, and give credit to all of your sources.
5. Any quotation of more than four lines in an MLA-style paper, or more than forty words in an APA-style paper, should be set off from the rest of the text. Begin a new line, indenting ten spaces to form the left margin of the quotation. The indentation means that you are quoting, so additional quotation marks are unnecessary in this case (except for quotations within the quotation).
6. Proofread your paper carefully. Typographical errors or careless mistakes in spelling or grammar can cause your audience to lose confidence in you. If your instructor allows ink corrections, make them as neatly as you can. Retype any page that has numerous or lengthy corrections.
7. If you have word-processed your paper, be sure to separate pages that have been printed on a continuous sheet. Whether your work is word-processed or typed, use a paper clip to bind the pages together.

IN CONCLUSION

The readings gathered in this book have demonstrated the importance of research in the world beyond the classroom. Extensive research is readily apparent in the articles by Mayo, Singer, and Shurr. But research also supports the arguments of O'Keefe, Horgan, Spitzer, Kates, Brookes, and Kohn—among others. None of these works could have been written if their authors had not taken the trouble to become well-informed on their chosen subjects.

Having studied these essays, you should be familiar with the way experienced writers use content notes to clarify various points in their arguments. Individual essays have also illustrated the major documentation styles. Deborah Mayo and Lisa Lemke use the APA author/year system, as does the team of writers headed by Anthony R. Perry. The essay by Tim Paetsch provides an example of a numbered system of references. Andrea Johnson, Patricia Lindholm, and Kim Bassuener all use the MLA author/work style.

For an example of the MLA author/work style in a longer paper, consider the following paper by Grace Reyes. You will find that it includes material from a range of sources that were located through the use of different tools: the main catalog for books, the *Essay and General Literature Index* for material published in anthologies, the *Readers' Guide* for articles in periodicals such as *Forbes,* and *The Education Index* for periodicals such as *Harvard Education Review.*

As you read the paper, note that it uses sources in order to support an argument. This argument shows that the author has ideas of her own and that her paper is more than a collection of notes. The paper as written, however, is different from the paper Grace originally envisioned. She began by intending to argue whether or not bilingual education is worthwhile, but she found that this topic was too big for her. She then tried to limit her work to the advantages of two-way bilingual programs only to find that she could not locate sufficient material on that topic. Her solution was to focus her paper upon the purpose of bilingual education, a topic that proved to be the right size for her. When you write a research paper of your own, be prepared to revise your focus when necessary. Although you may be able to write an excellent paper on the topic you set out to research, you could just as easily find it necessary to redefine that topic as your research proceeds.

Bilingual Education in a
Multicultural Nation

Thesis: The purpose of bilingual education needs to be clari-
fied if the controversy surrounding this issue is to
be resolved.

Introduction--why this topic is important
  I. History of bilingual education
     A. Role of federal government
        1. Languages used in bilingual education
        2. Students eligible for enrollment
     B. Range of programs offered
        1. Transitional Bilingual Education
        2. Immersion
        3. English as a Second Language
 II. Issues behind bilingual education
     A. Time necessary for learning language
        1. Quotation from Cardenas
        2. Quotation from Rodriquez
        3. Response to show who is right
     B. Importance of cultural diversity
        1. Languages spoken here
        2. Treatment of minorities
        3. America as a melting pot
III. Challenges facing bilingual education
     A. Segregated classrooms
        1. Integration through two-way programs
        2. Limits of two-way programs
     B. Increased needs
        1. Problems with funding
        2. Larger number of students needing help
     C. Multiple goals
        1. Instruction in English
        2. Instruction in other languages
        3. Instruction in culture
Conclusion--need to set priorities so we can cope with rising
needs

Reyes 1

Grace Reyes
Prof. Lewandowski
English 150
9 May 1991

Bilingual Education in a Multicultural Nation

Should American public-school children be taught in any
language besides English? Some people might think that this
question was answered a long time ago. After all, the federal
government has been funding bilingual education for over
twenty years. But there is still little agreement over what
"bilingual education" means and how it should be conducted.
Because language is so important in determining what a society is like, the outcome of this debate will affect all Americans, not just students. According to a recent article in
the New York Times, "What's at stake, then, is nothing less
than the cultural identity of the country" (Bernstein 52).

Most bilingual programs can be traced back to the Bilingual Education Act of 1968.[1] Although the original legislation
was designed to benefit Hispanic children, it was revised to
apply to all non-English speakers as the result of a compromise between Congress and the White House (Stein 31). Spanish
is now only one of 145 languages used for instruction in our
public schools (Thernstrom 46). And since 1974, bilingual
programs have been open to middle-class children whose primary language is English.

There is thus good reason to be confused about what
"bilingual education" means. This designation might be used
to describe a program designed to assimilate disadvantaged,
non-English speaking students into American society. It could
refer to a program designed to help middle-class students
maintain a language that is part of their ethnic background
even if they already speak English. Or it could describe a
program with a large number of English-speaking students
whose parents want them to learn a useful foreign language.
Some schools try to pursue all of these goals, and this leads
to another problem: Instruction can suffer when students with
different needs are placed together randomly or with a

Double space

Student estab-
lishes importance
of the topic

Reference to con-
tent note provid-
ing additional in-
formation

Student identifies
the problems that
concern her

teacher who is unprepared to help more than one type of
student.

In addition to enrolling students with different needs,
bilingual programs are organized in different ways. The most
common type of program is called "Transitional Bilingual Education." As its name suggests, TBE offers instruction in both
English and in a student's first language until he or she is
ready to make the transition into regular classes in which
English is the only language of instruction. Much of the debate over bilingual education has focused upon this type of
program, and since 1988 up to 25% of federal funds for bilingual education can be used for alternatives to TBE (Thernstrom 48). These alternatives include Immersion, or classes
in which a teacher speaks only English but nevertheless understands her students' language. (If the teacher occasionally uses the student's language to provide a hint, this is
called Structured Immersion.) Another alternative method of
instruction is teaching English as a Second Language. An ESL
class would normally include students who speak a number of
different languages, and instruction would be offered only in
English. Unlike Immersion, in which regular courses are
taught in English, an ESL class is devoted only to learning
how to read and speak English. Another difference is that
students taking ESL are usually pulled out of their regular
classes for part of the day.

Both proponents and critics of bilingual education agree
about the importance of learning English. The controversy
concerns how quickly English should be learned, and what type
of special instruction should be made available. Advocates of
TBE believe that it takes from five to seven years for students with limited proficiency in English to master the formal language necessary for understanding school work taught
in English. José A. Cárdenas, executive director of the In-
tercultural Development Research Association in San Antonio,
warns:

> Failure to allow sufficient language development
> before the transition will result in a child's

Student summarizes different types of bilingual education

Student identifies a source

Quotations more than four lines long are set off as a block. Indent ten spaces and do not add quotation marks.

Reyes 3

being unable to cope with anything but the most
shallow levels of learning and will affect that
child's future capability for learning. (362)

On the other hand, critics of bilingual education believe
that the use of another language in school can delay the
learning of English. In his memoir Hunger of Memory, Richard
Rodriquez writes:

Without question, it would have pleased me to hear
my teachers address me in Spanish when I entered
the classroom. I would have been much less afraid.
I would have trusted them and responded with ease.
But I would have delayed . . . having to learn the
language of public society. (19)

Ellipsis indicates an omission

Rodriquez is often cited as an authority on bilingual education, but he is speculating about what did not happen to him.

Student responds to a quotation

According to Jim Cummins, an internationally recognized expert on bilingual education, "language minority students instructed through the minority language . . . for all or part
of the school day perform as well in English academic skills
as comparable students instructed totally through English"
("Empowering" 20). If this is the case, then it would seem
that neither TBE nor Immersion is clearly preferable strictly
in terms of education.²

A shortened version of the title is included because the list of works cited includes more than one work by this author.

But bilingual education is a political issue as well as
an educational issue. Arguing that we need a common language
in order to hold together a society that is ethnically and
culturally diverse, critics of bilingual education often
characterize it as a threat to national unity (Banks 62;
Bernstein 48). According to this reasoning, anyone living
here should learn English as soon as possible, and loyalty to
another language can interfere with this goal. On the other
hand, cultural diversity can also be cited as a justification
for recognizing the importance of languages other than English. The United States "has always been a multilingual nation and indeed was characterized by multilingualism long
before it became a nation" (Paulston 485). Insisting that all
Americans speak English may make sense politically, but pre-

More than one source cited within the same parenthetical reference, indicating that both Banks and Bernstein support the point just made.

Student responds to an argument against bilingual education

tending that English is the only language ever spoken here means distorting the past and ignoring important parts of our national heritage.

Spanish has been spoken in North America since the six-teenth century, and Native American languages were spoken here even earlier. It's hard to justify denying anyone the right to speak the language of his or her ancestors, and it's especially hard to do so when the language in question has been spoken here for hundreds of years by people whose ances-tors became Americans as the result of military conquest. Some of the bitterness surrounding the debate over bilingual education can be understood when we realize that speakers of Spanish and Native American languages have been the victims of prejudice. Educators in Texas, for example, used to make uninvited home visits to persuade parents to stop speaking Spanish to their children. According to one such teacher:

An indirect quotation

"Their only handicap is a bag full of superstitions and silly notions that they inherited from Mexico . . . a lot depends on whether we can get them to switch from Spanish to English, when they speak Spanish they think Mexican" (qtd. in Stein 15). I hope that we now realize that it is racist to associ-ate thinking "Mexican" with "superstitions and silly no-tions." But even if more people are now prepared to recognize that the United States is a multicultural nation, racism seems to linger in some of the criticism of bilingual educa-tion. Just last year, for example, an article in Forbes maga-

As an alternative to using an ellip-sis, student uses her own words to link together two short quotations from the same paragraph.

zine defined bilingual education as a "strident political campaign for separate Spanish teaching," favored by a "loud minority of Hispanic politicians and leftish liberals" (Banks 62).

Student summa-rizes and re-sponds to another argument against bilingual educa-tion.

As for immigrants, opponents of bilingual education often emphasize that the United States was settled by people from many different countries. But they then argue that their parents or grandparents received no special treatment after arriving in the United States, so no one else should either. This argument implies that the future can never be better than the past. Late nineteenth-century immigrants were often crowded into unhealthy tenements and exploited in sweat

Reyes 5

shops. Child labor was common, and social services were
either minimal or nonexistent. Does this mean that we want
late-twentieth century immigrants to be subject to the same
hardships?

Critics of bilingual education often see the United
States as a "melting pot," implying that people from different cultures were once easily assimilated within the United
States—and that assimilation is being deliberately resisted
by recent arrivals. But I suspect that assimilation was always slow and painful. Even the image of a melting pot is
disturbing once you think about it. I don't think anyone
really wants to get <u>melted</u> <u>down</u>. The racism implicit in this
image can be seen in a pageant once held at the Ford Motor
Company. According to Colman Stein, Jr., a research analyst
who specializes in bilingual education, foreign-born workers
who had taken an "Americanization" program run by Ford carried signs identifying their national origin as they entered
a mock melting pot. Once in the pot, they were "cleaned" by
teachers with large scrub brushes before they could leave the
pot with new signs identifying them as American (5).

Student introduces a paraphrase with a reference to her source in order to show how much the subsequent page reference is meant to cover.

Understanding how minorities were treated in the past
should help us to recognize a fallacy in the argument that
bilingual education "sentences too many minority school leav-
ers, particularly Hispanics, to a second-class economic life"
(Banks 64). Minorities were sentenced to a second-class economic life long before the advent of bilingual education.
Bilingual programs may have failed to solve this problem, but
they should not be blamed for creating it. And we would certainly be better prepared to improve the quality of bilingual
education if we eliminated racism and misinformation from
this debate.

Student responds to another argument against bilingual education.

A more serious charge against bilingual education is
that it can become a type of segregated education once minority students are grouped together. According to one recent
critic:

There is often little that is integrated about the
education of these students. The students may dab-
ble in paints and dribble a ball together but, for

Reyes 6

Although the period usually goes after the parenthetical reference, it goes before the reference in block quotations.

most of the day, a bilingual classroom is a school
within a school——a world apart. (Thernstrom 48)
This is a problem that must be resolved. One possible solution is to integrate bilingual classrooms with English-speaking students who want to acquire a second language——whatever
their own ethnic heritage may be. In fact, one of the most
exciting developments in bilingual education is the "two-way"
program in which English-speaking students who want to acquire a second language are grouped with language-minority
students who are learning English. Although still fairly new,
"two-way programs seem to increase cross-cultural understanding and mutual respect among ethnic groups" (Crawford 172).
They may also help to improve the quality of foreign language
study in the United States, an area in which English-speaking
Americans have been traditionally weak. Unfortunately, there
is currently a much larger number of students needing to
learn English than students who are willing to learn a foreign language by enrolling in a bilingual program. Rosalie

Student makes a concession

Porter, a former member of the National Advisory and Coordi-
nating Council on Bilingual Education, estimates that two-way
programs would probably be able to enroll less than 10% of
language-minority children (157). Educators will need to explore other ways to make the bilingual classroom a multicultural classroom.

Another problem facing bilingual education is that funding has not kept pace with needs. Although the federal budget
for bilingual education has increased from $7,500,000 a year
in 1968 to $198,625,000 in 1989, funding never reaches many
school districts that need it (Porter 224-25).[3] And as the
United States becomes more ethnically diverse, bilingual programs are expected to serve an increasing number and variety
of students. According to sociologists Kenji Ima and Rubén G.

Student incorporates material from different sources within the same sentence, clearly revealing what information came from what source.

Rumbaut of San Diego State University, 48% of all immigrants
to this country during the 1980s came from Asia, and approximately 90% of them had limited proficiency in English. Their
needs have only begun to be addressed (54-55).

The number of Americans speaking a language other than
English is already higher than ever before in our history

(Bernstein 34), and it is expected to reach 39.5 million by the end of the century (Orvando 567), when approximately 20% of the school population will consist of language—minority children (Porter 5). We cannot ignore these children until they are ready to understand classes conducted exclusively in English, but we may not be able to make instruction available in every language spoken in every district. Although a large school district like that of New York City may be able to offer public education in Chinese, Greek, Haitian Creole, Kymer, Korean, Italian, Russian, and Vietnamese (Bernstein 34), many school systems lack the resources to guarantee instruction in every language spoken within the district.

The debate over bilingual education would not have lasted so long or become so bitter if there were a simple solution to the question of how to help students with special language needs. But if there is no simple solution to this problem nationwide, we should avoid policies that insist upon all school districts offering the same method of instruction. We must also avoid policies that would be so general that school districts could ignore the very real needs of students with limited proficiency in English. It would be one thing to encourage more flexibility in program design and to experiment with different types of instruction; it would be something else to go back to the days when students who could not understand English were allowed to either sink or swim.

Overall, the research is inconclusive regarding the various types of instruction currently offered students with limited proficiency in English. We need to keep this in mind when making future decisions. As Jim Cummins argued in <u>Language and Literacy in Bilingual Education</u>, a "rational policy in regard to the education of minority students must abandon conventional wisdoms and acknowledge what is known and what is not yet known" (6).

Since this is the case, the federal government should encourage individual school districts to find the type of instruction that best suits their needs. But the government can define the purpose of bilingual education, and that means establishing priorities among three separate goals. Bilingual

---

Student begins to move toward her conclusion.

Although the list of works cited includes two works by Cummins, the parenthetical reference includes only a page number since the work is identified in the text of the paper.

education can be used simply as a means of helping students with limited proficiency in English become assimilated within American society. It could become a way of helping all American students become bilingual. Or it could be used as a way of teaching about the history and value of different cultures.[4]

Ideally, it would be desirable to pursue all of these goals. But it is hard to do so in any one classroom, since students with different needs require different types of instruction. With limited resources and many students, we need to clarify what goal is our top priority. I believe that lessons in different cultures are important, but they can be incorporated into the regular curriculum in such classes as history and geography where all students would benefit from them. The purpose of bilingual education should be to improve skills in language. We should encourage English-speaking students to become bilingual by developing two-way programs wherever possible. But our first priority should be helping language-minority students to learn English through concentrated effort and dedicated teaching. If this goal became widely understood, the debate over bilingual education would come closer to being resolved.

Student reaches her conclusion.

1" —

Notes

[1]Crawford calls bilingual education "a forgotten legacy." He points out that cities like Cincinnati, Milwaukee, and St. Louis had German–English schools in the nineteenth century; Louisiana had French–English schools, and Spanish–English schools were authorized in New Mexico in 1848. But bilingual education declined during the early twentieth century, in part because learning in other languages seemed unpatriotic during and after the First World War. For additional information on the history of bilingual education, see the first chapter in Crawford and the first two chapters in Stein.

[2]Cummins argues that one of the most important factors in helping minority students succeed in school is the attitude educators convey on a daily basis. He also argues that parents need to get involved in their children's education. These factors may be more important than whether a school uses TBE or Immersion.

[3]Porter argues that the federal government should restructure the way it makes money available. She calls for block grants for every state with minority–language students instead of the current system which awards money in the form of grants to successful applicants.

[4]Lessons in culture that would improve the self–esteem of minority students were considered important when many current programs were founded. See Thernstrom.

Content notes supplement the paper and indicate where readers could get additional information.

Reyes 10

Works Cited

Double-space

Leave five spaces blank.

Banks, Howard. "Do We Want Quebec Here?" <u>Forbes</u> 11 June 1990: 62–64.

Bernstein, Richard. "In U.S. Schools a War of Words." <u>The New York Times Magazine</u> 14 Oct. 1990: 34+.

Cárdenas, José A. "The Role of Native–Language Instruction in Bilingual Education." <u>Phi Delta Kappan</u> 67 (1986): 359–63.

Crawford, James. <u>Bilingual Education: History, Politics, Theory, and Practice</u>. Trenton: Crane, 1989.

Student cites two works by the same author. Instead of repeating the author's name, type three hyphens followed by a period. In a case like this, arrange the works alphabetically by title.

Cummins, Jim. "Empowering Minority Students: A Framework for Intervention." <u>Harvard Educational Review</u>. 56 (1986): 18–36.

———. <u>Language and Literacy Learning in Bilingual Instruction</u>. Washington: GPO, 1983.

Ima, Kenji and Rubén G. Rumbaut. "Southeast Asian Refugees in American Schools: A Comparison of Fluent English–Proficient and Limited English–Proficient Students." <u>Topics in Language Disorders</u> 9.3 (1989): 54–75.

Orvando, Carlos J. "Bilingual/Bicultural Education: Its Legacy and Its Future." <u>Phi Delta Kappan</u> 64 (1983): 564–71.

Paulston, Christina Bratt. "Bilingualism and Education." <u>Language in the USA</u>. Ed. Charles A. Ferguson and Shirley Brice Heath. Cambridge: Cambridge UP, 1981.

Porter, Rosalie Pedalino. <u>Forked Tongue: The Politics of Bilingual Education</u>. New York: Basic, 1990.

Two spaces

Rodriquez, Richard. <u>Hunger of Memory</u>. 1982. New York: Bantam, 1983.

Stein, Colman Brez, Jr. <u>Sink or Swim: The Politics of Bilingual Education</u>. New York: Praeger, 1986.

Thernstrom, Abigail M. "Bilingual Miseducation." <u>Commentary</u> Feb. 1990: 44–48.

GLOSSARY OF USEFUL TERMS

◆

ad hominem argument: An argument that makes a personal attack upon an opponent instead of addressing itself to the issue that is under dispute.

allusion: An informed reference that an audience is expected to understand without explanation.

analogy: A comparison that works on more than one level, usually between something familiar and something abstract.

anticipating the opposition: The process through which a writer or speaker imagines the most likely counterarguments that could be raised against his or her position.

audience: Whoever will read what you write. Your audience may consist of a single individual (such as your history teacher), a particular group of people (such as English majors), or a larger and more general group of people (such as "the American people"). Good writers have a clear sense of audience, which means that they never lose sight of whomever they are writing for.

authority: A reliable source that helps support an argument. It is important to cite authorities who will be recognized as legitimate by your opponents. This means turning to people with good credentials in whatever area is under consideration. If you are arguing about the economy, cite a prominent economist as an authority—not the teller at your local bank.

begging the question: An argument that assumes as already agreed upon whatever it should be devoted to proving.

bibliography: A list of works on a particular subject. One type of bibliography is the list of works cited that appears at the end of a research paper, scholarly article, or book. Another type of bibliography is a work in itself—a compilation of all known sources on a subject. An annotated bibliography is a bibliography that includes a brief description of each of the sources cited.

bogus claim: An unreliable or false premise; a questionable statement that is unsupported by reliable evidence or legitimate authority.

claim: Any assertion that can or should be supported with evidence. In the model for argument devised by Stephen Toulmin, the "claim" is the conclusion that the arguer must try to prove.

cliché: A worn-out expression; any group of words that are frequently and automatically used together. In "the real world" of "today's society," writers should avoid clichés because they are a type of instant language that makes writing seem "as dead as a doornail."

concession   Any point in an opposing argument that you are willing to recognize as valid. In argumentation, concessions help to diffuse the opposition by demonstrating that you are fair-minded.

connotation: The associations inspired by a word, in contrast to *denotation* (see below).

data: The evidence that an arguer uses to support a claim. It may take the form of personal experience, expert opinion, statistics, or any other information that is verifiable.

deduction: The type of reasoning through which a general observation leads to a specific conclusion.

denotation: The literal dictionary definition of a word.

diction: Word choice. Having good diction means more than having a good vocabulary; it means using language appropriately by using the right word in the right place.

documentation: The references that writers supply to reveal the source of the information they have reported.

equivocation: The deliberate use of vague, ambiguous language to mislead others. In writing, equivocation often takes the form of using abstract words to obscure meaning.

evidence: The experience, examples, or facts that support an argument. Good writers are careful to offer evidence for whatever they are claiming (see *claim*).

focus: The particular aspect of a subject upon which a writer decides to concentrate. Many things can be said about most subjects. Having a clear focus means narrowing a subject down so that it can be discussed without loss of direction. If you digress from your subject and begin to ramble, you have probably lost your focus.

generalization: Forming a conclusion that seems generally acceptable because it could be supported by evidence. Argumentative writing demands a certain amount of generalization. It becomes a problem only when it is easily disputable. You have overgeneralized if someone can think of exceptions to what you have claimed. Be wary of words such as "all" and "every" since they increase the likelihood of overgeneralization.

hyperbole: A deliberate exaggeration for dramatic effect.

hypothesis: A theory that guides your research; a conditional thesis that is subject to change as evidence accumulates.

induction: The type of reasoning through which specific observations lead to a generally acceptable conclusion.

irony: A manner of speech or writing in which one's meaning is the opposite of what one has said.

jargon: A specialized vocabulary that is usually abstract and limited to a particular field, hence, difficult to understand for those outside the field.

loaded term: A word or phrase that is considered an unfair type of persuasion because it is either slanted or gratuitous within its context.

metaphor: A comparison in which two unlike things are declared to be the same; for example, "The Lord is my shepherd."

meter: The rhythm of poetry, in which stressed syllables occur in a pattern with regular intervals. In the analysis of poetry, meter is measured by a unit called a "foot," which usually consists of two or three syllables of which at least one is stressed.

non sequitur: Latin for "it does not follow"; a logical fallacy in which a writer bases a claim upon an unrelated point.

paradox: A statement or situation that appears to be contradictory but is nevertheless true; for example, "conspicuous by his absence."

paraphrase: Restating someone's words to demonstrate that you have understood them correctly or to make them more easily understandable.

personification: Giving human qualities to nonhuman objects; for example, "The sofa smiled at me, inviting me to sit down."

persuasion: A rhetorical strategy designed to make an audience undertake a specific action. Although there are many different types of persuasion, most involve an appeal to feeling that would not be part of a strictly logical argument.

plagiarism: Taking someone's words or ideas without giving adequate acknowledgment.

point of view: The attitude with which a writer approaches a subject. Good writers maintain a consistent point of view within each individual work.

post hoc, ergo propter hoc: Latin for "after this, therefore because of this"; a logical fallacy in which precedence is confused with causation.

premise: The underlying value or belief that one assumes as a given truth at the beginning of an argument.

rhetorical question: A question that is asked for dramatic effect, without expectation of a response.

rime scheme (or "rhyme"):   A fixed pattern of rimes that occurs throughout a poem.

simile: A direct comparison between two unlike things that includes such words as "like," "as," or "than"; for example, "My love is like a red, red rose."

stereotype: An unthinking generalization, especially of a group of people in which all the members of the group are assumed to share the same traits; for example, the "dumb jock" is a stereotype of high school and college athletes.

style: The combination of diction and sentence structure that characterizes the manner in which a writer writes. Good writers have a distinctive style, which is to say their work can be readily identified as their own.

summary: A brief and unbiased recapitulation of previously stated ideas.

syllogism: A three-stage form of deductive reasoning through which a general truth yields a specific conclusion.

thesis: The central idea of an argument; the point that an argument seeks to prove. In an unified essay, every paragraph helps to advance the thesis.

tone: The way a writer sounds when discussing a particular subject. Whereas point of view establishes a writer's attitude toward his or her subject, tone refers to the voice that is adopted in conveying this point of view to an audience. For example, one can write with an angry, sarcastic, humorous, or dispassionate tone when discussing a subject about which one has a negative point of view.

topic sentence: The sentence that defines the function of a paragraph; the single most important sentence in each paragraph.

transition: A link or bridge between topics that enables a writer to move smoothly from one subtopic to another so that every paragraph is clearly related to the paragraphs that surround it.

warrant: A term used by Stephen Toulmin for an implicit or explicit general statement that underlies an argument and establishes a relationship between the data and the claim.

COPYRIGHTS AND
ACKNOWLEDGMENTS

♦

EITZEN, D. STANLEY "The Dark Side of Competition in American Society" by D. Stanley Eitzen. From *Vital Speeches of the Day*, January 1, 1990. Reprinted by permission of the author.

ELSHTAIN, JEAN BETH "Why Worry about the Animals?" by Jean Beth Elshtain. From *The Progressive*, March 1990. Reprinted by permission from *The Progressive*, 409 E. Main St., Madison, WI 53703.

FITZGERALD, RANDY "Our Tax Dollars for This Kind of Art" by Randy Fitzgerald. Reprinted with permission from the April 1990 *Reader's Digest*. Copyright © 1990 by The Reader's Digest Assn., Inc.

FOSS, JOE "They Want to Take Our Guns" by Joe Foss. Reprinted by permission from *Conservative Digest*, September 1988.

FRIEDAN, BETTY "The Feminine Mystique" by Betty Friedan. Reprinted by permission of W. W. Norton & Company, Inc. Copyright © 1983, 1974, 1963 by Betty Friedan. Copyright renewed 1991 by Betty Friedan.

FROST, ROBERT "Stopping by Woods on a Snowy Evening" and facsimile of last three stanzas, by Robert Frost. Copyright © 1923, 1969 by Holt, Rinehart, and Winston, Copyright © 1951 by Robert Frost. Reprinted by permission of Henry Holt and Company, Inc.

GANDHI, MAHATMA "Brahmacharya" by Mahatma Gandhi. Reprinted by permission of the Navajivan Trust.

HITLER, ADOLF "The Purpose of Propaganda" translated by Ralph Manheim. From *Mein Kampf*. Copyright © 1943 and copyright © 1971 by Houghton Mifflin Co. Reprinted by permission of Houghton Mifflin Co.

HOLMES, JOHN "On Frost's 'Stopping by Woods on a Snowy Evening' " by John Holms. Excerpt, pp. 417–19, from *Preface to Poetry*. Copyright © 1943 by Charles W. Cooper, copyright © 1946 by Harcourt Brace Jovanovich, Inc. Reprinted by permission of the publisher.

HORGAN, JOHN "Test Negative" by John Horgan. From *Scientific American*, March 1990. Reprinted with permission. Copyright © 1990 by *Scientific American*, Inc. All rights reserved.

HUBBELL, JOHN G. "The 'Animal Rights' War on Medicine" by John G. Hubbell. Reprinted with permission from the June 1990 *Reader's Digest*. Copyright © 1990 by The Reader's Digest Assn., Inc.

HUKILL, CRAIG "Employee Drug Testing" by Craig Hukill. From *Monthly Labor Review*, November, pp. 75–76, 1989. Reprinted by permission.

INGERSOLL, BRUCE "Range War." Originally titled as "Small Minnesota Town Is Divided by Rancor Over Sugar Policies" by Bruce Ingersoll. From *The Wall Street Journal*, June 26, 1990. Reprinted by permission of The Wall Street Journal, copyright © 1990 Dow Jones & Company, Inc. All rights reserved worldwide.

JOSEPH, LAWRENCE E. "The Bottom Line on Disposables," by Lawrence E. Joseph. From *The New York Times*, September 13, 1990. Copyright © 1990 by The New York Times Company. Reprinted by permission.

KARPATI, RON "A Scientist: 'I Am the Enemy' " by Ron Karpati. From *Newsweek*, October 18, 1989. Reprinted by permission of the author.

KAUFMAN, IRVING R. "The Battle Over Drug Testing" by Irving R. Kaufman. Copyright © 1986 by the New York Times Company. Reprinted by permission.

KING, MARTIN LUTHER, JR.   "Letter from Birmingham Jail," from *Why We Can't Wait* by Martin Luther King, Jr. Copyright © 1963, 1964 by Martin Luther King, Jr. Reprinted by permission of HarperCollins Publishers.

KOHN, ALFIE   "Incentives Can Be Bad for Business" by Alfie Kohn. Reprinted from *Inc.* magazine with the author's permission.

KOOPMAN, ROGER E.   "Second Defense" by Roger E. Koopman. From *Outdoor Life*, February, 1990. Reprinted by permission of the author.

KOSOVA, WESTON   "The Future of ROTC" by Weston Kosova. Originally titled "ROTC Ya Later." From *The New Republic*, February 19, 1990. Reprinted by permission.

MACHIAVELLI, NICCOLÒ   "Should Princes Tell the Truth?" by Niccolò Machiavelli. From *The Prince* by Niccolò Machiavelli, translated by Luigi Ricci, revised by E. R. P. Vincent (1935). Reprinted by permission of Oxford University Press.

MANDELA, NELSON   "The Struggle Is My Life" by Nelson Mandela. Reprinted by permission of Pathfinder Press. Copyright © 1986 by Pathfinder Press.

MARWICK, CHARLES AND PHIL GUNBY   "Fighting Drug Abuse in the Military." Originally titled "Like Other Segments of Culture, Military Has Had to Come to Grips with Drug Abuse Problem," by Charles Marwick and Phil Gunby. From the *Journal of the American Medical Association*, May 19, 1989, vol. 261, pp. 2784–2788. Copyright © 1988/89, American Medical Association. Reprinted by permission.

McKIBBEN, WILLIAM   "The End of Nature" by William McKibben. Copyright © 1989 by William McKibben. Reprinted by permission of Random House, Inc.

MICHENER, JAMES A.   "Are There Limits to Free Speech?" by James A. Michener. From *Parade* magazine, November 18, 1990. Reprinted by permission of William Morris Agency, Inc., on behalf of James A. Michener. Copyright © 1990 by James A. Michener. Originally published in *Parade* magazine.

MILLER, KRYSTAL   "School Dress Codes." Originally titled "School Dress Codes Aim to Discourage Clothing Robberies" by Krystal Miller. From *The Wall Street Journal*, April 5, 1990. Reprinted by permission of *The Wall Street Journal*, copyright © 1990 Dow Jones & Company, Inc. All rights reserved worldwide.

MOORE, CURTIS A.   "Does Your Cup of Coffee Cause Forest Fires?" by Curtis A. Moore. From *International Wildlife*, March/April 1989. Reprinted by permission of the author.

MURPHY, MICHAEL E.   "What the Greenhouse Effect Portends" by Michael E. Murphy. Reprinted from *America*, December 30, 1989. Reprinted with permission of America Press, Inc. Copyright © 1989. All rights reserved.

NELSON, MARIAH BURTON   "Who Wins? Who Cares?" by Mariah Burton Nelson. Reprinted by permission of the author.

O'KEEFE, ANNE MARIE   "The Case Against Drug Testing" by Anne Marie O'Keefe. Reprinted with permission from *Psychology Today* magazine. Copyright © 1987 American Psychological Association.

PARELES, JON   "Legislating the Imagination" by Jon Pareles. From *The New York Times*, February 11, 1990. Copyright © 1990 by The New York Times Company. Reprinted by permission.

PERRY, A. R.   Perry, A. R., Kane, K. M., Bernesser, K. J., and Spicker, P. T. "Type A behavior, competitive achievement-striving, and cheating among college students." *Psychological Reports*, 1990, 66, 459–465.

AUTHOR–TITLE
INDEX

◆

A 1
B 2
C 3
D 4
E 5
F 6
G 7
H 8
I 9
J 0